Windows 2000
Performance Guide

Windows 2000
Performance Guide

Mark Friedman and Odysseas Pentakalos

O'REILLY®

Beijing · Cambridge · Farnham · Köln · Paris · Sebastopol · Taipei · Tokyo

Windows 2000 Performance Guide
by Mark Friedman and Odysseas Pentakalos

Published by O'Reilly & Associates, Inc., 1005 Gravenstein Highway North, Sebastopol, CA 95472.

O'Reilly & Associates books may be purchased for educational, business, or sales promotional use. Online editions are also available for most titles (*safari.oreilly.com*). For more information contact our corporate/institutional sales department: (800) 998-9938 or *corporate@oreilly.com*.

Editor:	Robert Denn
Production Editor:	Emily Quill
Cover Designer:	Ellie Volckhausen
Interior Designer:	David Futato

Printing History:

January 2002:   First Edition.

Library of Congress Cataloging-in-Publication Data

Friedman, Mark, 1951 June 13-
    Windows 2000 performance guide: help for Windows 2000 administrators / Mark Friedman
      & Odysseas Pentakalos.
        p. cm.
    ISBN 1-56592-466-5
    1. Microsoft Windows (Computer file) 2. Operating systems (Computers) I. Pentakalos,
      Odysseas. II. Title.

QA76.76.O63 F774 2001
005.4'4769--dc21   2001036167

[M]

Table of Contents

Preface

The book you hold in your hands originally arose from need. Professionally, we felt the need to answer both basic and not-so-basic questions about the performance of Intel-based computer systems running various versions of the Microsoft Windows 2000 operating system, including both Windows NT and Windows XP. We expect that most readers of this book are seeking answers to common questions about computer and operating system performance out of similar personal or professional curiosity. This book, in fact, evolved from a seminar intended to address such questions that one of the authors developed and taught over a number of years.

The material in the book is the result of research performed over the last five years on successive versions of the Windows NT operating system, beginning with Version 3.5 and continuing to the present day. (As this book was going to press, we were experimenting with early versions of Windows XP. As best we can currently determine, almost all of the information provided here regarding Windows 2000 performance can also be applied to the 32-bit version of Windows XP.) Much of the material here is original, derived from our observations and analysis of running systems, some of which may contradict official documentation and the writings and recommendations of other authorities. Rest assured that we carefully reviewed any findings reported here that run counter to the received wisdom.

While we strive to make the discussion here definitive, there are necessarily many places where our conclusions are tentative and subject to modification should new information arise. We expect readers to be willing to challenge our conclusions in the face of strong empirical evidence to the contrary, and urge you to communicate to us (via the publisher) when you discover errors of commission or omission, for which we assume full responsibility. If you observe behavior on one of your Windows 2000 machines that seems to contradict what we say in the book, please share those observations with us. With your help, we should be able to produce a subsequent version of this book that is even more authoritative.

Our research for the book began with all the standard sources of information about the Windows 2000 operating system. We frequently cite official documentation included in the operating system help files. We also refer to the extensive reference material provided in the Windows 2000 Resource Kit. David Solomon and Mark Russinovich's *Inside Windows 2000*, published by Microsoft Press, was another valuable source of inside information. The Windows 2000 platform System Development Kit (SDK) and Device Driver Development Kit (DDK) documentation, along with Microsoft Developer Network (MSDN) KnowledgeBase entries and other technical articles, also proved useful from time to time. Intel processor hardware documentation (available at *http://www.intel.com*) was helpful as well, particularly in writing Chapters 4 and 5. At many points in the text, we cite other reference material, including various academic journals and several excellent books. From time to time, we also mention worthy magazine articles and informative white papers published by various vendors. This book contains a complete bibliography.

Originally, we intended this book to serve as an advanced text, picking up where Russ Blake's outstanding *Optimizing Windows NT* left off. Unfortunately, Blake's book is currently out of print and woefully obsolete. Blake led a team of developers who implemented a performance monitoring API for the initial version of Windows NT 3.1, when the OS first became available in 1992. Russ's book also documented using Performance Monitor, the all-purpose performance monitoring application the team developed. We acknowledge a tremendous debt to Russ, Bob Watson, and other members of that team. Writing when he did, Blake had little opportunity to observe real-world Windows NT environments. Consequently, almost all the examples he analyzes are based on artificial workloads generated by an application called Performance Probe, which he also developed. (The Performance Probe program is no longer available in the Windows 2000 Resource Kit; it is available in earlier versions of the NT 3.5 and 4.0 Resource Kits.)

While we also experiment in places with artificial workloads running under controlled conditions, we were fortunate to dive into Windows NT some years after it first became available. That allowed us to observe and measure a large number of real-world Windows NT and Windows 2000 machine environments. One advantage of real-world examples and case studies is that they are more likely to resemble the environments that you encounter. We should caution you, however, that many of the examples we chose to write about reflect extreme circumstances where the behavior we are trying to illustrate is quite pronounced. However, even when the systems you are observing do not evidence similar exaggerated symptoms, you should still be able to apply the general principles illustrated.

Our focus is on explaining how Windows 2000 and various hardware components associated with it work, how to tell when the performance of some application running under Windows 2000 is not optimal, and what you can do about it. The presentation is oriented toward practical problem-solving, with an emphasis on understanding and interpreting performance measurement data. Many realistic examples of performance problems are described and discussed.

Intended Audience

We have tried to aim this book at a variety of computer systems professionals, from system administrators who have mastered the basics of installing and maintaining Windows 2000 servers and workstations, to developers who are trying to build high-performance applications for this platform, to performance management and capacity planning professionals with experience on other platforms. Although we presume no specific background or prior level of training for our readers, our experience teaching this material suggests that this is not a book for beginners. If you find the material at hand too challenging, we recommend reading a good book on Windows 2000 operating system internals or on basic operating system principles first. We try to pick up the discussion precisely where most other official documentation and published sources leave off. This includes the course material associated with obtaining MCSE certification, which provides a very limited introduction to this topic.

Computer performance remains a core topic of interest to experienced programmers, database administrators, network specialists, and system administrators. We wrote this book for professionals who seek to understand this topic in the context of Windows 2000 and the hardware environment it supports. At a minimum, you should have a working knowledge of Windows 2000. We recommend that you have read and are familiar with the section on performance in the Windows 2000 Professional Resource Kit, which introduces the topic and documents the basic tools. For best results, you should have ready access to a computer running Windows 2000 Professional or Server so that you can refer frequently to a live system while you are reading, and put the abstract concepts we discuss into practice.

We understand that many people will buy this book because they hope it will assist them in solving some specific Windows 2000 performance problem they are experiencing. We hope so, too. Please understand, though, that for all but the simplest applications, there may be many possible solutions. While we do try to provide specific and detailed answers to Frequently Asked Questions, our approach to problem diagnosis is more theoretical and general than the many books that promise that this sort of understanding is easily acquired. It is possible that we have chosen to illustrate a discussion of some topic of immediate interest with an example that looks remarkably similar to a problem that you currently face. We all get lucky from time to time.

Organization of This Book

This book consists of twelve chapters and a bibliography.

Chapter 1, *Perspectives on Performance Management*, introduces a broad range of best practices in computer performance and capacity planning.

Chapter 2, *Measurement Methodology*, describes the Windows 2000 performance monitoring API, which is the source of most of the performance data that is dealt with in subsequent chapters.

Chapter 3, *Processor Performance*, discusses the basics of processor performance monitoring at the system, processor engine, process, and thread levels. Since the thread, not the process, is the unit of execution in Windows 2000, we focus on thread scheduling and thread execution priority.

Chapter 4, *Optimizing Application Performance*, is organized around a description of a programming optimization exercise that compares and contrasts several popular CPU usage code-profiling tools.

Chapter 5, *Multiprocessing*, discusses performance considerations when you are running Windows 2000 Server, Advanced Server, and Datacenter on machines with two or more processors.

Chapter 6, *Memory Management and Paging*, discusses Windows 2000 virtual memory management and describes the techniques Windows 2000 uses to manage RAM and the working sets of active application processes.

Chapter 7, *File Cache Performance and Tuning*, tackles the Windows 2000 file cache, a built-in operating system service that is crucial to the performance of a number of important applications, including Windows 2000 network file sharing and IIS.

Chapter 8, *Disk Subsystem Performance*, introduces basic disk performance concepts.

Chapter 9, *Filesystem Performance*, looks at filesystem performance.

Chapter 10, *Disk Array Performance*, discusses the disk array technology used in most larger Windows 2000 servers.

Chapter 11, *Introduction to Networking Technology* is a survey of computer networking, with an emphasis on the TCP/IP support in Windows 2000.

Chapter 12, *Internet Information Server Performance*, focuses on the Microsoft web server application Internet Information System (IIS).

The bibliography contains a list of references for those who would like to pursue these topics in more depth.

Conventions Used in This Book

We have used the following conventions in this book:

- *Italic* is used for filenames, directories, URLs, and hostnames. It is also used for emphasis and to introduce new terms.
- Constant width is used for commands, keywords, functions, and utilities.
- *Constant width italic* is occasionally used for replaceable items in code.

This icon signifies a tip relating to the nearby text.

 This icon signifies a warning relating to the nearby text.

How to Contact Us

Please address comments and questions concerning this book to the publisher:

O'Reilly & Associates, Inc.
1005 Gravenstein Highway North
Sebastopol, CA 95472
(800) 998-9938 (in the United States or Canada)
(707) 829-0515 (international or local)
(707) 829-0104 (fax)

We have a web page for this book, where we list errata and any additional information. You can access this page at:

http://www.oreilly.com/catalog/w2kperf/

To comment or ask technical questions about this book, send email to:

bookquestions@oreilly.com

For more information about books, conferences, Resource Centers, and the O'Reilly Network, see O'Reilly's web site at:

http://www.oreilly.com

Acknowledgments

Both authors gratefully acknowledge the support and assistance of Robert Denn and his staff at O'Reilly, without whom the book you hold in your hands would never have been completed. We are especially grateful for Robert's steady hand and patience throughout the long gestation period for this book. At one point we thought that he might select an engraving of a sloth to adorn the front cover. We would also like to acknowledge the help of many other individuals who reviewed earlier drafts of the book, including Dave Butchart, Janet Bishop, Bob Gauthier, Todd Glasgow, Kitrick Sheets, Jim Quigley, and Rich Olcott. They all contributed to making the final text clearer and more readable. Any errors that remain are solely the responsibility of the authors.

Mark would like to acknowledge the support of Ziya Aral and George Teixiera of Datacore for allowing him to complete this book on their watch. He is grateful for the long and fruitful collaboration with Stets Newcomb, Phil Henninge, and Dave Steier, working out the details of the Windows 2000 performance monitoring API. Special thanks to Joanne Decker for watching over me during this period. Barry Merrill, in particular, was helpful in getting that project off the ground, and his enthusiastic encouragement over the years is greatly appreciated. Russ Blake and Bob Watson from Microsoft also provided valuable support and assistance when we were starting out. Bob Gauthier, Jim Quigley, Sharon Seabaugh, Denis Nothern, and Claude Aron all contributed useful ideas and practical experiences. Also, thanks to Jee Ping, Kitrick Sheets, Dave Solomon, and Mark Russinovich for sharing their knowledge of Windows 2000 operating system internals.

Mark would also like to recognize some of the many individuals who contributed to his understanding of the discipline of computer performance evaluation over the past twenty years of his deepening involvement in the field. Alexandre Brandwajn and Rich Olcott deserve special recognition for being stimulating collaborators over a long and fruitful period. Thanks to Jeff Buzen, Pat Artis, Ken Sevcik, Barry Merrill, Dick Magnuson, Ben Duhl, and Phil Howard for all nurturing my early interest in this subject. A belated thanks to Kathy Clark of Landmark Systems for allowing me the opportunity to practice what I preached in the area of mainframe performance. A nod to Bob Johnson for giving me the courage to even attempt writing a book in the first place and to Bob Thomas for encouraging my writing career. To Bernie Domanski, Bill Fairchild, Dave Halbig, Dan Kaberon, Chris Loosely, Bruce McNutt, Rich Milner, Mike Salsburg, Ray Wicks, Brian Wong, and many other friends and colleagues too numerous to mention from the Computer Measurement Group, I owe a debt of gratitude that I can never repay for having shared their ideas and experiences so freely.

Thanks to the folks at Data General for giving us access to the CLARiiON disk array, and the folks at 3Ware Corporation for letting Odysseas use their RAID adapters. Thanks also to Ed Bouryng, Burton Strauss, Avi Tembulkar, and Michael Barker at KPMG for getting Odysseas involved with their performance tuning effort.

Odysseas would like to thank Edward Lazowska, Kenneth Sevcik, and John Zahorjan, who got him started in the area of performance modeling of computer systems with their summer course at Stanford University. I appreciate the support of Yelena Yesha from the University of Maryland at Baltimore County, and Milt Halem at NASA's Center for Computational Sciences, who got me involved with modeling the performance of hierarchical mass storage systems and supported me throughout that effort. Special thanks to Dr. Daniel Menascé of George Mason University for taking me under his wing. Danny generously shared his extensive knowledge and experience in the field of performance evaluation and modeling. He was also instrumental in honing my technical writing and research skills.

I want to thank my mother and brothers for their love and support over the years. I owe sincere gratitude to my father who always believed in me. If he were still alive, he would have been proud to see this book. Last, but not least, I must extend my most sincere gratitude to my wife Yimin. Throughout the long gestation period in getting this book completed, she took care of our two wonderful kids, John and Sophia, while I disappeared down in the basement to finish that very last chapter or make that very last modification. Despite the extra effort that she had to exert to compensate for my absence, she was supportive throughout.

## CHAPTER 1

Perspectives on Performance Management

Our goal in writing this book is to provide a good introduction to the Windows 2000 operating system and its hardware environment, focusing on understanding how it works from the standpoint of a performance analyst responsible for planning, configuration, and tuning. Our target audience consists of experienced performance analysts, system administrators, and developers who are already familiar with the Windows 2000 operating system environment.

Taken as a whole, Windows 2000 performance involves not just the operating system, but also the performance characteristics of various types of computer hardware, application software, and communications networks. The key operating system performance issues include understanding CPU scheduling and multiprogramming issues and the role and impact of virtual memory. Key areas of hardware include processor performance and the performance characteristics of I/O devices and other peripherals. Besides the operating system (OS), it is also important to understand how the database management system (DBMS) and transaction-monitoring software interact with both the OS and the application software and affect the performance of applications. Network transmission speeds and protocols are key determinants of communication performance. This is a lot of ground to cover in a single book, and there are many areas where our treatment of the topic is cursory at best. We have compiled a rather lengthy bibliography referencing additional readings in areas that we can discuss only briefly in the main body of this book.

Windows 2000 Evolution

Before we start to describe the way Windows 2000 works in detail, let's summarize the evolution of Microsoft's premier server operating system. While we try to concentrate on current NT technology (i.e., Windows 2000), this book encompasses all current NT releases from Version 3.5 onward, including current versions of NT 4.0 and Windows 2000. Each succeeding version of Windows NT incorporates significant architectural changes and improvements that affect the way the operating system functions. In many cases, these changes impact the interpretation of specific performance data counters, making the job of writing this book quite challenging.

Of necessity, the bulk of the book focuses on Windows 2000, with a secondary interest in Windows NT 4.0, as these are the releases currently available and in wide distribution. We have also had some experience running beta and prerelease versions of Windows XP. From a performance monitoring perspective, the 32-bit version of XP appears quite similar to Windows 2000. The few remaining NT 3.51 machines we stumble across are usually stable production environments running Citrix's WinFrame multiuser software that people are not willing to upgrade.

A daunting challenge to the reader who is familiar with some of the authoritative published works on NT performance is understanding that what was once good solid advice has become obsolete due to changes in the OS between Version 3, Version 4, and Windows 2000. Keeping track of the changes in Windows NT since Version 3 and how these changes impact system performance and tuning requires a little perspective on the evolution of the NT operating system, which is, after all, a relatively new operating system. Our purpose in highlighting the major changes here is to guide the reader who may be familiar with an older version of the OS. The following table summarizes these changes.

New feature/change	Comment
Added/changed between NT 3.5 and NT 4.0	
New `diskperf -ye` option	Fix to monitor Physical Disk activity in a volume set or software RAID 0/5 set correctly.
Task Manager performance tabs	Makes it easier to find and kill looping programs.
Logical and Physical Disk Avg Queue Length Counters added	The % Disk Time Counters were mistakenly identified as measuring disk utilization.
Revised Perfmon User Guide documentation	Tones down extravagant claims that Windows NT is "self-tuning."
Symmetric (SMP) Multiprocessor Support	NT Version 3 supports only asymmetric multiprocessing. All interrupts are serviced on Processor 0. With SMPs, device driver code must be made "thread-safe."
Common Network Device Interface Specification (NDIS) across Win9x and Windows NT	As long as network card vendors have to rewrite NIC device drivers anyway for Version 4, at least they will work on Windows 95, too.
Win32.dll	Moving user and GDI functions into the NT Executive provides better Windows than Windows.
Added/changed between NT 4.0 and Windows 2000	
Sysmon.OCX MMC snap-in replaces Perfmon	Many Sysmon enhancements, including fonts and multiple log data formats. Some valuable features inexplicably dropped, including the Chart Export facility.
Logical and Physical Disk % Idle Time counter added	100% − Idle Time = disk utilization; mislabeled % Disk Time counters are retained.
Per Process I/O Counts added to Task Manager and Physical Disk objects	Requested by developers of analytic and simulation modeling packages. Unfortunately, the Windows 2000 counters track logical file requests, not necessarily correlated with Physical Disk activity.

New feature/change	Comment
New Printer Queue measurements	
Job Object with resource limits introduced	Intended to provide a means for IIS to throttle runaway CGI scripts.
Windows Measurement Instrumentation	Support for the WBEM standard. Provides an infrastructure for integrated configuration, operations, and performance reporting tools. Actually first introduced in NT 4.0 with Service Pack 4, but not widely deployed.
New kernel Trace facility	Provides the ability to trace page faults, I/O requests, TCP requests, and other low-level functions without hooking the OS.
_Total instance of the Processor object supersedes counters in System object	
Below Normal and Above Normal Priority Levels	Provides more choice in the Scheduler's dynamic range.
Two choices for the duration of the time-slice quantum.	Semantics behind Win32PrioritySeparation changed again! Choose either Professional's short time slice interval or Server's very long interval.
Queued Spin Locks enhance SMP scalability	Queued spin locks reduce internal processor bus contention because threads do not have to execute a busy wait.
Network Monitor driver replaces Network Monitor Agent	The Network Monitor Agent placed the NIC in promiscuous mode in order to capture packets for performance analysis. The new Network Monitor driver looks only at packets processed by the networking stack.
Integrated support for Terminal Server Edition (TSE)	WinFrame was developed independently by Citrix for Version 3.51. After purchasing the rights from Citrix for version 4.0, TSE was integrated on top of existing NT 4.0 service packs. Windows 2000 Terminal Server adds a new Session object. The User object in NT 4.0 TSE is dropped to maintain consistency.
Added/changed between Windows 2000 and Windows XP	
64-bit Windows	16 TB virtual address space.
Intel SpeedStep measurement support	Since processor MHz varies based on power source, processor time is accumulated in separate buckets.
Process Heap Counters	Set DisplayHeapPerfObject to enable.
Volume Snapshot service	Filesystem support for cache flush and hold writes.
Faster boot and application launch	Uses Logical Disk prefetching.

Writing a book on Windows 2000 performance is an interesting challenge. Many of the popular computer books featured at your local bookstore promise easy answers. There is the *Computers for Dummies* series, the *Teach Yourself Windows 2000 in 30 Days* style book, the bookshelf on Windows 2000 Server Administration that looks like it was produced and sold by the pound, and the one that promises that if you follow its expert recommendations you will never again have a problem. We do not believe that giving simple solutions is the most effective way to communicate ideas and issues relating to computer performance. We expect that readers of this book will likely find themselves in difficult situations that have no direct precedent. In those situations, you will have to fall back on the insight and knowledge of basic principles that we describe in this book.

Although we of course dispense friendly advice from time to time, we concentrate instead on providing the information and the conceptual framework designed to help you become your own Windows 2000 performance expert.

Tools of the Trade

Understanding the tools of the performance analyst's trade is essential for approaching matters of Windows 2000 performance. Rather than focus merely on tools and how they work, we chose to emphasize the use of analytic techniques to diagnose and solve performance problems. We stress an empirical approach, making observations of real systems under stress. If you are a newcomer to the Microsoft operating system but understand how Unix, Linux, Solaris, OpenVMS, MVS, or another full-featured OS works, you will find much that is familiar here. Moreover, despite breathtaking changes in computer architecture, many of the methods and techniques used to solve earlier performance problems can still be applied successfully today. This is a comforting thought as we survey the complex computing environments, a jumbled mass of hardware and software alternatives, that we are called upon to assess, configure, and manage today. Measurement methodology, workload characterization, benchmarking, decomposition techniques, and analytic queuing models remain as effective today as they were for the pioneering individuals who first applied these methods to problems in computer performance analysis.

Computer performance evaluation is significant because it is very closely associated with the productivity of the human users of computerized systems. Efficiency is the principal rationale for computer-based automation. Whenever productivity is a central factor in decisions regarding the application of computer technology to automate complex and repetitive processes, performance considerations loom large. These concerns were present at the dawn of computing and remain very important today. Even as computing technology improves at an unprecedented rate, the fact that our *expectations* of this technology grow at an even *faster* rate assures that performance considerations will continue to be important in the future.

In computer performance, productivity is often tangled up with cost. Unfortunately, the relationship between performance and cost is usually neither simple nor straightforward. Generally, more expensive equipment has better performance, but there are many exceptions. Frequently, equipment will perform well with some workloads but not others. In most buying decisions, it is important to understand the performance characteristics of the hardware, the performance characteristics of the specific workload, and how they match up with each other.

In a sea of change, computer performance is one of the few areas of computing to remain relatively constant. As computing paradigms shift, specific areas of concern to performance analysts are subject to adjustment and realignment. Historically, the central server model of mainframe computing was the focus of much performance analysis in the 1960s and early 1970s. Understanding the performance of timesharing systems with virtual memory motivated basic research. Today, the focus has shifted to the performance of client/server applications, two- and three-tiered architectures, web-enabled transaction processing applications, internetworking, electronic mail and other groupware applications, databases, and distributed computing. Windows 2000 is at the center of many of these trends in desktop, networking, and enterprise computing, which is why Windows 2000 performance remains a critical concern.

Performance Measures

To be able to evaluate the performance of a computer system, you need a thorough understanding of the important metrics used to *measure* computer performance. Computers are machines designed to perform work, and we measure their capacity to perform the work, the rate at which they are currently performing it, and the time it takes to perform specific tasks. In the following sections, we look at some of the key ways to measure computer performance, introducing the most commonly used metrics: bandwidth, throughput, service time, utilization, and response time.

Bandwidth

Bandwidth measures the capacity of a link, bus, channel, interface, or device to transfer data. It is usually measured in either bits/second or bytes/second (there are eight bits in a data byte). For example, the bandwidth of a 10BaseT Ethernet connection is 10 Mb/sec, the bandwidth of a SCSI-2 disk is 20 MB/sec, and the bandwidth of the PCI Version 2.1 64-bit 66 MHz bus is 528 MB/sec.

Bandwidth usually refers to the maximum theoretical data transfer rate of a device under ideal conditions, and, therefore, it needs to be treated as an *upper bound* of performance. You can rarely measure the device actually performing at that rate, as there are many reasons why the theoretical bandwidth is not achievable in real life. For instance, when an application transfers a block of information to the disk, various layers of the operating system (OS) normally need to process the request first. Also, before a requested block of data can be transferred across a channel to the disk, some sort of handshaking protocol is required to set up the hardware operation. Finally, at the physical disk itself, your request is likely to be delayed during the time it takes to position the read/write actuator of the disk over the designated section on the rotating magnetic platter. The unavoidable *overhead* of operating system software, protocol message exchange, and disk positioning absorbs some of the available bandwidth so the application cannot use the full rated bandwidth of the disk for data transfer.

To provide another example, in networking people are accustomed to speaking about the bandwidth of a LAN connection to transfer data in millions of bits per second.

Consider an application that seeks to transfer an IP packet using the UDP protocol on an Ethernet network. The actual packet, when it reaches your network hardware, looks like Figure 1-1, with additional routing and control information added to the front of the message by various networking software layers.

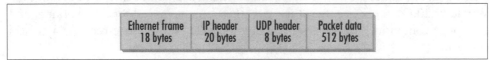

Figure 1-1. Typical Ethernet frame carrying a UDP packet

The datagram illustrated in Figure 1-1 is then passed to a network interface card (NIC) attached to the LAN. As the NIC generates the bit stream that it places on the LAN connection wire, it adds two error check bits for every eight data bits in the original payload. This 10/8 bit encoding scheme implemented at the Ethernet physical link layer reduces the effective bandwidth of the network connection proportionally. Assuming that nobody else is using the network when the packet arrives at the Ethernet interface, and that the full bandwidth is used for the transfer of this packet, we can calculate the actual bandwidth observed by the user for this particular data transfer using the following expression:

$$ObservedBandwidth = \frac{(Packet_{bytes} - Header_{bytes})}{Packet_{bytes}} \times RedundancyFactor \times MaxBandwidth$$

or:

$$\frac{(558 - 46)}{558} \times 8/10 \times 10 Mbps = 7.34 Mbps$$

The maximum effective bandwidth that can be observed by the user in this case is 7.34 Mb/sec. If there is congestion on the network, leading to *collisions* on an Ethernet network, the actual observed bandwidth might be substantially lower. As we will discuss in detail in Chapter 12, it is not unusual to expect the effective bandwidth of an Ethernet 10 Mb LAN to be less than 5 Mb/sec.

Throughput

Throughput measures the rate at which some sort of work is actually being done by the system; that is, the rate at which work is completed as observed by some application. Examples of throughput measurements include the number of reads per second from the filesystem, the number of instructions per second executed by the processor, the number of HTTP requests processed by a web server, and the number of transactions per second that can be processed by a database engine.

Throughput and bandwidth are very similar. Bandwidth is often construed as the *capacity* of the system to perform work, while throughput is the current observed rate at which that work is being performed. Understanding that the throughput of a particular system is starting to approach its effective capacity limits is something very important to know. It means, for example, that no amount of tweaking of esoteric tuning parameters is going to overcome the capacity constraint and allow the system to perform more work. The only effective solution that will allow you to perform more work is to upgrade the component of the system that is functioning at or near its effective bandwidth limits. Alternatively, you may be able to tune the application so that it runs more efficiently (i.e., utilizes less bandwidth) against the specific resource, or split the application somehow across multiple processing engines (processors, disks, network segments, etc.).

Service time

Service time measures how long it takes to process a specific request. Engineers also often speak of the length of time processing a request as the device's *latency*, another word for delay. Other related measures of service time are the *turnaround time* for requests, usually ascribed to longer running tasks, such as disk-to-tape backup runs, and the *round trip time*, an important measure of network latency because when a request is sent to a destination, the sender must wait for a reply.

There is no substitute for direct measurements of device or application service time. The service time of a filesystem request, for example, will vary based on whether the request is cached in memory or requires a physical disk operation. The service time will also vary depending on if it's a sequential read, a random read, or a write. The expected service time of the physical disk request also varies depending on the block size of the request. These workload dependencies demand that you measure disk service time directly, instead of relying on some idealized model of disk performance expectations.

The service time spent processing a web application request can be broken down into processing components: for example, time spent in the application script, time spent in the operating system, and time spent in database processing. For each one of these subcomponents, we might further decompose the application service time into time spent at various hardware components, the CPU, the disk, the network, etc. *Decomposition* is one of the fundamental techniques used in computer performance analysis to relate a workload to its various hardware and software processing components. To allow us to decompose application service times into their component parts, we must understand how busy various hardware components are and how specific workloads contribute to that utilization.

Utilization

Utilization measures the fraction of time that a device is busy servicing requests, usually reported as a percent busy. Utilization of a device varies between 0 and 1, where 0 is idle and 1 represents utilization of the full bandwidth of the device. It is customary to report that the CPU is 75% busy or the disk is 40% busy. It is not possible for a single device to ever appear more than 100% busy.

The utilization of a device is related directly to the observed throughput (or request rate) and service time as follows:

Utilization = Throughput × Service Time

This simple formula relating device utilization, throughput, and service time is known as the Utilization Law. The Utilization Law makes it possible to measure the throughput and service time of a disk, for example, and derive the disk utilization. For example, a disk that processes 20 input/output (I/O) operations per second with an average service time of 10 milliseconds is busy processing requests 20×0.010 every second, and is said to be 20% busy.

Alternatively, we might measure the utilization of a device using a sampling technique while also keeping track of throughput. Using the Utilization Law, we can then derive the service time of requests. Suppose we sample a communications bus 1000 times per second and find that it is busy during 200 of those measurements, or 20%. If we measure the number of bus requests at 2000 per second over the same sampling interval, we can derive the average service time of bus requests equal to $0.2 \div 2000 = .0001$ seconds or 100 microseconds (μsecs).

Monitoring the utilization of various hardware components is an important element of capacity planning. Measuring utilization is very useful in detecting system bottlenecks, which are essentially processing constraints due to limits on the effective throughput capacity of some overloaded device. If an application server is currently processing 60 transactions per second with a CPU utilization measured at 20%, the server apparently has considerable reserve capacity to process transactions at an even higher rate. On the other hand, a server processing 60 transactions per second running at a CPU utilization of 98% is operating at or near its maximum capacity.

Unfortunately, computer capacity planning is not as easy as projecting that the server running at 20% busy processing 60 transactions per second is capable of processing 300 transactions per second. You would not need to read a big, fat book like this one if that were all it took. Because transactions use other resources besides the CPU, one of those other resources might reach its effective capacity limits long before the CPU becomes saturated. We designate the component functioning as the constraining factor on throughput as the *bottlenecked device*. Unfortunately, it is not always easy to identify the bottlenecked device in a complex, interrelated computer system or network of computer systems.

It is safe to assume that devices observed operating at or near their 100% utilization limits are bottlenecks, although things are not always that simple. For one thing, 100% is not necessarily the target threshold for all devices. The effective capacity of an Ethernet network normally decreases when the utilization of the network exceeds 40–50%. Ethernet LANs use a shared link, and packets intended for different stations on the LAN can *collide* with one another, causing delays. Because of the way Ethernet works, once line utilization exceeds 40–50%, collisions start to erode the effective capacity of the link. We will talk about this phenomenon in much more detail in Chapter 11.

Response time

As the utilization of shared components increases, processing delays are encountered more frequently. When the network is heavily utilized and Ethernet collisions occur, for example, NICs are forced to retransmit packets. As a result, the service time of individual network requests increases. The fact that increasing the rate of requests often leads to processing delays at busy shared components is crucial. It means that as we increase the load on our server from 60 transactions per second and bottlenecks in the configuration start to appear, the overall response time associated with processing requests will not hold steady. Not only will the response time for requests increase as utilization increases, it is likely that response time will increase in a *nonlinear* relationship to utilization. In other words, as the utilization of a device increases slightly from 80% to 90% busy, we might observe that the response time of requests doubles, for example.

Response time, then, encompasses both the service time at the device processing the request and any other delays encountered waiting for processing. Formally, response time is defined as:

> *Response time = service time + queue time*

where queue time represents the amount of time a request waits for service. In general, at low levels of utilization, there is minimal queuing, which allows device service time to dictate response time. As utilization increases, however, queue time increases nonlinearly and, soon, begins to dominate response time.

Queues are essentially data structures where requests for service are parked until they can be serviced. Examples of queues abound in Windows 2000, and measures showing the queue length or the amount of time requests wait in the queue for processing are some of the most important indicators of performance bottlenecks discussed here. The Windows 2000 queues that will be discussed in this book include the operating system's thread scheduling queue, the logical and physical disk queues, the file server request queue, and the queue of Active Server Pages (ASP) web server script requests. Using a simple equation known as Little's Law, which is discussed later, we will also show how the rate of requests, the response time, and the queue length are related. This relationship, for example, allows us to calculate average response times for ASP requests even though Windows 2000 does not measure the response time of this application directly.

In performance monitoring, we try to identify devices with high utilizations that lead to long queues where requests are delayed. These devices are bottlenecks throttling system performance. Intuitively, what can be done about bottlenecks once you have discovered one? Several forms of medicine can be prescribed:

- Upgrade to a faster device
- Spread the workload across multiple devices
- Reduce the load on the device by tuning the application
- Change scheduling parameters to favor cherished workloads

These are hardly mutually exclusive alternatives. Depending on the situation, you may wish to try more than one of them. Common sense dictates which alternative you should try first. Which change will have the greatest impact on performance? Which configuration change is the least disruptive? Which is the easiest to implement? Which is possible to back out of in case it makes matters worse? Which involves the least additional cost? Sometimes, the choices are fairly obvious, but often these are not easy questions to answer.

One complication is that there is no simple relationship between response time and device utilization. In most cases it is safe to assume the underlying relationship is nonlinear. A peer-to-peer Ethernet LAN experiencing collisions, for example, leads to sharp increases in both network latency and utilization. A Windows 2000 multiprocessor implementing priority queuing with preemptive scheduling at the processor leads to a categorically different relationship between response time and utilization, where low-priority threads are subject to a condition called *starvation*. A SCSI disk that supports tagged command queuing can yield higher throughput with lower service times at *higher* request rates. In later chapters, we explore in much more detail the performance characteristics of the scheduling algorithms that these hardware devices use, each of which leads to a fundamentally different relationship between utilization and response time.

This nonlinear relationship between utilization and response time often serves as the effective capacity constraint on system performance. Just as customers encountering long lines at a fast food restaurant are tempted to visit the fast food chain across the way when delays are palpable, customers using an Internet connection to access their bank accounts might be tempted to switch to a different financial institution if it takes too long to process their requests. Consequently, understanding the relationship between response time and utilization is one of the most critical areas of computer performance evaluation. It is a topic we will return to again and again in the course of this book.

Response time measurements are also important for another reason. For example, the response time for a web server is the amount of time it takes from the instant that a client selects a hyperlink to the time that the requested page is returned and displayed on her display monitor. Because it reflects the user's perspective, the overall response time is the performance measure of greatest interest to the users of a computer system. It is axiomatic that long delays cause user dissatisfaction with the computer systems they are using, although this is usually not a straightforward relationship either. Human factors research, for instance, indicates that users may be more bothered by unexpected delays than by consistently long response times that they have become resigned to.

Optimizing Performance

Intuitively, it may seem that proper configuration and tuning of any computer system or network should attempt to maximize throughput *and* minimize response time simultaneously. In practice, that is often not possible. For example, system administrators that try to optimize throughput are apt to drive up response time to unacceptable levels as a result. Alternatively, minimizing response time by stockpiling only the fastest and most expensive equipment and then keeping utilization low in order to minimize queuing delays is not very cost-effective. In practice, skilled performance analysts attempt to achieve a balance between these often conflicting objectives:

- There is relatively high throughput leading to the cost-effective use of the hardware.
- Queuing delays are minimal, so users are satisfied with performance levels.
- System performance is relatively stable, consistent, and predictable.

To explain that these objectives are not so easy to reconcile, it may help to take an introductory look at queuing theory, a branch of operations research frequently applied to the analysis of computer systems performance.

Single-server model

Figure 1-2 shows the conventional representation of a queuing system, with customer requests arriving at a server with a simple queue. These are the basic elements of a queuing system: customers, servers, and a queue. Figure 1-2 shows a single server, but multiple-server models are certainly possible.

Figure 1-2. Simple model of a queuing system showing customer requests arriving at a single server

If the server is idle, customer requests arriving at the server are processed immediately. On the other hand, if the server is already busy, then the request is queued. If multiple requests are waiting in the server queue, the *queuing discipline* determines the order in which queued requests are serviced. The simplest and fairest way to order the queue is to service requests in the order in which they arrive. This is also called FIFO (First In, First Out) or sometimes First Come, First Served (FCFS). There are many other ways that a queue of requests can be ordered, including by priority or by the speed with which they can be processed.

Modeling assumptions

Figure 1-3 shows a simple queue annotated with symbols that represent a few of the more common parameters that define its behavior. There are a large number of parameters that can be used to describe the behavior of this simple queue, and we only look at a couple of the more basic and commonly used ones. *Response time* (W) represents the total amount of time a customer request spends in the queuing system, including both *service time* (W_s) at the device and *wait time* (W_q) in the queue. By convention, the Greek letter λ (lambda) is used to specify the *arrival rate* or frequency of requests to the server. Think of the arrival rate as an activity rate such as the rate at which HTTP GET requests arrive at a web server, I/O requests are sent to a disk, or packets are sent to a NIC card. Larger values of λ indicate that a more intense workload is applied to the system, whereas smaller values indicate a light load. Another Greek letter, μ, is used to represent the rate at which the server can process requests. The output from the server is either λ or μ, whichever is less, because it is certainly possible for requests to arrive at a server faster than they can processed.

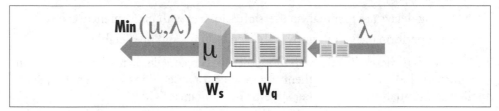

Figure 1-3. A queuing model with its parameters

Ideally, we hope that the arrival rate is lower than the service rate of the server, so that the server can keep up with the rate of customer requests. In that case, the arrival rate is equal to the completion rate, an important equilibrium assumption that allows us to consider models that are mathematically tractable (i.e., solvable). If the arrival rate λ is greater than the server capacity μ, then requests begin backing up in the queue. Mathematically, arrivals are drawn from an infinite population so that when $\lambda > \mu$, the queue length and the wait time (W_q) at the server grow infinitely large. Those of us who have tried to retrieve a service pack from a Microsoft web server immediately after its release know this situation and its impact on performance. Unfortunately, it is not possible to solve a queuing model with $\lambda > \mu$, although mathematicians have developed *heavy traffic approximations* to deal with this familiar case.

In real-world situations, there are limits on the population of customers. The population of customers in most realistic scenarios involving computer or network performance is limited by the number of stations on a LAN, the number of file server connections, the number of TCP connections a web server can support, or the number of concurrent open files on a disk. Even in the worst bottlenecked situation, the queue depth can only grow to some predetermined limit. When enough customer requests are bogged down in queuing delays, in real systems, the arrival rate for new customer requests becomes constrained. Customer requests that are backed up in the system choke off the rate at which new requests are generated.

The purpose of this rather technical discussion is twofold. First, it is necessary to make an unrealistic assumption about arrivals being drawn from an infinite population to generate readily solvable models. Queuing models break down when $\lambda \to \mu$, which is another way of saying they break down near 100% utilization of some server component. Second, you should not confuse a queuing model result that shows a nearly infinite queue length with reality. In real systems there are practical limits on queue depth. In the remainder of our discussion here, we will assume that $\lambda < \mu$. Whenever the arrival rate of customer requests is equal to the completion rate, this can be viewed as an *equilibrium assumption*. Please keep in mind that the following results are invalid if the equilibrium assumption does not hold; in other words, if the arrival rate of requests is greater than the completion rate ($\lambda > \mu$ over some measurement interval) simple queuing models do not work.

Little's Law

A fundamental result in queuing theory known as Little's Law relates response time and utilization. In its simplest form, Little's Law expresses an equivalence relation between response time W, arrival rate λ, and the number of customer requests in the system Q (also known as the *queue length*):

$$Q = \lambda \times W$$

Note that in this context the queue length Q refers both to customer requests in service (Q_s) and waiting in a queue (Q_q) for processing. In later chapters we will have several opportunities to take advantage of Little's Law to estimate response time of applications where only the arrival rate and queue length are known. Just for the record, Little's Law is a very general result that applies to a large class of queuing models. While it does allow us to estimate response time in a situation where we can measure the arrival rate and the queue length, Little's Law itself provides no insight into how response time is broken down into service time and queue time delays.

Little's Law is an important enough result that it is probably worth showing how to derive it. As mentioned, Little's Law is a very general result in queuing theory—only the equilibrium assumption is required to prove it. Figure 1-4 shows some measurements that were made at disk at discrete intervals shown on the X axis. The Y axis indicates the number of disk requests during the interval. Our observation of the disk is delimited by the two arrows between the start time and the stop time. When we started monitoring the disk, it was idle. Then, whenever an arrival occurred at a certain time, we incremented the arrivals counter. That variable is plotted using the thick line. Whenever a request completed service at the disk, we incremented the completions variable. The completions are plotted using the thin line.

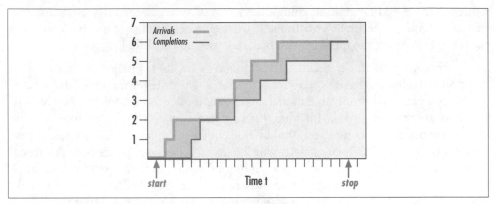

Figure 1-4. A graph illustrating the derivation of Little's Law

The difference between the arrival and completion lines is the number of requests at the disk at that moment in time. For example, at the third tick-mark on the X axis to the right of the start arrow, there are two requests at the disk, since the arrival line is at 2 and the completion line is at 0. When the two lines coincide, it means that the system is idle at the time, since the number of arrivals is equal to the number of departures.

To calculate the average number of requests in the system during our measurement interval, we need to sum the area of the rectangles formed by the arrival and completion lines and divide by the measurement interval. Let's define the more intuitive term "accumulated time in the system" for the sum of the area of rectangles between the arrival and completion lines, and denote it by the variable P. Then we can express the average number of requests at the disk, N, using the expression:

$$N = \frac{P}{T}$$

We can also calculate the average response time, R, that a request spends in the system ($W_s + W_q$) by the following expression:

$$R = \frac{P}{C}$$

where C is the completion rate (and $C = \lambda$, from the equilibrium assumption). This merely says that the overall time that requests spent at the disk (including queue time) was P, and during that time there were C completions. So, on average, each request spent P/C units of time in the system.

Now, all we need to do is combine these two equations to get the magical Little's Law:

$$N = \frac{P}{T} = \frac{C}{T} \times \frac{P}{C} = \lambda \times R$$

Little's Law says that the average number of requests in the system is equal to the product of the rate at which the system is processing the requests (with $C = \lambda$, from the equilibrium assumption) times the average amount of time that a request spends in the system.

To make sure that this new and important law makes sense, let's apply it to our disk example. Suppose we collected some measurements on our system and found that it can process 200 read requests per second. The Windows 2000 System Monitor also told us that the average response time per request was 20 ms (milliseconds) or 0.02 seconds. If we apply Little's Law, it tells us that the average number of requests at the disk, either in the queue or actually in processing, is 200 × 0.02, which equals 4. This is how Windows 2000 derives the Physical Disk Avg. Disk Queue Length and Logical Disk Avg. Disk Queue Length counters. More on that topic in Chapter 8.

 The explanation and derivation we have provided for Little's Law is very intuitive and easy to understand, but it is not 100% accurate. A more formal and mathematically correct proof is beyond the scope of this book. We followed the development of Little's Law and notation used by a classic book on queuing networks by Lazowska, Zahorjan, Graham, and Sevcik called *Quantitative System Performance: Computer System Analysis Using Queuing Network Models*. This is a very readable book that we highly recommend if you have any interest in analytic modeling. Regardless of your interest in mathematical accuracy, though, you should become familiar with Little's Law. There are occasions in this book where we use Little's Law to either verify or improve upon some of the counters that are made available in Windows 2000 through the System Monitor. Even if you forget everything else we say here about analytic modeling, don't forget the formula for Little's Law.

M/M/1

For a simple class of queuing models, the mathematics to solve them is also quite simple. A simple case is where the arrival rate and service time are randomly distributed around the average value. The standard notation for this class of model is M/M/1 (for the single-server case) and M/M/n (for multiple servers). M/M/1 models are useful because they are easy to compute—not necessarily because they model reality precisely. We can derive response time for an M/M/1 or M/M/n model with FIFO queuing if the arrival rate and service time are known using the following simple formula:

$$W_q = \frac{W_s \times u}{1 - u}$$

where u is the *utilization* of the server, W_q is the queue time, W_s is the service time, and $W_q + W_s = W$. As long as we remember that this model breaks down as utilization approaches 100%, we can use it with a fair degree of confidence.

Figure 1-5 shows a typical application of this formula for W_s = 10 ms, demonstrating that the relationship between the queue time W_q and utilization is nonlinear. Up to a point, queue time increases gradually as utilization increases, and then each small incremental increase in utilization causes a sharp increase in response time. Notice that there is an inflection point or "knee" in the curve where this nonlinear relationship becomes marked. (If you want an empirical description of the knee in the curve, find the inflection point on the curve where the slope = 1.) Notice also that as the utilization u → 1, the denominator term 1 − u → 0 where W_q is undefined. This accounts for the steep rise in the right-hand portion of the curve as u → 1.

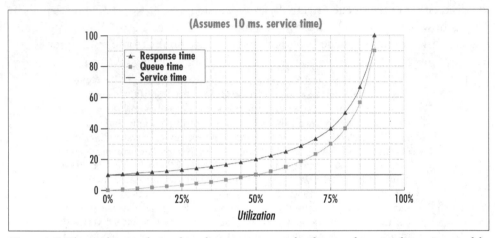

Figure 1-5. The nonlinear relationship of response time and utilization for a simple queuing model

The graph in Figure 1-5 illustrates the various reasons why it is so hard to optimize for both maximum throughput and minimal queue time delays:

- As we push a computer system toward its maximum possible throughput, we also force response time to increase rapidly.

- Reaching for maximum throughput also jeopardizes stability. Near the maximum throughput levels, slight fluctuations in the workload cause disproportionately large changes in the amount of queue time delay that transactions experience.

- Maintaining the stability of application response time requires low utilization levels, which may not be cost-effective.

Figure 1-5 strongly suggests that the three objectives we set earlier for performance tuning and optimization are not easily reconcilable, which certainly makes for interesting work. Having an impossible job to perform at least provides for built-in job security.

For the sake of a concrete example, let us return to our example of the wait queue for a disk. As in Figure 1-5, let's assume that the average service time W_s at the disk is

10 ms. When requests arrive and the disk is free, requests can be processed at a maximum rate of $1/W_s$ ($1 \div 0.010$) or 100 requests per second. That is the capacity of the disk. To maximize throughput, we should keep the disk constantly busy so that it can reach its maximum capacity and achieve throughput of 100 requests/sec. But to minimize response time, the queue should always be kept empty so that the total amount of time it takes to service a request is as close to 10 milliseconds as possible.

If we *could* control the arrival of customer requests (perhaps through scheduling) and could time each request so that one arrived every W_s seconds (once every 10 ms), we would improve performance. When requests are paced to arrive regularly every 10 milliseconds, the disk queue is always empty and the request can be processed immediately. This succeeds in making the disk 100% busy, attaining its maximum potential throughput of $1/W_s$ requests per second. With perfect scheduling and perfectly uniform service times for requests, we can achieve 100% utilization of the disk with no queue time delays.

In reality, we have little or no control over when I/O requests arrive at the disk in a typical computer system. In a typical system, there are periods when the server is idle and others when requests arrive in bunches. Moreover, some requests are for large amounts of data located in a distant spot on the disk, while others are for small amounts of data located near the current disk actuator. In the language of queuing theory, neither the *arrival rate distribution* of customer requests or the *service time distribution* is uniform. This lack of uniformity causes some requests to queue, with the further result that as the throughput starts to approach the maximum possible level, significant queuing delays occur. As the utilization of the server increases, the response time for customer requests increases significantly during periods of congestion, as illustrated by the behavior of the simple M/M/1 queuing model in Figure 1-5.*

Queuing Models in Theory and Practice

This brief mathematical foray is intended to illustrate the idea that attempting to optimize throughput while at the same time minimizing response is inherently difficult, if not downright impossible. It also suggests that any tuning effort that makes the arrival rate or service time of customer requests more uniform is liable to be productive. It is no coincidence that this happens to be the goal of many popular optimization techniques. It further suggests that a good approach to computer performance

---

* The simple M/M/1 model we discuss here was chosen because it is simple, not because it is necessarily representative of real behavior on live computer systems. There are many other kinds of queuing models that reflect arrival rate and service time distributions different from the simple M/M/1 assumptions. However, although M/M/1 may not be realistic, it is easy to calculate. This contrasts with G/G/1, which uses a *general* arrival rate and service time distribution, i.e., any kind of statistical distribution: bimodal, symptomatic, etc. No general solution to a G/G/1 model is feasible, so computer modelers are often willing to compromise reality for solvability.

tuning and optimization should stress *analysis*, rather than simply dispensing advice about what tuning adjustments to make when problems occur.

We believe that the first thing you should do whenever you encounter a performance problem is to *measure* the system experiencing the problem and try to understand what is going on. Computer performance evaluation begins with systematic empirical observations of the systems at hand.

In seeking to understand the root cause of many performance problems, we rely on a mathematical approach to the analysis of computer systems performance that draws heavily on insights garnered from queuing theory. Ever notice how construction blocking one lane of a three-lane highway causes severe traffic congestion during rush hour? We may notice a similar phenomenon on the computer systems we are responsible for when a single component becomes bottlenecked and delays at this component cascade into a problem of major proportions. Network performance analysts use the descriptive term *storm* to characterize the chain reaction that sometimes results when a tiny aberration becomes a big problem. Long before chaos theory, it was found that queuing models of computer performance can accurately depict this sort of behavior mathematically. Little's Law predicts that as utilization of a resource increases linearly, response time increases exponentially. This fundamental nonlinear relationship that was illustrated in Figure 1-5 means that quite small changes in the workload can result in extreme changes in performance indicators, especially as important resources start to become bottlenecks.

This is exactly the sort of behavior you can expect to see in the computer systems you are responsible for. Most computer systems do not degrade gradually. Queuing theory is a useful tool in computer performance evaluation because it is a branch of mathematics that models systems performance realistically. The painful reality we face is that performance of the systems we are responsible for is acceptable day after day, until quite suddenly it goes to hell in a handbasket. This abrupt change in operating conditions often begets an atmosphere of crisis. The typical knee-jerk reaction is to scramble to identify the thing that changed and precipitated the emergency. Sometimes it is possible to identify what caused the performance degradation, but more often it is not so simple.

With insights from queuing theory, we learn that it may not be a major change in circumstances that causes a major disruption in current performance levels. In fact, the change can be quite small and gradual and still produce a dramatic result. This is an important perspective to have the next time you are called upon to diagnose a Windows 2000 performance problem. Perhaps the only thing that changed is that a component on the system has reached a high enough level of utilization where slight variations in the workload provoke drastic changes in behavior.

A full exposition of queuing theory and its applications to computer performance evaluation is well beyond the scope of this book. Readers interested in pursuing the subject might want to look at Daniel Mensace's *Capacity Planning and Performance*

Modeling: From Mainframes to Client/Server Systems; Raj Jain's encyclopedic *The Art of Computer Systems Performance Analysis: Techniques for Experimental Design, Measurement, Simulation, and Modeling;* or Arnold Allen's very readable textbook on *Probability, Statistics, and Queuing Theory With Computer Science Applications.*

Exploratory Data Analysis

Performance tuning presupposes some form of computer measurement. Understanding what is measured, how measurements are gathered, and how to interpret them is another crucial area of computer performance evaluation. You cannot manage what you cannot measure, but fortunately, measurement is pervasive. Many hardware and software components support measurement interfaces. In fact, because of the quantity of computer measurement data that is available, it is often necessary to subject computer usage to some form of statistical analysis. This certainly holds true on Windows 2000, which can provide large amounts of measurement data. Sifting through all these measurements demands an understanding of a statistical approach known as *exploratory data analysis*, rather than the more familiar brand of statistics that uses probability theory to test the likelihood that a hypothesis is true or false. John Tukey's classic textbook entitled *Exploratory Data Analysis* (currently out of print) or *Understanding Robust and Exploratory Data Analysis* by Hoaglin, Mosteller, and Tukey provides a very insightful introduction to using statistics in this fashion.

Many of the case studies described in this book apply the techniques of exploratory data analysis to understanding Windows 2000 computer performance. Rather than explore the copious performance data available on a typical Windows 2000 platform at random, however, our search is informed by the workings of computer hardware and operating systems in general, and of Windows 2000, Intel processor hardware, SCSI disks, and network interfaces in particular.

Because graphical displays of information are so important to this process, aspects of what is known as *scientific visualization* are also relevant. (It is always gratifying when there is an important-sounding name for what you are doing!) Edward Tufte's absorbing books on scientific visualization, including *Visual Explanations* and *The Visual Display of Quantitative Information*, are an inspiration.* In many place in this book, we will illustrate the discussion with exploratory data analysis techniques. In particular, we will look for key relationships between important measurement variables. Those illustrations rely heavily on visual explanations of charts and graphs to explore key correlations and associations. It is a technique we recommend highly.

In computer performance analysis, measurements, models, and statistics remain the tools of the trade. Knowing what measurements exist, how they are taken, and how they should be interpreted is a critical element of the analysis of computer systems

---

* It is no surprise that Professor Tufte is extending Tukey's legacy of the exploratory data analysis approach, as Tukey is a formative influence on his work.

performance. We will address that topic in detail in Chapter 2, so that you can gain a firm grasp of the measurement data available in Windows 2000, how it is obtained, and how it can be interpreted.

Performance and Productivity

As mentioned at the outset, there is a very important correlation between computer performance and productivity, and this provides a strong economic underpinning to the practice of performance management. Today, it is well established that good performance is an important element of human-computer interface design. (See Ben Schneiderman's *Designing the User Interface: Strategies for Effective Human-Computer Interaction*.) We have to explore a little further what it means to have "good" performance, but systems that provide fast, consistent response time are generally more acceptable to the people who use them. Systems with severe performance problems are often rejected outright by their users and fail. This leads to costly delays, expensive rewrites, and loss of productivity.

The Transaction Model

As computer performance analysts, we are interested in finding out what it takes to turn "bad" performance into "good" performance. Generally, the analysis focuses on two flavors of computer measurements. The first type of measurement data describes what is going on with the hardware, operating systems software, and application software that is running. These measurements reflect both activity rates and the utilization of key hardware components: how busy the processor, the disks, and the network are. Windows 2000 provides a substantial amount of performance data in this area: quantitative information on how busy different hardware components are, what processes are running, how much memory they are using, etc.

The second type of measurement data measures the capacity of the computer to do productive work. As discussed earlier in this chapter, most common measures of productivity we have seen are *throughput* (usually measured in transactions per second) and *response time*. A measure of throughput describes the quantity of work performed, while response time measures how long it takes to complete the task. When users of your network complain about bad performance, you need a way to quantify what "bad" is. You need application response time measurements from the standpoint of the end user. Unfortunately, Windows 2000 is not very strong in this key area of measurement.

To measure the capacity of the computer to do productive work, we need to:

- Characterize end user interactions in identifiable units of work
- Measure and report how long it takes for the computer to process these units of work

Then, computer performance analysts try to determine why these processes are running slowly, and figure out how to speed things up. Sounds pretty simple, doesn't it?

There is an implicit assumption that computer processing can be broken into identifiable units for analysis when we talk about the performance and tuning of computer processing workloads in this fashion. Conceptually, we are using what is known as the *transaction model*. Transactions are *atomic* units of processing—you cannot break a transaction down into anything smaller without losing whatever it is that makes it a transaction. A transaction might involve executing SQL statements to query a database, applying a special effect in an image-processing program, scrolling a word-processing document from its beginning to the point where you left off editing, or recalculating a column of figures in a spreadsheet. These are all recognizable units of processing with a definite beginning and end. A transaction corresponds to some specific action that a user takes to initiate work. This correspondence is the critical link between the transaction response time and user productivity.

Let's look at some of the ways in which the transaction model is relevant to computer performance analysis. The performance of different configurations can be calibrated accurately by running any of the recognized industry benchmark streams that measure computer and network throughput, usually in transactions per second (or TPS). TPS is a common measure of throughput that is accepted across the industry. It is also possible to relate computer throughput to end user productivity, namely, how long it takes an individual to accomplish some computer-assisted task. Once we know how long it takes to process transactions, it may then be possible to determine what components are taking the most time (*decomposition*), why processing takes so long (*bottleneck analysis*), and what can be done to improve it (prescriptive *tuning*). These three analysis techniques are of fundamental importance, and we will revisit them many times in this book.

The transaction model also lends itself to the mathematical techniques associated with queuing theory. The two main elements of a queuing system are:

- A set of transaction-oriented workloads
- Networks of servers and queues

Many types of queuing systems can be analyzed mathematically if the arrival rate of transactions and their service demands are known. The theoretical model referred to back in Figure 1-3, for example, is based on very simple assumptions about the average rate in which new transactions are generated and the processing demands of these transactions.

Unfortunately, it is not always easy to group processing activities into distinct transactions in Windows 2000. An application running in the foreground (with the active title bar) processes mouse moves and keyboard events on a more or less continuous basis. It is hard to tell where a particular transaction begins or ends under these circumstances. Where work is not easily grouped into transactions, Windows 2000 does not measure and report transaction response time. In other cases, defining the boundaries of transactions is less problematic. In a client/server model, the point where the client application accesses a database on the server could easily mark the beginning of a transaction. When the server application finishes all its processing on behalf of the client request and returns control to the client application, the transaction is considered complete. An update transaction will issue a Commit command when it is finished processing, an unambiguous marker of the end of the transaction. If you are running client/server applications based on MS Exchange, MS SQL Server, or the Microsoft Transaction Server, it is possible to organize workloads into transaction units. It is disappointing that while these subsystems keep some transaction-oriented performance statistics, they generally do not report response time systematically.

Experienced performance analysts sorely miss having adequate transaction response time data to work with in Windows 2000. Without it, it is not possible to relate all the measurements about what is going on inside the computer to the work that people are doing with the computer. This complicates performance analysis, and it means that some of the best, proven methods cannot easily be applied to Windows 2000.

Designing for Performance

From the standpoint of an application developer, it is important to understand how to deliver software that performs well. A common fallacy is to measure system response time and equate it to productivity. While the two are related, they are far from the same thing. Consider a computer reservation system used by a trained operator. One implementation might break the task of making a reservation down into several subtasks, each of which is implemented to execute quickly. However, because the interaction with the computer requires a series of transactions, the actual process of making a reservation is long and complex. A second implementation might collapse all the user interactions into a single, more complicated transaction. It might take longer to process the bulkier transaction than several smaller transactions combined. According to objective measures of transaction response time, the first system is the better one. It is also the system people are apt to like better because it provides fast, consistent response. It just *feels* better.

Productivity is another matter. In this instance, productivity is measured as the number of reservations per day a skilled operator can perform. Under the second system, users may actually be able to perform more work, as measured objectively in reservations made per day per operator. The second system may also be cheaper to operate than the first because it does not process quite so many transactions, and it may even be able to support a heavier reservation load. Because workers are more productive using the second system, the company does not need quite so many operators and can be more profitable. User satisfaction with the second system, however, is probably somewhat lower than with the first alternative, presuming that it is possible to reduce these subjective feelings to an objective, quantitative scale.

Which system do you think your company will want to use? Which system do you think you would like to use? It is important to understand that any large-scale application system that you design and deliver is subject to very restrictive cost and performance constraints. All parties to the application development process, including the end user, must understand what these limitations are and accept them as *reasonable*.

If satisfaction is in the eye of the beholder, as a software developer you should look for ways to improve the performance of the second system to make it more acceptable. Perhaps procuring more expensive hardware can be justified. Alternately, there may be things that can be done to the design of the second system to make it more user-friendly without actually speeding it up. The psychological aspects of human-computer interaction are outside the scope of the book, but this is an area that experienced software designers should know something about. There are many simple design techniques and tricks that can make systems more palatable even when they are not lightning-fast.

Performance Management

Performance management remains one of the key system management disciplines performed by systems professionals of all stripes. For instance, as a LAN administrator, you may be responsible for setting up the hardware platform and operating system environment used to run the applications that your company needs to run its business. The performance aspects of this job include monitoring the hardware and software and making configuration changes and tuning adjustments to make things run better. To support capacity planning and budgeting, you may be called upon to provide measurement data to cost-justify hardware expenditures and as input to the capacity planning process that is designed to ensure that adequate resources continue to be available.

In a capacity planning role, you may be responsible for assuring that adequate resources are available over the long term. This may mean monitoring the current growth, factoring in new application projects, and trying to plan the hardware configuration that can supply adequate performance. This inevitably means that you will encounter your company's budget for new equipment purchases. You will be called upon to explain your recommendations in straightforward, nontechnical language. Perhaps your analysis will show that more hardware is needed to meet the performance objectives or else workers interacting with the system will not be fully productive. This is part of performance management, too.

Our approach to these and other performance management tasks is decidedly empirical. Remember, you cannot manage what you cannot measure. We recommend that you gather data from real systems in operation, analyze it, and make decisions based on that analysis. Those decisions may range from deciding how to configure a workstation running Windows 2000 Professional for optimal performance for a graphics-intensive application, to how to configure multiple Windows 2000 servers to support

Tricks of the Trade

Experienced application developers use many tricks to make long waits more acceptable to their users. For example, a status bar that provides feedback to a user is a friendlier way to process a long-running transaction than leaving the user in the dark about how long it will take. Status bars that estimate how long something like a file transfer will take are effective, but only if the prediction is halfway in the ballpark. The best technique is to make an estimate of the whole job based on the rate at which your program completes the first part of it, and update the estimate based on current activity rates.

While inexperienced users appreciate an application wizard that takes them through a new process step by step, experienced users are likely to find the extra steps tedious and annoying. Typically, you need to satisfy both groups. New users want to learn an application easily, without having to read the manual, and become productive quickly. Experienced users want the ability to execute complex, repetitive tasks quickly and easily. For inexperienced users, one approach is to provide wizards that walk them through a new task step by step. Meanwhile, experienced users need shortcuts like the macro-level ability to combine several commands into a new one, limiting the amount of user interaction required to perform command sequences that are executed repetitively.

Another programming trick is useful when there is a long processing delay, for example, when you are opening a file or retrieving a large number of records from a database. This trick is to display partial results as soon as you can while continuing with the long-running process in the background. This is a little trickier to program because you need to spawn a separate thread to process the long-running task in the background, and learn how to signal across threads running asynchronously. Inside the worker thread, be sure to communicate back to the main thread when you have accumulated enough data to display the first screen. Then, signal the main thread when the retrieval process has completed and terminate the worker thread if it is no longer needed. This trick exploits the difference between computer time and human interaction time to make your application look more responsive than it actually is.

distributed database or messaging applications. For systems under development, you may need to discuss hardware and software infrastructure alternatives with the programmers responsible for implementing the application. If you get an opportunity to influence the design of an important application under development, try to link decisions about design trade-offs to actual measurements of prototype code running under different conditions of stress. Before setting parameters and making tuning adjustments, review and analyze performance statistics from the system. Afterwards, verify that the changes you made are working by looking at similar measurement data.

Whatever the challenge, your approach should always be analytical. For example, before making a tuning adjustment, analyze the measurement data and develop a working hypothesis as to what the problem is and how to solve it. You will rely on a variety of analytical tools, mainly queuing models and statistical analysis. The analysis generates a working hypothesis, which is then tested against further observations. Does the adjustment you made improve the system's behavior in the way you expected? That is often convincing evidence that the working hypothesis you adopted was an appropriate one.

Rules of Thumb (ROTs)

The empirical approach we recommend contrasts with something we will call the Rule of Thumb approach. Rules of thumb (ROTs) are received wisdom passed down from professed experts to the masses. This sounds like a great approach since these self-appointed wizards appear to know much more about the sacred innards of Windows 2000 than you do. The problem with these pearls of wisdom is that they may not apply to your specific environment. We think you should find out how these great seers derived the rule being espoused, attempt to apply the same derivation to your environment, and determine for yourself if the rule is applicable. Quite possibly, after you have modified the rule to your specific environment, it may very well be relevant to your situation.

For example, our approach to evaluating whether or not to do a memory upgrade begins with the hypothesis that the amount of paging is related to an index of memory utilization we can calculate. The difference between a Windows 2000 server configured at 256 MB versus one configured at 512 MB might be a significant amount of money. If multiple Windows 2000 servers or workstations are involved, the dollars start to add up fast. The memory utilization index you need to calculate is the number of committed virtual memory bytes divided by the amount of hardware RAM installed. Look to find empirical evidence in the performance measurements that a relationship exists between the memory utilization index and paging activity. If this relationship does exist and you understand its behavior, you may be able to use it to estimate the benefits of a memory upgrade. This particular technique is discussed in greater detail in Chapter 6.

If we know that this relationship exists on many different systems, we might then distill the evidence into a general configuration rule. Without much further analysis, we might suggest that a good configuration rule of thumb is to provide at least 1 MB of RAM for every 2 MB of committed virtual memory. This is a very easy rule to apply because you can simply run the Task Manager application and access the Performance tab to determine the Commit Charge (K) total virtual memory peak (see Figure 1-6). Divide the Commit Charge (K) total by the Physical Memory (K) total field. If that ratio is 2 or more, it may be time to buy more memory for that machine. Remember, however, that your mileage may vary. Rather than just blindly applying this rule, we want you to understand how the rule was derived and be capable of adapting the method to your particular set of circumstances. We will discuss the empirical evidence used to derive this rule in Chapter 6, and try to explain how you can test to see whether this rule will work for you.

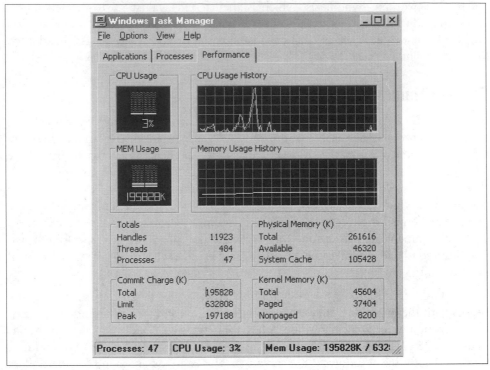

Figure 1-6. Task Manager Performance tab

Is Performance Tuning Obsolete?

Before proceeding further, there is a common notion that needs to be dispelled. This is the belief that performance considerations in the design and development of computer applications no longer matter because computing resources are so inexpensive. Advocates of this position concede that there *may* be a few instances where performance is still an important consideration today, but if you just wait a couple more years, these problems will be solved as the hardware keeps getting faster and cheaper.

We have heard this claim that "performance doesn't matter anymore" for at least 10 years, and we do not believe it is any truer today than it was a decade ago. First, though, we should admit that our perspective is warped because we are frequently the "outside expert" who is called in only during a crisis. Most people do not call the fire department until they have a fire. So we tend to see extreme situations where people are desperate for a solution and do not know where else to turn. Amazingly, many of these problems are very easy to diagnose and can often be solved right over the phone. On the other hand, some problems take weeks and months worth of effort to solve. And some of them, we are sorry to say, are never resolved to everyone's satisfaction. (There is a joke that no one ever said computer science was an *exact* science.)

Seeing only the more extreme cases tends to warp your perspective. However, we do see just as many of these problems today that we did ten years ago, so it does not seem reasonable to believe bigger and better hardware has solved all our performance problems. Computer performance is still a topic worthy of your consideration.

On the other hand, it is certainly true that the strides taken to improve the performance of hardware have been phenomenal. The PC that sits on our desktop today is a splendid piece of equipment. It costs considerably less money than you would have paid for a 640K PC/XT just 15 years ago. It has five hundred times more memory and about thousand times more disk space. It is lightning-fast at most tasks (although it is still painfully slow at others). Yes, hardware is improving rapidly, but it is important to realize that not all hardware advances at the same rate. For example, advances in disk performance have not been as rapid as instruction processing speeds. Moreover, even as the hardware gets cheaper and cheaper, there are always applications that demand even more resources than we have available.

In addition, computer performance continues to have a cost dimension to it that remains very significant. Many aspects of hardware design reflect cost/performance trade-offs, and it's important to understand what these are. A software developer still needs to understand how algorithms perform and especially how they scale as the problem space becomes larger or more users are added to the system. Finished designs for any nontrivial system are *always* compromises that aim for the best balance between performance and cost.

Bottleneck Analysis

To make the best planning decisions, a traditional approach is to try and understand hardware *speeds and feeds*—how fast different pieces of equipment are capable of running. This is much more difficult than it sounds. For example, it certainly seems like a SCSI disk attached to a 20 MB/second SCSI-2 adapter card should run much slower than one attached to an 80 MB/second UltraSCSI-3 adapter card. UltraSCSI-3 sounds as if should beat ol' SCSI-2 every time. But there may be little or no practical difference in the performance of the two configurations. (Perhaps the disk may only transfer data at 20 MB/second anyway, so the extra capacity of the UltraSCSI-3 bus is not being utilized.)

This example illustrates the principle that *a complex system will run only as fast as its slowest component*. Because there is both theory and extensive empirical data to back up this claim, we don't mind propagating this statement as a good rule of thumb. In fact, it provides the theoretical underpinning for a very useful analysis technique, which we will call *bottleneck analysis*. The slowest device in a configuration is often the weakest link. Find it and replace it with a faster component and you have a good chance that performance will improve. Sounds good, but you probably noticed that the rule does not tell you how to find this component. Given the complexity of many modern computer networks, this seemingly simple task is as easy as finding a needle in the proverbial haystack. Of course, replace some component *other* than the bottleneck device with a faster component and performance will remain the same.

In both theory and practice, performance tuning is the process of locating the bottleneck in a configuration and removing it. The system's performance will improve until the next bottleneck is manifest, which you again identify and remove. Removing the bottlenecked device usually entails replacing it with a newer, faster version of the same component. For example, if network bandwidth is a constraint on performance, upgrade the configuration from 10 Mb Ethernet to 100 Mb Fast Ethernet. If the network actually is the bottleneck, performance should improve.

A system in which all bottlenecks have been removed can be said to be a *balanced* system. All components in a balanced system are at least capable of handling the flow of work from component to component without delays building up at any one particular component. Visualize a network of computing components where work flows from one component (the CPU) to another (the disk), back again, then to another (the network), and back again to the CPU (see Figure 1-7). When different components are evenly distributed across the hardware, that system is balanced. It can even be proved mathematically that performance is optimal when a system is balanced in this fashion.

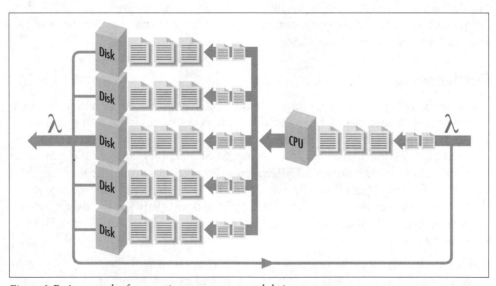

Figure 1-7. A network of computing components and their queues

We can visualize that the balanced system (and not one that is simply over-configured) is one where workload components are evenly distributed across the processing resources. If there are delays, the work that is waiting to be processed is also evenly distributed in the system. This work is illustrated by the shaded areas in Figure 1-8. Suppose we could crank up the rate at which requests arrive to be serviced (think of SQL Server requests to a Windows 2000 database server, for example, or logon requests to an Active Directory authentication server). If the system is balanced, we will observe that work waiting to be processed remains evenly distributed around the system as in Figure 1-8, but there is more of a backlog of requests that need distributing.

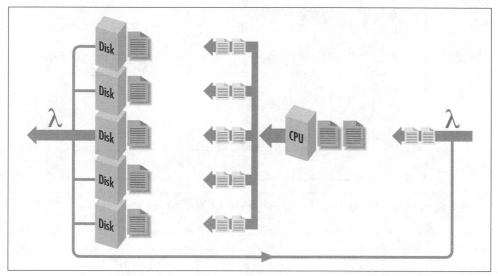

Figure 1-8. A balanced system where shaded areas indicate work queued for processing at different hardware components

If instead we observe something like Figure 1-9, where many requests are waiting behind just one of the resources, we can then say with some authority that that component is the bottleneck in the configuration. When work backs up behind a bottlenecked device, delays there may cascade, causing delays elsewhere in the configuration. Because the flow of work through the system is not a simple chain of events, but an interconnected network, the way that the delayed work impacts processing at other components may not always be obvious. Empirically, it is sufficient to observe that work accumulates behind the bottlenecked device at faster rates as the workload increases. Replacing this component with a faster one should improve the rate that work can flow through the entire system. So now you know that "computer performance analyst" is just a fancy term for a computer plumber who goes around clearing stopped-up drains!

Benchmarking

Unfortunately for us computer plumbers, it is not always easy to figure out where bottlenecks are or how to relieve them. Consider the nightly backup process that copies new and updated files to tape so that you can restore a user's environment when a hard disk crashes. Assume that when you first began backing up files on the computers attached to the LAN to the tape drive attached to the backup server, the

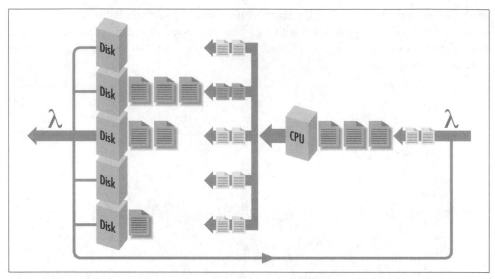

Figure 1-9. An unbalanced system where the second disk is the bottlenecked device

process took only four hours each night. Over time, because there are more users and more disks, the process takes longer and longer. Soon there are not enough hours during the evening to back up all the files that need to be backed up. What should be done about this situation?

First, you upgrade the tape drive to a newer model that the manufacturer promises is faster and more powerful. But that does not speed up the process. It is time to begin a search for the bottlenecked device. Unfortunately, there are many potential devices to be considered. Perhaps network bandwidth is the problem, and you need to update hubs, routers, and network interface cards. Perhaps the network is adequate (utilization is low and there are few collisions), but the network cards cannot pump data onto the line fast enough. Perhaps the cards are fine, but the networking software is slowing things down by waiting too long before transmitting the next request. (Maybe the TCP window size is not set correctly.) Perhaps the cards and the networking software are fine, but the client CPU is not able to push data out to the card because the internal bus connecting the card to the computer is not fast enough. Perhaps the hard disk where the files reside simply cannot move the data any faster because files are spread all over the disk instead of being located contiguously (i.e., the disk is fragmented). Perhaps this is not a problem that you are going to solve tonight.

Once you find irrefutable evidence of a bottlenecked device, you want to replace it with a faster component. How do we know that one component is actually faster than another? Will it actually be faster when it comes to *your* workload? Unfortunately, these questions are not easy to answer either. Worse, there is no general agreement or universally accepted standards of comparison among different machines, platforms, and architectures. This is due to the fact that there are so many workload-dependent factors. This leads us inevitably to the topic of building and executing comparative benchmarks.

Benchmarks are repeatable execution sequences that can be run on different computers at different times to form a basis of comparison. A benchmarking methodology is as follows. Develop a *representative* workload that can be executed over and over again. Run the workload on System A and again on System B (which is configured differently) and compare the results. Working hypothesis: Since the execution runs are otherwise identical, any time differences should be a function of differences in the operating environments. A benchmark establishes an apples-to-apples comparison between the performance of two or more systems.

Generally, there are two types of benchmark workloads: real and synthetic. *Real* (or *natural*) benchmark workloads are created by capturing actual system usage with a tool that is later used to play back the workload at a controlled rate or with more users. *Synthetic* benchmarks are sample applications or programs that you acquire purely for testing purposes. The fact that these synthetic applications exist and can be purchased off the shelf is particularly useful when the capacity planning exercise is for an application that remains to be built.

Benchmark applicability

The popularity of the benchmark approach, especially the test results reported extensively in consumer-oriented trade publications, should not be confused with its effectiveness in making configuration decisions. Decision-making based on benchmarks results, even with so-called industry-standard benchmarks, almost always generates serious questions about validity and interpretation. One important consideration is determining that the benchmark is relevant to the kind of work you eventually plan to perform. The fact that the benchmark load, in the case of both real or synthetic benchmarks, is *representative* of actual workloads is difficult to establish in practice, and once established, is subject to change over time. How can you determine that a given benchmark load is representative of your actual workload? Unfortunately, this is not a question with a simple answer.

Another problem is the assumption that the benchmark is repeatable across many different platforms. You are likely to find that benchmark measurements vary greatly in successive runs on the same configuration. Various cache loading effects are notorious in this regard, and cache techniques are in widespread use. (This is an enormously complicated technical topic that we will pursue in Chapters 6 and 7.) Manufacturers typically provide speed ratings of their equipment running standard benchmark suites in their development labs. When you attempt to measure performance levels in your own environment, inevitably they suffer by comparison. This leads immediately to the question, "What is different about my environment?" Again, not an easy question to answer. In the case of benchmark results published in the trade press, you may not be able to find out enough about the test configuration to ever make an apples-to-apples comparison to your workload.

Benchmark repeatability

These additional elements make benchmarking much more complicated in practice than in theory. Assessing the relative performance of two different processor architectures ought to be as simple as running the same benchmark test against each and evaluating the results. It isn't. Raw processor performance is typically measured by clock speed and the number of clock cycles needed per instruction. This leads to a standard measure of instructions executed per second (IPS) or Instruction Execution Rate (IER). But which instructions? Reduced Instruction Set Computers (RISC) may require three instructions to perform the same logical operation that a Complex Instruction Set Computer (CISC) can perform in one instruction. Both RISC and CISC computers typically also have pipelines and scalar processing facilities that enable them to execute some, but not all, instruction in parallel. Measurements of actual instruction execution rates vary significantly from workload to workload depending on the instruction mix.

By comparison, measurements of disk speed are relatively standardized. Disks are usually measured in terms of head seek time, rotational delay waiting to locate the desired sector while the device spins, and data transfer rates in bytes per second. However, under benchmark testing conditions, actual disk performance is affected by file placement, disk caching strategies, disk fragmentation, and many other considerations. Network access primarily depends on the speed of the wire, but is complicated by processing delays that occur as packets traverse the network of connections between local area and wide area segments. The network protocol in use also determines how many different messages are sent and received and what sorts of acknowledgments are required. In most realistic circumstances, network topology is so unique that only measurements gathered from the actual running system are trustworthy.

Benchmark engineering

Benchmarks are useful, but be careful in interpreting the results (the widely hyped test scores and ratings in articles and advertisements notwithstanding). Remember, for any of the popular, standardized benchmarks in widespread use, there is also a good deal of *benchmark engineering* going on back at the factory. The engineers that developed the equipment tested it constantly by running standard benchmarks to see if the latest engineering change yielded any improvement. This is standard practice. Vendors need ways to stress test products under development, and they naturally want to be able to advertise that their equipment received a better score than a competitor's on a well-known benchmark test.

Frequently, engineers will insert optimizations designed to speed up execution running a specific benchmark. The result of this process is equipment that is very good at running standard benchmark workloads, but may not be so good at running yours. There is nothing wrong with this practice, so long as the benchmark is in fact representative of actual workloads. But it does raise issues of interpretation. There is always the possibility that a particular optimization that accounts for a good benchmark score is not especially useful when it comes to your configuration and workload.

The ideal situation is performing empirical testing with the equipment running your workload. But building a realistic and representative benchmark-testing environment of your own is both expensive and time-consuming. Nor can you test all the different varieties and configuration permutations under consideration. Here, analytic techniques are useful for projecting the performance of proposed configurations from actual performance measurements. Understanding what the characteristics of the benchmark workload are and how they compare to your actual workloads is crucial in performing this type of analysis. *Workload characterization* is an essential first step in the analysis of both real and synthetic workloads.

Problems of Scale

As fast as hardware is improving, it still cannot always meet user expectations. Computer applications are growing more intelligent and easier to use. However, because of this, they also require more resources to run. Additionally, computer applications are being deployed to more and more people living in every part of the world. This inevitably leads to problems of scale: applications may run all right in development, but run in fits and starts when you start to deploy them on a widespread basis.

Problems of scalability are some of the most difficult that application developers face. There are three facets to scalability:

- The problems computers must solve get characteristically more difficult to compute as the number of elements involved grows.
- People often have unrealistically high expectations about what computer technology can actually do.
- There are sometimes absolute physical constraints on performance that cannot be avoided. This applies to long-distance telecommunications as much as it does to signal propagation inside a chip or across a communications bus.

We discuss these three factors in the following sections.

Software Scalability

There are "hard" problems for computers that have a way of getting increasingly more complicated as the problem space itself grows larger. A classic example is the traveling salesman problem, where the computer calculates the most efficient route through multiple cities. This can be accomplished by brute force with a small number of cities, for example, by generating all the possible routes. As the number of cities increases, however, the number of possible routes the computer must generate and examine increases exponentially. In the mathematics of computing, these problems are known as *NP-complete*. With many NP-complete problems, as the problem space grows more complicated, the computational effort using known methods explodes far beyond what even the fastest computers can do.

An application such as a search engine for the Internet provides a good example of something that works fine with a certain amount of data but collapses under the impact of more and more data points. No doubt, at one point in time, search engines seemed like a wonderful way to navigate the World Wide Web. Today, searching for web pages related to "Computer Performance" on AltaVista, we found 3000+ matches. Meanwhile, on Northern Lights we found 13,000+ matches. On Lycos we found matches with almost 9,000 web sites. Frankly, we are not sure whether it is better to find 3000 matches or 13,000; we certainly do not have time to look through thousands of search engine entries. Clearly, search engine technology has trouble dealing with the current scale of the Internet.

Commercial data processing workloads encounter similar problems of scalability. For example, it is well known that sorting algorithms, a staple of commercial workloads, scale exponentially. Building very large database applications that can scale to high volumes of activity and large numbers of users is also challenging, but in a different way. The performance issues that affect scalability in database and transaction processing workloads typically involve *serialization* and *locking*. When one transaction updates the database, the portions of the database affected by the update are locked. Other transactions that attempt to access the same portion of the database are delayed until the update completes. Updates can cause powerful parallel processing modes to revert back to much slower serial ones.

The implications of serialization and locking in the database world are very complicated. One update may trigger further activity when the indexes that speed access to the data themselves require updating. To ensure data integrity, certain update transactions may be forced to hold locks for long periods of time until several different portions of the database are updated. Database locking and serialization problems can typically be addressed only at the design stage. As an aside, when programmers attempt to use rapid application development (RAD) and other prototyping tools to speed the development process, transaction processing applications are often prone to these problems of scale. Using these development tools, the application is described in a logical fashion and then generated without regard to performance considerations. The application will demo well on a low volume of data, but user expectations are later shattered when the prototype does not scale beyond a small number of users, and the entire project then has to be rewritten by hand in C++.

Unrealistic User Expectations

The second aspect of the current application development environment that leads to performance problems is that expectations about what computer technology can and cannot do are often far removed from reality. It does not help that these inflated expectations are fueled by vendor claims of breakthroughs in applications such as handwriting analysis, speech recognition, and natural language processing. These are all activities that require years for humans to master, and none are easily translated into the logical, symbolic processing that computers excel at. No computer program is yet able to comprehend a simple bedtime story that we might read to our young children (let alone interpret the pictures). Even we may not completely understand some of these stories! A good tale's purposeful ambiguity certainly cannot be reduced to simple logic that a computer can process and understand.*

But because they can perform so many remarkable things—keeping track of the family finances, playing a good hand of bridge, or simulating an alternative universe—it is difficult for many people to accept that computers have limitations. Moreover, the pace of application development continues to be excruciatingly slow, frustrating the best intentions of the people who make software development tools. Consequently, the demand for new applications far exceeds the rate at which developers can supply them. In highly charged, competitive business situations where people are desperate for relief, it is not surprising that mistakes in judgment occur. Decision-makers are easily tempted to believe that there is a solution to their problems when, in fact, no technical solution actually exists.

Physical Constraints

Sometimes the constraints on what computers can do involve simple physical limitations. There are molecular limitations on how small the circuits on a silicon wafer can be fabricated or how close the magnetized bits on a rotating disk platter can be stored. An electromagnetic or optical signal carried through a wire travels at anywhere from 0.50 to 0.75 times the speed of light. Inside a computer it takes a minimum of 0.100 microseconds for the processor to signal a memory board located a mere 10 feet away. Signal propagation delay is one of the important reasons why processing speeds improve as semiconductor density increases.

Physical constraints limit the speed of long-distance communications, which affects networking applications that must traverse long distances. A 3000-mile data transmission over a wire requires about 25 milliseconds. But signals attenuate over long distances, and they are seldom transmitted from point to point. Every so often you need a repeater to process the signal, amplify it, and send it on, which means additional delays. If your signal is being routed over the public Internet backbone network, it can be routed from New York to Los Angeles via Atlanta, Denver, and San Francisco, easily traversing two or three times the distance of a direct point-to-point

---

* Simple bedtime story understanding belongs to a class of problems that evidently cannot be solved no matter how much computer power we throw at it. Much effort has been expended over the years debating whether certain problems that are apparently "solved" by humans with relative ease are even amenable to solution using the mathematical-logical processes inside a computer. Although very little progress towards finding a computerized solution to this class of problem has been made in some 50 years of research into Artificial Intelligence, many people devoted to the field are reluctant to give up just yet.

A Real-Life Scaling Problem

Some years ago, one of us had a job with one of the big long-distance telephone companies. There was a new Vice President of Information Technology (IT) on the scene, anxious to make his mark, who began to push a pet project to support online customer queries of their monthly telephone bills. Our unit was responsible for developing sizing estimates for the new application and participating in various design reviews and status meetings, primarily in a Quality Assurance role.

In order to respond to what were expected to be the most popular customer queries, the developers estimated that we needed to keep the last 6–8 weeks' worth of detailed customer billing data online. At the time, the MIS billing data centers, with an annual hardware budget exceeding $100 million per year, could only afford to keep about four days' worth of billing data online. At another status meeting, the database designers reported that the number of records in the online database being contemplated exceeded the limitations of the software by a factor of 10. Still, with the weight of the big boss behind it, the project plowed ahead.

From these status meetings, we developed anew an appreciation for the popular fairy tale known as "The Emperor's New Clothes." Anyone who attempted to leaven the planning discussions with a dose of reality was chastised for "not being with the program," as if the act of willing the system into existence was all that was required. As more and more evidence accumulated that the project would never be completed successfully, the status meetings began to take on a surreal quality. No one wanted to be the messenger who got shot for bringing the bad news.

For instance, because of the volume of updates involved, it was not feasible to update the query database in real time and keep it current. Nor was the nighttime batch window long enough to apply the updates daily to a read-only version of the online database. The VP agreed to let us look at the option of regenerating the query database on a weekly basis over the weekend. Under this option, the amount of disk space needed for the application, already prohibitive, tripled because during the weekend we needed space for three complete databases: the current online database; the current read-only query database, now one week out of date; and the new version of the query database. A benchmark of the database load that was constructed to allow us to obtain good sizing estimates ran for 72 hours for a quantity of data that was less than 10% of the projected production system.

Performance and capacity planning professionals who meddle with high-profile projects under development must be very careful. The development project is undoubtedly behind schedule and the beleaguered developers will resist any effort that is perceived as slowing things down even more. The best justification for your intervention is that it is necessary to ensure that the new application does not disrupt the Quality of Service of existing applications, achieved only as a result of a major performance and tuning effort sometime in the recent past. Instead of being perceived as standing in the way of progress, you need to adopt a statesman's like role preserving the painstaking achievements of the glorious past. Nicolo Machiavelli gave similar advice to worthies in the sixteenth century.

—continued—

The point of the story is that people's expectations (especially nonprogrammers who can be excused for not knowing any better) about what computers can do is extraordinarily high. Consider this typical scenario. Suppose some respected developer in your company publicly demonstrates prototype transactions for a new client/server application developed in VisualBasic, processing against a handful of customer accounts, executing within several seconds. When this prototype system is demonstrated to the users, they are wildly enthusiastic about its features and ease of use. Triumphantly, the developers prepare a full-scale demonstration with a test database close to its projected size. They are disappointed to learn that the server configuration they budgeted for can support only twenty concurrent users, instead of the 250 users they had envisioned. What a dilemma! The choice is to either increase the budget for the number of server PCs significantly, or delay deployment until the application can be rewritten in C++ and the databases redesigned for better performance. In one case like this that we were involved in, the decision was made to deploy the prototype system, but limit its use to one department until the application could be rewritten.

link. If you are sending a message via satellite, you must factor in the distance the signal must travel through outer space and back. Transmission delays over long distances simply cannot be avoided because the speed of light functions as an absolute upper bound on performance.

Cost/Benefit Analysis

Performance considerations are important in desktop systems, distributed and networked systems, and client/server applications today. Performance is one of the core system management disciplines, along with operations, storage management, change management, etc., and performance considerations play an important role in many system management decisions. One reason cost/performance considerations are important is that they can be quantified, unlike fuzzier concepts like ease of use. Because you can put a price tag on a system configured to achieve a particular level of performance, it is possible to do a cost/benefit analysis, which is a genuine aid to decision-making.

Consider an organization's decision to upgrade 1000 desktop PCs running Windows 95 to either Windows ME or 2000. Why not benchmark some of the proposed configurations running the applications that are normally in use? Comparing Windows ME to Windows 2000 Professional, you find that Windows ME outperforms Windows 2000 with 32 MB and 64 MB configurations. But at 128 MB and higher configurations, Windows 2000 Professional provides better performance. These results allow you to quantify the cost of moving to either alternative. While the cost of adding memory and, perhaps, disk space to a single machine may not amount to much, multiply by a factor of 1000 and the decision to upgrade involves six or seven figures. Clearly, performance is not the only criterion factored into the final decision, and it might not even be the most important factor. For instance, if Windows 2000 is not compatible with a critical piece of software, that might be enough to sway your decision towards Windows ME. On the other hand, there is a no-nonsense, bottom-line orientation in performance analysis that appeals to many executive decision-makers.

The Future of Performance Analysis

The horror stories of failed development projects that did not meet cost and performance specifications reflect the fact that expectations about what computer technology can do far exceed the reality. Large-scale application development is very demanding. In our judgment, even as hardware performance continues to improve over the next 10–20 years, development will not get easier. In the future, the computer industry will continue to be challenged to provide cost-effective solutions to even more difficult problems. For example, we expect that multimedia applications with voice, high-resolution graphics, and animation will continue to be plagued by performance issues in the decade ahead.

To take an example, we were recently asked to help size a medical imaging application for a large, state-wide health care organization. The size of these high-resolution imaging files ranged from 100–300 MB each. Physicians wanted to be able to access image files and discuss them with other specialists located in different parts of the statewide association. For each patient's case, the physicians might need to review multiple images before they could make a competent diagnosis. They wanted to be able to view the image files concurrently and make notes and annotate them interactively. Being very busy, they wished to be able to perform all these tasks in real time at locations convenient to them. Naturally, the budget for this new application was constrained by the realities of the health care financing system.

Of course, the physicians needed to view medical image files in a high-resolution mode to make a competent diagnosis. Immediately, we encounter capacity constraints because digital imaging and display technology today runs at a much lower resolution than hardcopy x-ray photographs, for example. Taking this application, which demonstrably runs fine on a dedicated high-powered workstation, and adding the element of long-distance file access creates distinct difficulties. The core of the problem is that very large, high-resolution image files created in one location needed to be copied very rapidly and transmitted across existing telecommunication links. So, while this application seems like something that ought to be pretty simple, especially after viewing the vendor's standalone workstation demonstration, there is more to it than meets the eye.

While techniques like caching recently used images on a local server's disk could improve performance of the application once the image is loaded, there is no avoiding the fact that moving files that large across a wide-area network (WAN) link is slow. Either the organization must upgrade its communications links, or the users of the system must learn to accept some reasonable limitations on the type of service that this application can deliver. An example of those limitations is that the consultation session be subject to some advance notice, say one hour, with a setup procedure to identify the images to be transferred.

Various cost/performance alternatives are customarily called *service levels,* where a process of negotiation between the user departments and the technical support team is used to reach a *service level agreement.* Such an agreement formalizes the expected relationship between system load, response time, and cost for a given application. We will have more to say on this subject later in this chapter.

Often, when the system is too slow and the productivity of the end users is negatively impacted, it is back to the drawing board to overhaul the application. Under these circumstances, it may be the performance analyst's job to persuade the users that these are, in fact, reasonable limitations consistent with the cost to run the application and the current state of technology. When people understand that there is a price tag associated with their dream system, they tend to adopt a more sensible attitude. A few simple charts can be used to express the relationship between file transfer time and file size across various communication links. Then the costs associated with using the existing T1 network links, upgrading to DSL or DDS-3, or resorting to some other more exotic and expensive alternative can be compared and contrasted. If the performance analyst does a good job of laying out these alternatives, an agreement can usually be reached amicably.

If unsatisfactory performance is the result of poor design decisions, the performance analyst may be called upon to assist the developers responsible for re-engineering the application. In any event, it is during these times of perceived performance problems that the performance analyst is challenged to help the organization cope with adversity. There will be difficult decisions to be made in this hour of crisis that will benefit from concise and objective analysis.

Internet Capacity Planning

The best argument for the continued relevance of performance analysis today is the Internet. Growth in the use of the Internet is one of those phenomena that few predicted. What started out as a network of interconnected computers tied together as a way for researchers at the Department of Defense and various universities to communicate has within a few short years become a major public access network that everyone with a computer and a modem can use. That explosive growth has led to extremely serious capacity problems heightened by the highly visible nature of this network. It is front-page news in *USA Today* or the *Wall Street Journal* when major performance problems on the Internet are exposed.

Internet traffic is processed by a set of backbone service providers who switch packets onto the public phone system. In 1996, digital traffic on the public phone system exceeded analog voice traffic for the first time. Moreover, Internet data traffic has continued to grow at an unprecedented rate, doubling approximately every two to three months, according to some experts. Obviously, network capacity planning in the Internet Age is a considerable challenge.

Designated Internet service providers (ISPs) use banks of routers to examine packets and switch them accordingly. The underlying network protocol used to support the Internet is known as TCP/IP, which is being used today in ways its original designers could not have anticipated; for example, voice and video data streaming traffic over TCP/IP was not even contemplated when the protocol was conceived. In router design, if there is an overload, IP packets are simply dropped rather than queued at the router. This technique relies on the fact that TCP will ultimately recover and retransmit the information. Meanwhile, neighboring routers are sensitive to the fact that packets dropped at one node may seek alternative routes. The net result is that an isolated, overloaded resource sometimes causes *flares* or even more widespread *storms* that can impact service regionally, which is how these disruptions in service levels are characterized.

Identifying the root cause of these problems is neither easy nor straightforward. Many different vendors, including various telephone companies and ISPs, "own" portions of the Internet backbone. Even as these vendors are scrambling to add capacity to fix these problems, there is considerable jockeying among these vendors as to the root causes of the problem and how to pay for fixing them. Aspects of web server design, web browser design, and the TCP/IP protocol itself have been identified as contributing factors.

The flat-fee arrangements most users have with consumer-oriented ISPs for access privileges also contribute to the problem. People browsing the Internet are the only class of consumer on the public-access telephone network that do not pay for service based on the traffic they generate. As Internet users run more bandwidth-hogging applications like MP3 audio, telephony, and on-demand video streaming, this structural problem interferes with the ability of ISPs to make rational resource allocation decisions, undercutting the industry's Quality of Service (QoS) initiatives.

The performance problems that the Internet faces today are classic problems of scalability:

- Technology that worked extremely well in prototype environments but has difficulty adapting to larger-scale workloads
- Outrageous user expectations about web browser performance, with multimedia applications attempting to squeeze large amounts of data across low-speed modem links
- The simple physical constraints involved in long-distance communications

However, the most interesting aspect of the plague of Internet performance problems is their high profile and visibility. Most of the performance problems we encounter are private, confined to a single company or user population. However, the Internet is a public network with tens of millions of users, and problems on the Internet are visible to the multitudes. In spite of the evident questions and concerns, there are a large number of companies that rely on the Internet to host basic business and commercial services. Given that a company with a web site has little influence over the factors that determine performance for customers who access that web site, the prudent thing to do is to hedge your bets. Many experts recommend augmenting the public network with private lines and switching gear that can be monitored and controlled with more precision.

If there is any lesson in all this, it is that performance management and capacity planning problems are not disappearing despite the miraculous improvements in computer hardware. If anything, larger-scale application deployment, the dispersion of applications across wide-area communication networks and heterogeneous systems, and an increased rate of change are making performance problems even more difficult to diagnose and solve today. Chapters 11 and 12 provide an in-depth discussion of large-scale networking and Internet performance issues, respectively. Satisfied that our time invested in understanding computer performance issues will be worthwhile in the years ahead, we can profitably turn our attention to the practical matter of assessing and using the tools of the trade.

Performance Tools

We should consider ourselves lucky that so much attention has been paid to the discipline of computer performance evaluation by so many talented people over the years. There is a small but very active Special Interest Group of the Association of Computing Machinery called SIGMETRICS (see *http://www.sigmetrics.org*) devoted to the study of performance evaluation. There are many good university programs where topics in performance evaluation are taught and Ph.D. candidates are trained. For practitioners, there is a large professional association called the Computer Measurement Group (*http://www.cmg.org*) that sponsors an annual conference in December. The regular SIGMETRICS and CMG publications contain a wealth of invaluable material for the practicing performance analyst.

It is also fortunate that one of the things computers are good for is counting. It is easy to augment both hardware and software to keep track of what they are doing, although keeping the measurement overhead from overwhelming the amount of useful work being done is a constant worry. Over time, most vendors have embraced the idea of building measurement facilities into their products, and at times are even able to position them to competitive advantage because their measurement facilities render them more manageable. A system that provides measurement feedback is always more manageable than one that is a black box.

Users of Windows 2000 are fortunate that Microsoft has gone to the trouble of building in extensive performance monitoring facilities. We explore the use of specific Windows 2000 performance monitoring tools in subsequent chapters. The following discussion introduces the types of events monitored in Windows 2000, how measurements are taken, and what tools exist that access this measurement data. The basic measurement methodology used in Windows 2000 is the subject of more intense scrutiny in Chapter 2.

Performance Monitors

Measurement facilities are the prerequisite for the development of *performance monitors*, the primary class of tool. Performance monitoring began as a hardware function, something that continues to thrive in many circumstances, including network line monitors or sniffers, which insert a probe at an appropriate spot on the network. Performance monitoring today is usually associated with extensions to the set of base operating systems software services. Vendors generally accept the notion that the OS should collect measurement data and access additional measurement data collected by hardware.

Performance objects and counters

Windows 2000 is well instrumented, and you can access a wealth of information on its operation and performance. Windows 2000 keeps track of many different events, including interactions that occur between hardware and systems software. It makes extensive use of event *counters*, operating system functions that maintain a running total of the number of times some event has occurred. For example, interrupt processing is augmented by a simple procedure to count the number and types of interrupts or traps being serviced. It is also possible to obtain a count of virtual memory page faults that occur in a similar fashion. Windows 2000 also adds instrumentation to count the number and types of filesystem requests that are issued. Event counters that are updated continuously can also be called *accumulators*.

The duration of requests to disks and other peripherals can also be measured by recording the start time of the original request and the end time of its completion. In Windows 2000, the operating system data structures used to serialize access to resources like the processor and the disks are instrumented. (Windows 2000 gives lip service to the ideal of object-oriented programming, so these data structures are called objects.) Instrumentation also makes it possible to determine the number of requests waiting in a disk queue, for instance. These are "right now" types of measurements: instantaneous counts of the number of active processes and threads, or numbers that show how full the paging datasets are or how virtual memory is allocated. These instantaneous measurements are more properly considered to be *sampled,* since typically in Windows 2000 you are accessing individual observations.

When you use Windows 2000's built-in System Monitor application, accumulators and instantaneous counter fields are all lumped together as counters, but they are actually very different types of data. The distinction is critical because it is based on how the measurement data is collected, which affects how it can be analyzed and interpreted. The kind of field also affects the way collection data must be handled during subsequent summarization. We pursue this topic in Chapter 2.

Once per interval, a performance monitor application like the System Monitor harvests the collection data maintained by Windows 2000, gathering up the current values for these counters. Notice that the overhead associated with performance monitoring when the operating system is already maintaining these event counters is minimal. The only additional work that the application must perform is to gather up the data once per interval, make appropriate calculations, and store or log the results. In Windows 2000, collection agents are linked to performance objects. Windows 2000 operating system services are responsible for collecting base measurements for the principal resources like memory, disks, and the processor. Windows 2000 also provides instrumentation that records resource utilization at a process and thread level. Core subsystems like the network browser and redirector are also instrumented. The performance monitoring facilities are extensible; subsystems like Microsoft Exchange Server and Microsoft SQL Server add their own objects and collection agents. An overview of Windows 2000 performance monitoring is presented in Chapter 2, while subsequent chapters delve into various measurements and their uses.

At what rate should the data be collected? Capacity planners who deal with longer-term trends are ordinarily quite content with interval measurements every 15, 30, or 60 minutes. When you are trying to project seasonal or yearly changes, that level of detail is more than sufficient. On the other hand, if you are called upon to perform a *post mortem* examination to determine the cause of a performance problem that occurred on the network yesterday, more detail is apt to be required. By increasing the rate of data collection, a finer-grained picture of system activity emerges that may make it possible to perform a more detailed problem diagnosis. But this also increases the overhead proportionally—usually the most significant aspect of which is the increased overhead in post-processing, e.g., more disk I/O to the log file, and larger log files that must be stored and moved around the network. Since the accumulators involved are maintained continuously, the duration of the collection interval does not affect the amount of overhead in the measurement facility itself.

In our experience, summary data collected at one-minute intervals is adequate for diagnosing many performance problems. Problems that fall through the cracks at that level of granularity are probably so transitory that it may be very difficult to account for them anyway. Logging data at even more frequent intervals also means a proportionate increase in the size of your collection files. Still, there will be times when you need to know, and the only way to find out is to collect detailed performance or trace data at a fine level of granularity. For example, when you are developing an important piece of code and you want to understand its performance, collecting performance data at very high rates may be the only way to gather enough detail on short-running processes to be useful.

Event tracing

Where formal measurement facilities do not exist, it is sometimes possible to substitute diagnostic traces and other debugging facilities. Debugging facilities typically trap every instance of an event, and, thus, the data collection methodology they use is properly called *event-oriented*. There is an entry in a diagnostic trace every time an event occurs.

In Windows 2000, there are three event logs that contain information useful in a performance context: one used by the system; one used by applications, and one used for security. Events in the Windows 2000 log are timestamped so you can tell when something happened. When two events are related, you can easily tell how much time has elapsed between them. Sometimes this information is all you have to go on when you are reconstructing what happened. For instance, you can tell when someone logged onto the system, and that an application crashed or a connection was lost. Compared to a user's recollection of what happened, of course, you can always rely on the accuracy of data recorded in the log.

Windows 2000 also contains a powerful operating system kernel tracing facility called the Windows Management Instrumentation, or WMI. Kernel events that can be traced include Active Directory commands, TCP commands, page faults, and disk I/O requests. WMI is designed to assist in the detailed analysis and diagnosis of performance problems. Because of the volume of trace data that can be generated and the overhead associated with widespread event tracing, this facility needs to be used cautiously. WMI is a new feature in Windows 2000, so there has not been much time to produce killer performance tools that exploit it. But this facility has a great future.

Another powerful tracing tool available in Windows 2000 is the Network Monitor driver. Network Monitors are known generically as "sniffers" after the brand name of the most popular hardware version. The Windows 2000 Network Monitor driver captures communications packets, tracing network activity without specialized hardware probes. While it is designed primarily for diagnosing network problems, the Network Monitor is useful in performance analysis. A fuller discussion of the Network Monitor and the use of Network Monitor traces to diagnose network performance problems is provided in Chapter 11.

Marshaling what are primarily debugging tools to solve performance problems can be difficult because debugging tools have different design criteria. In a debugging environment, the emphasis is on problem determination, not performance monitoring. Moreover, the overhead in running debuggers can be quite significant. In addition, many debuggers are intrusive, i.e., they actually modify the operating environment to obtain the diagnostic information they require. There is nothing more frustrating to a developer than a program that runs to completion successfully in debugging mode, but fails in its normal operating environment. The other problem with using debugging facilities like the event log is the lack of good data reduction tools to create the summarized statistical data used in performance analysis.

Code profilers

Somewhere between general-purpose performance monitors and debugging facilities are application-oriented *code profilers* designed to help developers understand the way their code operates. A profiler inspects a process as it executes and keeps track of which programming statements and routines are running. The developer then examines the results, using them to zero in on the portions of the program that execute for the longest time. If you are trying to improve the performance of an application, it is usually worthwhile to concentrate on the portion of the program that appears to be running the longest. Profilers can be integrated with compilers so that developers can resolve performance problems at the level of the module or statement. We will take a close look at these tools in Chapter 4.

Performance Databases

Performance monitors excel at real-time monitoring. What happens when a performance problem occurs and you are not there to watch it? Unless you are capturing performance statistics to a file, you missed what happened and may not be able to reconstruct it. Even if you are attempting to watch what is going on in the system in real time, there is a limit to how many different variables you can monitor at once. Screen space is one limiting factor, and another is your ability to make rapid mental calculations as whatever phenomenon you are watching whizzes by. Capturing data to a file means you can pursue your *post mortem* examination under less stringent time constraints.

The Microsoft Windows 2000 System Monitor can log data to a file, which meets the minimum requirements for a performance database. Experienced performance analysts and capacity planners probably have in mind a more extensive facility to capture long-term trends spanning weeks, months, and even years. Commercial software to build and maintain performance databases originated from the need to charge back and finance the purchase of expensive mainframe equipment during the 70s and 80s. Historically, these performance databases were implemented using SAS, a so-called 4GL with strong statistical and charting capabilities. The disadvantage of SAS was that a working knowledge of the language was required to use these packages. As a result, a number of later performance databases were implemented using proprietary databases and reporting facilities. Recently, both types of software packages have been extended to Windows 2000.

Because they support a variety of analytic techniques, performance databases add a whole new dimension to the pursuit of Windows 2000 performance and tuning. With performance databases, the emphasis can shift from real-time firefighting to armchair studies that focus on strategic problems. It is possible to anticipate problems instead of merely reacting to them. In the right hands, performance databases can be extremely valuable tools for workload characterization, management reporting, and forecasting.

Workload characterization

In general, the type of statistical analysis of computer performance measurement data that is performed is known as *workload characterization*. Analysts look for ways of classifying different users and developing a resource profile that describes a typical user in some class. Application developers might be lumped into one class and clerical employees in the accounting office into another based on patterns of computer usage. For instance, users in one class might run different applications than users in another—not too many people in the accounting department execute the C++ compiler. Even when they do use the same applications, they may use them in different ways. Workload characterization leads to the development of a *resource profile*, which associates an average user in one class with typical computer resource requirements: processing cycles, disk capacity, memory, network traffic, etc. Understanding the characteristics of your workload is a necessary first step in analyzing computer performance for any modeling study or other capacity planning exercise.

Reporting

The performance data captured to a file is useless unless it is made visible to you and other interested parties through reporting. Some form of management reporting is usually required to provide your organization with a sense of what areas are under control and where problems exist. There are two effective approaches to day-to-day management reporting that parallel recognized management strategies:

- Management by Objective
- Management by Exception

Save detailed analysis reports for yourself—it is not likely that too many other people are interested in the statistical correlation between memory caching and the response time of particular SQL transactions.

To implement Management by Objective reports, you first have to develop management objectives. If the computer systems being monitored play an integral part in daily work, then your organization undoubtedly has goals for system availability and performance even if no one has expressed them explicitly. These goals or objectives need to be translated into something that can be quantified and measured on the computer. Then reporting can be developed that documents actual availability and performance levels against these objectives.

Management by Exception entails reporting on only those instances where performance objectives are not met. When faced with managing tens, hundreds, or thousands of Windows 2000 computers, the Management by Exception approach helps organizations cope with the potential volume of information they must sift through on a daily basis. Exception reporting alerts key personnel that something serious is afoot at a specific place and time. Much exception reporting attempts to encapsulate "expert" opinions and rules of thumb about which metrics and their values warrant concern. Since experts themselves often disagree, this reliance on received wisdom can be problematic, to say the least. One of our goals in writing this book is to empower you to perform your own "expert" analysis about what is important in your environment.

Exception alerting can also break down when too many exception thresholds are exceeded, with the result that beepers are ringing at the help desk at an annoying frequency. It is important to ensure that alerts truly reflect exceptional conditions that support personnel should be informed of immediately. One approach to managing alerts is statistical. An informational alert based on a 95th percentile observation in a representative baseline measurement can be expected to occur once every 20 measurement observations. If this alert is currently generated 10 times every 20 measurement intervals, then the current system is manifestly different from the baseline interval. One virtue of the statistical approach is that it can be easily calibrated to control the rate at which alarms occur. This approach effectively highlights differences over time, identifying gross changes in measurement observations in the absence of expert opinions about what such changes might mean empirically. The significance of the change is another question entirely, which, of course, may also be problematic.

Graphical reports are certainly the most effective way to communicate the technical issues associated with computer performance. A good reporting tool will allow you to manipulate the raw performance data you collected so that you can present it cogently. Figure 1-10 illustrates a typical management report where the data was massaged extensively prior to presentation. In this example, detailed information on per-process CPU consumption was summarized by hour, and then filtered so that only large consumers of CPU time over the interval are displayed. For the sake of accuracy, processes that were smaller consumers of CPU were grouped into an "Other" category. The stacked bar chart presents detailed and summarized information visually. The results are displayed against a Y axis scale that extends to 400% busy for a multiprocessing system containing 4 CPUs.

To support Management by Objective, your main tool is *service-level reporting*. Users care primarily about response time: how long it takes for the computer to generate a response once the user initiates an action, like clicking OK in a dialog box. Response time goals can be translated into service objectives that show the relationship between the user or transaction load and system responsiveness. Referring to the theoretical

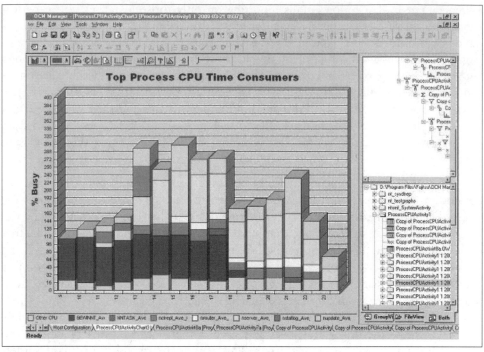

Figure 1-10. A graphical report summarizing technical information

relationship predicted in queuing theory illustrated back in Figure 1-3, performance tends to degrade at an increasing rate as more and more users are added to the network.

In any organization where one group provides technical support and other systems management functions for others, formal service level agreements can be adopted. These communicate the anticipated relationship between load and responsiveness, and establish reasonable expectations that as the load increases without a corresponding increase in hardware capacity, performance levels can be expected to decline. In these situations, regular reporting on compliance with service level agreements is obviously very useful. For example, when technical support is outsourced to a third party, reporting on service objectives is absolutely essential to assess contract compliance.

In the absence of formal service level agreements, informal ones based on user expectations usually exist. People can sense when the system they are accustomed to using is slower than normal, and when that happens, they complain. Whether or not formal service level agreements are in place, performance analysts are called upon to investigate the complaints and remedy them. What if the solution is to upgrade or add hardware and there is no money available to buy more equipment? Reporting on the current configuration's capacity to achieve specific objectives can document the situation so that all parties can see where the problems lie.

As mentioned previously, for all its sophistication, Windows 2000 performance monitoring sorely lacks an orientation towards measuring and monitoring end-to-end transaction response time. Windows 2000 also lacks the ability to track the flow of work from client to server and back at a transaction level. When transaction response time cannot be monitored from end to end, transaction-based service level reporting is not possible. As the platform matures, no doubt this deficiency will be eliminated, but with few exceptions, this is the sorry state of affairs with most Windows 2000 applications today.

It is possible to monitor service levels in Windows 2000 at a somewhat higher level than the transaction with existing measurement facilities. Subsystems like Exchange and SQL Server do report the number of logged-on users, the total number of transactions processed in an interval, and other broad indicators of load. A weaker, but still effective form of service level reporting can be adopted that documents the relationship between the user load measured at this macro level and the ability to achieve service level objectives.

For Management by Exception, *exception reporting* is what you need. With all the metrics available from a typical Windows 2000 machine, it can be a challenge deciding which to report. Windows 2000 literally can supply data on more than a thousand different performance counters. Instead of reporting on the mundane, exception reporting details only events that are unusual or irregular and need attention.

Deciding which events are mundane and which are problematic is key. Frequently, exceptions are based on reporting intervals where measurements exceeded established threshold values. Chapter 2 summarizes the System Monitor counters and our recommended threshold value for exception reporting. Subsequent chapters provide the rationale behind these recommendations. For example, all intervals where processor utilization exceeds 90% busy can be reported. However, it makes better sense to generate an alarm based on an actual indicator of delay at the processor, not just crossing a utilization threshold. It is more informative to send an alarm when the processor utilization exceeds 90% *and* the processor queue length exceeds four threads per available processor.

Trending and forecasting

The performance database is also the vehicle for longer-term storage of performance measurement data. Detailed data from log files can be summarized into daily, weekly, monthly, and even yearly files. Keeping data on resource utilization over longer periods of time makes it possible to examine trends and forecast future workload growth. A combination of forecasting techniques can be employed. In the absence of input from other parts of the business, current trends can be extrapolated into the future using simple statistical techniques such as linear regression.

If a correlation can be found between an application's resource profile and underlying business factors, then historical forecasts can be amplified based on business planning decisions. An example of this *business-element*-based forecasting approach is an insurance claims system where activity grows in proportion to the number of policies in effect. You then need to develop a resource profile, for example, that shows the computer and network load for each insurance claim, on average. Once the average amount of work generated per customer is known, it is straightforward to relate the need for computer capacity to a business initiative designed to increase the number of customers.

Baselining

Another popular technique worth mentioning is *baselining*. Baselining refers to the practice of collecting a detailed snapshot of computer and network activity and saving it to use later as a basis of comparison. This technique is particularly useful in network monitoring where the amount of detailed information that can be collected is enormous, and the structure of the data does not lend itself readily to summarization. Instead, performance analysts often choose to archive the entire snapshot. Later, when problems arise, a current snapshot is taken and compared to the baseline data in the archive. The comparison may show that line utilization has increased or the pattern of utilization has changed. It is good practice to periodically update the old baseline with current data, perhaps every six months or so.

Modeling

The final class of performance tools in widespread use is *predictive models*. Predictive models can be used to answer "what if?" questions to assess the impact of a proposed configuration or workload change. You might be interested in knowing, for example, whether increasing the load on your Internet Information Server will cause the system to bog down, whether adding 50 more users to a particular LAN segment will impact everyone's performance, and what kind of hardware you should add to your current configuration to maintain service objectives. Modeling tools for Windows 2000 include very detailed simulations of network traffic to very high-level approximations of transaction traffic in a distributed client/server database application.

The first warning about modeling is that these powerful tools are not for novices. Using modeling tools requires a broad foundation and understanding of both the underlying mathematics and statistics being applied, along with a good grounding in the architecture of the computer system being studied. In skilled hands, modeling tools can make accurate predictions to help you avoid performance and capacity-related problems. In the wrong hands, modeling tools can produce answers that are utter nonsense.

Modeling technology is divided into two camps, one that uses simulation techniques and one that uses analytic techniques (i.e., solves a series of mathematical equations). In simulation, a mathematical description of the computer system is created and studied. Transactions enter the system and are timed as they execute. If one transaction can block another from executing, that behavior can be modeled precisely in the system. This type of modeling is sometimes called *discrete-event* simulation because each transaction or component of a transaction is treated as a discrete element. *Monte Carlo* techniques refer to the use of random number generators to create workloads that vary statistically. *Trace-driven* simulations capture current workload traffic and play it back at different rates. At the conclusion of the simulation run, both detailed and summary statistics are output.

The advantage of simulation is that any computer system can be analyzed by someone who knows what they are doing. Commercially available modeling packages contain comprehensive libraries of model building blocks that are ready to use. The disadvantage of simulation is that the models that are constructed can be very complex. One part of the model can interact with another in ways that cannot easily be anticipated, and it is easy to produce behavior that does not match reality. Debugging a detailed simulation model can be very difficult.

Analytic modeling also begins with a mathematical description of the computer system, but there the similarity to simulation ends. Analytic modeling relies on mathematical formulas that can be solved. The trick in analytical modeling is knowing what formulas to use and knowing how to solve them. Fortunately for the rest of us, analytical models and their solutions can be programmed by mathematicians and packaged into solutions that can be applied by skilled analysts.

Central Server model

The analytic framework for computer performance modeling was pioneered in the 1960s with applications for both centralized computing and computer networks. For example, one of the leading architects of the ARPAnet networking project back in the 1970s, the forerunner of today's Internet, was a renowned performance modeler named Dr. Leonard Kleinrock of UCLA. An approach known as the Central Server model was developed during that same period for modeling transaction processing workloads. The Central Server model represents a computer system as a series of interconnected resources, mainly the processor and the disks, as Figure 1-7 illustrated. Transactions enter the system by visiting the CPU, accessing one of the disks, returning to the CPU, etc., until the transaction is processed.

The Central Server model is a convenient abstraction, but of course it does not resemble the way real systems are put together. "Where is memory?" is a common question. The answer is that paging activity to disk as a result of memory contention is usually incorporated into the model indirectly as another disk I/O component. A model is intended only to capture the essence of the computer system, and it is surprisingly effective even when many details are conveniently ignored. The key in modeling, however, is that some details are too important to be ignored and must be reflected in the model if it is going to behave properly.

If the system is capable of processing multiple transactions concurrently, any single transaction is likely to encounter a busy resource where it must first wait in a queue before processing. Multiuser computer systems are inherently more complex to understand because of the potential for resource contention leading to queuing delays. If there are multiple users waiting for a resource, a combination of the scheduling algorithm and the queuing discipline determines which user is selected next for service. To understand the Central Server model it is necessary to know the rate at which transactions arrive at each of the different resources and how long it takes to process each request. The model can then be solved, using either analytical techniques or simulation, to calculate the total round-trip time of a transaction, including the time spent waiting for service in various queues, based on the scheduling algorithm and queuing discipline.

Mean value analysis

The best-known branch of analytical modeling for computer systems is known as mean value analysis (MVA). Jeff Buzen discovered an exact solution technique for the MVA equations generated by a Central Server model when he was working on his Ph.D. degree at Harvard University during the 1970s. Dr. Buzen later became one of the founders of BGS Systems, where he worked to commercialize the modeling technology he developed. This work led to the BEST/1 family of modeling tools. Now manufactured and distributed by BMC Software, BEST/1 was recently extended to support Windows 2000.

Several years ago, Dr. Buzen published a critique of the measurement data available in Windows NT and described how it should be enhanced to provide a better basis for modeling in the future. Reviewing Dr. Buzen's critique, it is apparent that Windows 2000 does not yet support modeling studies of the rigor that Buzen envisions, whether simulation or analytic techniques are used. One of Dr. Buzen's major laments is the lack of transaction-based response time reporting in Windows 2000, a point we touched upon earlier.

Extending modeling technology

Over the years, the basic approaches to modeling computer systems pioneered in the 1960s and 1970s were refined and extended to more complex system configurations. Some of these extensions allow models to incorporate key details of the processor scheduling algorithms being used, represent fine details of the I/O subsystem, and incorporate network traffic. A few of these extensions are described here.

The simplest queuing discipline and one of the most common is FIFO, which stands for First In, First Out. Most computer operating systems implement priority queuing at the processor allowing higher-priority work, such as interrupt processing, to preempt lower-priority tasks. Windows 2000 implements priority queuing with preemptive scheduling at the processor based on priority levels that are adjusted dynamically by the OS. There are a number of ways to approach modeling priority queuing.

Priority schemes are just one of the issues facing detailed disk I/O models. SCSI uses a fixed-priority scheme based on device addresses to decide which of multiple requests will gain access to the shared SCSI bus. SCSI disks that support tagged command queuing implement a shortest-path-first queuing discipline that schedules the next I/O operation based on which queued request can be executed quickest. Other key I/O modeling issues concern the use of disk array technology and RAID, and the ubiquitous use of caching to improve disk performance.

Both local-area networking (LAN) and wide-area networking (WAN) technology introduce further complications. Ethernet uses a simple, non-arbitrated scheme to control access to shared communications media. When two or more stations attempt to transmit across the wire at the same time, a *collision* occurs that leads to retransmission. Most high-speed IP routers make no provision for queuing. When they become overloaded, they simply drop packets, which forces the TCP software responsible for reliable data communication to retransmit the data.

It is possible to extend the concepts honed in developing the Central Server model to Windows 2000 networks and distributed systems. Figure 1-11 shows a scheme proposed by Dr. Mike Salsberg of Fortel that extends the Central Server model to networks and client/server systems. From the standpoint of the client, there is a new I/O workload that represents remote file I/O. The delays associated with remote file access are then decomposed into network transmission time, remote server processing, and remote server disk I/O activity. Salsberg's approach captures the bare essentials of distributed processing, which he proposes to solve using conventional simulation techniques.

Modeling studies

Modeling studies take one of two basic forms. One route is to study a system that is currently running to predict performance in the future when the workload grows or the hardware characteristics change. A *baseline model* of the current system is built and validated against the actual system. In *validation*, the model is prepared and then solved to obtain predicted values, such as the utilization of various resources or the predicted transaction response time. The model outputs are then compared to actual measurements of the system under observation. The model is valid for prediction when the predicted values are approximately equal to the observed values. Obviously, it is not safe to use an invalid model for prediction, but the sources of error in an invalid model can be very difficult to track down.

The second form of modeling studies is for a system under construction. Instead of measurements from an actual running system, there is instead only a set of specifications. These specifications are translated into a resource profile of the proposed system, and then the model is built in the usual way and solved. Obviously, the intermediate step where specifications are transformed into resource profiles of the proposed workload is prone to errors. However, as the system is actually being built,

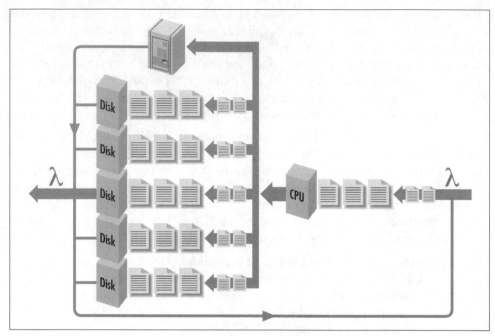

Figure 1-11. Salsberg's approach of extending the Central Server to incorporate network traffic

it should be possible to generate successively more accurate models based on collecting actual measurements from running prototype code. Incorporating modeling studies into application development projects is also known as *software performance engineering*. Practitioners who rely on software performance engineering techniques early and often during application development have a much better chance of success than those who ignore performance concerns until it is too late.

## CHAPTER 2

Measurement Methodology

Microsoft Windows 2000 comes equipped with extensive facilities for monitoring performance, and these have been available in the operating system since its inception. The Windows 2000 performance monitoring API is the name we coined to describe the built-in facilities for monitoring system activity in Windows 2000. In this chapter, we take a thorough look at this API, which is the main source of the performance statistics that system administrators and application developers utilize.

Performance Monitoring on Windows

The performance monitoring statistics available in Windows 2000 are quite extensive. At a basic level, they report on processor, memory, disk, and network usage, for example. Windows 2000 also measures and reports on the utilization of these system resources by application processes and execution threads. The extensive set of performance metrics collected is designed to assist system administrators and application developers, both of whom need to understand the impact of their decisions on overall system performance.

For example, the Windows 2000 32-bit application programming interface (the Win32 API) provides a complex set of operating system services for application developers to use, including thread scheduling, process virtual memory management, and file processing. The performance statistics Windows 2000 provides are complementary—they help programmers use these operating system services efficiently. Some applications written for Windows 2000, as we shall see, attempt to adjust automatically to their runtime environment. For instance, they may allocate a specific number of execution threads per processor, allowing the application to scale efficiently on multiprocessor machines. Or they may allocate memory-resident buffers for caching frequently used disk objects based on the amount of available RAM. These simple heuristics designed to allow an application to adjust automatically to its runtime environment neglect one vital element in computer performance, namely, the specific characteristics of your workload. To allow applications to scale across different hardware configurations and different workloads requires additional flexibility.

Many applications developed specifically for Windows 2000 provide external controls that allow system administrators to adjust the values of configuration and tuning parameters. Tuning knobs that determine how many threads to create or how much RAM to allocate impact application scalability and other aspects of its performance. We discuss a number of these tuning parameters later in this book. These parameters often focus on the application runtime services that the Win32 API specifies and the Windows 2000 operating system implements. Setting tuning parameters that influence the execution behavior of key applications requires a knowledge and understanding of the various performance statistics available.

As the operating system has matured, so have its performance monitoring facilities. Each successive version of Windows NT has featured significant changes and improvements in the performance data and tools included with the OS. Because you may have to run and support Windows NT and 2000 systems running different versions, it is helpful to understand the major operating system–level differences. Chapter 1 summarized the major changes in Windows 2000's evolution that affect performance monitoring so that you can easily reference these OS-level changes.

Because the built-in performance monitoring facilities are extensible, major applications that run on Windows 2000—file and print services, MS Internet Information Server (IIS), SQL Server, Exchange Server, Lotus Notes, Oracle, etc.—also produce extensive performance information. These complex, multiuser server applications exploit many of the special Win32 operating system services designed to boost application performance. The performance statistics they produce during runtime are designed to provide feedback to system administrators, and to complement the many application-specific tuning parameters that are available to adjust performance.

The operating system includes several useful applications for viewing and analyzing the performance data collected. The most important performance tools are Task Manager (Taskman) and the new Windows 2000 System Monitor (Sysmon) application, which replaces the Performance Monitor (Perfmon) application from earlier versions of Windows NT. In this chapter we review these basic tools and look at how they work. (Unless explicitly stated otherwise, the System Monitor features and facilities discussed also apply to earlier versions of Performance Monitor.)

The tools provided with Windows 2000 are adequate for many purposes, but more sophisticated users like hardware planners with an enterprise-wide outlook will doubtless require better solutions. There are many third-party tools that tap into the same underlying measurement data sources that Sysmon exploits. If you are using any of these third-party performance tools, you will probably find that our description of the way Sysmon works applies to them, too.

No matter which tool is being used, both the Microsoft software and third-party products harvest performance data from a standardized common source. By far the most important of these is the Windows 2000 performance monitoring API, which we describe in great detail. The statistics available through the Windows 2000 performance monitoring API are the cornerstone of Windows 2000 performance monitoring, performance tuning, and capacity planning. The information provided here is also intended to help programmers who want to add performance instrumentation to their applications. Understanding the capabilities and limitations of the performance monitoring API is critical to providing useful metrics about your application.

Before we plunge into using the Windows 2000 performance monitoring statistics for bottleneck analysis and capacity planning in earnest, it will prove helpful to learn how this measurement interface works. In this chapter, we concentrate on the measurement data itself—how it is derived and how it should be interpreted. Along the way, we will also discuss a number of other central concerns in Windows 2000 performance monitoring, including the cost of performance monitoring and important data collection overhead considerations. By the way, if you need help in running the System Monitor application, Part 6 of the Windows 2000 Professional Resource Kit serves as the user manual for this and other performance-oriented tools.

There are, of course, additional sources of valuable information over and above the statistics available using Sysmon. Some of these include the Windows 2000 Registry, the event logs, other application-specific logs from programs like IIS and Exchange, and network packets captured by the Network Monitor or other network sniffer products. We do not spend much time with these in this chapter, but will deal with them as they arise in the appropriate context in later sections of this book.

The fact that Windows 2000 can collect a prodigious amount of performance-oriented data is both a blessing and a curse. The good news is that if you are experiencing a performance problem, there is probably some measurement data available somewhere that is relevant to your problem. Toward the end of this chapter, we discuss a set of standard performance counters that we recommend for getting started in Windows 2000 performance monitoring. The bad news is that there is so much potential data to sift through that the job of performance analysis is rarely easy. People often ask us to give them some simple formula or rules of thumb for determining where their problems lie. Unfortunately, Windows 2000 is a complicated piece of software, as are applications like MS SQL Server or Lotus Notes that run on top of it. We wish that we could make this topic simpler (and we have tried to make it as simple as we can), but we probably cannot.

Performance Monitoring API

Windows 2000 provides two distinct sets of performance monitoring services. The first is an interface for managing the collection and reporting of performance data objects. (Although Windows 2000 calls various sets of related performance statistics "objects," you may feel more comfortable thinking about them as records or record types.) Associated with each object is a set of related *counters*, in effect, numerical data fields. The Windows 2000 operating system kernel is extensively instrumented, and a wide range of detailed performance data is available on hardware resource usage, operating system activity, and active processes and threads across this interface. Besides the kernel, the I/O manager and the various networking services like TCP/IP are also instrumented.

The performance monitoring interface also defines a callable facility that allows a performance monitoring application (like the System Monitor) to retrieve the performance statistics that are collected. The API defines a set of data structures that are used to pass the performance statistics from the data collectors to performance monitoring applications.

The Win32 performance monitoring interface is both *open* and *extensible*. That makes it possible for key applications and subsystems to add to the pool of available performance metrics. And, in fact, many of Microsoft's internally developed applications already exploit this extensible interface, having added their own performance statistics to those maintained by the operating system kernel. These applications include MS SQL Server, Exchange Server, Internet Information Server, and others. Many applications developed on or ported to Windows 2000 by other vendors also utilize this interface for performance data collection. As of this writing, we are aware of some 200 distinct performance objects that are available, with literally thousands of different performance data counters.

A good reason for using the standard facilities for Windows 2000 performance data collection is that the data provided is immediately accessible by the second set of services: the applications that Microsoft and other vendors provide for collecting and viewing performance data. While the Microsoft Windows 2000 Resource Kit mentions a dozen different performance tools that are available, these boil down to two principal tools. One is the Windows 2000 Task Manager, which beginning in NT Version 4.0 provides a compact, real-time view of system activity. The second and more complete and comprehensive tool is System Monitor (or Performance Monitor in NT 4.0), which has the capability to display all the available performance data in both graphical and tabular views, log performance data to a file, and generate alerts. Let's begin by familiarizing ourselves with these essential tools first.

Task Manager

The Task Manager application is a convenient tool you can use from your desktop to monitor the status of the system interactively. If the system is behaving sluggishly or erratically, it is often possible to understand why using Task Manager. A Ctrl-Shift-Esc key combination launches Task Manager. At a glance, you can access system-wide CPU and memory performance statistics, as in Figure 2-1.

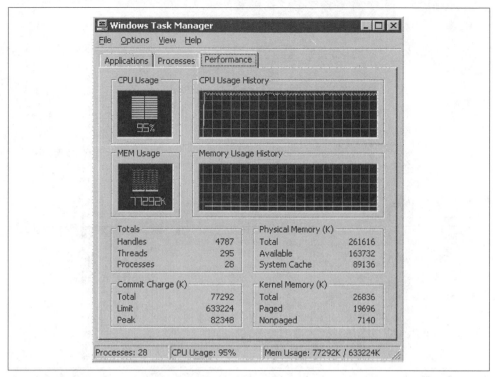

Figure 2-1. The Performance tab of the Task Manager

If a runaway process has gone into a loop and is consuming an excessive amount of CPU time, you can see that under the Processes tab, illustrated in Figure 2-2. The Process tab displays a grid showing resource usage by process. Using the View → Select Columns menu option, you can customize this grid to display the fields that are of interest. For instance, we routinely like to view the CPU Usage, Memory Usage, and Page Fault Delta fields in this display. You can sort the Processes View simply by clicking on the appropriate column label. If you determine that a runaway process is looping by watching the CPU Usage and Page Fault Delta fields, for example, you can then terminate the process by right-clicking on it and accessing the End Process pop-up menu option. (If the runaway process is running as a service, you have to use the Services applet in the Control Panel to put it out of its misery.) When you are done with the Task Manager, minimizing it sends it to the desktop system tray at the lower right-hand corner of the screen. The minimized display is a color-coded histogram for CPU utilization. Positioning the mouse over the minimized Task Manager icon pops up the message "CPU Usage: xx%." Very handy!

The Task Manager is largely unchanged between Windows 2000 and Windows NT 4.0. The only enhancement of note is that several additional columns are available under the Processes tab. These new columns provide logical I/O activity counts at the process level. Because these columns reflect cumulative I/O activity rather than

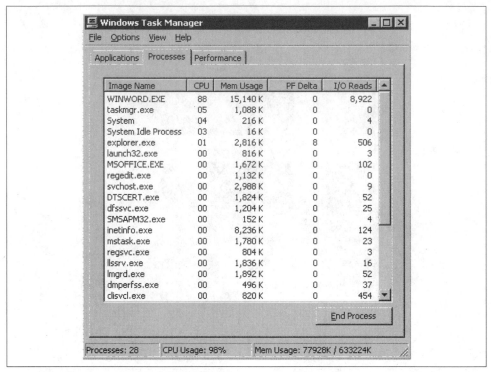

Figure 2-2. The Processes tab of the Task Manager

interval deltas, you will probably find that they are not very good at characterizing what is happening on the system *right now*. The ability to display an interval delta showing the current I/O rate per process would have been more useful.

System Monitor

Although it is fast and convenient, the Task Manager is capable of displaying only a very limited set of performance metrics. It is also limited in that it can only display them in real time. For both real-time and historical data gathering, Microsoft provides another tool. This is the System Monitor (or Perfmon in Windows NT), the heavyweight tool in the Microsoft arsenal of performance monitoring utilities. It features a straightforward graphical user interface designed for exploring and diagnosing performance problems interactively. Perfmon was developed initially for NT Version 3 and carried forward to NT 4.0 virtually without changes. Microsoft subsequently replaced Perfmon with a new System Monitor (Sysmon) application in Windows 2000 (although you can still find a copy Perfmon in the Windows 2000 Resource Kit). In many ways very similar to Perfmon, Sysmon also features some distinct differences and improvements. We will explore these differences later in this chapter. Since Sysmon provides a superset of the capabilities available in Perfmon, the discussion here focuses on features common to both utilities.

You launch the System Monitor from the Administrative Tools menu. By default, System Monitor displays performance statistics in time series using a simple line chart format. See Figure 2-3 for an example. In Chart View, click on the + button to add specific performance counters to the chart, which are then collected and plotted over time. Under Properties, you can customize the graphical display. Among other options, you can specify the collection interval that you want to use to drive data collection. (The default collection interval is once per second.) In the Chart View, this also corresponds to the rate in which the display updates. You can also customize the chart by selecting line colors and widths. In addition, there are scaling options that make it possible to mix different types of information on a single display.

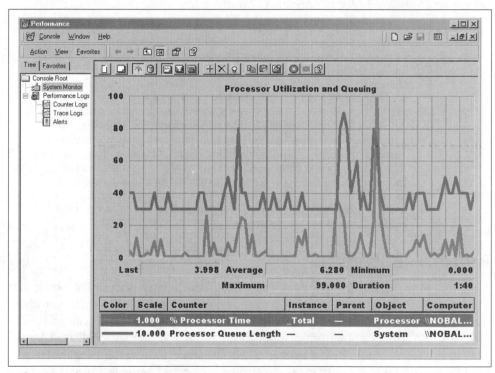

Figure 2-3. System Monitor displaying performance statistics

Windows 2000 also contains a data logging service called *smlogsvc.exe*, which can collect performance data and log it to a file. The logging feature of System Monitor is very useful, allowing you to select and write a large quantity of performance statistics to a file, which you can then analyze later using the System Monitor displays. If you choose to log data in a text file format, you can import performance data into tools like MS Excel to analyze it further. We rely on the logging features of System Monitor throughout this book to illustrate various Windows 2000 performance topics.

Although a capable tool for problem-solving, Sysmon also has many built-in limitations. For instance, Sysmon supports only one way to view the performance data it collects: as a series of line charts plotted against a horizontal time axis. While certainly useful, the two-dimensional time series view is inherently limited. Furthermore, there are so many performance data elements to view and analyze that using Sysmon quickly becomes very tedious and time-consuming. You will find that a System Monitor chart starts to appear very cluttered when you add more and more counters to the visual display. With all the performance data available, it is easy to see why the Windows 2000 environment is such a fertile ground for third-party tools. Many of the examples discussed in this book were illustrated using popular third-party Windows 2000 performance tools.

 Notice that the System Monitor horizontal X axis is unmarked! That is because it might not be a consistent value throughout its length. The chart display is wide enough to plot 100 data points. If you decide to change data collection intervals in the middle of a display, System Monitor simply adds the new series of points to the old ones, so that the X axis reflects both time intervals. The Duration value reflects the current collection interval, which does not match the X axis if data points from more than one collection interval are displayed. If there are fewer than 100 data points to graph, the line graphs are truncated. If you are looking at data in real time, the display wraps around back to the beginning once you accumulate more than 100 data points. If there are more than 100 data points from a log file to display, the System Monitor Chart skips every *n/100* intermediate points so that the graphed line fills out the display area.

Performance Objects

Both the Microsoft System Monitor and various third-party performance tools rely on the same underlying set of performance data collection facilities. A distinguishing feature of Windows 2000 is a standard data collection mechanism developed specifically for performance monitoring applications to retrieve statistics collected by the operating system and other subsystems. Performance statistics are organized into objects, according to the hardware or software component being measured. This section discusses how the performance statistics in Windows 2000 are organized.

Windows 2000 performance data can be accessed internally using any of three very similar interfaces. The original interface queries the Registry. This is the oldest and best-known interface, and also the most complex. In Windows NT 4.0, Microsoft introduced the second interface, the Performance Data Helper (PDH) API, which simplifies access to the performance statistics. Because it is easier to use for harvesting a few select metrics at a time, the PDH API has proved very successful. Finally, in

Windows 2000, Microsoft provides a new Windows Measurement Instrumentation (WMI), which the new Sysmon application can use. The new WMI interface is being developed with an eye for the future and may eventually diverge from the others. WMI is based on the WBEM* standard, which is endorsed by the Desktop Management Task Force (DMTF), an organization to which Microsoft, Intel, Compaq, HP, and other major computer industry vendors belong.

For the moment, Windows 2000 continues to support all new and old interfaces. All three interfaces provide similar facilities. Since our purpose here is merely to describe the capabilities of the measurement interface, it does not matter too much which one we choose. With that in mind, we will discuss the oldest Registry interface because it remains the one people are most familiar with.

The Registry interface

The Registry interface provides a convenient way to access the available performance data. The Windows 2000 Registry is a repository of configuration data used to record the current status of the system. It is a tree-structured file (actually stored as a series of files, or *hives,* on disk to provide a degree of fault tolerance) in which data is stored under specific key values. If you are not familiar with the Registry, run the *regedit.exe* program from a command line to bring up the Registry Editor. We often refer to information stored in the Registry throughout this book.

HKEY_PERFORMANCE_DATA is the Registry key that programs use to access the performance objects and counters from the Registry. You can't find these fields in the Registry Editor, though; it ignores these key values because they are not available for a user to modify. Unlike the rest of the static configuration information available from the Registry, the Windows 2000 performance statistics are not actually stored in the Registry files, and unlike other data stored in the Registry, the data associated with various performance counters is not persistent. Consequently, when you run the Registry Editor application, the performance statistics are hidden from view. However, using standard Win32 programming services, you can write a program to retrieve data from the Registry, including the performance statistics. Using the existing Registry interfaces makes it relatively easy for any application to retrieve performance statistics. Since an application can access the Registry remotely, performance monitoring applications like System Monitor are network-enabled. They are not limited, as Task Manager is, to looking only at local system performance statistics.

---

* WBEM, which stands for Web Based Enterprise Management, is an initiative endorsed by a number of large hardware and software vendors to unify disjoint computer and network management reporting standards. Originally proposed by BMC Software in 1996 to unite SNMP, DMI, and Microsoft's Registry-based performance monitoring standards using a Common Information Model (CIM), WBEM is endorsed by Microsoft, Intel, Compaq, Dell, Cisco, and others. A white paper from Microsoft providing an overview of WBEM is available at *http://eu.microsoft.com/windows2000/library/howitworks/management/WMIOverview.asp*. The Desktop Management Task Force (DMTF) is currently responsible for defining the WBEM standard, which can be accessed at *http://www.dmtf.org/spec/wbem.html*.

So, if the performance data you can view in System Monitor is not actually stored in the Registry, where is it? Behind the specific calls to the Registry interface to retrieve performance statistics, there is a simple mechanism to identify and call performance data providers. These providers are the system software routines that gather up the performance data upon request. Notice that there are multiple providers of performance data on any Windows 2000 system. When an application like the System Monitor issues a RegQueryValueEx call to access current values of the HKEY_PERFORMANCE_DATA Registry key to retrieve performance data fields, the call is redirected to the specific performance monitoring data provider responsible for collecting and maintaining those statistics. These program modules are known as Perflib DLLs (dynamic link libraries).

When a performance monitoring application calls the Registry interface, an underlying function identifies and loads the Perflib DLLs that are available on the target system. These Perflib DLLs are loaded into the address space of the calling program, an active performance monitoring application (such as Sysmon). Working behind the scenes, the Perflib DLLs perform the real meat-and-potatoes work in Windows 2000 performance monitoring.

Enumerating Perflib DLLs

When you press the + button in Sysmon to add counters, it triggers a mechanism behind the scenes that enumerates all the performance objects and counters available on the specified computer system. One distinguishing characteristic of the Windows 2000 performance monitoring interface is that the set of performance monitoring objects and counters available at any one time is quite dynamic. Performance data providers plug into this interface when the applications they are associated with are installed. A runtime mechanism discovers the available objects and counters by first determining the Perflib DLLs that are installed, then calling the specified Perflib DLL initialization routines to find out what objects and counters they provide.

The Registry Editor can be useful in visualizing this dynamic calling mechanism. Services and device drivers install their customization parameters under the HKLM\SYSTEM\CurrentControlSet\Services key. Applications that want to collect performance statistics add a Performance subkey under their main application key, as illustrated in Figure 2-4. Here MS SQL Server 2000 (internally known as Version 8) has set up the Performance subkey that the performance monitoring interface requires. To install its set of performance counters, an application sets the value of Library to the name of the module that is responsible for data collection. The SQL Server 8.0 Perflib DLL responsible for collecting the SQL Performance Data Object in this case is *SQLCTR80.dll*. The Performance subkey also specifies the name of the Perflib DLL initialization routine to call to enumerate the objects and counters it provides, the actual data provider routine to call each collection interval, and a termination routine. The Registry values for First Counter and Last Counter show the index values for the counters that *SQLCTR80.dll* is responsible for reporting. (By the way, on your system the First Counter and Last Counter IDs are liable to be different. Object and counter IDs for *extended counters* like the SQL Server 8.0 ones are parceled out on a first come, first served basis, as Perflib DLLs are installed.)

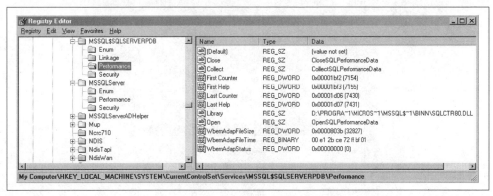

Figure 2-4. The Performance subkey in MS SQL Server, shown in the Registry Editor

A performance monitor application that wants to retrieve SQL Server statistics issues a call to RegQueryValueEx looking for those specific counters under the HKEY_ PERFORMANCE_DATA key. The performance monitoring interface identifies *SQLCTR80.dll* as the keeper of these counters, and the request is routed to that program. *SQLCTR80.dll* fills in the counter values that have been defined, and eventually the data makes its way back to the original requestor.

A Resource Kit tool called Extensible Counter List (illustrated in Figure 2-5) performs an enumeration of the Perflib DLLs that are installed. This Resource Kit utility, mostly of interest to developers, produces a diagnostic report listing all the Perflib DLLs that are installed and showing any modules that cannot be located. This can be useful in figuring out what is going on when an application removes its Perflib DLL but fails to remove its corresponding Services Performance subkey that registers the Perflib module (not an uncommon occurrence). As illustrated, basic Windows 2000 counters are maintained by four separate Perflib DLLs: *perfdisk.dll*, *perfnet.dll*, *perfos.dll*, and *perfproc.dll*.

The meaning and usage of all the Performance subkey fields are documented in the Resource Kit's Registry help file documentation (to which we refer often in this book). Of particular interest are several fields that standard entries for modules like *perfdisk.dll* and *perfnet.dll* contain, but Perflib DLLs developed by people far removed from the development and maintenance of the Windows 2000 performance monitoring software often do not. These document a number of new facilities added to the performance monitoring API in Windows 2000 to improve its security and integrity.

Because the performance monitoring interface is documented in the platform DDK (Device Driver Development Kit), any software developer can plug into it relatively

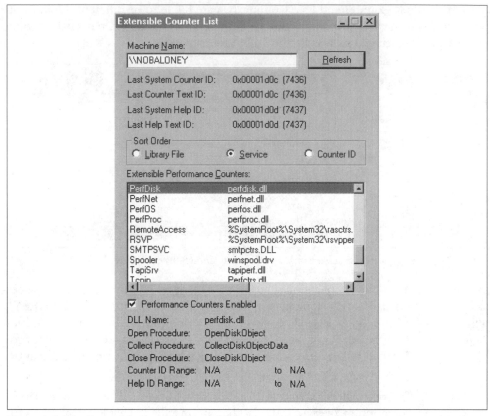

Figure 2-5. The Extensible Counter List tool from the Resource Kit

easily, almost too easily on an open platform like Windows 2000. Sometimes this leads to third-party Perflib DLLs that are quite buggy. These problems are only manifest when you run a performance monitoring application like System Monitor that indirectly accesses one of these "rogue" Perflib DLLs. Since problems with rogue Perflib DLLs tend to be reported to the Microsoft team responsible for System Monitor, Windows 2000 contains some new facilities to insulate System Monitor from these problems.

These performance monitoring integrity features include Open, Timeout, and Collect Timeout fields, which the performance monitoring interface uses to safeguard the integrity of system monitoring applications that encounter rogue Perflib DLLs behaving badly, i.e., hanging or going into an infinite loop. Evidently, the Microsoft developers of *SQLCTRS80.dll* were not familiar with this innovation because the fields were not added when SQL Server 2000 installed its Perflib DLL. However, do not despair. If necessary, you can always add them manually to the Registry using the Registry Editor (being careful to specify them *exactly* as documented).

The Resource Kit's Registry help file also documents a new Performance subkey field called Disable Performance Counters. When the performance monitoring interface detects a badly behaved Perflib DLL (i.e., one that does not return prior to its Time-out value), the facility adds this key automatically to the appropriate Performance subkey so that problems do not recur in subsequent performance monitoring sessions. If you are ever wondering why some performance counters that you expect are not appearing in System Monitor, check the Performance subkey and see if Windows 2000 has disabled that set of counters. Then contact your vendor to resolve the problem, which presumably involves replacing the current, malfunctioning version of the Perflib DLL with a repaired version. After you have resolved the problem, you can remove the Disable Performance Counters flag. When you restart the System Monitor, you should see the wayward counters you were looking for.

As another bulwark against rogue Perflib DLLs damaging system integrity, Microsoft added a new field in the current key called ExtCounterTestLevel. If you set ExtCounterTestLevel to its highest possible level, which is 1, the performance monitoring interface tests the validity of memory buffers processed by Perflib DLLs, then copies the data they contain into a new buffer before it is returned to the calling performance monitoring application. The default is that no Perflib DLL integrity checking is performed. This was the only option under earlier versions of Windows NT, too, and it led to the occasional problem when a less-than-vigorously tested Perflib DLL was installed.

Base performance objects

Performance data in Windows is organized into *objects*, the equivalent, perhaps, of records to a COBOL programmer or rows of a table to a DBA. (Object-oriented programming, or OOP, is currently in vogue, and Windows 2000 uses OOP terminology pervasively.) The operating system kernel collects performance data for a set of basic objects. In alphabetical order, these base counters include the following objects that are installed by default: Cache, Job, IP, Logical Disk, Memory, Objects, Paging File, Physical Disk, Print Queue, Process, Processor, Redirector, Server, Server Work Queues, System, TCP, and Thread. Most of these performance objects are self-explanatory. They present the utilization levels and status of the system's CPU, memory, and disk resources. Some of the objects require some further discussion and clarification. We attempt to do a bit of that here, while postponing the bulk of the discussion describing the most useful objects and counters and how they are derived and interpreted for later chapters.

The Objects object counts the number of kernel objects in existence—events, mutexes, processes, critical sections, semaphores, and threads. Each kernel object requires some amount of non-pageable memory, so there is some justification for the category. The developers of the operating system kernel are quite interested in these metrics, but you will rarely need to take an interest in them.

The Server object reflects networked file activity, which the Server Work Queues object plumbs in greater detail. The Redirector is the component of Windows 2000 that routes requests that reference a remote file (rather than a local one) over the network to the Server component running on the corresponding computer. If Windows 2000 is being used primarily as a file and print server, the Redirector statistics provide a view of file server activity from the standpoint of its network clients. We say more about the file server application in Windows 2000 and its network client, the Redirector, in later chapters.

In Windows 2000, a *process* is the basic unit of work associated with an executing program. Windows 2000 establishes a unique *context* for virtual addressing for each *instance* (more OOP terminology) of a running process. The execution *context* of a process includes, for example, the page tables used by the processor hardware for virtual memory address translation. (The OS manages and maintains page tables on behalf of every running process.) The OS monitors and reports the memory, paging activity, and CPU resources used by processes. Inside a process, one or more *threads* represent the dispatchable units that execute instructions and perform I/O. Each process has at least one thread; many processes utilize multiple threads. Thread measurements primarily concern consumption of CPU cycles and dispatching priority. Each process is a separate object instance, as is each thread within a process.

The Processor object contains statistics on systemwide CPU consumption. Windows 2000 uses a straightforward mechanism for determining overall processor utilization without having to rely on specific hardware instrumentation, which may or may not be available. When there is no work waiting for processing, the operating system dispatches an *Idle thread*. Overall processor utilization is calculated every collection interval simply by subtracting the utilization of the Idle thread from 100%. Processor statistics calculated in this fashion are reported under the Processor object. In a multiprocessor, there are multiple Processor object instances, which are summarized in a _Total instance of the Processor object. In prior versions of Windows NT, the System object contains the corresponding summarized system-level CPU utilization measurements. Don't be confused; these are the same measurements, just labeled differently. By the way, the Idle thread is not really a thread—think of it as a bookkeeping mechanism. The Idle thread is actually implemented in the Hardware Abstraction Layer (HAL)* because there may be hardware-dependent operations that need to be performed when the processor is idle.

---

* The Hardware Abstraction Layer (HAL) is a low-level component of the Windows 2000 operating system responsible for processor hardware-specific services like interrupt handling, task switching, interprocessor signaling, and serialization. In Win2k, processor-specific routines are confined to a single routine, *hal.dll*. Concentrating its hardware-specific support in a single machine language module greatly enhances the portability of the Windows 2000 OS. If you are not familiar with the HAL and the overall organization of the Windows 2000 operating system, refer to *Inside Windows 2000* by David Solomon and Mark Russinovich, especially Chapter 2.

Monitoring disk performance

You can access performance statistics for both logical disks (filesystems) and physical disks (hardware entities). Disks are monitored by a measurement program inserted between the filesystem driver and the disk driver called *diskperf.sys*. Historically, disk monitoring was disabled due to its potential for generating significant overhead. That is hardly a concern today for most Windows 2000 systems, which is why Windows 2000 enables physical disk monitoring by default. Two copies of diskperf need to be loaded simultaneously in Windows 2000 to maintain statistics for both logical disks (or partitions) and physical disks. To enable logical disk monitoring, issue the following command, which will take effect the next time the system is restarted:

```
diskperf -yv
```

On NT 4.0 systems, disk performance monitoring is disabled by default. To ensure that disk performance monitoring is turned on, issue the following command:

```
diskperf -y
```

Monitoring will be enabled the next time you restart the computer. If diskperf is not enabled, the logical and physical disk counters will show zero values. It is important to set diskperf to measure your disks automatically in advance, rather than waiting until a problem occurs. If diskperf is not running and you are experiencing a performance problem, no disk statistics are available to help you diagnose the problem.

The disk performance monitoring functions view all disk I/O requests and keep track of how long they run. diskperf maintains counters for the number of I/O requests per disk, the bytes transferred, and whether they are reads or writes. From these basic disk counters, additional measures are derived, including the average request size and average response time. Windows 2000 also keeps track of disk % Idle Time. Similar to the way Windows 2000 calculates processor utilization, the % Idle Time counter can be used to calculate disk utilization.

The diskperf counters kept for both logical and physical disks have a legacy with many twists and turns. A fundamental problem surfaced in the original Windows NT Version 3 implementation when the disk performance counters that purported to report disk utilization, a critical measure, were calculated incorrectly. Windows NT 4.0 addressed the problem, but did not resolve it. For Windows 2000, the developers instituted a more satisfactory resolution, which was the introduction of the % Idle Time counter. Unfortunately, the original counters that were calculated incorrectly still remain to sow confusion; better they were eliminated entirely.

A second problem arose in Windows NT version 3 due to complexity introduced by a function called the fault-tolerant disk driver (*ftdisk.sys*), which supports disk mirroring, striping, and striping with parity (RAID 5). Using the Disk Management applet, it is possible to invoke ftdisk volume manager functions and set up a logical disk that consists of multiple partitions spread across two or more physical disks.

With ftdisk enabled, more complicated relationships between logical volumes and physical disks can be created than were ever possible with diskperf. Using ftdisk can result in some confusing-looking disk performance statistics where the logical disk activity does not match the physical disk activity. NT 4.0 fixes this problem, but only if the disk performance collector is set up to monitor activity after *ftdisk.sys* has sorted out the mapping between logical and physical disks using an extended option setting called diskperf -ye. This installs the *diskperf.sys* performance monitoring layer below the fault-tolerant disk driver, *ftdisk.sys*, in the I/O stack. Unfortunately, this is not a wholly satisfactory resolution, since *diskperf.sys* running below *ftdisk.sys* leads to inaccurate logical disk measurements.

The Windows 2000 version of diskperf resolves this problem definitively by allowing two copies of diskperf to be loaded simultaneously, one above and one below ftdisk. The Windows 2000 version of diskperf also references the logical disks associated with each physical disk in the instance name reported. Rather than attempt an even lengthier explanation of the logical and physical disk counters and their checkered history here, we defer that discussion until Chapter 8.

Network counters

As noted earlier, many Microsoft software components take advantage of the performance data collection interface. This includes the standard TCP/IP networking software support. (In Windows NT 4.0, the summary statistics for TCP and IP are only available when you install the SNMP networking service.) If you install the Network Monitor driver, a standard feature of the operating system, several additional network monitoring objects are enabled for display in System Monitor. The Network Monitor driver is inserted into the NDIS (Network Device Interface Specification) layer of networking software to record performance information about network packets prior to them being processing by higher-level protocols like IP and TCP. The corresponding NT 4.0 version of the Network Monitor Agent, known internally as Bloodhound, is a protocol analyzer that traces packets moving across the network segment. It captures data transmission packets from each individual network interface cards (NICs) running in promiscuous mode, and reports on them. With the Bloodhound Perflib DLL, *bhmon.dll*, installed, you can collect performance counters on network segment traffic, including packets sent and received, bytes transferred, line utilization, and error statistics.

Extensible counters

The performance monitoring API is extensible, allowing applications like MS SQL Server, MS Exchange Server, and the MS Internet Information Server to add performance statistics to the mix. The advantage of having these applications write extensible performance objects is twofold. First, the performance data they gather is immediately available for use by existing tools like Sysmon. Second, application-oriented data is synchronized in time with complementary hardware- and operating system–level statistics. The application data can be combined with these statistics to provide a more complete picture of overall system activity.

Each application that reports performance data using the performance monitoring API includes a Perflib DLL that is installed with it. These Perflib DLLs gather statistics and return them to performance monitoring applications like Sysmon. This is not necessarily easy to accomplish. The Perflib DLL module is loaded into the performance monitoring application's address space. The Perflib DLL may need to access performance data that resides in the monitored application's address space. For example, *SQLCTR80.dll* running inside Sysmon's MMC (Microsoft Management Console) process accesses performance data stored inside the *sqlserver.exe* address space using a named pipe interprocess communication (IPC) service. There are circumstances when *SQLCTR80.dll* cannot connect to the sqlserver address space (maybe it is too busy with other work) across this interface, and data collection is interrupted. When this occurs, you might see an error message in the event log like the one illustrated in Figure 2-6.

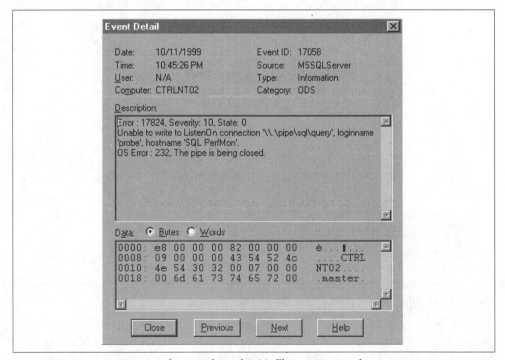

Figure 2-6. An error message indicating that sqlctr80.dll cannot respond to requests

Figure 2-7 pictures an Extensible Counter List display illustrating the complex monitoring structure that the MS Exchange Server application uses involving five different Perflib DLLs. Exchange uses multiple Perflib DLLs because Exchange itself consists of several components running as separate processes. For instance, the

Exchange Information Store Counters provided by *mdbperf.dll* monitor database activity occurring within the principal Information Store process called *store.exe*. A different Perflib DLL called *perfdsa.dll* monitors activity to Exchange folders and address books occurring within the Directory Services process called *dsamain.exe*.

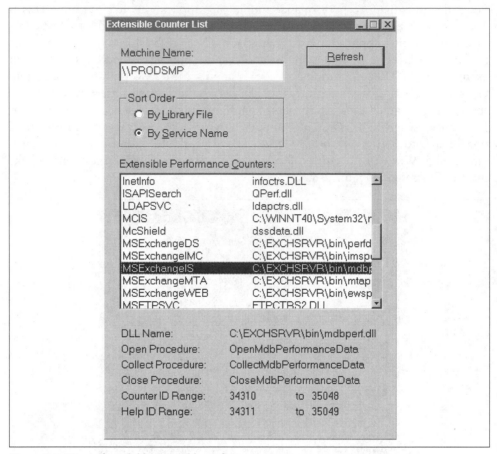

Figure 2-7. View of available extensible performance counters

Instances of objects

For many types of objects, multiple *instances* are collected each interval. For example, each process running in the system represents a separate instance of the Process object in Sysmon. The Task Manager display in Figure 2-1 shows a Windows 2000 system that currently has 28 processes running with a total of 295 threads. If you want to look at all the Process and Thread performance data that is available, that would involve looking through all 323 instances collected each collection interval—potentially lots and lots of data. Many performance objects are instanced. There is one instance for each physical disk and each logical disk that is defined. When you are running on a symmetric multiprocessor (SMP), there is one Processor object instance for each CPU and one Paging File object instance for each paging file.

Object instances are named so that you can identify them. Processor objects are given instance names of 0, 1, 2, etc., depending on the number of CPUs installed. Processes are identified by the name of their executable image file, e.g., *word, taskmgr,* or *services.* The process instance name is not guaranteed to be unique. If you have several copies of Word running, you will see several process instances named *word.* Each process, however, does have a unique ID that can be used to differentiate among multiple instances of the same image. Logical disk instances are identified by drive letter, e.g., *C:* or *D:.* (Performance stats are maintained only for local hard drives.) Physical Disks are numbered 0, 1, 2, and so on; likewise with a process's threads. Since threads can be created and destroyed during the course of program execution, there is no guarantee that the thread 7 appearing now is the same thread 7 that was active ten minutes ago.

Sysmon lets you add data to a chart for just those instances you want to watch. Working with an object like Process or Thread, where there are lots of instances, can be very cumbersome. In this case, it is useful to first create a report listing activity from every instance, and then return to the Chart View to add just the instances and counters that look interesting. Figure 2-8 shows the System Monitor Add Counters dialog box that allows you to select specific object and counter instances and add them to a chart or report. Unfortunately, Sysmon does not make this operation especially easy because you cannot sort a report by value or print it. Back in the original Performance Monitor, you could export chart data to a comma-delimited file, which you could then import and process using something like Excel. Once the report data is loaded into a spreadsheet, you could sort columns by value. Unfortunately, the Export option is not available with the Windows 2000 Sysmon application. Your only Import/Export option with Sysmon is to log the data in text format.

Special _Total instances for some objects make it easier to monitor larger configurations. There are _Total instances for Processor, Process, and Thread objects, the Paging File, and the Logical and Physical Disk objects, for example. The associated Perflib DLLs manufacture these instances by totaling up all the individual instances. They are needed because System Monitor itself cannot perform any arithmetic calculations. On a multiprocessor, the Processor object contains an instance for each hardware CPU element. Despite its name, the _Total instance of the Processor % Processor Time counter reports averages, not totals. In NT 4.0, no _Total instance of the Processor object was created. Instead, processor utilization is summarized in counters available under the System object. What is confusing is that these counters are called % Total Processor Time, for example, although they actually represent an *average* over all processor instances. In Windows 2000, the familiar System object counters that summarize overall CPU utilization are gone.

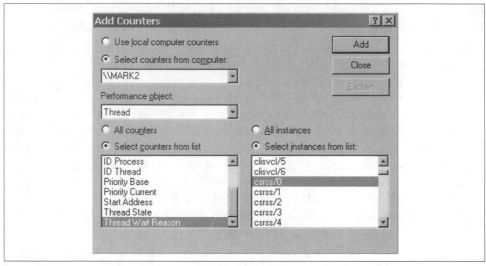

Figure 2-8. Sysmon's Add Counters dialog box

Parent-child relationships

The performance monitoring interface supports one other wrinkle: a parent-child relationship between an instance from one object with an instance from another. Currently, Windows 2000 defines only one parent-child relationship among base performance objects: the relationship between a process and its threads. Processes reflect the virtual address space created for a running program, which might be a service running in the background with no user interface, or a full-blown Windows application running on your desktop. The *executable unit* of a process is the thread; this means that the thread contains the program code that is actually dispatched by the operating system and executed. Each process has at least one thread, thread 0, which is created when the process is created. As a thread executes, it can spawn additional threads within the same process address space. All the threads associated with a process are identified with that process instance name, which is designated as the thread's parent. Inside System Monitor, the notation csrss => 0 associates a specific thread 0 instance with a parent process, in this case, *csrss.exe*. The only other example of a parent-child relationship that did exist was between a logical disk volume and the physical disk where it resides. However, that relationship is no longer specified explicitly in Windows 2000. To date, there are no extended counters that implement parent-child relationships.

Performance Counters

Each object or record has one or more counters, which are essentially numeric fields reflecting some measurement data. Specific counters are available that can tell you how busy the system processor is, how memory is allocated, how busy the disks and network connections are, etc. Others show you how much free disk space is available in each filesystem or how long the system and various processes have been up and running. Still others help you pinpoint performance bottlenecks at the CPU, memory, or disk that are impacting performance levels.

Figure 2-8 illustrated the Add Counter dialog box used to select the computer you are interested in monitoring and to add specific counters associated with some object (or object instance) to a Sysmon chart, report, or logging file. (The Perfmon counter selection dialog box is quite similar.) Even on simple systems, there are hundreds of counters from which to choose. Understanding what counters are available and what they mean is at the heart of Windows 2000 performance monitoring, tuning, and capacity planning. This book provides detailed explanations and usability notes for all the important Windows 2000 performance counters.

Explain Text

Figure 2-9 shows Explain Text, which is a sentence or two about the counter and what it refers to. This is static text supplied by the performance data collector when it installs its counters. These text fields are also accessed dynamically using the Registry (or equivalent) interface. For many fields, that smidgeon of Explain Text is the only clue that reveals what a particular counter is good for. The Windows 2000 Resource Kit documentation provides some additional help in several chapters devoted to the use of the System Monitor.

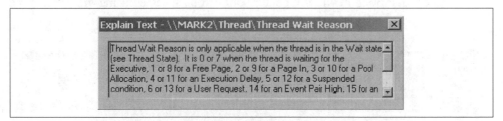

Figure 2-9. Explain Text provides additional information about a particular counter

The Resource Kit Performance Monitor usage notes have an interesting history. Russ Blake, the software architect primarily responsible for the development of the original NT Performance Monitor, wrote a book to document Perfmon entitled *Optimizing Windows NT*. (Note that Sean Dailey's excellent book on NT performance bears the same title.) Prior to NT 4.0, Blake's *Optimizing Windows NT* was packaged as Volume 4 of the Resource Kit, an entire book devoted to performance monitoring and NT's built-in performance tools, mainly Perfmon. Like some other deities, Blake chose to rest after his labors developing Perfmon and ultimately retired from Microsoft several years ago. Quite a few chapters from Blake's original book were updated and incorporated into the Professional version of the Windows 2000 Resource Kit. His documentation about Perfmon internals, including a copy of the Version 3 Perfmon source code, was moved first to the Win32 SDK and subsequently to the Windows 2000 Device Driver Kit (DDK). Our advice is to keep Blake's original book around, if you can still find it, despite the fact that changes to later OS versions render some of the information obsolete. He does an admirable job in making an arcane and complex technical topic accessible to a wide audience.

The current documentation for the System Monitor is contained within the Professional version of the Resource Kit documentation, including material describing the key 4.0 changes. Some of the chapters from Blake's original book are no longer published in the same form. Appendixes A and B, more than 200 pages listing all the performance counters and Registry parameters with performance implications, are among the missing. No doubt, this information was considered both too bulky and too dynamic to warrant republishing in book form. Instead, documentation on the specific performance counters and Registry settings, many of which can impact performance, was moved to two compiled help files that are contained in the Resource Kit CD: *Counters.chm* and *Regentry.chm*, respectively. These are both worthwhile sources of information.

The Resource Kit's *Counters.chm* help file consolidates all the Explain Text available for the many built-in operating system and networking objects and counters; see Figure 2-10. To find this help file, install the Resource Kit and access the performance counters documentation. Because the operating system developers supervise the development of the *Counters.chm* file, it contains little Explain Text for extended counters, which, in any event, is usually quite skimpy. It also documents several costly objects that Sysmon will not collect, but can be accessed using other Resource Kit tools.

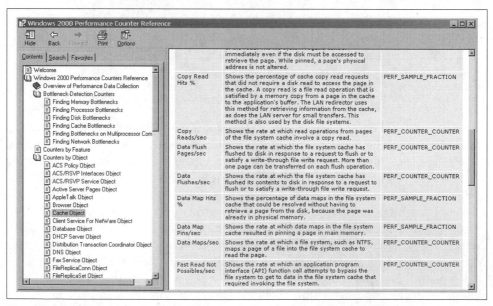

Figure 2-10. The Counters.chm help file documents performance objects and counters

The *Regentry.chm* help file is another useful tool, a massive compendium of Registry settings that influence many aspects of system operation. It is an indispensable source of authoritative information on the many Registry tweaks that can affect application and system performance. The sheer amount of information it contains is forbidding; Figure 2-11 illustrates just some of the runtime parameters associated with the Windows 2000 file server client component. Even so, *Regentry.chm*, like *Counters.chm*, is limited to documenting core operating system services. For help with the many tuning performance parameters associated with IIS, MS Exchange, or SQL Server you must look elsewhere.

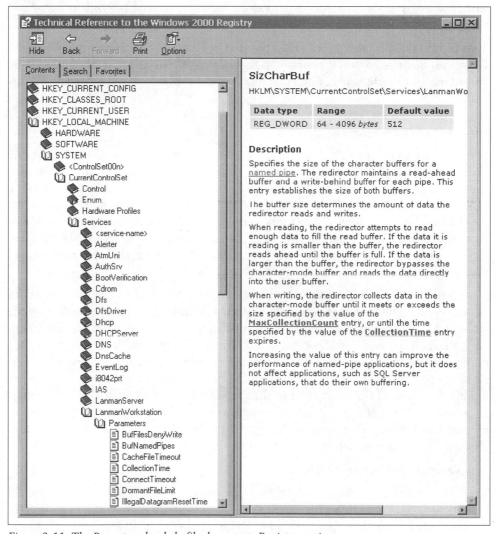

Figure 2-11. The Regentry.chm help file documents Registry settings

Counter types

Understanding how the various performance counters are derived at a detailed level each collection interval is a prerequisite to using them correctly and helps in understanding which counters can be summarized at higher-level intervals. The *counter type* definition identifies the form of the raw data to a performance monitoring application like Sysmon, and defines any calculations that Sysmon should perform to transform the metric into a valid measurement statistic. The counter type also implicitly defines the summarization logic that applies to the field if you are keeping a record of what is happening on your systems for longer-term capacity planning. Suffice to say that some counter types can be summarized readily, while others resist almost any summarization; we discuss this topic shortly.

A wide variety of counter types are supported, with over 20 different types defined. These can be distilled into three basic categories: *difference* or *accumulator* counters, *instantaneous* or *right now* counters, and *compound* counters that use predefined formulas.

Difference and time difference counters

The most common counter type is a *difference* or *accumulator* value, a continuously maintained counter field that literally counts events as they occur. Some difference counter types count events, while others keep track of time or count bytes sent to the disk or across a network. Two examples of events that the operating system counts are the number of hardware interrupts that occur and the number of paging operations that the operating system initiates. This type of instrumentation works quite simply: each time a hardware interrupt occurs, for example, the operating system maintains a counter that is incremented by one.

It is up to a performance monitoring application (i.e., Sysmon) to transform the continuously maintained counter variables that the OS maintains into rates reflecting the amount of activity that occurred in a given collection interval. The Perflib DLL supplies the current value of the counter each collection interval to the performance monitoring application, which normalizes it to produce a rate, like pages/sec or network packets/sec. To accomplish this, the performance monitoring application retains the value of the counter from the previous interval and calculates the difference, reflecting the amount of activity associated with the current collection interval. Finally, this interval delta value is divided by the length of the collection interval to create a rate per second where the Duration is calculated as $t_1 - t_0$:

$$(Counter_{t1} - Counter_{t0}) / (Duration)$$

The most common variety of difference counter is a simple 4-byte (32-bit) field known as a PERF_COUNTER_COUNTER. For counting very large numbers of events, there is a 64-bit variant called a PERF_COUNTER_LARGE_COUNTER.

There are a variety of time-oriented difference counters, including PERF_COUNTER_100NSEC_TIMER and PERF_ELAPSED_TIME, which function in a similar fashion. They differ from an ordinary difference counter in that they maintain a continuous count in clock ticks, not events. A HAL function transforms hardware-specific clock interrupts into a normalized virtual clock that interrupts the operating system every 100 nanoseconds. This becomes the Windows 2000 system clock used for timing all events in the system at the granularity of 100-nanosecond units.

The PERF_ELAPSED_TIME counter provides the basis for simple availability reporting at both the system and process level. Elapsed time is constructed from a retained value of the system clock that marks the start of a process. The performance monitoring application retrieves the current clock value, makes the difference calculation, and converts Windows 2000 timer ticks to wall-clock time for display purposes. The System Up Time metric is calculated from a similar retained clock value marking the time the operating system initialized.

The execution time of threads is also measured in timer ticks. Each time the Scheduler dispatches a thread, the operating system captures the current time in 100 nanosecond unit clock ticks. When the thread finishes using the CPU, the current clock value is obtained again. The difference, which is the amount of time the thread was running, is calculated. This value is accumulated and stored in a field in the Thread Information Block associated with that thread. Then, during performance data collection, the *perfproc.dll* Perflib DLL responsible for process and thread statistics inventories the current threads and returns the current value of this retained clock timer value to the performance monitoring application. Sysmon matches up the various threads of the process, compares the current value to the previous one, and calculates the difference. This calculated value is the amount of CPU time the thread has consumed during the last measurement interval. The PERF_COUNTER_100NSEC_TIMER counter definition then specifies a calculation to report this timer value as a % CPU Busy. This is accomplished by dividing the accumulated CPU usage in 100-nanosecond clock ticks by the total number of clock ticks in the measurement interval. The formula for calculating % Busy is:

$$(Timer_{+t1} - Timer_{t0})/Duration \times 100$$

where all the timer values, including the Duration field, are in 100-nanosecond units. The % Processor Time counters in the Process and Thread objects are both PERF_COUNTER_100NSEC_TIMER counters.

When there are no threads requesting CPU service, Windows dispatches an Idle thread. As noted previously, this is not an actual thread; it is a HAL function that serves as a bookkeeping mechanism. There is one Idle thread per processor to keep track of each processor element separately. The Scheduler dispatches the Idle thread to record the number of unused CPU cycles. Windows 2000 accumulates clock ticks for the Idle thread in the same fashion as any other thread. The "inverse" part of the

PERF_100NSEC_TIMER_INV counter type definition specifies that this CPU % Busy value should be subtracted from 100% to measure the amount of time the processor was busy performing real work. Thus, Windows 2000 does not directly measure how busy the CPU engines are; it measures the amount of time they are idle and calculates the inverse.

Instantaneous counters

The second and simplest type of counter is a *raw* or *instantaneous* counter. A raw counter is the value of some performance metric *right now*. No calculations need to be performed on this kind of counter field: the performance monitoring application simply displays the current value as is. Moreover, a raw counter is always an integer value, reflecting the current state of the machine. It represents a single observation or measurement sample. When looking at Explain Text, you can be sure that it is a raw counter if you see the following sentence: "This is an instantaneous count, not an average over the time interval." Beginning in Windows NT 4.0, Microsoft added this language to the documentation to distinguish this type of counter from the others. A raw counter is designated a PERF_COUNTER_RAW internally. A wider 8-byte PERF_COUNTER_BULK_COUNT is used when the counter is liable to overrun a 4-byte field.

A good example of a raw counter is the Processor Queue Length counter in the System object. This is the current number of threads in the processor dispatching Ready Queue. If you are collecting System objects once per minute, then once a minute you know the current value of the Processor Queue Length. This does not provide any information about what happened *during* that minute; all you can tell is that at the *end* of the minute, the value of the counter is such and such. A raw counter gives you one observation about the state of the system per measurement interval. It represents the current state of the system, for example the number of available bytes of memory or the current thread count for a process.

Figure 2-12 shows an example of the System Monitor tracking the Processor Queue Length over the last 100 seconds. This counter value is a PERF_COUNTER_RAW, so it is the number of threads that are ready to run at the moment that the data was collected: here, every second. Notice that the value of the Processor Queue Length counter is always an integer.

Compound counters

Difference counters and raw counters make up the bulk of all Windows 2000 performance monitoring metrics, but there are also a few specialty counters that are harder to categorize. Many of these are *compound* fields based on predefined formulas. Compound counters are used to derive values calculated from more basic measurement data. Examples include the PERF_AVERAGE_TIMER, PERF_RAW_FRACTION, PERF_SAMPLE_FRACTION, and PERF_AVERAGE_BULK counters. Compound

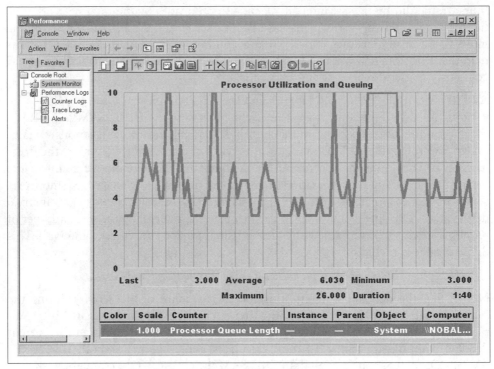

Figure 2-12. A raw (instantaneous) counter

counters package together the multiple data fields System Monitor needs to make a predefined calculation. The specific formula used is based on the counter type.

In the case of a PERF_RAW_FRACTION, the counter is presented as a fraction to be calculated. A good example is the % Free Space counter in the Logical Disk object that reports the amount of space occupied on a logical disk partition as a percentage of the total disk partition capacity. The *perfdisk.dll* Perflib DLL supplies both the numerator (bytes allocated) and denominator (total capacity of the partition in bytes) of the fraction for Sysmon to calculate. System Monitor simply performs the specified calculation and displays the result. From the standpoint of summarization, a PERF_RAW_FRACTION behaves like a raw counter in that it is a single measurement performed at a specific instant in time.

The % Broadcast Frames counter is an example of a PERF_AVERAGE_BULK type in the Network Segment object (available only in Windows NT Version 4). It is a compound counter produced from two continuously maintained event counters. Conceptually, it is a hybrid of a difference counter and a raw fraction. In this case, the continuously maintained event counters measure the total number of frames and broadcast frames sent and received across a network segment from the point of view of the measured system. The performance monitoring application preserves the frame count from the previous interval and calculates the difference, which represents the frame traffic during the last interval. Then Sysmon divides by the total network traffic in frames, and the result is displayed as a percentage of the total traffic for the interval. Because Windows expects that a continuously maintained frame counter field that monitors network traffic can grow quite large, the PERF_AVERAGE_BULK counter type uses doublewidth 64-bit words.

A PERF_SAMPLE_FRACTION is similar, except that 32-bit words are supplied. The various % Cache Hits counters in the Cache object use the PERF_SAMPLE_FRACTION counter type. Both the numerator and denominator are continuously maintained event counters. The numerator reflects a cumulative count of the total number of cache hits that occurred; the denominator is a cumulative count of the total number of file read operations handled by the Cache Manager. Sysmon preserves both measurements from the previous interval and calculates the two interval delta values. Dividing the number of cache hits in the interval by the total number of requests in the interval yields the desired hit rate for the current interval. This derived value is then displayed:

$$(Hits_{+t1} - Hits_{t0}) / (Total\ requests_{+t1} - Total\ request_{t0}) \times 100$$

Notice that the denominator reflecting the total amount of file activity during the interval is subject to change based on current activity levels. In its Chart View, Sysmon displays minimum, maximum, and average values of the points in the current display. The average values Sysmon calculates and displays for both the PERF_AVERAGE_BULK and Cache Hits PERF_SAMPLE_FRACTION counters is subject to error because the calculation performed for the Chart View is based on averaging average values. A cache hit ratio for a low-activity interval is averaged with a high-activity interval. This is a mistake made by both Sysmon and Perfmon—a weighted average based on the activity rate needs to be calculated instead.

Figure 2-13 illustrates this problem. Both the MDL Read Hits % counter and the MDL Reads/sec activity rate are shown. Perfmon calculates and displays an average hit rate value for the MDL Read Hits % field of 37.069. Charting the MDL Reads/sec counter reveals that the MDL cache activity rate varies considerably over the measurement interval. The average value displayed is incorrect because it is the unweighted average of all the interval delta fields. Figure 2-14 shows that the Perfmon Report View calculates a different value for the MDL Read Hits % over the interval. In this case, this value, which is the correct weighted average, is 65.558. It is calculated using the first and last numerator and denominator counter values reported, so it is weighted by activity. As this example illustrates, calculating the average of averages can lead to serious errors.

A limited number of predefined calculations are defined. This is an important consideration if you are developing a Perflib DLL to add extensible counters: you must be sure to fit your measurement data into the preexisting counter types available. Unfortunately, many extended counter Perflib DLL developers do not appreciate this step.

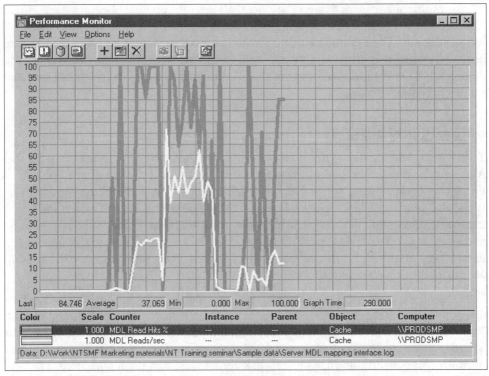

Figure 2-13. This calculation of the MDL Read Hit % value is incorrect

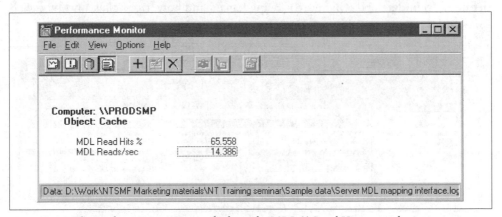

Figure 2-14. The Perfmon Report View calculates the MDL % Read Hits correctly

Performance Data Logging

While designed primarily for interactive use, Sysmon (and Perfmon) also supports basic data logging facilities. Data being collected can be captured to a log file, which in turn can be used as input to the program's online display facilities. It is also possible to run multiple copies of Sysmon at once. While one copy is collecting data in real time, you can start another copy and examine a log file from a background data collection session. The Sysmon chart utility functions exactly the same way in real time as it does when it is displaying data from a file, except that the data you are viewing does not scroll off the screen, and you have additional commands to control the time range of the data you display.

Data Logging Sessions

To create a new log file using the System Monitor, select the Performance Logs and Alerts folder on the left side of the screen, and then access the Counter Logs folder. From the Action menu, select New Log Settings. After you name the new log settings, the Counter Log Properties Dialog Box appears. The Add button brings up a familiar Add Counters dialog that allows you to select the object, object instances, and counters you want to view. You also specify the collection interval, which can be in seconds, minutes, hours, or days. The shortest collection interval that System Monitor allows is one second.

Figure 2-15 expands the Performance Logs and Alerts node on the Microsoft Management Console that is used to anchor performance monitoring in Windows 2000. Two counter logs are shown. One is the System Overview performance data log that Microsoft configures by default. This logging file tracks three metrics that report overall processor utilization, physical disk contention, and paging activity. The second log file entry describes a background performance monitoring session that we defined. To understand what data is being logged and how, right-click on MyLogSettings and access the logging session properties.

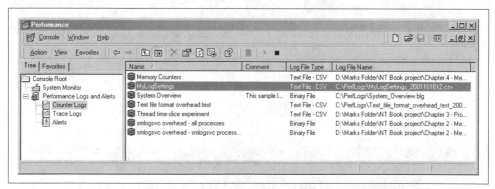

Figure 2-15. The Microsoft Management Console showing counter logs

Figure 2-16 shows the MyLogSettings properties, which are spread across three display tabs: General, Log Files, and Schedule. The General properties are illustrated here, and define the specific objects and counters you want to collect and how often you want to collect them. The Add button is used to add specific objects and counters to a logging file set. Sysmon allows you to monitor all the instances associated with specific performance objects, or select specific instances and counters.

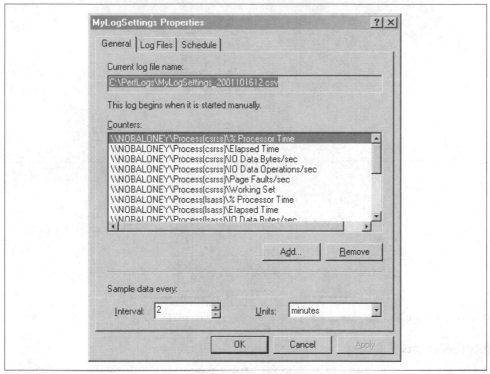

Figure 2-16. The General tab of the MyLogSettings properties

The Log Files and Schedule tabs allow you to specify the logging file format (binary or text) and limit the size of the files the System Monitor creates. Sysmon, for example, allows you to specify a maximum size for a binary circular logging file. Once Sysmon logging reaches the end of a binary circular file, the program automatically returns to the start of the file and begins overriding the oldest performance data. The option we selected was to spin off new comma-delimited log files regularly, adding a timestamp to the filename to identify the log file uniquely. To do this, you need to specify that Sysmon should start a new log file immediately after closing the current active log file, as illustrated in Figure 2-17.

Comma- or tab-delimited log files are suitable for post-processing using applications like Microsoft Excel or Access. The Office applications can perform further analysis and reporting on the performance data you have collected. When you have specified all the properties of the log session, you are ready to start the logging operation.

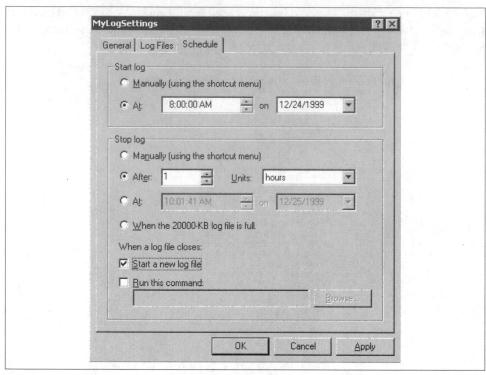

Figure 2-17. The Schedule tab can be used to specify continuous data logging

Log file formats

System Monitor allows you to choose between two log file formats. The first is a binary file format that outputs data very efficiently. The second is a text file format that allows for data interchange with applications like Excel and Access. Text format should be used cautiously because the logging application consumes substantially more processor resources when it is creating text files, as will be discussed in more detail next. System Monitor allows you to specify a size limit to the log file you create. The binary format circular file option illustrated in Figure 2-18 wraps around to the beginning of the file and begins overwriting data once you have reached the specified log file size limit. This option assures that you will always see the most recent data when you view the log file without consuming excessive amounts of disk storage.

Depending on how often you log data and which objects and object instances and their counters you choose to collect, System Monitor logging files can grow quite rapidly. The size of the performance log file you create also depends on the file format you select. Collecting every counter for every process and thread instance, for example, usually approximates worst-case behavior of the log file because there are so many instances of Process and Thread data. We ran an experiment to illustrate how fast the log file can grow by logging every Process and Thread counter on a system with 40 active processes and 325 threads. After just 7 minutes ($7 \times 60 = 420$ collection

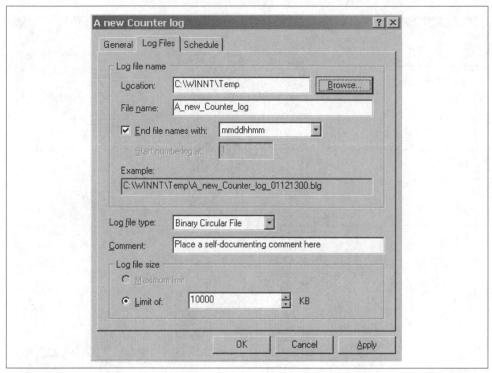

Figure 2-18. Setting up a new counter log in System Monitor

intervals), the binary log file grew to just over 92.5 MB, more than 2 MB per collection interval. As illustrated in Figure 2-19, the System Monitor log service *smlogsvc. exe* consumed between 4–6% of the processor on an 800 MHz Pentium III while it was gathering performance data and writing this binary log file.

By comparison, when we switched to the text file format, the size of the file created was reduced to about 14 MB. However, the CPU consumption of the *smlogsvc* process increased drastically. Creating a text file format log of Process and Thread data, *smlogsvc* absorbed fully 60% of the capacity of an 800 MHz processor during data collection.

Scheduling background data collection

Having a tool like the Windows 2000 System Monitor logging key performance metrics continuously is inherently valuable, assuming you have a good handle on the two overhead considerations: file size and CPU consumption. Suppose a performance problem occurs when you are not available to watch what is happening. A background data collection session might be able to capture the statistics you need to diagnose a problem that occurred in the recent past. Suppose a user reports a performance problem that occurred several hours ago. A continuous background data collection

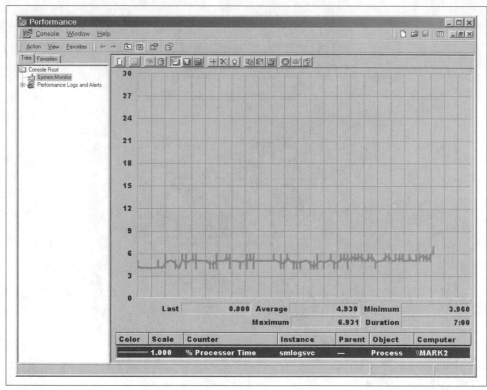

Figure 2-19. The overhead of logging Process and Thread counters using the binary file format

session on the afflicted computer could capture data that allows you to diagnose the condition after the fact.

The System Monitor scheduling functions allow you to automate the performance data collection process. These include the ability to specify when a data logging session should start and stop. You can also specify that the logging service immediately resume data collection after it closes a log file so that you can log data continuously, as illustrated back in Figure 2-17. In addition, the System Monitor logging service automatically generates unique names for all the log files it creates, either by numbering them consecutively or appending a timestamp to the filename telling you when the file was created.

Figure 2-20 shows the Source tab of the Systems Monitor properties using the log file from the little experiment just described. Using the Time Range control, you can narrow down a large log file for charting or reporting. While setting a Time Range allows you to home in on a narrow view of the collection file, working with a large binary format file in System Monitor can still be frustrating. System Monitor currently does not support the Export function from Perfmon that allowed you to transfer data from a performance monitoring session to an application like Excel or

Access for further analysis. Using the System Monitor, the only way to create data that these applications can process is to write a text format log file. As observed, you must be very careful when you log data in text format because the amount of CPU time consumed can be excessive.

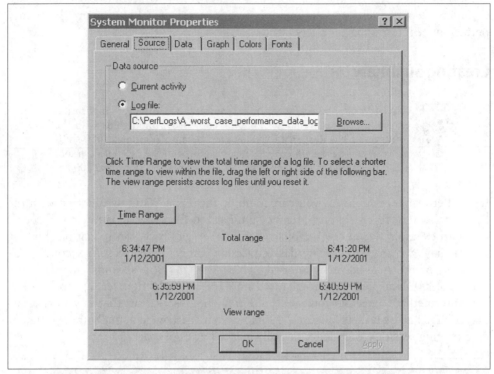

Figure 2-20. System Monitor's Time Range controls can vary the time window of a chart

If Windows 2000 supports critical business functions at your company, it makes sense to implement regular procedures for monitoring the performance of those systems. Continuous background performance monitoring has the obvious advantage that when a performance problem occurs, you already have the performance data required to diagnose it. Naturally, the more types of performance problems you want to be able to diagnose, the more performance data you want to collect automatically in the background. For example, if you want to detect and diagnose processor, memory, disk, and network bottlenecks, you need to collect the System, Processor, Memory, Cache, Logical Disk, Physical Disk, and various networking performance objects, at a minimum. To understand what applications are contributing to a performance problem, you will also want to collect process-level data and any application-specific extended counters that are available from applications like Exchange, SQL Server, or IIS.

Consequently, continuous background performance data logging inevitably involves some compromise between how much performance data you want to collect, and how much you are able to collect without impacting system performance. The ability to limit the size of the performance data logging files by collecting limited object and counter instances is significant, and keeping your performance data logging files from overrunning the available disk storage space is important. The new features of the Windows 2000 System Monitor application allow you to accomplish these goals. Comparable scheduling and automation functions are available in many third-party performance monitoring products.

Creating Summary Data

 This section applies only to the Performance Monitor application available prior to Windows 2000. A copy of Perfmon ships with the Windows 2000 Resource Kit. However, because Windows 2000 ships with several new counter types not supported in the NT 4.0 Perfmon, the older application does not function flawlessly on Windows 2000.

Using Performance Monitor, you can combine the Time Window function with the Relog capability to create and archive summarized files. We illustrate this process using an example. Figure 2-21 depicts a Chart View of processor utilization showing several days worth of data. The data collection interval used was 15 seconds. The duration of the measurement interval, which was 247,865 seconds, suggests that some 16,000 data points were collapsed into 100 by skipping over (approximately) 160 intermediate intervals for each measurement observation that is actually displayed. This is misleading. Figure 2-22 shows that there were actually three different data logging sessions, each automatically marked by bookmarks.

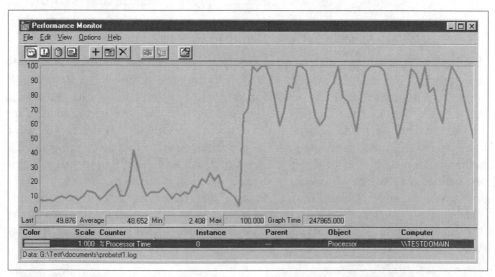

Figure 2-21. A Chart View of processor utilization from three different logging sessions

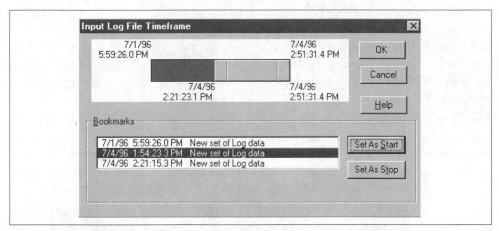

Figure 2-22. The Time Window showing the start and end of the three logging sessions

The first measurement interval covered approximately seven hours before we stopped the log. The second bookmark was selected as the start point to produce the view in Figure 2-23. That allows you to zoom in on the interval with the most activity, a period of about one half hour. During this period, Figure 2-23 indicates that there were actually six cycles of activity that occurred. (Each cycle of activity corresponds to a benchmark run when we were trying to stress the disk configuration.)

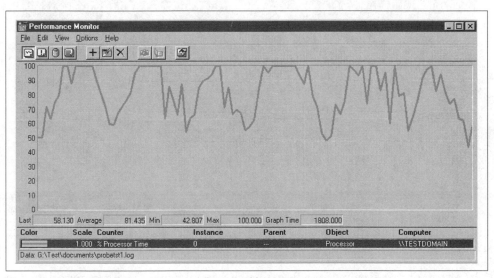

Figure 2-23. The Chart View starting at the second logging session

The value being charted, % Processor Time, is derived from a delta time counter field, which summarizes correctly when intermediate points are dropped. Notice the effect of speeding up the measurement collection interval in the second logging session. The seven hours monitored by the first session fill half the chart in Figure 2-21, while a half hour's worth of data from the second session fills the other half. There is also no indication on the chart that there was a lull for almost two days in which no measurement data was collected. Because there are no labels on the X axis at the bottom of the chart to indicate the date and time, the Chart View makes it appear that the measurements are both contiguous and continuous. If you are building your own reporting, this is not the way to do it.

Notice that Figure 2-23 reveals more detail than Figure 2-21 because not so many intermediate data points are skipped. The peaks and valleys are more craggy in this close-up view. Figure 2-23 shows that the time interval for this chart is 1808 seconds, or 120 measurement intervals of approximately 15 seconds duration. To create this Chart view, Perfmon simply dropped 20 of these measurement intervals.

Next, we relogged the data from Figure 2-21 using a 30-second interval to reduce the size of the file log for long-term storage. The result is Figure 2-24, which shows a loss of detail from Figure 2-23 (and a loss of 30 seconds because an interval at the end was dropped). Because there are now fewer than 100 data points, Perfmon truncates the graph. Now compare Figures 2-21, 2-23, and 2-24, noting the subtle differences. The six major processing cycles are distinct in each view, but there are telltale differences in the craggy peaks and valleys.

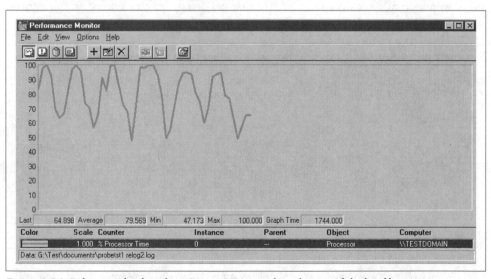

Figure 2-24. Relogging the data from Figure 2-21 to reduce the size of the log file

The lesson of this example is to be extremely careful working with historical data in Perfmon. It is easy to misinterpret Perfmon charts, especially when different logging sessions are combined into one. It is especially easy to get fooled when data from different sessions with different measurement intervals is combined into one. This is something to be aware of both in real time and in viewing data from a log. (If you change the measurement interval in a real-time session you get the same effect, at least until the display wraps.) The Relog function provides quick and dirty summarization for interval delta counters, but the Chart View obscures what the actual measurement interval is and does not indicate if and when it changes.

Summarization

Summarization of detailed performance data is necessary to reduce the volume of information that must be stored to capture longer-term usage trends. From summarized data, it is possible to use statistical techniques to project future workload demands and predict when serious performance bottlenecks are likely to surface. This discussion should clarify what happens when you use the Relog function in the NT 4.0 Perfmon application. Since Microsoft dropped the Relog function from the Windows 2000 System Monitor, this discussion is also helpful for anyone interested in summarizing Windows 2000 performance data outside of the System Monitor application, which does not provide summarization directly.

The following discussion briefly describes the mechanics of collecting performance counters and touches upon very simple statistical concepts. Since we will be dealing with many average value calculations, it is helpful to understand how to calculate, use, and interpret them. This topic usually sends people scrambling to unearth their old college textbooks, but never fear. The authors also slept through Statistics 101 during freshman year. Consequently, the following excursion is mercifully brief and basic; besides, now that there is something useful to relate the study of statistics to, you might find the subject less painful! To make the subject more concrete, we focus on some of the key disk performance measurements taken by the Windows 2000 diskperf filter driver.

Once an interval, a performance monitor application like Sysmon harvests the disk performance measurements maintained by diskperf, gathering up the current values for these counters. Using the current value of an accumulator or difference type counter, an *interval delta* value is calculated by subtracting the value of the counter saved from the previous interval. One example is a calculation that properly yields the number of disk accesses during the current interval:

[1] $IOevents_n \Delta = IOevents_n - IOevents_{n-1}$

Dividing the interval delta value by the duration of the interval yields a rate:

[2] $IO_{rate} = IOevents_n \Delta / interval\ duration$

Formulas [1] and [2] together correspond to the calculation Sysmon makes to calculate the Disk transfers/sec counter in the Logical and Physical Disk objects. This rate is an average over the interval. It tells us nothing about the *distribution* of I/O activity during the interval; for instance, it is conceivable that all the activity occurred in the very first second of the current interval and the disk was idle thereafter.

To make the example concrete, consider an I/O event counter that holds the value 351,923 this interval and 351,359 at the last collection interval. The duration of the interval is 60 seconds. 351,923 – 351,359 = 564 I/O events that occurred during the interval. Dividing 564 by 60 yields an average I/O rate of 9.4 per second.

Measurement of disk I/O response time proceeds along identical lines. The operating system instrumentation is a bit more elaborate because at least two items of interest need to be maintained, and the accumulator used is incremented not by one, but by a distinct, measured value. The operating system must initially store a clock value representing the start time of an I/O operation that is in flight. When the I/O operation is completed, the current clock value is again retrieved. diskperf uses a unique identifier from the IO Request Packet (IRP) to keep track of individual I/O requests because many disk devices (and disk arrays) can process multiple I/O requests at a time. The response time for an individual request is calculated by subtracting the start time from the end time:

[3] $IOevent\ time_n\ \Delta = end\ time\ -\ start\ time$

This event duration time value is then added to an accumulator:

[4] $IOtime\ Accumulator = IOtime\ Accumulator + IOevent\ time_n\ \Delta$

As a result, this accumulator field now holds a time value that represents the duration of all I/O operations that occurred while the diskperf measurement facility was active. An additional wrinkle is that this accumulator field, frequently a time value, must be maintained in a finite number of bits, so that it is subject to wrapping. The performance monitoring software that harvests the data on an interval basis must be able to detect and compensate for this condition.

As before, the performance monitor accesses the current value of the accumulator and subtracts the previous value to obtain an interval delta. This delta value represents the total elapsed time for the I/O requests that completed during the interval:

[5] $IOtime_n\ \Delta = IOtime_n\ \Delta - IOtime_{n-1}\ \Delta$

For instance, assuming the time value kept in the accumulator is maintained in milliseconds, the current value is 5,727,868, the value at the end of the previous interval was 5,621,777, and the number of milliseconds that I/O requests were active during the interval is 5,727,868 – 5,621,777 = 6091 milliseconds.

Dividing by the number of I/O operations (from Formula [2]) yields the average I/O response time during the interval. In statistics, the average is also known as the mean, or the first moment. It is considered the best single value that can be substituted for a range of observations of that value. Computationally, it is very easy to maintain interval delta counters and calculate mean values at the end of some measurement interval. This enables powerful measurement tools to be built which do not absorb lots of system overhead.

[6] $AverageIOtime_n = IOtime_n\ \Delta\ /\ IOevents_n\ \Delta$

Returning to our example, the average I/O response time is 6091/564 or about 10.8 ms. This corresponds to the counter called Avg. Disk sec/Transfer. Again, this represents an average value over the interval and tells us nothing about the underlying distribution of I/O response time during the interval.

Notice that the overhead associated with performance monitoring when the operating system is maintaining these event counters anyway is minimal. In this design, the performance monitoring application needs to perform some additional work, namely gathering up the data once an interval, making the appropriate calculations, and storing or logging the results.

If you understand the mechanism being used, you should see that the same basic method works for interval delta counters whether the collection interval is 1 second, 1 minute, or 24 hours. At what rate should the data be collected? Capacity planners who deal with longer-term trends are ordinarily content with interval measurements every 15, 30, or 60 minutes. When you are trying to project seasonal changes or yearly growth trends, that level of detail is more than sufficient. On the other hand, if you are performing a *post mortem* examination to determine the cause of a performance problem that occurred yesterday, more detail is apt to be required. By increasing the rate of data collection, a finer-grained picture of system activity emerges that may make it possible to perform a more detailed problem diagnosis. But this also increases the overhead proportionally, the most significant thing being the increased overhead in post-processing, e.g., more disk I/O to the log file, larger log files that must be stored and moved around the network.

Since the accumulator-type counters involved are maintained continuously, the duration of the collection interval does not affect the overhead in the measurement facility itself. This is a key point. The embedded instrumentation is collecting information as events occur whether anyone is gathering the information or not. This means that you should be able to choose the collection interval that meets your requirements without regard to its impact on system operations. However, running a System Monitor logging session, you can hardly be impervious to overhead considerations, as observed previously.

In our experience, summary data collected at one-minute intervals is adequate for diagnosing many performance problems. The data that falls through the cracks at that level of granularity is probably so transitory that it may be difficult to account for anyway. Logging data at even more frequent intervals also means an increase in the size of your collection files. Still, there will be times when you need to know, and the only way to find out is to collect detailed performance or trace data at an even finer level of granularity. For example, developers concerned about the performance of their applications running on Windows 2000 normally require a more detailed snapshot to properly determine the impact of a programming change. In an application stress test, you may want to see detailed data available as frequently as once per second, which is the shortest collection interval that the *smlogsvc* currently supports.

To summarize, interval delta counters, which provide mean value calculations, are easy to maintain if the proper operating system interfaces are monitored. Average values can then be calculated without having to consume an inordinate amount of resources. This is the primary method used to instrument Windows 2000.

Using a method of simply ignoring intermediate observations, however, you can summarize accumulator or difference counters and transform detailed data into summarized data. Let's revisit the Perfmon Relog function and see how it summarizes interval delta measurement data. Each collection interval, Perfmon writes the current value of the accumulator field used to calculate the Disk transfers/sec counter. The binary format log file contains successive values for this counter. To continue with the previous example: 351,359 the first interval; 351,923 the next; followed by 352,017, 352,788, 352,941, and 353,212. To change the collection data from its original one-minute interval to five-minute intervals, Relog drops the intermediate observations. This leaves only an initial value for this counter of 351,359 and a final value of 353,212. Perfmon calculates the Disk transfers/sec counter using Formulas [1] and [2], just as before. The interval delta value is 1853, the number of I/O events that occurred in this five-minute interval. The number of I/O events is divided by the duration between collection intervals, which is 300 seconds. The result is 6.177, the average rate of I/O requests during the five-minute interval.

The final point to be made in this context is that raw counters (any field the Explain Text identifies as an instantaneous count) cannot be summarized in this fashion. When you relog data using Perfmon, which causes intermediate measurement points to be dropped, these measurements of raw counter values are simply removed from consideration. Perfmon retains only the values of raw counters for the measurement intervals that are preserved. If you need to summarize instantaneous or raw counters outside of Sysmon, for example, you should calculate simple summary statistics to represent each historical measurement interval: the average, maximum, minimum, and perhaps even the standard deviation, a useful indicator of the distribution of raw counter observations.

Performance Monitoring Overhead

Now that we understand how the Windows 2000 performance monitoring interface works, we can tackle the issue of overhead. "What does all this Windows 2000 performance monitoring cost?" is a frequent question. Naturally, you want to avoid any situation where performance monitoring is so costly in its use of computer resources that it drastically influences the performance of the applications you care about. Performance monitoring must be part of the solution, not part of the problem. As long as the overhead of performance monitoring remains low, we can accept it as part of the cost of doing business. With performance monitoring, when something goes wrong, we at least have a good chance of finding out what happened. However, as we have already observed, logging performance data to a text file using System Monitor can be very CPU-intensive. When a logging session that is writing a text format data file is active, it can consume so much CPU time that it affects the performance of other applications you are trying to run.

Understanding how much overhead is involved in Windows 2000 performance monitoring is not a simple proposition. It helps to break up the overhead considerations into three major areas of concern:

- The overhead involved in measuring Windows 2000
- The overhead involved in gathering performance monitor data
- The overhead involved in analyzing and other post-processing of the measurement data

We discuss these three areas of concern in the following sections.

Instrumentation Overhead

The overhead of instrumentation refers to the system resources used in collecting performance measurements as they occur. With a few exceptions, the overhead of collecting both base and extended counters is built into Windows 2000. This overhead occurs whether or not there is a performance monitoring application like Sysmon actually looking at the information being collected. For example, Windows 2000 provides instrumentation that keeps track of which processes are using the CPU and for how long. This instrumentation is integral to the operating system; it cannot be turned off. Consequently, the overhead involved in making these measurements cannot be avoided.

The developers of Microsoft Windows 2000 are naturally concerned with these inherent overhead issues. Rest assured that the basic difference and raw counters were designed to minimize the overhead to instrument various portions of the operating system. Maintaining a difference counter when some event that is instrumented occurs adds only a few simple instructions to the execution code path: just enough to load the previous counter field, increment it, and store it back. For many raw counters, there is virtually no overhead impact on the system except when a performance monitoring application explicitly requests data collection. The Perflib DLL only needs to access some memory-resident data structure that the operating system maintains anyway to derive a current value for many of the raw counters. For example, the *perfos.dll* module traverses the three memory management list structures that make up Available Bytes—the Standby list, the Free list, and the Zero list—when Sysmon specifically requests data for the Memory object.

The Windows 2000 developers have also taken steps to allow you some degree of control over the amount of overhead that measurement consumes automatically. In particular, instrumentation in the disk and network interface drivers to collect measurement data is optional because there can be relatively high overhead associated with collecting the data in these two areas. For example, unless the option is explicitly set, Windows disk drivers do not automatically collect I/O measurements describing logical disk activity. Only Physical Disk monitoring is enabled by default. Issuing the diskperf command with the -yv switch enables data collection for the optional Logical Disk measurements. When disk performance measurement data collection is not enabled, the logical disk performance counters are all zero values. To enable the logical disk measurements, you must first run diskperf -yv and then restart the computer. Similarly, to collect statistics on network resource utilization, it is necessary to explicitly install the Network Monitor Driver networking service to collect the Network Interface Object, for example.

Data Collection Overhead

While there is normally little you can do about the overhead of Windows 2000's performance instrumentation, you do have the ability to determine how much overhead is consumed in collecting and processing performance statistics. For example, in Windows 2000, Microsoft separated the performance collection engine, which runs unattended as a service, from the Sysmon GUI, which saves on resources. In Windows NT 4.0, you might choose to run the Perflog or Datalog utilities in the Resource Kit that perform data collection with less overhead than the Perfmon GUI. Without the overhead of running the GUI, you can generally assume that the overhead of data collection is proportional to the data you are collecting and how much of it there is. We illustrate these considerations shortly.

As discussed earlier, there is a specific Perflib DLL associated with each performance data object. Collecting information about each object requires a separate call to its associated Perflib program. You can minimize collection overhead by limiting the number of objects you collect. For objects that have a parent-child relationship, things are a bit more complicated. A parent-child relationship is defined between Process and Thread object instances. All data associated with parent and child objects is collected together with a single call to the appropriate Perflib program. Data collection for Thread data automatically collects information on all Process objects instances at the same time.

From an overhead perspective (always an important consideration in performance monitoring), once you enable one counter, the data collection overhead inside the Perflib DLL is the same as if you had enabled all the counters associated with the object. The module responsible for data collection is called once for the object, and it returns with all the fields and object instances. When the Perflib DLL finishes gathering up the data for a request, it returns to the calling application, i.e., the System Monitor. At that point, additional processing occurs inside the performance monitoring application. For example, System Monitor filters out the counters and instances that were not requested, and then writes the data associated with the request to the logging file. When you are writing a binary log file, System Monitor processing is roughly proportional to the amount of data that is written.

To understand the overhead of running the System Monitor, try running a simple experiment on your computer. Start a System Monitor logging session to create a log file produced on a 400 MHz machine running Windows 2000 Server collecting all instances and all counters of the Process object. We collect this performance data once per second on a system with 49 active processes, as illustrated in Figure 2-25. Since we are collecting the Process object, we are able to record the resources the smlogsvc service consumed collecting this basic set of information. Figure 2-25 illustrates that the smlogsvc CPU consumption averaged 1.2% busy over the duration of the experiment. This is a relatively trivial amount of CPU overhead to add to any of your Windows 2000 servers.

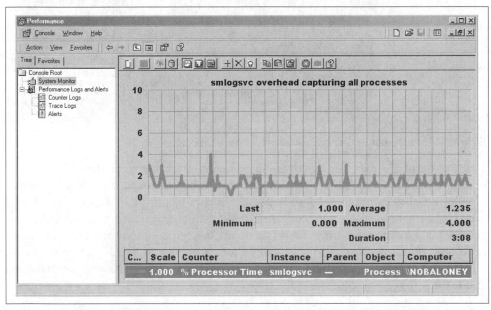

Figure 2-25. Overhead of smlogsvc CPU consumption with 49 processes

However, collecting all the instances of the Process object and writing them to the log file causes the log files to grow quite large quite fast. In this experiment, the log file reaches its 10 MB limit in just over three minutes. The log file covers 188 one-second collection intervals, or over 50K per interval. In general, you have to watch out for objects like Process, Thread, (Terminal Server) Session, and SNA Server that usually have many instances. Selecting specific object instances for logging reduces the size of the log file substantially, and the overhead involved in data collection proportionally. Figure 2-26 shows that CPU consumption for smlogsvc drops to under 0.1% when counters from only a single process are logged. (Those of you using Perfmon under NT 4.0 will discover that the program logs every instance of an object when the object is selected for data collection.)

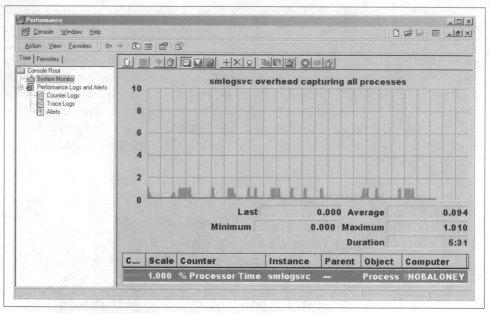

Figure 2-26. Vastly reduced overhead with only a single process

There is naturally more overhead associated with collecting some data objects than others. Detailed thread-level data, for example, requires more processing than simple high-level system information. Because Thread objects are in a parent-child relationship with Process objects, collecting information on threads involves collecting process data at the same time. If you are really concerned about measurement overhead, you might decide not to collect any Process or Thread data. The problem with doing this, of course, is if there is a performance problem, you have no information about the applications running at the time.

GUI overhead

Compared to exercising the graphical Chart View of System Monitor in real time, background monitoring sessions using the smlogsvc service are much less resource-intensive. Figure 2-27 illustrates a rather extreme case where the System Monitor is attempting to report on all the Process counters for 39 instances. While the usefulness of this is doubtful, to say the least, the point of the experiment is to call attention to the potential overhead impact of the Sysmon GUI. Figure 2-27 highlights the MMC (Microsoft Management Console) process that hosts the System Monitor application. Notice that the MMC process is consuming 15% of a 400 MHz CPU as it paints the display once per second. Obviously, when the System Monitor is utilized in a more practical fashion, the overhead of running the GUI application is not of grave concern.

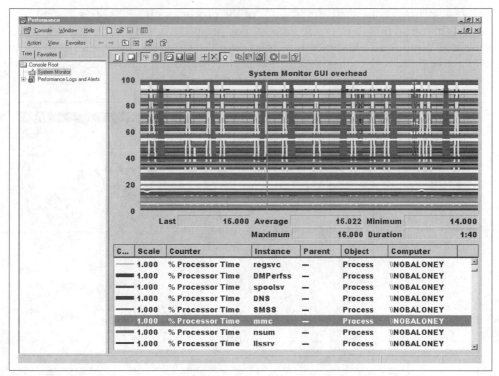

Figure 2-27. Overhead of Sysmon GUI in an extreme case

Text file log format

When you opt for the convenience of the text file format (*.TSV* or *.CSV*), the overhead of logging performance data using the smlogsvc is significantly higher. This is because the smlogsvc performance data logging program must calculate all the statistics you request at runtime. There is additional computational overhead associated with calculating the interval delta values for any accumulator type counters that you choose to log. How much overhead is a function of the objects and counters you select. Again, collecting Process and Thread instances causes the most overhead. Unless you are very selective about which objects, object instances, and counters you want to log, you may find that the overhead consumed by the smlogsvc program to output text format files is prohibitive. The processing overhead is mainly associated with matching up current and previous counter values to make the necessary accumulator counter calculations, a process discussed in more detail in Chapter 4.

Figure 2-28 illustrates these overhead considerations. It shows smlogsvc process CPU utilization during a data collection session in which we logged Process and Thread counters to a comma-separated text file (CSV). We selected all Process and Thread instances and counters for data logging and then logged them once per second. Reading the logging file back into the System Monitor, Figure 2-28 reveals that the smlogsvc process consumed almost 90% of the processor on a 400 MHz system running Windows 2000 during this session. For perspective, the system was an otherwise idle Windows 2000 server, but it did have about 30 running processes and over 300 active threads. Needless to say, it is prohibitive to run the Windows 2000 data logging service in this fashion. You must be very careful with text file format log files.

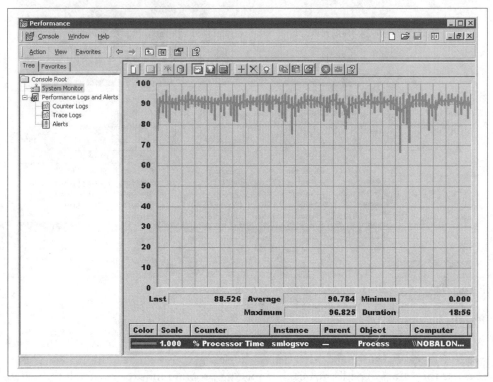

Figure 2-28. Logging data to a CSV format file can be prohibitively expensive

Monitoring remote systems

Another aspect of performance monitoring overhead to be aware of is collecting data from remote systems. This System Monitor function is very useful for connecting to remote systems and looking at what is happening there. However, overhead considerations dictate that this function should be used very carefully, too. The major concern is the network traffic that this function can generate. The amount of traffic generated is a function of the objects being collected. Because the underlying Perflib DLL collection services return all object instances that currently exist, there can be substantial network traffic associated with collecting objects like Process and Thread that have many instances.

Figure 2-29 shows the Windows 2000 System Monitor monitoring two remote computers. Here, Sysmon is pointing to two different Windows 2000 servers on our local area network (LAN) 100 Mb Ethernet network segment that was otherwise idle. We set Sysmon to collect one Process counter and one Thread counter from each of these two machines. The network traffic from Sysmon collecting this data alone measures 130,000 bytes per collection interval (in this case, once per second). The reason for all this traffic is that performance counters for *all* process and thread objects are passed from the remote system across the network back to Sysmon, which then (and only then) filters out the process and thread instances we didn't ask for. As a matter of interest, the *PRODSMP* server has 624 active threads; the smaller *NTTEST* server has only 301. Monitoring the *PRODSMP* server alone involved 83K bytes of network traffic per second. The network traffic scales proportionately to the amount of performance data collected at the remote system and passed back over the network.

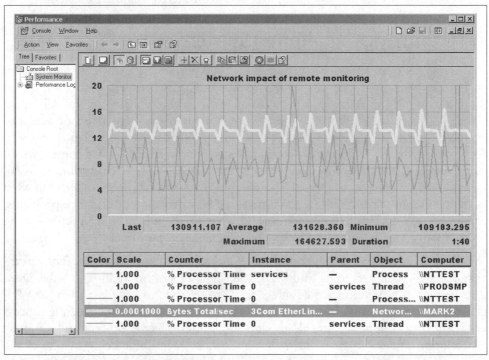

Figure 2-29. Sysmon monitoring two remote systems

Naturally, as long as you are careful about what objects you monitor, running Sysmon remotely is not a problem.

Post-Processing Overhead

Because Windows 2000 is so well instrumented and there is so much performance data that can be logged, designing effective monitoring and collection procedures that scale across a large network of machines can be challenging. For instance, we know of a large banking company that uses a Windows 2000 server in over one thousand bank branch offices across the country. Collecting some Windows 2000 performance data on these servers is necessary to ensure the smooth operation of the bank's business. Simply transferring that data back to performance analysts at the bank's headquarters each night is challenging enough, but then that data must be processed and analyzed. The point is to detect performance and operational problems associated with an out-of-capacity machine or a machine running short of disk space before they happen. Obviously, this is a big, complicated operation. Hopefully, the benefits of such a proactive performance monitoring strategy outweigh the significant costs of performing all this processing. In the case of this one company, at least, being able to manage the performance of a large number of Windows 2000 servers with a tiny central office support staff is considered well worth the effort.*

A Performance Monitoring Starter Set

We recognize that with so many Windows 2000 performance objects and counters to choose from, it is easy to be overwhelmed. To help readers who want to get started in Windows 2000 performance monitoring without having to read all the in-depth chapters that follow, we now present a set of recommended objects and counters that you can use to begin collecting performance data at regular intervals for your important Windows 2000 machines, shown in Table 2-1. Of course, we do not want to discourage you from reading the rest of the book; this simple list of counters will certainly not provide enough information to help you understand what is happening inside a Windows 2000 machine experiencing performance problems. Subsequent chapters of this book explain what these and other counters mean in some detail and show how to use them to solve practical performance problems.

We also include a brief discussion of some of the performance counters. The recommended set of counters to monitor include System, Processor, Memory, Cache, Disk, and networking performance counters that are relevant to a wide variety of Windows 2000 server and workstation machines. We also recommend collecting process data for critical applications, along with application-specific objects and counters where appropriate. For example, for a Windows 2000 machine being used as a web server, the Internet Information System Global object provides invaluable performance and tuning information.

The Usage Notes column accompanying the entries in the Windows 2000 performance monitoring starter set describe some convenient rules of thumb for detecting specific performance bottlenecks based on the associated counter value. In other

---

* For more information, see the article by Stan Dylnicki entitled "Monitoring 2000+ Windows NT in a WAN/ LAN environment," published in the CMG 2000 *Proceedings*, available from the Computer Measurement Group, Turnersville, NJ.

cases, the Usage Notes discuss some popular misconceptions associated with specific Windows 2000 performance counter fields that sound like they mean one thing, but actually measure something else entirely. We understand that these Usage Notes may disagree with the recommendations of other authorities and even the official Windows 2000 Explain Text. Rest assured that we do not contradict the official Microsoft sources without good reason. You will find those reasons documented in ample detail in the body of this book. Useful new counters available only in Windows 2000 are also noted.

Table 2-1. Windows 2000 objects and counters

Object name	Counter name	Usage notes
System	Processor Queue Length	Probable bottleneck when Processor Queue Length $> 3 \times$ # CPUs.
	% Total Processor Time	As Processor % busy approaches 75–95%, the Processor Queue Length tends to increase nonlinearly.
	% Total User Time	Among the counters moved to _Total instance of Processor object in Windows 2000.
	% Total Privileged Time	Operating system functions running in Ring 0 or kernel mode run in Privileged mode.
	% Total DPC Time	Included in % Total Privileged Time. Deferred Procedure Calls represent Interrupt-related processing performed after the CPU is re-enabled for interrupts. DPCs are scheduled to run at higher priority than all kernel or user threads. See Chapter 3.
	% Total Interrupt Time	High-priority Interrupt Service Routines perform device-dependent processing while lower-priority device interrupts are masked.
	System Up Time	Used to track system availability.
	Context Switches/sec	INT instructions that trap to Ring 0 kernel mode from Ring 3 count as context switches in Intel architecture. Unfortunately, context switches that flush processor cache TLBs due to reloading the TSS cannot be broken out separately.
Memory	Available Bytes	Process Working Set growth becomes constrained when Available Bytes < 4 MB (approximately); the system is under severe stress when Available Bytes < 1 MB.
	Pool Nonpaged Bytes	The system's nonpageable (fixed) memory.
	Pool Paged Resident Bytes	The operating system's pageable memory that is currently resident in RAM.
	System Code Resident Bytes	Covered in Chapter 6.
	System Driver Resident Bytes	Total System Resident Bytes = Pool Nonpaged Bytes + Pool Paged Resident Bytes + System Code Resident Bytes + System Driver Resident Bytes + System Cache Resident Bytes.
	System Cache Resident Bytes	The current amount of RAM used for the file cache; limited to 512 MB in NT 3-4, about 960 MB maximum in Windows 2000.
	Page Faults/sec	Can be a grossly misleading number. Page Faults/sec = "soft" Transition Faults + application file Cache Faults + demand zero faults + hard page faults.

Table 2-1. Windows 2000 objects and counters (continued)

Object name	Counter name	Usage notes
Memory	Page Reads/sec	Hard page fault rate!
	Page Writes/sec	Updated "dirty" pages must be flushed to disk before they can be reused by a different application.
	Committed Bytes	Represents virtual memory pages backed in either RAM or secondary storage (paging files). Calculate a virtual:real memory contention index = Committed Bytes / Total RAM. Consider adding RAM when this ratio starts to approach 2:1.
	Commit Limit	Maximum number of virtual memory pages that can be allocated without extending the paging file(s).
	% Committed Bytes in Use	Committed Bytes / Commit Limit. Consider adding RAM when consistently > 70% on a server. On a workstation, close some applications.
	Cache Bytes	Actually, the system address space working set, but includes the file cache. The sum of Pool Paged Resident Bytes + System Code Resident Bytes + System Driver Resident Bytes + System Cache Resident Bytes.
	Transition Faults/sec	"Soft" page faults resolved without having to access the disk. Interesting number to track, but there is nothing you can do about the Transition Fault rate. Consider them a byproduct of the Windows 2000 page stealing algorithm, discussed in Chapter 6.
	Cache Faults/sec	Normal application file I/O operations are diverted to use the paging subsystem. Each file cache fault leads to a physical disk read I/O operation.
	Demand Zero Faults/sec	The rate at which applications require brand new pages.
	Write Copies/sec	Private Copy on Write pages from shared DLLs.
	Pages Input/sec	Calculate the bulk paging rate: Pages Input/sec / Page Reads/sec.
	Pages Output/sec	Try to limit Pages Input/sec + Pages Output/sec to 10-20% of total disk bandwidth, if possible. Disk bandwidth absorbed for paging operations is unavailable for application processes.
	Pool Paged Bytes	Calculate a virtual:real memory contention index = Pool Paged Resident Bytes / Pool Paged Bytes. Compare to Page Reads/sec to anticipate real memory bottlenecks.
Cache	Copy Reads/sec	Inefficient Copy interface used by (most) applications not specifically designed for Windows 2000.
	Copy Read Hits %	Target > 80% for efficient application file processing. However, if application files resist caching, there is little you can do about it.
	Lazy Write Flushes/sec	The Lazy Write algorithm used to cache disk file updates in memory means that you should never leave a critical Windows 2000 server unprotected without an Uninterruptible Power System (UPS).
	Lazy Write Pages/sec	Covered in Chapter 7.
	Data Maps/sec	Cache mapping interface used primarily by NTFS and Redirector.
	Data Map Hits %	Target > 90% for efficient NTFS processing.
	Data Map Pins/sec	Covered in Chapter 7.

Table 2-1. Windows 2000 objects and counters (continued)

Object name	Counter name	Usage notes
Cache	Pin Reads/sec	Covered in Chapter 7.
	Pin Read Hits %	Target > 90% for efficient NTFS file metadata update processing.
	Data Flushes/sec	The rate at which NTFS requests pages containing file metadata be written to disk.
	Data Flush Pages/sec	Covered in Chapter 7.
	MDL Reads/sec	Efficient cache interface used by networking applications like (file) Server and IIS.
	MDL Read Hits %	Target > 90% for efficient IIS static HTML, GIF, and JPEG file processing.
	Read Aheads/sec	Sequential prefetching triggered by a detected pattern of forward sequential access. Disk prefetching justifies regular use of the built-in disk defragmenter utility.
	Fast Reads/sec	NTFS supports Fast Read interface that bypasses the IO Manager on Read hits.
Process	% Processor Time	Per Process CPU usage; capped at 100% by default.
	Page Faults/sec	Indirect indicator of per Process I/O activity in NT 4.0; but includes "soft" transition fault activity.
	IO Data Bytes/sec	New in Windows 2000. Tracks logical requests, so do not expect to match these new per Process IO counters with disk activity measurements.
	IO Data Operations/sec	New in Windows 2000.
	% User Time	Covered in Chapters 3, 6.
	% Privileged Time	Covered in Chapters 3, 6.
	Virtual Bytes	Per Process contribution to Committed Bytes. Cautionary note: shared DLL virtual bytes are not counted as part of the Virtual Bytes of each associated Process.
	Working Set	Pages from resident shared DLLs are counted as part of the Working Set of each associated Process.
	Elapsed Time	Used to track application availability.
Thread	% Processor Time	Covered in Chapter 3.
	Thread State	State = 1 means thread is ready and waiting in the system's Processor dispatching queue.
	Thread Wait Reason	Typically, most waiting threads are waiting for a component of the NT Executive: Wait State Reason Code = 7.
Logical Disk, Physical Disk	Avg. Disk sec/Read	Measured response time of disk read requests.
	Avg. Disk sec/Write	Measured response time of disk write requests.
	Avg. Disk sec/Transfer	Overall measured average response time of all disk requests.
	Disk Reads/sec	Poor response time matters only if disks are active. SCSI disks with on-board cache buffers paradoxically tend to have faster read service times as I/O rates increase.

Table 2-1. Windows 2000 objects and counters (continued)

Object name	Counter name	Usage notes
Logical Disk, Physical Disk	Disk Writes/sec	Covered in Chapter 8.
	Disk Transfers/sec	Covered in Chapter 8.
	Avg. Disk Queue Length	Calculated average number of active disk requests = Disk Transfers/sec $\times$ Avg. Disk sec/Transfer. Note: this is Little's Law formula. Consequently, this calculated field is invalid for any interval in which the Little's Law equilibrium assumption does not hold. Check the values of Current Disk Queue Length for the previous and current interval to determine if $\lambda > C$ (see Chapter 1.)
	Avg. Disk Read Queue Length	Calculated average number of active disk requests = Disk Reads/sec $\times$ Avg. Disk sec/Read.
	Avg. Disk Write Queue Length	Calculated average number of active disk requests = Disk Writes/sec $\times$ Avg. Disk sec/Write.
	Current Disk Queue Length	Instantaneous count of queued I/O requests. Systematically undersampled on a uniprocessor, but a good number to compare to the calculated value for the Avg. Disk Queue Length.
	% Disk Read Time	Misleading indicator of Disk Busy, capped at 100%. Calculated as the product of Disk Reads/sec $\times$ Avg. Disk sec/Read. Same as Avg. Disk Read Queue Length, except offset by two decimal points.
	% Disk Write Time	Misleading indicator of Disk Busy, capped at 100%. Calculated as the product of Disk Writes/sec $\times$ Avg. Disk sec/Write. Same as Avg. Disk Write Queue Length, except offset by two decimal points.
	% Idle Time	New in Windows 2000. Used to calculate: Disk utilization = 100 − % Idle Time. Disk service time = Disk utilization / Disk Transfers/sec. Disk Queue time = Avg. Disk sec/Transfer − Disk service time
	Disk Read Bytes/sec	Disk read throughput, normally limited to about 50% of SCSI bus capacity.
	Disk Write Bytes/sec	Disk write throughput, normally limited to about 50% of SCSI bus capacity.
	Avg. Disk Bytes/Read	Calculated average block size = Disk Read Bytes/sec / Disk Reads/sec.
	Avg. Disk Bytes/Write	Calculated average block size = Disk Write Bytes/sec / Disk Writes/sec.
Processor	% Processor Time	With symmetric multiprocessing, individual processor statistics tend *not* to vary significantly.
	% User Time	Covered in Chapter 3.
	% Privileged Time	Covered in Chapter 3.
	Interrupts/sec	Watch for sudden increases; could be a malfunctioning device or device driver.
	% Interrupt Time	Covered in Chapter 3.
Network Interface	Total Bytes Received/sec	Covered in Chapter 11.
	Total Bytes Sent/sec	Covered in Chapter 11.

Table 2-1. Windows 2000 objects and counters (continued)

Object name	Counter name	Usage notes
Network Interface	Packets Received/sec	Covered in Chapter 11.
	Packets Sent/sec	Covered in Chapter 11.
	Current Bandwidth	Calculate % Network utilization = (Total bytes received/second + Total bytes sent/second)/ Current Bandwidth. Shared Ethernet network segments tend to saturate at > 30–50% busy; switched segments can run at close to 90% utilization without degradation.

For file and print servers

Object name	Counter name	Usage notes
Server	Bytes Received/sec	Covered in Chapter 5.
	Bytes Transmitted/sec	Covered in Chapter 5.
	Server Sessions	Covered in Chapter 5.
	Work Item Shortages	Increase MaxWorkItems if Work Item Shortages > 0, unless Processor % Processor Time is also > 80%
	Context Blocks Queued/sec	The rate of individual file server requests sent by networking clients
Print Queue	Jobs	Helpful new performance object in Windows 2000. Current number of jobs in a print queue.
	Bytes Printed/sec	Covered in Chapter 3.
	Total Jobs Printed	Covered in Chapter 3.
	Total Pages Printed	Covered in Chapter 3.

For network clients using NT Server's file and print sharing services

Object name	Counter name	Usage notes
Redirector	Bytes Received/sec	Covered in Chapter 11.
	Bytes Transmitted/sec	Covered in Chapter 11.
	Read Bytes Network/sec	Measures the network traffic from networked file read requests.
	Write Bytes Network/sec	Measures the network traffic from networked file write requests.
	Current Commands	Counts the number of commands queued for network file processing. Should never be more than one per NIC.
	File Data Operations/ sec	The total rate of individual networked file requests sent by this client.

For machines using Microsoft's IIS Web server

Object name	Counter name	Usage notes
Internet Information Services Global	File Cache Hits %	Caching HTML file handles in memory saves on disk I/O and improves performance. Static HTML files are cached in system's file cache using the efficient MDL interface.
	Current Files Cached	Covered in Chapter 12.
	Current File Cache Memory Usage	Covered in Chapter 12.
	BLOB Cache Hits %	Caching Binary Large Objects (BLOBs, GIFs and JPEGs associated with HTML requests) in memory saves on disk I/O and improves performance.
	Current BLOBs Cached	Covered in Chapter 12.
	Total Blocked Async I/O Requests	These represent requests blocked by the bandwidth throttling feature. See Chapter 12.

Table 2-1. Windows 2000 objects and counters (continued)

Object name	Counter name	Usage notes
Web Service	Total Method Requests/sec	The HTTP Method defines the type of HTTP request. This is the total web service request rate per web site.
	Get Requests/sec	GET is the HTTP method used to request static HTML pages and embedded GIF and JPEG requests.
	CGI Requests/sec	CGI scripts are involved in many forms-processing applications.
	ISAPI Extension Requests/sec	ISAPI requests predate Microsoft's Active Server Pages server host scripting facility to support dynamic HTML pages.
	Current Connections	Covered in Chapter 12.
	Current CGI Requests	Covered in Chapter 12.
	Current ISAPI Extension Requests	Covered in Chapter 12.
	Service Uptime	Uptime for each web site instance for tracking availability.
Active Server Pages	Request Execution Time	Execution time for the last ASP request (in milliseconds).
	Request Queue Time	Queue time delay for the last ASP request (in milliseconds).
	Requests Executing	Covered in Chapter 12.
	Requests Queued	Covered in Chapter 12.
	Requests/sec	Calculated average response time = (Requests Executing + Requests Queued) / Requests/sec (from Little's Law). Compare this value to the reported Request Execution Time + Request Queue Time, which reports the execution and queue time of the last completed ASP request only.
	Transactions/sec	Covered in Chapter 12.
	Transactions/pending	Covered in Chapter 12.

## CHAPTER 3

Processor Performance

At the heart of any computer is a Central Processing Unit (CPU), or simply the *processor* for short. The processor is the hardware component responsible for computation: a machine that executes arithmetic and logical instructions presented to it in the form of computer programs. In this chapter we look at several important aspects of processor performance in a Windows 2000 system.

The processor hardware is capable of executing one set of instructions at a time, yet computers are loaded with programs that require execution concurrently. Generally, there are two types of programs that computers execute: systems programs and applications programs. An operating system like Windows 2000 is a systems program. It is a set of computer instructions like any program, but it is designed to interface directly with the computer hardware. The operating system, in particular, is responsible for controlling the hardware: the CPU, memory, network interface, and associated peripheral devices. The operating system is also responsible for determining what other programs actually get to run on the computer system. There is a very strong performance component to this aspect of operating systems software. The Windows 2000 designers are trying to make the experience of using their computing platform as pleasant as possible. This includes running applications fast and efficiently.

Like other operating systems, Windows 2000 includes a Scheduler component that controls what application programs the processor executes and in what order. We discuss the functions performed by the Windows 2000 Scheduler first, but limit our scope to the uniprocessor environment initially. Multiprocessors introduce a number of complications, which we address in Chapter 5.

Windows 2000 Design Goals

Before diving into the subject of the Windows 2000 Scheduler, it is good idea to highlight two of the major design goals behind Windows 2000. These goals are *portability* and *simplicity*, and they are important to understand because they have influenced the decisions that were made about what features to put into the OS.

Portability

Portability means that the operating system should be able to run (and run well) on a very broad range of computing environments, from standalone workstations to very large, clustered systems. This is challenging to accomplish because the hardware and the workloads run on such a wide range of computing alternatives are, well, wide-ranging. From its inception, Windows NT, and now Windows 2000, was committed to accomplishing this goal without making too many major platform-specific optimizations. This is a carefully calculated and thoughtful stance, in our view.

Concessions to specific hardware features can definitely show a big payoff in the short term, which makes it very tempting for OS designers to make them. These same concessions are apt to be a drag on performance over the longer term, however. This is significant, since operating systems have a long shelf life. (MS-DOS is now over twenty years old, the original Unix kernel was developed twenty-five years ago, and there are elements of the IBM MVS mainframe operating system originally developed in 1960 still running today. Remember that some of the vaunted "New Technology" in Windows NT/2000 is already over ten years old.)

Building Windows 2000 for the long haul and avoiding hardware-specific optimizations is important from the standpoint of portability. The Windows 2000 designers relied on the fact that over the long term, the power of the hardware used to run Windows 2000 would catch up and ultimately overcome any limitations of the OS. No sense succumbing to the temptation of making short-term, hardware-specific concessions when these features are not likely to endure.

Today, however, Windows 2000 runs only on Intel-compatible processor hardware. The situation is far different from the past when NT ran on MIPS, PowerPC hardware, and the Digital (now Compaq) Alpha microprocessors. (It was the hardware manufacturers who stopped supporting NT on MIPS, PowerPC, and Alpha platforms, by the way, not Microsoft.) Today, it makes sense for Microsoft to optimize Windows 2000 for the Intel platform, and this has started to happen.

Simplicity

The second goal is to keep the user interface to the operating system simple. This Windows 2000 design goal translates into the mantra *No Knobs*, which is frequently invoked by Microsoft developers. In reality, the operating system is not simple, so the trick is to make the user's interface into the operating system *appear* uncomplicated. Having a great stock of parameters to tweak performance in this direction or that certainly collides with this idea. Therefore, whenever there are lots of tuning knobs available, it is common for the manufacturer to establish reasonable default values to make it easier to get up and running right away. Windows 2000 contains many default parameter values that are set at the factory. Depending on whether you are running the Professional flavor of Windows 2000 or Server, for example, some of these parameters will have different default values. But No Knobs means more than having a bunch of reasonable default parameters to start with. It also means that if these default values are wrong or inappropriate, the operating system itself should detect the situation and correct it.

This is very ambitious. Windows 2000 not only has to perform well under a wide variety of circumstances, but when it is *not* performing well, it should be able to detect the situation and correct matters. Unfortunately, this is not a simple problem, and no OS, including Windows 2000, can deliver completely on this score. Since Windows 2000 cannot detect and correct performance problems on its own, the No Knobs policy effectively means that there is often no way for *anyone* to regulate the system when it is under stress. Since this is not acceptable, Microsoft is exposing more tuning knobs for Windows 2000 over time. The term *expose* in this context is programmer-speak meaning that these knobs represent parameter settings that were always there, but their values were controlled by the system. When these parameters are exposed, it means you can start having fun manipulating them directly.

The No Knobs policy definitely does not extend to what Win32 applications written with Windows 2000 in mind can do. Win32 applications have extraordinary capabilities to exploit high-performance features of Windows 2000, *if* they choose to. Where the Windows 2000 developers have selected not to build some control function into the OS, they often provide documented interfaces into Windows 2000 that application developers and third-party developers can take advantage of. Throughout this book, you will see examples where third-party developers have exploited some specific performance-oriented function that the OS supports. Note that many of these Win32 API functions are very advanced and should not be invoked lightly.

With this background in mind, we are ready to approach the topic of processor performance in Windows 2000. First, we look at the component of Windows 2000 that interfaces to the processor hardware. This component is the Windows 2000 thread Scheduler. As the name implies, the Scheduler is responsible for managing the processor workload, which consists of program *threads* that need to execute. Consistent with the goals of portability and simplicity, the Scheduler is designed to adapt to many different types of workloads and to require a minimum of user intervention to set up and use. Programmers can interact with the Windows 2000 Scheduler using the Win32 application programming interface (API) to set thread priorities. Consistent with the No Knobs approach, very few thread scheduling controls are actually provided for system administration. Large server configurations with the need to balance a varied workload mix may require additional tuning knobs, but the Scheduler provides few built-in controls for administering these large, mixed-workload, multiprocessor configurations.

Following this chapter's detailed look at the Windows 2000 Scheduler, we discuss processor hardware performance considerations in Chapter 4, emphasizing the Intel IA-32 architecture that dominates the world of Windows 2000 today. We also review the tools an application programmer can use to analyze processor utilization for Windows 2000 applications in development. Then, in Chapter 5, we look at symmetric multiprocessor (SMP) hardware, which dominates the hardware environment for large-scale Windows 2000 Servers, again focusing on the Intel microprocessors. At that point, we review the Windows 2000 Scheduler's multiprocessing support, and look at a third-party tool that enhances the Windows 2000 Scheduler, particularly in SMP configurations.

The Thread Execution Scheduler

The component of Windows 2000 that interacts with the processor hardware is known as the Scheduler. Task scheduling is a fundamental part of any operating system and resides in the OS kernel, *ntoskrnl.exe*, for reasons that should become apparent during this discussion. The Windows 2000 thread scheduler supports foreground/background execution, multiprogramming, multiprocessing, and preemptive scheduling with priority queuing. It functions similarly to other major operating systems such as Compaq's OpenVMS, Unix V, and IBM's MVS. If you are familiar with task scheduling in one of these OSes, you should not have any trouble understanding how the Windows 2000 Scheduler works too. On the other hand, if you have prior exposure only to MS-DOS and Windows, you may find many new topics being introduced.

Multiprogramming

Windows 2000 is a *multiprogramming* operating system, which means that it manages and selects among multiple programs that can all be active in various stages of execution at the same time. The *dispatchable unit* in Windows 2000, representing the application or system code to be executed, is the *thread*. (Unix terminology is identical. NT Versions 4.0 and higher also support a lightweight variant of threads called *fibers*, but that is a detail we can ignore for now.) The Scheduler running inside the Windows 2000 operating system kernel keeps track of each thread in the system and points the processor hardware to threads that are ready to run.

The basic rationale for multiprogramming is that most computing tasks do not execute instructions continuously. After a program thread executes for some period of time, it usually needs to perform an input/output (I/O) operation like reading information from the disk, printing characters on a printer, or drawing data on the display. While the program is waiting for this I/O function to complete, it does not need to hang on to the processor. An operating system that supports multiprogramming saves the status of a program that is waiting, restores its status when it is ready to resume execution, and finds something else that can run in the interim.

Because I/O devices are much slower than the processor, I/O operations typically take a long time compared to CPU processing. A single I/O operation to a disk may take 10 milliseconds, which means that the disk is only capable of executing perhaps 100 such operations per second. Printers, which are even slower, are usually rated in pages printed per minute. In contrast, processors might execute an instruction every one or two clock cycles, with Intel processors capable of running at 500–2000 *million* cycles per second. During the time one thread is delayed 10 milliseconds during an I/O operation, the processor could be executing some 50,000,000 instructions on behalf of another thread.

Figure 3-1 illustrates the way multiprogramming is generally designed to work, with different application programs sharing a single processor. In a multiprogrammed operating system, programs execute until they *block*, normally because they are waiting for an external event to occur. When this awaited event finally does occur, interrupt processing makes the program ready to run again. The figure illustrates how the Windows 2000 Scheduler runs multiple application threads concurrently. Five application threads are depicted, plus the system's Idle thread, which is dispatched when there is no other work ready to run. Threads are shown in one of three possible states: running, blocked (waiting), and queued (or ready) to run.

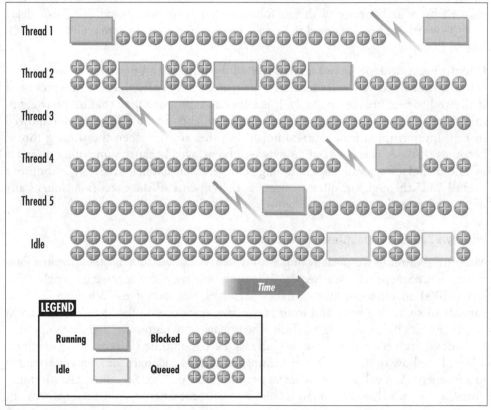

Figure 3-1. Thread multiprogramming

As illustrated, Thread 1 executes until it blocks because it issued an I/O request to a device (for example, to retrieve data from a file on a disk drive). The Scheduler then selects Thread 2, which was queued for execution. Subsequently, an interrupt from some device forces Thread 2 to return to the processor Ready Queue. Once initiated, I/O operations are normally carried out asynchronously and independently of the processor, interrupting the processor only when completed. Typically, there is a blocked thread waiting for the I/O operation to complete. During interrupt processing, Thread 3, which was waiting for the I/O that just completed, has its priority boosted. Because Thread 3 is now a higher-priority task than Thread 2, the Scheduler dispatches Thread 3 next, after the interrupt is serviced. When Thread 3 blocks (to initiate another I/O request), the Scheduler redispatches Thread 2, which runs until the next interrupt occurs.

Multiprogramming introduces the possibility that a program will encounter delays waiting for the processor while some other program is running. In Windows 2000, following an interrupt, the thread that was notified that an event it was waiting on occurred usually receives a priority boost from the Windows 2000 Scheduler. The result is that the thread that was executing when the interrupt occurred is often preempted by a higher-priority thread following interrupt processing. This can delay thread execution, but does tend to balance processor utilization across CPU- and I/O-bound threads.

Due the great disparity between the speed of the devices and the speed of the processor, individual processing threads are usually not a very efficient use of the processor if allowed to execute continuously. It is important to understand that multiprogramming actually *slows down* individual execution threads because they are not allowed to run uninterrupted from start to finish. In other words, when the waiting thread becomes ready to execute again, it may well be delayed because some other thread is in line ahead of it. Multiprogramming represents an explicit trade-off to improve overall CPU throughput, quite possibly at the expense of the execution time of any individual thread.

Windows 2000 Server multiuser environments

Multiprogramming is especially important when Windows 2000 is operating in a multiuser environment, i.e., as a server. When multiple users are accessing a single Windows 2000 machine—a file or database server, for example—Windows 2000 is capable of switching back and forth between various user-initiated tasks. As long as ample processing capacity is available, the impact of dynamically sharing the processor among multiple processes on overall task execution time is normally quite minor. We will see how to determine if processing capacity is adequate for your environment in a moment. We will also see what steps the Windows 2000 Scheduler takes to minimize the delays a thread encounters in an environment where the processor is shared.

Foreground/background execution

Multiprogramming is a less critical function in single-user workstations, where the needs are different. At a single-user workstation, the workload is characterized as either *foreground* or *background*. The thread executing in the foreground is the one the user is currently interacting with using the mouse or keyboard. From the standpoint of the Win32 API, this process is said to have the *input focus*—this identifies the specific process message loop that Windows 2000 routes current keyboard and mouse events to. To make the experience of using the application as pleasant as possible, the operating system must ensure that processing messages corresponding to user interactions with the foreground application are expedited. Later in this section, we look at how the Windows 2000 Scheduler, which implements priority-based multithreading in general, incorporates elements of foreground/background execution priority scheduling.

In a multiprogrammed operating system like Windows 2000 that uses *priority queuing* and *preemptive scheduling*, background tasks need a minimum level of service, too. For instance, suppose that Internet Explorer was managing a nice long download of a Windows 2000 Service Pack in the background. The operating system needs to ensure that this background task gets service, too. This is important for background communications threads that have to maintain some level of dispatchability in order to keep a session going, for example. The technical term is that a background thread can get *starved* when it does not receive at least minimal service over some length of time. There is potential for starvation in any priority-based scheduling scheme like the one Windows 2000 employs. But the Windows 2000 Scheduler takes specific measures to ensure that a starving thread does get fed every so often.

Even when you are not running a long-running background task explicitly, Windows 2000 typically is switching back and forth among multiple programs. For example, bring up the Windows 2000 Task Manager by typing Ctrl-Shift-Esc. Under the Applications tab (see Figure 3-2), you can see all the Windows programs that are eligible to execute in the foreground. These are the desktop applications that can set the input focus and receive and process keyboard and mouse events. Windows 2000 allows you to initiate several applications at once and switch back and forth between them. Switch To, in this context, means to change which active program has the input focus. The ability to switch back and forth freely between applications is common to both Windows and Windows 2000. But because it implements priority queuing with preemptive scheduling, the thread Scheduler in Windows 2000 is much more sophisticated than the Windows 95, 98, or ME flavors, which were designed strictly for desktop systems. Windows 2000 needs a more complex Scheduler due to the more stringent requirements of Windows 2000 server systems, which are explicitly multiuser environments.

The Processes tab (Figure 3-3) lists *all* the processes that are actually running at the moment. You will notice that there are lots more programs running than just the

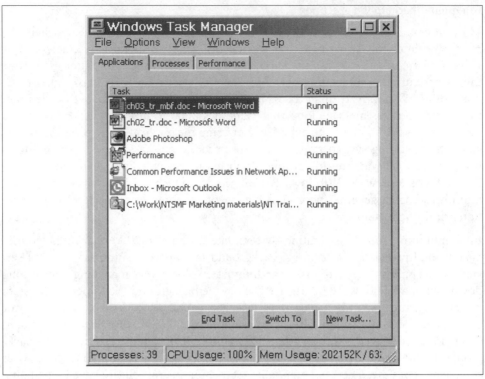

Figure 3-2. The Windows 2000 Task Manager Applications tab

ones you explicitly started. Many of these programs are Windows 2000 *services*, programs started automatically by the Windows 2000 Service Control Manager that, by design, cannot interact with the desktop. (The Services node, accessed from the Computer Management administrative tool, is a user interface of sorts to the Service Control Manager to manage things like which services start automatically and which start manually.)

Since you may not have noticed until now that Windows 2000 has been switching back and forth between all these processes, you might conclude that multiprogramming is a very effective strategy in general. It works because most active programs are really only executing for very small periods of time. For example, Figure 3-3 shows that outside of *WINWORD.exe*, the application with the input focus, and a System Idle Process, which does not sound like it is doing anything important, no other programs are currently executing. (We sorted on the CPU column, which corresponds to spending time in an execution state during the last Task Manager snapshot.) Task Manager can be customized to reveal the number of threads per process, which is also illustrated. As mentioned previously, the thread is the dispatchable unit in Windows 2000, not the process. Every thread represents an instruction stream that is eligible to execute on the processor.

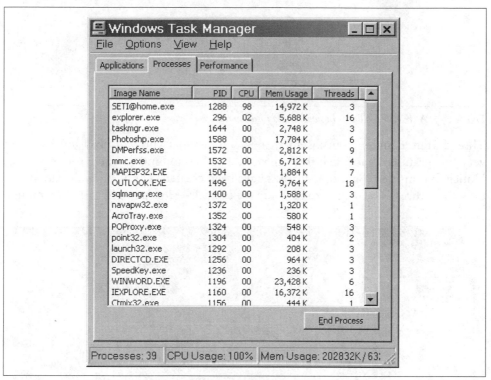

Figure 3-3. The Windows 2000 Task Manager Processes tab

Thread State

As we now know, a multiprogramming operating system switches the processor back and forth between all the program threads that are executing. When the current thread *blocks*, usually due to I/O, the Windows 2000 Scheduler finds another thread that is ready to run and schedules it for execution. If no threads are ready to run, Windows 2000 schedules a thread associated with the System Idle process to run instead. When an I/O operation completes, a blocked thread becomes eligible to run again. This scheme means that threads alternate back and forth between two states: a *ready* state, where a thread is eligible to execute instructions, and a *blocked* state. A blocked thread is waiting for some system event that signals that the transition from waiting to ready can occur. Logically, the thread state transition diagram in Figure 3-4 models this behavior.

Let's illustrate this behavior by using the Windows 2000 System Monitor to watch threads as they change from state to state. Take an application like the MS Internet Explorer and watch as it executes. After it initializes, start up Sysmon and find the Thread object. Select all instances of the IEXPLORE thread and track the value for Thread State. You should see a display that looks something like Figure 3-5. The

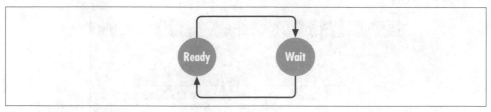

Figure 3-4. A thread oscillates between ready and waiting

Thread State counter is an instantaneous counter that you will need to observe at very fine granularity to catch this behavior. The Sysmon interval here is one second. Notice that inside IE, multiple threads have been created. The Sysmon display shows only the 8 threads belonging to IE; there are typically 13 or more IE threads running.

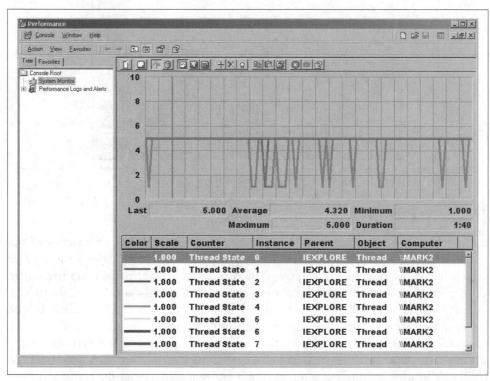

Figure 3-5. Monitoring the Thread State counter for MS Internet Explorer

The value of the Thread State counter corresponds to the state indicated in Table 3-1. (There are some additional thread state values that we have not discussed, but you are not likely to encounter them watching Sysmon. A thread in an unknown execution state is probably in trouble!) Notice that Thread 0 in Figure 3-5 bounces back and forth between being ready to run (Thread State = 1) and waiting (Thread State = 5).

Table 3-1. Values for the Thread State counter

Value	State
0	Initializing
1	Ready
2	Running
3	Standby
4	Terminated
5	Waiting
6	Transition
7	Unknown

The Wait Reason can be discerned by tracking a counter called Thread Wait Reason. The Thread Wait Reason codes are shown in Table 3-2. For instance, if you find threads blocking frequently due to paging (Wait Reasons 1–3, 8–10), this is a cause for concern. (We discuss virtual memory and paging in Chapter 6.)

Table 3-2. Values for the Thread Wait Reason counter

Value	Reason
0	Waiting for a component of the Windows NT Executive
1	Waiting for a page to be freed
2	Waiting for a page to be mapped or copied
3	Waiting for space to be allocated in the paged or nonpaged pool
4	Waiting for an Execution Delay to be resolved
5	Suspended
6	Waiting for a user request
7	Waiting for a component of the Windows NT Executive
8	Waiting for a page to be freed
9	Waiting for a page to be mapped or copied
10	Waiting for space to be allocated in the paged or nonpaged pool
11	Waiting for an Execution Delay to be resolved
12	Suspended
13	Waiting for a user request
14	Waiting for an event pair high
15	Waiting for an event pair low
16	Waiting for an LPC Receive notice
17	Waiting for an LPC Reply notice
18	Waiting for virtual memory to be allocated
19	Waiting for a page to be written to disk
20+	Reserved

Not having written any of this application code, we are forced to speculate on what some of the threads inside Internet Explorer might be doing. Thread 0 may be responsible for maintaining the user interface, responding to keyboard events and mouse moves. This is a high-priority task because the results are immediately visible to the user manipulating the keyboard; the other tasks that IE is trying to accomplish in parallel to this one might be designated as lower in priority. These unglamorous but no less important tasks are sometimes designated as *housekeeping* chores. One housekeeping thread might be responsible for maintaining contact with the networking communication TCP/IP sockets interface to send and receive data. Another might be responsible for maintaining the history log of pages being visited, and still another might be responsible for maintaining the Temporary Internet Files disk-resident cache where recently accessed HTML pages and web graphics files are stored.

These housekeeping chores are distinguished by the fact that they are long running, and they run in threads separate from the screen handling thread for the sake of performance. By consigning these tasks to background threads, the programmer makes the user interface (UI) application thread appear more responsive. Because the UI thread does not get tied up performing long-running disk or network I/O functions, the thread associated with handling the user request is available to respond immediately when a keyboard request is made. It is a classic case of division of labor, and a good example of keeping up appearances. Long-running background tasks are accomplished below the surface and out of view. Meanwhile, very visible processing associated with direct human-computer interaction is executed at high priority.

Before anyone gets the wrong idea, we should mention that developing multi-threaded applications is not a panacea. It is much harder to write and debug a computer program that runs as 10 different threads than it is to write a program that is single threaded.

You should also notice in Figure 3-5 that no IE thread is ever observed in the running state (Thread State = 2). IE threads seem to transition from the ready state directly to the waiting state. Of course, we know that Internet Explorer is doing some work during this interval because it is maintaining communication with the Windows sockets TCP/IP stack and repainting the screen. Is it just bad luck that we did not catch any of the IE threads in the running state? The answer is no, it is not just bad luck. To watch these measurements, we needed to run the Sysmon application. One of the MMC application threads associated with Sysmon is in the running state *every* time a measurement is taken, as Figure 3-6 clearly shows. This is the thread responsible for performing Windows 2000 performance data collection, so it is always running when the instantaneous values of the Thread State counters are captured. This is an interesting example of the Heisenberg Uncertainty Principle as applied to computer measurement. Running the System Monitor application distorts the system behavior you are trying to observe, since it is a process with dispatchable threads that requires resources like any other process. Note that in a multiple processor configuration, there *is* an opportunity to observe threads other than the one from System Monitor in the running state.

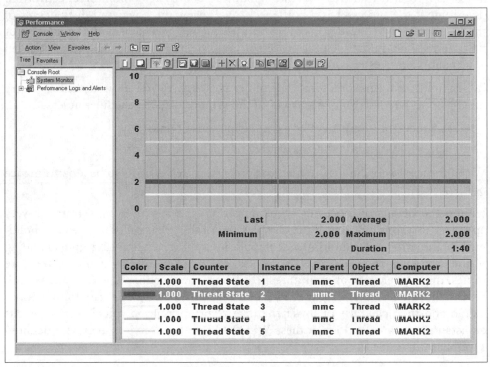

Figure 3-6. *When Sysmon is running, one thread can always be observed in the running state*

 Werner Heisenberg was a German-born physicist whose dictum about the difficulties inherent in making accurate measurements of quantum-level phenomena became known as the Uncertainty Principle. Referring to attempts to measure the position, motion, and velocity of subatomic particles, Heisenberg wrote, "The more precisely the position is determined, the less precisely the momentum is known." (Momentum is mass times velocity.) In quantum physics, this uncertainty arises because the act of measurement influences the physical phenomena being observed. This problem is inherent in many sorts of computer performance measurements, too. Heisenberg's formulation of the Uncertainty Principle famously lead some to question the premises underlying the notions of causality and determinism in classical physics and other areas of modern science. See Roger Penrose's *The Emperor's New Mind: Concerning Computers, Minds, and the Laws of Physics*, for a contemporary perspective on these issues in the context of the prospects for computer intelligence. To learn more about Professor Heisenberg and his famous formulation, see *http://www.aip.org/ history/heisenberg/*.

Processor Performance Monitoring

We will now learn how to use the Windows 2000 System Monitor effectively to determine if the processor is a bottleneck. We review the down-and-dirty details of the Windows 2000 thread scheduling priority queuing mechanism in a moment, but first we provide an overview of processor performance monitoring so that you can detect simple processor bottlenecks.

In general, from a performance and tuning perspective, you do not need to worry much about the underlying mechanics of the Windows 2000 Scheduler unless:

- The processor is very busy for extended periods of time
- There are many ready threads waiting to run

When these two conditions are true, the processor itself is likely to be a performance bottleneck.

Hiding the details of processor scheduling from the system administrator is very appropriate in our view, given the complexities of the subject. For a developer building a high-performance multithreaded application, however, a greater understanding of the Windows 2000 Scheduler is necessary. Thread scheduling is one of the core topics that developers of multithreaded Win32 applications should understand. Essentially, a developer using the Win32 API establishes a base priority for her application and then can raise or lower the relative priority of individual threads as circumstances dictate. We look at these Win32 API runtime services in greater detail in a moment.

Measurement methodology

For performance monitoring, we need to understand the basic mechanism to measure CPU usage at the thread, process, and processor level in Windows 2000. Each time a thread is dispatched (including the Idle thread), the Scheduler records the current time. When the running thread relinquishes control of the processor, the Scheduler again records the time. Subtracting the two timestamps yields the amount of processor time the thread consumed. This value is maintained in 100-nanosecond clock ticks, as discussed in Chapter 2, and stored in the thread's ETHREAD (Thread Environment) block, an internal operating system housekeeping area. Thread processor busy is also summarized across all the threads in the process to yield a measure of per-process processor consumption. An executing thread can gain access to the thread- or process-level CPU time it has accumulated using the GetThreadTimes and GetProcessTimes Win32 API calls.

Processor hardware utilization measurements are made using a variation of this basic bookkeeping mechanism. Windows 2000 accumulates processor busy time for the Idle thread dispatched when there are no ready threads to run in the same way it does for other threads. Since the Idle thread runs only when no other threads are ready to run, how busy the processor is can be calculated by subtracting the amount of processor time the Idle thread absorbed from 100%:

Processor$_n$ % Processor Time = 100% – Idle Thread$_n$ % Processor Time

% Processor Time in the Processor object is maintained in this fashion using one Idle thread per processor. Finally, a systemwide average of the % Processor Time per processor is calculated as:

Processor _Total instance =
Σ Processor % Processor Time / # of processor instances

This average value is reported in the _Total instance of the Processor object in Windows 2000. The measurement methodology associated with the % Processor Time counters is summarized in Table 3-3. Notice that in Windows NT Versions 3 and 4 the System object contains a % Total Processor Time counter that corresponds to the _Total instance calculation performed in Windows 2000. In both cases, while the official names of the systemwide processor utilization counters refer to a *total* value, what is actually reported is an *average* computed across all hardware engines.

Table 3-3. Derivation of processor utilization counters in Windows NT/2000

Object	Counter	Derivation
Thread	% Processor Time	Windows 2000 Scheduler calculates based on the duration of the running state
Process	% Processor Time	Σ Thread % Processor Time
Processor *n*	% Processor Time	100% – Idle Thread *n* % Processor Time
_Total Processor	% Processor Time	Σ Processor % Processor Time / # of processors
System (NT 3 & 4)	% Total Processor Time	Σ Processor % Processor Time / # of processors

The processor utilization counters report the data in the form of % busy, although the counters were all derived from the timing facility built into the Windows 2000 Scheduler, which keeps tracks of 100-nanosecond clock ticks. To convert % Processor Busy to Processor Time, simply multiply by the duration of the measurement interval. For example, for a machine observed to be 86% busy over a five-minute interval, calculate:

Processor time = 0.86 $\times$ 300 = 258 CPU seconds

Normalizing CPU time

Another issue is that both % utilization and processor time measurements are relative to the processing power of the hardware. "Percent of what?" is the next logical question. This is because we expect a program running on a 100 MHz Pentium to use three times the amount of processor time as the same program running on a 300 MHz Pentium machine. For comparisons across hardware, normalizing CPU seconds based on a standard hardware platform can be useful. We suggest normalizing using a 100 MHz baseline Intel processor. Fortunately, AMD and Intel chips identify their clock speed to the initialization NTDETECT routine. This clock speed value is stored in the Registry under HKLM\HARDWARE\DESCRIPTION\System\ CentralProcessor. For example, in the case of the 299 MHz chip illustrated in Figure 3-7 (nominally, a 300 MHz Pentium II or P6), multiply 258 CPU seconds by three to normalize processor consumption to generic 100 MHz processing units. This is a very useful technique for capacity planning and can help you anticipate how your current workload running on a four-way 400 MHz system will perform when you move to a new server that uses 1.2 GHz engines.

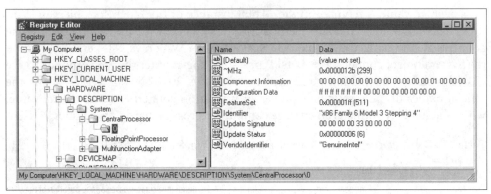

Figure 3-7. The Central Processor signature stored in the Registry shows the processor speed

Processor state

For each object in Table 3-3, processor utilization can be further broken down into time spent executing in user mode (Intel Ring 3) or in privileged mode (Ring 0), two mutually exclusive states. Applications typically run in the more restricted user mode, while operating system functions run in privileged mode. Whenever an application implicitly or explicitly calls an operating system service (e.g., to allocate or free memory, or perform some operation on a file), a *context switch* occurs as the system transitions from user to privileged mode and back again. The portion of time that a thread is executing in user mode is captured as % User Time; privileged mode execution time is captured in the % Privileged Time counter.

Processor time usage in Windows 2000 is broken out into two additional subcategories. % Interrupt Time represents processor cycles consumed in device driver interrupt service routines (ISRs), which process interrupts from attached peripherals such as the keyboard, mouse, disks, network interface card, etc. This is work performed at very high priority, typically while other interrupts are disabled. It is captured and reported separately not only because of its high priority, but also because it is not easily associated with any particular user process. Windows 2000 also tracks the amount of time device drivers spend in deferred procedure calls (DPCs), which also service peripheral devices but run with interrupts enabled. DPCs represent higher-priority work than other system calls and kernel thread activity. Note that % DPC Time is already included in the % Privileged Time measure. We discuss both ISRs and DPCs further when we describe the priority queuing mechanism in Windows 2000.

The Scheduler's thread timing function is notified whenever any context switch occurs, and dutifully records the processing time for the completed function in the appropriate bucket. The context switch might involve going from one user thread to another, a user thread to a kernel function, or a kernel thread to an ISR, followed by a DPC. The Scheduler instruments each variety separately. This enables us to produce the processor utilization histogram illustrated in Figure 3-8, which breaks out processor utilization into its four separate components. In this example, the bulk of the time the process is busy is spent in user mode (light gray). There is a sustained burst of DPC time (darker gray) in the lower right-hand corner, beginning shortly after 23:00 hours. Be sure to subtract % DPC Time from % Privileged Time to create this kind of histogram correctly.

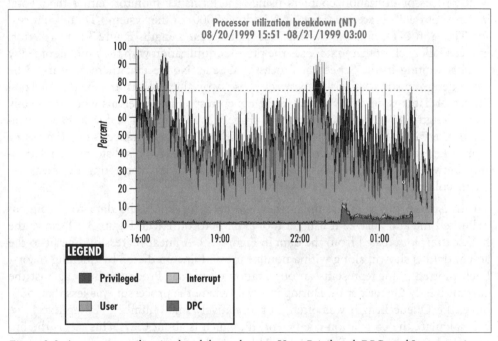

Figure 3-8. A processor utilization breakdown showing User, Privileged, DPC, and Interrupt time

The Processor Ready Queue

The Processor Queue Length counter in the System object (illustrated in Figure 3-9) is an extremely important indicator of processor performance. It is an instantaneous peek at the number of Ready threads that are currently waiting to run. Even though reporting processor utilization is much more popular, the Processor Queue Length is actually a more important indicator of a processor bottleneck. It shows that work is being delayed, and the delay is directly proportional to the length of the queue.

The chart in Figure 3-9 reports the Processor Queue Length and the System % Total Processor Time (this is an NT 4.0 server) for the same overburdened machine illustrated in Figure 3-8. The overall processor utilization is plotted for reference. Since there is one Scheduler Dispatch Queue that services all processors, the Queue Length counter is only measured at the System level. The Thread State counter in the Thread object indicates precisely which threads are waiting for service at the processor(s). In other words, the Processor Queue Length counter indicates how many threads are waiting in the Scheduler dispatcher Ready Queue, while the Thread State counter tells which threads are in the queue. A good working assumption is that when the processor is very busy, queuing delays impact the performance of executing threads. The longer the queue, the longer the delays that threads encounter.

Next, let's look at how processor utilization and queue length are related. To check for the presence of a CPU bottleneck, we capture the values of the two important system-wide processor utilization counters using a performance monitor: either the _Total instance of the % Processor Time (in Windows 2000) or the System _Total % Processor Time (in NT), and the System Processor Queue Length. Figure 3-9 is a Performance Gallery chart that juxtaposes the processor utilization with the number of ready threads waiting in the Scheduler Processor Queue. Notice that there appears to be some deterministic relationship between these two values. When the System % Total Processor Time is near 100% busy, there are corresponding intervals when the Ready queue length grows, too. Keep in mind that we are comparing a continuously measured interval delta counter (% Processor Time) with an instantaneous one (Processor Queue Length) that is measured at a specific point in time. This distorts the relationship between the two counters, so we must be careful in interpreting the measurements collected.

To investigate this relationship further, we need to export the data to a comma-delimited file and analyze it using a tool like Microsoft Excel. Figure 3-10 shows the X-Y scatterplot created from the data in Figure 3-9. A linear regression line fit to the actual data is shown, along with a nonlinear trend line predicted by queuing theory. Each plotted point represents an observation of average Processor Busy against the current Ready Queue depth. During intervals where the processor was less than 50% busy, the Queue Length was often 0 or a relatively small number.* Using Excel, we can calculate the correlation coefficient, r2, which is about 0.27. This yields the linear trend line shown in Figure 3-10. Although the relationship is far from perfect, there is solid evidence that as the Processor Busy increases, so does the size of the Ready Queue. Above 90% busy, Queue Length values in the range of 5, 10, 20, or more ready and waiting threads are commonplace. This is a large number of delayed threads and would likely have a severe performance impact. A convenient rule of thumb is that more than two or three threads in the Ready Queue per processor is

---

* Since we already know that the performance monitor was running at the time the Processor Queue Length counter was recorded, a value of 1 indicates one other thread ready to run.

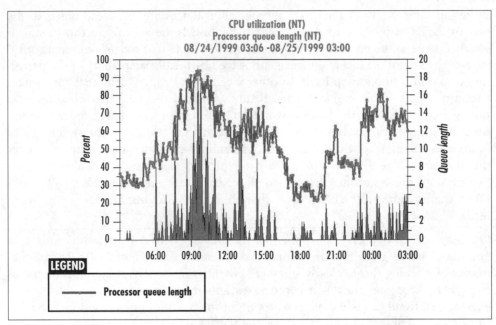

Figure 3-9. Comparing the processor utilization to the processor queue length

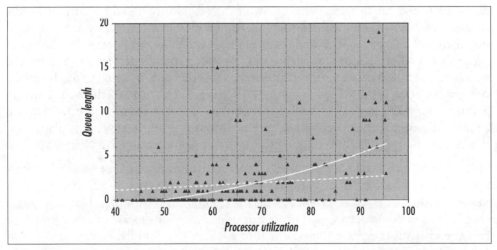

Figure 3-10. An X-Y scatterplot of the data shown in Figure 3-9

probably a sign of trouble. This four-way machine frequently reports as many as five threads per processor in the Ready Queue during peak processing loads. (This example is a Lotus Notes email server, where peak loads correspond to morning activity when everyone arrives at work, and after midnight when replication runs.) That represents a big backlog of work certain to delay threads that are queued for service at the processor.

By monitoring the Thread State counter for all instances of the Thread object at the same time, it is possible to determine which threads are waiting in the Processor Ready Queue at the time measurements are taken. Note that the instantaneous measure of the size of the Ready Queue is influenced by the dispatchability of the performance monitor application itself. In other words, the Ready Queue that the System Monitor reports is the *residue* of the Ready Queue at the time the Scheduler was finally able to dispatch the System Monitor measurement thread. The System Monitor runs at high priority, but by no means at the highest priority in the system. (This is another example of the Heisenberg Uncertainty Principle applied to computer measurement. The System Monitor is *never* able to measure the Processor Queue Length until the system has dispatched all ready threads, including ISRs, APCs, and DPCs that execute at a higher priority than the System Monitor measurement thread itself.)

Queuing theory predicts an exponential relationship between processor utilization and queue length more like the second trend line plotted in Figure 3-10. The mathematics of queuing theory clearly show the potential for serious delays at the processor when there are many active processes and the processor is very busy. This exponential trend line is actually a better fit for the behavior observed in Figure 3-10. But be careful about relying on a mere mathematical description of processor queuing behavior; the complexity of the priority-based scheduling scheme used in Windows 2000 and the dynamic adjustment of thread priority based on current events resists a simple mathematical representation. In addition, the system you are observing likely differs from an idealized mathematical model. Most importantly, the maximum depth of the processor queue you are monitoring is always limited by the number of active processes (and their dispatchable threads). Where the model might predict a queue depth of 50 or more, as shown in Figure 3-10, the actual queue length never rises above 35 because there are never more than 35 threads that are capable of running concurrently in the measured workload. Real systems place constraints on the upper bounds of the observable queue, as discussed in Chapter 1.

Still, this theoretical relationship between processor busy and queue length is sobering. On a very active server with many, many active threads, the queue length is likely to grow as the model predicts. There is a nonlinear relationship between queue length (and queuing delays) and processor utilization. This means that when delays become evident, they have the potential to escalate very rapidly. Checking the Processor Queue Length counter regularly is the best way to determine if your system is experiencing these delays.

Priority scheduling is the general solution designed to cope with situations where the processor is very busy. Priority scheduling orders the Ready Queue, ensuring that under conditions of scarcity, the highest-priority work gains favored access to the resource. The Windows 2000 Scheduler implements an elaborate and dynamic priority scheme, which we will review in a moment. The advantage of priority-based dispatching is that favored workloads gain access to the processor even when the processor is very busy. However, the disadvantage is that low-priority work may receive little or no service as the system approaches saturation. Priority queuing represents *unfair scheduling* in the sense that low-priority work can be delayed (or subject to *starvation*) indefinitely if there is only enough capacity to service the high-priority work. More on this topic later.

Measurement inconsistencies

Inevitably, computer performance measurements contain logical inconsistencies. In this section we look at two anomalies that arise in the Windows 2000 processor utilization measurements we have been discussing. The first is a common problem that results from measurement data collection serialization. The second is known as the *capture ratio* problem and is also quite common.

One manifestation of the serialization problem is that the size of the Ready Queue reported in the System Processor Queue Length counter will likely not match the number of threads reported in the ready state in the Thread object. These measurements are taken separately at two different points of time. Even though the time difference is tiny in human terms, inside your computer it may be significant, especially on very busy systems. As discussed in Chapter 2, performance monitors harvest the measurement data associated with different objects one at a time. Since there is one measurement thread active in an application like the System Monitor, measurements for different objects are necessarily taken at different times. Between the time that the System object is measured, which returns the current processor queue length, and the time the current threads are inventoried to determine thread state, many events can happen that impact the dispatchability of the performance monitor measurement thread. Higher-priority device interrupts may occur that need to be processed, which delay the measurement thread. The result of interrupt processing, in turn, may make additional threads ready for execution. These ready threads may also execute at higher priority than the measurement thread, delaying the return of the thread measurement data even further. It should come as no surprise, then, that these two sets of measurements—taken at two different points in time—are likely to be out of sync.

Because a performance monitoring application is affected by the environment in which it is dispatched, it may not be able to capture consistent and complete information. The *capture ratio* problem is a broad category that subsumes many similar types of measurement data anomalies. This problem is important in capacity planning due to the desire of performance analysts to associate processor utilization with some identifiable user workload. When the processor is busy, we want to know who did it. Sometimes, we know the processor is busy (because the Idle thread was not dispatched), but we cannot tell which user or system process is responsible.

Logically, the thread scheduling mechanism that is used to capture the measurements of processor utilization (see Table 3-3) that Windows 2000 captures suggests the following equivalence relationship:

Σ *Thread % Processor Time =*
Σ *Process % Processor Time =*
Σ *(Processor % Processor Time - Idle Thread Processor Time) =*
Σ *(_Total Processor % Processor Time $\times$ # of processors)*

This means that the sum of the processor busy measurements for all the threads of a process should be equal to the processor busy reported for the process, and that the sum of processor busy measurements for all the processes running should equal the processor busy reported for the processors. In a perfect world, all these measurements, derived from a single collection mechanism inside the Windows 2000 Scheduler, would be perfectly consistent. It should be possible to work your way up from the Thread processor time measurements to the Process measurements, and from the Process measurements to the processor measurements, after the Idle thread CPU consumption is removed.

But, in fact, you are likely to find that these measurements are inconsistent when they are examined during a given interval. When you add up all the Process % Processor Times reported, you often obtain a number that is considerably *less* than what is reported under the Processor (or System) object. You may also find that when you add up all the Thread % Processor Times, you have a number that is *more* than is reported for the Process % Processor Time. This should occur only on a multiprocessor, as we explain shortly. There are one minor and two major sources for these capture ratio anomalies. The minor reason is the granularity of the Windows 2000 virtual clock, which is limited to measuring events in 100-nanosecond increments. This can lead to minor rounding errors when there are very fast processors and dispatchable units of brief duration.

The major reasons for capture ratio problems in Windows 2000 are:

- Transient threads and/or processes
- A truncation rule built into the way the % Processor Time counter is calculated

These two anomalies are discussed in more detail in the following sections.

Transient threads and processes

The performance counters that were maintained by the Windows 2000 Scheduler in the internal operating system Executive Process (EPROCESS) block for a certain process (or thread) and that kept track of how much CPU time it absorbed are destroyed after a process (or thread) terminates. At the next System Monitor collection interval, it is as if that process or thread never existed. The consistency problem comes about when the terminated process contributed to the processor CPU busy during its last interval. Let's assume Thread 0 of Process Foo was running at t1. Prior to t2, when System Monitor data collection occurs, Foo terminates. While Thread 0 of Foo was running, the Idle thread was not running. So the calculation of the Processor % Processor Time counter made at t2 reflects the CPU Time that Process Foo absorbed. But the Foo Process object is no longer around at t2, so the sum of all Process % Processor Time counters, represented by the _Total instance, is less than the amount of CPU busy reported at the Processor level.

A second anomaly results from a truncation rule associated with the Process % Processor Time counter. It is not possible for a processor to be more than 100% utilized: 100% is everything it has to give. By definition, the PERF_100NSEC_TIMER_INV counter type is constrained so that it can never report a value greater than 100% busy. This is consistent with the way one would want the Processor % Processor Time counter to work, at the thread level, at least. Process % Processor Time is a PERF_100NSEC_TIMER counter type, too, and it is calculated from the sum of all its Thread % Processor Time counters because, after all, the thread is the unit of dispatchability (and, therefore, of CPU resource usage accounting). Consider a busy four-way multiprocessor running MS SQL Server, which has 36 different threads capable of executing concurrently, as illustrated in Figure 3-11. Four active processors means that there is actually $4 \times 100\%$ or 400% total CPU busy available for consumption. With 36 potentially active threads, SQL Server can be active on several processors at once and is, in fact, capable of absorbing most of the 400% available CPU time. If that should actually happen, System Monitor rules for the PERF_100NSEC_TIMER process counter require that it report no more than 100% Processor Time. If you add up all the SQL Server Thread % Processor Time counters, however, it is possible to recover any additional Process CPU Busy and report it accurately. A more systematic way to deal with this potential problem is with a Registry override. Adding a Registry value named CapPercentsAt100 to the key HKCU\Software\Microsoft\PerfMon with a value of zero turns off this default truncation rule.

These capture ratio problems in the % Processor Time measurements are annoying, to say the least, and they cause problems for anyone attempting to account rigorously for processor utilization. The resource load measured at the system level is *uncaptured* when we cannot account for it at the process or workload level. What to do with this uncaptured CPU utilization is problematic when we are projecting workload growth: as the workload expands, will this uncaptured CPU utilization grow along with it?

CPU utilization lost due to transient processes is the more serious offense because the lost data is not recoverable by any other means. A partial remedy is to decrease the amount of time between System Monitor measurement intervals, which narrows the window of exposure. Increasing the rate of data collection has overhead considerations, though, so be careful.

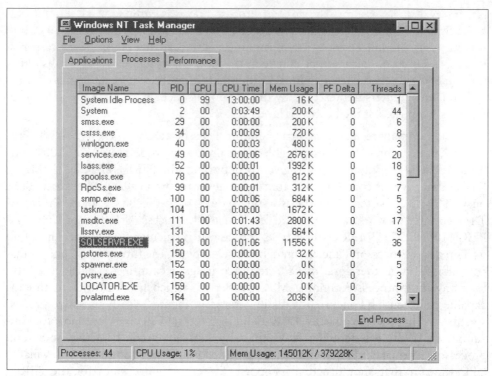

Figure 3-11. An application such as SQL Server can consume more than 100% Processor Time

On the other hand, as long as you are aware of it, the PERF_100NSEC_TIMER truncation anomaly is something you can adjust for during reporting. There is an overhead concern in that this requires collecting thread measurement data, which may be prohibitive because of the sheer quantity of data that results. However, a process that consumes more than 100% Processor Time and happens to have transient threads leads to a situation where it is not possible to recover a correct measurement value at all for the process's CPU utilization in this fashion. All in all, the Registry setting that turns off this default truncation rule is your best bet. We recommend making that part of your standard configuration.

Managing the Ready Queue

Think of priority scheduling as the set of rules for ordering the Ready Queue, which is the internal data structure that points to the threads that are ready to execute. A ready thread (from Internet Explorer or any other application) transitions directly to the running state, where it executes if no other higher-priority ready threads are running or waiting. If there is another ready thread, the Windows 2000 Scheduler selects the highest-priority thread in the Ready Queue to run. We will now flesh out the simple thread state transition diagram sketched in Figure 3-4. Figure 3-12 adds some details to the picture. It shows the Ready Queue, where threads that are ready to execute wait until selected by the Scheduler. It also illustrates the conditions that cause the running thread to transition to either the wait state or back to the Ready Queue. Finally, it shows the role of interrupt processing in the transition of threads from various wait states back to ready.

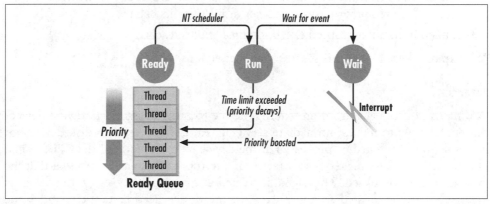

Figure 3-12. A more complete thread state transition diagram

Hiding the details of processor scheduling from the system administrator may be appropriate, given the complexities of the subject. Windows 2000 system administrators have limited built-in capabilities to control the scheduling priorities of applications. There are, however, third-party utilities that provide more extensive administrative controls. On the other hand, for a developer building a high-performance multithreaded application, a fundamental understanding of the Windows 2000 Scheduler is necessary. Thread scheduling is one of the core topics that developers of multithreaded Win32 applications should understand.*

Essentially, using the Win32 API, a developer establishes a base priority for his application, and then can raise or lower the relative priority of individual threads as circumstances dictate. What we attempt to do here is provide a fundamental understanding of how the Windows 2000 Scheduler works from a performance standpoint. A developer of a complex Windows 2000 multithreaded application might also consider exposing an external parameter that allows the user of the application to control its scheduling priority. Later in this chapter we look at several applications that do just that.

---

* Since the systems-oriented aspects of the Win32 API are amply documented in books like *Programming Applications for Microsoft Windows* by Jeffrey Richter (Microsoft Press), there is no need to go into the details here. Part II of Richter's text discusses Windows 2000 processes and threads and provides numerous examples of how these APIs work.

Once a thread is running, it executes continuously on the processor until one of the following events occurs:

- An external *interrupt* occurs
- The thread *voluntarily* relinquishes the processor, usually because it needs to perform I/O
- The thread *involuntarily* relinquishes the processor because it incurred a page fault, which requires the system to perform I/O on its behalf
- A maximum uninterrupted execution *time limit* is reached

We explore these four events in the following sections.

Interrupts

An *interrupt* is a signal from an external device to the processor. Hardware devices *raise* interrupts to request immediate servicing. An I/O request to a disk device, for example, once initiated, is processed at the device independently of the CPU. When the device completes the request, it raises an interrupt to signal the processor that the operation has completed. This signal is treated as a high-priority event: the device is relatively slow compared to the processor, the device needs attention, and some other user may be waiting for the physical device to be free. When the processor recognizes the interrupt request, it:

- Stops whatever it is doing immediately (unless it is already servicing a higher-priority interrupt request)
- Saves the status of the current running thread (including the current values of processor registers, e.g., the Program Counter showing the next instruction to be executed and the Stack Pointer pointing to the program's working storage) in an internal data structure called the Thread Context
- Begins processing the interrupt

The thread that was running when the interrupt occurred returns to the Ready Queue, and it might not be the thread the Scheduler selects to run following interrupt processing.

Interrupt processing likely adds another thread to the Ready Queue, namely the thread that was waiting for the event to occur. In Windows 2000, one probable consequence of an interrupt is a reordering of the Scheduler Ready Queue following interrupt processing. The device driver that completes the interrupt processing supplies a *boost* to the priority of the application thread that transitions from waiting to ready when the interrupt processing completes. Interrupt processing juggles priorities so that the thread made ready to run following interrupt processing is likely to be the highest-priority thread waiting to run in the Ready Queue. Thus, the application thread waiting for an I/O request to complete is likely to receive service at the processor next. We look at the priority boost a waiting thread receives when it transitions to ready in more detail in a moment.

Voluntary wait

A thread voluntarily relinquishes the processor when it issues an I/O request and then waits for the request to complete. Other voluntary waits include a timer wait or waiting for a serialization signal from another thread. A thread issuing a voluntary wait enters the wait state, causing the Windows 2000 Scheduler to select the highest-priority task in the Ready Queue to execute next. The Thread Wait Reason for a thread in a voluntary wait state is 7, waiting for a component of the Windows 2000 Executive (see Table 3-1).

Involuntary wait

Involuntary waits are most frequently associated with virtual memory management. For example, a thread enters an involuntary wait if the processor attempts to execute an instruction referencing data in a buffer that is currently not resident in memory. Since the instruction cannot be executed, the processor generates a *page fault* interrupt, which Windows 2000 must resolve by allocating a free page in memory and reading the page containing the instruction or data into memory from disk. The currently running process is suspended and the Program Counter reset to reexecute the failed instruction. The suspended task is placed in an involuntary wait state until the page requested is brought into memory and the instruction that originally failed is executed. At that point, the virtual memory manager component of Windows 2000 is responsible for transitioning the thread from the wait state back to ready. As mentioned earlier, there are several Thread Wait Reasons that correspond to various virtual memory delays, making it possible to diagnose paging problems very precisely. We return to this topic in Chapter 6.

Time allotment exceeded

A thread that does not need to perform I/O or wait for an event is not allowed to monopolize the processor completely. Without intervention from the Scheduler, some very CPU-intensive execution threads will attempt to do this. A program bug may also cause the thread to go into an infinite loop, in which it attempts to execute continuously. Either way, the Windows 2000 Scheduler eventually interrupts the running thread if no other type of interrupt occurs. If the thread does not relinquish the processor voluntarily, the Scheduler eventually forces it to return to the Ready Queue. This form of processor sharing is called *time-slicing*, and it is designed to prevent a CPU-bound task from dominating the use of the processor for an extended period of time. Without time-slicing, a high-priority CPU-intensive thread could delay other threads waiting in the Ready Queue indefinitely. The Windows 2000 Scheduler implements time-slicing by setting a clock timer interrupt to occur at regular intervals to check on the threads that are running.

When a thread's allotted time-slice is exhausted, the Windows 2000 Scheduler interrupts it and looks for another ready thread to dispatch. Of course, if the interrupted thread happens to be the highest-priority ready thread (or the only ready thread), the Scheduler selects it to run again immediately. However, Windows 2000 also lowers the priority of a thread that executes for the entire duration of its time-slice to reduce the likelihood that a CPU-intensive thread will monopolize the processor. This technique of boosting the relative priority of threads waiting on device interrupts and reducing the priority of CPU-intensive threads approximates a *mean time to wait* algorithm, a technique for maximizing throughput in a multiprogramming environment.

Interrupt Processing

Interrupts are subject to priority. The interrupt priority scheme is hardware-determined, but in the interest of portability it is abstracted by the Windows 2000 HAL. During interrupt processing, interrupts from lower-priority interrupts are *masked* so that they remain pending until the current interrupt processing completes. Following interrupt processing during which interrupts themselves are disabled, the operating system returns to its normal operating mode with the processor reset once more to receive interrupt signals. The processor is once again *enabled* for interrupts.

Strictly speaking, on an Intel processor, there is a class of interrupts used for switching between the user level and privileged operating system code. Although this involves interrupt processing on the Intel microprocessor, we are not referring to that type of interrupt here. Switching privilege levels does not necessarily cause the executing thread to relinquish the processor. However, Windows 2000 does classify these OS supervisor call interrupts as *context switches*, which is discussed in more detail in Chapter 5.

In Windows 2000, hardware device interrupts are serviced by an *interrupt service routine*, or ISR, which is a standard device driver function. Device drivers are extensions of the operating system tailored to respond to the specific characteristics of the devices they understand and control. The ISR code executes at the interrupt level priority, with interrupts at the same or lower level disabled. An ISR is high priority by definition since it interrupts the regularly scheduled thread and executes until it voluntarily relinquishes the processor (or is itself interrupted by a higher-priority interrupt).

The ISR normally signals the device to acknowledge the event, stops the interrupt from occurring, and saves the device status for later processing. It then schedules a *deferred procedure call* (DPC) to a designated routine that performs the bulk of the device-specific work associated with interrupt processing. DPCs are a special feature of Windows 2000 designed to allow the machine to operate enabled for interrupts as much as possible. DPC code executes at a higher priority than other operating system privileged modes, but one that does not disable further interrupts from occurring and being serviced. See Figure 3-13 for an illustration of the overall priority scheme Windows 2000 uses. It shows, in order of priority, the Interrupt Request level priorities, the special Active Dispatch level where DPC and APC (operating system Asynchronous Procedure Calls) routines run, and the Passive Dispatch levels controlled by the Windows 2000 thread Scheduler. The so-called passive priority levels controlled by the Scheduler are further divided into two groups, real-time (or fixed) and dynamic priority levels.

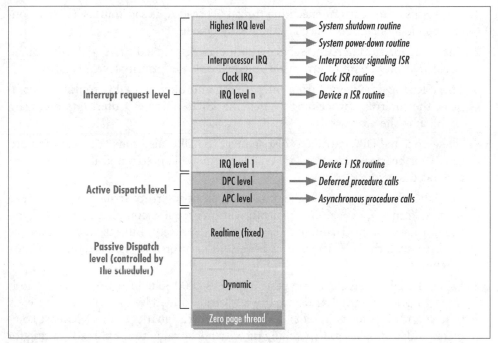

Figure 3-13. The overall Windows 2000 dispatching priority scheme

The DPC mechanism in Windows 2000 keeps the machine running in a state enabled for interrupts as much as possible. This architecture is especially useful with Intel PC hardware where many devices connected to a single PCI bus can share the same Interrupt Request Queue (IRQ) level. DPC routines execute from a separate DPC dispatcher queue, which Windows 2000 empties before it calls the Scheduler to redispatch an ordinary kernel or application thread. A typical function carried out by a DPC routine is to reset the device for the next operation and launch the next request if one is queued. When the DPC completes, a high-priority kernel or device driver thread then marks the I/O function complete. At the end of this chain of events, a waiting thread transitions to the ready state, poised to continue processing now that the I/O it requested has completed.

When an interrupt occurs, the thread executing loses control of the processor immediately. When the DPC performing the bulk of the interrupt processing completes, the Windows 2000 Scheduler checks the Ready Queue again and dispatches the highest-priority thread. The interrupted thread does not necessarily regain control following interrupt processing because a higher-priority task may be ready to run. This is variously known as *preemptive scheduling, preemptive multithreading,* or *preemptive multitasking.*

To summarize, the sequence of events when a device interrupt is processed is as follows:

1. The status of the current executing thread (Thread A) is saved in its Thread Context block. Thread A is placed in the Ready Queue.

2. The appropriate interrupt service routine is dispatched. The ISR runs at an *elevated priority*, with interrupts at an equal or lower priority level disabled.

3. The ISR stops the device from interrupting and queues a DPC routine to complete the interrupt processing. When the ISR terminates, interrupts are again enabled on the processor.

4. The associated DPC routine is dispatched. The DPC also runs at an elevated priority, but because interrupts are enabled, it may be preempted if another interrupt occurs before it completes.

5. The DPC routine completes the processing of the interrupt request and notifies a waiting kernel or device driver thread with the request completion status. Typically, a kernel thread running at a high fixed priority, but still lower than the level at which the DPC runs, receives this notification and is placed on the Ready Queue.

6. When the DPC queue is empty, the Windows 2000 Scheduler is invoked. It finds the high-priority kernel or device driver thread notified by the DPC in the Ready Queue and dispatches it. This device driver thread marks the I/O request complete. It also supplies a dispatching priority boost value to the thread waiting for the I/O request. This priority boost is returned to the I/O Manager, an operating system component of the Windows 2000 Executive.

7. Assuming that no more high-priority DPC, kernel, or device driver threads are queued to run, the Scheduler dispatches an I/O Manager thread. The I/O Manager signals application Thread B waiting for the I/O operation to complete, which causes that thread to transition from the wait state to the ready state. The I/O Manager applies the priority boost passed from the device driver to the waiting application.

8. Eventually, when no other higher-priority threads are pending, the Scheduler selects the highest thread waiting in the Ready Queue to be dispatched. (This could be either Thread A or Thread B.)

The processing indicated in Steps 1–7 runs at a higher priority than any performance monitoring application. The % Interrupt Time and % DPC Time counters are maintained automatically during these processing steps. The Windows 2000 System Monitor can then harvest this measurement data when its collection thread is eventually dispatched.

Complicated as it seems, the sequence of events involved in interrupt processing described here is seldom even that simple in real life on a busy machine. For example, while one ISR is dispatched, a higher-level IRQ can be raised and interrupt it! Furthermore, imagine a machine with multiple processors where several engines are involved in processing interrupt requests concurrently. On a multiprocessor, for example, the DPC invoked by the ISR can be dispatched on a different processor, where it can begin execution *before* the ISR itself actually completes.

When it ultimately regains control at the Passive Dispatch level following an interrupt, the Windows 2000 Scheduler examines the Ready Queue, selects the highest-priority ready thread, and instructs the processor to begin executing it. Thread dispatching priority in Windows 2000 is represented by a five-bit number ranging from 0 to 31: the higher the number, the higher the priority. (The thread dispatching priority scheme is illustrated in Figure 3-13.) Zero is the lowest priority and is reserved for use by the system. The values between 1 and 31 are divided into two sections. Priority values in the range of 16 to 31 are reserved for real-time scheduling and are generally unused by normal applications. The real-time priorities are more properly understood as fixed values. Threads using real-time priorities have higher dispatching priority than many Windows 2000 operating system services, so real-time should be used only by applications that know what they are doing.*

The priority values between 1 and 15 are known as the dynamic priority range, and are subject to dynamic adjustment by Windows 2000. The Win32 API provides a programming interface that further divides the dynamic range into five priority classes: Idle, Below Normal, Normal, Above Normal, and High, as shown in Figure 3-14. (The Below Normal and Above Normal classes are new in Windows 2000.) Each priority class corresponds to a *base priority,* which can be set by a process using the SetPriorityClass Win32 API function call. Processes that do not call SetPriorityClass default to the normal priority class.

Notice in Figure 3-15 that several processes running on this desktop machine are set to run at high priority. These include Task Manager, which explains how Task Manager always seems to gain control even when some other process is in a CPU loop. Also included are *winlogon.exe*, which provides security and authentication services for the desktop, and *csrss.exe*, the client/server runtime subsystem that provides services like menus, dialog boxes, and window management for desktop applications. This illustrates one of the most important principles of priority scheduling: *service provider processes should be placed in a higher dispatching priority class than consumers of those*

---

* While Windows 2000 is capable of hosting real-time applications, it has limitations that make it impractical for many time-critical applications, like an airplane flight controller. The DPC mechanism introduces a degree of variability in the time it takes to process interrupts that many time-critical tasks simply cannot afford. For more information, see "Real-Time Systems and Microsoft Windows NT," under Backgrounders, Platform Articles, Kernel-base in the MSDN library. *WinRT*, developed by Bsquare under license from Microsoft, is a version of embedded Windows NT suitable for building real-time applications.

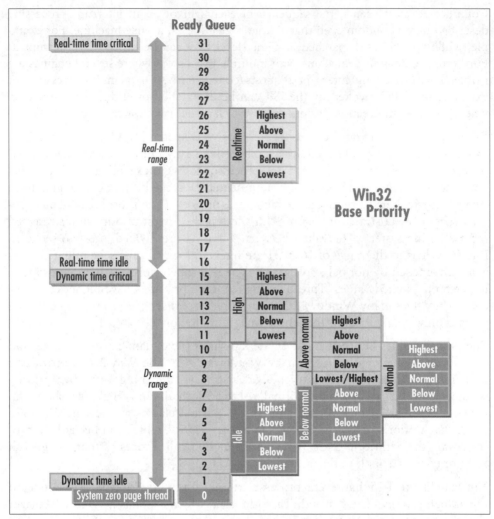

Figure 3-14. The Win32 dispatching priority

services. This ensures that service providers get dispatched in a timely manner when their services are requested by consumers.

The Idle priority class seems intended for applications like screen savers, which run only when no other application threads are ready.* The new Windows 2000 Below Normal and Above Normal priority classes are underutilized at the moment, too.

---

* The *SETI@home* peer-to-peer computing program that analyzes radio signals captured from deep space for signs of intelligent extraterrestrial life is one of the few processes we know about that run at Idle priority by design. *SETI@home* allows anyone with a computer and an Internet connection to take part in the project. Written in the form of screensaver, the *SETI@home* program searches for extraterrestrial signals while the computer is idle.

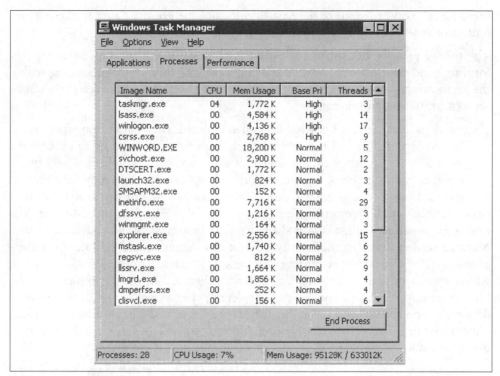

Figure 3-15. The Base Priority of active processes can be viewed in Task Manager

Thread Priority Adjustments

Threads inherit the base priority of their parent process when they are created, but they can adjust their priority upwards or downwards dynamically during runtime. Within each dynamic priority class, there are five priority adjustments that can be made at the thread level by calling SetThreadPriority. These adjustments are Highest, Above Normal, Normal, Below Normal, and Lowest. They correspond to +2, +1, +0, −1, and −2 priority levels above or below the base level, as illustrated in Figure 3-14. The base priority and the adjustments map to the dispatch priority levels in a straightforward way. The High, Above Normal, Normal, Below Normal, and Idle base priorities correspond to normal priority levels of 13, 10, 8, 6, and 4. The adjustments add or subtract a value of 1 or 2 from the normal base, as illustrated in Figure 3-14. Notice that the priority levels of different base classes overlap. The Win32 API also provides for two extreme adjustments within the dynamic range: *time-critical*, or priority 15, and *idle*, or priority 1. Priority 0 is reserved for the operating system's zero page thread, which is, as the name suggests, a thread that stuffs zeros into free memory pages. The Idle thread, which is a bookkeeping mechanism rather than an actual execution thread, has no priority level associated with it. At the thread level, you can monitor the Base Priority and the Priority Current (the last current priority level of the thread), which reflects any adjustments.

The thread priority adjustments allow an application designer to give threads performing time-critical work higher dispatching priority than other processing within the application. Threads performing longer-running background processes should be set to priorities below normal.

To gain an accurate picture of what is happening inside the system being monitored, the System Monitor should run at a relatively high priority. Needing to observe the Processor Queue Length with any degree of accuracy, for example, suggests that a performance monitoring application should be High priority. You may have noticed in Figure 3-15 that the System Monitor is conspicuously absent from the list of processes running at High priority. (The Version 3 and 4 NT Performance Monitor does run at High priority.) Figure 3-16 sheds light on this mystery, illustrating a System Monitor session watching the Priority Current thread counter for the Microsoft Management Console, which is hosting the System Monitor applet. MMC Thread 2, which was identified as the collection thread in Figure 3-6, runs at priority 15, the highest priority in the dynamic range. Evidently, the System Monitor performance data collection thread issues a SetThreadPriority call to boost its priority to the time-critical setting. This allows the System Monitor to collect more accurate performance statistics.

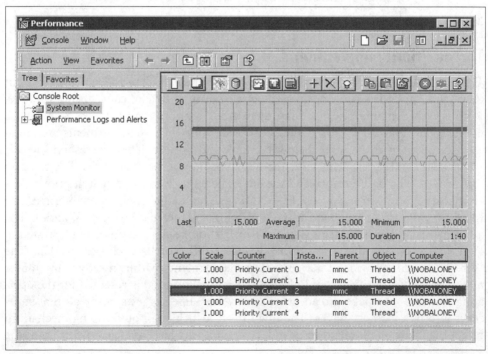

Figure 3-16. The System Monitor watching the Priority Current thread counter for the MMC

Following an interrupt, the Windows 2000 Scheduler simply scans the thread dispatcher Ready Queue, which is ordered by priority. The highest-priority ready thread is scheduled to run next. Within a priority level, ready threads are ordered in a FIFO (First In, First Out) queue. The type of scheduling within the priority level is also called *round-robin*. Multithreaded applications that need to set thread dispatch priority appropriately should keep in mind the priority scheduling principle cited earlier: place service provider threads in a higher dispatch priority level than the threads that are consumers of those services. This ensures that threads that provide service are dispatched in a timely manner when their services are requested by consumers of those services. Setting a good example, Microsoft developers tend to place their applications in the normal priority class, but then boost threads responsible for service tasks to time-critical priority. A look at the Remote Access Services (RAS) Manager program supporting dial-up networking, for example, shows ten threads idling at the normal priority level. As illustrated in Figure 3-17, as soon as the application is activated, several threads are raised to time-critical priority by calling the SetThreadPriority interface.

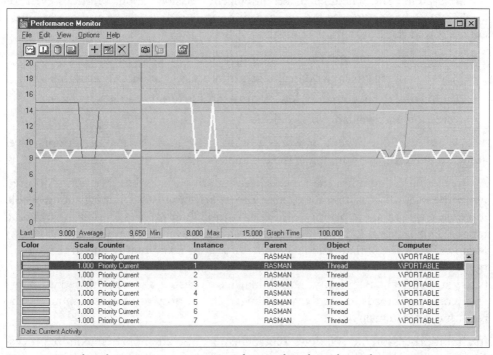

Figure 3-17. When the RAS Manager is activated, some threads are boosted

These multithreaded programming techniques need to be used carefully. Application designers should avoid placing threads performing long-running, CPU-intensive tasks at a higher priority level than other threads. To ensure that time-critical threads perform the minimum amount of processing required at high priority, offload longer-running tasks to lower-priority threads wherever possible. If a thread needs to run at high priority, make sure it is not dependent on resources held by a lower-priority task—this can lead to a situation called a *deadlock* or *deadly embrace*. A deadlock occurs when a high-priority thread cannot get to the resources it needs because they are held by a low-priority thread, which in turn can never get dispatched. The high-priority thread might execute a spin lock, testing a lock repeatedly in an attempt to acquire it. A deadly embrace occurs when the lock never becomes free because the lower-priority thread holding the lock is forced to wait in the Dispatch Ready Queue. In these situations, developers should use the Win32 API synchronization objects (the Critical Section object for intraprocess communication, and mutex objects for IPC) because they avoid spin locks that consume excessive CPU time.

Dynamic Priority Adjustments

Priorities in the 1–15 range are called *dynamic* because the Windows 2000 Scheduler automatically raises or lowers thread priorities based on what is currently happening on the system. The Scheduler makes intelligent decisions about priorities even for applications that do not use the SetThreadPriority interface. There are several different goals that the OS attempts to juggle:

- Making foreground applications appear as responsive as possible
- Load balancing typical workload mixes of processor- and I/O-bound threads
- Minimizing the potential for low-priority threads to suffer from starvation
- Detection and avoidance of deadlocks

The Windows 2000 Scheduler works toward these goals by making priority level adjustments to threads running in the dynamic range.

A thread that relinquishes the processor voluntarily usually has its priority boosted when the event it is waiting for occurs. Boosts are cumulative, but it is not possible to boost a thread above priority 14, the next-to-highest priority level in the dynamic range. (This leaves priority 15 in the dynamic range available for time-critical work.) Meanwhile, a thread that relinquishes the processor involuntarily due to the expiration of its time-slice often has its priority *decremented*, although it will not be pushed below its original base priority. As you may have guessed, these priority adjustments apply only to threads in the dynamic range. The priority of threads running in the real-time range remain fixed.

In a multiprocessor, the Windows 2000 Scheduler also attempts to maximize processor throughput by incorporating processor affinity into the decision-making process.

Priority boost following an interrupt

Interrupt processing supplies a priority boost to a thread that has just been awakened by an external event such as an I/O completion or an IPC signal. The scheme

Windows 2000 uses to boost the priority of threads following an interrupt is shown in Table 3-4.

Table 3-4. Dynamic adjustments to thread priority following an interrupt

Interrupting device	Priority boost
Sound card	+8
Mouse, keyboard	+6
Network card, named pipe, serial port, mailslot	+2
Disk, CD-ROM, parallel port, video card, event, semaphore	+1

This boost is temporary because it decays over time. A thread responding to a keyboard or mouse event has its priority temporarily boosted by 6. This means that the foreground application thread responsible for handling keyboard or mouse input is automatically boosted to near time-critical level. A thread awakened because of a disk I/O completion has its priority boosted by 1. This increases the likelihood that an I/O-intensive thread is dispatched soon after the I/O interrupt occurs. Priority boosts are also cumulative. A thread executing at normal priority 8 that gets boosted to 9 when an I/O it is waiting on completes will be boosted again to priority 10 when it receives a NIC interrupt. As previously mentioned, the only limitation is that Windows 2000 will not boost priority into the priority 15 time critical level at the high end of the dynamic range. Once a thread is boosted to priority 14, it is not boosted any higher.

These automatic adjustments make thread priority within the dynamic range *very* dynamic. Figure 3-18 illustrates what happens to the priority of some of Internet Explorer's many threads as a result of a variety of web-surfing user input and I/O completions. The priority of the highlighted thread is quite dynamic, and it is not the only thread in the IE process that is subject to frequent adjustments. This event-based, priority boosting scheme helps Windows 2000 manage those applications that do not otherwise take advantage of the Win32 thread scheduling services. Once applied, priority boosts decay over time, eventually causing the thread to return to its base priority. We look at that specific behavior in a moment.

The policy of automatically boosting the priority of threads based on the last interrupt helps interactive applications that do not exploit the advanced thread scheduling services of the operating system to run well on Windows 2000 machines. Unfortunately, the policy does have two unpleasant side effects. The first affects applications that actually do try to exploit Windows 2000 multithreading services. The second affects applications that scan large disks.

Disabling dynamic adjustments

The dynamic adjustment policy means that programmers developing complex multi-threaded applications can never be exactly sure of the current priority of executing

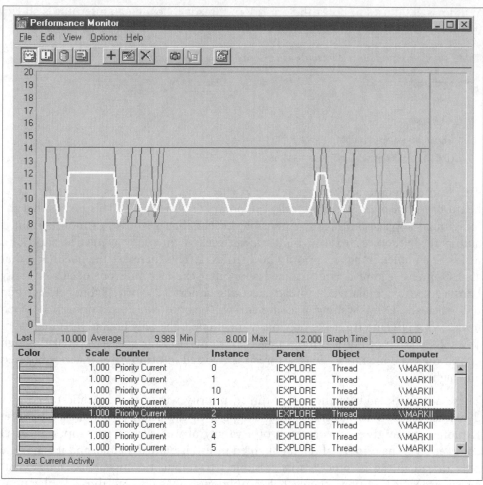

Figure 3-18. Priority adjustments in the dynamic range

threads. The problem especially afflicts experienced programmers used to statically assigned dispatching priorities in other operating systems. The SDK documentation describing the SetPriorityClass and SetThreadPriority API calls gives programmers a false sense of security. It is easy to think that you have absolute control over the dispatching priority of threads in your application, when, in fact, the operating system adjusts the priorities of threads executing in the dynamic range continuously.

Suppose the Windows 2000 application being developed consists of a server thread and several worker threads. Since worker threads require services from time to time from the server thread, the programmer developing the application uses the SetThreadPriority function to establish the dispatching priority of the server thread at +2 over the process base used by the worker threads. Because of dynamic adjustment, there is no guarantee that the server thread will remain at a higher dispatching priority when the application executes. In fact, it is possible for Windows 2000 to boost the priority of worker threads to a level higher than the server thread. This may cause a variety of logical and/or performance-related problems, as the inadvertently lower-priority server thread is unable to service worker thread requests responsively enough. The application may even suffer from a deadlock or deadly embrace as a result of this inversion of the expected relative priority scheme. This happens when a worker thread needs to acquire a resource from the server thread, but the higher-priority worker thread prevents the server thread from executing. Compounding the problem, which is difficult enough in any case to diagnose, the application programmer may not realize the extent to which dynamic thread priority adjustments take place.

Windows 2000 provides two ways for programmers to deal with this potentially thorny problem. The first is the GetThreadPriority API call that can be issued inside your program to determine the current priority of a thread. This is not a wholly satisfactory solution, however, because thread priorities change constantly. Consequently, Windows 2000 introduces a new function to disable dynamic priority boosts at either the process or thread level. These two new API calls are SetProcessPriorityBoost and SetThreadPriorityBoost, respectively.

I/O-bound threads

The second effect impacts efficient, long-running I/O-bound threads like the ones that scan your hard drive. These include the infamous Microsoft Office FindFast function, most virus scan programs, and disk defragmentation utilities. The FindFast function developed for Microsoft Office is probably the most notorious example since it is a Microsoft-developed application. You would think they would have known better.

The FindFast utility scans your hard drives to create an index that is used to speed up the Advanced Find file search utility used in applications like Word and Excel. FindFast is automatically installed with Office applications up until Office 2000. By default, it schedules an automatic scan of your hard drive partition every two hours to keep its index file current. If FindFast is installed on your system, you will see a Control Panel applet that looks like Figure 3-19. This applet is used to regulate the behavior of this utility. You can change the rate FindFast scans your hard drive or turn off its regularly scheduled disk scans completely. You will also see a large file named *ffastun0.ffx* on your logical drive. That file contains the FindFast index that is built and maintained by scanning your hard drive.

The FindFast scan can take a long time to run and is very disruptive. The bigger the hard drive partition it has to index, the longer it runs. The FindFast application itself executes efficiently and rapidly; that is not the problem. Because the indexing thread is I/O bound, it has its priority boosted following every I/O interrupt so that it reaches a high priority level. At this point it tends to monopolize your whole system. Because it gets such good dispatching priority, FindFast monopolizes both the processor and

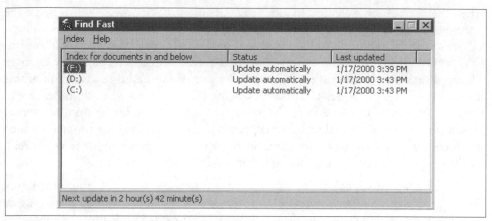

Figure 3-19. The MS Office FindFast applet is installed in the Control Panel

the hard drive partition it is scanning. Figure 3-20 illustrates what goes on when the FastFind indexing functions run. FastFind creates a process with two threads. Thread 0 appears to perform the actual disk I/O, and is dispatched at priority 14. Thread 0 hands off data to Thread 1, which is a CPU-bound thread dispatched at priority 8. With one thread monopolizing the disk and another thread grabbing the processor, it is very hard to get any other work done on your machine while this function is executing. Since FindFast was installed automatically with MS Office applications, problems arose because so many people were unaware that something so disruptive was running periodically on their system. FindFast is not alone in this regard: almost any application that scans your hard drive periodically has a similar impact on performance in Windows 2000, an undesirable side effect of the priority boost mechanism.

Recognizing the problem, Microsoft dropped the FindFast function from Office 2000. The Windows 2000 developers then went to a great deal of trouble to develop an alternative Advanced Search facility based on the company's web-oriented Index Server technology. The Index Server-based Advanced Search utility exploits two new specific Windows 2000 features, NTFS sparse files and the NTFS change journal file.

Time-Slicing

Threads that have their priority boosted are subject to *decay* back to their current base. The priority decay mechanism is incorporated into the Scheduler's time-slicing function. Recall that time-slicing is a Scheduler function that eventually forces CPU-intensive threads to relinquish the processor involuntarily. Time-slicing makes it more difficult for a CPU-intensive thread to monopolize the processor.

In Windows 2000, the maximum duration of a thread's time-slice running on the processor is based on something called a *quantum*, which is a hardware-specific time interval. The quantum in Windows 2000 determines the amount of time between

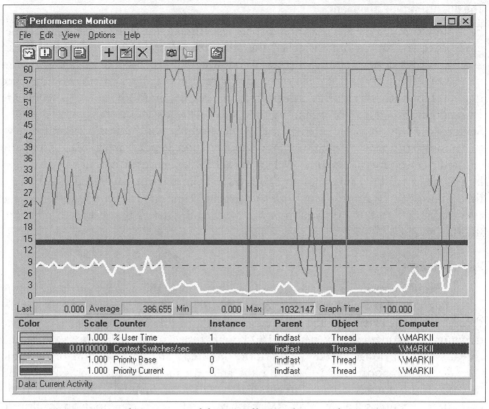

Figure 3-20. Monitoring the execution of the MS Office FindFast application

regularly scheduled timer interrupts. When one of these timer interrupts occurs, the Scheduler gains control of the system and:

- Reduces the priority level of a running thread that had previously been boosted if that thread is still running above its base priority
- Forces a running thread that has consumed its entire processor time allotment (its time-slice) to return to the Ready Queue

These Scheduler interventions allow the operating system to detect CPU-intensive threads and intercede to give other threads a better opportunity to get dispatched.

The rate at which the Scheduler generates timer interrupts to examine the state of the system is machine-specific. On faster machines, the Windows 2000 Scheduler intervenes at a faster rate. For instance, for a 100 MHz machine, the Scheduler interrupts occur every 20 milliseconds. On a 300 MHz machine, the rate is just 15 milliseconds. On a 600 MHz machine, the rate is once every 10 milliseconds. As Intel machines get faster, we can expect that Microsoft will continue to increase the rate of Scheduler interventions accordingly.

The quantum time allotment

Each time the Scheduler selects and dispatches a thread, the thread is assigned a specific processor time allotment called the *quantum value*. The value that the thread receives varies depending on whether Windows 2000 Professional or Server is running. On Windows 2000 Professional, each thread is initially allotted two time-slice quanta. However, threads of a foreground process (the one with the input focus) are allotted an elongated six quantum time-slice. Threads associated with Terminal Server User sessions are treated as if they were running on Professional and receive the same two time-slice quanta. On Windows 2000 Server, each thread is initially allotted twelve time-slice quanta. When the Scheduler gets control following its regularly scheduled timer interrupt, it subtracts 1 from the current executing thread's time allotment. If a thread continues to execute continuously, the quantum value eventually falls to zero, at which point the Scheduler forces the thread to return to the Ready Queue.

Priority decay

At each timer interrupt, the Scheduler also decrements the priority of the currently executing thread if that thread was previously subject to a dynamic boost, i.e., if the thread's current priority is above its base. Using this priority decay mechanism, the dynamic adjustment policy detects I/O-bound threads that turn into CPU-bound threads that no longer need their priority boosted. The combination of dynamic thread priority boosts for I/O-bound threads and priority decay for CPU-bound threads approximates a *mean-time-to-wait* (MTTW) scheduling algorithm. Many computer scientists believe MTTW provides optimal throughput in multiprogrammed computer systems. This approximate MTTW scheduling algorithm maximizes throughput without sacrificing overall application responsiveness. Because mechanical peripheral devices are so slow compared to the processing speeds achieved in semiconductor devices like the processor and RAM, it makes to sense to favor I/O-bound threads. While I/O-bound threads wait for slow devices to respond, there are plenty of cycles to spare for lower-priority compute-bound work.

Tuning the time-slice value

Windows 2000 uses default time-slice values that are somewhat arbitrary and not always optimal for a given workload. In effect, the time-slice value is tuned to be one of two values, depending on the expected workload. The Server default value is chosen with larger multiple processor configurations running server applications like MS SQL Server in mind. This may not be optimal for other types of server workloads. The duration of a time-slice is relatively high on Server, which means compute-bound threads have more of an opportunity to monopolize the processor when you are running Server. The smaller time-slice value that Windows 2000 Professional uses should be suitable for most (but not all) interactive workloads. Consequently, Microsoft carries the Professional time-slice defaults forward to Terminal Server sessions where multiple users are running interactive workloads on a central server. Overall, we believe the defaults Microsoft establishes are sound choices, and you need compelling reasons to change them.

Windows 2000 does allow you to choose between the two ways Windows 2000 time-slicing can be set up. Accessing the System applet from the Control Panel, selecting the system, choosing the Advanced tab, and clicking Performance Options brings up the dialog box illustrated in Figure 3-21. This presents you with a choice. Optimizing performance for applications means running with the shorter time-slice values assigned in Windows 2000 Professional by default. Choosing background services runs the longer Windows 2000 Server default time-slices.

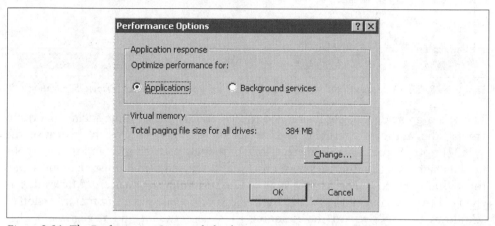

Figure 3-21. The Performance Options dialog box

Behind this Control Panel applet is a Registry setting called Win32PrioritySeparation under HKLM\SYSTEM\CurrentControlSet\Control\PriorityControl that the Performance Options dialog manipulates. Figure 3-22 illustrates the value of Win32PrioritySeparation that corresponds to the Windows 2000 Server default time-slicing value. Windows 2000 Server defaults to a value of x'18', which is interpreted as follows. Transform the hex code into binary and you get '011000'b. Working from the left two bits at a time, Win32PrioritySeparation encodes:

1. Whether short (Professional) or long (Server) time-slice intervals are used

2. Whether fixed or variable time-slice intervals are used

3. The degree of time-slice quantum stretching performed on behalf of the foreground application, similar to quantum stretching under Windows NT 4.0

The '011000'b encoding translates into the long (Server) time-slice value, fixed-length intervals, and no quantum stretching for the foreground application. Changing the parameter to optimize performance for applications (as in Figure 3-21) changes the Win32PrioritySeparation code to x'26'. This translates into a short (Professional) time-slice value, variable-length intervals, and stretching the quantum of the foreground application by a factor of 3.

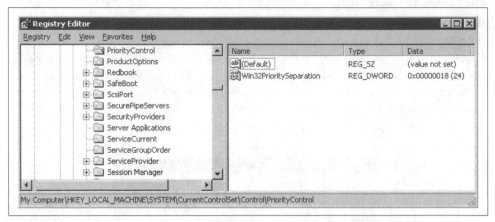

Figure 3-22. The Windows 2000 Server default time-slicing value for Win32PrioritySeparation

There is a great deal of confusion about the Windows 2000 time-slicing algorithm among the authors of articles and books on the subject. Possibly because the Win32PrioritySeparation parameter is one of the few performance and tuning knobs in plain sight, some authorities have mistakenly assumed that it must be doing something dramatic. In most cases, it is not. Further confusing matters, Microsoft has changed the meaning of the Win32PrioritySeparation value in every major version of Windows NT. We regard the Resource Kit's *Regenty.chm* and *Regentry.hlp* files' description of the Win32PrioritySeparation parameter as definitive.

In his authoritative book *Programming Applications for Microsoft Windows*, Jeffrey Richter writes that Windows 2000 developers have been hesitant to document the Scheduler fully because they do not want developers to rely on features that may be changed in future releases. There would certainly be less confusion if Microsoft documented its time-slicing implementation in clear, unambiguous language. According to Microsoft documentation (see the article entitled "Priority Inversion and Windows NT Scheduler," Article ID: Q96418 in the Microsoft Knowledge Base), a time-slice in NT is two quanta, or 30 milliseconds on x86 hardware. As discussed previously, that is true for Windows 2000 Professional (and NT Workstation), but not for Server, and only for processor hardware running at a certain speed. Other Microsoft documentation takes pains *not* to disclose the length of the time-slice quantum because it varies from processor to processor based on clock speed.

Authorities with access to Windows 2000 source code have attempted to document the Scheduler more fully. David Solomon's excellent book *Inside Windows 2000* describes the Scheduler in more detail than the official documentation, which is scattered across MSDN articles and the SDK documentation. Our discussion here hews closely to Solomon's description of the time-slicing algorithm in Windows 2000, except that Solomon appears unaware that the quantum value chosen is proportional to the speed of the processor.

Mark Russinovich, co-author of *Inside Windows 2000* and a regular contributor to *Windows 2000 Magazine*, is especially interested in the time-slicing quantum and has written several articles on the subject. Russinovich is a proponent of tweaking the time-slice quantum. He and his partner Bryce Cogswell developed a Quantum Frobber* applet for Windows NT (be careful! This applet causes a blue screen on Windows 2000) that allows you to examine the current time-slice value and change it. This freeware applet is illustrated in Figure 3-23. It can be downloaded from Russinovich's web site *http://www.sysinternals.com*.

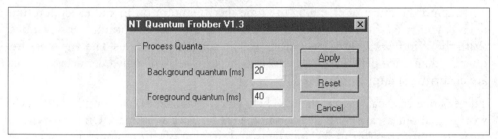

Figure 3-23. The Quantum Frobber applet developed by Mark Russinovich and Bryce Cogswell

The duration of a processor time-slice is a parameter that many operating systems let users manipulate. How to set a time-slice duration parameter to be optimal for your workload is actually a very difficult question. Answering the question requires knowing your workload quite well. Returning to Figure 3-1 for inspiration, what you need to know to devise an optimal time-slice duration value is how long threads from different applications execute before they voluntarily relinquish the processor. Time-slicing punishes CPU-bound threads that execute for longer intervals than the time-slice duration. You have to figure out which threads these are and whether it is a good idea to punish them. Typically, you would not want to punish an important processor-intensive job by interrupting it too frequently. But on the other hand, you also would not want to let a processor-bound application monopolize the processor to the extent that other threads receive little or no service.

---

* The name Russinovich chose for the utility can be taken as a cautionary note regarding its usage. From the Hacker's Dictionary:

frobnicate: /frob'ni-kayt/ vt. [Poss. derived from {**frobnitz**}, and usually abbreviated to {**frob**}, but "frobnicate" is recognized as the official full form.] To manipulate or adjust, to tweak. One frequently frobs bits or other 2-state devices. Thus: "Please frob the light switch" (that is, flip it), but also "Stop frobbing that clasp; you'll break it." One also sees the construction "to frob a frob'. See {tweak} and {twiddle}.

Usage: frob, twiddle, and tweak sometimes connote points along a continuum. "Frob" connotes aimless manipulation; "twiddle" connotes gross manipulation, often a coarse search for a proper setting; "tweak" connotes fine-tuning. If someone is turning a knob on an oscilloscope, then if he's carefully adjusting it, he is probably tweaking it; if he is just turning it but looking at the screen, he is probably twiddling it; but if he's just doing it because turning a knob is fun, he's frobbing it.

However, to put this whole matter into perspective, the time-slice duration decision may be fun to talk about, but it is not very consequential unless:

- The processor is very busy for extended periods of time
- There are many ready threads backed up on the Ready Queue

The Windows 2000 Scheduler's dynamic priority scheme makes the time-slice decision even more difficult. With dynamic adjustments, the relative priority of threads is subject to constant change. Further complicating matters, it is difficult to acquire the detailed performance measurement data relevant to a time-slicing decision in Windows 2000. If you monitor the Context switches/sec counter in the System object, you will get some idea of just how frequently Scheduler decisions are made. To understand the effect of changing the time-slice quantum on thread execution time delays, you need to collect lots of thread state and current priority observations. With the Windows 2000 System Monitor, you cannot collect this data any more frequently than once per second, a grossly macro-level view of Scheduler decisions that are occurring at a microscopic level.

There is one easy calculation that can help you assess whether or not it is worth even worrying about arcane time-slicing parameters for your workload. On a per-process basis, monitor the Thread % User Time and the rate of thread context switches, as illustrated in Figure 3-24. Convert Thread % Processor Busy to CPU time per second by dividing by 100. Then divide the thread CPU time by the number of context switches to calculate the average thread execution time. This is a good approximation of the total number of voluntary waits that the process incurred. Finally, analyze the results. How many times does the average thread execution time exceed the value of its time-slice allotment?

Figure 3-25 is a chart that analyzes two workloads of interest running on a Windows 2000 Professional workstation. We collected the Thread % User Time and Context switches/sec counters for the two processes once per second over a period of several minutes. Exporting the data into an Excel spreadsheet, we then calculated the average thread execution time each interval. One of the workloads shown is the Pinball game that ships with Windows 2000. This application does not need to perform any disk I/O operations before its time-slice expires. Games like this that feature spiffy real-time graphics often use every bit of available processing power. Because it is CPU-intensive, Pinball is an application whose performance could easily be affected by the duration of a processor time-slice. Judging from the performance data we collected, while it does not perform disk I/O, Pinball appears to issue frequent calls to the DirectX graphics interface, which results in a high rate of context switches per second.

From Figure 3-25, we can see that threads from both applications being monitored rarely execute longer than 4 milliseconds before a context switch occurs. Since the time-slice value on the machine where this example was collected was 20 milliseconds

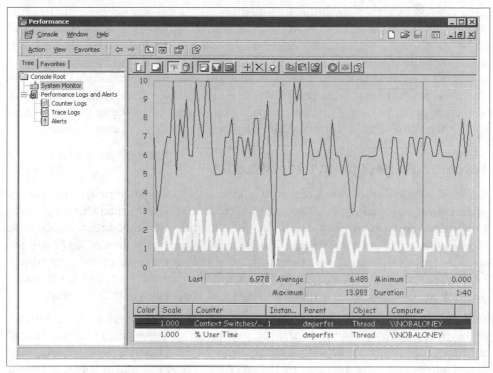

Figure 3-24. Monitoring the Thread % User Time and the rate of thread context switches

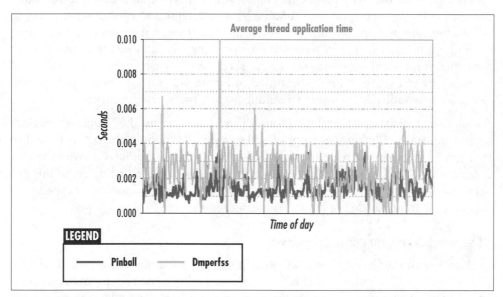

Figure 3-25. The average thread execution time for two applications

(2 multiplied by a 10-ms quantum for Windows 2000 Professional on a 400 MHz Pentium III), Pinball's main CPU-intensive processing thread rarely executes long enough to be cut short by the Scheduler. Here we have a CPU-bound process that is barely affected by the short time-slice used in Windows 2000 Professional. We suspect that if you apply this analysis to the applications and workloads you are interested in, you will find that very short thread execution times are the rule rather than the exception. The great majority of application threads are not impacted by the time-slice interval, even when the shorter Windows 2000 Professional time-slice duration is involved.

Foreground/Background Adjustments

Windows 2000 favors the foreground application in an attempt to improve the apparent responsiveness of the system, an illusion that benefits interactive users. The foreground application is by definition the one with the input focus, or, in other words, the application to which Windows 2000 currently directs keyboard and mouse events. All other desktop applications in the normal priority class are considered background applications. Depending on the level of the Windows 2000 operating system, Windows 2000 favors the foreground application in different ways.

In Windows 2000, the big priority boost a foreground thread receives when a mouse or keyboard interrupt is processed is the primary mechanism for enhancing the performance of the foreground application. The priority boost associated with keyboard and mouse interrupts propels the receiving thread to near the top of the Ready Queue. This boost also makes machines running Windows 2000 Server more responsive to the logged-on user running various foreground applications, trying to administer the system, for instance. At the same time, on Professional the foreground application is subject to quantum stretching—it can execute at this priority for triple the normal quantum-based time-slice value. By performing the analysis of average thread execution times illustrated in Figure 3-25 on many different applications, we conclude that quantum stretching usually has very little effect.

As another general assist, any foreground thread waiting on the Windows message loop is automatically boosted to priority 14 when a Windows message is posted to that thread from any source. Only foreground applications that interact with the keyboard, mouse, and video display contain a message loop in the first place, so this priority boost targets foreground applications, too. Background threads associated with services, for example, do not contain a message loop.

NT Version 3.51 foreground priority boost

Back in Version 3.51, Windows NT used to provide an additional priority boost for foreground applications. In 3.51, NT automatically drops the priority of background applications in the normal priority class one priority level. The normal base priority for an application running in the background is thus reduced to 7. Meanwhile, NT automatically boosts the base priority of the foreground application one priority level to 9. Relative to a background application thread, foreground application threads are then separated by two priority levels. In other words, a thread executing in a background application at the highest priority level runs at priority 9, the same as a foreground application thread running at the normal level. A foreground application's priority boost remains in effect for all its associated threads as long as that process holds the input focus. With preemptive scheduling operating, the effect of this adjustment is that foreground applications run to completion at high priority, while background applications are permitted access only to residual processing capacity. See Figure 3-26 for an illustration of this scheme.

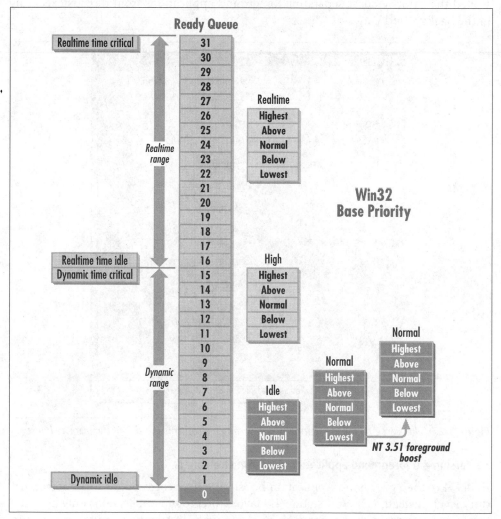

Figure 3-26. NT 3.51 priority levels showing the foreground application boost

The foreground application boost increases the apparent responsiveness of the system to an interactive user, but also increases the likelihood that background applications will suffer from starvation. This is why Microsoft developers introduced the Foreground Application Boost tuning parameter. This parameter controls the size of the priority boost of the foreground application. There is an interface to set the Application Performance Boost using the Performance tab in the System applet in the Control Panel (illustrated in Figure 3-27). This setting determines whether the priority of foreground applications is boosted two (the default as illustrated in Figure 3-26), one, or no priority levels. The Registry value associated with this tuning is Win32PrioritySeparation. Back in NT Version 3, Win32PrioritySeparation controlled the priority boost separating foreground applications from threads executing in the background.

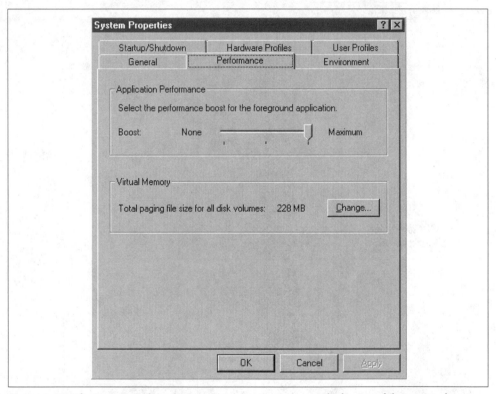

Figure 3-27. The Foreground Application Boost parameter controls the size of the priority boost

NT Version 4.0 foreground application quantum stretching

In NT 4.0, the Foreground Application Boost no longer corresponds to a boost in priority level. Instead, NT Workstation 4.0 favors foreground applications only by granting them a longer time-slice interval. This is known as *quantum stretching*, a feature that Windows 2000 retains. The applet to change the boost parameter was not changed, but the meaning of the Win32PrioritySeparation parameter did. A value of 0 means that foreground applications have a time-slice equal to two quanta, the same as all other applications. The default value of 2 corresponds to a time-slice value of six quanta for the foreground application. An intermediate value of 1 gives the foreground application a time-slice of four quanta. Given that few applications run for an entire time-slice before they voluntarily relinquish the processor (because they need to perform an I/O operation, for example), the boost parameter in NT 4.0 Workstation has very little effect on most applications. As a practical matter, NT 4.0 relies instead on the dynamic priority adjustment mechanism that boosts thread priority immediately following receipt of an interrupt, as previously discussed. This provides all the priority boost a foreground application ordinarily needs.

The boost parameter has a different effect under Windows NT Server Version 4.0. Foreground applications are given a brief priority boost, similar to what happens under Version 3.51, except the boost does not remain in effect for the entire time that the application may have the focus. The tuning parameter is used to determine the magnitude of this temporary boost.

In general, this parameter can be useful when you are running NT Workstation with:

- A relatively low-powered processor
- One or more foreground applications that are CPU-bound (e.g., a 3D drawing program or other graphics-intensive application)
- Critical background applications like a communications task that show evidence of starvation (e.g., timeouts that constantly cause the telecommunications line to drop)

Under circumstances like these, reducing the priority boost for the foreground application should allow background applications greater access to the processor. The trade-off is that the lower priority boost might make the foreground applications appear less responsive. Be advised that in most circumstances, manipulating this tuning parameter will have little or no impact on overall system performance.

Starvation Avoidance

Every three seconds, a Windows 2000 kernel thread associated with the Balance Set Manager (discussed in Chapter 6) scans the Ready Queue looking for threads in the queue that have received *no processor service* during the interval. If Windows 2000 finds any such threads, they are immediately boosted to the top of the dynamic priority range and allowed to execute for twice the usual time-slice duration. This favored treatment is short-lived, however. Once these threads complete their execution cycle, they return to their original priority immediately.

Deadlock Detection and Avoidance

Consider a situation where Thread A holds a resource like a mutex or semaphore that Thread B is waiting for. Meanwhile, Thread B holds a different resource that Thread A is waiting for. When neither A or B can proceed because each holds a lock on a resource that the other is requesting, we say that A and B are *deadlocked* or in a *deadly embrace*. One particular kind of locking mechanism with implications for processor scheduling is called a *spin lock* or a *busy wait*. In this type of lock, a thread seeking to enter a critical section tests a lock variable to see if it is set. Once the lock variable is free, the thread continues. But if the lock is held by a different thread, the first thread continues to loop through the section of code where it tests for the availability of the lock. As discussed earlier, if the lock is held by a lower-priority thread, the first thread is devoted to wasting processing cycles.

The availability in Windows 2000 of kernel-mode objects for thread synchronization eases the task of the operating system trying to detect deadlock conditions and unwind them. When a thread requests a locked kernel-mode resource such as a critical section or a mutex that is unavailable, the system waits for 500 milliseconds for the resource to free up. If the resource is still unavailable, the system boosts the priority of the thread holding the resource to speed its completion and waits four seconds. If the resource becomes available before this time expires, the timing stops, and the resource is released to the waiting thread. Otherwise, the request is canceled with an error code indicating a timeout. The Registry value ResourceTimeoutCount under the subkey HKLM\SYSTEM\CurrentControlSet\Control\Session Manager can be used to increase the amount of time that Windows 2000 waits before canceling a request for a resource.

As long as applications rely on Windows 2000 kernel-mode synchronization objects, multithreaded applications can communicate efficiently without running the risk of deadlocks. For example, on a uniprocessor, spin locks protecting critical section objects are automatically converted to semaphores so there is no need for an application to perform a busy wait. Critical section spin locks do burn cycles on multiprocessors, however, and deadlocks of the type discussed can still occur. Programs written in assembler that implement their own synchronization facilities can also deadlock. To avoid deadlocks of this type, Windows 2000 randomly inverts the priority of low-priority threads, according to a note in the Windows 2000 Knowledge Base entitled "Priority Inversion and Windows 2000 Scheduler" (ID# Q96418).

Thread Scheduling Tuning

As we have seen, Windows 2000 provides an extensive set of facilities to set the dispatching priority of an application's executing threads. Applications like Internet Explorer, RAS, System Monitor, and SQL Server take full advantage of Windows 2000 thread scheduling priority internally. For applications that do not take full advantage of these facilities, the Windows 2000 thread Scheduler adjusts thread priorities dynamically to increase the system's responsiveness, maximize throughput, and prevent thread starvation. Applications like SQL Server and Exchange expose external tuning parameters that allow the administrator to configure the number of threads started and their priority, and system applications like the Windows 2000 Spooler and the file server component also have tuning parameters that control the number and priority of threads the process initiates. Windows 2000 itself also exposes some tuning options for adjusting the number of worker threads it creates and runs.

Clearly, the inside of a specific application is *not* the best vantage point from which to make tuning decisions that can impact system performance globally. In this area, Windows 2000 provides very little support to a system administrator who needs to adjust the relative priorities of different applications running on the same system, When sufficient processing capacity is available and the Ready Queue never backs up, an external mechanism to adjust dispatch priority is not necessary. But when these conditions do not hold, some form of tuning intervention is desirable. Keep in mind that Windows 2000 needs to operate over a wide range of processing environments where processing power varies from a single processor of various speeds to four and eight-way multiprocessor configurations. No set of default parameters will be adequate across such a broad range of computing power.

In this section we review the Windows 2000 Scheduler adjustments that can be made externally by a system administrator or performance analyst. This is a relatively brief section because the options available are limited. This has created an opportunity for third-party developers to extend the set of controls available for processor scheduling. We describe the use of one third-party tool that has risen to this challenge, and discuss a new operating system interface introduced in Windows 2000 that will make it easier to build administrator controls to regulate thread scheduling in the future.

As a general rule, before making any adjustments, the performance analyst should first determine if they are appropriate. To begin, look to see if the processor is extremely busy. Then, determine which applications are monopolizing processor resources. Finally, investigate which threads are delayed in the Scheduler Ready Queue. If critical application threads are discovered delayed in the Ready Queue, priority adjustments may be appropriate. If processing resources are available, increasing the number of threads available to an application may improve its responsiveness. Increasing the number of threads available for processing is something to consider in a large-scale server environment, especially one that takes advantage of multiprocessing hardware.

Task Manager Adjustments

The most straightforward way to adjust priorities in Windows 2000 is with the Task Manager. Right-clicking on a process in the Processes tab pops up a menu that allows you to change the base priority of a process. This function would be considerably more useful if it also worked for services, but it does not. When you try to change the priority of any process started by the Service Control Manager, the error message in Figure 3-28 is displayed. Thanks to an excellent short article by Jeffrey Richter published in the March 1998 issue of the *Microsoft Systems Journal*, we learned that this "Access is denied" error message is due to the fact that the Task Manager application is not authorized to deal with services, since they operate under a different security context. This security issue can be surmounted using a small program wrapper Richter created that gives Task Manager the appropriate access authority. With it, you can use Task Manager to adjust the base priority of any process, including services.

Figure 3-28. The "Access is denied" error message

Task Manager is an excellent utility program for managing your system interactively. It can be used to kill a process that has gone into a loop or to adjust dispatch priorities when system performance is not adequate. On a server, you may find that the desktop is unresponsive because applications are consuming so many processing cycles in the background. Use Task Manager to boost the foreground application you are running to the High priority class, and you will find the desktop is much more responsive. Or, you can reassign a background service like Backup (if you install Richter's Taskman wrapper program) that is sucking up all available cycles to the Idle priority class so that other applications can execute more readily. This makes desktop applications easier to access, while Backup threads continue to absorb residual CPU cycles.

Task Manager is limited in that it only lets you change the priority class of a process. Consider Process CPUhog that issues SetThreadPriority to set specific threads to Time Critical priority. Using Task Manager to reset the base priority of CPUhog does not affect any of its threads running at the Time Critical level.

Task Manager must also be manipulated manually by someone operating the machine in question. Adhering to the No Knobs philosophy, Windows 2000 does not have a parameter file that takes effect at system initialization that determines the relative dispatching priority of different application processes when they execute. Microsoft might develop something like this in the future as the operating system continues to evolve.

WarpNT

For people who cannot wait for Microsoft to provide the tuning knobs they crave, there is a product called WarpNT that does the trick. WarpNT is a grab bag featuring several administrative tuning controls that Microsoft decided not to include in Windows NT and 2000. In the area of thread scheduling, WarpNT contains controls to set both the priority and the time-slice quantum for individual processes. Figure 3-29 illustrates the interface WarpNT uses to regulate the time-slice quantum and dispatching priority of running processes. In contrast to Task Manager, the application is authorized to manipulate background services, and the settings themselves remain in effect after rebooting the system.

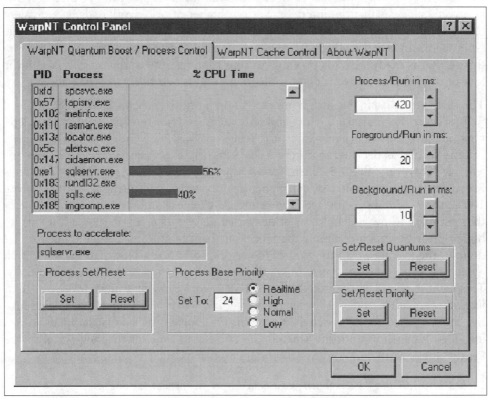

Figure 3-29. The WarpNT Control Panel

Having the controls begs the question of how to manipulate them effectively. Again, note that manipulating the dispatching priority has very little effect, unless the processor is very busy and the Ready Queue is backed up. When that is the case, *priority queuing schemes combined with preemptive scheduling subject low-priority applications to a significant risk of starvation*. If threads of important processes are suffering from starvation, you face a *capacity* problem that cannot be overcome by mere tuning. But tuning thread priorities can be an effective strategy for regulating bursty workloads or large servers where you are trying consolidate several workloads on a single machine.

The key to developing an effective priority scheme is understanding what the effect of priority queuing and preemptive scheduling is on lower-priority workloads. Whenever a high-priority thread is ready to run, it preempts the execution of a lower-priority thread that is already running, forcing it to wait in the Ready Queue until the higher-priority thread enters the wait state. In effect, the CPU consumption of higher-priority workloads interferes with the execution of lower-priority workloads and slows them down. Furthermore, the execution time impact on lower-priority work is *proportional* to the CPU consumption of all higher-priority threads. One approach suggests that the interference from higher-priority workloads is equivalent to lower-priority work executing on a proportionally slower machine. For example, when a machine is already 50% busy running higher-priority work, a low-priority thread that is ready to run is preempted from running 50% of the time. It is as if the low-priority thread is executing on a processor that is effectively only half as fast.

The first step in using this insight for setting up a priority scheme is to collect Thread % Processor Time measurements and sort them by Priority Current. For completeness, include high priority % Interrupt Time and % DPC Time work at the highest priority levels, as depicted in Figure 3-13. Summarize % Processor Time by priority level as shown in Table 3-5. Then, for each priority level, calculate the amount of % Processor Time consumed by all higher-priority work. Subtract this number from 100%, then compute its inverse. The result is a CPU execution time *elongation factor* that estimates how much lower-priority threads are delayed in execution due to higher-priority work preempting the processor. For example, an elongation factor of 2 doubles the average execution time of lower-priority threads. Notice in Table 3-5 that when the processor gets quite busy, the elongation factor increases exponentially. This technique will give reasonable results on a machine with a single processor, but, like other queuing models, the elongation factor calculation becomes extremely sensitive as the processor approaches saturation. Of course, this is what happens in real life, too, when lower-priority threads are subject to indefinitely long waits in the Ready Queue until the Windows 2000 starvation avoidance mechanism kicks in.

Table 3-5. Calculating the elongation factor of lower-priority application threads

Process thread	Priority current	% Processor time	Sum (Higher priority CPU time)	Elongation factor
Interrupt time		8%		none
DPC time		4%	8%	1.09
System	Realtime	4%	12%	1.14
System	15	4%	16%	1.19
inetinfo	14	12%	20%	1.25

Process thread	Priority current	% Processor time	Sum (Higher priority CPU time)	Elongation factor
sqlserve	14	20%	32%	1.47
services.exe	14	5%	52%	2.08
rasman	14	5%	57%	2.33
YourApp1	8	20%	62%	2.63
YourApp2	6	10%	82%	5.56
Total CPU time		92%		

Now compare the elongation factors impacting YourApp1 and YourApp2 when their relative priority is reversed in Table 3-6. We can easily see that the bigger CPU consumer YourApp1 has more of an impact on the performance of YourApp2 than the other way around. This analysis suggests a good organizing principle for any priority scheme subject to preemptive scheduling: *heavy consumers of the resource disproportionately impact light users; therefore, place heavy consumers at lower priority than light users.*

Table 3-6. Reversing the relative priority of two applications

Process thread	Priority current	% Processor time	Sum (Higher priority CPU time)	Elongation factor
YourApp2	8	10%	62%	2.63
YourApp1	6	20%	72%	3.57

It is worth noting that the approximate mean-time-to-wait scheduling policy implemented by Windows 2000 operates according to the same basic principle. That is why it rarely pays to override the decisions made hundreds and thousands of time per second by the Scheduler on relatively simple configurations.

Windows 2000 System Thread Priority

As mentioned, administrator controls are helpful because inside the application is not the best point from which to make configuration and tuning decisions that have a global impact on system performance. Moreover, from an application's point of view, there is not always a simple way to make effective use of processor resources. In fact, there are a number of factors, including the processing capacity of the current system, the number of processors on the current system (we tackle multiprocessor concerns in Chapter 5), and the demands of other workloads on the system. Given these complications, the experienced application developer can often devise no better solution than to expose the Win32 process and thread scheduling API and allow the Windows 2000 system administrator to shoulder some of the burden. Accordingly, Windows 2000 itself and some Windows 2000 applications provide options and parameters that permit system administrators to adjust and control CPU dispatching.

The total number of threads associated with the operating system kernel and the Executive is governed by the flavor of the operating system (Server or Professional), the amount of memory, and the number of available processors. On Windows 2000 Server, for example, you can expect about 40 system kernel threads to be initialized. See Figure 3-30 for an illustration. Of these, one thread each runs at priority levels 23 and 18. Several additional threads run at priority 17 and 16 in the real-time priority range. Notice that none runs higher than level 23. Allowing for the system zero page thread running at priority level 0, the remaining kernel threads execute in the dynamic range. On an NT 4.0 Server system running on a dual processor with more than 64 MB of memory, we observed 47 threads associated with the operating system. Expect an additional 20 threads or so per processor. The number of kernel threads you will find also depends on the specific device drivers installed.

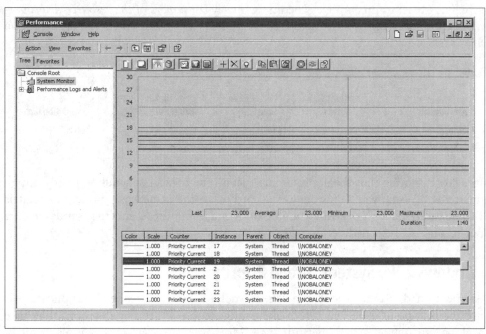

Figure 3-30. Priority of kernel threads in Windows 2000 Server

Within Windows 2000, the system's default threading behavior can be adjusted using the two Registry parameters illustrated in Figure 3-31. Critical OS worker threads perform time-critical tasks like page stealing that delay the execution of application tasks. These threads run at priority level 16. The delayed worker threads handle tasks that are not considered time-critical, running at priority level 12. Time-critical application threads running in the dynamic range execute at a higher priority than these delayed worker threads. One intriguing aspect of this AdditionalCriticalWorkerThreads tuning knob is that no performance data is available to help you determine if you need it. Consider that there is no way for the System Monitor measurement thread running at priority level 15 to ever catch a high-priority OS critical worker thread in the Ready Queue.

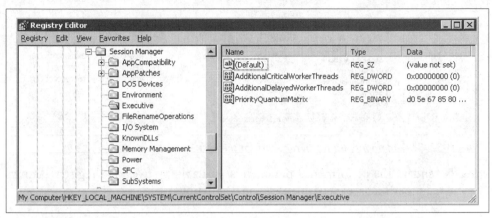

Figure 3-31. The Registry tuning parameter that lets you create additional threads

File and Print Services

When Windows 2000 is deployed primarily as a file and print server, the system applications associated with these functions may be more critical to maintaining a responsive system than the OS kernel services. Printing under Windows 2000 is handled by the spooler service, *spoolsv.exe*, while file services are the responsibility of the Server service, which is incorporated into *services.exe*. The Registry value for Priority-Class under subkey HKLM\SYSTEM\CurrentControlSet\Control\Print determines the priority of the *spoolsv.exe* process. It defaults to NORMAL_PRIORITY_CLASS. There are also SchedulerThreadPriority and PortThreadPriority parameters, which set the priority of these spooler threads relative to the base PriorityClass. Besides watching for print spooler threads backed up in the Ready Queue, Windows 2000 lets you monitor printer performance. The Print Queue object reports print throughput statistics on a printer-by-printer basis, which can be very useful in this context. See Figure 3-32.

Consistent with the usual practice for adjusting tuning parameters, begin by watching the results using a performance monitor. Figure 3-33 illustrates a monitoring session watching the thread priority of the print spooler on an NT 4.0 machine using Performance Monitor (when the process was named *spoolss.exe*). Notice that the priority of the highlighted Thread 6 is subject to dynamic priority boosts because it is responsible for driving I/O to the active printer. These automatic priority adjustments allow spooler threads waiting on the printer to respond quickly as soon as the device is ready. Dynamically boosting the priority of I/O-bound print spooling

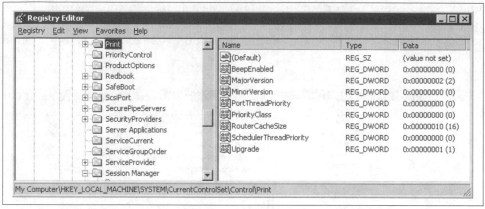

Figure 3-32. Thread priority tuning parameters for the print spooler service

threads renders the performance parameters available by tweaking registry settings somewhat superfluous, except in exceptional situations.

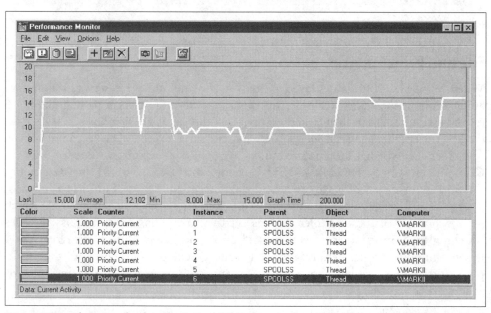

Figure 3-33. Observing the thread priority of the print spooler with Performance Monitor

The options to control the performance of file services are much more elaborate. These tuning parameters are all located under HKLM\SYSTEM\CurrentControlSet\ Services\LanmanServer\Parameters. The LanmanServer Registry key is a legacy of Windows 2000's heritage as the jointly developed IBM OS2 LAN Manager file server. On the client side, file accesses are redirected by the Workstation service to a network resource and passed across the network using the Server Message Block (SMB) protocol. The Server network service is the component of Windows 2000 that fields these file requests when they are received by the target system. To make things even more confusing, both Workstation and Server network services are installed under systems running either Windows 2000 Professional or Server. Both services are among those executed by threads running within the *services.exe* process. (The Windows 2000 developers could probably make this more confusing, but we do not see how.)

The ThreadPriority parameter specifies the priority of all server service threads in relation to the normal base priority of the *services.exe* process. The default value of 1 allows server threads to run at one priority level higher than the *services.exe* base. Values of 0 (to lower the priority of server threads to equal the priority base) and 2 (to boost priority two levels) are also supported. A ThreadPriority value of 15 sets Server threads to run at the time-critical range, above all other applications. If Windows 2000's performance as a file server is critical, this setting is worth considering. File server performance options also include the ability to set the number of file server threads. Under NT 3.51 use the CriticalThreads, BlockingThreads, NonBlockingThreads, and ThreadCountAdd parameters. Under Windows 2000 and NT Version 4.0, matters are much simpler. The operative file server thread tuning parameter is MaxThreadsPerQueue, which determines the maximum number of threads the server creates to service its per-processor queue of work requests. The default value is 30 per processor, which probably needs to be adjusted only if you observe server work item shortages using Sysmon. The server dynamically adjusts the number of threads available to service client requests, using the smallest number of threads possible to achieve maximum server throughput. We describe the architecture of this type of thread pooling server application in detail in Chapter 5.

To use any of these file server tuning options effectively, you should understand the structure of SMB processing. Session-oriented file server requests are taken off the network stack and placed on a FIFO work queue. File server threads take work items off the queue and process them as soon as possible. To exploit multiprocessing, file server services use multiple processors when they are available. A separate Work Item Queue is maintained per processor. A separate queue is also maintained for blocking requests, which are requests likely to tie up a thread for an extended period of time. (I/O operations block the execution of the worker thread. An I/O request to retrieve a directory list from a remote disk, for example, results in a blocking request because the remote file server must retrieve the data requested from the appropriate disk.)

The Server Work Queues object provides the measurement data used to fine-tune the file server environment. Of particular importance are the Available Work Items and the current Queue Length at each work queue. Additional measurements of the number of active and available threads per work queue are useful, too. If file server requests are not being processed quickly enough so that either the number of Available Work Items remains close to zero or the current queue length is frequently greater than 1, consider adjusting the parameters controlling the number of threads and work items upwards. As an aside for those who are contemplating implementing network file sharing without acquiring a Windows 2000 Server license, Windows

2000 Professional is restricted to a maximum of 64 server work items. Under Windows 2000 Server, up to a total of 64K file server work items can be allocated.

Server Applications

Multiuser server applications like Microsoft Exchange, Lotus Notes, Internet Information Server (IIS), and SQL Server all provide some ability to control the number of threads used to process client requests. Except for an extended discussion of IIS in Chapter 12, details of these complicated applications are beyond the scope of this book. We do, however, discuss the architectural elements common to thread pooling server applications in Chapter 5, along with a general performance monitoring and tuning strategy for this type of application. We also discuss their use of memory-resident disk caching in Chapter 7.

Because creating more processing threads in the application consumes CPU time and memory, it is never a good idea to increase the number of threads arbitrarily. A basic strategy for determining whether or not to increase the number of processing threads in any multiuser server application is outlined here:

1. If the average Processor % Busy is approaching saturation or the Processor Queue Length is growing, you are experiencing a capacity constraint, not a performance problem that you can eliminate by tweaking some parameters. You need more or faster hardware. Adding more processing threads in the application moves the bottleneck around, but does not eliminate it. You should check to see if the capacity constraint is impacting the applications you care about by collecting and analyzing Thread State. If important threads are frequently waiting in the Ready Queue, do not hesitate to place that hardware order immediately. If, on the other hand, significant spare CPU processing resources are available, increasing the thread count may do some good. Go to Step 2.

2. Is the number of processing threads acting as an artificial constraint on application performance? If the application reports the number of queued requests, review that metric to see if a bottleneck is evident. This is the easiest way to determine if work is backed up in the application, and may strongly suggest that more processing threads will provide some benefit. Both File Server and IIS provide indicators of queued requests, as we shall see in Chapter 5. Be careful in MS Exchange and Lotus Notes. Mail requests can be queued for a variety of reasons that have little to do with performance.

3. Thread pooling applications generally create and release worker threads only when they are needed. When these applications are running at or near their maximum thread setting, there is a good chance having more processing threads available will boost throughput, absent some other throughput constraint. This is the best way to determine if the number of threads processing concurrent requests is a potential bottleneck when a direct measurement of request queuing is missing.

MS SQL Server

Historically, MS SQL Server has offered more OS-specific performance and tuning options than any other MS-developed server application. Microsoft had initially contracted with Sybase to port their flagship Database Management System (DBMS) to Windows NT back in Version 3. Apparently, Sybase developers were not imbued with the same No Knobs philosophy. SQL Server tuning parameters abound up until the SQL Server 7.0 release, where many esoteric tuning options were eliminated. However, even the leaner Version 7.0 release retains basic tuning knobs to control both the number of threads and thread dispatching priority. Again, these options are important because of the variety of workloads and configurations that run the application. It is simply not possible for any default set of parameters to work well across a wide range of environments.

The SQL Server Version 6 and 6.5 options that determine the number of threads are Max worker threads, RA (Read Ahead request) worker threads, and backup threads. RA threads are specifically used to perform asynchronous tables scans when necessary, while backup threads are dedicated to database dump and bulk load operations. Additional threads to perform these operations should be created only if the workload justifies it. SQL Server 7.0 and SQL Server 2000 (nominally Version 8.0) consolidated these threading parameters into a single control over the number of worker threads created, as illustrated in Figure 3-34.

Selecting Boost SQL Server priority is possible on either a uniprocessor or SMP computer. When selected on a uniprocessor, SQL Server runs at priority 15, which is high but within the dynamic class of priorities that range from 1 through 15. When selected on an multiprocessor, SQL Server runs at priority 24, which is midway into the real time class of priorities and a higher priority than the operating system kernel threads we looked at before. The control limiting the specific processor that SQL Server threads can execute on is designed to work in tandem with this option. We discuss these options further in Chapter 5. They are not recommended outside of highly specialized conditions.

MS Exchange Server

The MS Exchange Server is a complex application that contains several interrelated processes. Since Exchange handles email message delivery traffic, the most important measures of performance are message throughput and response time. Fortunately, Exchange provides a series of Messages Delivered/min performance counters and also reports average delivery time and the length of various I/O message queues. You should be prepared to monitor the MSExchangeIS Private and MSExchangeIS Public objects with their message arrival rate, message send and receive queue length, and Average Local Delivery Time metrics if you are considering adjusting the number of processing threads. Figure 3-35 illustrates a sample performance monitoring session that looks at those specific Exchange counters.

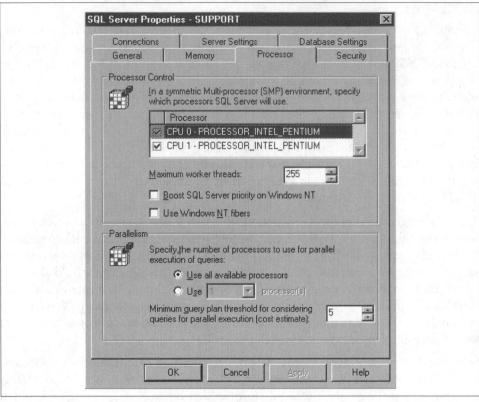

Figure 3-34. SQL Server tuning options control the number and priority of threads

Be careful with the average local delivery time measurements that Exchange provides in the MSExchangeIS Private and MSExchangeIS Public objects—they are calculated based on a moving average of the last 10 messages delivered. Delivery time is expressed in tens of milliseconds: in other words, a delivery time of 100 equals 1 second. (See KnowledgeBase entry Q188684.)

You must also be careful about interpreting the queue length measurements in Exchange, because the send and receive queues can back up for reasons that have nothing to do with performance. For instance, if your Internet connection is down for any reason, Internet mail messages will stack up in the output queue. Unfortunately, the average delivery time metric is not definitive because it is cumulative. For detailed performance analysis of Exchange message delivery times, you must turn to its transaction log files, which are an excellent source of detailed information on message size and delivery.

The workhorse application process inside Exchange is usually the database, where all the mail and attachments are stored. The Exchange database is associated with a process named *store.exe*. There is a tuning parameter that lets you set both the minimum and maximum number of *store.exe* database threads. If you run the Exchange

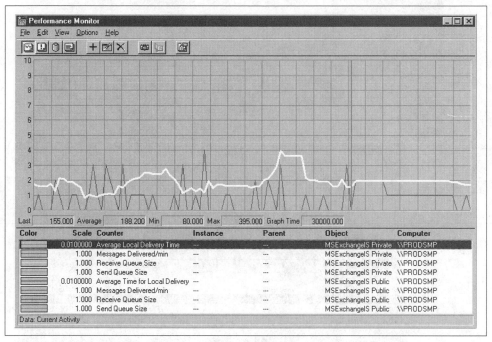

Figure 3-35. Monitoring the MSExchangeIS Private and MSExchangeIS Public objects

Performance Optimizer *perfwiz.exe*, you can access and change these parameters. Meanwhile, Address Book queries and processing related to background replication is controlled by the Directory Services component of Exchange, *dsamain.exe*. perfwiz allows you to set the number of dsamain processing threads, too. Figure 3-36 illustrates a Performance Monitor session where we are watching the Process % Processor Time and Thread Count for both store and dsamain. We are also monitoring an Exchange-specific counter called Threads in Use associated with the MSExchangeDS (referring to the Directory Services component) object. When the number of threads in use approaches its maximum value, it is worth considering raising the application's thread limit.

The Exchange Message Transfer Agent (MTA) component is responsible for moving mail messages back and forth between the database and Exchange clients or interconnections (for Internet Mail, for instance). Exchange has tuning parameters that let you set the number of MTA send and delivery threads for both public and private folders, too.

MS Internet Information Server (IIS)

Similar to other multiuser server applications we have been discussing, IIS also provides tuning parameters to control the number of threads available to process incoming Internet (or intranet) requests. The maximum number of threads IIS allocates

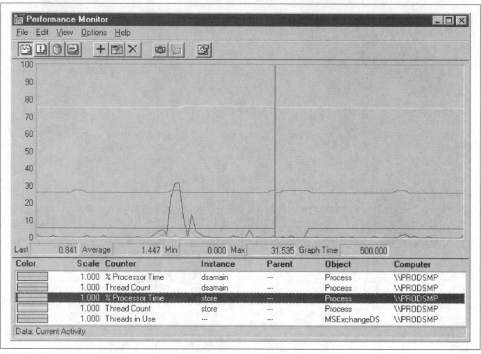

Figure 3-36. Performance Monitor session observing % Processor Time and Thread Count

defaults to two threads per MB of physical memory, but can be controlled directly using the PoolThreadLimit parameter. IIS releases a maximum of 10 active threads per processor, but this number can be raised by setting the MaxPoolThreads parameter. Both these parameters need to be added to the HKLM\SYSTEM\CurrentControlSet\Services\InetInfo\Parameters Registry key. As discussed with Exchange, monitoring the inetinfo process Thread Count is the best way to determine if the default maximums are inadequate. IIS performance and tuning is discussed in more depth in Chapter 12.

Job Resource Limits

The final topic in this chapter concerns a new kernel object in Windows 2000 called a Job, which is used to enforce resource limits against one or more processes. Processes assigned to Jobs can have execution time limits, for example: a process in a Job that exceeds its user mode CPU time execution can be automatically canceled. You can also control both the scheduling priority and time-slice quantum for processes assigned to Jobs. If the Job has a priority class limit, attempts to set process or thread priority above that limit are ignored. In addition, processes assigned to a Job are not subject to dynamic priority boosts. Jobs can also enforce processor affinity restrictions on multiprocessors and real memory usage (working set) limits.

Unfortunately, you have to write your own programs to create any Jobs you want to use, to assign processes to Jobs, and to monitor the execution of those processes. Job kernel objects in Windows 2000 do provide the capability to build powerful administrator controls to manage resource usage by processes, but right now, Jobs are just a building block added to the already extensive Win32 API for Windows 2000. Microsoft or third-party developers will probably one day develop a set of standard resource-limited Jobs that you can assign executing processes to and restrict their execution time behavior.

Jobs are particularly well suited to an application like IIS that spawns other processes, namely CGI scripts, from time to time. If the CGI script is not particularly well behaved—imagine a script with a programming bug that goes into an infinite loop—a Job is a handy construct to keep that runaway process from degrading overall system performance. Setting a reasonable JOB_OBJECT_LIMIT_PROCESS_TIME value for the CGI scripts assigned to a Job allows an application like IIS to detect runaway CGI scripts and cancel them automatically. However, it is not as easy to use Job objects to regulate the CPU consumption of other long-running processes. You can set a *total* CPU usage execution limit time, but you cannot restrict one process to using, say, no more than 10% of a processor each execution interval. You have to specify this execution limit in 100-nanosecond timer ticks. Your program also has to be smart enough to set a CPU time limit proportional to the speed of the processor, but, of course, now you know where in the Registry your program can find this information.

You can use Jobs to enforce a relative priority scheme or tweak the Scheduler's default time-slice values. Using the Job SchedulingClass parameter, you can establish a wide range of time-slice values for processes assigned to a Job, ranging from 2 to 20 quanta. The Job SchedulingClass parameter is not enforced on Windows 2000 Professional, only Server.

If you do decide to develop a program to create Jobs and assign processes to them, you will find that Microsoft has added the necessary instrumentation to track Jobs and the processes in them. There is a new Job object performance object, along with Job object detail counters that let you see each process assigned to the Job. The Job object counters make it easy to track Jobs that impose resource limits on the processes they contain. The Job Object Detail counters merely regurgitate statistics that are already available for Process object instances.

The steps involved in building a Job control monitor are relatively straightforward. The CreateJobObject API call is used to create the Job and establish its security context. Security is very important concern because an unauthorized program could create a Job object, assign winlogon to it, and then kill that process, which would cause Windows 2000 to hang. Once a Job is created, you call SetInformationJobObject to set up the various resource and other limits that a Job can enforce. Finally, you call AssignProcessToJobObject, referencing the appropriate process and Job handles. It is also desirable to set up a Job execution monitoring program that receives various notifications, for example, when a process running within a Job exceeds its execution time allotment. At that point, your Job execution monitor can access Job-related statistics and decide whether or not to grant the process a reprieve. This aspect of the Job API is reasonably complex, so we leave this discussion to other sources.

## CHAPTER 4

Optimizing Application Performance

The best medicine for most performance problems is invariably prevention. Despite advances in software performance engineering,[*] developing complex computer programs that are both functionally correct and efficient remains a difficult and time-consuming task. This chapter specifically looks at tuning Windows 2000 applications running on Intel hardware from the perspective of optimizing processor cycles and resource usage. Fine-tuning the execution path of code remains one of the fundamental disciplines of performance engineering.

To bring this topic into focus, we describe a case study where an application designed and developed specifically for the Microsoft Windows 2000 environment is subjected to a rigorous analysis of its performance using several commercially available CPU execution profiling tools. One of the development tools we used requires an understanding of the internal workings of Intel processors, and justifies a lengthy excursion into the area of Intel processor hardware performance.

The performance of Intel processor hardware is the focus of the second half of this chapter. We will look inside an Intel x86 microprocessor to dissect the complex mechanisms employed to execute computer instructions. You may encounter situations where a background and understanding of Intel processor hardware is relevant to solving a performance or capacity problem. This chapter also introduces a set of Intel processor hardware performance measurements that can be extremely useful in troubleshooting CPU performance problems. While the first part of this chapter should appeal to developers responsible for applications that need to run efficiently under Windows 2000, the second part should have wider appeal. The technical

---

[*] Integrating performance considerations into application design and development is associated with *software performance engineering*, a name originally popularized by Dr. Connie Smith in her 1990 textbook *Performance Engineering of Software Systems*. For a more recent (and less academic) survey of the field, see Chris Loosely and Frank Douglas, *High-Performance Client Server*, published in 1998 by John Wiley and Sons. Unfortunately, while many professional developers endorse the goals of performance engineering, few put the principles enumerated by these authors into practice.

discussion of the Intel processor architecture lays the groundwork for our treatment of multiprocessor performance considerations in Chapter 5.

Background

The application that is the target of this analysis is a C language program written to collect Windows 2000 performance data continuously on an interval basis. Since the application is designed primarily for use as a performance tool, it is very important that it run efficiently. A tool designed to diagnose performance problems should not itself be the *cause* of performance problems. Moreover, the customers for this application, many of whom are experienced Windows 2000 performance analysts, are a very demanding group of users.

The application's structure and flow is straightforward. Following initialization, the program enters a continuous data collection loop. Inside this loop, Windows 2000 services are called to retrieve selected performance data across a well-documented Win32 interface. The program consists of a single executable module called *dmperfss.exe* and two adjunct helper dynamic load libraries (DLLs); it simply gathers performance statistics across this interface and logs the information collected to a local disk file. The optimization of the code within this inner loop was the focus of this study.

Some additional details about the dmperfss application's structure and logic are important to this discussion. To a large extent, the program's design is constrained by the Windows 2000 Win32 performance monitoring Application Programming Interface (API) discussed in Chapter 2 that is the source of the performance data being collected. The performance data in Windows 2000 is structured as a set of *objects*, each with an associated set of *counters*. (Individuals not accustomed to object-oriented programming terminology might feel more comfortable thinking about objects as either *records* or rows of a database table, and counters as *fields* or columns in a database table.) There are more than 200 different performance objects defined in Windows 2000: *base* objects, which are available on every system, and *extended* objects, which are available only if specific application packages like MS SQL Server or Lotus Notes are installed. Within each object, specific performance counters are defined. Approximately 20 different types of counters exist, but generally they fall into three basic categories: accumulators, instantaneous measures, and compound variables, as described in Chapter 2.

The *dmperfss.exe* application retrieves designated objects one at a time by making a call to the Win32 function RegQueryEx(). Having collected a data sample, the program then makes the appropriate calculations for all the counter variables of interest, and writes the corresponding counter values to a comma-delimited data collection file. In some cases, there are multiple *instances* of an object that need to be reported. For example, a computer system with four processors reports four instances of the processor object each collection interval, plus a synthesized _Total instance. A parent-child relationship is defined for some object instances; threads are associated with a parent process. This means that both the parent and child object instances are retrieved using a single call to the performance monitoring interface.

At the time of the study, there were no apparent performance problems with the dmperfss data collection application. The program is most often used to retrieve a carefully crafted subset of the available data using collection intervals ranging from 1 to 15 minutes, with one-minute intervals being the recommended setting. At those rates of data collection, the overhead of dmperfss data collection was uniformly much less than 1% additional processor utilization during the interval. Nevertheless, a good overall assessment of the performance of an application is almost always valuable in guiding future development. Furthermore, there are good reasons to run data collection at much more frequent intervals than current customer practice.* Consequently, we wished to investigate whether it was feasible to build a monitoring program that would collect certain data at much more frequent intervals—perhaps as frequently as once per second, or even more frequently.

The performance analysis of this application was initiated at a point in the development cycle where the code was reasonably mature and stable. Once a software program under development is functioning correctly, it is certainly appropriate to tackle performance optimization. But it should be stressed that performance considerations should be taken into account at *every* stage of application design, development, and deployment.

The Development Tools

This case study focuses on analyzing the code execution path using commercially available profiling tools. CPU profiling tools evaluate a program while it is executing and report on which sections of code are executing as a proportion of overall execution time. This allows programmers to focus on routines that account for the most execution time delay. This information supplies an otherwise sorely missing empirical element to performance-oriented program design and development. Without reliable, quantitative information on code execution paths, programmers tend to rely on very subjective criteria to make decisions that affect application performance. These tools eliminate a lot of idle chatter around the coffee machine about why a program is running slowly and what can be done to fix it. Profilers provide hard evidence of where programs are spending their time during execution.

---

* For instance, accumulator values, which are running totals, and instantaneous values are both collected at the same rate. Would it be possible to collect instantaneous values more frequently and then summarize these sample observations? See also Chapter 3's discussion of transient processes for at least one other good reason for running data collection at short intervals.

A code profiler also provides data to help evaluate alternative approaches to speeding up program execution. The data might tell you which compiler optimization options are worthwhile, which sections of code should be targeted for revision, and where inline assembler routines might prove most helpful. In planning for the next cycle of development, the results of a code execution profile improve the decision-making process.

The code in the program under analysis, as with most programs written for the Windows environment, makes extensive use of the Win32 application programming interface and C runtime services. One desirable outcome of code profiling is a greater understanding of the performance impact of various system services, where many Windows programs spend the majority of their time during execution. The time spent inside these calls to system services is like a black box, which means the programmer generally has little knowledge of the performance characteristics of these runtime services. Understanding their performance impact at least helps the programmer use these system services more efficiently when there are no viable alternatives to using them.

The following profiling tools were investigated during the course of this study:

- The profiler option in the Microsoft Visual C++ compiler Version 5
- The Rational Visual Quantify execution profiler
- The Intel VTune version optimization tool

All three are popular commercial packages. In selecting these specific tools, no attempt was made to provide encyclopedic coverage of all the code profiling options available for the Windows 2000/Intel environment. Instead, we focused on using a few of the better-known and widely available tools for Windows 2000 program development to solve a real-world problem.

The Microsoft Visual C++ optimizing compiler was a natural choice because all the code development was performed using this tool. It is a widely used compiler for this environment, and its built-in code profiling tool is often the first choice for developers who might be reluctant to buy an additional software package. The Rational Visual Quantify program is one of the better-known profiler tools for C and C++ language development. Rational is a leading manufacturer of developer tools for Unix, Windows, and Windows 2000. The Visual Quantify program features integration with the Microsoft Visual Studio development environment and is usually reviewed in surveys of C++ development tools published in popular trade publications. Finally, we used the Intel VTune program because this has garnered wide acceptance within the development community. It is an optimization tool developed by Intel specifically for programs that run on Intel hardware. VTune is a standalone program and, we discovered, is more oriented toward assembly language development than typical application development using C or C++.

The Application Tuning Case Study

In this section we compare and contrast the three code profilers that we used to examine the application's consumption of processor cycles. All the tests were made on a Windows NT 4.0 Server installation, but the results apply to the Windows 2000 environment with almost no modification. Overall, we found both compiler add-on packages to be extremely useful and well worth the modest investment. Visual Quantify provides a highly intuitive user interface. It extends the CPU profiling information available through the built-in facilities of MS Visual C++ by incorporating information on many system services, and it greatly increased our understanding of the code's interaction with various Windows 2000 system services. VTune supplemented this understanding with even more detailed information about our code's interaction with the Windows 2000 runtime environment. VTune's unique analysis of Intel hardware performance provides singular insight into this critical area of application performance.

Visual C++ Profiler

The first stage of the analysis used the code execution profiler built into MS Visual C++. This is a natural place for any tuning project to begin given that no additional software packages need to be licensed and installed. Runtime profiling is enabled from the Link tab of the Project, Settings dialog box inside Developer Studio, which also turns off incremental linking. Profiling can be performed at either the function or line level. Function-level profiling counts the number of calls to the function and adds code that keeps track of the time spent in execution while in the function. Line profiling is much higher impact and requires that debug code be generated. In this exercise, we report only the results of function profiling.

Select Profile from the Tools menu to initiate a profiling run. Additional profiling options are available at runtime. The most important of these allow the user to collect statistics on only specific modules within a program or to restrict line profiling to certain lines of code. At the conclusion of the run, a text report is available in the Output window under the Profile tab. You can view the report there or import the text into a spreadsheet where the data can be sorted and manipulated. The first few lines of the function-level profile report are shown here. The output is automatically sorted in the most useful sequence, showing the functions in order by the amount of time spent in the function.

```
Module Statistics for dmperfss.exe
----------------------------------
    Time in module: 283541.261 millisecond
    Percent of time in module: 100.0%
    Functions in module: 155
    Hits in module: 11616795
    Module function coverage: 72.3%
```

Func Time	%	Func+Child Time	%	Hit Count	Function
248146.507	87.5	248146.507	87.5	249	_WaitOnEvent (dmwrdata.obj)
8795.822	3.1	8795.822	3.1	393329	_WriteDataToFile (dmwrdata.obj)
4413.518	1.6	4413.518	1.6	2750	_GetPerfDataFromRegistry (dmwrdata.obj)
3281.442	1.2	8153.656	2.9	170615	_FormatWriteThisObjectCounter (dmwrdata.obj)
3268.991	1.2	12737.758	4.5	96912	_FindPreviousObjectInstanceCounter (dmwrdata.obj)
2951.455	1.0	2951.455	1.0	3330628	_NextCounterDef (dmwrdata.obj)

The data is from a profiling run of the dmperfss program that lasted about six minutes. The program was set to collect a default collection set once a second and write this information to a file. The following performance objects are included in this collection set: System, Processor, Memory, Cache, Logical Disk, Physical Disk, Process, Redirector, Server, and Network Segment.

The profiling report itself is largely self-explanatory. The amount of time spent in the function, the amount of time spent in the function and its descendants, and a Hit Count are tabulated. The specific function is identified by name, with the name of the object module that exports it in parentheses.

Interpreting the report is equally straightforward. The profiling statistics indicate that the program spent 87.5% of its execution time in a function called WaitOnEvent. In this function, the program is waiting for the Windows 2000 Timer event that signals that it is time to collect the next data sample. Notice that the Hit Count for this function, which represents the number of times this function was entered, is just slightly less than the number of seconds in the execution interval. This no doubt reflects some delay in initialization. It seems safe to assume that the program is actually executing the other 12.5% of the time. The WriteDataToFile function, which was entered 393,329 times, accounts for close to 25% of the program's actual execution time. It appears that this function is called over 1,000 times for each collection interval.

The only noticeable difficulty in working with the Visual C++ profile report is that it does not identify the function call parent-child relationships. Notice that the function call FindPreviousObjectInstanceCounter is executing 1.2% of the time (about 10% of the program's actual active time). When functions called by FindPreviousObjectInstanceCounter are factored in, the function call is executing 4.5% of the time. Unfortunately, it is not possible to identify the child functions called from a parent function by glancing at the report. Since the programmer creating the execution profile has access to the source code, it should be reasonably simple to trace the function's execution using the debugger, for example, to determine what calls the FindPreviousObjectInstanceCounter function makes to other helper functions. But in practice, for a program as complex as dmperfss, this is not a trivial exercise.

While the built-in execution profiler is not as robust as other available tools, it did help us identify the program modules that had the greatest impact on performance. The C++ profile report was consistent with later analysis results that honed in on the same relatively small set of modules that were responsible for a disproportionate amount of CPU time consumption. While not as comprehensive as the other tools, the Microsoft Visual C++ profile option proved both easy to use and effective.

Visual Quantify

Rational Visual Quantify is an add-on code profiling tool for Windows 2000 that works with Microsoft Visual C++, Visual Basic, and Java running on Intel hardware. It addresses the major usability limitations we encountered with the profiler built into the Microsoft C++ compiler. First and foremost, it has an intuitive GUI interface that makes it easy to navigate through the profiling output. But Visual Quantify (or VQ, for short), we found, is more than just a pretty face. The profiling data it collects extends to an impressive number of system modules and services. VQ measures the performance impact associated with third-party ActiveX and DLL-based components that your program links to dynamically. It also captures the amount of processor time spent inside a surprising number of Win32 API calls. Acquiring profiling information on the overhead of the dmperfss program during function calls to external modules *outside* the executable was of great benefit in this context.

Like the Visual C++ profiler, VQ gathers information at the level of either the function or the line, and also provides options that allow you to specify when you want the profiling data collection effort to begin. This lets you bypass initialization code and focus on the application's inner loop, for example. Another nice feature is the ability to compare two or more profiling runs of the same program. This is useful during the iterative process of implementing code changes to ensure that the changes have the desired effect.

Loading modules

VQ obtains profiling information on dynamically loaded modules called from the target application at runtime. It runs the application in its address space and watches as it calls other modules. As long as the external function being called is associated with a shareable DLL, VQ can instrument it. (Fortunately, most DLLs and OCXs *are* shareable.) It does this by copying the module being called into the VQ process address space and inserting its measurement hooks into this copy of the code. Rational calls this technique Object Code Insertion, which it claims to have patented.

The first noticeable thing about running Visual Quantify is how long it takes to get started. This is because the process of intercepting dynamic program loads, loading a private copy of the module into the VQ process address space, and inserting the instrumentation hooks is quite lengthy. Commonly accessed DLLs like *MCVSRT50. dll* are normally resident in the system when a program begins execution and do not have to be loaded. In the case of the dmperfss program, VQ initialization took over 20 minutes before program execution was able to proceed unimpeded. VQ keeps you entertained during this startup delay with two displays that show the progress of initialization. The Threads display, illustrated in Figure 4-1, shows the status of the profiling run. The Threads display is a histogram showing activity by thread. We are not certain why so many threads are displayed here—the application itself only has two, corresponding to main_66 (top) and thread_17f (the grayish squares in the middle of the screen). It seems plausible that VQ spawns a separate thread to load each DLL. Gray squares in the main_66 thread indicate VQ delays to load the modules and insert its hooks.

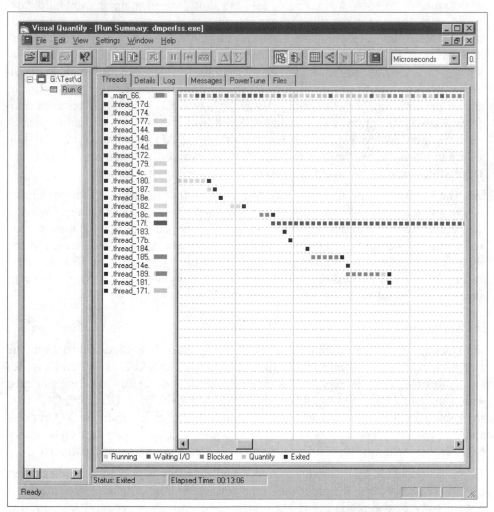

Figure 4-1. The VQ Run Summary Threads tab shows the status of all running threads

The Log display illustrated in Figure 4-2 is quite informative. VQ logs each load module as it encounters it in the course of program execution. Here we see *dmperfss.exe* being instrumented, followed by *NetApi32.dll*, *MSVCRT.dll*, *NETRAP.dll*, *SAMLIB.dll*, etc. When VQ encounters a module that it cannot instrument, like *authperf.dll*, a warning message is printed. Obviously, following the trail of the modules called from the main application program, loading them, and instrumenting them is very time-consuming. One of VQ's execution-time options copies instrumented load modules to a disk cache. On subsequent VQ runs, the program checks first to see if a current copy of the load module is available from the disk cache, speeding up processing on subsequent profiling runs considerably.

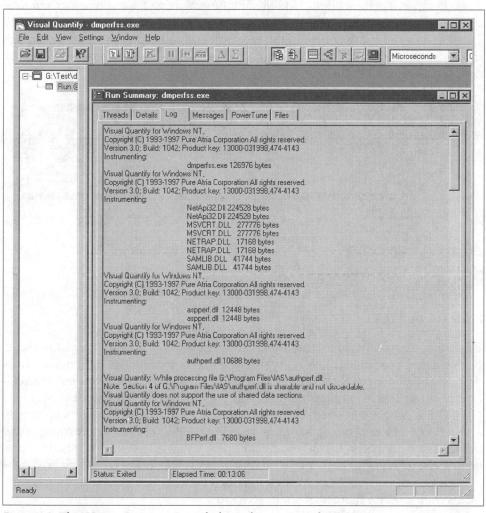

Figure 4-2. The VQ Run Summary Log tab shows the sequence of DLLs

Figure 4-3, which displays the dmperfss functions ordered by the amount of time spent in execution, shows how effective VQ is in instrumenting third-party code. Notice that the program is spending most of its time in operating system runtime module. These include Timer waits and waiting for other events to occur when the program is asleep between collection intervals. Where the Microsoft VC++ profiler collected data on 155 function calls, VQ provides data on 616. Eight out of the first eleven modules are functions embedded in *KERNEL32.dll*. VQ shows precisely how long these Win32 API calls take. The first `dmperfss` function to make the list is $10_ OUTPUT, which is responsible for only 0.03% of the total execution time. The information VQ provides changed our perspective from fine-tuning the code in `dmperfss` to improving the way the code interacts with Windows 2000 system services. Because it gathers all this additional information, VQ's intuitive user interface is even more important. You can open several different windows at one time, each focusing on a different segment of the program, and you can navigate easily through the code execution path. The screen shots here cannot do justice to just how well designed the interface is.

Function	Calls	Function time	F+D time	F time (% of .Root.)	F+D time (% of .Root.)	Avg F time	Min F time	Max F time	Module
WaitForMultipleObjects	349	347517543.03	347517543.03	31.98	31.98	995752.27	993688.55	1003975.42	KERNEL32.DLL
Sleep	3569	29401724.49	29401724.49	2.71	2.71	8238.08	6.02	140468.80	KERNEL32.DLL
HeapReAlloc	11513	14353892.17	14353892.17	1.32	1.32	1246.75	12.60	8948.48	KERNEL32.DLL
WriteFile	507795	12091304.16	12091304.16	1.11	1.11	23.81	14.80	246696.47	KERNEL32.DLL
RegQueryValueExW	15361	5275120.85	55098825.43	0.49	5.07	343.41	3.75	20518.29	ADVAPI32.DLL
LoadLibraryA	14	5118472.23	5431646.54	0.47	0.50	365605.16	104.18	1549919.15	KERNEL32.DLL
CollectP5PerformanceData	3839	1717419.33	2066004.45	0.16	0.19	447.36	293.75	2586.96	p5ctrs.dll
HeapAlloc	6121	855347.03	855347.03	0.08	0.08	139.74	0.58	3049.33	KERNEL32.DLL
NtFsControlFile	60	756794.60	756794.60	0.07	0.07	12613.24	296.33	288093.46	NTDLL.DLL
CloseHandle	7	747194.58	747194.58	0.07	0.07	106742.08	7.63	746408.95	KERNEL32.DLL
HeapFree	5851	561729.66	561729.66	0.05	0.05	96.01	0.86	4264.30	KERNEL32.DLL
NtDeviceIoControlFile	3863	351209.84	351209.84	0.03	0.03	90.91	32.87	2145.86	NTDLL.DLL
$10_OUTPUT	221332	323989.34	1784090.10	0.03	0.16	1.46	0.16	2.81	dmperfss.exe
BhCollectPerformanceData	15349	247183.75	274304.80	0.02	0.03	16.10	6.24	2154.90	bhnon.dll
WaitForSingleObjectEx	18	229501.09	229501.09	0.02	0.02	12750.06	7.19	65450.04	KERNEL32.DLL
IsPreviousNoParentSameInstance	1727001	224958.62	264989.87	0.02	0.02	0.13	0.07	1.27	dmperfss.exe
GetDiskFreeSpaceW	348	217145.95	217145.95	0.02	0.02	623.98	488.14	1563.02	KERNEL32.DLL

Figure 4-3. The VQ Function List is sorted by Function Time

Of course, this added level of information comes at a price in additional overhead. Notice that the function call WaitForMultipleObjects accounts for 32% of the execution time. This is the *KERNEL32.dll* function, which is called from the WaitOn-Event routine located in *dmwrdata.obj* that the C++ profiler found was consuming fully 87.5% of the time! Because of the measurement overhead, it is important to accept VQ's function timing statistics as *relative* indicators of performance, rather than absolute numbers. In other words, the proportion of the time the `dmperfss` program spent in WaitOnEvent compared to WriteDataToFile was consistent across the MS VC++ profiler and VQ. We describe the effort made to validate the measurements from all three sources later in this chapter.

The overhead associated with the VQ measurement technology was enough of a factor to limit the types of program execution scenarios that we could realistically gather performance information about. In particular, we wanted to assess the impact of collecting different Windows 2000 performance objects. The easiest way to do that was to set up a data collection set that included *all* available objects, overriding the program's default collection set to use the Master Collection set instead. However, when we ran VQ with `dmperfss` collecting all available objects, there was so much measurement overhead that we were unable to collect data at frequent enough intervals to gather data in a systematic fashion. We worked around the problem easily enough by creating subsets of the program's Master Collection set and analyzing them. The overhead associated with VQ profiling is the one consideration to be aware of when you are using the program and interpreting its results.

VQ excelled in illuminating the execution path associated with the Win32 services that were routinely called by the dmperfss program and were responsible for much of the execution time. Figure 4-4 shows the Function Detail display obtained by zooming in on the RegQueryValueEx function, which is the oldest and most commonly used interface to collect performance data in Windows 2000. (For more information, refer back to Chapter 2.) The Function Detail screen displays the program functions that called RegQueryValueEx and the functions called *from* RegQueryValueEx. (You can navigate back and forth in the Function Detail screen to trace the execution path forward and back.) In the absence of the information VQ provides, the interface to RegQueryValueEx is a black box. The calls to RegQueryValueEx are well documented in the Win32 System Development Kit (SDK). Microsoft also supplies a code sample in the SDK that shows how to support extended counters across this interface, but the actual program flow of control is not documented. VQ opens up this black box so that we can get a good look inside.

The Windows 2000 performance monitoring interface

Performance objects in Windows 2000 are associated with a Perflib DLL that responds to three function calls: Open, Close, and Collect. Figure 4-5 illustrates the Registry entries that a Perflib DLL must create. A performance monitor application like the Windows 2000 System Monitor, the NT Performance Monitor, or dmperfss scans the Windows 2000 Registry looking for these entries in order to see what collection data is available on a particular machine. The performance monitoring application calls the Open function for the performance DLL initially to enumerate the objects and counters that it can report. The Collect function is then performed at regular intervals to retrieve data. The metadata retrieved from the Open call is used to process the data buffers retrieved by the Collect function. The Close function is used to perform any necessary cleanup inside the Perflib DLL.

Figure 4-4 showed that RegQueryValueExW is called from two places by dmperfss, 15,350 times from GetPerfDataFromRegistry, and just three times from GetTextFromRegistry. GetPerfDataFromRegistry is called from the dmperfss data collection loop once an interval for each performance object, while GetTextFromRegistry is called only at initialization to retrieve the performance object metadata. Yet the three initialization calls are almost as time-consuming as the interval data collection calls, according to the VQ measurement data.

VQ then breaks down the time spent in RegQueryValueEx according to the functions it calls, most of which are Open, Close, and Collect calls embedded in Perflib DLLs.

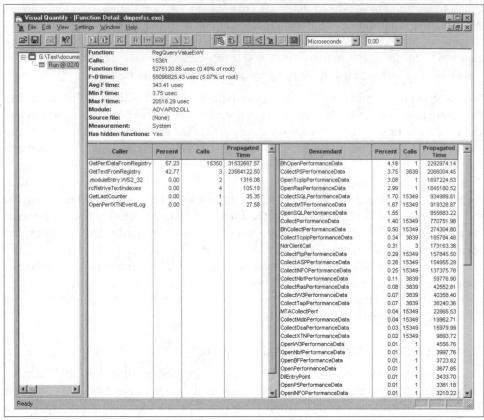

Figure 4-4. Function detail display showing calls to and from ReqQueryValueEx; the Descendent calls reference Open and Collect routines in Perflib DLLs

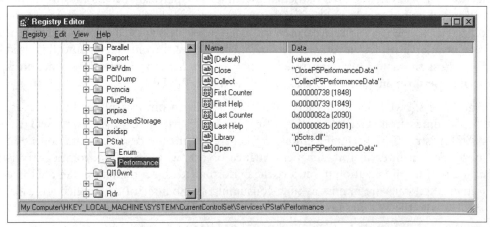

Figure 4-5. Performance subkeys under Services Registry key point to Perflib DLLs and their entry points for performance data collection

From the number of function calls executed, we see a one-to-one correspondence between calls to RegQueryValueEx and a number of Perflib DLL Collect functions. What we found surprising was that functions like CollectSQLPerformanceData, which is associated with the collection of MS SQL Server performance data, were being called implicitly. MS SQL Server was installed on this machine, but the dmperfss program did *not* explicitly reference the SQL Server performance objects. As expected, the Perflib DLL Open calls are made just once. Several of the Open calls are very time-consuming, possibly due to serialization delays associated with interprocess communication. But since the Open calls are made just once, the time spent waiting for the Perflib DLL to initialize is acceptable. (Besides, there is nothing we can do to improve someone else's code.)

Figure 4-6 shows a view of the execution profile that VQ creates called the Call Graph. The Call Graph traces the subfunctions called from function GetPerfData-FromRegistry in the *dmperfss.exe* program. The thickness of the line connecting two functions represents relative amount of time spent traversing that particular logical path. This display clearly identifies the program's critical path of execution, which is useful for zeroing in on what sections of code need work. Recall that with the Microsoft VC++ profiler, it was not possible to measure the execution time in any modules called from GetPerfDataFromRegistry because they were outside the range of the instrumented program. With VQ, you can see deeply into modules other than your own. In this instance, at least, we found the insight gained into the workings of these system interfaces extremely valuable. The program's execution time profile gives us important information that is simply unavailable from any other documented source.

Overall, we gave the Rational Visual Quantify program very high marks in usability. It extends the execution time analysis so that you can look inside many system calls and interfaces. The user interface is exceptionally well designed, allowing the user to cope with all the additional information presented.

Intel VTune

Intel's VTune product is a CPU execution profiling tool aimed at helping the programmer create code that is optimized for Intel hardware. VTune samples system-wide activity using a methodology that runs off the hardware's high priority clock interrupt. During clock interrupt processing, VTune figures out what process was executing immediately prior to the interrupt occurring. Then VTune maps the program counter for the thread that was running into the process virtual address space to figure out what module and code are being executed. Later, when it has finished collecting data, VTune post-processes the information to produce a detailed report on just about every routine running on the Windows 2000 system. Because the clock IRQ is such high priority (refer to the discussion of IRQ priority in Chapter 3), almost every Windows 2000 system routine is visible to VTune.

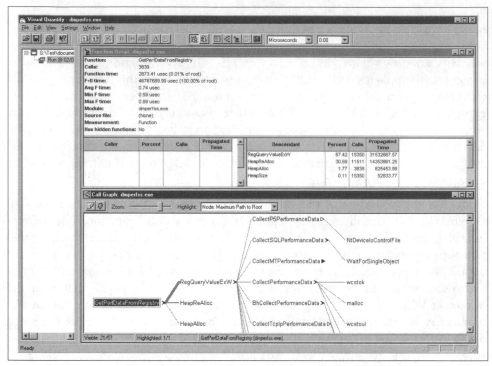

Figure 4-6. The Call Graph reveals the critical path through your code during execution

There are several distinct advantages to this approach. First of all, it generates very low overhead. We made our first run with VTune using the same setup as under VQ; the `dmperfss` application was set to collect the default collection set once per second. During this run, VTune identified that 90% of system activity occurred in a module called *Hal.dll*. HAL is the hardware-specific Windows 2000 Hardware Abstraction Layer. Apparently, the code for the system Idle thread, which Windows 2000 dispatches when there is no other work for the system to perform, resides here.

We conclude that with the default collection set being harvested once per second, the system was cruising at less than 10% busy with VTune running. This highlights another advantage of VTune: namely, that the profiling program captures just about all system activity, even code executing inside the Windows 2000 operating system kernel and the HAL. Because these operating system modules are not shareable DLLs, they are not visible to tools like Visual Quantify. Finally, this measurement methodology is the only way to get good performance data on complex applications involving multiple process address spaces, interprocess communication, etc. In other words, VTune may be the best way to gain insight into web site applications that interact with back-end databases, or COM-based applications that run within the context of the Microsoft Transaction Server.

In reacting to the initial results reported by VTune, we decided it would be helpful to try and accumulate more samples related to dmperfss activity, and less involving the operating system's Idle thread function. Consequently, we changed the collections parameters for dmperfss to collect all available performance objects once per second. Remember that under VQ, overhead considerations made it impractical to profile the program under those circumstances. Using the more efficient, timer-based VTune data collection mechanism, this scheme worked just fine.

Figure 4-7 illustrates the available VTune output reports. A Modules Report is shown from an interval where dmperfss was executing, collecting the full Master Collection set once per second during an approximately five-minute interval. All the modules detected in execution during that interval are listed on the left side of the chart in alphabetical order. The chart is a histogram showing the amount of CPU time spent inside each module. Each vertical bar represents 10% CPU consumption.

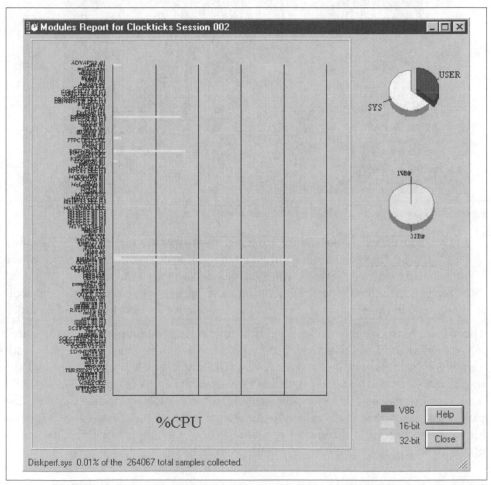

Figure 4-7. The Vtune Modules Report shows all the active modules in the system

This VTune report is so detailed that it is quite hard to read. By clicking on a section of the chart, you can zoom in to see more detail; see Figure 4-8. There are no other sort options for this display, which also contributes to the difficulty in manipulating the display. Figure 4-8 zooms in on the portion of the chart where two modules consuming a good deal of CPU time are sorted together. These modules are operating system routines, *ntdll.dll* and *ntoskrnl.exe*. Neither of these was visible using any of the other profiling tools.

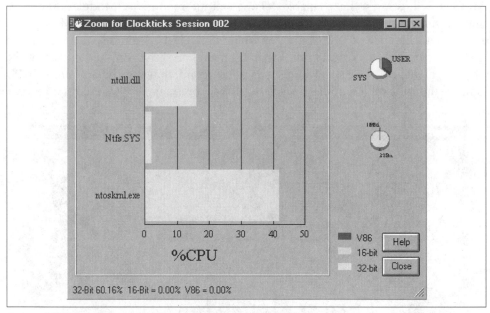

Figure 4-8. Zooming in on low-level operating system modules

Figure 4-9 illustrates VTune's ability to zoom in on specific modules. This is a picture of the dmperfss executable in virtual storage, showing the code addresses where VTune detected activity, which are then mapped to program modules. Here the interface is a bit more flexible, with various sort options available for program hotspot analysis. In this view, modules are sorted by relative address in the load module.

The VTune hotspot analysis identified two functions inside dmperfss that accounted for more than 70% of the activity inside the process address space. These two modules were NextInstanceDef and IsPreviousAndParentSameInstance. These VTune results correlate well with the original MS C++ profiler and VQ runs. MS C++ found high activity inside NextInstanceDef and FindPreviousObjectInstanceCounter, the parent function that calls IsPreviousAndParentSameInstance internally. VQ also identified IsPreviousAndParentSameInstance as one of the most heavily utilized modules with an extremely high number of function calls.

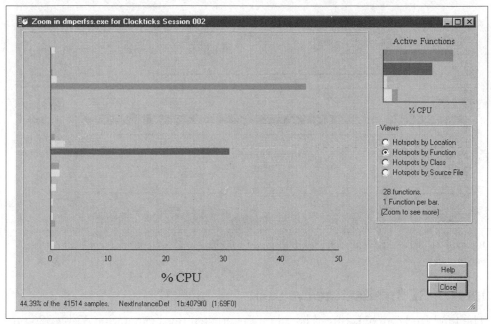

Figure 4-9. Zooming in on functions inside dmperfss

Figure 4-10 shows the detailed analysis VTune performed on the code being executed in the NextInstanceDef module. Here, execution time is mapped to the actual machine code generated by the C++ compiler. This is the area in which VTune stands above the crowd. There are six machine instructions associated with this routine, accounting for fully 44.39% of the CPU time consumed by the process. You can see how VTune breaks down the CPU consumption instruction by instruction. Making full use of the report output in Figure 4-10, we discovered, requires becoming familiar with the Pentium hardware and its performance characteristics. We will return to a discussion of this VTune report after an excursion into the realm of Intel Pentium and Pentium Pro hardware performance.

Intel Processor Hardware Performance

VTune, we discovered, is targeted specifically for programs that execute on Intel hardware, and provides a very detailed and informative analysis of program execution behavior on the Intel Pentium processor family. It turns out that this analysis is not as useful for programs executing on newer Intel hardware, such as the Pentium Pro, Pentium II, Pentium III, or Pentium IV. However, learning how to use this detailed information requires quite a bit of understanding about the way that Pentium (and Pentium Pro) processor chips work.

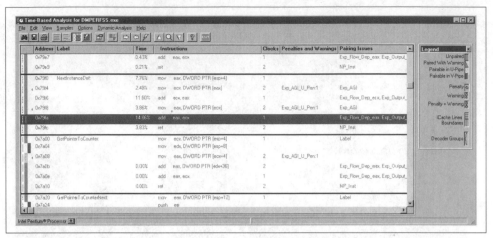

Figure 4-10. VTune code analysis report pinpoints specific hardware optimizations that can be performed

Intel IA-32 Architecture Evolution

The Intel IA-32 architecture is based on the original third-generation 32-bit 386 processor family. Today, the Intel 32-bit architecture is associated with Pentium (P5) and Pentium Pro, Pentium II, Pentium III, and Pentium IV processors (these four correspond to the P6 generation of Intel microprocessors). For example, the Pentium IV is a sixth-generation microprocessor (P6) running the Intel x86 instruction set. Hardware designers refer to the Intel x86 as a CISC (Complex Instruction Set Computer), a style of hardware that is no longer in vogue. Today, hardware designers generally prefer processor architectures based on RISC (Reduced Instruction Set Computers). The complex Intel x86 instruction set is a legacy of design decisions made twenty years ago at the dawn of the microprocessor age, when RISC concepts were not widely recognized. The overriding design consideration in the evolution of the Intel x86 microprocessor family is maintaining upward compatibility of code developed for earlier-generation machines produced over the last twenty years.

Table 4-1 summarizes the evolution of the Intel x86 microprocessor family starting with the 8080, first introduced in 1974. As semiconductor fabrication technology advanced and more transistors were available to the designers, Intel's chip designers added more and more powerful features to the microprocessor. For example, the 80286 (usually referred to as the 286) was a 16-bit machine with a form of extended addressing using segment registers. The next-generation 386 chip maintained compatibility with the 286's rather peculiar virtual memory addressing scheme while implementing a much more straightforward 32-bit virtual memory scheme. In contrast to the 16-bit 64K segmented architecture used in the 286, the 386 virtual addressing mode is known as a "flat" memory model.

Table 4-1. The evolution of the Intel x86 microprocessor family

Processor	Year	Clock speed (MHz)	Bus width (bits)	Addressable memory	Transistors
8080	1974	2	8	64 KB	6,000
8086	1978	5-10	16	1 MB	29,000
8088	1979	5-8	8	1 MB	29,000
80286	1982	8-12	16	16 MB	134,000
80386	1985	16-33	32	4 GB	275,000
486	1989	25-50	32	4 GB	1,200,000
Pentium (586)	1993	60-233	32	4 GB	3,100,000
Pentium Pro (686)	1995	150-200	32	4 GB	5,500,000
Pentium II (686)	1997	233-333	64	4 GB	7,500,000
Pentium III (686)	1999	400-800	64	64 GB	> 15,000,000
Pentium IV (686)	2001	1200-1700	64	64 GB	40,000,000

Pipelining

The extra circuitry available in the next-generation 486 processors introduced in 1989 was utilized to add architectural features to create even higher performance chips. The 486 microprocessor incorporated floating-point instructions (available in an optional coprocessor during the days of the 386) and a small 8K Level 1 code and data cache. Including a small cache memory meant that the 486 could also speed up instruction using *pipelining*. Pipelining is a common processor speedup technique that exploits an inherent parallelism in the process of decoding and executing computer instructions. The 486 breaks instruction execution into five stages, as illustrated in Figure 4-11:

- Prefetch. During Prefetch, the next instruction to be executed is copied from cache memory to the CPU.
- Instruction Decode, Part 1 (op code interpretation).
- Instruction Decode, Part 2 (operand fetch).
- Execution.
- Write Back. Registers and memory locations are updated.

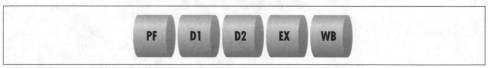

Figure 4-11. The five stages of an instruction execution cycle in the 486 processor

Since an instruction will spend at least one clock cycle in each stage of execution, a 486 instruction requires a minimum of five clock cycles to execute. In other words, a

486 processor running at a clock speed of 100 MHz should be able to execute 100,000,000 ÷ 5 = 20,000,000 instructions per second. The Level 1 processor cache memory, first available among the Intel family of microprocessors in the 486 machines, is critical to the performance of a pipelined CPU. As long as the addresses and data areas referenced in the instruction are resident in the CPU cache, the microprocessor executes each instruction stage in one clock cycle. On the other hand, there is a significant performance penalty if data or instructions have to be fetched from main memory. The CISC architecture used in the Intel x86 family of microprocessors is also a significant performance factor because many 486 instructions require more than one clock cycle in the Execute stage. (The essence of pure RISC designs is that only simple instructions that can execute in a single clock cycle are implemented.)

Separate pieces of hardware circuitry in the processor are responsible for carrying out the processing associated with each stage in the execution of a machine instruction. The specific logic circuitry associated with executing each stage of an instruction is idle during other stages of instruction execution in simple, nonpipelined processors. The idea behind a pipeline is to utilize this hardware by attempting to overlap instruction execution. As illustrated in Figure 4-12, the 486 pipeline has the capacity to execute five instructions in parallel: as soon as Instruction 1 completes its prefetch stage, the prefetch hardware can be applied to the next instruction in sequence. When the 486 pipeline is working optimally, even though each individual instruction still takes five clock cycles to execute, an instruction completes *every clock cycle*! The behavior of a pipelined processor architecture leads quite naturally to measuring its performance according to the number of clocks per instruction (CPI). Pipelining boosts the actual instruction rate of a microprocessor from 5 CPI for the nonpipelined version to 1 CPI for the pipelined processor (under ideal circumstances, as we shall see).

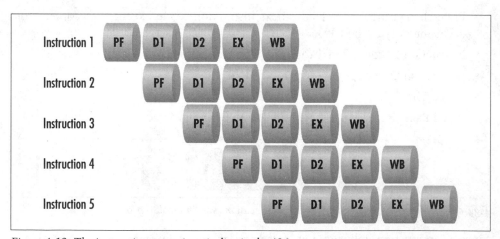

Figure 4-12. The instruction execution pipeline in the 486

Pipeline Stalls

In practice, CPIs in the range of one clock per instruction are not achievable even in the very best textbook examples of RISC processor design. Some of the problems are endemic to the technology. Various instruction sequences result in pipeline *stalls* that slow down instruction execution rates; branch instructions that change the sequence of instruction execution cause the wrong instructions to be loaded and decoded when the branch that changes the sequence is executed. Consequently, processors like the Pentium and Pentium Pro use *branch prediction* strategies to keep track of when branches were taken in the past and to load the pipeline with instructions out of sequence based on history.

Mispredicted branches are not the only source of pipeline stalls. Often it is necessary to stall the pipeline because the output from one instruction is required by the next instruction. When one instruction updates a register and the instruction that follows uses that same register to address data, it is necessary to stall the pipeline in the address generation stage for the second instruction. A pipeline stall with a dependent relationship between instructions that execute near each other is known as an *interlock*.

Pipeline stalls due to mispredicted branches and interlocking instruction dependencies are common to both RISC and CISC machines. Intel's experience with speeding up the 486's instruction execution rate using simple pipelining floundered for a different reason: the x86 complex instruction set. Complex x86 instructions require more than one clock cycle in the execution stage. Reviewing the specifications in Intel's documentation, you can see that the basic commands in the integer instruction set require between one and nine clock cycles. The rep prefix used in the commonly used bulk memory Move instructions alone requires four clocks, for example. A 32-bit far call, used for branching to and from a subroutine, can require as many as 22 clock cycles. This variability in instruction execution time plays havoc with the 486's five-stage pipeline, causing frequent stalls in the EX stage, as depicted in Figure 4-13. The drawing illustrates a 486 pipeline stall because Instruction 1's EX cycle requires five clocks to complete. You can see how a stall in one instruction backs up the entire pipeline. Because some complex instructions require many clock cycles to execute, the 486's instruction execution rates fell well short of optimal performance.

P5 Superscalar Architecture

As the next-generation semiconductor fabrication technology became available, Intel's chip designers faced a quandary. Some pipelining performance issues can be readily addressed with more hardware, so the P5 or Pentium chip gained separate code and data caches as well as branch prediction logic. (The Pentium's use of branch prediction was subject to a well-publicized patent infringement suit brought

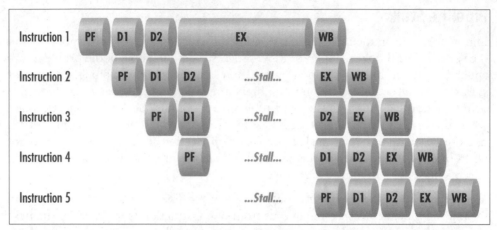

Figure 4-13. A pipeline stall: a complex instruction delays all following instructions

by Digital. The litigation was settled out of court in 1998.) But the performance issues related to the x86 complex instruction set resisted a simple hardware solution.

The Pentium introduced a *superscalar* dual pipeline architecture that allows, under the right circumstances, two instructions to be completed in a single clock cycle. The Pentium dual pipeline is illustrated in Figure 4-14. The Pentium contains a single Prefetch engine capable of operating on dual instructions in parallel. The Pentium can then load the two instruction execution pipelines in parallel. Where a pipeline computer is theoretically capable of executing instructions at a rate of one CPI, a superscalar machine such as the Pentium is capable of an instruction execution rate that is *less than* one CPI. The top pipeline in the Pentium superscalar pipeline is known as the *U pipe*, and its execution characteristics are identical to those of the 486. The bottom pipeline is called the *V pipe* and is loaded only under special circumstances.

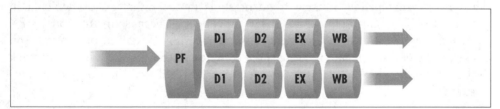

Figure 4-14. The Pentium dual pipeline

The Pentium Prefetch stage follows arcane *instruction pairing rules* that determine whether the second instruction in an instruction pair can be loaded in the V pipe and executed in parallel. The rules for loading the V pipe are fairly complex. Two simple, single-cycle execution instructions can almost always be paired and executed in parallel. Some authorities have observed that the Pentium instruction pairing rules identify a subset of RISC instructions inside the full, complex instruction set that can be executed in parallel. This characterization is a bit simplistic, however. Any instructions that use immediate operands or addresses (i.e., the data the instruction operates on is embedded in the instruction) can never be paired. Furthermore, if the second instruction operates on any of the same registers as the first, it cannot be executed in parallel. This is a particularly strict requirement in the x86 environment, where there is a legacy of only eight General Purpose Registers. The small number of registers available to instructions leads to a few registers being referenced repeatedly, which leads to pipeline instruction dependency interlocks.[*]

Optimizing instruction streams for the Pentium

Like pipelining, the superscalar architecture in the Intel 586 borrowed techniques in widespread use in the computing industry. The hardware manufacturers that introduced superscalar architectures in the late 1980s also developed their own systems software, including the compilers that generated code optimized to run on these machines. These RISC hardware manufacturers relied on their compilers to generate code that would run optimally in a parallel environment and take full advantage of the specific hardware architecture. An optimizing compiler, for example, may resort to inserting placeholder instructions into the instruction sequence or rearranging instructions to avoid sequences with direct dependencies between successive instructions.[†]

In the open PC environment, Intel holds an enviable position as the developer of the hardware used in most PC desktop, workstation, and server machines. However, Intel develops very little of the systems software that run on its hardware, including the most popular operating systems and high level language compilers. Intel's challenge when it introduced the Pentium superscalar architecture was to promote the use of this hardware among third-party systems software developers, including the leading developer of compilers and operating systems for the Intel platform, which is Microsoft.

Intel's approach to promoting the Pentium architecture was to provide two types of tools for use by third-party developers. The first was to build into the processor a measurement interface that third-party software could tap into. The measurement interface for the Pentium and subsequent machines provides extensive instrumentation on internal processor performance. It includes the ability to measure the actual CPU instruction execution rate (not just how busy the processor is, as in native Windows

---

[*] Contemporary RISC designs deal with this problem by adding lots more registers for programmers to choose from. Intel designers ultimately addressed this problem in the P6 from a direction that would *not* require rewriting (or recompiling) existing applications. The use of pseudo-registers in the P6 architecture is discussed later in this chapter.

[†] For a thoughtful discussion of these and other RISC processor design decisions, see Hennessey and Patterson's *Computer Architecture: A Quantitative Approach*. Professor Hennessey, who is currently the president of Stanford University, was also a co-founder and Chief Scientist at MIPS Computers, where he designed the first generation of commercial RISC machines.

2000 measurements), the number of paired instructions that executed in the V pipe, and various metrics that deal with pipeline stalls. The hardware measurement interface lets you collect just two of the available metrics at a time.

A utility called CPUMON, available from *http://www.sysinternals.com*, allows you to enable the Pentium counters and access them using the Windows System Monitor. Pentium performance counters can also be accessed under Windows NT by installing the P5 counters, using software Microsoft distributes as part of the Windows NT 4.0 Resource Kit. We illustrate some of the uses of these Pentium counters in the next chapter in the context of multiprocessing, where they are especially useful. As of this writing, Microsoft has not released a version of its Resource Kit software to access the Pentium counters that runs on Windows 2000.

The second tool Intel provides is VTune, which performs two key functions that developers can use to optimize the code they develop. The first provides a very usable interface to the built-in Pentium measurement interface. Using this interface, VTune can be used to collect internal Pentium performance statistics on a program as it executes. The second key aspect of VTune is the capability to analyze code sequences and make recommendations on how to write code that is optimal for the Pentium. Among other things, VTune computes the CPI for an instruction sequence and calculates the utilization of the V pipe; see Figure 4-15.

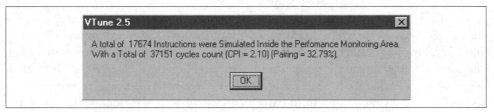

Figure 4-15. VTune computes the CPI for an instruction sequence and calculates V pipe utilization

Using VTune to identify instruction execution hotspots

With this background, we can now return to VTune's analysis of the NextInstance-Def subroutine that was identified as a hotspot within the dmperfss program, as depicted back in Figure 4-10.

The Microsoft Visual C++ compiler generated the six lines of very tight machine code for this subroutine from the following C language statements:

```
PERF_INSTANCE_DEFINITION * NextInstanceDef
            ( PERF_INSTANCE_DEFINITION *pInstance )
{
    PERF_COUNTER_BLOCK  *pCtrBlk;
    pCtrBlk = (PERF_COUNTER_BLOCK *)
      ((PBYTE)pInstance + pInstance->ByteLength);
    return    (PERF_INSTANCE_DEFINITION *)
      ((PBYTE)pInstance + pInstance->ByteLength + pCtrBlk->ByteLength);
}
```

This C language helper function advances a pointer inside the buffer of data returned by RegQueryEx from the beginning of one object instance to the next occurrence of an instance. When dmperfss is retrieving instanced data, particularly data associated with processes and threads, this code is called repeatedly to parse the performance data buffer. As we have seen, all three performance profiler products identified this segment of code as an execution hotspot in the program. In the VTune analysis of dmperfss, the NextInstanceDef code segment was executed even more frequently because both process and thread data was being collected. The profiling data strongly suggests that the efficiency of the program can be optimized by improving the performance of this specific segment of code.

The code generated by the Microsoft compiler to carry out these C language statements is a sequence of admirably compact machine language instructions:

```
00408D40    mov     ecx,dword ptr [esp+4]
00408D44    mov     edx,dword ptr [ecx]
00408D46    mov     eax,dword ptr [ecx+edx]
00408D49    add      eax,ecx
00408D4B    add      eax,edx
00408D4D    ret
```

The code analysis VTune performs on the machine language instructions in NextInstanceDef (illustrated in Figure 4-10) indicates that *none* of these frequently executed instructions is capable of being executed in parallel on a Pentium. The total lack of parallelism comes despite the fact that these are all simple one and two cycle instructions. The screen legend in the right-hand corner of the VTune display in Figure 4-10 decodes the visual clues the program provides to instruction execution performance. Instructions that can be paired and executed in parallel are clearly indicated, as are the boundaries of code cache lines. The P5 optimization switch on the VC++ compiler generates NO OP instructions to line up code on cache line boundaries, as shown here.

This code is unable to take advantage of the Pentium's parallelism. VTune informs us that the machine code instructions generated by the compiler stall the U pipe. The column marked "Penalties and Warnings" indicates that the second and fourth MOV (move) instructions cause an address generation interlock (AGI) that stalls the U pipe. Notice that each instruction in this routine is executed once and only once each time through the routine. There are no branches. However, the instruction timings VTune reports, based on its sampling of the program as it was running, show a wide variation in the execution time of the individual instructions in this code sequence.

The instruction execution timings VTune reports clearly show the performance impact of stalling the pipeline. The second MOV instruction, requiring two clock cycles to execute, is found in execution 2.48% of the time. This instruction copies the value at the address pointed to by the EAX register into the ECX work register. The previous instruction sets up the EAX address using a parameter passed on the stack pointer (ESP). There is an obvious dependency between these two instructions. The next instruction adds a value to ECX. The code is doing arithmetic on another address pointer and uses this value in the MOV instruction that follows. Because the first MOV stalls the pipeline, the ADD instruction that follows is found to be in execution 11.6% of the time. Continuing the analysis, we see how pipeline stalls propagate through the instruction sequence. The next MOV instruction (another two-cycle instruction) is in execution 3.86% of the time, while the single one-cycle ADD that follows it was found to be in execution 14.86% of the time!

Faced with this situation, a programmer working in assembly language can rework the machine instructions to avoid the address generation interlock problem easily enough by adding a third work register. The more complicated code sequence actually runs several times faster than the original. VTune provides detailed advice to the assembly language programmer concerning Pentium-specific instruction execution performance issues, as illustrated in Figure 4-16. The ADD instruction analyzed has an obvious problem due to the interlock with the previous instruction. But it also occasionally requires the data referenced by the EAX register to be refreshed from memory, rather than using the copy that was found in the data cache.

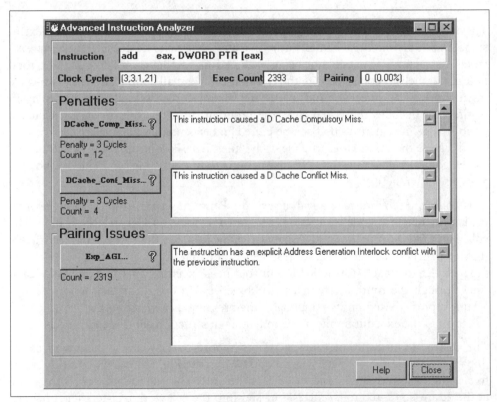

Figure 4-16. VTune's Advanced Instruction Analysis describes the stalls encountered

Code optimization strategies

To take advantage of all the detailed performance information on instruction execution that VTune provides, an application programmer working in a C++ language development environment faces three choices. The first and easiest option is to tell the compiler to generate code optimized for the Pentium processor. Naturally, we tried that route first, recompiling the program with the P5 optimizing switch. Afterwards, running VTune again, we noted some changes in the sequence of instructions generated for this routine, but nothing was an extensive enough restructuring of the program logic to show any appreciable improvement. Figure 4-17 summarizes a run we made after instructing the compiler to generate code optimized for the Pentium. The CPI shows a slight reduction compared to Figure 4-15, although, curiously, the percentage of paired instruction execution actually dropped. Of course, CPI is the more important indicator of performance.

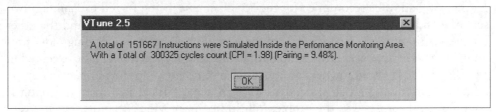

Figure 4-17. Summary of instruction execution results

The second option is to replace the code generated by the compiler with an inline assembly language routine. We did experiment with that option in this instance and were very satisfied with the performance improvements that resulted, despite the fact that adding another work register made the code longer and somewhat more complicated. This counterintuitive outcome is not unusual for a RISC machine, which can often execute longer code sequences faster than shorter, more compact ones. The third option is to recode the original C language routine, which is the route we believe was suggested in this instance to address the number of times this helper function is being called. We tackled the lengthy code restructuring project in the next development cycle, and we continue to rely on Rational Visual Quantify and Intel VTune to measure the impact of those improvements.

Intel P6 Microarchitecture

As complicated as the superscalar, parallel processing, pipelined P5 hardware is, Intel's current generation of P6 Pentium Pro, Pentium II, Pentium III, and Pentium IV hardware is even more complicated. The simple parallel U and V pipelines of the Pentium are replaced by a complex *microarchitecture* that addresses x86 instruction execution issues from an entirely different direction. The P6 microarchitecture attempts to perform instruction coding optimizations automatically during instruction execution, reducing the need to perform Pentium-style instruction sequencing manually (or automatically during compiler code generation). This change of direction suggests that the use of VTune to fine-tune instructions was neither as widespread or as successful as Intel had hoped.

The Intel 686 family of microprocessors were also the first models explicitly designed with advanced multiprocessor configurations in mind. We take up the topic of multiprocessing in the next chapter. Intel also expanded the range of hardware performance measurements available on the P6 machines to support more complex multiprocessor configurations.

Instruction execution parallelism

As discussed previously, instruction pairing in the Pentium was limited to a relatively small subset of the available instruction set. To get the most mileage out of the Pentium hardware, compilers had to be revised, and C language programs that ran on the 486 had to be recompiled for the P5. Of course, being forced to maintain two separate and distinct sets of load modules, one optimized for the 486 and the other for the Pentium, is problematic, to say the least. But without recompiling older programs to make more use of the simple RISC-like instructions that can be executed in parallel on the Pentium, owners of Intel machines do not reap the full benefits of the new and potentially much faster hardware. A second issue in generating optimal code for the Pentium was the problem illustrated in previous sections. Having very few General Purpose Registers to work with makes it difficult to write x86 code that does not stall the pipeline and can take full advantage of the superscalar functions.

Increased logic capacity in newer generation chips makes a more complex parallel processing architecture possible in the P6, PII, PIII, and PIV. The limitations imposed by the original x86 instruction set forced a change in direction. Without fundamental changes, Intel would not have succeeded in further boosting the Instruction Execution Rate (IER) of its next-generation chips beyond what can be achieved by simply increasing clock speed. Among other things, the P6 microarchitecture was designed to address specific performance limitations that arose in the P5 generation of machines, allowing the Intel legacy CISC architecture to keep pace with current advances in RISC processor technology.

The P6 microarchitecture addresses some of these specific performance issues to permit an even greater degree of parallel execution of instructions. Figure 4-18 illustrates the major elements of the P6 instruction execution pipeline, which is considerably more complex than the P5 structure. Additional parallelism is introduced because as many as three instructions at a time can be decoded in parallel during a single clock cycle. The level of parallelism that can be achieved still depends on the instruction execution sequence because, as depicted, the P6 contains two simple instruction decoders and one complex instruction decoder, all designed to work in parallel. Since the complex instruction decoder can decode simple instructions (but not vice versa), a sequence of three simple instructions can be decoded in a single clock cycle. On the other hand, a sequence of three complex instructions requires three clock cycles to decode because there is only one set of complex instruction decoder logic on board the chip.

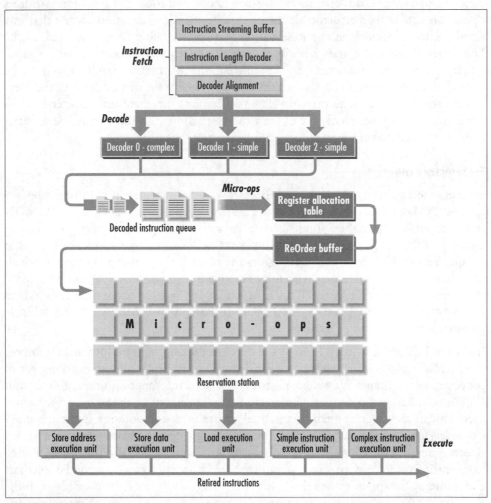

Figure 4-18. The major elements of the P6 instruction execution pipeline

Micro-ops

In the P6 architecture, decoding instructions means translating them into a RISC-like set of fixed length micro-operations, or *micro-ops*. Most micro-ops are designed to execute in a single clock cycle. To augment the limited number of GPRs available to the machine language programmer, these micro-ops can draw on 40 internal work registers, or *pseudo-registers*. After unwinding CISC machine instructions into RISC-like instructions, micro-ops are stored in a pool called the Reservation Station from which they can be executed in any order.* The dispatch unit of the processor, which can execute up to five micro-ops in parallel in a single clock cycle, contains five different functional execution units, as shown. A simple micro-op instruction, a complex micro-op, a Load operation, a Store Data operation, and a Store Address operation can all be performed in parallel. Out-of-order execution means that any Load micro-op waiting in the Reservation Station is eligible to be executed by the Load execution unit if it is free. When all the micro-ops associated with a given machine language instruction are completed, the instruction itself is said to be *retired*. Retiring instructions also means that any results are written back to the computer's registers and cache memory. The processor's retirement unit can retire up to three instructions per clock cycle, with the restriction that these must be in strict order according to the original instruction execution stream.

Performance counters

Intel engineers extensively reworked the hardware performance monitoring interface for the P6 family of microprocessors. Figure 4-19 illustrates using the CPUMON freeware utility available from *http://www.sysinternals.com* to turn on the P6 counters. Like the P5 facility, the P6 allows you to look at only two measurements at a time. Figure 4-19 illustrates turning on a counter that measures the rate at which instructions are retired, along with a measurement of internal activity resource stalls that reflects pipeline efficiency. This Instructions Retired/sec counter corresponds to the processor's internal Instruction Execution Rate, a straightforward and valuable measurement of processor performance.

It should be apparent from Figure 4-19 that the P6 hardware performance monitoring interface provides a wealth of performance statistics on almost every aspect of processor performance. Various aspects of the cache, internal bus, floating-point unit (FPU), etc., are instrumented. Understanding what many of these arcane measurements mean may require a trip to the Intel processor documentation library at *http://www.developer.intel.com*. The meaning of the specific performance counter we selected here, Instructions Retired, ought to be obvious from the preceding discussion of the P6 microarchitecture. You probably know enough about the P6 microarchitecture at this point to use the Instructions Decoded metric, or possibly even the Resource Stalls counter, which reports the number of clock cycles where no instructions could be retired due to various types of execution pipeline stalls.

---

* The major innovation distinguishing the latest-generation Intel Pentium IV processors is a special internal cache for recently translated micro-op code sequences. Apparently, Intel architects discovered that the complicated logic to convert CISC instructions into micro-ops was a major internal bottleneck, leaving the Reservation Station understocked with micro-instructions to be executed. See "The microarchitecture of the Pentium 4 processor" by Hinton, et. al., available at *http://developer.intel.com/technology/itj/q12001/articles/art_2.htm* for details.

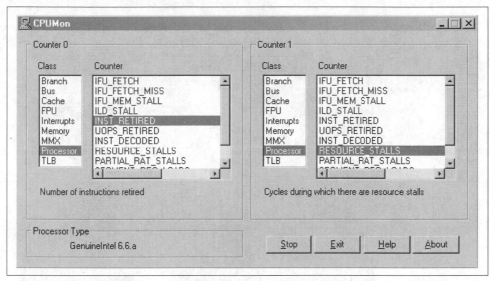

Figure 4-19. Enabling the P6 performance counters using the CPUMON shareware utility

Figure 4-20 illustrates using System Monitor to track the Instruction Execution Rate of a 400 MHz Pentium II machine. Inside System Monitor, we selected Counter 0 and Counter 1 under the CPUMON object, corresponding to the Instructions Retired/sec and Resource Stalls/sec hardware measurements. We used the Pinball game application (again, an excellent CPU load generator) to generate a load on the system that drove processor busy to 100%, as shown. With the processor running at 100% busy, this machine is executing (or *retiring*) approximately 200,000,000 instructions per second, or about two clocks per instruction. During a peak interval, as many as 440,000,000 instructions per second executed, depending on the specific program routines that were running. Despite some variation, IER certainly appears to be well correlated with the measure of % Processor Time CPU busy that Windows 2000 reports conventionally. In this example, when IER dips, there is a corresponding dip in % Processor Time. Naturally, the IER you measure on your machines is a function of the specific instruction stream being executed—if you run Pinball, you are liable to make a similar CPI calculation. But different workloads with different instruction mixes will yield very different results.

The P6 microarchitecture is designed to construct automatically the sort of optimized code sequences that the programmer had to craft by hand using VTune. In fact, VTune cannot perform the kind of analysis illustrated here on code instruction sequences for the much more complicated P6. How effective the complex P6 architecture actually is in optimizing code sequences remains an open question. The dmperfss performance data collected by VTune that was reported in Figure 4-10 was collected on a Pentium Pro running at 200 MHz. From these results, it is evident that the P6 did not parallelize this instruction sequence very successfully. The P6 microarchitecture apparently could not eliminate the pipeline stalls caused by address generation

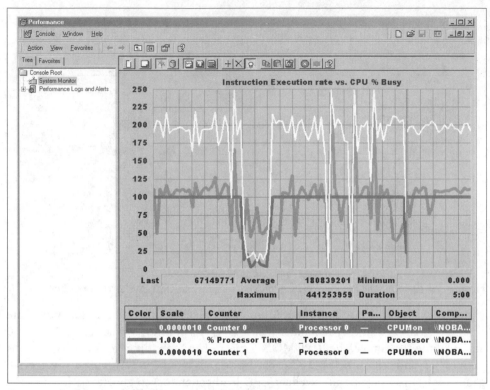

Figure 4-20. Comparing the IER to Processor % Processor Time

interlock in this code sequence. This is a clear indication that VTune will continue to play a valuable role in helping programmers optimize the performance of Windows 2000 applications.

IA-64

As this book is going to press, Intel is beginning to introduce seventh-generation P7 microprocessors that are capable of executing native 64-bit instructions, clocked at 1 Ghz and higher speeds. The first P7 64-bit chips are called Itanium processors. The Intel IA-64 P7 architecture is, naturally, even more complicated than the P6. The Itanium microprocessor chip incorporates three levels of cache memory, not just two like the P6 does. It provides 128 internal pseudo-registers. It is designed to support an even greater level of parallel processing than the P6 machines, with a ten-stage pipeline and four distinct integer and four MMX instruction execution units, all capable of executing instructions in parallel. Like the P6, the P7 contains separate Load and Store engines, too. It has four separate floating-point instruction execution engines, and is designed to fetch and process up to six instructions in parallel each clock cycle. And, of course, the Itanium processors retain full binary instruction compatibility with the previous-generation 32-bit architecture.

## CHAPTER 5

Multiprocessing

As discussed in the last chapter, one sure route to better performance is to buy denser microprocessor chips, which have more logic packed into less space and therefore run faster. Intel founder Gordon Moore's Law, which says that microprocessor density and speeds will double every 18–24 months or so, has not let us down over the last 20 years. If you wait long enough, perhaps your performance problems will just go away with the next generation of computer chips! Another proven technique is *multiprocessing*, building computers with two, four, or more microprocessors, all capable of executing the same workload in parallel. Instead of waiting another 18 months for processor speed to double again, you might be able to take advantage of multiprocessing technology to double or quadruple your performance today. If you have a workload that is out of capacity on a single-processor system, a multiprocessor configuration running Windows 2000 may be the only reasonable alternative that offers you any hope of relief from these capacity constraints today.

Multiprocessing technology lets you harness the power of multiple microprocessors running a single copy of the Windows 2000 operating system. Enterprise-class server models with multiple CPUs abound. When is a two- or four-way multiprocessor solution a good answer for your processing needs? How much better performance should you expect from a server with multiple engines? What sorts of workloads lend themselves to multiprocessing? These are difficult questions to answer, but we try to tackle them here. For even bigger problems, you might even want to consider more exotic solutions where multiple multiprocessors are *clustered* to work together in parallel to power your web site, for example. However, clustered Windows 2000 solutions are beyond the scope of this book.

In this chapter, we introduce the performance considerations relevant to multiprocessors running Windows 2000. Per our usual method, we attempt to construct a conceptual framework that will allow you to formulate answers to these performance and capacity planning questions *for your workload*. First, we introduce multiprocessor technology and see how it works, then discuss how it is implemented in Windows 2000 and what performance trade-offs are involved. We also introduce the measurement data available under Windows 2000 that focuses on multiprocessor performance, and look at those applications that can best take advantage of multiprocessing for better performance. Finally, we discuss configuration and tuning options that are available for Windows 2000 multiprocessors.

Although many applications take good advantage of multiprocessors under Windows 2000 Professional, we concentrate on Windows 2000 Server workloads exclusively in this chapter, as that is where multiprocessing configurations are most common. These also tend to be relatively expensive systems, so understanding the performance ramifications of multiprocessors has a bottom line component associated with it. Again, we focus specifically on Intel hardware (although most of the general discussion applies no matter what your hardware platform is). By their very nature, multiprocessors are not simple systems, and, consequently, the issues and performance trade-offs that need to be understood can be quite complex. Unfortunately, there is no way to avoid complexity here, and frankly, the performance considerations for multiprocessing and parallel processing systems are so involved that we only scratch the surface of this fascinating topic. Many people have devoted their professional careers to the design of high-performance parallel systems, and there is a great body of published research and literature available to anyone with an interest in this subject. Suggestions for further reading are included in the bibliography.

Multiprocessing Basics

Very powerful multiprocessor (MP) hardware configurations are widely available today from many PC server manufacturers. Beginning as far back as the 486 processors, Intel hardware has provided the basic capability required to support multiprocessing designs. However, it was not until the widespread availability of the P6, known commercially as the Intel Pentium Pro microprocessors, that Intel began making processors chips that were specifically built with multiprocessing servers in mind. The internal bus and related bus mastering chip sets that Intel built for the P6 were designed to string up to four Pentium Pro microprocessors together. As we write this chapter, hardware manufacturers are bringing out high-end microprocessors based on the Intel Pentium III, specifically using the flavor of microprocessor code-named Xeon that is designed for 4-, 8-, and 16-way multiprocessors. Anyone interested in the performance of these large-scale, enterprise-class Windows 2000 Servers should be aware of the basic issues in multiprocessor design, performance, and capacity planning.

Shared-Memory Multiprocessing

The specific type of multiprocessing implemented using P6, Pentium II, III, and IV chips is generally known as *shared-memory* multiprocessing. (There is no overall consensus on how to classify various parallel processing schemes, but, fortunately, most authorities at least can agree on what constitutes a shared-memory multiprocessor!) In this type of configuration, the processors operate totally independently of each other, but they do share a single copy of the operating system and access to main memory (i.e., RAM). A typical dual processor shared-memory configuration is illustrated in Figure 5-1, with two P6 processors that contain dedicated Level 2 caches. (They each have separate built-in Level 1 caches, too.) A two-way configuration simply means having twice the hardware: two identical sets of processors, caches, and internal buses. Similarly, a four-way configuration means having four of everything. Having duplicate caches is designed to promote scalability, since the cache is so fundamental to the performance of pipelined processors.

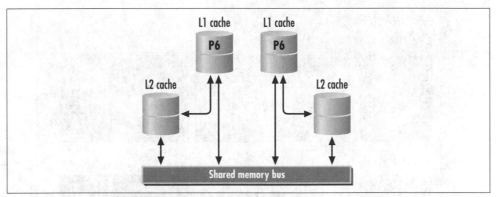

Figure 5-1. A shared-memory multiprocessor

The processors also share a common bus that is used to access main memory locations. This, obviously, is not so scalable, and according to experienced hardware designers, this shared component is precisely where the bottleneck in shared-memory designs is often found.

The idea behind shared-memory multiprocessors looks pretty simple, and if it were not for the complex, internal pipelined microarchitecture of these processors, it would be. We recall that memory locations have to be loaded into cache memory before they can be accessed by the microprocessors in the usual, pipelined fashion. As a practical matter, data from memory can be resident in more than one processor cache at the same time. This leads to problems maintaining the integrity of shared data stored in memory. For instance, if Thread A running on CPU 0 changes location x'f00a 0dc4' in memory, then Thread B, executing on CPU 1 and trying to retrieve this data, must be able to access the most current copy from shared memory, rather than use a stale version from its private cache. This is generally known as the *cache coherence* problem, and it has several important performance implications, discussed in a moment.

Operating system support

Each processor in a multiprocessor is capable of executing work independently of the others. Separate, independent threads may be dispatched, one per processor, and run in parallel. Only one copy of the Windows 2000 operating system is running, controlling what runs on all the processors. From a performance monitoring perspective, you will see multiple instances of the processor object reported in both Taskman (as illustrated in Figure 5-2) and System Monitor.

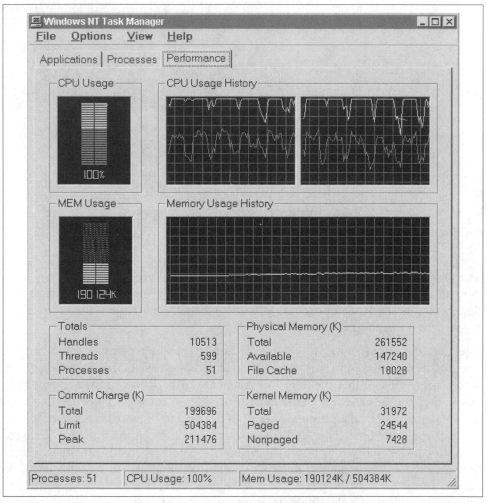

Figure 5-2. Measurement support for multiprocessors in Task Manager

The specific type of multiprocessor support offered beginning in Windows NT 4.0 is known as *symmetric multiprocessing*, often abbreviated as SMP. Symmetric in this context, means that every thread is eligible to execute on any processor. Prior to NT

4.0, Windows NT supported only *asymmetric multiprocessing*. In an NT 3.5x machine, interrupts could only be processed on CPU 0. CPUs 1, 2, 3, could only run user and kernel code, never interrupt service routines (ISRs) and Deferred Procedure Calls (DPCs). This asymmetry ultimately limits the scalability of NT 3.5x multiprocessor systems, because the CPU 0 engine is readily overloaded under some workloads while the remaining microprocessors are idling. In an SMP, in theory, all the microprocessors should run out of capacity at the same time. One of the key development projects associated with the NT 4.0 release was changes to the kernel to support SMPs. In addition, the development team fine-tuned the OS code to run much better in a multiprocessing environment. (Later in this chapter, we discuss some of the coding techniques that are appropriate in a multiprocessing environment.) Windows 2000 also incorporates further improvements inside the operating system to boost performance on large n-way multiprocessor configurations.

The SMP support available in Windows NT 4.0 and above normally allows any processor to process any interrupt, as illustrated in Figure 5-3. This performance data depicts a two-way symmetric multiprocessor system running NT 4.0 Server. (Be careful: the vertical axis scale was adjusted down to a maximum of 30 to make the chart data easier to decipher.) The two processor instances of % Privileged Time and % Interrupt Time counters are shown. CPU 0 and 1 Privileged Time are the top two lines. You have to look carefully to see that these are two lines because they are so nearly identical on this SMP. CPU 0 and 1 Interrupt Time are shown at the bottom; again, these two lines are virtually identical. The processing workload is roughly balanced across both processors, although the load does bounce back and forth a bit, depending on what threads happen to be ready to run.

As should be evident from these pictures, threads are dispatched independently in Windows 2000 so that it is possible for a multithreaded application to run in parallel on separate processors. Applications designed for Windows 2000 take advantage of this architecture by creating multiple threads, as we saw in Chapter 3. The operating system creates separate Idle threads that are dispatched on the appropriate idle processor when there is no other work to do, so that it can account for processor utilization on a per-processor basis. The mechanism for keeping track of processor usage at the thread and process levels is essentially unchanged. No matter what processor is selected, a thread's CPU time is maintained when dispatched. The various Thread % Processor Time counters are then rolled up to the Process % Processor Time counter in the same fashion. By default, System Monitor will not report a value for the Process % Processor Time counter that is greater than 100%. But the default behavior of Sysmon can be modified by specifying a CapPercentsAt100 value of zero under the Registry key HKEY_CURRENT_USER\Software\Microsoft\PerfMon to allow Sysmon to report values of the Process % Processor Time greater than 100%. You should make this change on all multiprocessors.

The bottom of Figure 5-3 shows the amount of CPU time consumed servicing interrupts on the two processors. The amount of time spent processing interrupts per processor is roughly equal, though there is some degree of variation that occurs naturally. This is not always the most efficient way to process interrupts, by the way. Having one type of ISR or DPC directed to a single processor can have a positive impact on performance if the processor that runs the DPC code, for instance, is able to keep it in cache, rather than being forced to fetch instructions from memory. Similarly, the Windows 2000 Scheduler tries to dispatch a ready thread on the same processor where it recently ran for that very same reason. A thread is said to have an *affinity* for the processor where it was most recently dispatched. Processor affinity in a multiprocessor is discussed later.

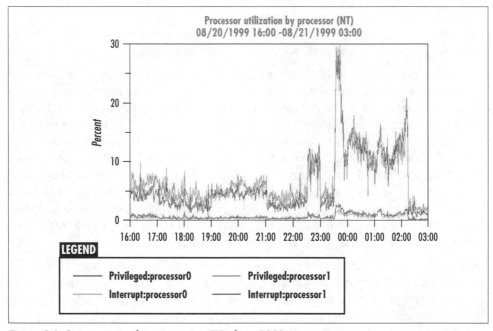

Figure 5-3. Symmetric multiprocessing in Windows 2000

Thread scheduling

Since multiple programs are loaded in Windows 2000 memory anyway, it seems like it should be a relatively simple matter for Windows 2000 to run two (or three or four or eight) programs at a time. Unfortunately, shared-memory and coordination issues associated with the need to maintain cache coherence make things considerably more complicated. Even though the separate processors operate largely independently of each other, there are some occasions where the hardware must communicate and coordinate. There are also times when it is necessary to prevent multiple independent processors from running in parallel. Indeed, shared memory multiprocessors require some mechanism to ensure that threads execute *serially* as they access and update global shared-memory data structures. A brief look at how the Windows 2000 Scheduler works in a multiprocessor configuration will illustrate the data integrity concerns. It will also serve both to highlight the cache coherence problem and put the performance implications of multiprocessing into perspective.

The Windows 2000 OS kernel is multithreaded, which means it is capable of working in parallel if the hardware is available. During installation, the presence of a multiprocessor is detected and a multiprocessing version of *ntoskrnl.exe*, the OS kernel, is loaded. During OS initialization, about 20 additional kernel threads are allocated for each additional processor that is detected. Windows 2000 internal data structures provide native support for up to 32 processing engines. Meanwhile, Windows 2000 maintains a single copy of the Scheduler's dispatching queue for ISRs, DPCs, and kernel and normal program threads that is shared across all processors. There is only one Dispatcher Ready Queue, even on a multiprocessor.

Processor affinity

Logically, the structure of the Ready Queue and the relative priority of threads waiting to execute is identical whether Windows 2000 is executing on an single processor or on multiple processors. The main difference is that multiple threads can run *concurrently* on a multiprocessor, a little detail that leads to many complications. In the regular course of events, the Windows 2000 Scheduler selects the highest priority waiting thread to run on each available processor. In addition, certain execution threads may have an affinity to execute on specific processors. Windows 2000 supports both *hard affinity,* where a given thread is eligible to run *only* on specific processors, and *soft affinity*, where Windows 2000 favors scheduling specific threads on specific processors, usually for performance reasons.

Hard affinity is specified at the process and thread level using a processor affinity mask. The Win32 API calls to accomplish this are straightforward. First, a thread issues a GetProcessAffinityMask call referencing a process handle, which returns a 32-bit SystemAffinityMask. Each bit in the SystemAffinityMask represents a configured processor. Then, the program calls SetProcessAffinityMask with a corresponding 32-bit affinity mask that indicates the processors that threads from the process can be dispatched on. Figure 5-4 illustrates the use of this function in Taskman, which allows you to set a process's affinity mask dynamically, subject to the usual security restrictions that allow Taskman to operate only on foreground-eligible processes by default. There is a corresponding SetThreadAffinityMask call to override the process settings for specific threads. Once hard affinity is set, threads are eligible to be dispatched only on specific processors. This chapter concludes with a section discussing when setting a processor affinity mask for certain applications can be very desirable for performance reasons. Along the way, it is necessary to tackle several related multiprocessing topics to consider this important configuration and tuning strategy.

Suppose that following an interrupt, an application program thread becomes ready to run, and multiple processors are idle. First, Windows 2000 must select the processor on which to run the ready thread. This decision is based on performance. If the

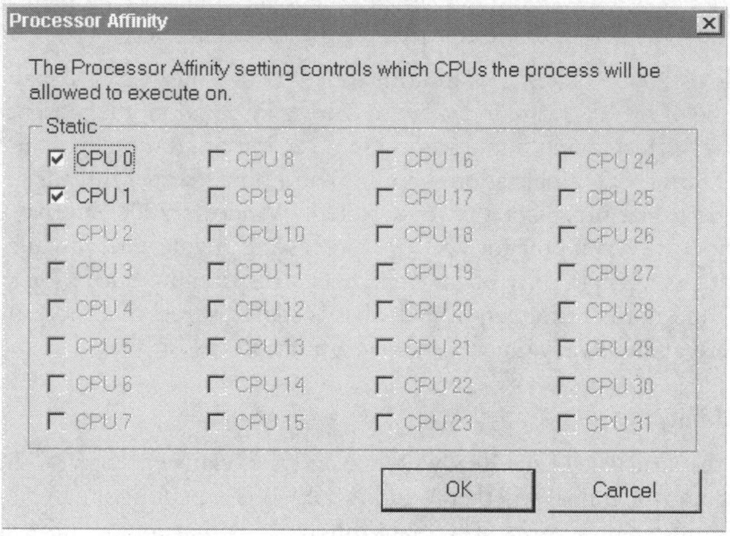

Figure 5-4. Setting a process's processor affinity mask using Taskman

thread was previously dispatched within the last Scheduler quantum (you remember the Scheduler time-slice quantum, don't you?), Windows 2000 attempts to schedule the thread on that processor, which works as long as the current thread has a higher priority than the thread that is already running there or the ideal processor happens to be idle. This is known as soft affinity. By scheduling the thread back on the same processor where it just ran, Windows 2000 hopes that a good deal of the thread's code and data from the previous execution interval are still present in that processor's cache. The difference in instruction execution rate between a cache "cold start," when a thread is forced to fault its way through its frequently accessed code and data, and a "warm start," when the cache is preloaded, can be substantial. However, Windows 2000 is willing to schedule the waiting thread on a different processor if the desired processor is busy with a higher-priority task.

Serialization and locking

The Scheduler code in Windows 2000 can run in multiple threads concurrently. Therefore, Windows 2000 must ensure that two processors do not try and run the same ready thread at the same time. This is just one example of a more general integrity issue in a multiprocessor. Because shared-memory data structures can be accessed by multiple threads concurrently, a *serialization* or *locking* mechanism is necessary to ensure that independent processors do not, for example, select the same thread off the Ready Queue at the same time. To prevent this, the shared-memory locations associated with the Windows 2000 Scheduler's dispatching queue are locked so that threads are only added or removed from the Ready Queue one at a time. We look at this serialization mechanism more closely in a moment. Serialization services are one of the key functions performed by the Windows 2000 operating system. (The current fashion in OS design is that about the *only* function performed in the low-level operating system microkernel is serialization. That is how fundamental serialization and locking are!) Windows 2000 must ensure that kernel threads running on multiple processors serialize before accessing its shared internal data structures. Windows 2000 also provides serialization services to application programs with similar requirements.

Shared-memory multiprocessor programming model

One reason shared-memory multiprocessors are so popular is that, with minor exceptions, programs that run on uniprocessors can run unmodified on shared-memory multiprocessors. In addition, almost any multithreaded application will likely benefit from having a choice of processors to run on—any thread can run on any available processor in an SMP. However, extreme care must be exercised to prevent multiple threads in your application from accessing and changing shared data structures in parallel. To help developers, the Windows 2000 operating system provides a complete set of platform-independent serialization services, courtesy of the HAL, for use by both application programs and kernel mode drivers. These thread synchronization services are used to ensure that Windows 2000 applications are "thread-safe," i.e., capable of executing correctly on a multiprocessor. This set of thread synchronization services allows programmers to implement complex, multithreaded applications without having to understand the underlying hardware mechanisms on a multiprocessor, which are platform-specific. Understanding the performance ramifications of shared-memory multiprocessors does require some knowledge of the hardware, however.

Let's look at the execution of a multithreaded program running on a multiprocessor. Each ready and waiting thread runs independently, acquiring a processor when one is free and the specific thread is the highest priority task in the dispatcher Schedule Ready Queue. Threads from within a single process may need to communicate with each other from time to time and are likely to share access to common, global variables. While one thread is actively changing global values, it is necessary to block other threads from accessing them until after the modifications are complete. Imagine a program like the one illustrated in Figure 5-5 that operates on some common list structures and shares a copy of a common piece of code to access and update these shared data structures. Programmatically, it is necessary to *serialize* access to common data structures that can be referenced by multiple threads executing in parallel. Using serialization, one thread at a time gains exclusive access to these data structures in order to change them, potentially forcing other threads to wait if they require access to the data structures being changed. Serialization services are used to protect shared data structures so that modifications to shared data on a multiprocessor proceed one at a time. In Figure 5-5, Thread 1 obtains the lock to a critical section and proceeds to execute it, while Thread 2 blocks waiting for the lock.

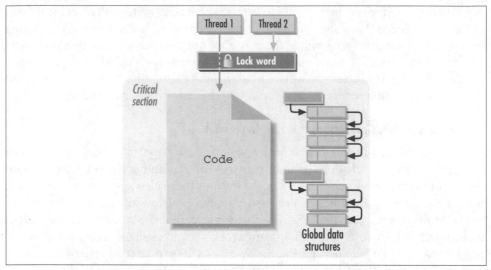

Figure 5-5. Critical sections

Serialization services to ensure that only one thread at a time can access shared-memory locations are at the heart of Windows 2000, just like any multiprocessor operating system kernel. The precise mechanism for serialization is processor-specific, located within the HAL. The Intel instruction set provides a LOCK prefix, which indicates that the instruction that follows serializes *across* all processing engines. From a hardware perspective, the LOCK prefix wraps a shared-memory bus LOCK# signal around successive memory fetch and store commands. The LOCK prefix is designed to be coded along with an instruction like CMPXCHG (which works on a memory word) or BTS (which operates on a bit) to test and set a value in memory in a single instruction execution cycle. (The frequently used XCHG serializing instruction for operating on shared memory has an implicit LOCK associated with it.) Instructions coded with the LOCK prefix are guaranteed to run uninterrupted and gain exclusive access to the designated memory location for the duration of the operation.

In programming terms, serialization is commonly referred to as *locking* a particular section of code involved in updating shared data structures so that it can only be executed by one thread at a time. A shared code fragment that requires locking because it updates shared memory is called a *critical section*. To gain access to the code inside a critical section, a thread must first acquire the *lock word* associated with it. This is a designated memory location that, for example, contains a zero value if no thread is executing the code, and a nonzero value if some thread is.

A thread attempting to enter a critical section first tests the value of the lock, not a trivial matter when a multiprocessor is serving two or more threads independently. If the thread determines that the critical section is not locked, it is free to enter and execute the critical section of code. As the thread enters a critical section, it sets the lock word. The fact that the lock word is set acts as a signal to any other thread trying to gain access to the routine.

The LOCK prefix in front of a CMPXCHG instruction allows a program to test and set a lock value in memory in a single instruction. On a multiprocessor, this memory read and update is guaranteed to be *atomic*. That means the instruction runs uninterrupted and is immediately visible to all other processors with access to shared memory when it is executed. Another thread attempting to gain access to the locked critical section must wait until the lock is released.

When a thread holding the lock has completed its update, it issues another locked XCHG instruction to reset the lock word and allow blocked threads to enter the protected code. What to do about a thread that terminates while it holds a lock is one of the big problems programmers developing multithreaded applications face. It is easy to imagine scenarios where a thread executing a critical section fails, leaving the lock set. Surviving threads remain blocked and the entire process hangs. This is not a pretty sight.

Windows 2000 serialization services

The Windows 2000 HAL abstracts several serialization primitives that rely on the LOCK prefix, coded with a suitable instruction like CMPXCHG or XCHG. Programs running under Windows 2000 that need to lock data structures call OS systems services to perform serialization on their behalf so that programmers do not need to understand the underlying processor hardware details. Windows 2000 supports three Win32 serialization objects: *critical sections* (called just "sections" in System Monitor), *semaphores*, and *mutexes*. Using System Monitor, you can keep track of the number of sections, semaphores, and mutexes that have been created by looking at the corresponding counters in the Object object. Figure 5-6 illustrates the synchronization objects created when we launched Internet Explorer, Excel, Word, and Outlook from a desktop PC running Windows 2000 Professional. If you are writing your own applications that perform sophisticated multithreading, these counters may be of interest. Otherwise, you are unlikely to ever need to monitor these counters.

The Windows 2000 serialization services make it relatively easy for a programmer to write code that will execute correctly on a multiprocessor. Not only does the programmer not have to deal with the underlying hardware, but the code is also portable across different hardware environments. A *critical section* object in Windows 2000 can be used to synchronize access to a shared code segment among multiple threads from a single process. A *mutex* (an abbreviation for *mutual exclusion*) object is a similar construct that can be used to synchronize threads from *different* processes. Mutexes are owned by threads and support behavior to signal any remaining threads that an owning thread has terminated without releasing the mutex, allowing for application recovery in this environment. Windows 2000 calls a mutex held by a terminated thread *abandoned*. Your stranded thread receiving a call-back when a

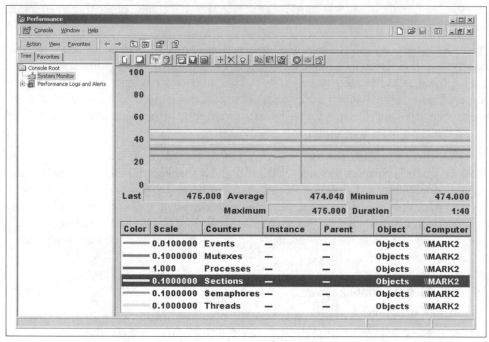

Figure 5-6. Monitoring sections, semaphores, and mutexes using Performance Monitor

mutex is abandoned allows your application to recover from this sort of catastrophic failure, which would otherwise cause it to hang. Finally, counting *semaphores* implement slightly more complicated semantics to keep track of, for example, multiple readers accessing shared data while a writer thread waiting for exclusive control of the critical section waits until the resource is totally free.

While the serialization services Windows 2000 provides make it easier to program multithreaded applications that execute correctly on a multiprocessor, building such applications is never easy. It is very difficult for most programmers to deal with multiple threads executing at the same time, and independent threads can interact in such complex ways that it is hard for even experienced programmers to anticipate them in advance.

Shared-Memory Multiprocessor Scalability

Shared-memory multiprocessors running SMP operating systems are the most common breed of multiprocessor. A great deal is known about hardware performance in this context. As discussed previously, any multithreaded application will likely benefit from having a choice of processors to run on, and in an SMP any thread can run on any available processor. Even single-threaded applications may benefit, since multiple applications can run in parallel. Because a dual processor system running Windows

2000 can dispatch two threads at a time, not just one, it seems reasonable to assume the dual processor configuration is twice as powerful as having a single engine to do the work. To see why this isn't exactly so, we will need to investigate a few aspects of shared-memory multiprocessor *scalability*.

Shared-memory multiprocessors have some well-known scalability limitations. They seldom provide perfect linear scalability. Each time you add a processor to the system, you do get a corresponding boost in overall performance, but with each additional processor the boost you get tends to diminish. It is even possible to reach a point of diminishing returns, where adding another processor actually reduces overall capacity. In this section we discuss several fundamental issues that impact multiprocessing scalability, including:

- The overhead of multiprocessor synchronization
- Multiprocessor-related pipeline stalls caused by cache coherence conflicts
- Cycles wasted by code executing spin locks

Understanding these sources of performance degradation in a shared-memory multiprocessor will help us in examining and interpreting the measurement data available on a Windows 2000 multiprocessor.

One thing to be careful about is that the processors in an SMP may look busy, but if you look inside the processors, you will find they are not performing as much productive work as you thought. The way to look inside, of course, is to use the Pentium counters. In the last chapter, we saw that the internal measurements of instruction execution rate (IER) generally track Processor % Processor Time very well on a single engine system. However, on a multiprocessor, internal IER and external processor busy measures may not correspond in the same expected way.

Figure 5-7, taken from a two-way multiprocessor, illustrates this essential point. The screen on the left shows the Task Manager histogram of processor utilization on this machine. Notice that both engines are running at near 100% utilization. This configuration contains two 200 MHz Pentium Pro machines. Remember, on a uniprocessor, a good rule of thumb is to expect performance at or near two machine cycles per instruction (CPI). This translates into capacity of about 100,000,000 instructions per second on a 200 MHz P6. The screen on the right shows actual measurements for one of these engines at only 12,345,000 instructions per second, or a CPI of about 16.7. This machine is delivering only about 12% of its rated performance—notice over 146 million resource-related stalls, too. Making sure that an expensive four- or eight-way multiprocessor server configuration is performing up to its capacity is not a trivial affair.

Speed-up factors

When we talk about scalability in the context of either multiprocessors or parallel processors, we are referring to our basic desire to harness the power of more than

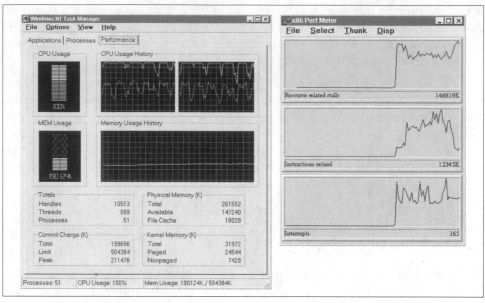

Figure 5-7. Multiprocessor scalability issues force you to look inside the processor

one processor to solve a common problem. The goal of a dual processor design is to apply double the CPU horsepower to a single problem and solve it in half the time. The goal of a quad processor is to apply quadruple the processing power and solve problems in one quarter the time. The term *speed-up factor* refers to our expectation that a multiprocessor design will improve the amount of time it takes to process some multithreaded workload. If a multiprocessing design achieved a speed-up factor of 1, then two processors would provide fully twice the power of a single engine. This would be perfect linear scalability, something shared-memory multiprocessors are just not capable of. A reasonable expectation is for a speed-up factor in the range of about 0.85. This means that two Intel processors tied together would be able to function at only about 85% efficiency. Together, the two would provide 1.7 times the power of a standalone processor. An improvement, but certainly a more marginal and less cost-effective one than the ideal. It turns out that Windows 2000 running on Intel hardware provides MP scalability in that range.

What happens when you add a third, fourth, or even more processors? The best models of shared memory multiprocessor performance suggest that the machines get progressively less efficient as you add more processors to the shared bus. However, with proper care and feeding, multiprocessor configurations with quite good scalability can be configured, although this requires skill and effort. We explore the configuration and tuning of multiprocessing workloads later in this chapter.

Microsoft reported in 1996 that the symmetric multiprocessing support built for Windows NT Version 4.0 sported a speed-up factor of 0.85. Figure 5-8 compares the theoretical prospects for linear speed-up in a multiprocessor design to the actual (projected) scalability of Windows NT Version 4.0 based on the measurements reported by Microsoft. The projection used here is a guess, of course, and your mileage may vary, but it is based on the formula Gunther[*] recommends for predicting multiprocessor scalability, and is consistent with a number of published benchmarking results.[†] Actual performance is very workload-dependent, as we discuss shortly. Figure 5-8 illustrates that actual performance of a multiprocessor running Windows NT falls far short of the ideal linear speed-up. In fact, beyond four multiprocessors, the projection is that adding more engines hardly boosts performance at all. Many published benchmark results of Windows NT multiprocessors evidence similar behavior. Moreover, after a certain point (more than 12 processors), adding additional engines actually degrades overall performance. The Windows NT multiprocessor scalability is typical of general-purpose operating systems—no worse, no better. To achieve anywhere near linear scalability requires highly engineered, special-purpose parallel processing hardware and complementary operating system services to match. We review some of the factors impacting shared-memory multiprocessor scalability in more detail later.

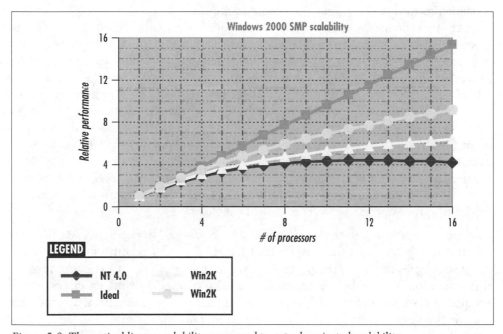

Figure 5-8. Theoretical linear scalability compared to actual projected scalability

---

[*] Neil J. Gunther, *The Practical Performance Analyst*. New York: McGraw-Hill, 1998.

[†] For instance, see the review article on eight-way scalability in the September 1998 *Windows NT Magazine* at *http://winntmag.com/Magazine/Article.cfm?IssueID=58&ArticleID=3781*.

Windows 2000 incorporates some further enhancements designed to improve multi-processor scalability. Microsoft implemented a new HAL function called *queued spin locks* that exploits a new Intel instruction on the Pentium III. It is not clear just how much this new function will help on large-scale 8- and 16-way machines. Figure 5-8 suggests two possibilities, both reflecting a relatively marginal increase in multiprocessor scalability to 0.90 or possibly even 0.95.

To summarize, it is simply not possible to string processor after processor together and double, triple, quadruple, etc., the amount of total processing power available. The principal obstacle of shared-memory designs, which are quite simple from the standpoint of the programmer, is that they typically encounter a bottleneck in accessing shared-memory locations using the shared system memory bus. To understand the nature of this bottleneck, let's proceed to a discussion of the sources of performance degradation in a multiprocessor. We now look at the performance impact of serializing instructions, as well as other multiprocessor cache effects, including the extra cycles consumed by spin lock code.

Serializing instructions. The first noticeable multiprocessor effect is the performance impact of serializing LOCKed instructions. Instructions coded with the LOCK prefix are guaranteed to run uninterrupted and gain exclusive access to the designated memory locations. Locking the shared-memory bus delays any threads executing on other processors that need access to memory locations not currently resident in cache. In addition, there are a number of hardware-oriented operations performed by the operating system that implicitly serialize by locking the shared-memory bus on an Intel shared-memory multiprocessor. These include setting the active task state segment (TSS), which is performed during a context switch of any type. Intel hardware also automatically serializes updates of the Page Directory Entries and Page Table Entries that are used in translating virtual memory addresses to real memory locations. (This impacts the page replacement algorithm that Windows 2000 uses on Intel multiprocessors, as we will see in the next chapter.)

Intel documentation (see the *Intel Architecture Software Developer's Guide: Volume 3, System Programming Guide*, especially Chapter 7) describes some specific serializing instructions that force the processor executing them to drain the entire instruction execution pipeline before executing the instruction. Following execution of the serializing instruction, the pipeline is started up again. These serializing instructions include privileged operations that move values into internal Control and Debug Registers, for example. Serializing instructions also have the effect on the P6 of forcing the processor to re-execute out-of-order instructions. The performance impact of draining the instruction execution pipeline and re-executing micro-ops ought to be obvious.

As discussed in the previous chapter, current-generation Pentium and Pentium Pro Intel processors are pipelined, superscalar architectures. The performance impact of executing an instruction serialized with the LOCK prefix includes potentially stalling the pipelines of other processors executing instructions until the instruction that requires serialization frees up the shared-memory bus. As you can imagine, this can be a fairly big performance hit, too, which is solely a consequence of running your program in a multiprocessor environment. The cost of both sorts of instruction serialization contribute to at least some of the less-than-linear scalability that we can expect in a multiprocessor. This cost is very difficult to quantify, and certainly workload-dependent. Moreover, there is also very little one can do about this source of degradation. Without serializing instructions, multiple processors would simply not work reliably.

A final source of multiprocessor interference is interprocessor signaling instructions. These are instructions issued on one processor to signal another processor, for example, to wake it up to process a pending interrupt. Interprocessor signaling is quite expensive in performance terms.

Cache effects. In Chapter 4, we discussed how essential on-board CPU caching is to the performance of pipelined processors. Intel waited to introduce pipelining until there was enough real estate available on its 486 chips to incorporate an on-board cache. It should not be a big surprise to learn that one secondary effect of multiprocessor coordination and serialization is that it makes caching less effective. This, in turn, reduces the processor's instruction execution rate. To understand why SMPs impact cache effectiveness, we soon take a detour into the realm of cache coherence. From a configuration and tuning perspective, one intended effect of setting up an application to run with processor affinity is to improve cache effectiveness and increase the instruction execution rate. Direct measurements of both instruction execution rate and caching efficiency, fortunately, are available via the Pentium counters. A freeware tool called CPUmon, available at *http://www.sysinternals.com/ntw2k/ freeware/cpumon.shtml*, supports the Pentium counters under Windows 2000.*

Spin locks. If two threads are attempting to access the same serializable resource, one thread will acquire the lock, which then blocks the other one until the lock is released. But what should the thread that is blocked waiting on a critical section do while it is waiting? An application program in Windows 2000 is expected to use a

---

* Several examples in this chapter illustrate the use of the older Pentium counter tool Microsoft provided in the NT 4.0 Resource Kit. This utility is no longer available in the Windows 2000 Resource Kit—in fact, the 4.0 version blue-screens on a Windows 2000 machine. The Pentium counter tool in the NT 4.0 Reskit did not always work as designed anyway. There were many environments where you could not succeed in getting the *P5ctrs.dll* Perflib DLL to report on Pentium counters through Perfmon. On a multiprocessor with multiple engines, the *P5stat.sys* device driver was supposed to enable P6 measurements on multiple processors, reporting multiple instances for the various counters. Using the x86 Perf Meter program, *P5perf.exe*, however, you are only able to look at one processor at a time, and you cannot tell which one. As a Resource Kit tool sold "as is" with no support, Microsoft was under no obligation to fix these deficiencies. When Microsoft dropped support for its Pentium counters tool in Windows 2000, it was fortunate that Version 2 of CPUmon that interfaces to the performance monitoring API was available from another supplier.

Win32 serialization service that puts the application to sleep until notified that the lock is available. Win32 serialization services arrange multiple threads waiting on a shared resource in a FIFO queue so that the queueing discipline is fair. This suggests that a key element of designing an application to run well on a shared-memory multiprocessor is to minimize the amount of processing time spent inside critical sections. The shorter the time spent executing inside a locked critical section of code, the less time other threads are blocked waiting to enter it. Much of the re-engineering work Microsoft did on NT 4.0 and again in Windows 2000 was to redesign the critical sections internal to the OS to minimize the amount of time kernel threads would have to wait for shared resources.

If critical sections are designed appropriately, then threads waiting on a locked critical section should not have long to wait! Moreover, while a thread is waiting on a lock, there may be nothing else for it do. For example, a thread waiting on the Windows 2000 Scheduler lock to acquire a ready thread to dispatch can perform no useful work until it has successfully acquired that lock. So, consider any blocked thread waiting on a lock that is a kernel thread. The resource the thread is waiting for is required before any other useful work on the processor can be performed. The wait can be expected to be of very short duration. Under these circumstances, the best thing to do may be to loop back and test for the availability of the lock again. We have already seen an example of code that tests for availability of a lock, then enters a critical section by setting the lock using a serializing instruction. If the same code finds the lock is already set and branches back to retest the lock, this code implements a *spin lock*. If you were able to watch this code's execution, it would appear to be spinning back and forth within a very tight loop of just a few instructions.

Spin locks are used in many, many different places throughout the operating system in Windows 2000, since operating system code waiting for a critical section to be unlocked often has nothing better to do during the (hopefully) very short waiting period. In addition, device drivers are required to use spin locks to protect data structures across multiple processors. Windows 2000 provides a standard set of spin lock services for device drivers to use in ISRs and kernel threads outside of ISRs. (See the DDK documentation on, for example, KeInitializeSpinLock, IoAcquireCancelSpinLock, and related services for more detail.) These standard services allow device drivers written in C language to be portable across versions of Windows NT running on different hardware. In Windows 2000, where these portability concerns are no longer present, these ready-made HAL runtime services still serve to insulate C language programmers from the intricacies of Intel's multiprocessing support.

In Windows NT Version 4.0, you can use the Thunk function in the x86 Perf Meter application in the Resource Kit (*pperf.exe*—the same application used to access the Pentium counters) to observe spin lock activity. For example, from the Thunk menu, select the *ntfs.sys* filesystem driver module, using *hal.dll* as the target module. Then select the KfAcquireSpinLock and KfReleaseSpinLock for monitoring, as illustrated in Figure 5-9. If you then generate some ntfs file metadata activity, like emptying the

Recycle bin, you will observe ntfs driver code using the HAL spin lock function to protect critical sections of code. Now consider a 2-, 4-, or 8-way multiprocessor with an ntfs filesystem. *ntfs.sys* functions can be executed on any processor where there is an executing thread that needs access to disk files. In fact, in multiprocessors it is likely that ntfs functions will execute concurrently (on different processors) from time to time. As Figure 5-9 illustrates, *ntfs.sys* uses HAL spin lock functions to protect critical sections of code, preserving the integrity of the filesystem in a multiprocessor environment.

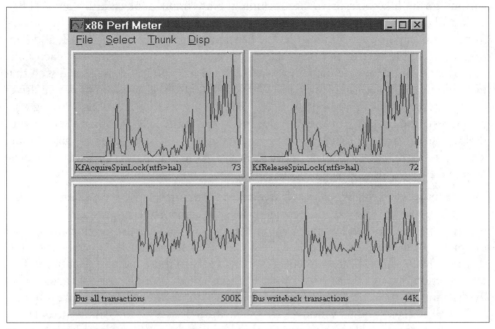

Figure 5-9. The Thunk function can be used to monitor spin lock activity

Spin lock code is effectively dormant when run on a single-processor system, but can consume (or waste, depending on your point of view) a significant number of processor cycles on a multiprocessor. Again, the use of spin locks is, to a large degree, unavoidable. The performance implication of spin locks is that processor utilization increases, but no useful work is actually being performed. In this way, simple measures of processor utilization can be misleading. Windows 2000 client applications care about throughput and response time, which may be degraded on a multiprocessor even as measurements of CPU utilization look rosy.

The combined impact of serializing instructions, interprocessor signaling, diminished cache effectiveness, and the consumption of processor cycles by spin lock code limit the scalability of shared-memory multiprocessors in Windows 2000 and other shared-memory multiprocessing operating systems. Furthermore, each additional processor added to the configuration amplifies these multiprocessor scalability factors. These factors make sizing, configuring, and tuning large-scale n-way Windows 2000 multi-processors a very tricky business. Just how tricky should become more apparent after considering the cache coherence problem in the next section.

Cache Coherence

The cache effects of running on a shared-memory multiprocessor are probably the most salient factors limiting the scalability of this type of computer architecture. The various forms of processor cache, including Translation Lookaside Buffers (TLBs), code and data caches, and branch prediction tables, all play a critical role in the performance of pipelined machines like the Pentium, Pentium Pro, Pentium II, and Pentium III. For the sake of performance, in a multiprocessor configuration each CPU retains its own private cache memory, as depicted in Figure 5-10. We have seen that multiple threads executing inside the Windows 2000 kernel or running device driver code concurrently can attempt to access the same memory locations. Propagating changes to the contents of memory locations cached locally to other engines with their own private copies of the same shared-memory locations is a major issue, known as the *cache coherence* problem in shared-memory multiprocessors. Cache coherence issues also have significant performance ramifications.

Maintaining cache coherence in a shared-memory multiprocessor is absolutely necessary for programs to execute correctly. While independent program execution threads operate independently of each other for the most part, sometimes they must interact. Whenever they read and write common or shared-memory data structures, threads must communicate and coordinate accesses to these memory locations. This coordination inevitably has performance consequences. We illustrate this side effect by drawing on the example discussed earlier, where two kernel threads are attempting to gain access to the Windows 2000 Scheduler Ready Queue simultaneously. A global data structure like the Ready Queue that may be accessed by multiple threads executing concurrently on different processors *must* be protected by a lock on a multiprocessor. Let's look at how a lock word value set by one thread on one processor is propagated to cache memory in another processor where another thread is attempting to gain access to the same critical section.

In Figure 5-10, Thread 0 running on CPU 0 that has just finished updating the Windows 2000 Scheduler Ready Queue is about to exit a critical section. Upon exiting the critical section of code, Thread 0 resets the lock word at location mem1 using a serializing instruction like XCHG. Instead of locking the bus during the execution of the XCHG instruction, the Intel P6 operates only on the cache line that contains mem1. This is to boost performance. The locked memory fetch and store that the instruction otherwise requires would stall the CPU 0 pipeline. In the Intel architecture, if the operand of a serializing instruction like XCHG is resident in processor cache in a multiprocessor configuration, then the P6 does not lock the shared-memory bus.

This is a form of *deferred write-back caching*, which is very efficient. Not only does the processor cache hardware use this approach to caching frequently accessed instructions and data, but so do Windows 2000 systems software and hardware cached disk controllers, for example.

In the interest of program correctness, updates made to private cache, which are deferred, ultimately must be applied to the appropriate shared-memory locations *before* any threads running on other processors attempt to access the same information. Moreover, as Figure 5-10 illustrates, there is an additional data integrity exposure because another CPU can (and frequently does) have the same mem1 location resident in cache. The diagram illustrates a second thread that is in a spin loop trying to enter the same critical section. This code continuously tests the contents of the lock word at mem1 until it is successful. For the sake of performance, the XCHG instruction running on CPU 1 also operates only on the cache line that contains mem1 and does not attempt to lock the bus because that would probably stall the other processor's instruction execution pipeline. We can see that unless there is some way to let CPU 1 know that code running on CPU 0 has *changed* the contents of mem1, the code on CPU 1 will spin in this loop forever. The Intel P6 processors solve this problem in maintaining cache coherence using a method conventionally called *snooping*.

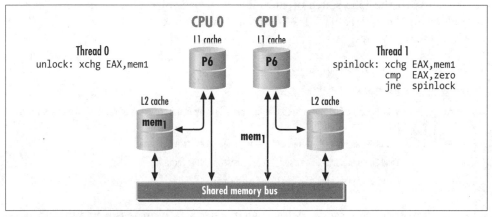

Figure 5-10. The cache coherence problem

MESI Snooping Protocol

Snooping protocols to maintain cache coherence have each processor listening to the shared-memory bus for changes in the status of cache resident addresses that other processors are operating on concurrently. Snooping requires that processors place the memory addresses of any shared cache lines being updated on the memory bus. All processors listen on the memory bus for memory references made by other processors that affect memory locations that are resident in their private cache; thus the term *snooping*. The term *snooping* also has the connotation that this method for keeping every processor's private cache memory synchronized can be performed in the background (which it is) without a major performance hit (which is true, but only up to a point). In practice, maintaining cache coherence is a complex process that interferes substantially with normal pipelined instruction execution and generates some serious scalability issues.

Let's illustrate how the Intel snooping protocol works, continuing with our Ready Queue lock word example. CPU 1, snooping on the bus, recognizes that the update to the mem1 address performed by CPU 0 *invalidates* its cache line containing mem1. Then, because the cache line containing mem1 is marked invalid, CPU 1 is forced to refetch mem1 from memory the very next time it attempts to execute the XCHG instruction inside the spin lock code. Of course, at this point CPU 0 has still not yet updated mem1 in memory. But snooping on the shared-memory bus, it discovers that CPU 1 is attempting to read the current value of mem1 from memory. CPU 0 intercepts and delays the request. Then CPU 0 writes the cache line containing mem1 back to memory. Then, and only then, is CPU 1 allowed to continue refreshing the corresponding line in its private cache and update the lock word.

The cache coherence protocol used in the Intel architecture is denoted *MESI*, which corresponds to the four states of each line in processor cache: *modified*, *exclusive*, *shared*, or *invalid* (see Table 5-1). At any one time, a line in cache is in one and only one of these four states.

Table 5-1. The states of the MESI cache coherence protocol

State	Description
Modified	Valid line, modified, guaranteed that this line only exists in this cache, the corresponding memory line is stale
Exclusive	Valid line, unmodified, guaranteed that this line only exists in this cache
Shared	Valid line, unmodified, line also exists in at least one other cache
Invalid	An invalid line that must be refreshed from memory

The MESI protocol very rigidly defines what actions each processor in a multiprocessor configuration must take based on the state of a line of cache and the attempt by another processor to act on the same data. The previous scenario illustrates just one set of circumstances that the MESI protocol is designed to handle. Let's revisit this example using the Intel MESI terminology.

Suppose that Thread 1 running in a spin lock on CPU 1 starts by testing the lock word at location mem1. The 32 bytes containing this memory location are brought into the cache and flagged *exclusive* because they are currently contained only in the CPU 1 cache. Meanwhile, when CPU 0 executes the first part of the XCHG instruction on mem1 designed to reset the lock, the 32 bytes containing this memory location are brought into the CPU 0 cache. CPU 1, snooping on the bus, detects CPU 0's interest in a line of cache that is currently marked exclusive and transitions this line from exclusive to shared. CPU 1 signals CPU 0 that it too has this line of memory in cache, so CPU 0 marks the line shared, too. The second part of the XCHG instruction updates mem1 in CPU 0 cache. The cache line resident in CPU 0 transitions from shared to modified as a result. Meanwhile, CPU 1, snooping on the bus, flags its corresponding cache line as *invalid*. Subsequent execution of the XCHG instruction within the original spin lock code executing on CPU 1 to acquire the lock finds the cache line invalid. CPU 1 then attempts to refresh the cache line from memory, locking the bus in the process to ensure coherent execution of all programs. CPU 0, snooping on the bus, blocks the memory fetch by CPU 1 because the state of that memory location in CPU 0 cache is *modified*. CPU 0 then writes the contents of this line of cache back to memory, reflecting the current data in CPU 0's cache. At this point, CPU 1's request for memory is honored, and the now current 32 bytes containing mem1 are brought into the CPU 1 cache. At the end of this sequence, both CPU 0 and CPU 1 have valid data in cache, with both lines in the shared state.

The MESI protocol ensures that cache memory in the various independently executing processors is consistent no matter what the other processors are doing. Clearly, what is happening in one processor can interfere with the instruction execution stream running on the other. With multiple threads accessing shared-memory locations, there is no avoiding this. These operations on shared memory stall the pipelines of the processors affected. For example, when CPU 0 snoops on the bus and finds another processor attempting to fetch a line of cache from memory that is resident in its private cache in a modified state, then whatever instructions CPU 0 is attempting to execute in its pipeline are suspended. Writing back modified data from cache to memory takes precedence because another processor is waiting. Similarly, CPU 1 running its spin lock code must update the state of that shared line of cache when CPU 0 resets the lock word. Once the line of cache containing the lock word is marked invalid on CPU 1, the serializing instruction issued on CPU 1 stalls the pipeline because cache must be refreshed from memory. The pipeline is stalled until CPU 0 can update memory and allow the memory fetch operation to proceed. All of this results in time-consuming delays that reduce the CPU instruction execution rate on *both* processors.

One not-so-obvious performance implication of snooping protocols is that they utilize the shared-memory bus heavily. Every time an instruction executing on one processor needs to fetch a new value from memory or update an existing one, it must place the designated memory address on the shared bus. The bus itself is a shared resource. With more and more processors executing, the bus tends to get quite busy. When the bus is in use, other processors must wait. Utilization of the shared-memory bus is likely to be the most serious bottleneck impacting scalability in multiprocessor configurations of three, four, or more processing engines.

Pentium Pro Hardware Counters

The measurement facility in the Intel P6 or Pentium Pro processors (including Pentium II, III, and IV) was strengthened to help hardware designers cope with the demands of more complicated multiprocessor designs. By installing the CPUmon freeware utility available for download at *http://www.sysinternals.com*, system administrators and performance analysts can access these hardware measurements. While the use of these counters presumes a thorough understanding of Intel multiprocessing hardware, we hope that the previous discussion of multiprocessor design and performance has given you the confidence to start using them to diagnose specific performance problems associated with large-scale Windows 2000 multiprocessors. The P6 counters provide valuable insight into multiprocessor performance, including direct measurement of the processor instruction rate, Level 2 cache, TLB, branch prediction, and the all-important shared-memory bus.

CPUmon, a freeware Pentium counter utility, lets you enable and then disable the Pentium counters for a specific interval, as illustrated in Figure 5-11. The CPUmon user interface, which separates the various counters that are available into different classes, is user-friendly. (CPUmon assigns the counters different names from the ones the x86 Perf Meter application does, which is confusing. Even more confusing, some of the available P6 counters are missing entirely from the program.) Once the Pentium counters you select are enabled, Version 2 of CPUmon provides a Perflib DLL that lets you view them continuously using System Monitor, as illustrated in Figure 5-12.

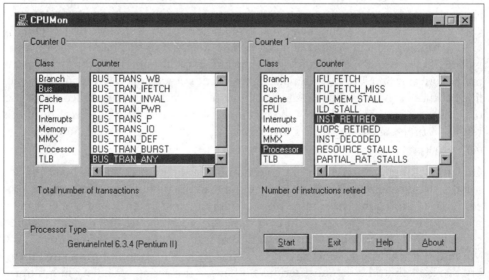

Figure 5-11. The CPUmon freeware utility is used to access the Pentium counters

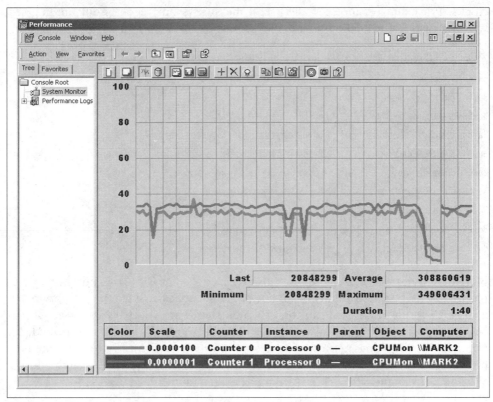

Figure 5-12. CPUmon lets you view Pentium counter measurements using System Monitor

Shared-Memory Bus Utilization Measurements

The shared-memory bus measurements can often shed the most light on multiprocessor performance. Table 5-2 lists the various P6 bus measurement counters, using the Microsoft counter names from the NT 4.0 Reskit's *counters.hlp*. The first observation we make looking at these counter names and their (unilluminating) Explain Text is that many of them are arcane and esoteric. To understand what "Bus DRDY asserted clocks/second" means might send us scurrying to the Intel architecture manuals, which, unfortunately, are of little use. A second observation, which may be triggered by viewing the counters under controlled conditions, is that some of them probably do not mean what they appear to. For example, the Bus LOCK asserted clocks/sec counter consistently appears to be zero on both uniprocessor and multiprocessor configurations. Not much help there. The shared-memory bus is driven at the processor clock rate, and some counter names use the term *cycles* while others use the term *clocks*. The two terms are interchangeable. Although not explicitly indicated, some counters that mention neither clocks nor cycles are also measured in clocks. For example, an especially useful measure is Bus requests outstanding/sec, which measures the total number of clocks the bus is busy.

Table 5-2. P6 shared-memory bus hardware measurements

Bus all transactions/sec	Bus invalidate transactions/sec
Bus BNR pin drive cycles/sec	Bus IO transactions/sec
Bus burst read transactions/sec	Bus LOCK asserted clocks/sec
Bus burst transactions (total)/sec	Bus memory transactions (total)/sec
Bus clocks receiving data/sec	Bus partial transactions/sec
Bus CPU drives HIT cycles/sec	Bus partial write transactions/sec
Bus CPU drives HITM cycles/sec	Bus read for ownership trans/sec
Bus deferred transactions/sec	Bus requests outstanding/sec
Bus DRDY asserted clocks/sec	Bus snoop stalled cycles/sec
Bus instruction fetches/sec	Bus writeback transactions/sec

Bus memory transactions and Bus all transactions measure the number of bus requests. The bus measurements are not processor-specific, since the memory bus is a shared component. If you run the CPUmon shareware utility, you can see all processors report nearly identical values for BUS_TRAN_ANY, while, as expected, the number of instructions retired is processor-specific (see Figure 5-13). The memory bus that the processors share is a single resource, subject to the usual queuing delays. We will derive a measure of bus queuing delay in a moment.

Now, let's look at some more P6 measurement data from a multiprocessor system. A good place to start is with Bus all transactions/sec, which, as noted, is the total number of bus requests. Figure 5-14 shows that when the bus is busy, it is usually due to memory accesses. Bus memory transactions/sec represent over 99% of all bus transactions. The measurement data is consistent with our discussion suggesting that bus utilization is often the bottleneck in shared-memory multiprocessors that utilize snooping protocols to maintain cache coherence. Every time any processor attempts to access main memory, it must first gain access to the shared bus.

Larger Level 2 caches help reduce bus traffic, but there are diminishing returns from caches that are, in effect, too big. Each time a memory location is fetched directly from a Level 1 or Level 2 cache, it is necessary to broadcast the address on the bus. At some point, larger caches do not result in significant improvements in the rate of cache hits, yet they increase the management overhead necessary to maintain cache coherence. In this regard, both the rate of Level 2 cache misses and the number of write-back memory transactions are relevant, as both actions drive bus utilization (see Figure 5-15). The P6 Level 2 cache performance measurements are especially useful in this context for evaluating different processor configurations from Intel and other vendors that have different amounts of Level 2 cache. By accessing this measurement data, you can assess the benefits of different configuration options directly.

Figure 5-13. CPUmon results for two separate processors

This is always a better method than relying on some rule-of-thumb value proposed by this or that performance expert, perhaps based on a measurement taken running a benchmark workload that does not reflect your own.

The Bus snoop stalled cycles/sec counter has intrinsic interest on a multiprocessor. A high rate of stalls due to snooping is a direct indicator of multiprocessor contention. See Figure 5-16, which again was measured on a two-way multiprocessor. The number of snooping-induced stalls is low here. Even though as a percentage of the total resource stalls they are practically insignificant here, this is still a measurement that bears watching.

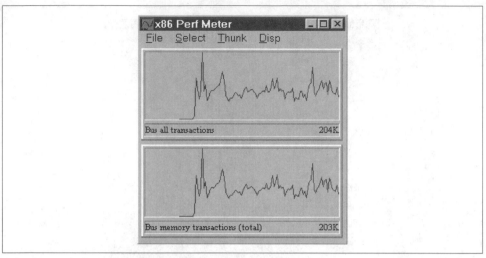

Figure 5-14. Memory transactions often represent over 99% of all bus transactions

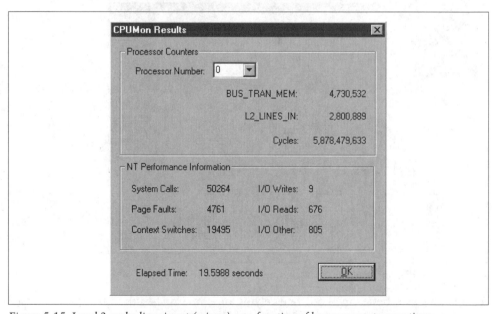

Figure 5-15. Level 2 cache lines input (misses) as a function of bus memory transactions

Next, consider the Bus requests outstanding counter, which is a direct measurement of bus utilization in clocks. By also monitoring Bus all transactions, you can derive a simple response time measure of bus transactions measured as the average clocks per transaction:

Average clocks per transactions = Bus requests outstanding ÷ Bus all transactions

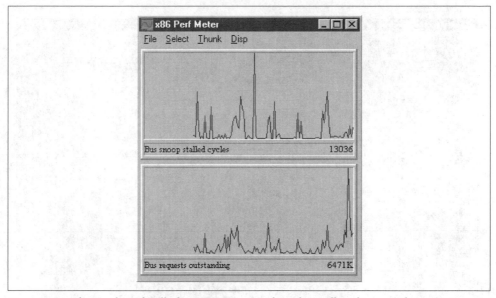

Figure 5-16. The number of stalls due to snooping is relatively small in this example

Assuming that contention for the shared-memory bus is a factor, saturation of the bus on an n-way multiprocessor will likely drive up bus transaction response time, measured in clocks per transaction on average. Figure 5-17, a Perfmon screen shot, provides a uniprocessor baseline for this calculation. Since Perfmon cannot perform any arithmetic calculations, we exported the chart data to a file so that it could be processed in an Excel spreadsheet. Using Excel, we divided Bus requests outstanding by Bus all transactions to derive the average number of clocks per transaction. (Bear in mind that we can access only two counters at a time. Since memory transactions typically represent more than 99% of all bus transactions, it is safe to assume that clock cycles calculated using this formula genuinely do reflect the time it takes the processor to access memory.) The average clocks per bus transaction in this example generally fall in the range of 10–30 clocks, with an average of about 18 clocks per transaction. These calculations are summarized in the chart shown in Figure 5-18. In the case of a uniprocessor, the memory bus is a dedicated resource and there is no contention. Now compare the uniprocessor baseline in Figure 5-18 to the two-way multiprocessor in Figure 5-19. Here the average clocks per transaction is about 30, coming in at the high end of the uniprocessor range. The average number of clocks per bus transaction increases because of queuing delays accessing the shared-memory bus in the multiprocessor. In a multiprocessor, there is bus contention. By tracking these P6 counters, you can detect environments where adding more processors to the system will not speed up processing any because the shared-memory bus is already saturated. Bus contention tends to set an upper limit on the performance of a multiprocessor configuration, and the P6 counters let you see this.

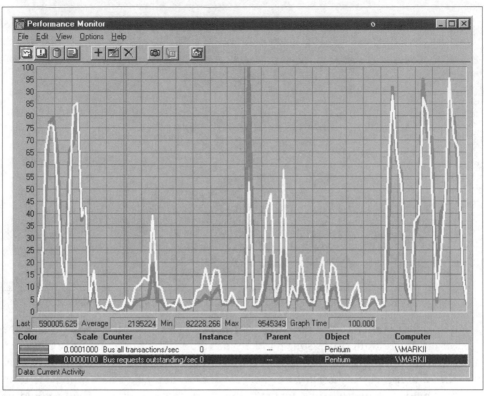

Figure 5-17. Tracking P6 bus measurements on a uniprocessor using Performance Monitor.

With the Pentium III, Intel introduced a new instruction called PAUSE, which reduces the bus contention that results from repeatedly executing spin lock code. The Windows 2000 HAL adds a new queued spin lock function that exploits the new hardware instruction where available. Device driver code trying to enter a critical section protected by a queued spin lock issues the PAUSE instruction, referencing the lock word protecting that piece of code. PAUSE halts the CPU until the lock word is changed by a different executing thread running on another processor. At that point, the PAUSEd processor wakes up and resumes execution.

The PAUSE instruction was designed to eliminate the bus transactions that occur when spin lock code repeatedly tries to test and set a memory location. Instead of repeatedly executing code that tests the value of a lock word to see if it is safe to enter a critical section, queued spin locks wait quietly without generating any bus transactions. Since saturation of the shared memory bus is an inherent problem in shared-memory multiprocessors, this innovation should improve the scalability of Windows 2000. At the same time, Intel designers also boosted the performance of the Pentium III system bus significantly, which should also improve multiprocessor scalability under Windows 2000.

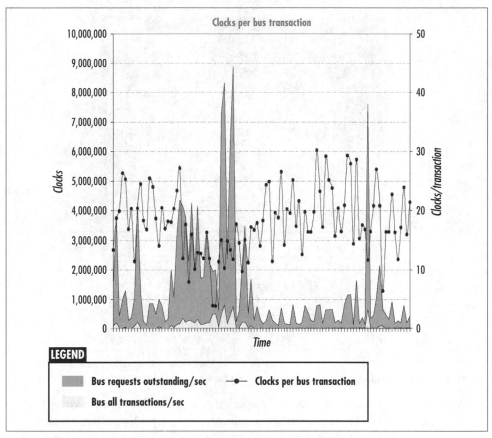

Figure 5-18. Average clocks per bus transaction on a uniprocessor

Optimization and SMP Configuration Tuning

Having identified the major issues in multiprocessor scalability and performance, it is now time to turn our attention to what can be done about them. In this section we address some of the important performance issues that developers of scalable server applications must face when confronted with multiprocessors. Our discussion here is cursory, as we cannot do this complex subject justice in this brief space. Suffice to say that building large, complicated application software for any platform is very difficult, and Windows 2000 is no exception. Hopefully, we will succeed in laying down some basic helpful guidelines.

Then, we review the steps that system administrators can take to get the most out of large, multiprocessor configurations. Unfortunately, very few applications provide tuning knobs that are useful in a multiprocessing environment beyond the ability to control the number of threads they create. Since only a multithreaded application can take advantage of multiple processors, being able to control the number of

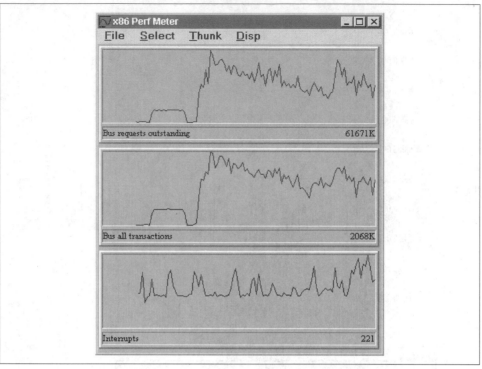

Figure 5-19. Average clocks per bus transaction on a two-way multiprocessor

threads created by the application is something, at least. There are two important exceptions, however. There are tuning parameters to control threading, priority, and processor affinity that influence the performance of SQL Server running on a multiprocessor. We also look at a useful processor affinity setting for network interface cards. However, because most applications lack the appropriate tuning knobs, we then turn to a discussion of a third-party package that assists in multiprocessor configuration and tuning. The NCR SMP Utilization Manager add-on to Windows 2000 provides valuable assistance in configuring very large, n-way multiuser Windows 2000 servers.

Configuring Server Applications for Multiprocessing

The programming model used in Windows 2000 is designed around execution threads and processes, where threads are scheduled by the operating system, not by the process that created them. If you are writing a server application in Unix, a call to fork( ) or vfork( ) creates a child process that runs independently of the parent. The same application written for Windows 2000 would probably call CreateThread to create independent processing threads. (Of course, you can continue to use multiple processes in Windows 2000. The Win32 API call CreateProcess corresponds to the standard Unix fork call to spawn a child process.) Many applications ported to Windows 2000 from Unix betray their operating system heritage and use fork instead of CreateThread. This is partially because it is a big effort to rewrite code that already works. Moreover, developers trying to maintain some degree of cross-platform compatibility with their applications are understandably reluctant to introduce platform-specific optimizations. Nevertheless, to achieve the best results on Windows 2000, programmers should adopt Windows 2000's programming model that relies on multiple threads running within a process. Generally, wherever multiple processes are used in Unix, the Win32 programmer should use multiple threads.

Multithreaded Applications

A key advantage of threads is that they share the 4 GB virtual memory address space of the parent process (more about virtual memory management in Windows 2000 in Chapter 6), so they require less work for the operating system to create and destroy. Sharing an address space means that running multiple threads within the same process is also safer, since those threads can communicate using private virtual memory. This tends to be significantly safer than using shared memory for interprocess communication (IPC), which Windows 2000 also supports. A bug that fatally overruns an array or a list structure in private virtual memory damages the application only and is easily recovered by the OS. A similar bug in shared memory can damage other applications and, potentially, the operating system itself.

Having decided to use threads, the next question is, "How many threads does my application need?" There are no hard-and-fast rules for creating scalable server applications, but some practical performance guidelines can be discussed. Even though creating multiple threads entails less overhead than creating multiple processes, and there is no practical limit on the number of threads a server application can create, managing multiple threads does require *some* system overhead. For example, system and application memory is required for every thread that is created, so you should not create lots of unnecessary threads. But consider a server application that supports multiple clients. How many clients can your application support on a Windows 2000 server with a single 200 MHz processor and 64 MB of memory? How about on a Windows 2000 server with eight 400 MHz processors and 1 GB of memory? Not only does the second system use processing engines that are twice as fast, there are eight times as many of them, with plenty more memory to boot. You will likely need lots of threads for your server application to take advantage of all this extra computing capacity. For instance, unless it can run eight threads concurrently, the application cannot utilize all the processing resources that the bigger server has to offer. On the other hand, the right number of threads on the eight-way server will probably overwhelm the smaller-scale, one-processor server system.

Normally, because Windows 2000 systems scale across such a wide range of environments, you must establish useful defaults that scale with the number of processors, but ultimately let the system administrator override these defaults by providing a tuning knob. Consider, for example, the approach taken in Microsoft Internet Information Server (IIS) to setting performance and tuning options. The Performance tab in the WWW Service Master Properties dialog box is illustrated in Figure 5-20. The dialog box simply asks the system administrator to specify the number of HTTP hits per day expected: fewer than 10,000, fewer than 100,000, or more than 100,000. Presumably, IIS does the rest: allocating the right number of threads and the right amount of memory for caching HTML pages based on this setting.

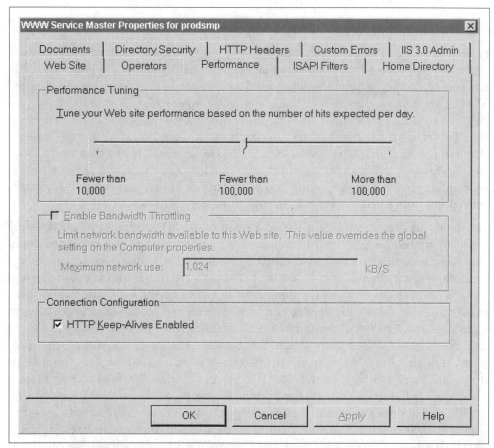

Figure 5-20. IIS threading and memory usage is automatically adjusted using this dialog box

This kind of sweeping tuning control knob introduces some obvious problems. For instance, what is the best setting to use if you expect only 20,000 hits per day? Or what if you expect 2 million hits? This simplistic tuning knob also ignores basic issues involving workload characterization that are crucial to performance and tuning of this server application: how large are the HTML files, what is the distribution of their access, can they be cached effectively, etc. It also ignores the hardware environment: the processor, memory, disk, and networking resources available to process this workload. Happily, IIS, like many other Windows 2000 server applications, has several Registry settings designed to configure and control the performance of the application with considerably greater precision.

The first consideration for a server application that needs to scale across such a wide range of computing hardware is to create more worker threads on larger systems. One approach is to examine the hardware environment by looking at the Registry during initialization to see how many engines are available, and then create threads accordingly. Another is to provide an external parameter that permits an administrator to fine-tune the number of threads that your application creates. We have already seen a number of well-behaved Windows applications that have such controls, including the Windows 2000 File Server function in *services.exe*, MS SQL Server, MS Exchange, and even the Windows 2000 kernel itself.

Thread Pooling

A more dynamic method of scaling applications is to create a *pool* of worker threads, automatically increasing or decreasing the number of threads depending on the demand. This is how many server applications are built. Often, worker threads structured as a pool are dispatched from an internal queue as units of work arrive, as depicted in Figure 5-21. As work requests arrive, the application:

1. Wakes up a Receiver thread, which
2. Associates the unit of work with a work item on the available queue, then
3. Wakes up a worker thread sleeping on the available thread queue to begin processing the request.
4. If no worker threads are available, the Receiver thread queues the work item and signals a Control thread to create an additional worker thread.
5. Meanwhile, any worker thread that completes its processing on behalf of some unit of work posts the Sender thread, and
6. Checks the work queue prior to going back to sleep.

Usually, control-oriented Sender and Receiver threads are simple programs that manage the input and output queues, and the worker threads perform the bulk of the actual application-related processing. Increasing the number of worker threads created in the pool (and the number of available work items) is one way to make sure the application scales on multiprocessors. With all these different threads potentially executing concurrently on a multiprocessor, it is easy to see how complicated the interaction between threads can get. Obviously, using Windows 2000 synchronization objects to manage shared data structures like the work unit queues and the thread pool itself is critical to ensure the application runs correctly on a multiprocessor.

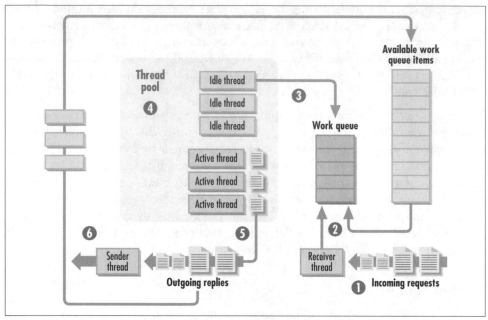

Figure 5-21. The structure of a thread pooling application

Given this application architecture, how many worker threads should be created? To find the answer, view the application as an M/M/n queuing system. The optimal number of processing threads, n, depends on the rate at which work arrives, the average amount of time a worker thread spends processing a request, and the capacity of the machine to perform the work involved. (In this chapter, we are concerned only with CPU resources, but memory, disk, and networking resources all need to be considered.) Each worker thread available represents only an *opportunity* to receive service because the resource needed (the processor, the disk, the database) may itself be overloaded. But it is safe to assume that if the number of items waiting in the work queue is greater than one per processor, and the processors are less than, say, 60% utilized, increasing the number of worker threads will not do any harm and may actually do some good.

If increasing the number of available threads results in increased processor utilization (a good enough measure of application throughput for now), then you are on the right track. It may seem counterintuitive, but you can then continue to increase the number of threads until the processor saturates at close to 100% busy. Of course, at this point you have worker threads waiting in the Ready Queue for CPU service, but this is merely changing where the work requests are queued: from the application work queue to the processor Ready Queue. From a pure performance standpoint, it does not make much difference *where* application work units are queued. What may happen, though, is that other workloads on the same system suffer because the processors are overloaded. That consideration may force you to throttle back the thread pooling application so it does not overwhelm all other work on the system.

When a unit of work arrives requesting some service and no worker threads are available, the thread pooling application creates a new thread to process it. Just in case the entire thread pool gets backed up waiting for some resource (and because the overhead of thread creation is not completely negligible), server applications usually establish some upper limit on the total number of worker threads that can be created. Of course, if an existing thread is available, it is used instead. Normally, threads created during a period of heavy demand are retained for some time afterwards, even though they are idle. It is more efficient to keep a few idle worker threads alive than for your application to be constantly creating and destroying threads.

To summarize, multithreaded Windows 2000 server applications that operate a thread pool dynamically create threads as needed, up to some user-defined upper limit. As a general rule, if the application is currently running at or near its maximum allotment of threads, the work queue is backed up, and processor resources are available, then it is time to increase the limit on creating new threads. This rule of thumb is far from foolproof, unfortunately. If worker threads are consistently blocked at the disk, for example, adding more processing threads is not likely to provide any performance relief. Once the work item queue is depleted, the thread pooling application is likely to respond to further work requests with an error condition, which is also something that can be avoided by increasing the size of the work item pool.

Monitoring Thread Pooling Applications

An application that relies on thread pooling must provide feedback on its performance so the administrator can set a reasonable thread upper limit. The thread pooling application should monitor the rate at which work requests arrive, the current size of the request queues, the current number of threads in use, and the number of available threads. Of course, direct measurement of request wait time and execution time is extremely useful, too. Instrumentation added to the application should report some of the following useful performance metrics, ideally using a Perflib DLL, so that the application measurements can be correlated with other aspects of system activity:

- The current number of worker threads in use
- The maximum number of worker threads in use
- The number of times the application needs to create a new worker thread but is already running at the maximum thread allocation limit
- The current number of the available (free) and occupied (busy) work queue items
- The number of times arriving work is delayed or deferred because there were no work items on the available queue

With applications that do not report response time metrics, you can compute average response time using Little's Law if you know the transaction arrival rate and the number of transactions in the system (namely, the number of busy work queue items, including requests waiting in the work queue). As discussed in Chapter 1, Little's Law postulates:

$$Queue\ Length\ =\ Arrival\ Rate\ \times\ Response\ Time$$

Under the right circumstances, we can apply Little's Law to calculate response when measures of the arrival rate and the number of concurrent work requests in the system are available. The Microsoft Exchange Message Transport component, for example, provides performance counters that measure the rate of incoming and outgoing messages, the length of the work queue, and the number of concurrent threads in use. It does not report response time, but you can estimate it using Little's Law.

With these basic reporting requirements in mind, let's look at some other Windows 2000 server applications that utilize thread pooling and see how they stack up. Table 5-3 summarizes the thread pooling measurement statistics that IIS Active Server Pages and Windows 2000 networked file services supply. These two thread pooling applications are extensively instrumented, as discussed in detail in the next sections.

Table 5-3. ASP and file server thread pooling application performance counters

Measurement statistic	Active Server Pages counters	Server and Server Work Queues Counters
Active worker threads	Requests Executing	Active threads, per Server Work Queue
Maximum worker threads		Active Threads + Available Threads, per Server Work Queue
Work items in use	Requests Executing	Max(Available Work Items) – Available Work Items, per Server Work Queue
Work queue depleted	Requests Rejected	Work item shortages, Blocking Requests Rejected
Work request rate	Requests/sec	Context Blocks Queued/sec
Active requests	Requests Executing	
Queued requests	Requests Queued	Queue Length, per Server Work Queue

IIS Active Server Pages

IIS has two tuning parameters that control the size of its thread pool: PoolThread-Limit, which defaults to two threads for each MB of physical memory, and Max-PoolThreads, which controls the number of threads IIS allows to run concurrently. The default is 10 active threads per processor, which applies to all active IIS connections, including both HTTP and FTP connection requests. These tuning parameters are located at HKLM\SYSTEM\CurrentControlSet\Services\InetInfo\Parameters. Figuring out how to set these IIS threading parameters is difficult, though, because IIS does not report statistics on activity within the thread pool. Only data on the number of concurrent connections for the various IIS services is available from the System Monitor measurements.

IIS with Active Server Pages is a little different. Active Server Pages are *scripted*, which means they represent code that is executed by IIS at runtime to create the web page to display dynamically, rather than referencing static HTML pages (files) that are simply transmitted across the wire. ASP is frequently used when it is necessary to access a SQL Server or Oracle database containing information to be displayed. Not surprisingly, ASP runtime services are configured as a thread pool, as are the ODBC connections to SQL Server or some other database. There are two Registry settings for IIS Active Server Pages that impact the performance of ASP on a multiprocessor: ProcessorThreadMax and RequestQueueMax. These settings are added to the Registry at the following location: HKLM\SYSTEM\CurrentControlSet\Services\W3SVC\ ASP\Parameters. Using the Windows 2000 System Monitor, you should monitor the number of ASP Requests/sec, the number of Requests Executing, and the number of Requests Queued. ASP also reports measures called Request Wait Time and Request Execution Time, which reflect the amount of time the *last* request processed spent waiting in the queue and executing.

It is useful to compare the Request Execution Time and Wait Time values to the average response time of requests calculated using the Little's Law formula:

Requests Executing + Requests Queued = Requests/sec × Average Response Time

This calculation is illustrated in an example shown in Figures 5-22 through 5-24, which report on measurement data collected from a busy e-commerce web site running IIS and ASP. There are several caveats about the validity of using Little's Law to calculate ASP request response time from the available measurement data, however. Little's Law requires very few assumptions, as discussed in Chapter 1. But the one assumption it does require is that the system being measured is in a state of equilibrium, where the number of requests entering service is equal to the number of requests exiting the system. When this assumption cannot be satisfied because the system is blocked, the Little's Law calculation is meaningless. Another important assumption is that the ASP request rate itself must be sufficiently high to justify this statistical approach. Little's Law can normally be applied successfully when several transactions per second are processed, but not when only a few transactions per hour are processed. Finally, keep in mind that the Requests/sec counter is a continuously measured value reflecting all activity during the interval, while the number of Requests Executing and Requests Queued are instantaneous values measured at the end of the current interval. With measurement intervals longer than a minute or so, it is easy for these two types of measurements to be out of sync. However, with these warnings in mind, you should find it extremely useful to calculate ASP average response time, instead of relying solely on the direct service and queue time measures that the System Monitor reports that apply only to the last ASP request processed in the interval.

Figure 5-22 shows the ASP request rate (on the right-hand axis) and the values of the Requests Executing and Requests Queued counters (shown as a stacked bar chart graphed against the left-hand axis). In this example, the ASP request execution rate peaks at about five requests per second, which serves as an upper limit of the capacity of this system to field web requests. Requests arriving at a higher rate lead to a large number of queued requests, as illustrated. Notice the large quantity of queued requests at several times during the day, with the largest spike at 15:00 when the ASP queue exceeds 120 work requests.

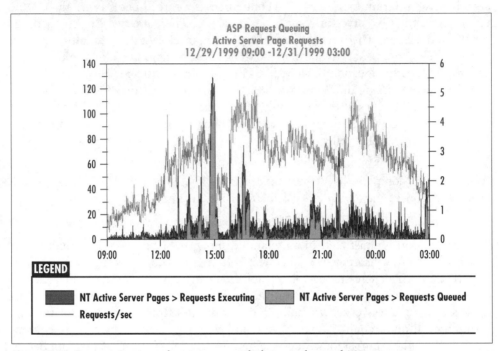

Figure 5-22. Requests/sec is not keeping pace with the arrival rate of ASP requests

Figure 5-23 shows the measured Request Execution Times and Wait Times reported over the same interval. Remember that both the Request Execution Time and Request Wait Time reported represent processing time for only the last request processed. Nevertheless, we can see that some of the times reported are quite large, particularly during intervals that correspond to large spikes in the number of ASP requests queued for processing in Figure 5-22.

Finally, Figure 5-24 shows the results of making the Little's Law calculation to derive a measure of response time for this IIS ASP application. The calculated average response time is usually below five seconds, except for several spikes that correspond to periods where there was a large backlog of requests in the ASP processing queue. These calculated measures are reasonably consistent with the actual measurements for the last ASP request processed shown in 5-23. Most of those requests were processed in less than five seconds, too. It is always worthwhile to compare a direct measure of response time against a value calculated using Little's Law.

Since ASP requests issuing database calls can block inside your back-end Oracle or SQL Server database, tuning a large-scale ASP environment is not as simple as increasing the ASP request processing level. It may also entail understanding and

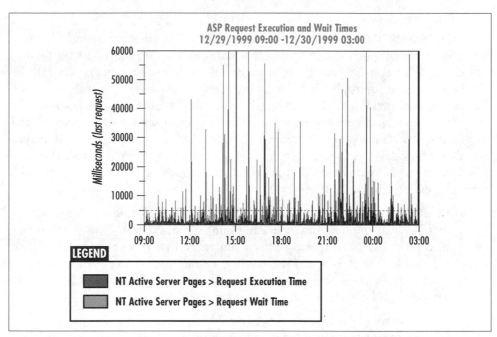

Figure 5-23. The measured Request Execution Times and Wait Times reported

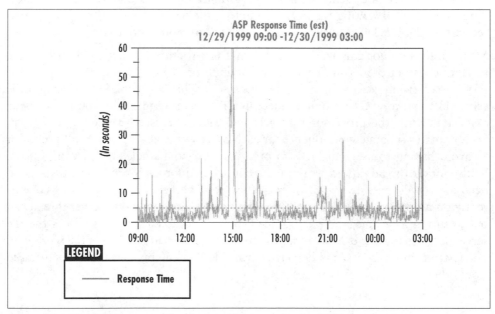

Figure 5-24. The ASP Response Time estimated here applies Little's Law

tuning your database configuration. We discuss the performance of IIS and Microsoft's Active Server Pages technology in more detail in Chapter 12.

File Server

The Windows 2000 Server service, which provides file services to network clients, is a venerable thread pooling application that dates back to Windows 2000's heritage as OS2 LanManager. Server tuning options still reside in the Registry key HKLM\SYSTEM\CurrentControlSet\Services\LanmanServer\Parameters. The File Server service consists of several threads running within *services.exe*. (To see which *services.exe* threads are associated with Server, try stopping the Server service while you are monitoring the *services.exe* process threads.) Network clients accessing files and directories that reside on a file server generate work requests. (Server is installed on NT Workstation and Windows 2000 Professional, too, which can both serve quite nicely as peer-to-peer networked file servers.)

Network file sharing remains a mainstay application in Windows 2000, and the application has elaborate performance and tuning options that are worthy of its stature. It also produces lots of performance counters so that you can monitor it effectively. Knowing that it is a thread pooling application is extremely helpful in understanding the various performance options and performance data that the Server application provides. Here's how the application works.

As file requests are received, a free work item is allocated, which is handed off to a worker thread to process. Since many networked file requests involve doing I/O to disk (many others are cached), threads performing this function can block. While a request is blocked waiting for I/O to complete, the Server worker thread parks that request on the Blocking Queue and looks around for more work to do.

Meanwhile, nonblocking work requests that are waiting are assigned to separate work queues per processor. This symmetric multiprocessor support spreads the file server load evenly across all available processors. This is accomplished using a file server ISR and a DPC that queues incoming file server requests on the work queue associated with the processor that accepted and processed the network request. Server creates separate work queues for each processor available on a multiprocessor to avoid having to use spin locks to protect access to a single shared work queue. With worker threads and a work queue constructed for each processor, there is no need to protect these dedicated work queues from worker threads executing concurrently on a different processor. Within a processor, since only one server thread can be executing at a time, there is no need for spin locks either. This allows the file server services to scale extremely well as more processors are added. If the work item queue from one processor is depleted, available work items can then be *borrowed* from other processor work queues.*

---

* Note that borrowing a work item on occasion from another processor's queue complicates the per-processor work queue implementation. The borrowing thread must gain access to the work queue using a spin lock, of course. This necessitates building a critical section that protects the processor queue for all accesses that change its status. But since borrowing is a rare occurrence, normally only one thread at a time is ever executing the critical section.

This information about how File Server works should clarify the performance counters that are produced. The Server object contains global counters, while the server work queues contain separate instances for each processor work queue (numbered 0, 1, 2, etc.) and a Blocking Queue instance. Some of the key performance measures were identified in Table 5-3.

File Server tuning options include Registry settings for MaxThreadsperQueue, MaxRawWorkItems, and others, and the important Size parameter, which is used to specify the amount of internal memory allocated. The Server Size default is Large. If file requests are received but Server has no available Work Items, the request is rejected. By monitoring the Work Item Shortages and Blocking Requests Rejected counters in the Server performance object, you can detect any instances where File Server dropped requests due to resource shortages. You should then determine where Work Items are being queued by looking at the Server Work Queues object. Statistics for each processor queue are reported as separate instances, as illustrated in Figure 5-25. This is done to help with scalability and to avoid having to use a spin lock to control access to a shared work queue.

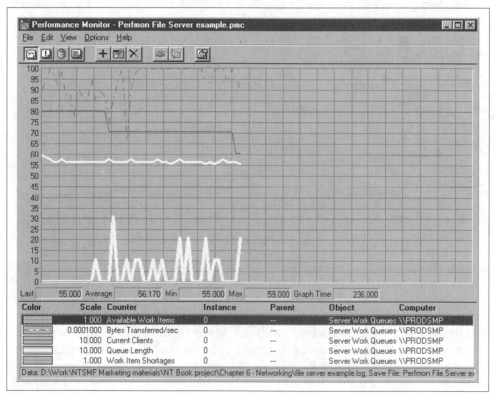

Figure 5-25. Monitoring File Server performance

The number of both available Server threads and active Server threads is reported per queue. These are instantaneous counters. All the items on the Blocking Queue represent active Work Items, so Server zeros all of the queue length statistics out for that instance of the Server Work Queue object. One thread per processor is assigned to the Blocking Queue to service I/O requests as soon as possible. If file requests are received and all available threads are busy, Server will start additional threads up to the value of MaxThreadsperQueue. The default value is 10 threads per queue in Windows 2000, and 30 threads per queue in NT 4.0. As noted in Chapter 3, there is also an option to adjust File Server thread priority.

File Server does not report response time or service time metrics, but, fortunately, you can calculate the average response time using Little's Law. Context Blocks Queued/sec represents the arrival rate of File Server requests. The number of requests in the system equals MaxRawWorkItems (which the System Monitor does not report directly) minus Available Work Items (which is available in the System Monitor). In other words, each active Work Item represents an active request. Unless you specifically set MaxRawWorkItems, the number created can vary significantly across configurations, as illustrated in Table 5-4. But even though MaxRawWorkItems is not directly available, you can observe the maximum value for Available Work Items, especially during a period of no file server activity. In Figure 5-25, for example, the maximum Available Work Items reported was 59.

Table 5-4. Maximum Raw Work Items for different OSes with different amounts of memory

OS	# of engines	MB	Max Raw Work Items
NTW 4 SP3	1	128	2
NT Server 4 SP4	1	128	127
NT Server 4 SP3	2	256	80
NT 2000 Server	1	256	127

With this information you can compute the average Server response time:

$$RT = (MaxWorkItems - Available\ Work\ Items) \div Context\ Blocks\ Queued/sec$$

For example, from the sample data illustrated in 5-25, the estimated response time values are calculated and displayed in Figure 5-26. We can see that the average File Server request here is processed in about 20 milliseconds. Note that the Available Work Items counter is an instantaneous value, while Context Blocks Queued/sec is an interval delta value. If the load on the file server is relatively steady and the measurement interval is quite small (we used 5 seconds in this example), the resulting calculation is trustworthy. Over intervals with much more variation in the number of Available Work Items, the calculated result is dubious because the necessary equilibrium assumption that Little's Law requires is violated. As always, be careful.

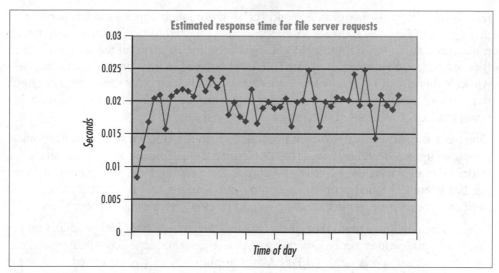

Figure 5-26. Using Little's Law to calculate the average response time for File Server requests

Transaction Server

With so many server applications utilizing thread pooling to achieve scalability, Microsoft initiated a development project to build a runtime environment suitable for most types of transaction-oriented client/server applications. Microsoft developers recognized that if they could prepackage a thread pooling interface into an appropriate set of runtime services, it might greatly accelerate the development of client/server application software for the Windows 2000 platform. This impulse ultimately led to the development of MTS, the Microsoft Transaction Server, now bundled into both Windows NT and Windows 2000. MTS runtime services include automatic thread pooling for both applications and ODBC database connections, plus a variety of shared (private) memory communication services that server applications typically employ. MTS also provides transaction back-out and recovery services.

Essentially, MTS offers built-in services to provide the basic building blocks that complex client/server applications normally require. With the availability of MTS, which has been absorbed into the COM+ development effort in Windows 2000, the number of thread pooling server-side applications available to run under Windows 2000 is expected to increase rapidly. Assuming that appropriate measurement data is available for MTS transaction processing applications, a tuning methodology similar to thread pool monitoring can be used to fine-tune performance of these applications over a wide range of hardware environments.

Coding practices

With MTS COM+ runtime services making it easier than ever to develop scalable thread pooling server applications for Windows 2000, it becomes necessary to say a few words about the performance and scalability of such applications. It is not surprising that Windows 2000 Server applications projected to run on large scale n-way multiprocessors often do not scale well. System administrators all too frequently find that, even though ample processing resources (as well as memory, disk I/O and networking bandwidth) are available, there are evident response time or throughput bottlenecks. Finding out where and why these applications bottleneck, and then figuring out how to fix those bottlenecks is not trivial.

One frequent source of performance problems in multithreaded server applications is poorly designed critical sections. If multiple threads are forced to wait excessively for critical section locks, the application will not scale well to large n-way multiprocessing hardware. The first problem is finding out whether this is a factor in the poor performance of your application. The second problem is figuring out how to fix it.

Diagnosing locking performance problems associated with large-scale, multithreaded applications can be difficult. For device driver code, Microsoft supplied the Thunk function within the x86 Perf Meter application that is also used to set and view Pentium counters. The Thunk function turns on instrumentation inside Windows NT device driver services, including kernel spin lock functions, as illustrated back in Figure 5-9. At the device driver level, you can use Thunk to select the specific NT kernel service that you want to observe. Excessive spin lock cycle consumption is also liable to drive overall processor utilization up and effective instruction execution rates down.

For multithreaded server applications that use Win32 synchronization services like critical sections and mutexes, monitor the application's threads while it is running using the System Monitor. Win32 synchronization services avoid utilizing spin locks on multiprocessors. You will probably need to run the System Monitor at very short intervals, perhaps collecting data once per second. Examine the Thread State and the Thread Wait State Reason. Threads waiting for a critical section or a mutex have a Wait State Reason of 7, Waiting for a Component of the NT Executive. Unfortunately, that is a very common Thread Wait State Reason. Judging from how little processor time threads consume based on the Thread's % Processor Time counter values and the frequency that you find threads in Wait State Reason 7, you may conclude that lock contention is a serious performance concern.

Profiling tools like Visual Quantify and vTune, discussed in the previous chapter, can also be used to pinpoint runtime locking bottlenecks. Visual Quantify works well for multithreaded single-process applications. You may have to rely on vTune for applications that span process boundaries. VTune can also find performance problems in device driver code. One overt symptom of lock contention problems is that processor utilization is relatively low and processor resources are readily available, yet increasing the number of threads does not boost application throughput. If your multithreaded application is instrumented and exports performance monitoring counters as described in Table 5-3, you will also be able to recognize that work queues are backing up while this is all happening.

Finding these performance problems is tough enough, but fixing them may be even tougher. Conceptually, threads queue up waiting for locks due to the rate of locking requests and the duration of those requests. Thread serialization and locking is a classic queuing problem. Optimization solutions along the lines of reducing the rate and duration of locking requests immediately suggest themselves. If requests for acquiring some pooled resource are queued, you may be able to reduce the rate of requests by allowing bulk requests.* Instead of acquiring these resources one at a time, you may be able to acquire them two, five, or even one hundred at a time. If making bulk requests cuts down on the rate of lock requests without making the duration of locking requests significantly longer, the overall impact on the performance of your application is beneficial.

With an eye towards reducing the duration of locking requests, you will want to examine the code inside critical sections very carefully, fine-tuning it to ensure that it can execute as quickly as possible. Breaking monolithic locking structures into finer-grained ones can solve many locking-related performance problems. Look for opportunities to replace a single lock that is heavily used by three, four, or more separate locks. In extreme cases, you may even need to do away with shared-memory data structures that are subject to heavy contention and replace them with separate per-processor data structures that do not require cross-processor locking, as Microsoft did with File Server.

Partitioning Multiprocessors

Beyond controlling multithreaded applications, another important tuning option for system administrators is *partitioning* large-scale multiprocessors to handle heterogeneous workloads. As we have seen, Windows 2000 shared-memory multiprocessors face serious scalability hurdles. As more processing engines are added to the system, the efficiency of the overall system diminishes due to the overhead of maintaining cache coherence and contention for the shared-memory bus. As we suggested at the outset, it makes sense to run Windows 2000 systems as dedicated application servers for a number of reasons, including some of the scalability and performance issues discussed in this chapter. But most shops would prefer not to have to maintain quite so many machines. For ease of administration, it is certainly advantageous to consolidate Active Directory and Domain controllers with machines performing file and print services so that each new redirected filesystem request does not require authentication from an entirely different machine on the network. Running messaging applications like MS Exchange or Lotus Notes on a few large-scale machines may result in reduced

---

* Update transactions delayed in a queue waiting to receive a unique serial identification number is the classic example. One well-known solution is to create intermediate brokers that acquire groups of IDs in bulk. Instead of transactions queuing for a single component that assigns IDs serially, transactions request a unique ID from one of the brokers. Having multiple brokers, in effect, establishes multiple queues, which removes the bottleneck.

administration costs and less complex replication processing to manage. Partitioning offers a way to carve up large-scale multiprocessors into two or more logical machines that can be managed more efficiently than an undifferentiated n-way server machine.

Partitioning is accomplished in Windows 2000 Server by assigning specific processes to specific processors using the Win32 hard processor affinity API. We have seen that the Windows 2000 Thread Scheduler implements soft affinity by default. If the processor where the thread was last dispatched is free or currently running a thread with a lower priority, the thread in question is dispatched on that processor, known as its *ideal processor*. The reason for selecting the thread's ideal processor is performance. When the thread was last executed there, it began to accumulate its code and data in the processor cache. Once the thread has established its working set in processor cache, the instruction execution rate (IER) can be expected to be several times faster. The IER for a thread subject to a cache cold start is potentially only 10–20% of the IER expected when the same thread benefits from a warm start in cache. (The specific benefit of a cache warm start is, of course, workload-dependent, but the potential speed-up factor is considerable.) Because many program segments have very tight working sets, programs usually do not need lots of processor cache, either, once they get started. By dispatching a thread on the processor on which it ran last, Windows 2000 is automatically attempting to optimize for processor performance.

Now imagine a situation where you deliberately restrict an important application so that it can only run on a small number of processors using hard affinity. This is a particularly attractive option when you are configuring a large four-, six-, or eight-way multiprocessor. Restricting the threads of a process to a small number of processors increases the likelihood that when the threads are dispatched, they are dispatched on a processor that retains cached data from that process address space. In an extreme (but by no means unusual) case, you might consider restricting a process to run on only one of the available processors. In this case, the process's threads are always dispatched on the same processor, so it is highly likely that at least some portion of the process working set is still resident in cache when its threads resume execution. Remember that concentrating threads on a processor tends to improve the instruction execution rate. Consequently, it would not be unusual for a process that absorbed 80% busy across all eight available processors to need only 40% of one processor when its threads are all concentrated on that processor. Because the IER is boosted, the application actually runs twice as fast.[*]

---

[*] Cache effects like this are notorious for creating havoc in workload characterization and benchmarking, as exemplified in trying to obtain repeatable performance benchmark results. Because of cache effects, increasing the rate work arrives often leads to processing efficiencies where the amount of work consumed per transaction actually decreases. Consider a workload transaction that runs in isolation. It is subject to a cache cold start and takes duration N to process. A second transaction that can share the cached data associated with the first transaction benefits from a cache warm start, and only takes a fraction of the time N to process. Throughput is doubled while average service time actually decreases. Due to cache, processing efficiency may continue to increase as the arrival rate of transactions increases. Contrasting cold versus warm start cache performance in processors is hardly the only place where we see this counterintuitive phenomenon.

Improving the IER of specific process threads on a multiprocessor is the rationale behind partitioning. Partitioning is used to counteract some of the multiprocessor scalability effects described earlier. It is an important technique for improving the cost-effectiveness of large n-way shared-memory multiprocessors.

NDIS PfsrocessorAffinityMask

Concentrating device driver interrupt handling code onto one specific processor is particularly attractive because performance issues associated with spin locks disappear. Device drivers must use spin locks to guard shared-memory data structures that can be accessed from separate threads running on different processors at the same time. We saw that a thread spinning in a busy wait queue waiting for another thread to finish processing inside a critical section may execute many instructions, but it is not actually doing any useful work. The innovative use of queued spin locks in Windows 2000 reduces shared memory bus contention during spin lock execution, but does not actually reduce the amount of time an application might wait for a spin lock to become free.

Now consider what happens when a device driver interrupt handler DPC is always dispatched on the same processor. There will never be any contention for the spin locks that protect shared-memory data structures. Because only one driver thread at a time can be executing, only one thread at a time will ever try and enter a critical section. The code that loops testing the lock word over and over again until it is free is never executed; since no other thread is in the critical section, the lock is acquired without delay!

For this reason, the Windows 2000 NDIS (Network Device Interface Specification) driver that controls your network interface cards (NICs) supports a hard processor affinity setting. At HKLM\SYSTEM\CurrentControlSet\ServicesNDIS\Parameters, you can code a ProcessorAffinityMask value, which is used to associate specific NIC cards with specific processors. When the NDIS parameter is nonzero, the deferred procedure calls (DPCs) that process NIC card interrupts are confined to a specific processor, one per card. You can code a simple 32-bit processor affinity mask of x'FFFFFFFF' (the system default value) and let the operating system set the processor affinity of each NIC card driver, or set a specific mask yourself. Under the default processor affinity mask, the system assigns the first NIC card to the highest number CPU in the system (CPU 7 on an eight-way, for example), then works its way down until all NIC cards have been assigned different processors.

The NDIS processor affinity mask was introduced in NT 3.5 when the operating system confined interrupt processing to CPU 0. The processor affinity mask allowed you to force DPC processing to other processors, lessening the load on CPU 0, which was the likely bottleneck. The NDIS driver processor affinity option that confines DPCs that process network interrupts can still be a useful setting on a Windows

2000 Server running symmetric multiprocessing where interrupts can be processed on any available processor. Suppose the Windows 2000 Server is serving as a high speed networking hub. Because DPCs are dispatched at a higher priority than any normal task, setting processor affinity virtually ensures that the DPC code stays resident in the processor cache, assuming there are frequent enough interrupts. This makes the NDIS DPC code execute very fast!

However, there is a drawback when DPCs are processed on a different processor from the one that processed the original interrupt. For example, assume that the NDIS DPCs have a hard affinity setting assigning them to CPU 3 in a four-way SMP. Whenever an NDIS interrupt occurs that is processed on a processor other than CPU 3 (say CPU 1), then CPU 1 must signal CPU 3 when it schedules the DPC. Interprocessor signaling, as we indicated previously, is an expensive operation. In addition, any data associated with the NDIS interrupt processing retained in CPU 1 cache must be flushed.

From the standpoint of processor instruction execution efficiency, better results are obtained when *both* the NDIS interrupts and the associated DPCs are dispatched on the same engine. This can be done, but requires a third-party package, for instance, the NCR SMP Utilization Manager.* Using the NCR SMP Utilization Manager, you can assign processor affinity to specific interrupts, as illustrated in Figure 5-27. In this example, the IRQs associated with the Intel 8042 10/100 Ethernet card are assigned hard processor affinity for CPU 1, the same processor assigned to NDIS DPCs, by default. Using the NCR package, we also configured interrupts associated with the Adaptec SCSI card on this NT 4.0 server to CPU 0 to balance the interrupt processing workload a bit. This configuration option works best when a server with multiple PCI buses is used, so that SCSI interrupts assigned to one of the buses can be processed concurrently with NDIS interrupts assigned to a different PCI bus.

Setting hard processing affinity in this manner runs counter to the spirit and intent of symmetric multiprocessing. The resulting configuration becomes *asymmetric*, which means that the workload is no longer balanced across processors. Figure 5-28 illustrates the imbalance that occurs on this machine when NIC interrupts are concentrated on CPU 1. % Interrupt Time is substantially higher on CPU 1 (the topmost line) because NIC interrupts are processed there exclusively. Since our goal was to concentrate the NIC interrupts and DPCs by isolating them to CPU 1, Figure 5-28 indicates we have achieved the desired result. The obvious danger of setting hard affinity is that confining any process to too few processors restricts its performance. This is not very risky in the case of binding DPC execution to a single processor because % DPC Time is normally quite low, and NIC interrupts only occur one at a time.

---

* As of this writing, the NCR SMP Utilization Manager is not available to run under Windows 2000.

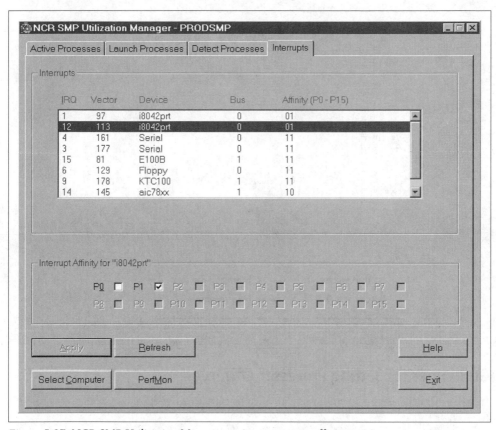

Figure 5-27. NCR SMP Utilization Manager assigns processor affinity to interrupt servicing

However, this is a risky strategy for any workload that might overrun the processors assigned to serve it. If there are not enough processors assigned (or the processors are not big enough), the workload will back up inside the system. Problems arise when you start to find critical application threads delayed in the Ready Queue even though overall processor utilization is low. The shape of the problems should become clear when you analyze individual processor-level statistics. You may find that the processors where constrained workloads are confined are quite busy, while others are relatively idle. Creating a severely imbalanced configuration is one of the serious risks of manually partitioning SMPs, and avoiding this requires a commitment to regular performance monitoring to ensure that resources dedicated to specific critical workloads remain adequate to the task. The next section discusses this issue in greater depth.

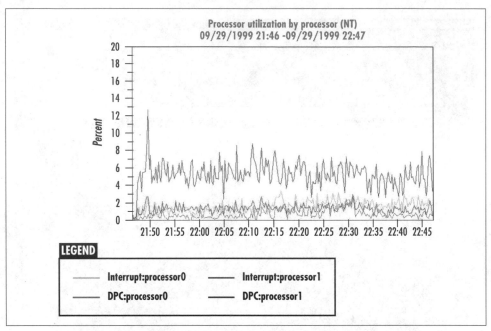

Figure 5-28. Hard processor affinity for Interrupts and DPCs leads to an unbalanced configuration

Guidelines for Setting Processor Affinity

In general, utilizing hard processor affinity to partition workloads on the system calls for:

- Understanding the CPU requirements of your application during both normal and peak loads
- Configuring enough processors to safely absorb the application's CPU processing requirements without causing excessive queuing
- An ongoing commitment to monitor the system to detect changes in the workload pattern

Let's take a look at all three areas of concern.

Understanding the CPU requirements of any specific application entails monitoring its associated Process % Processor Time counters. You can learn about longer-term CPU usage patterns and trends by monitoring the application over several weeks at regular intervals. If processor utilization peaks at predictable hours, monitor those periods closely to understand the characteristics of those peak periods. You need to configure the system so that there are enough processor resources available to it for both normal and peak loads. Consider monitoring peak periods in even greater detail, for instance, at one-minute intervals instead of five, to gain additional insight into the application's resource requirements.

Deriving a *peak:average ratio* is a very useful metric for understanding the application's processing requirements, where the peak period is the busiest one- or five-minute interval over a typical processing shift, as compared to the average measured during the shift. The greater the variability in processor requirements, the higher the peak:average ratio. Workloads with a peak:average ratio of over 2 or 3 are very inconsistent and need to be watched extra carefully.

You also need to factor in some additional system overhead requirements beyond what is specifically consumed at the process level. No doubt, the application in question will require some additional system resources performed on its behalf. Server applications like SQL Server or Oracle, which attempt to bypass most Windows 2000 system services once they are initialized, usually require another 10–20% of additional system overhead. Other applications may require 20–40% more processor resources in the form of various system memory and I/O services.

Once you understand the processor requirements for a given workload, you can establish a partitioning scheme. To ensure that the system remains responsive to the workload in question, configure enough processors so that the projected average application load, including system overhead, puts the configured CPUs in the range of 20–60% busy. The rationale behind this rule of thumb is as follows. Below 20% utilization, the application is probably not dispatched frequently enough on its dedicated processors to benefit much from cache warm starts. Above 50% utilization, there may not be sufficient processor resources to handle peak loads (assuming a 2:1 peak:average ratio) without excessive queuing. Of course, you should also monitor the system object Processor Queue Length counter and periodically check to ensure that threads from the application you are concerned with are not delayed waiting in the Ready Queue (Thread State = 1).

To ensure that lengthy processing queues do not develop during peak loads, configure enough processors to keep projected peak load usage below 75% busy. If it is only possible to hit one of these two targets because of extremely high variability in the workload's processor requirements, then the peak load target is normally the more important one. You do not want users to experience serious response time problems during normal peak periods.

Once you establish the processor requirements for your applications, you usually also need to restrict other workloads that might conflict with your critical applications to processors other than the ones assigned to your preferred workload. To make life easier, narrow the field to only those workloads with significant processing requirements and assign them hard processor affinity on different processors.

Finally, using hard processor affinity settings to partition a large n-way Windows 2000 server requires a commitment to monitor that system continuously to ensure that changes in the workload do not render your carefully planned configuration inadequate. You must remain vigilant. If the workload changes in such a way that critical applications are being starved of processing resources they need, then you must adjust hard processor affinity settings accordingly. Once you set up hard processor affinity restrictions, the Windows 2000 Thread Scheduler can no longer balance processing across all available CPUs. One indication that a system with hardcoded processor affinity is out of balance is that the dispatcher Ready Queue gets longer even though average processor utilization remains low. On the other hand, you may find, by examining the threads waiting in the ready state, that this behavior is exactly what you intended. If threads from preferred applications are being executed promptly while threads associated with lower-priority applications are delayed, that is precisely the behavior you want.

SQL Server

Among Windows 2000 packaged applications, only SQL Server supports a processor affinity mask. Up through Version 6.5, use either the Configuration tab of the Configure dialog in the Enterprise Administrator application, or the sp_configure stored procedure. Note, the Show Advanced Options flag must be turned on to see these options. The processor affinity mask option is designed to complement the other advanced processor tuning parameters available in SQL Server. These include the ability to boost SQL Server threads to real-time priority above even OS kernel threads, to define the duration of a SQL Server thread time-slice, and to control the level of SQL Server thread concurrency.

On a multiprocessor, setting priority boost lets SQL Server threads run at priority 24 in the real-time range, higher priority than any OS kernel threads. When priority boost is coded along with a processor affinity mask, Microsoft documentation refers to this as SQL Server's *dedicated SMP support* because it allows SQL Server threads to run at higher priority than anything else in the system except ISRs, DPCs, and APCs. This is worth trying on an n-way multiprocessor *only* if you also set a processor affinity mask to enable the operating system and threads from other applications to get access to other processors not dedicated to SQL Server, as illustrated in Figure 5-29.

The SMP concurrency setting under SQL Server 6.5 controls the number of threads that SQL Server will release to Windows 2000 for execution. See Figure 5-30. By default, the value of the SMP concurrency parameter is set to 0, which means SQL Server releases $n - 1$ threads, where n is the number of processors detected. (On a uniprocessor, SQL Server is set to release only one thread at a time anyway.) If a processor affinity mask is set, SMP concurrency is set by default to -1, which means to release one less than the number of configured dedicated processors. There are many situations where you might need to restrict SQL Server running on an n-way multiprocessor even further. Again, analyze SQL Server's CPU requirements and set a processor affinity mask and an SMP concurrency value accordingly.

Together, the processor affinity mask, the priority boost, and SMP concurrency parameters can modify dramatically the performance of SQL Server running on a

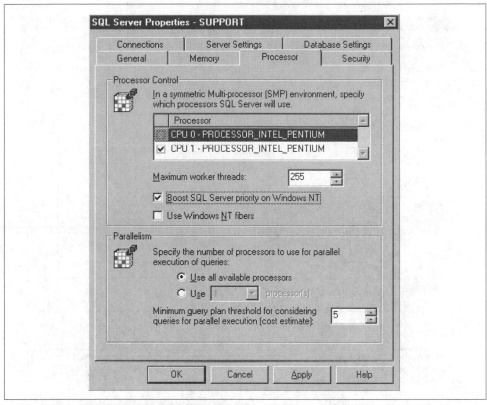

Figure 5-29. SQL Server 2000 can boost SQL Server thread priority into the real-time range

multiprocessor. None of these parameters should be set without first analyzing SQL Server's CPU processing requirements, as described previously in the "Guidelines for Setting Processor Affinity" section. A number of Windows 2000 professionals report having great success using these tuning options, especially in benchmark environments where the workload is very controlled. These parameters are one reason that SQL Server can run TPC-C benchmarks so well. When your Windows 2000 server is dedicated to running SQL Server, these advanced tuning options can be used in concert with the NDIS processor affinity mask. On the other hand, when you are trying to run SQL Server as one of several server applications sharing a large n-way multiprocessor, using these options can easily do a great deal of harm. In the rough-and-tumble world of real-life workloads, it is necessary to proceed much more conservatively because of the potential impact on real customers and their service levels.

NCR SMP Utilization Manager

To make any headway at all using partitioning on a large n-way Windows NT server outside of the realm of dedicated SQL Server machines, you probably need NCR's

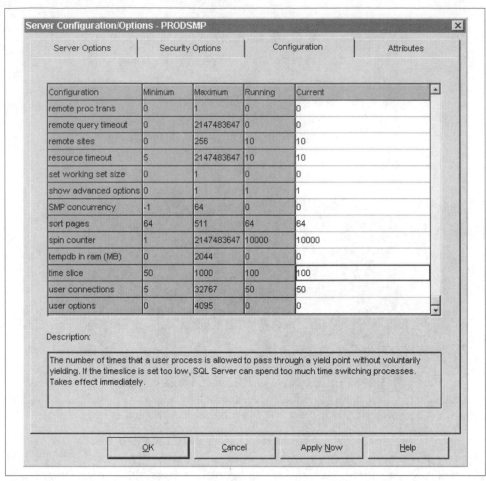

Configuration	Minimum	Maximum	Running	Current
remote proc trans	0	1	0	0
remote query timeout	0	2147483647	0	0
remote sites	0	256	10	10
resource timeout	5	2147483647	10	10
set working set size	0	1	0	0
show advanced options	0	1	1	1
SMP concurrency	-1	64	0	0
sort pages	64	511	64	64
spin counter	1	2147483647	10000	10000
tempdb in ram (MB)	0	2044	0	0
time slice	50	1000	100	100
user connections	5	32767	50	50
user options	0	4095	0	0

Description:

The number of times that a user process is allowed to pass through a yield point without voluntarily yielding. If the timeslice is set too low, SQL Server can spend too much time switching processes. Takes effect immediately.

Figure 5-30. SQL Server Version 6.5 advanced options include processor affinity mask, the priority boost, and SMP concurrency parameters

SMP Utilization Manager (SUM). This utility was originally designed to accompany NCR's high-end Worldmark server hardware, which can be configured with multiple Intel processors. Initially, NCR found it difficult to run its largest server configurations efficiently under NT Version 3. It developed the SUM utility program to add administrator controls to the NT Thread Scheduler. The program remains just as useful in an NT 4.0 symmetric multiprocessing environment in case you want to consolidate several workloads and you configure three, four, or more engines. (A good deal of the collective NCR wisdom on running large-scale NT servers is condensed in Curt Aubley's *Tuning and Sizing Windows 2000 for Maximum Performance*, from Prentice Hall Computer Books, 2001.) Currently, the SMP Utilization Manager is available from NCR in a bundle called Enterprise Pack, which includes some other tools designed to help administer very large-scale Windows 2000 systems. Meanwhile, the

SUM program itself has evolved into an effective tool for partitioning any large n-way NT Server. (As we were going to press, the NCR SUM program was still not available for Windows 2000.)

As illustrated previously in Figure 5-27, the SUM utility can be used to assign hard processor affinity to different IRQs and their associated ISRs. This can be used, as illustrated, to direct interrupts from SCSI cards and NICs to separate processors, or, along with the NDIS ProcessAffinityMask, to assign both interrupt processing and DPCs associated with specific NIC cards to a specific processor. As a more general-purpose partitioning tool, the program can be used to set both the priority and processor affinity of any service or application process. Figure 5-31 illustrates the capability of the program to create a static configuration file to detect specific processes at initialization and assign them designated priority or processor affinity settings. As of this writing, the program is unique in providing this valuable capability to assist NT system administrators in configuring and controlling a large multiprocessor NT server.

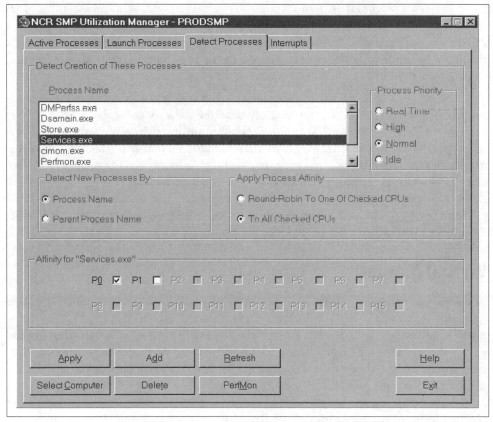

Figure 5-31. The NCR SMP Utilization Manager Detect Processes tab

## CHAPTER 6

Memory Management and Paging

Windows 2000 is a demand paged, virtual memory operating system. It currently supports 32-bit virtual memory addresses on Intel-compatible processors. This chapter describes the virtual memory management features of Windows 2000 and its implications for performance monitoring and capacity planning. Because Windows 2000 runs on PC architectures that often have limited I/O bandwidth, making sure that there is ample physical memory is one of the most important configuration and tuning considerations.

The first section of this chapter provides an overview of the Windows 2000 Virtual Memory Manager. The second section describes the page replacement policies implemented in Windows 2000. The third section describes the memory management performance measurement data that Windows 2000 provides, and also discusses practical strategies for sizing and tuning Windows 2000 memory. In this chapter we also share our perspective on a number of hotly debated topics in Windows 2000 performance: how to tell when your system needs more RAM, how many paging files to define and where to place them, and whether or not you should let Windows 2000 extend your paging files automatically.

Virtual Memory

Random access memory (RAM) is an essential element of your computer, and is used to store both code and data during program execution. Each memory location is unique, allowing the information stored in memory to be accessed directly and updated. Programs are loaded from disk into RAM and executed from memory. Data files stored on the disk are loaded into RAM, manipulated, and updated. While a program is executing, it allocates working storage in memory. Program instructions manipulate physical memory locations at the byte (8 bit) level, double byte or word (16 bit) level, or double word (32 bit) level, where each byte of memory is individually and uniquely addressable.

Generally speaking, only specific operating system kernel threads access and operate directly on physical memory locations. Application programs use *virtual memory* instead, addressing memory locations indirectly. One advantage of virtual memory addressing is that separate application programs all loaded into RAM concurrently are isolated from each other when they run. The operating system creates a separate virtual address space for each individual process. Threads associated with a process can only reference the real memory locations that correspond to its assigned range of virtual memory addresses. This makes it harder for a bug in one program to affect other executing programs.

Virtual memory addresses are assigned to physical memory locations *on demand*, which has a number of implications for the performance of virtual memory machines. Since their introduction in the late 1960s, virtual memory architectures quickly came to dominate the computing world due to their flexibility compared to the fixed memory partitioning schemes that preceded them. Because available RAM is allocated for active pages on demand, virtual memory systems use RAM much more efficiently than real memory partitioning schemes.

Virtual Addressing

Virtual memory is a feature supported by most advanced processors. Hardware support for virtual memory includes a hardware mechanism to map from logical (i.e., virtual) memory addresses that application programs reference to physical (or *real*) memory hardware addresses. When an executable program's image file is first loaded into memory, the logical memory address range of the application is divided into fixed-size chunks called *pages*. These logical pages are then mapped to similar-sized physical pages that are resident in real memory. This mapping is dynamic, in that frequently referenced logical addresses tend to reside in physical memory (also known as RAM, real memory, or main memory), while infrequently referenced pages are relegated to paging files on secondary disk storage. The active subset of virtual memory pages associated with a single process's address space currently resident in RAM is known as the process's *working set*, because they are the active pages referenced by the program as it executes.

Virtual addressing is designed to be transparent to application programs, allowing them to be written without regard to specific real memory limitations of this or that computer. This is a great boon to application developers. Virtual addressing even makes it possible for an executing program to reference an address space that is larger than the amount of physical memory installed on a particular computer. Virtual memory addressing allows a programmer to exploit what looks like a virtually infinite-sized computer memory where *each* individual process can address up to 4 GB of virtual addresses. Naturally, there are some performance ramifications if the program attempts to reference more memory locations than can actually fit inside real memory.

Virtual memory systems work surprisingly well because executing programs seldom require all the associated code and data areas they allocate to be resident in physical memory concurrently in order to run. With virtual memory, only the active pages associated with a program's current working set remain resident in real memory. On the other hand, virtual memory systems can run very poorly when the working sets of active processes greatly exceed the amount of physical RAM that the computer contains. It is important to understand the logical and physical memory usage statistics available in Windows 2000 in order to recognize and diagnose cases where virtual memory addressing leads to the serious performance problems that arise when real memory is over-committed.

Page fault resolution

For all its virtues, virtual memory can raise some serious performance issues. Chief among them is execution delays encountered by programs whenever they reference virtual memory locations not in the current set of memory-resident pages. This is known as a *page fault*. A program thread that incurs a page fault is halted during *page fault resolution*, the time it takes the operating system to find the specific page on disk and restore it to real memory.

When a program execution thread attempts to reference an address on a page that is not currently resident in real memory, a hardware interrupt occurs that halts the executing program. An operating system interrupt service routine (ISR) gains control following the interrupt and determines that the address referenced is valid, but is not currently resident. (If a program accesses an invalid memory location due to a logic error, e.g., referencing an uninitialized pointer, a similar hardware error occurs. It is up to the ISR to distinguish between the two conditions.) The operating system then must remedy the situation by locating a copy of the desired page on secondary storage, issuing an I/O operation to the paging file, and copying the designated page from disk into a free page in RAM. Once the page has been copied successfully, the operating system redispatches the temporarily halted program, allowing the program thread to continue its normal execution cycle.

Performance Concerns

A pervasive concern of virtual memory schemes is that the performance of application programs may suffer when there is a shortage of real memory and too many page faults occur. Windows 2000 maintains a pool of available (free) real memory pages to resolve page faults quickly. Whenever the pool is depleted, Windows 2000 replenishes its buffer of available RAM by *trimming* older (i.e., less frequently referenced) pages of active processes and by *swapping* the pages of idle foreground applications to disk. If the supply of real memory is ample, executing programs seldom encounter page faults that delay their execution, and the operating system has no difficulty maintaining a healthy supply of free pages. If the system is short on real memory (relative to the memory required to back concurrently referenced pages with actual physical memory pages), a high rate of page faults may occur, slowing the performance of executing programs considerably. Obviously, the operating system may not be able to maintain an adequate pool of available real memory when there is not enough real memory to go around.

In a virtual memory computer system, some page fault behavior—for instance, when a program first begins to execute—is inevitable. From a configuration and tuning perspective, what you are seeking is *not* to eliminate paging activity completely, but to prevent *excessive* paging from impacting performance. You want to avoid three types of performance problems that can occur when there is too little real memory:

- *Too many page faults.* Having too many page faults leads to excessive program execution delays during page fault resolution. This is the most straightforward performance problem associated with virtual memory addressing.

- *Disk contention.* Virtual memory systems that are subject to a high page fault rate may also encounter disk performance problems because of the extra disk I/O workload generated to resolve page faults. In systems where the paging file (or files) is located on the same disk (or disks) as application data files, I/O to the paging file can limit the ability of applications to access their own data files. A possible secondary effect of disk contention is elongation of page fault resolution time, further delaying the programs affected when page faults do occur.

- *Competition for memory.* Because real memory is allocated to executing programs on demand, there is another potential pitfall. In virtual memory systems, programs resident in memory *compete* for access to available physical memory. The inevitable result of competition when memory is scarce is that the memory access pattern of one program can unduly influence other running programs.

A severe shortage of real memory can seriously impact performance. Moving pages back and forth between disk and memory consumes both processing and disk capacity. A system forced to use too many CPU and disk resources on virtual memory management tasks and too few on the application workload is said to be *thrashing*. The image this conjures up is of a washing machine so overloaded that it expends too much energy sloshing laundry around without getting the clothes very clean. In the section ""Memory Capacity Planning," we review the real and virtual memory performance statistics Windows 2000 provides to assist in diagnosing machines that are experiencing performance problems due to excessive paging.

Inevitably, the solution to a paging problem is to install more real memory capacity. Alternatively (and less definitively), it may help to improve page fault resolution time by focusing on disk I/O performance. This typically involves some combination of (1) defining additional paging files across multiple (physical) disks, (2) reducing disk contention by removing other heavily accessed files from the paging file physical disks, or (3) upgrading to faster disks. Disk performance is the subject of subsequent chapters, so we avoid discussing it in depth here.

Naturally, being able to predict which systems are becoming memory-constrained and are likely to encounter performance problems due to excessive paging offers the possibility of heading off serious performance problems before they occur. In the final section of this chapter, ""Memory Capacity Planning," we discuss a simple technique that can often reliably forecast the onset of paging problems.

Operating system support

Virtual memory addressing makes life easier for application programmers, but it is decidedly not transparent to operating systems. The OS must perform a number of critical functions to enable the scheme to work. One OS responsibility is constructing and maintaining per-process address space virtual-to-real memory translation tables that the hardware refers to in the course of executing instructions. These *page tables* map logical program virtual addresses to real-memory locations, as illustrated in Figure 6-1. The operating system also must manage the contents of real memory effectively. This requires implementing a *page replacement policy* to ensure that frequently referenced pages remain in real memory. Windows 2000 attempts to maintain a pool of free or available memory to accommodate the rapid resolution of the page faults that inevitably occur. Whenever there is a shortage of available real memory, Windows 2000 triggers its page replacement policy to replenish its supply of free pages.

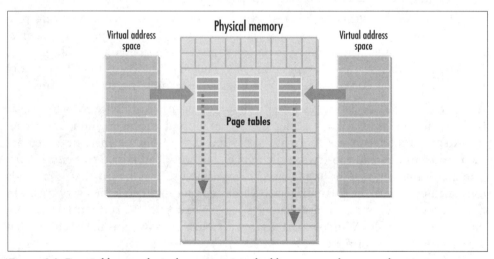

Figure 6-1. Page tables map logical program virtual addresses to real-memory locations

Committed Pages

Windows 2000 builds page tables on behalf of each process created. A process's page tables are built on demand as virtual memory locations are allocated, potentially mapping the entire 32-bit-wide 4 GB virtual process address space depicted in Figure 6-1. The Win32 `VirtualAlloc` API call provides both for *reserving* contiguous virtual address ranges and *committing* specific virtual memory addresses. Reserving virtual memory does not trigger building page table entries because you are not yet using the virtual memory address range to store data. Your application might want to reserve a range of virtual memory addresses in advance for a data file intended to be mapped into virtual storage. Only when the file is accessed are those virtual memory pages actually allocated (or committed). Since reserving virtual memory is a unique Windows 2000 feature, programmers must code a call to the Win32 VirtualAlloc routine to reserve memory, instead of a standard C runtime malloc call to allocate virtual memory.

In contrast, *committing* virtual memory addresses causes the Windows 2000 Virtual Memory Manager (VMM) to construct a page table entry to map the address into physical RAM, or, alternatively, to one or more paging overflow files that reside on disk. All other unreserved and unallocated virtual memory addresses associated with a process address space are termed *free*.

Commit Limit

There is a hard limit in Windows 2000 on the number of page table entries the operating system will build. Windows 2000 maintains a virtual memory *Commit Limit* that prohibits page tables from being built for virtual memory pages that will not fit in either physical RAM or the paging files. The Commit Limit is the sum of physical memory and the allotted space on the paging files. Windows 2000 currently supports a maximum of 16 paging files, each of which must reside on distinct logical disk partitions. Page files named *pagefile.sys* are always created in the root directory of a logical disk. Each paging file can accommodate up to one million pages, so each can be as large as 4 GB on disk. That amounts to a 64 GB upper limit on the amount of virtual memory that can ever be allocated, plus the amount of RAM installed on the machine. A single page file configured when the operating system was installed is the more normal environment. For such systems, the size of the paging file and the amount of RAM installed serves as the upper limit on how much virtual memory Windows 2000 allows programs to allocate.

Memory leaks

Once the Commit Limit is reached, subsequent program calls to allocate virtual memory will fail. An executing program that contains a logic flaw known as a *memory leak* can create a dangerous situation as Windows 2000 approaches the Commit Limit.

A program with a memory leak allocates virtual memory for some (usually temporary) work area and then "forgets" to free it when it is done. If permitted to execute long enough, such a program will eventually allocate all available virtual memory, ultimately causing the system to either lock up or crash. Unfortunately, many memory leak bugs are subtle and difficult to find. Moreover, a program can leak memory in areas of virtual memory shared by many different processes, making it extra difficult to find the culprit. Later, we illustrate the virtual memory usage statistics you can collect that can help you detect and diagnose memory leaks.

Paging file extension

Before the Commit Limit is reached, Windows 2000 will alert you to the possibility that virtual memory may be exhausted. Whenever a paging file becomes 90% full, Windows 2000 issues the distinctive warning message illustrated in Figure 6-2. Following the instructions in the message directs the operator to the Performance tab of the system applet in the Control Panel, where additional paging file space can be defined on the fly or existing paging files can be extended (assuming disk space is available and the page file does not already exceed 4 GB). A Windows 2000 system event message in the system log with an ID of 26 is also generated that documents the condition. •

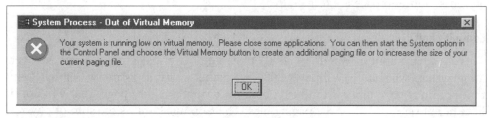

Figure 6-2. The warning message issued when any paging file is 90% full

Windows 2000 creates an initial paging file automatically when the OS is installed. It is built on the same logical drive where Windows 2000 is installed, with a minimum allocation equal to the amount of physical memory plus about 15 MB. It is defined by default so that it can extend to approximately two times the size of RAM. The Virtual Memory paging file dialog box illustrated in Figure 6-3 allows for defining a range of allocated paging file space for each paging file created. After several seconds of processing above the 90% allocation level without an operator intervention occurring, Windows 2000 extends the affected paging file automatically, subject to space being available on the specified logical disk.

Unfortunately, extending the paging file usually causes it to *fragment* so that it no longer occupies contiguous disk sectors. The authorities are in virtually complete agreement that such a unilateral action jeopardizes the performance of the system, forcing subsequent paging file operations to cross noncontiguous segments of the paging file, which in turn leads to time-consuming embedded disk seek operations. It is worth asking yourself whether you should allow this to happen. You can easily prevent paging files from being extended automatically by setting the Maximum Size of the paging file equal to its Initial Size.

Other authors on Windows 2000 performance topics recommend that paging file allocations be strictly limited so that the allocation cannot be extended. This presumes that initially paging file allocations themselves acquire a set of physically contiguous disk sectors. This is often a safe assumption for the original paging file built by the Windows 2000 installation program on the same logical disk partition as the operating system itself, when the logical disk is in a pristine state; it may not be a

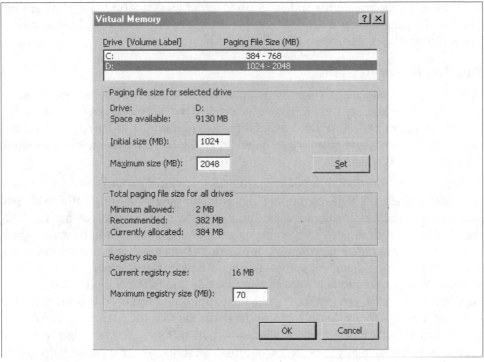

Figure 6-3. The Virtual Memory dialog box used to define and modify paging file extents

good assumption for paging files added subsequently, which are likely to be subject to fragmentation.

We disagree with the conventional wisdom in this area. While in no way minimizing the performance impact of a fragmented paging file, we invite readers to consider the alternative. Not being able to extend the paging files when the system approaches the Commit Limit exposes running programs to the possibility of virtual memory allocation failures, a contingency that few programs allow for. Not allowing paging files to expand under stress redirects that stress onto applications, some of which will surely fail as the absolute Commit Limit looms. So long as the virtual memory allocation peak itself is transient, allowing the paging files to expand at least ensures that the system stays up. For our money, maximizing system availability is nearly always of paramount importance, even at a sacrifice of optimal performance levels.

Even if the extension is permanent, the situation is still not guaranteed to lead to a serious performance problem, the profusion of expert advice to the contrary. For instance, you can try to minimize the long-term performance impact of a paging file extension by later running the disk defragmenter utility to consolidate the paging file back into a single, contiguous disk extent. But a fragmented paging file may not be a serious performance liability in the first place. Because your paging files coexist on physical disks with ample amounts of application data, some disk-seek back and forth between the paging file and application data files is unavoidable. Having a big hunk of the paging file surrounded by application data files may actually reduce average seek distances for your overall disk I/O workload.

Virtual memory shortage alerts

We readily concede one problem with Windows 2000 extending a paging file automatically when allocation on a paging file crosses the 90% threshold, which is that waiting until the 90% threshold may be too late, especially on any system configured with a single paging file. We recommend taking remedial action long before the 90% threshold is reached.

Figure 6-4 is an illustration of what virtual memory allocation looks like on a system that has reached the 90% paging file allocation threshold. It shows that both real memory and the paging file are quite full by the time the system reaches the 90% threshold. Not only are there few available virtual memory slots, what slots are available may be very scattered, preventing applications from allocating large blocks of virtual storage. The system is approaching the Commit Limit where simple calls to VirtualAlloc can start to fail. Applications may begin to fail because they cannot allocate virtual memory. For instance, the system application responsible for sending the warning message to the console and to the event log that the paging file is 90% full sometimes fails because it cannot allocate virtual memory, so you might not even receive notification that the event has occurred. In short, by the time the 90% paging file allocation threshold is reached, it may already be too late to take corrective action.

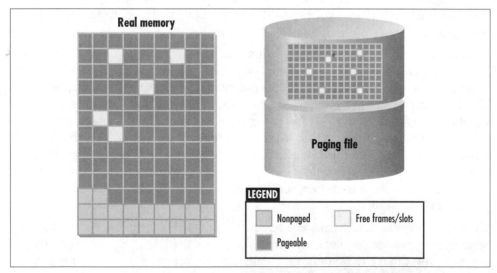

Figure 6-4. Virtual memory allocation at the 90% paging file allocation threshold

A more proactive approach uses continuous performance monitoring to generate an alert when % Committed Bytes exceeds, say, a 70% threshold value. If you are operating a system above this level of virtual memory utilization consistently, it is time to explore longer-term remedial measures that might involve adding more physical memory, defining additional paging file space, or both. Computers systematically exceeding 70–80% Committed Bytes may suffer from serious performance degradation due to excessive demand paging activity anyway.

Multiple paging files

In light of the fact that Windows 2000 supports up to 16 paging files, it is worth discussing the possible advantages and disadvantages of having multiple paging files. From a performance standpoint, having multiple paging files translates into increased bandwidth for paging I/O operations. Theoretically, to maximize paging file throughput, defining a separate paging file per physical disk is probably optimal, although not always, strictly speaking, necessary. The Windows 2000 configuration constraint is that only one paging file can be defined per logical disk. Here Windows 2000 is constrained by the filesystem, which will not permit multiple files with the same name in a folder. Nevertheless, the performance benefit of defining more than one paging file is dependent on being able to access multiple physical disks, not necessarily multiple logical disks. Multiple paging files configured on the same physical disk only leads to increased disk contention.

Of course, what looks like a single physical disk to Windows 2000 may in fact be an *array* of disks controlled by a hardware disk array controller of some sort. Again, the rule of thumb of allocating no more than one paging file per physical disk applies. A 4+1 RAID 5 disk array with four data disks and one parity disk can accommodate up to four paging files. Remember that you must define multiple logical disk partitions for this scheme to work.

A good way to think about how many paging files you need is to consider that any I/O activity to a paging file reduces the effective capacity of the physical disk where the paging file resides to perform application I/O operations. Once the amount of paging I/O to a physical disk consumes more than 10–20% of the disk's total I/O capacity, it is probably time to consider some remedial action to reduce the relative I/O load from paging. The most straightforward way to accomplish this is to add real memory, but if you are unable to add RAM to the system for any reason, defining additional paging files, one per physical disk, will help spread the paging I/O load across multiple disks. Later in this chapter we review some of the performance statistics you can collect that help you determine when it might be a good time to add another paging file for performance reasons.

Clustered paging I/O

A feature of Windows 2000 paging that encourages you to configure multiple paging files is its reliance on *clustered paging* file I/O. When a page fault occurs, Windows 2000 does not just bring the requested page into memory. Instead, depending on both the type of page and how much RAM is installed on the system, the operating system arranges to bring in one or more nearby pages in a single I/O operation.

Details on Windows 2000's clustered paging algorithm are shown in Table 6-1. For example, whenever a page fault occurs because of a program accessing a code page that is not in RAM, Windows 2000 is not satisfied to retrieve that single 4K page from the disk. Instead, it copies the page specifically requested along with the next seven pages associated with that program image file. The "Other" category in Table 6-1 includes page faults that can occur accessing page tables, for example, during virtual address translation. (Windows 2000 can differentiate between code pages and data pages because code pages are write-protected. Windows 2000 can also tell from consecutive page table entries (PTEs) where code and data segments end so that the operating system does not attempt to prefetch pages that are outside the process address space boundary.)

Table 6-1. Number of pages read from the paging file

Memory size	Page fault type		
	Data	Code	Other
Small (< 20 MB)	2	3	5
Medium (20<MB<64)	2	3	5
Large (>64)	4	8	8

Instead of simple *demand paging*, clustered paging file I/O adds an element of *anticipatory paging* to the Windows 2000 scheme. The rationale behind anticipatory paging is that page faults are not isolated events. These are computerized logic programs executing, after all, not random events. Individual page accesses are part of a systematic pattern of virtual memory access that the operating system can exploit. Computer scientists call this phenomenon *locality of reference*, which is the high probability that an executing program that just accessed code page n is likely to access code page n+1 in the near future. Locality of reference characterizes memory accesses of all kinds, which is what makes caching strategies so effective across many different types of computer technology. After all, caching strategies are deployed successfully in processors, database management systems (DBMS), and disk controllers. And it is certainly appropriate to view RAM as a cache for virtual memory in systems that use virtual memory management, providing one more example where caching is also very effective.*

---

* The term *locality of reference* is more of a logical tautology than an explanation for the effectiveness of caching strategies across a wide range of digital information retrieval modes. It is even tempting to characterize the organization of human memory in the same way. Physiologically, human brains appear to have a short-term memory cache that is just one component in a hierarchically organized storage system in the brain. Consider the great variety of human behavior that can be characterized as habit-forming, patterns of behavior that are retrieved and executed so quickly that we are unconscious of ever even "thinking" about them. Habit-forming behavior patterns are stored in long-term memory and are retrieved and executed unconsciously. The hierarchical organization of the human brain apparently may rely on something analogous to caching strategies to optimize human information storage and retrieval. The units of human memory caching are what the evolutionary biologist Richard Dawkins calls *memes*, identifiable units of human cultural behavior.

Part of the rationale behind clustered paging is that individual disk I/O operations to the paging file are time-consuming. After spending considerable time positioning the disk arm over the correct disk sector, it makes sense to grab several related pages from the disk in one continuous operation. Ultimately, this saves time compared to returning again and again to the paging file disk to retrieve subsequent pages for the address space, assuming a large enough proportion of prefetched pages are actually accessed within a relatively short period of time.

Anticipatory paging turns individual on-demand page read requests into bulk paging operations. This is the same rationale behind your decision to add a few extra items to your shopping cart when you make an emergency visit to the supermarket, avoiding a second time-consuming visit to the store later in the day. It takes so long (relatively speaking) to get to the disk in the first place that it makes sense for Windows 2000 to grab a few extra pages while it is there (assuming they are contiguous to the page being accessed). After all, these pages are likely to be used in the near future.

Of course, just like the impulse buys you make on your shopping expedition, there is no guarantee that the executing program that took the page fault will need to access these extra pages any time soon. As Table 6-1 suggests, the likelihood of these extra pages wasting precious RAM is something Windows 2000 attempts to take into account. It is more aggressive about bringing in extra code pages (programs often access code pages sequentially) than it is about program data structures, for example. The operating system also performs more aggressive anticipatory paging when there is more memory installed on the system. All these precautions are necessary because anticipatory paging strategies are, in fact, wasteful. They are throughput-oriented optimizations that tend to increase both disk and memory utilization. They explicitly trade off throughput against page fault resolution time, which is likely to increase.

Clustered paging elongates page read operations. Because it is handling bulk paging requests, the paging file disk is busier longer than it would be if it were just performing individual on-demand page read operations. (Keep in mind that if the anticipatory paging strategy proves successful, something which is highly workload-dependent, overall paging file disk utilization may be reduced.) Having more time-consuming paging file requests normally does not affect the thread currently delayed waiting for a page fault to be resolved. Indeed, this thread may directly benefit from Windows 2000 correctly anticipating a page access. However, *other* executing threads that encounter page faults that need to be resolved from the same paging file disk can be impacted. These threads are forced to wait until the previous bulk paging operation completes before Windows 2000 can resolve their page faults. Because the bulk paging file read operations Windows 2000 issues execute longer than single page on-demand requests, page fault resolution time for executing threads that encounter page faults subsequently can increase. In other words, anticipatory paging is a throughput-oriented optimization, not a response-oriented one.

The parameters in Table 6-1 that Windows 2000 uses to decide how much anticipatory paging to perform are hardcoded and cannot be changed. However, it is important to take note that clustered paging occurs and configure your system appropriately. When you see signs that clustered paging file operations are contributing to a disk bottleneck, one thing you can do to quickly relieve the situation is define another paging file on another physical disk. Having a second (or third or fourth) paging file allocated increases paging file I/O parallelism. While one paging file disk is busy with a bulk paging operation, it may be possible for Windows 2000 to resolve a page fault for a second thread—if it is lucky enough to need a page from a different paging file than the one that is currently busy. The section ""Memory Capacity Planning" later in this chapter looks at the memory performance counters you should monitor so that you can tell when it may be a good time to add paging files to mitigate the impact of clustered paging operations.

Moving the paging file

Another concern is the potential disk contention that results from locating the primary paging file on the same logical disk where the operating system files are installed (*%root*). This is the configuration the Windows 2000 setup installation routine builds, and it takes some doing to change it. Since most people expect the *%root* drive where system modules and common DLLs are located to be pretty busy, having the paging file located on the same logical drive will lead to disk contention. In practice, most system modules are loaded into RAM during system initialization. Consequently, accessing them does not usually generate many physical disk I/O requests once the system is up and running, so long as there is an ample supply of physical memory. But this is also the same logical drive where temporary files are stored by default and where many applications store key files, so disk contention using the default Windows 2000 configuration can be a concern.

Changing the default configuration to move the paging file to a different logical disk is a two-step process. First, define the new paging file. Once you have defined a second paging file, Windows 2000 will let you delete the original paging file on the *%root* disk. Naturally, this change requires rebooting because Windows 2000 is currently using the default paging file. Following a reboot, the change you requested will take effect, and the paging file on the *%root* disk will be gone.

When you instruct Windows 2000 to remove the default *%root* paging file, the warning message shown in Figure 6-5 appears. In order to create a crash dump in the event of a system failure, Windows 2000 requires a paging file on the *%root* disk where the operating system is installed that is large enough to hold the entire contents of RAM. Removing the paging file from the *%root* disk (or reducing its size below the amount of RAM installed) means that you will not be able to create a crash dump showing the complete contents of RAM when there is a system failure (blue screen). Depending on the importance of being able to create a crash dump, this may not be a risk worth running.

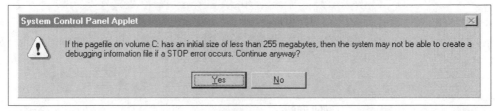

Figure 6-5. The warning message when you attempt to remove the paging file from the %root disk

If you do create additional paging files (or decide to move the original paging file), there is a good reason to create a paging file on a dedicated logical disk partition. Windows 2000 maintains no paging file performance statistics beyond monitoring the amount of space consumed (the %Usage and %Usage Peak counters in the Paging File object). There are no performance counters that show the amount of paging activity to individual paging files or measure the time it takes to resolve page faults by reading the disk. The only way in Windows 2000 to determine the amount of paging activity per paging file is to dedicate a paging file on a logical disk and use the Logical Disk performance statistics instead. While performance monitoring considerations may suggest moving the paging file to its own, dedicated logical disk, the necessity of obtaining a good crash dump may oblige you to retain the original paging file configuration built on the *%root* disk.

Process Virtual Address Spaces

The operating system constructs a separate virtual memory address space on behalf of each running process, potentially addressing up to 4 GB of virtual memory. Each Windows 2000 process virtual address space is divided into two equal parts, as depicted in Figure 6-6. The lower 2 GB of each process address space (the user address space) consists of private addresses associated with that specific process, and refers to pages that can only be accessed by threads running in that process address space *context*. Each per-process virtual address space can range from '0x0001 0000' to address '0x7fff ffff', spanning 2 GB, potentially. (The first 64K addresses are not used.) Each process gets its own unique set of user addresses in this range. Furthermore, no thread running in one process can access virtual memory addresses in the private range associated with a different process.

Shared addresses

The upper half of each per-process address space in the range of '0x8000 0000' to '0xffff ffff' consists of system addresses common to *all* virtual address spaces and that are commonly addressable from all running processes. This feat is accomplished by combining the system's page tables with each unique per-process set of page tables.

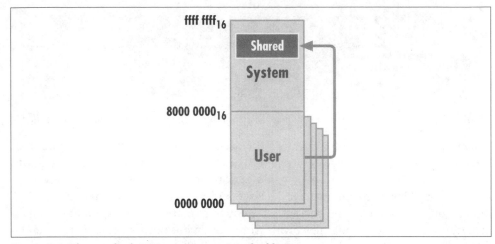

Figure 6-6. The standard 4 GB per-process virtual address space

While addresses in the system range are commonly accessible from threads running in each and every process, system virtual addresses are allocated using supervisor authority (Ring 0 on Intel hardware), which restricts memory access to threads running in privileged mode. Because shared system virtual memory addresses can only be accessed by threads running in privileged mode, application program threads running in user mode are unable to access commonly addressable virtual memory locations associated with the operating system directly. However, any system call made by an application execution thread that results in a trap into kernel mode (implemented as INT Interrupt instructions on Intel processors) routinely changes the system state from User Ring 3 to Privileged Ring 0 and permits access to these system virtual memory areas.

Commonly addressable system virtual memory locations play an important role in interprocess communication, or IPC. Specific virtual memory management API functions can be used to allocate portions of commonly addressable system areas to share data between two or more distinct processes, as illustrated in Figure 6-6. For example, the mechanism Windows 2000 uses that allows multiple process address spaces to access common modules known as *dynamic link libraries* (DLLs) utilizes this form of shared memory addressing. (DLLs are library modules that contain subroutines and functions, which are called dynamically at runtime, instead of being linked statically to the programs that utilize them.)

One widely used technique for sharing information between processes in Windows 2000 is for one process to allocate memory in the commonly addressable system area and then point one or more additional processes to the shared memory segment. This method of performing IPC is quite popular among Windows programmers. This is unfortunate, as it does not provide any of the integrity checking built into more sophisticated ways to communicate between processes, like named pipe services or COM.

Extended addressing

Both Windows 2000 Advanced Server and Datacenter permit a different partitioning of user and system addressable storage locations that extends the private user address range to 3 GB and shrinks the system area to 1 GB, as illustrated in Figure 6-7. The 3 GB user address space option is enabled by adding the /3GB switch to *boot.ini*. Only programs linked with the /LARGEADDRESSAWARE option can utilize this extended 3 GB user address space. For example, MS SQL Server is capable of exploiting an extended 3 GB user address space, and can use this extended private area to allocate more database buffers to boost performance.

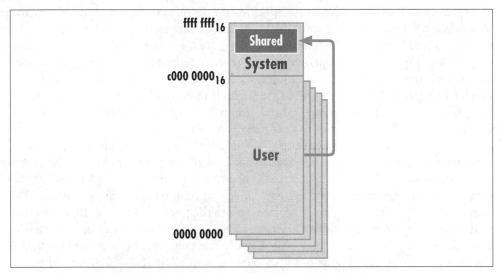

Figure 6-7. Extended 3 GB user address space

Virtual address translation

During instruction execution, virtual addresses are translated into physical (real) memory addresses. This *virtual address translation* takes place inside the instruction execution pipeline internal to each processor. For example, during the Prefetch stage of instruction execution discussed in Chapter 4, the pipeline translates the logical address of the next instruction to be executed, pointed to by the program counter (PC) register, into its corresponding real address. Similarly, during the instruction Decode phases, virtual addresses pointing to instruction operands are translated into their corresponding real addresses.

The precise mapping function used to translate a running program's virtual addresses into real physical memory locations is hardware-specific. Hardware specifications include:

- The mechanism by which the specific virtual translation context is established for the current address space
- The format of the virtual-to-physical address translation tables used
- The method for notifying the operating system that page faults have occurred

We review the Intel-specific hardware requirements for building and maintaining page translation tables in the following section.

Page tables

Intel's IA-32 processor architecture specifies the format of the page tables that the Windows 2000 operating system must build and maintain to enable the computer to perform virtual-to-real address translation. Figure 6-8 shows the IA-32 hardware-specific mechanism for translating virtual to real addresses. (Most machines that support virtual addressing use a similar scheme.) IA-32 uses a 4K page. (So-called large 1 MB pages are also supported, something that Windows 2000 uses for mapping the operating system kernel.) Intel employs a two-level, hierarchical indexing scheme using a Page Directory, which then points to the page tables themselves, as illustrated. The Page Directory resides in a single 4K page that is always resident in memory while the process executes. Internal Control Register 3 points to the origin of the Page Directory. Page tables, also 4K in size, are built on demand as virtual memory locations are accessed. These consist of 32-bit page table entries (PTEs) that contain the physical memory address where the page of virtual addresses is currently mapped. Each page table can map 1024 4K pages (a 4 MB range), while the Page Directory can point to 1024 page tables. The combination supports the full 4 GB addressing scheme. Figure 6-8 also illustrates the Windows 2000 virtual memory mapping scheme for shared operating system addresses and individual user address spaces.

As the processor instruction execution hardware encounters virtual addresses, representing either instructions or data areas, it performs a table look-up. The first 10 bits of the virtual address are used as an index into the page table directory to locate the page table associated with that specific 4 MB range. The second 10 bits are used to index into the designated page table to find the PTE. The PTE entry then contains the high order 20 bits of the real memory address of the page—its corresponding address in RAM. If the page is invalid, the entry specifies a paging file address where it can be found. The 20-bit real memory address contained in the PTE replaces the first 20 bits of the original virtual address. The low order 12 bits from the original virtual address, capable of representing offsets 0–4095 into the page, are retained. These 12 bits are added to the 20 bits in the PTE entry to form the complete 32-bit real memory address.

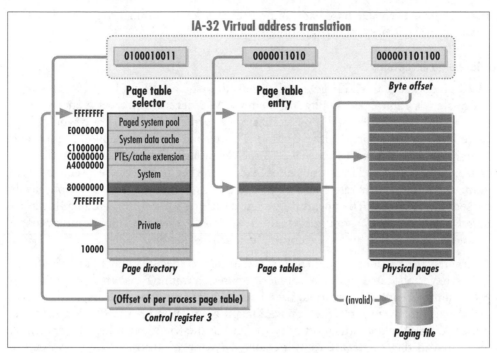

IA-32 Virtual address translation

0100010011 0000011010 000001101100

Page table selector — **Page table entry** — **Byte offset**

FFFFFFFF
E0000000 — Paged system pool
C1000000 — System data cache
C0000000
A4000000 — PTEs/cache extension
— System
80000000
7FFEFFFF

Private

10000

Page directory **Page tables** **Physical pages**

(Offset of per process page table)

Control register 3

(invalid) →

Paging file

Figure 6-8. The workings of Intel IA-32 virtual address translation

As required by the hardware, Windows 2000 builds and maintains one set of page tables capable of accessing the full 4 GB range of virtual addresses per process. Because each process is a separate and distinct *address space*, each execution thread inherits a specific address space *context*. A thread can access only virtual addresses associated with its specific process address space, with the exception of common system virtual addresses accessible by any thread with the appropriate security level. Any code that attempts to access a memory location that is not valid for that process context references an invalid PTE and causes an access violation. This memory protection mechanism eliminates many sorts of errors that occur when a thread in one process context inadvertently attempts to modify memory locations that belong to another process.

Since virtual address translation is a repetitive task, significant performance benefits are achieved by buffering these mapping tables in very fast cache memory on board the processor chip. Like other computer architectures that support virtual memory, Intel processors provide hardware Translation Lookaside Buffers (TLBs) to speed up virtual address translation. The TLB is a small, dedicated cache containing the most recent virtual:real address translations performed by the processor. When Control Register 3 is reloaded to point to a new set of per-process page tables, a *context switch* occurs. This has performance implications. A context switch flushes the TLB, slowing down instruction execution for a transitional period known as a cache *cold start*. There is even a P6 hardware counter that tracks the number of Instruction TLB misses/sec, if you are interested in observing this mechanism.

Addressing exceptions

The PTE contains a Valid page flag that indicates whether or not the virtual memory address has a counterpart in physical memory. Whenever the processor encounters a PTE with the invalid bit set in the course of performing virtual memory addressing, there is an address translation exception. This terminates instruction execution and generates an interrupt. It is then up to the operating system to determine the root cause of the virtual address translation exception. For instance, the executing program may have merely referenced a virtual address that exists, but is not physically present (a *page fault*). The operating system is then responsible for fetching the designated page from the paging file where it is stored, copying it into some available physical memory slot, and re-executing the failed instruction.

Alternately, due to a program logic error, the address specified may not be valid, i.e., it was never allocated in the first place. Upon determining that this very common programming error has occurred, the operating system performs a diagnostic memory dump and terminates the application program. Windows 2000, for example, writes Access Violation diagnostics to the end of the Dr. Watson log file, *drwtsn32.log* stored in the *%system32* root directory. Or, you can instruct Windows 2000 to dump the contents of real memory to disk when a program error like this occurs.

To assist in trapping common programming mistakes, Windows 2000 deliberately designates x'0001 0000' as the starting point for all process address spaces, marking the first 64K process virtual memory addresses as invalid. A common programming error is to reference an inadvertently uninitialized pointer, leading to an address calculation that generates a reference to a low virtual memory address. By flagging the page table entries for the first 64K of each process address space as invalid, Windows 2000 is able to catch many of these errors before they can do serious damage. The 64K boundary, by the way, is a legacy of Intel's 64K segmented virtual addressing scheme for the original 80286 processors where address pointers were 16 bits wide. If you examine a Dr. Watson log, you will typically see one or more Access Violations involving low storage virtual addresses where Windows 2000 has succeeded in catching programs with that kind of common programming bug in the act.

Memory status bits

For a valid page, the high order 20 bits of the PTE reference the address of the physical memory location where the page resides, which is used in virtual address translation. As illustrated in Figure 6-9, an Intel IA-32 page table entry points to either a real page in memory if the page is valid, a location in the paging file, or a Virtual Address Descriptor (VAD). The Intel IA-32 hardware PTE also maintains a number of status bits that reflect the current status of the virtual memory page. Bit 0 of the

PTE is the "Present" bit, the valid bit that indicates whether of not the virtual address currently resides in physical memory. If the Present bit is not set, an Intel processor ignores the remainder of the information stored in the PTE. If Bit 0 is set, the interpretation of the other bits is determined as shown.

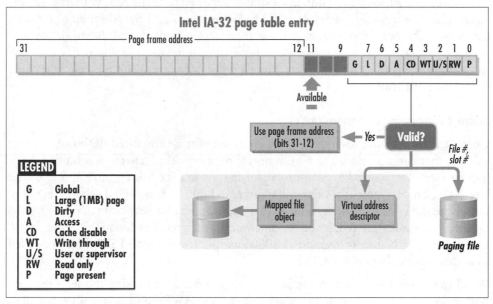

Figure 6-9. The workings of Intel IA-32 page table entry

The status bits 1–6 are used by the hardware to maintain additional status information about the real memory page. Bit 2, for example, is an authorization bit set to prevent programs executing in user mode (Ring 3) from accessing operating system memory locations allocated by kernel threads running in Ring 0. The "Dirty" bit 6 is set whenever the contents of a page are changed. The operating system refers to the Dirty bit during page replacement to determine if the copy of the page on the paging file is current. Bit 5 is an "Access" bit that the hardware sets whenever the page is referenced. It is designed to play a role in page replacement, and it is used for that purpose by Windows 2000 under circumstances that we describe shortly. Likewise, Windows 2000 turns off the Read/Write bit to protect operating system and process code pages from being overwritten inadvertently by executing programs. Windows 2000 does not utilize the Intel hardware status bits 3 and 4, which are "hints" designed to influence the behavior of the processor cache. Windows 2000 does use 1 MB Large pages to load sections of the operating system, which cuts down on the number of PTEs that need to be defined for the system virtual memory areas.

The page table format used in the Digital Alpha, which Windows NT also supports, is conceptually similar, but somewhat different in its implementation because the processor hardware requirements are different. In 32-bit addressing mode, the Alpha uses 8K pages. The Alpha's Page Directory lookup uses the first 8 bits of a virtual address, while the next 11 bits are an offset into the page table entries. These architectural differences between processors were crucial to the design of the NT page replacement policy, which was intended to function on both Intel and Digital Alpha hardware. The Alpha also maintains a similar set of page status bits, with at least one striking difference: there is no Access bit. When deciding how to replace pages on the Alpha, the operating system gets no information from the hardware on an executing program's pattern of reference to its virtual addresses. The Alpha does not use separate Write protection and Dirty bits either; it uses one Write bit that essentially serves both functions.

Address Windowing Extensions (AWE)

Current Intel Pentium III and IV Xeon chips support an enhanced 36-bit addressing scheme that can address up to 64 GB of real memory. This scheme is a bit of a stop-gap between the 32-bit P6 microprocessor family and the full 64-bit P7s due out in late 2001. This support allows manufacturers to build high-powered servers that contain more than 4 GB of addressable RAM. Accessing addresses above the 32-bit 4 GB boundary requires the PSE36 driver software from Intel, downloadable from *http://www.intel.com*. Naturally, Windows 2000 incorporates the Intel PSE36 driver needed to address more than 4 GB of RAM.

Windows 2000 supports this peculiar 36-bit extended addressing mode. This support is known as Address Windowing Extensions (AWE), and it is a little peculiar, too; see Figure 6-10. Under Windows 2000, applications can only access addresses above the 32-bit line indirectly by calling the AWE API routines. The AWE Win32 API allows a programmer to define an extended addressing window into the real memory above the 4 GB line and manipulate data stored there. The OS only lets you access these extended addresses using 36-bit real memory addresses, so that Windows 2000 does not have to create 36-bit page table entries. There are AWE routines to access and store data using real 36-bit addresses. These 36-bit addresses must be mapped into conventional 32-bit virtual addresses before your Win32 program running in user mode can manipulate them.

There are probably not many programmers who will take advantage of this ability to access memory above the 4 GB line. Not many processes need more than the 4 GB of virtual memory addressability that Windows 2000 offers conventionally. Programmers responsible for applications that are virtual memory–constrained today may be better off waiting for the full 64-bit addressing that Intel's next-generation P7 Itanium processors offer.

Win64

Win64 refers to a forthcoming version of Windows XP that supports Intel's new Itanium processors and their IA-64 architecture. As of this writing, Microsoft has

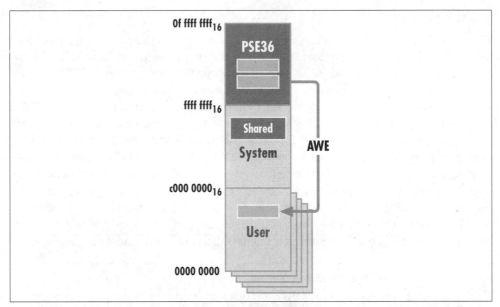

Figure 6-10. Windows 2000 supports the 36-bit extended addressing mode with AWE

released many of the specifications for its Win64 support, explaining to developers how to take advantage of Intel's latest architectural advances. Unquestionably, Windows XP's 64-bit support is designed for massive machines where the amount of virtual memory available per process is 16 terabytes (16,000,000,000,000 bytes)! To give you an idea of just how massive Win64 machines could be, consider that the 64-bit flavor of the operating system allows for 128 GB worth of page table entries to support these potentially huge process virtual address spaces.

Microsoft has also explained that we can expect the 64-bit version of Windows XP to retain the same look and feel as the current 32-bit version. While 64-bit Windows will use 64-bit PTEs and address pointers, the Virtual Memory Manager functions of 64-bit Windows XP probably will not look much different from the way the operating system works today.

Frankly, there is little experience across the computer industry with virtual memory systems on this scale, which makes it difficult to say exactly how such systems might used. One possibility is that these systems will retain huge amounts of data in RAM, which suggests that extended availability, reliability, and fault tolerance will be key attributes. Another salient characteristic of such massive systems is that it will take so long to load large amounts of data into memory that it will be counterproductive to take them down for any reason.

Invalid PTEs

When the PTE Present bit 0 is not set, the hardware ignores the remaining contents of the PTE, and the operating system is free to use this space any way it sees fit. Of primary importance, Windows 2000 uses the empty space in an invalid PTE to store essential information about where a paged-out page can be located on the paging file. This information is stored in an invalid PTE, as shown in Figure 6-11. Invalid PTEs reference a paging file number (PFN) and offset to identify the location on disk where the page is stored. The PFN is a 4-bit index that is used to reference up to 16 unique paging files. It is cross-indexed to the HKLM\SYSTEM\CurrentControlSet\Control\ Session Manager\Memory Management Registry key, where information about the paging file configuration is stored in the PagingFiles field. The 20-bit paging file offset then references a specific page file offset up to x'f ffff', or 1 million. A transition bit is maintained by the operating system for determining which pages in a process working set are active. Its role in page replacement is discussed in the next section.

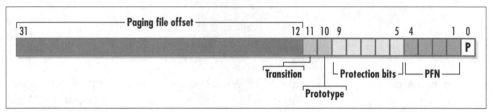

Figure 6-11. If a page is invalid, information about where it is located is stored in the PTE

Windows 2000 also builds prototype PTEs, identified as shown. The prototype PTE is the mechanism used for mapping shared memory pages into multiple process address spaces. Windows 2000 executables frequently access shared code organized in DLLs. DLL modules are loaded once by the operating system into an area of commonly addressable storage backed by a real PTE. When referenced by individual processes, the operating system then builds a prototype PTE that points to the real PTE. Using the prototype PTE mechanism, a DLL is loaded just once, but can be referenced by many different process address spaces. Prototype PTEs also play a role in the Windows 2000 file cache, which is the operating system's general-purpose means of mapping application files into virtual memory for faster access. Further details of prototype PTEs are beyond the scope of the current discussion, but we take up the subject of the built-in file cache in Chapter 7.

Page Replacement

Before we delve into the available Windows 2000 memory and paging measurements, it is important to understand the page replacement policy Windows 2000 uses. Following a policy of allocating real memory page slots *on demand* as they are referenced inevitably fills up all available physical memory. A common problem virtual memory operating systems face is what to do when a page fault occurs, a valid page must be retrieved from the paging file, and there is little or no room left in physical memory for the referenced page. When real memory is fully allocated and a new page is referenced, something has to give. A *page replacement policy* decides what to do when this happens.

Available Bytes

You can watch real memory filling up in Windows 2000 by monitoring Available Bytes, which represents free, unallocated RAM. Available Bytes counts the number of free pages in RAM at any particular time; it is the all-important buffer of free pages the OS maintains in order to resolve page faults quickly. The Available Bytes counter, like all the real memory allocation counters in Windows 2000, reports the amount of RAM currently not allocated to any process in bytes. The use of bytes is a legacy from earlier versions of Windows NT, when both 4K Intel pages and 8K Digital Alpha pages were supported. Since you might not necessarily know whether the measurements came from an Intel or an Alpha processor, Microsoft decided to report the data in bytes rather than pages. If you monitor Available Bytes using the System Monitor application, you will find that the number of Available Bytes is always evenly divisible by 4096, the number of bytes per page.

Try a simple experiment where you start and stop some application processes. As you do this, watch Task Manager to monitor virtual and physical memory usage. On the Task Manager Performance tab (illustrated in Figure 6-12), the MEM Usage and Memory Usage History graphs refer to virtual memory Committed Bytes. The value charted corresponds to the Commit Charge (K) Total field in the lower-left quadrant. The Task Manager Commit Charge field reports on virtual memory allocations in 1024 kilobyte (KB) segments; the corresponding Committed Bytes counter in the System Monitor counts bytes, which accounts for the difference between the two measurements. The current virtual memory Committed Bytes Limit is also shown. The Memory Usage History graph charts Committed Bytes against the Commit Limit, which serves as the maximum value for the Y axis.

In the upper-right text quadrant (immediately below the Memory Usage History timeline), Task Manager shows Total system memory (the amount of installed RAM), Available, and System Cache, all denominated in 1000 bytes. The Task Manager Available field corresponds exactly to the System Monitor Available Kbytes counter, by the way.

As you open new applications on your desktop, watch as virtual memory Committed Bytes increases while Available Bytes decreases in tandem. For example, in Figure 6-12, we are looking at a system with 256 MB of RAM installed. It currently has 208 MB of virtual memory committed, with 26 MB free memory remaining (about 10%). As a general rule of thumb, a 5–10% cushion of Available Bytes is normally ample. This system has sufficient physical memory to run this workload.

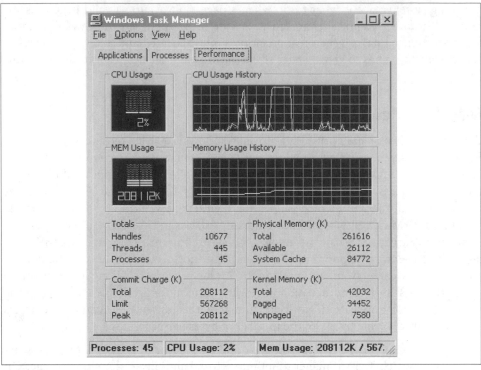

Figure 6-12. The Performance tab tracks virtual memory allocations and available RAM

If you are able to start enough application programs, you will eventually observe that the number of Committed Bytes begins to exceed the amount of physical RAM installed. This is the first indication that real memory might be filling up. As long as Committed Bytes is less than the amount of RAM installed, every virtual memory page requested by application processes can fit in RAM. That means the amount of RAM installed is sufficient for this workload. However, just because Committed Bytes is greater than the amount of RAM installed does not mean that RAM is completely allocated. Some application committed pages that have not been referenced in a long time may not be currently resident in real memory. Idle pages are subject to being paged out of the system, so RAM may still not be completely allocated.

Windows 2000 continues to permit applications to allocate more virtual memory up to the Committed Bytes Limit. If your applications continue to add more Committed Bytes to the system, at some point all those active virtual memory pages will not fit easily into physical RAM and you will start to notice an impact on system performance. At this point, when you click on an application that you have not accessed in a while, you are likely to hear the hard disk grinding away. Windows 2000 is performing paging I/O to the disk, taking older pages in memory and writing them to the paging file to make room for current pages that it must read back into memory from the paging file disk. As you continue to open new applications and drive Committed

Bytes higher, the slowdown in system performance will eventually become acute. Congratulations, you have induced *thrashing* on your computer.

When the number of virtual memory Committed Bytes starts to exceed the amount of physical RAM installed, you can probably also observe that the number of Available Bytes begins to stabilize at approximately 4 MB. Windows 2000 attempts to maintain a 4 MB cushion of Available Bytes in order to service application requests for new pages quickly. If the working sets of active processes exceed the size of physical memory, there is contention for real memory. In Windows 2000 you can often observe signs of this contention when the system's pool of Available Bytes reaches about 4 MB. At approximately 4 MB of available RAM, Windows 2000 crosses a threshold where the behavior of its virtual memory management policy changes. If Windows 2000 has difficulty maintaining a 4 MB pool of available RAM and the demand for virtual memory continues to increase, you will likely observe telltale signs of thrashing.

Portability Goals

When RAM is full and an executing program encounters a page fault, Windows 2000 must make room for the new page. The approach to page replacement that Windows 2000 employs was designed to satisfy processor-specific hardware requirements while retaining a large degree of hardware-independence. Even though Windows 2000 runs on x86 Intel processors exclusively, over its lifetime, versions of Windows NT have been developed that support quite different MIPS, PowerPC, Digital Alpha, and Intel IA-32 processor architectures. Even today, the operating system remains highly portable, at least in theory.

The goal of portability distinctly influenced the page replacement policy that Windows 2000 employs to manage virtual memory. The Windows 2000 page replacement policy was designed to work with almost any processor hardware, including models such as the Digital Alpha that do not maintain a hardware Access bit. Initially, early versions of the Microsoft operating system ignored the hardware Access bit completely, even where it was available (which was on Intel processors). Later releases of NT, beginning with Version 4.0, do make use of the Intel hardware Access bits under limited circumstances, the inevitable result of Microsoft's decision to optimize Windows 2000 for its dominant hardware platform.

Maintaining a high degree of portability across a wide variety of processor architectures means ignoring opportunities to exploit unique processor-specific hardware features. This is a temptation that developers of operating systems developed and maintained by hardware manufacturers are usually unable to resist, something that has undermined the goal of portability espoused by the original developers of Unix. What Windows 2000 may sacrifice in performance by not being optimized around any specific computing hardware, it gains in portability. Of course, with the availability of Intel-compatible processors spanning a wide range of cost and performance, porting Windows 2000 to other computing platforms does not appear to matter much today.

The extent to which Microsoft operating system developers will be tempted to sacrifice their portability goals in favor of supporting unique Intel processor-specific optimizations in the future will probably be determined by:

- The extent to which Linux exploits some of the unique Intel processor-specific features that Microsoft ignores
- How successful these processor-specific optimizations prove in dislodging Microsoft Windows 2000's dominant position atop the Intel server and desktop market

These developments bear watching over the next few years. Consider that there is little need today to port the Windows 2000 operating system to any alternative hardware platform, with the exception of the newer IA-64 processors, which are upward compatible with the IA-32 instruction set. In the foreseeable future, we may never see Windows 2000 running on any other processor architectures again, rendering much of the admirable OS kernel architecture Microsoft developed to promote hardware portability superfluous.

Virtual memory management is an area where the Microsoft Windows 2000 developers might be tempted to compromise their principles and exploit some of Intel's proprietary hardware features, but not necessarily because the operating system is not effective today. On the contrary, experience shows that the page replacement policy implemented by Windows 2000 is quite effective. However, the fact that it is somewhat unconventional and, consequently, poorly understood does lead to some problems. Systems professionals who come to the Windows 2000 platform with a background in some other operating system architecture (other than VAX/VMS, which is quite similar) find themselves on unfamiliar ground, with paging statistics that do not mean what they customarily mean on other platforms.

In the next section, we discuss the page replacement strategy that most systems professionals are familiar with: LRU (which stands for Least Recently Used). Then we compare and contrast the Windows 2000 policy, which implements LRU in an unconventional way in that it does not rely on hardware Access bits being available. Once you understand how Windows 2000 implements page replacement, you should have no difficulty interpreting the memory and paging counters provided by the operating system to measure the performance of its virtual memory management policies. Finally, we discuss ways in which more conventional elements of LRU are creeping back into the OS, which may also prove reassuring.

LRU

The page replacement policy most often adopted by operating system designers involves identifying currently resident memory pages that have not been referenced recently and removing them from memory. (Before "dirty" pages containing changed data can be removed, the operating system must first copy their contents to the paging file.) This popular solution to the page replacement problem is called Least Recently Used or LRU, which captures the overall flavor of the strategy. LRU tries to identify "older" pages and replaces them with new ones, reflecting current virtual memory access patterns of executing programs.

Intuitively, an LRU page replacement policy that uses information about historical patterns of virtual memory page accesses to predict future reference patterns seems like the right approach. Nevertheless, despite its popularity, LRU is not optimal. Its performance can be improved upon substantially, for example, if an executing program provides "hints" about its expected pattern of memory reference. However, in the absence of specific hints from the program, which are seldom forthcoming, LRU generally performs well over a wide range of circumstances. Moreover, its behavior is very well understood because it is practiced in a variety of contexts, not just virtual memory management. Most cache management routines rely on LRU in one form or another.

How LRU works

In general, LRU maintains an ordering of resident virtual memory pages from Most Recently Referenced to Least Recently Used. When real memory is full and an executing program references a page that is not currently resident in memory (i.e., a page fault occurs), the Least Recently Used page in real memory is replaced with the current Most Recently Referenced page. Older pages, by inference, are less likely to be referenced again soon by executing programs, so they are the best candidates for page replacement. Older pages selected for replacement are effectively removed from memory—the next time they are referenced they must be retrieved from a paging file. If the page in memory was modified, the operating system must first update the copy on the paging file before it is definitively removed.

In practice, many LRU virtual memory implementations, including the one found in Windows 2000, attempt to maintain some pool of free pages in RAM. This pool of Available Bytes allows the OS to schedule an I/O to the paging file to resolve the page fault immediately. Then, when this pool becomes depleted, a round of *page stealing* is triggered, which replenishes the pool of free pages before it is completely exhausted. (Windows 2000 prefers the more polite designation of page *trimming*.) Windows 2000 uses page trimming on a regular basis to maintain its pool of free pages (reported as Available Bytes). In this approach, LRU is used to identify candidates for page stealing—the "older" pages in RAM.

The challenge in Windows 2000 is to identify older pages without relying on specific processor hardware support. This is accomplished by trimming pages from process working sets provisionally. After trimming pages aggressively from active processes, Windows 2000 adds them to the pool of Available Bytes, but tags them initially as being in a provisional state. They are not immediately removed from RAM. The next time threads from active processes are scheduled to run, they reference the pages that are active, and these stolen pages are allowed to transition back into the process working set. So-called *transition faults* or *soft page faults* are handled quickly, with a minimum of overhead. Eventually, what is left behind in the pool of Available Pages are older, unused pages that are good candidates to be replaced.

Figure 6-13 provides an overview of this procedure. Trimmed process working set pages are placed initially in the Standby List, where they are allowed to transition fault back into their process working set the next time they are referenced. Transition faults are distinguished from *hard page faults*, which must be satisfied by reading the paging file disk. Pages in the Standby List that are unreferenced long enough are eventually moved to the Free List. As illustrated, so-called "dirty" or changed pages in the Standby List must be copied to the paging file before they can move to the Free List. When the System Zero Page Thread executes, it zeros out the contents of pages on the Free List, which allows them to move to the Zero List. Pages from the Zero List are allocated whenever either a hard page fault occurs or a process references a brand new page (also known as Demand Zero page faults). Together, the size of the Standby List, the Free List, and the Zero List are added together and reported as Available Bytes.

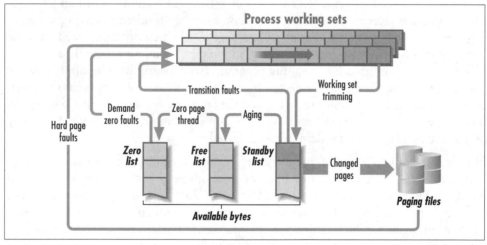

Figure 6-13. Page trimming

The page trimming procedure is threshold-driven. Page trimming is invoked when one or more of the List structures that make up the pool of Available Bytes is depleted. In addition, Windows 2000 schedules writes to the paging file when the number of changed pages exceeds a threshold value. Modified pages are written in bulk to disk by Modified Page Writer threads, again based on threshold values being exceeded. In *Inside Windows 2000*, Solomon and Russinovich report that when the number of changed pages on the Standby List exceeds 300, then Windows 2000 attempts to flush 75 dirty pages in bulk to disk. If the Zero List is ever depleted and the system is too busy with other work to schedule the Zero Page Thread, it is not a big deal. The operating system simply zeros out a page from the Free List in real time so that security is never compromised.

Measurement support

Figure 6-13 also illustrates the points where this process is instrumented. The Transition Faults/sec counter in the Memory object reports the rate at which soft page faults occur. Similarly, Demand Zero Faults/sec reports the rate at which new pages are being created. Pages Output/sec shows the rate at which changed pages have been copied to disk. By implication, since real memory is a closed system:

Pages trimmed/sec = Transition Faults + Demand Zero Faults + Hard page faults

plus any change in the size of the Available Bytes buffer from one interval to the next. The individual sizes of the Standby, Free, and Zero lists are not reported. Nor does Windows 2000 report the rate at which the Balance Set Manager's page trimming routine runs, nominally at least once per second.

The Pages Read/sec counter corresponds to the rate of hard page faults requiring the operating system to retrieve a page from disk. The fact that Pages Input/sec is usually larger than Pages Read/sec reflects the use of anticipatory paging. Pages Input/sec is the actual number of pages retrieved from disk. Calculating:

Pages per page fault = Pages Input/sec / Pages Read/sec

reports the average number of pages retrieved per page fault. Similarly, the Pages written/sec counter shows the number of page write operations that were initiated, and Pages output/sec counts the number of physical 4K pages actually written. As Figure 6-14 indicates, there is a tendency for the operating system to make greater use of bulk paging whenever there is an increased paging load. As either input or output paging operations get backed up, Windows 2000 attempts more clustered paging operations to improve paging I/O throughput. Thus, the onset of an abundance of clustered paging operations suggests a potential paging I/O bottleneck.

When the average number of pages read or written to disk is consistently above two pages per page fault or page write operation, *and* more than 10–20% of all I/Os to the disk are the result of paging operations, it is probably time to add another paging file, if possible. Adding a second paging file spreads the paging I/O load across another physical disk and usually improves page fault resolution time substantially.

Windows 2000 supplies one other important measurement of overall paging activity, namely Page Faults/sec. Unfortunately, interpreting how the Page Faults/sec counter relates to the other paging activity counters is problematic. Page Faults/sec includes both Transition (soft) Faults/sec and hard page faults (Pages Read/sec). It evidently also includes the number of Cache Faults/sec due to the normal diversion of application I/O to the paging subsystem (the operation of the Windows 2000 File

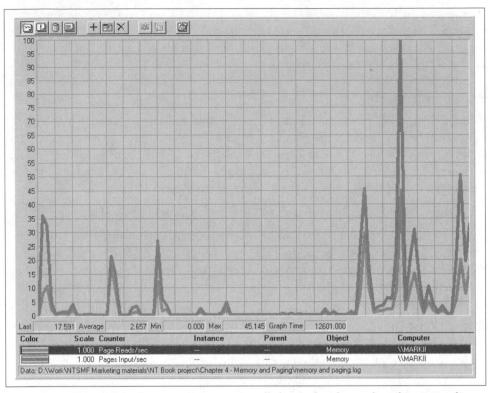

Figure 6-14. The number of Pages Input/sec is normally larger that the number of Pages Read/sec

Cache is discussed in Chapter 7). There is strong evidence that it also includes the number of Demand Zero Faults/sec:

Page Faults/sec = Cache Faults/sec + Demand Zero Faults/sec
+ Pages Read/sec + Transition Faults/sec

but that evidence is not conclusive. Figure 6-15 offers a typical example. The stacked bar chart sums Cache Faults/sec, Demand Zero Faults/sec, Pages Read/sec, and Transition Faults/sec from a Windows 2000 Server. This sum is compared to the Page Faults/sec counter for the same interval, marked by an *. For some measurement intervals, the number of Page Faults/sec reported does correspond to the sum of the other four counters. Intervals where the number of Page Faults/sec reported is most consistent with the other counters appear to correspond to intervals where Demand Zero Faults/sec is high and there are few Transition Faults/sec. In intervals where there is a lively mixture of the four different categories of page faults, the number of Page Faults/sec reported disagrees with the number of page faults reported in the four distinct categories—sometimes by as much as 30%! Unfortunately, official Microsoft sources provide no explanation for this discrepancy.

Next, let's evaluate the effectiveness of the Windows 2000 page replacement policy. There is a tendency for systems professionals accustomed to other operating systems

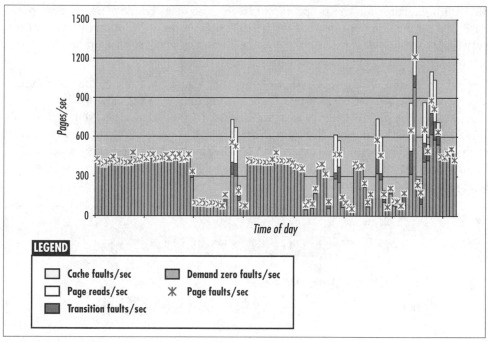

Figure 6-15. Comparing Page Faults/sec to other counters

to view the Windows 2000 LRU implementation critically. Perhaps it just takes a little getting used to. To begin with, LRU is seldom practiced in its pure form; maintaining a total ordering of pages by their time of last reference is a prohibitively high overhead function. (Imagine the rate at which real memory pages are accessed, normally at least once or twice *per instruction*.) Computer hardware evolved to support LRU memory aging by supplying a function that automatically updates reference bits as virtual addresses are translated into real ones. As discussed previously, the Intel IA-32 architecture maintains these reference bits (the access bit) in the PTE.

The Clock algorithm

A popular variant of LRU for virtual memory page replacement utilizes hardware-maintained access bits. Many people are familiar with this variation, known as the "Clock" algorithm, because it is practiced in both MVS and Unix. Every clock interval, an OS memory management function scans and resets all the hardware access bits, and accumulates information about how long pages resident in physical memory have gone unreferenced. This aging information about resident pages is then used to order them by the approximate time of their most recent reference. Using this ordering, page replacement proceeds by replacing the oldest resident pages whenever physical memory is depleted.

The Clock variant of the LRU strategy has its known limitations, too, not the least of which is its difficulty scaling to very large memory configurations. The aging algorithm executes in time proportional to the size of its resident page frame database. An optimization introduced in the IBM mainframe MVS operating system for very large memories, for example, varies the frequency of Clock updates based on the age of the oldest page in the system.*

On uniprocessors, Windows 2000 implements a degenerate form of the Clock aging algorithm that uses the PTE access bit to distinguish between new and old pages. When it is time to steal pages (on a uniprocessor), the Balance Set Manager kernel thread responsible for page trimming scans each process working set and examines each PTE, as illustrated in Figure 6-16. The illustration shows a process working set before, during, and after the regularly scheduled Balance Set Manager working set scan designed to age pages.

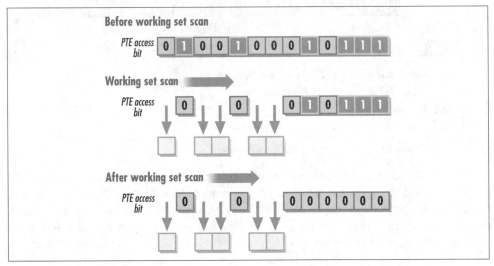

Figure 6-16. The Balance Set Manager scans the process working set

The Balance Set Manager scans the process working set and trims pages that the access bit indicates have not been referenced in the interval since the last time the working set scan routine was run. If the hardware access bit is set, then the page is designated as a "new" page and allowed to remain in the process working set. Then the Balance Set Manager resets the hardware access bit in the PTE. In this scheme, a new page is one with its access bit set; any other page is old and, therefore, a candidate for page stealing. Note that not every page where the access bit was not set is trimmed from the process working set. The Balance Set Manager only trims enough pages from each process working set to replenish the Available Bytes pool.

---

* For a discussion of the scalability of page replacement policies in large-scale IBM mainframes, see "MVS Memory Management," published in the 1991 *Proceedings* of Computer Measurement Group's annual conference.

The Balance Set Manager thread that performs the process working set scans is scheduled to run once per second. Whenever Available Bytes falls below some threshold, page trimming is also scheduled. As illustrated, page trimming is halted when a certain number of pages are trimmed from the working set and the pool of Available Bytes is replenished. Even after the Available Bytes free pages pool is stocked, the Balance Set Manager working set scan continues to reset the PTE access bits of pages in each process working set in anticipation of the next working scan and page trimming cycle.

This is not quite the whole story in Windows 2000, but it is how Windows 2000 uses the Intel PTE access bit to identify older pages in a process working set that are good candidates for page stealing. Obviously, the only way for the Balance Set Manager to find a page with its access bit set is if some process execution thread accessed the page sometime *after* the last time the Balance Set Manager kernel was dispatched. This degenerative form of LRU has the advantage that it executes a steal cycle quickly because it is easy to locate "old" pages that are candidates for stealing. However, it does have the disadvantage that it does not distinguish among "older" pages to any great degree.

Multiprocessor effects

This simple approach to LRU page aging runs into grave difficulty on IA-32 multiprocessors, which is why Microsoft restricts its use to single processor systems. Consider a four-way processor designed to execute a homogenous SQL Server workload, for example. The operating system's Balance Set Manager page trimming thread gets dispatched on Processor 0. Meanwhile, Processors 1–3 are busy executing SQL Server threads processing against the database. When the Balance Set Manager running on CPU 0 processes the SQL Server process address space, it resets the access bits in the process's page table entries (PTEs). Remember that only one set of PTEs is built per process, even on a multiprocessor. The PTE updates that the Balance Set Manager thread running on Processor 0 makes invalidate any SQL Server process PTEs that are cached in the TLBs on board Processors 1–3. Because the Balance Set Manager running on processor 0 updates these PTEs, SQL Server threads executing on processors 1–3 are delayed while current PTE entries are fetched from RAM. The effect of the Balance Set Manager's updating of a process's PTE-resident access bits is to flush the TLB on every other processor where the application's threads are active. Not only does this TLB flush degrade multiprocessor performance, it has the extra unpleasant effect that the performance degradation gets worse with more processors.[*]

---

[*] Consider that this TLB flush behavior significantly impacts the performance of a dedicated SQL Server machine trying to execute a TPC-C benchmark, for example. Executing a TPC-C benchmark, it would not be unusual for 6 of 8 CPUs in an 8-way configuration to be executing SQL Server threads. Updating the PTEs would result in TLB flushes anywhere SQL Server threads were executing, severely impacting Instruction Execution Rate.

For this reason, Windows 2000 restricts PTE access bit manipulation to uniprocessor systems. On multiprocessors, Windows 2000 never interrogates or resets the hardware access bits that reside in the process PTEs. The trade-off in the loss of page trimming efficiency is more than offset by the gain in multiprocessor scalability, especially when such systems are configured with ample amounts of RAM in the first place.

Putting It All in Focus

Experience shows that, peculiar as it may be, the Windows 2000 page replacement policy is normally quite effective. The transition fault mechanism ages trimmed pages, allowing active pages to return to process working sets. Over time, pages left on the Standby List are correctly identified as older, unreferenced pages. These can be safely moved from the Standby List to the Free List and made available for new virtual memory allocations.

The key to the transition fault mechanism being able to effectively identify good candidates for page stealing is allowing trimmed pages to remain on the Standby List long enough. What is "long enough" is relative, depending on the memory access pattern of your workload and the capacity of your system to move pages to and from the disk. Notice that there is no minimum length of time that trimmed pages remain on the Standby List, Free List, and Zero List, nor is there any measurement data that reports how old pages are when they are replaced with newer ones. As in most virtual memory management systems, the best indicator of performance problems is a high rate of hard page faults, those satisfied by reading the disk. Consequently, it is very important to monitor the Pages Read/sec counter that reports hard page faults. These are the page faults that impact thread execution time in Windows 2000.

One criticism of the current Windows 2000 page replacement policy is that several critical aspects do not scale to systems with very large amounts of RAM. In particular, the size of the Available Bytes buffer of free pages is the same whether your system has 64 MB of RAM or 1 GB of RAM. The size of the Available Bytes buffer should scale with the size of RAM. You must do this manually in Windows 2000 by monitoring real memory utilization and ensuring that Available Bytes seldom dips below approximately 5% of the total RAM installed.

The transition fault mechanism, which is used to identify older, unused pages in Windows 2000, is unavoidable. It is not unusual for the rate of transition faults processed to be extremely high, even when there is plenty of free RAM available. Moreover, in the absence of a shortage of Available Bytes, a high rate of transition faults does *not* necessarily mean that you are experiencing a paging problem. Figure 6-17 is a graph showing the Transition Faults/sec and Demand Zero Faults/sec counters from a four-way Windows 2000 Server running a large Oracle database application. Transition faults are occurring at the rate of some 6000 per second, but the system evidently has ample amounts of free RAM (Available Bytes is shown, graphed by a solid line against the left Y axis). Meanwhile, there are over 2000 Demand Zero page faults occurring per second, too. On the system on which all this virtual memory management is occurring, the number of Available Bytes exceeds 250–300 MB at all times. (This particular system was configured with 2 GB of RAM.) Transition faults and Demand Zero pages faults evidently do not just go away when you add RAM to your system.

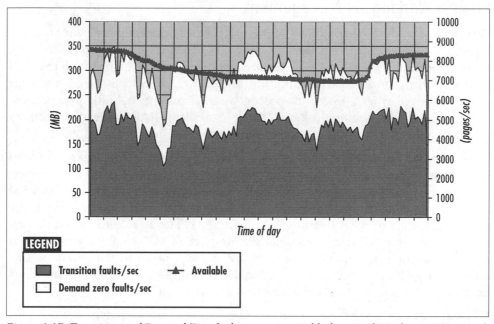

Figure 6-17. Transition and Demand Zero faults are an inevitable feature of Windows 2000 virtual memory management

Calling these transition faults "soft" faults tends to cushion any concern with the high amount of overhead associated with transition fault processing. True, transition faults are handled swiftly compared to hard page faults, which require an I/O to the paging file. Since the page is still resident, RAM is already allocated, and the PTE data is preserved, the amount of operating system processing involved is minimal. However, transition fault processing is hardly free. Each transition fault is associated with an addressing exception, which, in turn, generates an interrupt. Undeniably, the system shown in Figure 6-17 is forced to service an additional 8000 interrupts/sec, compared to some other operating system running the same Oracle database application. As systems with larger and larger amounts of RAM become commonplace, one optimization that would reduce unnecessary transition faults would be to slow down the rate of page trimming based on the amount of Available Bytes. When ample memory is available, the operating system should not have to work so hard trying to manage it.

The multiprocessor effect described previously when PTE-resident access bits are reset is a serious problem. As long as Intel processors utilize access bits located in ordinary RAM there is no way to avoid flushing processor TLBs when PTEs are updated. This problem can probably be resolved only by adding some new hardware function.

Process Working Set Management

Due to page stealing, one program's pattern of memory access can influence the performance of other executing programs since they all share a common memory pool. More generally, this is the trade-off between a policy of *global LRU*, which treats all process virtual address spaces uniformly, and *local LRU*, which applies the page replacement policy on a process-by-process basis. Under a global LRU policy, a single program with a memory leak can absorb all available RAM, generating memory contention that will slow the execution of other running programs.

While it has some global aspects and remains vulnerable to memory leaks, Windows 2000 decisively practices a localized per-process working set management policy. Each process has a designated *working set maximum*, initially set by default by the operating system. This is the maximum number of pages associated with any single process that the operating system will keep in RAM. The default maximum process working set size is 345 pages, or slightly more than 14 MB, on any system with at least 64 MB of RAM installed. Any process running at its maximum value that attempts to reference a new page finds that the Virtual Memory Manager removes an existing page *before* adding the new one to the process working set.

Of course, this designated maximum working set size value is a purely arbitrary one. The dynamic aspect of Windows 2000's working set management allows processes that need more RAM to increase their working sets as long as there are at least 4 MB of available RAM. When physical memory is available, the working set maximums of all processes running at their maximums are adjusted upward by the Balance Set Manager when it runs once per second. This allows processes that need more memory to add pages to their designated maximums and increase their working sets over time. Working set maximum adjustments occur once per second as long as the pool of memory available for new allocations (memory counter Available Bytes) is approximately 4 MB or more. As long as this cushion of available memory exists, process working set maximums for any process currently running at its maximum value are increased 20 pages each time the Balance Set Manager thread runs.

This dynamic adjustment mechanism allows each process working set to drift upwards to find its natural level. However, if Available Bytes drops to 4 MB, process working set growth is stunted. Processes may not be able to acquire all the real memory they require, and performance can suffer.

By default, a process acquires a minimum working set of 50 pages. Windows 2000 will trim pages from a process working set below its minimum value only when the system is under stress, defined as when the number of Available Bytes falls below 1 MB.

Windows 2000 also provides an application programming interface (API) to allow individual processes to specify their real memory requirements to the operating system and take the guesswork out of page replacement. Some applications developed specifically for Windows 2000, including Microsoft SQL Server and Internet Information Services, utilize a SetProcessWorkingSetSize Win32 API call to inform Windows 2000 of their physical memory requirements. SQL Server 2000, for instance, has a tuning parameter that can establish working set minimum and maximum values for the *sqlserver.exe* process address space. As illustrated in Figure 6-18, you can tell SQL Server to call SetProcessWorkingSetSize to set the process working set minimum and maximum values so they are equal. This restricts Windows 2000 from stealing pages from the *sqlserver.exe* process address space unless Available Bytes falls below 1 MB.

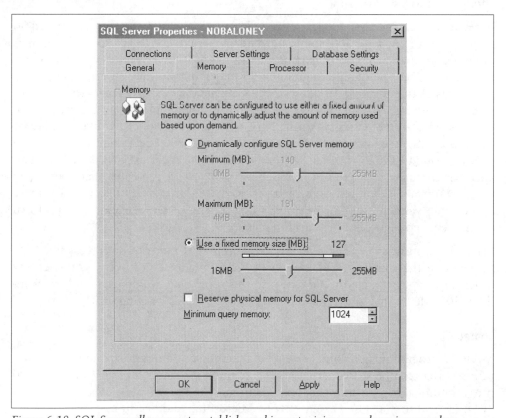

Figure 6-18. SQL Server allows you to establish working set minimum and maximum values

The problem with controls like the SetProcessWorkingSetSize Win32 API call is that they are static. Meanwhile, virtual memory management is very much a dynamic process that adjusts to how various running programs are currently exercising memory. One undesirable side effect of dynamic memory management is that the amount of memory one process acquires can affect what else is happening on the system. As an antidote, setting a static limit on the number of real pages an application can utilize requires constant vigilance to ensure the value specified is the correct one. If you set the wrong value for the process working set, it is all too easy to have the system run *worse* than if you had allowed Windows 2000 to retain the default settings. For example, if you do not reserve enough real memory for a cherished application to run effectively, calling SetProcessWorkingSetSize to set the process working set could have a negative impact on its performance because it will encounter too many page faults. On the other hand, if you reserve too much memory on behalf of the application, you can negatively impact the performance of other processes that need to run concurrently. If you wall off too much RAM for one application, there may not be enough memory to go around.

Because virtual memory usage is dynamic, a control like the one illustrated in Figure 6-18 to set a suitable minimum and maximum range for an application is often useful. If you click the "Dynamically configure SQL Server memory" radio button, you can set appropriate minimum and maximum working sets for your workload. This setting instructs Windows 2000's dynamic memory management routines to use a working set range for SQL Server that is more appropriate than the system defaults. This kind of setting is particularly helpful for an application like SQL Server that has an appetite for more RAM than the Windows 2000 default maximum of 345 pages (about 14 MB). Of course, as long as Available Bytes exceeds 4 MB, the Balance Set Manager adjusts the maximum working set of processes that need more memory upwards. But these adjustments take place slowly over time. Setting a more appropriate value for the maximum working set size of a process at the outset can eliminate lots of unnecessary transition faults.

Naturally, you need to determine a good working set range for a process like SQL Server: one that minimizes SQL Server paging, but does not overly constrict any other important workloads. We return to this topic once we understand how Windows 2000 determines the number of pages in a process's working set.

Shared DLLs

Modular programming techniques encourage building libraries containing common routines that can be shared easily among running programs. In the Windows 2000 programming environment, these shared libraries are known as *dynamic link libraries* or DLLs, and they are used extensively by Microsoft and other developers. The widespread use of shared DLLs complicates the bookkeeping Windows 2000 performs to figure out how many resident pages are associated with each process working set. If *explorer.exe*, *iexplore.exe*, and a dozen other processes (including services) all access the same copy of the Microsoft VC++ Foundation Classes runtime library *mfc42u.dll* loaded into shared memory, how should Windows 2000 account for the resident pages of the *mfc42u.dll* image file? Before you answer, consider that it is simply not possible for Windows 2000 to determine which resident pages of shared DLLs have been accessed by which running processes.

Perhaps you could count the current resident pages of the DLL against the working set of the application that originally loaded the DLL. Of course, it does not seem fair to charge for resident pages that the specific process may never have touched. Furthermore, accounting for the resident pages in this fashion becomes impossible once the original process terminates, yet DLL pages remain resident in memory because other active processes are accessing them.

On the other hand, perhaps Windows 2000 should not count those pages as being in any process working sets at all. Given the extent to which modern modular programming techniques utilize shared library DLLs, this would greatly understate the size of some process working sets.

Windows 2000's solution to this conundrum is to count *all* the resident pages associated with shared DLLs as part of *every* process working set that has the DLL loaded. All the resident pages of the DLL, whether the process has recently accessed them or not, are counted against the process working set maximum. This has the effect of charging processes for resident DLL pages they may never have touched, but at least this overcounting is performed consistently across all processes that have the DLL loaded. In Windows 2000, the Process Working Set bytes counter includes all resident pages of all shared DLLs that the process currently has loaded.

Unfortunately, this working set accounting procedure makes it difficult to account precisely for how real memory is being used. It also leads to a measurement anomaly that is illustrated in Figure 6-19. For example, because the resident pages associated with shared DLLs are included in the process working set, it is not unusual for a process to acquire a working set larger than the number of committed virtual memory bytes that it has requested. Notice the number of processes in Figure 6-19 with more working set bytes (Mem Usage) than committed virtual bytes (VM Size). None of the committed virtual memory bytes associated with shared DLLs are included in the Process Virtual Bytes counter even though all the resident bytes associated with them are included in the Process Working Set counter.

System working set

Windows 2000 operating system functions also consume RAM, so the system has a working set that needs to be controlled and managed like any other process. In this section we discuss the components of the system working set and look at how it is managed.

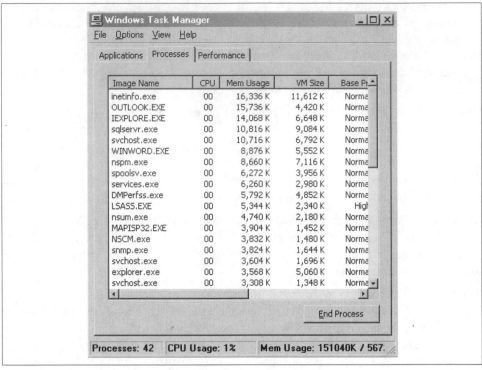

Figure 6-19. Task Manager reports on Memory Usage and committed virtual memory

Both system code and device driver code occupy memory. In addition, the operating system allocates data structures in two areas of memory: a pool for non-pageable storage and a pool for pageable storage. Data structures accessed by operating system and driver functions when interrupts are disabled *must* be resident in RAM at the time they are referenced. These data structures are usually allocated from the non-pageable pool so that they reside permanently in RAM. The Pool Nonpages Bytes counter in the Memory object shows the amount of RAM currently allocated that is permanently resident in RAM.

Mainly, though, most system data structures are pageable: they are created in a pageable pool of storage and subject to page replacement like the virtual memory pages of any other process. The Windows 2000 operating system maintains a working set of active pages in RAM that are subject to the same page replacement policy as ordinary process address spaces. The Cache Bytes counter provides the total number of resident pages in the current system working set. Cache Bytes is the sum of the System Cache Resident Bytes, System Driver Resident Bytes, System Code Resident Bytes, and Pool Paged Resident Bytes counters. The operating system's working set is known as the cache because it also includes resident pages of the Windows 2000 file cache, the operating system function that typically consumes more RAM than any other. (The Windows 2000 file cache is the subject of Chapter 7.)

The system working set is subject to the same local page replacement policy as ordinary process working sets. By default, the system cache has a minimum working set of about 4.8 MB and a maximum working set (on Windows 2000 Professional) of a little more than 2000 pages, or about 8 MB. Just like ordinary processes, when the operating system is running at its maximum working set value and it references a page that is not currently resident (causing a page fault), the new page displaces an older page from the system cache and the older page is moved to the Standby list. Just like ordinary processes, when the Balance Set Manager thread responsible for page trimming detects that the operating system is running at its current working set maximum and at least 4 MB of RAM are available, it adjusts the system working set upwards 20 pages at a time.

A registry parameter called LargeSystemCache (illustrated in Figure 6-20)* can be set to change the system working set maximum value. When the LargeSystemCache is turned on, the system working set maximum size is set to approximately 80% of the total amount of RAM installed. For example, on a Windows 2000 server with 256 MB of RAM installed (closer to 261,616,000 bytes, according to Task Manager), turning the LargeSystemCache setting on raises the system working set maximum value to 210,940 KB, according to the CacheSet utility available for downloading from *http://www.sysinternals.com.* (Note: the Windows 2000 Resource Kit's Registry entry help file contains several errors. It reports that the LargeSystemCache can expand to the size of physical memory, minus about 4 MB. This more extreme behavior is the way things used to work under Windows NT Versions 3 and 4, but no longer holds under Windows 2000. It also reports that LargeSystemCache is enabled by default under Server, but that is not true either. The NT 4.0 *Regentry.hlp* file contained a similar error.)

Turning on the LargeSystemCache setting, which boosts the value of the system's maximum working set size, favors the system working set over the working sets of other processes. It allows the working set of the system, which includes the Windows 2000 file cache, to grow relatively unconstrained in relation to other process working sets and to absorb the bulk of the system's installed RAM. In Chapter 7, we look in much greater detail at the impact of the LargeSystemCache parameter on system performance.

---

* Figure 6-20 also shows a Memory Management Registry parameter called SecondLevelDataCache that a number of authorities recommend setting. This setting has almost no impact on performance—you should leave it alone. The operating system can do very little to impact the operation of the Level 1, 2, and 3 processor caches when they are available. For more information, see KnowledgeBase article Q183063. Even the performance results Microsoft reports here (+2% or –0.4%) are more likely to be normal benchmark variations due to cache loading effects than substantiative improvements or degradations in overall system performance due to changing this parameter.

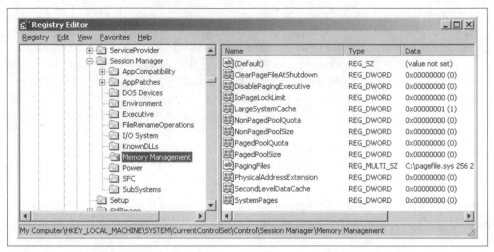

Figure 6-20. The LargeSystemCache parameter changes the system working set maximum value to approximately 80% of the total amount of RAM installed

Accounting for RAM usage

The five counters previously cited—Pool Nonpaged Bytes, System Cache Resident Bytes, System Driver Resident Bytes, System Code Resident Bytes, and Pool Paged Resident Bytes—account for the operating system's use of RAM. Adding Available Bytes to these five counters and creating a chart like the one illustrated in Figure 6-21 is an effective way to see how operating system functions are currently using RAM. You may recall that Available Bytes represents the sum of three lists, the Zero List, the Free List, and Standby List. Windows 2000 does not report the number of pages on these three list structures separately. In this representation, we stacked all six counters, with Available Bytes positioned at the bottom of the chart, to make it easy to determine how much RAM is free. In this example, the Pageable Pool resident bytes (in light gray) and the file cache (in medium gray) are consuming the most amount of RAM, which is typical.

If you subtract the sum of the six counters charted in Figure 6-21 from the total amount of RAM installed, you can calculate the amount of RAM that process working sets currently occupy. For instance, Figure 6-21 reports memory allocation counters for a system with 128 MB installed. Consequently, the working sets of running processes occupy about 40 MB in Figure 6-21, on average.

Adding process working sets to the six system memory allocation counters reported in Figure 6-21 should complete the picture of RAM usage on a Windows 2000 system. Unfortunately, the picture that results is fuzzy. Adding the Working Set counter from the _Total instance of the Process object to the six counters in Figure 6-21 yields the chart in Figure 6-22. (The Process _Total Working Set bytes are a dark band added underneath Available Bytes.)

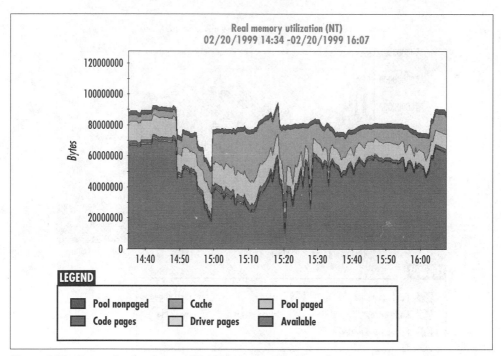

Figure 6-21. Accounting for the use of RAM by operating system functions

The chart illustrated in Figure 6-22 takes on an unexpected look. If Windows 2000 could account precisely for the way in which RAM is utilized, the seven counters charted would sum consistently to 128 MB, since there is 128 MB of RAM installed. As illustrated, that is not how these counters work. The reason for this anomaly, as noted earlier, is due to the manner in which process working sets are calculated, leading to double-, triple-, and quadruple-counting shared memory pages from DLLs. As discussed previously, a resident page in a DLL is counted against the working set of each and every process that has it loaded.

You can see that it is not easy in Windows 2000 to calculate *exactly* how RAM is allocated. Sometimes, as in Figure 6-22, the Memory counters inexplicably sum to less than the amount of installed RAM, suggesting that some amount of memory is not being used at all. At other times, adding up these counters yields a value greater than the amount of RAM installed, suggesting more widespread use of shared DLLs. Either way, the picture of RAM usage presented by the available performance counters is disconcertingly confused. Since the chart in Figure 6-22 requires a footnote to explain why the numbers do not sum consistently to 128 MB, we prefer creating the chart in Figure 6-21 and reporting process working sets separately.

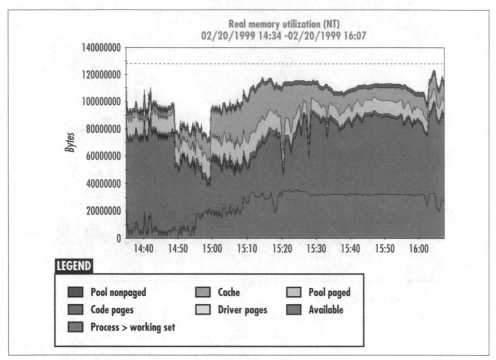

Figure 6-22. Accounting for real memory usage

Detecting memory leaks

While the Windows 2000 memory counters cannot precisely account for RAM utilization, they are still effective for many other purposes, including detecting memory leaks. Memory leaks are caused by programs that allocate virtual memory that they mistakenly fail to free after they are finished with it. Memory leaks are nasty program bugs that are sometimes difficult to find. A program containing a memory leak bug often executes to completion and produces the correct results, so the presence of the bug is not always detected. In fact, as long as the program containing the memory leak does not impact other executing processes, the bug can go undetected for a long time. A program with a slow memory leak might execute continuously over an extended period of days, weeks, or even months before anyone even notices that there is a problem.

The telltale sign of a memory leak is that Committed Bytes at the system level and/or Virtual Bytes at the process level are continuously increasing. Eventually, a program with a memory leak exhausts the system's supply of virtual memory, which can cause other running programs and even system code to fail as the system runs up against the virtual memory Committed Bytes limit. Depending on the rate at which the defective program leaks memory and the amount of excess virtual memory available, it can be a long time before any dire effects are evident.

A program that is leaking memory by allocating and then failing to free some private virtual memory areas is relatively easy spot because the process Virtual Bytes counter is continuously increasing. It is often harder to detect programs that allocate shared memory from the system's Pageable Pool and fail to release that. Because virtual memory allocated in the shared memory region of the Pageable Pool is not associated with any specific process, finding the offending program can be difficult. Often, it is necessary to use the process of elimination to find the offender. For example, Figure 6-23 shows a system that has a memory leak where the defective program is allocating virtual memory from the system's Pageable Pool and not releasing it. Here, it is easy to see that the Pageable Pool is expanding continuously over a long period of time until it is abruptly released. Luckily, in this case, the pattern of virtual memory growth and release could be associated with the start and stop of a specific process, which made it possible to find and fix the offending program.

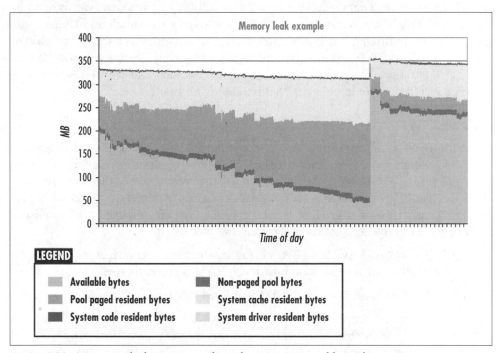

Figure 6-23. A program leaking memory from the system's Pageable Pool

Memory Capacity Planning

The previous sections of this chapter discussed the manner in which Windows 2000 manages real memory and the performance statistics that describe what is happening to both process virtual memory and physical RAM on a Windows 2000 system. With this background, we can now move on to tackle a more demanding set of questions.

This section discusses Windows 2000 server and workstation memory capacity planning. How can you tell when a system needs more RAM? When is a system undergoing excessive paging? Finally, how can you forecast demand for RAM so that you can stay ahead of your hardware requirements?

Measuring Memory Utilization

We have seen that Windows 2000 reports two types of memory utilization statistics. It reports several instantaneous measures of real memory allocation (Available Bytes, Cache Bytes, per-process Working Set Bytes), and several indicators of virtual memory management–oriented paging activity (Transition Faults/sec, Page Reads/sec, Page Writes/sec, and Demand Zero Pages/sec). In this section, we further explore the relationship between memory allocation and paging activity, with an eye to interpreting the measurement data available in Windows 2000. In particular, we want to be able to detect when a Windows 2000 system is paging too much and needs more memory. By monitoring hard page fault rates, for instance, you should be able to identify Windows 2000 systems that are paging excessively. In this section, we provide an illustration of a system that is paging excessively, and try to describe with some precision the system behavior that frequently results.

Available Bytes

Available Bytes is an instantaneous counter that measures real memory allocation, and is the single most important measure of memory utilization available in Windows 2000. The Available Bytes counter reports the current size of the Standby, Free, and Zero lists. The Standby list contains pages recently trimmed from executing process working sets. New pages that processes request are created from the Zero list of aged pages, or, if the Zero list is empty, from the Free list.

The current number of Available Bytes is fundamentally a measure of memory occupancy. By implication, it reports on how much RAM is currently free:

$$Real\ Memory\ allocated = sizeof(RAM) - Available\ Bytes$$

However, as discussed previously, this is not always a safe assumption in Windows 2000 because there are some anomalies in the way memory allocations are accounted for. A good configuration rule of thumb is to maintain a buffer of Available Bytes equal to approximately 5–10% of total RAM. Maintaining an ample supply of Available Bytes is necessary so that page faults can always be resolved quickly.

It is also important to monitor the number of Available Bytes against two thresholds that trigger a change in the Windows 2000 page replacement policy. At approximately 4 MB of Available Bytes, process working sets are no longer allowed to expand above their current maximum values. Any system running consistently at or near 4 MB of Available Bytes is real memory–constrained to some degree. If you are monitoring your critical application and file servers on a minute-by-minute basis, for example, the percentage of time that Available Bytes measures 4 MB ± 20% is a worthwhile metric to track. A system that occasionally runs at or near 4 MB of Available Bytes (< 5% of the time) is probably not a problem. On the other hand, a system that runs consistently at or near 4 MB of Available Bytes (> 40% of the time) is probably suffering from a real-memory constraint.

Windows 2000 has a second Available Bytes threshold value that alters the page replacement policy. When Available Bytes reaches about 1 MB, pages below the process working set minimum are no longer exempt from page trimming. Any system running at or below 1 MB even occasionally (> 10% of the time) is dangerously memory-constrained.

Even though Available Bytes is the single most important metric concerned with memory and paging, you should not be content to monitor it in isolation. Because it directly impacts thread execution time, it is also important to monitor the hard page fault rate (the Page Reads/sec counter) in tandem. In fact, the reason to look at the Available Bytes counter is the likely relationship between memory contention and demand paging. As long as process working sets are allowed to grow, processes that need more memory will be able to acquire those resources. However, at or below the 4 MB threshold, working set growth is constrained and some processes may feel the shortage. When memory is constrained, we can expect to see more demand paging.

Figure 6-24 illustrates the expected relationship between Available Bytes and demand paging (the Page Reads/sec counter) during an experiment in which we overloaded the memory of a Windows 2000 Professional system by, among other things, massaging a huge Excel spreadsheet. The exponential trend line in Figure 6-24 indicates that paging increases as Available Bytes approaches the 4 MB threshold. Notice, moreover, that Available Bytes remains at about the 4 MB threshold even when paging rates are quite high—Windows 2000 attempts to maintain that amount of free RAM at all times. This behavior makes it important to note the percentage of time that Available Bytes is observed hovering near the 4 MB threshold.

Physical disk constraints

Figure 6-24 illustrates that the Windows 2000 page replacement policy sets a lower limit on the value of Available Bytes. There is also an inherent upper limit to the amount of paging back and forth to disk. In general, the disk configuration that holds the paging file serves as the upper limit on the rate of demand paging activity that the system can sustain. For example, Figure 6-24 shows a simple, one-disk system. The upper limit on paging activity on this one-disk system is the capacity of a single disk to perform I/O. In this example, this single-disk system seems to be limited to about 700–1000 paging operations per second, the maximum paging rate

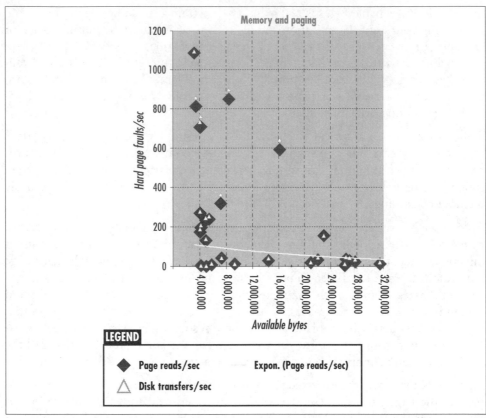

Figure 6-24. The relationship between Available Bytes and demand paging (Page Reads/sec)

observed during any one interval.* The total physical disk activity to the C: drive holding the paging file is also displayed in Figure 6-24. Notice that demand paging represents the bulk of all I/O operations during the experiment. The example illustrates a crucial point, namely, that a virtual memory constraint is manifest indirectly

---

* A more informed reading of the data charted in Figure 6-24 based on an understanding of hard drive technology suggests there are two operating regions for current disk hardware, a subject discussed in more detail in Chapters 8-10. Under ideal conditions where most disk accesses are sequential, disk hardware performance can reach 1000 operations per second or better. Sequential access benefits from the disk's built-in buffer so that subsequent I/Os to a disk track can be retrieved from the disk's internal cache without incurring a motion seek or rotational delay. In addition, on a disk buffer hit, data can be transferred at full interface speed. The capacity of a single disk to perform (mostly) sequential disk accesses establishes an absolute upper bound on paging activity. Paging I/O can sometimes have a surprisingly high sequential component, depending on how space on the paging files get allocated to specific process virtual memory addresses. The more usual case is that disk activity generated by demand paging is more random. In the case of more random disk access patterns, disk performance is confined to a much lower operating range. In the case of the single disk system observed in Figure 6-24, the upper limit on disk performance when the workload is random appears to be closer to 200 I/Os per second, again a function of the disk used in this example. Besides several observations in the 800-1200 I/Os per second range, there is a cluster of observations near the 200 I/O operations per second mark.

---

as a disk I/O problem. The most visible aspect of a real memory shortage is excessive I/O activity to the paging file.

Whatever the disk configuration–related capacity constraint is, it also serves as an upper limit on the amount of paging operations the system can perform. As we will see when we discuss Windows 2000 I/O performance in Chapter 8, it is not always easy to figure out the capacity of a specific disk configuration. For the single-disk subsystem in Figure 6-24, what matters most are the capabilities of the disk hardware. However, on a system with multiple disks, there are more factors to consider. The SCSI bus that connects the disk to processor board may be the configuration constraint that limits the amount of I/O that the system can do. On servers configured with multiple SCSI or fibre channel adaptors, PCI bus capacity might be the configuration constraint that limits the amount of I/O that the system performs. We will try to sort out these disk performance issues in Chapters 8 through 10.

Paging file configuration guidelines

This inevitably brings up the matter of determining an optimal number of hard page faults for a particular environment. Rather than merely providing the usual answer, which is "It depends," let's try to see what it might depend on. Any usable configuration guideline that attempts to quantify the number of hard page faults a particular Windows 2000 configuration can perform should consider the following:

- The number of physical disks available for paging, since each disk is a single server with some finite I/O throughput capability
- The speed of these disks
- Other I/O capacity constraints, such as the speed of the bus connections or the fact that disk I/O competes with other peripherals for access to the shared PCI bus
- The fact that any paging to those disks reduces proportionally their availability to satisfy normal file I/O requests

Given that most PC-based server architectures have limited I/O bandwidth, it is advisable to keep paging I/O traffic to a minimum, perhaps confined to 10–20% of overall disk bandwidth. This configuration guideline suggests that the bulk of a disk configuration's I/O processing capacity should be reserved for the applications running on the system, instead of being consumed by operating system virtual memory management overhead functions that can easily be avoided by adding RAM to the system.

Memory Contention

Considering the way Windows 2000 virtual memory management works, it should be apparent that real memory utilization cannot be measured in the same way that processor, disk, or network line utilization is measured. For instance, real memory capacity is not consumed in quite the same way that processor capacity is.* Real memory is allocated on demand and occupied continuously until it is either abandoned by its original user or replaced by a more recent consumer. That means that at any time there may be some memory locations that are allocated but are not being actively used. For example, there are often infrequently accessed resident pages of a process working set that occupy real memory even as these pages go unreferenced for some period of time. The fact that infrequently accessed virtual memory pages can often be replaced by currently referenced pages with very little impact on performance is ample evidence that these memory locations are not being actively utilized.

Memory allocation statistics may show that real memory is full, but that is not a foolproof indicator of a real memory constraint. Worse, the goal of any virtual memory management scheme is to utilize all available real memory. Consequently, virtual memory systems often report (close to) 100% memory occupancy on a continuous basis. Some of these real memory locations typically are occupied by infrequently referenced virtual pages, while others contain pages in continuous use.

Over and above the fact that real memory may be 100% allocated, the performance of virtual memory systems becomes a concern only when real memory is over-committed and high paging rates result. This situation results when the size of active process working sets overflows the amount of physical RAM installed. The fact that real memory is allocated on demand and that 100% memory occupation is the rule rather than the exception suggests that we need additional measures that capture the dynamic aspect of virtual memory management. Something that measures the *intensity* with which a segment of RAM is accessed would be ideal. Lacking direct measurements on memory access intensity, however, we will have to make do with the Windows 2000 measurements in hand.

The root cause of a system that is paging excessively is that there is too little real memory to support the range of virtual addresses that executing processes are routinely accessing. Instead, of memory allocation statistics, we need measures of *memory contention* that can reveal the extent of real memory demand generated by executing virtual memory address spaces. Windows 2000 does not directly report on memory utilization in this sense. Instead, the available measurements that we have described merely report how much real memory is currently allocated and which

---

* One trenchant way to make this point is to show that virtual memory management processes cannot be fairly represented using a queuing model, in spite of the best efforts of many in the field over many years. The dynamic way that page replacement algorithms manage physical RAM does *not* correspond to the standard elements of a queuing system. While process virtual address spaces can stand in for customers, and instruction memory accesses could plausibly represent service requests, notice that memory access has no separate service time component distinct from instruction execution latency. Neither is it reasonable to construe instruction execution memory accesses delayed in a queue of any conventional sort. In fact, the manner in which the Central Server model of computing that was discussed in Chapter 1 is extended to incorporate virtual memory is to add an extra I/O workload component associated with paging to the conventional formulation. Since a real memory shortage is manifest as a disk I/O performance problem, this approach allows queuing models to incorporate virtual memory considerations, albeit indirectly.

processes or parts of the system working set are occupying it at the moment. Nevertheless, it is possible to derive two measures of memory contention in Windows 2000 that can be useful in predicting the onset of a real memory constraint. Let's look at these two measures and how they might be used to predict the onset of a serious paging problem.

Committed Bytes: Installed RAM

Besides monitoring virtual memory allocation statistics, physical memory occupancy, and paging activity, it is also useful to develop predictive measures. One useful calculation is to derive a *memory contention index* that correlates with the level of paging activity observed. As we have seen, the Available Bytes counter correlates with hard paging activity until the system reaches the 4 MB Available Bytes threshold that triggers a change to the dynamic page replacement policy. Since Windows 2000 attempts to maintain a 4 MB Available Bytes cushion at all times, monitoring Available Bytes alone cannot reliably predict the rate of hard paging activity once the system reaches that threshold. Imagine System A, where process working sets grow enough to just graze the 4 MB threshold. System A stabilizes at or near the 4 MB Available Bytes threshold without suffering from performance degradation due to excessive paging. In contrast, System B running at the 4 MB Available Bytes threshold is destabilized, sustaining a hard page fault rate near the capacity of the disk subsystem. These two obviously distinct cases cannot be distinguished by monitoring the level of Available Bytes alone.

A useful working hypothesis for developing a memory contention index is that demand paging activity is generally caused by virtual memory address spaces contending for limited physical memory resources. Consider, then, a memory contention index computed as the ratio of *virtual* memory allocated to the amount of *real* memory installed. This *V:R ratio* is easily computed in Windows 2000 by dividing Committed Bytes by the amount of installed RAM:

$$V:R = Committed\ Bytes\ /\ Installed\ RAM$$

One clear virtue of this memory contention index is that it is easily computed and has a straightforward interpretation. It measures the full range of virtual addresses created dynamically by process address spaces and compares it to the static amount of RAM configured on the system.

Consider the case where V:R is 1 or less. This means that for every Committed Byte of virtual memory that processes have allocated, there is a corresponding 4K page available in RAM to hold that virtual memory location. Under these circumstances, very little demand paging activity will normally occur. When V:R is near 1, Windows 2000 hard paging rates are usually minimal. The demand paging activity that does occur is usually confined to processes creating (and later destroying) new pages, reflected in the rate of Demand Zero Pages/sec that you are able to observe. Since there is room in RAM for just about every virtual memory page that processes allocate, we expect to see very little hard page fault processing. There is very little memory contention. Of course, even when there is little or no memory contention, you may still see large amounts of transition (soft) faults due to Windows 2000 memory management, cache faults (depending on the type of application file processing that is occurring) and demand zero page faults (depending on the applications that are running).

Installing enough RAM for every process virtual memory page to remain resident in real memory is a bit extreme. Since some virtual memory addresses are usually inactive at any one time, it is not necessary to keep infrequently accessed virtual memory pages in real memory all the time for performance reasons. Some amount of hard page fault activity is certainly acceptable. However, when processes begin to allocate more virtual memory pages than can fit comfortably in RAM, the page replacement algorithms of Windows 2000 are forced to juggle the contents of RAM more, trimming inactive pages from these applications and not allowing those process working sets to grow. At this point, the number of Committed Bytes is greater than the amount of RAM, which is why Windows 2000 memory management routines need to work harder. Since all the virtual memory pages allocated by currently executing processes exceeds the amount of RAM installed, the likelihood increases that executing processes will access pages that are not currently resident in real memory, causing hard pages faults. Naturally, when the number of hard page faults becomes excessive, it is time to add more RAM to the system.

Even the simple V:R ratio described here, computed as Committed Bytes:Installed RAM, can have surprising predictive value. Moreover, it is relatively easy to trend the V:R ratio as process virtual memory loads increase, allowing you to anticipate the need for a memory upgrade. For Windows 2000 systems with their limited I/O bandwidth, we generally recommend confining the amount of paging activity performed on physical disks shared with application data files to 10–20% of I/O processing. On systems where you maintain a V:R ratio of 1.5:1 or less, you will normally observe paging activity that is well within these configuration guidelines. Furthermore, we recommend monitoring the V:R ratio on a regular basis and intervening (where possible) to add RAM when the memory contention index passes 1.5:1 and before it reaches a value of 2:1. In this manner you can ensure that paging activity to disk remains at acceptably low levels.

Unfortunately, trending V:R is not a foolproof technique for predicting paging activity. One problem is that applications like SQL Server protect their working sets from Windows 2000 memory management and perform their own equivalent virtual memory management. Another problem is that some applications perform predominantly static virtual memory allocations, often allocating overlarge blocks of virtual memory at initialization instead of allocating only what they need on demand. In these cases, Committed Bytes remains static, failing to reflect the dynamic aspect of virtual memory accesses accurately.

However, the technique works well enough in the general case that it will keep you out of major trouble on most Windows 2000 systems. We find it frustrating that this simple memory contention index cannot be computed directly using tools like the built-in Windows 2000 System Monitor. System Monitor does not report static configuration information like the amount of RAM installed, nor, as we have seen, is it possible to calculate the amount of RAM installed reliably from the Memory counters that are available. Alternatively, making a Win32 API call to the GlobalMemoryStatus routine returns the amount of RAM currently configured minus the current amount of Nonpaged Pool Bytes. This method can be used to determine the amount of RAM available programmatically.

Pool Paged Bytes:Pool Paged Resident Bytes

Fortunately, another memory contention index can be calculated in Windows 2000. Besides being computable from existing memory counters, this memory contention index is also more likely to reflect the dynamic aspects of virtual memory demand than the simple Committed Bytes:Installed RAM ratio. Calculate:

V:R Ratio = Pool Paged Bytes / Pool Paged Resident Bytes

The system's pageable pool is the source for all allocations that operating system services, including device drivers, make for virtual memory that does not need to reside permanently in RAM. Pool Paged Bytes reports the current amount of virtual memory allocated within the system's pool of pageable virtual memory. Pool Paged Resident Bytes reports the current number of pages within that pool that are resident in RAM.

The Pool Paged Bytes:Pool Paged Resident Bytes ratio reports the amount of committed virtual memory allocated by operating system services, compared to the amount of physical memory those pages currently occupy. Pool Paged Bytes over and above the number of Pool Paged Resident Bytes represents committed operating system virtual memory pages that are currently stored on the paging file. As this ratio increases, operating system services are likely to encounter increased contention for physical memory, with higher paging rates the likely result.

One advantage of this memory contention index is that operating systems services tend to be better Windows 2000 citizens than your average application program. Well-behaved users of virtual memory in Windows 2000 allocate memory only on demand. Thus, the Pool Paged Bytes:Pool Paged Resident Bytes ratio is likely to be a good indicator of current memory contention, albeit limited to operating system services. Since working storage for shared DLL library routines is also often allocated from the system's pageable pool, the index also reflects some degree of per-process virtual memory demand.

Let's look at how this memory contention index behaves, especially with regard to its ability to predict demand paging rates. In Figure 6-25, we calculated the Pool Paged Bytes:Pool Paged Resident Bytes memory contention index for the same set of measurement data reported in Figure 6-24. Figure 6-25 shows that this memory contention index is well correlated to the actual demand paging activity observed. The exponential trend line also happens to be quite representative of virtual memory systems. Figure 6-25 identifies three distinct operating regions for this workload. When the Pool Paged Bytes:Pool Paged Resident Bytes ratio is approximately 1.5, the great majority of virtual memory pages allocated in this pool fit readily into available RAM. This corresponds to intervals where there are not many hard pages faults occurring. When the Pool Paged Bytes:Pool Paged Resident Bytes ratio rises above 3, greater memory contention and substantially higher paging rates are observed, clustered around 200 hard page faults processed/sec. Finally, at even higher Pool Paged Bytes: Pool Paged Resident Bytes ratios, the amount of paging varies drastically, reaching a maximum observed value above 1000 hard page faults/sec. This suggests that a system is destabilized or thrashing due to excessive virtual memory management.

A memory utilization curve relating memory contention to paging activity can have predictive value, especially when the trend line is well correlated with the underlying data, as in Figure 6-25. For example, this trend line could be used to justify a memory upgrade for machines running similar workloads as the contention index begins to approach 3. Since this memory contention index is also easy to trend, you can use it to forecast future virtual memory demand. For instance, if you project that a growing system workload will reach an undesirable level of paging sometime in the next three months, you can schedule a memory upgrade in anticipation of that event.

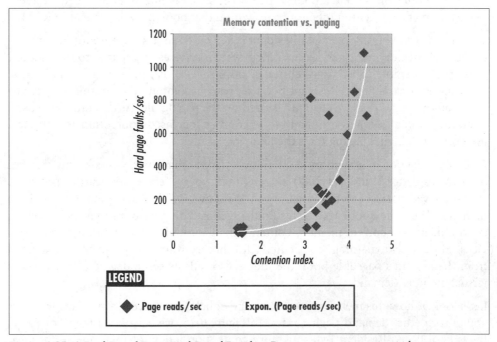

Figure 6-25. A Pool Paged Bytes:Pool Paged Resident Bytes memory contention index

## CHAPTER 7

File Cache Performance and Tuning

The built-in Windows 2000 file cache is essential to the performance of Windows 2000 file servers. It is also an important factor in the performance of Microsoft Internet Information Server (IIS) as well as many other applications. The file cache is a specific, reserved area of virtual storage in the range of system memory addresses, as discussed in Chapter 6. As the name implies, it operates on files, or, more specifically, sections of files. When file sections are referenced, they are *mapped* into this area of virtual memory by the Cache Manager. This mapping occurs transparently to the application that is trying to read or write the file in question. (The everyday meaning of the word *cache* refers to it being a hidden storehouse. Caching functions are hidden from the applications.) The memory used for the file cache is managed just like any other area of real memory allocated within the system working set, subject to the same Windows 2000 virtual memory management page replacement policy discussed in the previous chapter. Frequently referenced files tend to remain in cache memory automatically, so no external tuning parameters need to be set to initiate caching under Windows 2000 on either Professional and Server.

The idea behind memory-resident file cache is to speed up access to data that is otherwise stored permanently on disk. Access to any file segments that are resident in memory is much, much faster than having to retrieve the file from a disk or CD-ROM. It is important to realize, however, that caching does not speed up file access unconditionally. For example, the performance benefit of caching a file that is read once from start to finish by a single application is minimal. The data blocks associated with the file still have to be accessed serially from the disk, copied into RAM, and stored there. The Windows 2000 file cache does attempt to improve upon the *apparent* responsiveness of this serial, sequential disk file activity by *prefetching* blocks from the disk in anticipation of the next disk file I/O request. This helps the responsiveness of foreground applications like Microsoft Word because the Windows 2000 Cache Manager automatically reads ahead in the file being opened. By the time the user of the application presses the Page Down key, the file data needed to refresh the display has already been retrieved from disk and is resident in memory.

Once a file is read again, the benefits of memory caching become evident. As long as the data block requested remains resident in memory, subsequent file I/O requests are resolved directly from memory without ever having to access the disk. A file that is shared among multiple users (being accessed across the network, for example) is stored just once in the cache. The original user of the file responsible for initiating the file access causes the data to be *staged* from disk into memory. All subsequent users of the file benefit from the data being held in cache memory through faster access. Typical single-user applications like MS Office products do not normally derive a great deal of benefit from this aspect of the Windows 2000 file cache, but many multiuser server-based applications can and do. The Microsoft IIS application is a good example of a server application that benefits from the built-in file cache. HTML and GIF files frequently accessed by users of the IIS web publishing service, for example, tend to remain in memory, allowing IIS to process them without having to perform physical disk accesses.

Another way that application performance benefits from caching is by buffering writes in memory and deferring the update of the physical disk. This form of file caching is known as *deferred write-back cache*, also frequently referred to as *lazy write*. Deferring writes has two potential benefits. The first is that the application may re-write the same data block. If this occurs before the write is flushed from cache to disk, it is no longer necessary to perform the original write. Having been deferred, there is now an I/O operation that no longer needs to occur at all, resulting in a net savings. Consider, for example, an editing session using a typical word processing application like MS Word. Often the user edits and re-edits the same section of the file repeatedly. Deferred write-back cache reduces the number of physical disk operations that need to take place whenever subsequent updates overlay a current change residing in the cache.

The second benefit of deferred write-back caching is that by waiting, disk writes can often be flushed to disk in bulk I/O operations that may be more efficient than the way the original application specified. In Windows 2000, deferred writes are allowed to accumulate in cache memory until a threshold value for the number of dirty file pages in cache is reached. An operating system thread to flush dirty file pages resident in the cache to disk using efficient bulk I/O operations is then dispatched.

Using lazy write cache management means that Windows 2000 must be shut down gracefully. Pulling the plug on the computer abruptly strands numerous file updates parked temporarily in cache memory, which is why Windows NT issues that "Please wait while the system writes unsaved data to the disk" message during shutdown. During an orderly shutdown of the operating system, all dirty pages in the file cache are flushed to disk before the signal is sent that it is OK to power off the machine. This means that important Windows 2000 server machines should always be connected to an uninterruptible power system (UPS) to prevent data loss due to dirty file pages that have not yet been written to disk accumulating in the file cache.

The basic principles behind the use of a memory-resident file cache in Windows 2000 are no different from the other examples of caching discussed in earlier chapters. These include the Level 1 and Level 2 caches inside the processor, and the caching of active virtual address pages in RAM that is the essence of virtual memory management. When the active segments of frequently accessed files are held in RAM, access to them is considerably faster than having to retrieve them from disk (or from CD-ROM or from across the network). The size of the file cache in Windows 2000 is managed like any other process working set—it just happens to be part of the system working set and, in fact, is normally a major component of it. There are no tuning knobs or parameters in Windows 2000 to configure the minimum or maximum file cache beyond the architectural limitation that it can be no larger than 960 MB. If more memory is available and file access demands it, the file cache will expand in size. If there is a shortage of real memory available and application processes are more demanding, the file cache will shrink. In Windows NT, the file cache is limited to 512 MB of virtual memory.

The size of the file cache is adjusted dynamically according to load, using the basic page trimming algorithm discussed in Chapter 6. One tuning knob, LargeSystem-Cache, is available that affects cache sizing. What it does is quite extreme, making it effective only in isolated instances. In Windows NT, the tuning knob available produces even more extreme behavior, rendering it almost useless. We discuss this tuning knob near the end of this chapter.

File Cache Sizing

The Windows 2000 file cache is similar in function to the file caches built into most commercial versions of the Unix operating system. The Windows 2000 file cache stores segments of active files in RAM in anticipation of future requests. This function speeds access to files that are used by multiple users and applications. Besides accelerating access to shared files, the Windows 2000 file cache also performs anticipatory *read aheads* for sequentially accessed files. In addition, the file cache provides for buffering writes in memory, using deferred write-back caching, or lazy write. When writes are issued for cached files, data is first written into memory-resident file buffers. The permanent update to disk, requiring a time-consuming physical disk operation, is deferred until some later time. The caching read ahead and lazy write functions are typically effective at improving the performance of most Windows 2000 applications.

Transparently to applications, I/O requests to files are diverted to check the file cache prior to accessing the disk. If the data requested is already resident in the file cache memory, it is not necessary to access a relatively slow disk drive to read the data requested. The operation becomes a *cache hit*. If the section of the file requested is not in memory, there is a *cache miss*, which ultimately is passed back to the filesystem to resolve by reading the information requested from disk into the cache. The best single indicator of cache performance is the *cache hit ratio*, reported as the percentage of total file I/O requests satisfied from the cache.

The single most important issue in file cache performance is sizing the cache so that it is large enough to be effective. If the cache is too small, access to disk files is slower. On the other hand, having too large a file cache means that the machine is configured more expensively than necessary.

It is difficult to determine in advance what size cache will deliver what kind of hit ratio for your workload. In general, as cache size increases, so does the cache hit ratio, usually in a nonlinear fashion. Figure 7-1 illustrates the theoretical relationship between cache size and hit ratio for a given workload. The curve in Figure 7-1 is broken down into three distinct regions. Cache performance can usually be characterized according to these three regions. Initially, very small increases in the size of the cache result in very dramatic increases in cache hit ratios. This area is indicated on the chart as Region 1. Here, performance is quite sensitive to minor changes in the cache size (or minor changes in the workload). Because cache effectiveness is very volatile in this region, this is not a desirable configuration. Eventually, caches are subject to diminishing returns as they get larger and larger, as illustrated by the area of the curve marked as Region 3. Here, adding more memory only marginally increases cache effectiveness, so this is not desirable either. That leaves Region 2 as the most desirable configuration, probably leaning toward Region 3 for the sake of stability, but not too far for the sake of efficiency. Understanding this trade-off between cache size and cache effectiveness in the context of your specific workload is crucial.

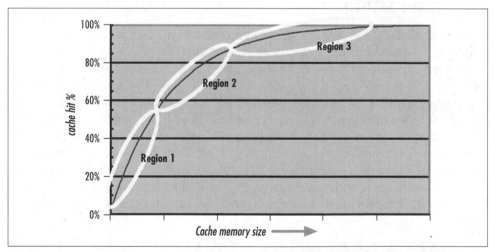

Figure 7-1. The theoretical relationship between cache size and cache effectiveness (hit ratio)

The actual amount of memory the Windows 2000 file cache consumes is determined dynamically based on system activity, so this theoretical model of cache effectiveness does not provide much practical guidance for the Windows 2000 systems administrator. Windows 2000 provides no external parameters that control the size of the file cache directly. (As mentioned, there is *one* cache size tuning parameter available that must be used very carefully.) In Windows 2000, the current size of the file cache is a function of the amount of system RAM installed, the number and size of the files currently in use, and the contention for memory from other applications that are also running. It is important to remember that the file cache competes for access to the same real memory resources as all other applications.

Cache Performance Counters

For performance monitoring, there is a Cache performance object and a full set of performance measurement counters that provide a great deal of information about the Cache Manager and related cache activity. To monitor cache effectiveness, there are counters that report on cache memory size, activity, and the various cache hit ratios. As we describe the various file caching mechanisms, we also discuss the relevant performance counters that are available to measure cache effectiveness.

Cache Size

Following Figure 7-1, it is important to monitor both the size of the file cache and the cache hit ratio. The real memory pages that the file cache occupies are counted as part of the system working set, subject to normal page trimming. The Memory object performance counter System Cache Resident Bytes reports the amount of real memory currently in use by the file cache. As the number of System Cache Resident Bytes increases, we normally expect that the various measures of hit ratio will also increase. Moreover, the cache size can grow simply as a function of the size of the files that are currently in use and their pattern of access. If there is little contention for real memory, the file cache grows in direct proportion to the rate of requests for new files (or new sections of currently open files). However, since the file cache must compete for real memory with other applications, what the other applications running in the system are doing at the same time influences the growth of the file cache. As other applications make demands on real memory, relatively inactive pages from the file cache are subject to Windows 2000 page trimming.

The Windows 2000 file cache is allocated within the system's virtual address range. This range of addresses spans only 960 MB of virtual storage (512 MB in Windows NT 4.0), setting an upper limit on the size of the file cache that is available in Windows NT and Windows 2000. Buy as much RAM as you want, but it is not possible for the file cache in Windows 2000 to be any larger than 960 MB. The 960 MB range of virtual storage reserved for use by the cache is divided into consecutive 256 KB sections. Files are mapped into the cache region using 256 KB logical segments defined from the beginning of each individual file's byte stream. The file cache interacts with the Windows 2000 Virtual Memory Manager using the generic mapped file support described in Chapter 6.

As file segments are cached, the Cache Manager simply allocates the next available 256 KB slot until the cache is full. The Cache Manager keeps track of which files are actively mapped into the cache virtual memory so that when a file is closed (and no other application has the same file open), the Cache Manager can delete it from virtual storage. In case more than 960 MB worth of file segments ever needs caching, the Cache Manager simply wraps around to the beginning of the cache to find inactive segments. In this fashion, a new file request replaces an older one.

The Cache Resident Bytes counter reports the amount of real memory the file cache is currently occupying. The Cache Bytes counter, which sounds like it might tell you the size of the cache, actually reports the full system working set, which includes Cache Resident Bytes and several other real memory areas. In a Windows 2000 file server (remembering Windows 2000's heritage as the follow-on to the joint IBM/ Microsoft-developed OS2 LAN Manager), the file cache so dominates the system working set that internal documentation frequently refers to the entire system working set as the cache. This usage carries over to tools like Task Manager, which labels the system working set as the System Cache in the Performance tab, illustrated in Figure 7-2. The Windows NT version of Task Manager called this field File Cache, which is probably just as misleading. Curiously, the number of bytes in the System Cache reported by Task Manager does not correspond exactly to the Cache Bytes counter in the System Monitor.

The file cache relies on the standard Windows 2000 page replacement policy to control the amount of real memory available for caching files. As you might expect, this has its good and bad points. The fact that system administrators do not have to tweak a lot of cache sizing parameters is a benefit. When the rate of file access increases, the dynamic nature of virtual memory management allows the file cache to expand accordingly. On the other hand, there is no way to set a minimum cache size, below which Windows 2000 will not steal file cache pages. This means that when real memory is under stress, it is entirely possible for the Windows 2000 file cache to be squeezed out of real memory entirely. This means that you must monitor Windows 2000 file servers and IIS machines to ensure that they always have enough memory to cache their file workloads effectively.

Chapter 6 discussed the virtual memory management page replacement policy implemented in Windows 2000 that relies on an operating system component called the Balance Set Manager to trim the working sets of active processes. The resident pages in the file cache are considered part of the system working set for purposes of page trimming. By default, the system working minimum and maximum working set values are approximately 4 and 8 MB, respectively. (Refer back to Chapter 6.) These values are used to regulate the size of the file cache in Windows 2000 since the file cache is part of the system working set. The system maximum working set is also subject to gradual upward adjustment whenever the working set is at its maximum value but there is ample free memory available (Available Bytes > 4 MB). In the

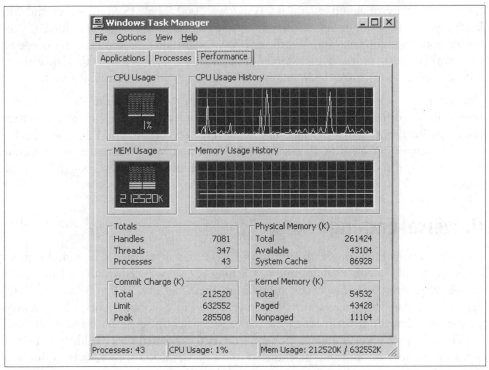

Figure 7-2. The memory that Taskman reports is allocated for the file cache is not limited to the file cache

"Cache Tuning" case study reported later in this chapter, you will be able to see quite clearly this upward adjustment mechanism in action.

One final sizing consideration is that the Windows 2000 file cache is not limited to use by disk requests. Files stored on CD-ROM, a DVD disk, or a networked disk are all diverted to use the same built-in file cache.

Cache Hit Ratio

Most file I/O is directed through the Cache Manager. Later, we discuss two sets of Cache Manager interfaces specifically designed for Windows 2000 system applications. For instance, one of the major users of the file cache is the file server service, which utilizes a special interface that was defined with it in mind. Only a few applications that run on Windows 2000 take advantage of the two special interfaces.

The default behavior of Windows 2000 subjects all files to cache management, although it is possible to turn off caching for specific files. At the time the file is opened, it is possible to specify that caching should be disabled. Bypassing cache management, however, forces the application to code its own low-level I/O routines. Consequently, bypassing the Cache Manager is done only by some server applications specifically designed to run on Windows 2000, like MS SQL Server and MS Exchange. On the other hand, anyone developing an application intended to run under both Windows 9x and Windows 2000, for instance, is unlikely to choose to perform this extra work. This extends to applications like Microsoft's Office suite, whose applications utilize the Windows 2000 file cache in the normal manner.

There are four Cache performance object counters that report the cache hit ratio based on the different filesystem Cache Manager interfaces. The hit ratio counters are Copy Read Hits %, Data Map Hits %, MDL Read Hits %, and Pin Read Hits %. The differences between the Copy, Mapped Data, and MDL interfaces to the Cache Manager are discussed in the later section "How the Windows 2000 File Cache Works."

Universal Caching

The file cache is built into both Windows 2000 Professional and Server, and it functions identically in either environment. Caching is everywhere! An interesting aspect of the Windows 2000 file cache stems from this ubiquity. When Windows 2000 Server file servers are accessed by Windows 2000 Professional clients, files accessed across the network are subject to memory-resident caching on *both* the server and the client side! With caching everywhere, frequently accessed files are likely to be resident in memory on multiple machines. From one standpoint, this leads to duplication and adds to the memory requirements of Windows 2000 machines. On the other hand, all this file caching is very effective from a performance standpoint, so there is an overall benefit.

On systems configured to run as file servers or Internet web servers, for example, one of the major consumers of real memory is the file cache. Since even large-scale PC servers generally have limited I/O bandwidth compared to enterprise-scale servers, configuring an adequate amount of memory for use as a file cache is important. You should consider that any memory-resident disk cache is an explicit trade-off of memory for disk activity. Normally, in PC workstations and servers, this trade-off yields significant performance benefits. When we discuss disk I/O performance in the next three chapters, we quantify the performance benefit of cache versus disk access more definitively.

Caching and Disk Activity Statistics

Another aspect of the file cache that should be noted is its relationship to the performance counters that measure physical I/O operations to disk. Whenever there are performance problems and you find an overloaded disk, it is natural to want to know which application processes are responsible for that physical disk activity. The operation of the Windows 2000 file cache makes it very difficult to determine this.

The cache statistics that are maintained count *logical* file requests issued by various applications, encompassing all the different Windows 2000 filesystems at the system level. Operations that are cache hits eliminate the need for physical disk operations to occur. The cache statistics are global; how individual applications that are running are using the cache cannot be determined. Meanwhile, logical (and physical) disk statistics count physical I/O operations. Since the great majority of logical file requests are handled through the file cache, logical and physical disk counters reflect those logical file requests that *miss* the cache. Cache misses generate synchronous physical disk operations.

One additional process at work here needs to be understood. Caching *transforms* some logical file I/O operations from synchronous requests into asynchronous disk requests. These transformations are associated with read ahead requests for sequential files and lazy write deferred disk updates. As the name implies, read ahead requests are issued in anticipation of future logical I/O requests. (These anticipated future requests may not even occur. Think about the number of times you open a document file in MS Word but do not scroll all the way through it.) Lazy write deferred disk updates occur sometime *after* the original logical file request. The update needs to be applied to the physical disk, but the required physical disk operation is usually not performed right away. So what is happening at the physical disk *right now*, as expressed by the current logical and physical disk statistics, is usually *not* in sync with logical file requests. This is the influence of caching. Caching makes it almost impossible to determine which applications are causing a physical disk to be busy except under very limited conditions (when very few applications are using the disk, for example).

Windows 2000 introduces a series of per-process file I/O counters that keep track of Reads, Writes, and Bytes at the process level. These new counters can be accessed from both the System Monitor, as illustrated in Figure 7-3, and Task Manager (not illustrated; the Windows 2000 Task Manager reports only cumulative values for these counters, so its usefulness in debugging a performance problem that is occurring right now is limited). As illustrated, per-process I/Os are separated into three basic categories: Reads, Writes, and Other Operations. The fourth category, Data Operations, is derived from the sum of the Reads and Writes. Both I/O operations and bytes are counted.

These new counters account for I/O operations (and bytes) at the process level, prior to the influence of the cache. While they certainly provide interesting and useful information on running processes, the new counters do *not* solve the problem of being able to relate physical disk activity back to the individual process. Since the new counters count *logical* file operations, because of cache effects, it is still not possible to see the load that individual applications are putting on the disk hardware. Nor do we expect that this problem will be alleviated in future releases of the Windows 2000 operating system. Due to lazy write caching, for example, it is never easy to associate an application process with the physical disk activity that occurs because cached operations decouple these otherwise logically related system events.

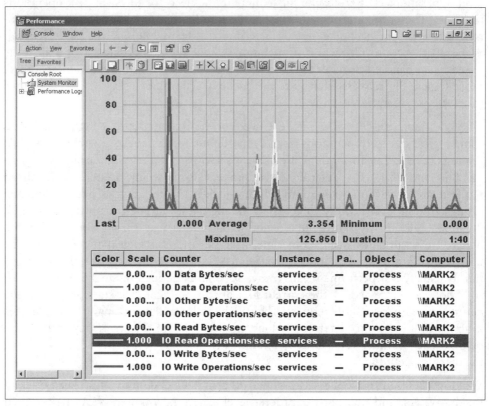

Figure 7-3. Per-process I/O counters track operations at the process level

Cache Loading Effects

One final point about the ubiquitous Windows 2000 file cache is that whenever there is any significant interaction with the file cache, it is difficult to run repeatable benchmark tests. Cache loading effects are notorious for their impact on benchmarks. At the beginning of a benchmark when the cache is empty, most of the file accesses are direct to disk. (This is known as a cache *cold start*.) Later on, when all the files have been loaded into the file cache, very few accesses are direct to disk. (When the cache is already populated with the working set of objects being managed, it leads to cache *warm starts*.) Two otherwise identical benchmarks runs, one executed from a cache cold start and the other from a warm start, will yield very different results.

Both the pervasiveness of the Windows 2000 file cache and its impact on local and networked requests make it difficult to factor in the effect of caching when you attempt to run repeatable benchmark workloads. Commercial-grade benchmarking programs are aware of these difficulties and provide specific mechanisms to allow for cache loading effects. For any benchmark runs you decide to initiate yourself, *caveat emptor*. The examples discussed later in this chapter should provide you with adequate guidance to help interpret the various cache object statistics, and will help you understand the nature and extent of any cache loading effects present during your specific benchmark test.

How the Windows 2000 File Cache Works

The Windows 2000 file cache works by converting (most) normal file I/O requests into requests for virtual memory mapped files. The Cache Manager interfaces to applications in several different ways. The standard interface is the *Copy interface*. Because it is entirely transparent to applications, the Copy interface is used by most applications. As the name implies, the Copy interface copies file data from a buffer inside the file cache to an application data file buffer on a read, and copies data in the opposite direction on a write.

Two other standard interfaces to the Windows 2000 file cache use memory more efficiently than the Copy interface: the *Mapping interface* and the *MDL interface*. Applications that want to take advantage of these Cache Manager interfaces must contain significant amounts of Windows 2000–specific code. The Windows 2000 file server service, Redirector, NTFS, and IIS use these more efficient interfaces.

The Copy Interface

Figure 7-4 diagrams in simple terms how the Copy interface functions for read hit requests. An application file read request calls the appropriate filesystem driver in Windows 2000, where the request is immediately routed to the Cache Manager. The Cache Manager maps each open file into the virtual memory reserved for the cache. This mapping is performed on 256 KB sections of a file at a time. Responding to the read request, the Cache Manager locates the block of data specified and copies it into an application-provided data buffer. This satisfies the original file request, and the application thread resumes its normal processing. At this point, the file data requested resides in two places concurrently, which is an inefficient use of computer memory. However, this is the only way to plug the file cache function into existing applications transparently, without requiring extensive modifications to allow the application to accept a *pointer* to file data resident in the system cache.

Figure 7-5 illustrates what happens when a cache miss occurs. The Cache Manager incurs a page fault when it attempts to access a file segment that is not resident in the cache. The Windows 2000 Virtual Memory Manager is then invoked to resolve the page fault. VMM determines that the page fault falls within the scope of a mapped file virtual address range. VMM accesses the virtual address descriptor (VAD) associated

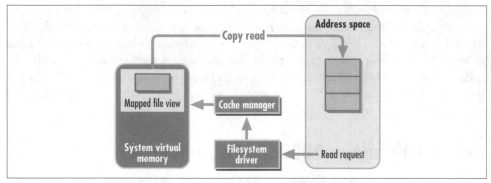

Figure 7-4. The Copy interface copies data from the system cache into an application file buffer

with the virtual address, which, in turn, points to the file object mapped into that specific 256 KB cached file segment block. VMM then issues a callback to the appropriate filesystem driver, which generates and processes a physical disk I/O request. This disk request copies data into Cache memory, not the application's virtual address space. At this point, the page fault is resolved and the Cache Manager processing resumes. As on a hit, the data in cache is then copied into the application data buffer provided.

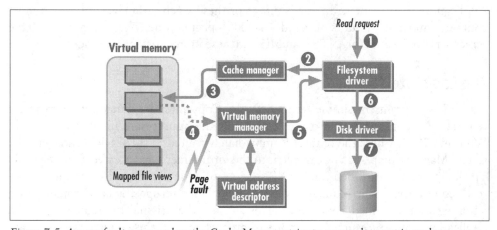

Figure 7-5. A page fault occurs when the Cache Manager tries to access data not in cache memory

The Copy Reads/sec and Copy Read Hits % counters measure file cache activity that uses the Copy interface, which applies to most normal applications, such as MS Word.

There is a variation of the Copy interface called the *Fast Copy interface* that bypasses the filesystem and goes directly to cache. The Redirector service used to resolve networked file requests uses the Fast Copy interface routinely, as does the file server service for smaller sized requests. NTFS requests can use the Fast Copy variation, while FAT16 requests cannot. The Fast Copy interface is more efficient that the plain Copy interface because it avoids the processing overhead associated with the initial call to the filesystem. It still maintains two copies of the file data in memory, so it is not any more efficient in that respect. The Fast Reads/sec counter measures file cache activity that uses the Fast Copy interface. Fast Reads are included in the Copy Reads/sec counter, and the Copy Read Hit % counter also includes Fast Read Hits.

Lazy Write

File write requests across the Copy interface are subject to deferred write-back caching, or lazy write. The Copy interface copies data from the application's file buffers into virtual storage locations associated with the cache. Dirty pages in the cache are backed with real memory, as illustrated in Figure 7-6, which again means that a copy of the current data resides in two separate memory locations: in the application and in the system working set. Sometime later, dirty pages in the system cache are flushed to disk by lazy write system worker threads. Cached file write requests subject to lazy write mean that the logical I/O request returns almost immediately after copying data into the system cache. Windows 2000 counts these logical write operations on a per-process basis (as illustrated in Figure 7-3). In earlier versions of Windows NT, the rate of logical write operations per process is unreported.

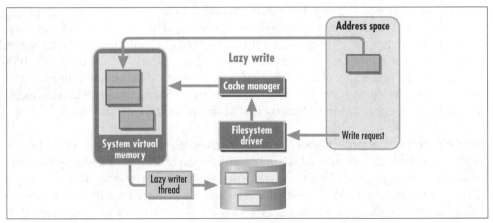

Figure 7-6. Dirty pages in the system cache are written to disk by lazy write system worker threads

Physical disk updates

The file cache lazy writer must apply updates to disk eventually. In Windows 2000, there are three mechanisms that accomplish this. The first mechanism writes to disk when the disk is idle. If the disk is very busy and too much changed data backs up in the file cache, it eventually triggers the second mechanism, a lazy write flush. This attempts to write data back to disk in bulk. A third mechanism is required in case the file cache lazy writer does not keep up with the demand for virtual memory. It depends on the normal real memory page trimming algorithm used in Windows

2000. File cache pages residing in the system working set are subject to page trimming, like any other hunk of virtual memory. When the demand for virtual memory exceeds the supply, file cache pages from the system working set can be stolen. A dirty file cache page that is stolen must then be processed by a mapped page writer kernel thread before it can be made available for reuse. We discuss these three mechanisms in the following sections

Disk Idle writes. If the disk is idle, the lazy writer leisurely writes back earlier write requests to disk. The file cache can determine that the disk is idle when there are no file cache requests that trigger synchronous disk operations. Since the disk update must be applied eventually, it makes sense to send write commands to the disk if it is idle anyway. In practice, it is never easy for the Cache Manager to determine when the disk is idle. About the only way for the lazy writer to determine this is to schedule an I/O to the disk and see what happens. (There may be applications using the disk that bypass the Cache Manager. Resolving hard page faults is one such application.)

An older Cache Manager utility, which can be downloaded from *http://www. sysinternals.com/cacheman.htm*, documents some of the internal constants that the Windows NT Cache Manager uses. (Be careful. Cache Manager does not work on current systems, including Windows 2000. It only executes on NT 4.0 at the level of service pack 3.0 and below.) The Cache Manager program documents a series of constants that are used in the lazy write algorithm. These include CcFirstDelay, which delays writes three seconds after their first access; CcIdleDelay, which triggers writes one second into an idle period; and CcCollisionDelay, which triggers a 100-millisecond delay if a speculative lazy write encounters a disk busy condition. As of this writing, it is not certain if these parameters that control Cache Manager operation were carried forward into Windows 2000, but it seems likely they were.

Threshold-triggered lazy write flushes. Just in case the disk is never idle, it would not do to allow dirty file cache pages to accumulate in the cache forever. At some point, lazy write flushes are triggered by a threshold value when too many dirty file cache pages have accumulated in RAM. Threshold-driven lazy write flushes are the second mechanism used to update the physical disks. The System Internals Cache Manager utility reveals a constant called CcDirtyPageThreshold, which is set by default to 1538 pages. When the number of dirty pages in cache reaches this threshold, it triggers a lazy write flush. A second constant called CcDirtyPageTarget is set to 1153 pages, 75% of the value of CcDirtyPageThreshold. When a lazy write flush is triggered, Windows 2000 attempts to flush one quarter of the current dirty pages to disk each time. In *Inside Windows 2000*, Solomon and Russinovich report that the dirty cache page threshold that triggers a flush to physical disk is equal to 3/8 the size of RAM. It makes sense that as the potential size of the file cache grows, this threshold value is adjusted upwards proportionally.

The activity from both idle disk flushes and threshold-triggered lazy write flushes are grouped together in a single set of performance counters available for monitoring file cache performance. Lazy Write Flushes/sec is the rate of both idle disk and threshold-triggered lazy write flushes. Because threshold-triggered dirty file pages are flushed to disk in bulk, be sure to monitor Lazy Write Pages/sec, too. This counter reports the total number of physical disk transfers associated with file cache–initiated writes. In lightly loaded file servers, file cache pages are flushed one at a time using the idle disk mechanism. But in more heavily accessed systems, the impact of threshold-driven bulk lazy write flushes should be apparent, as illustrated in the performance monitor data displayed in Figure 7-7.

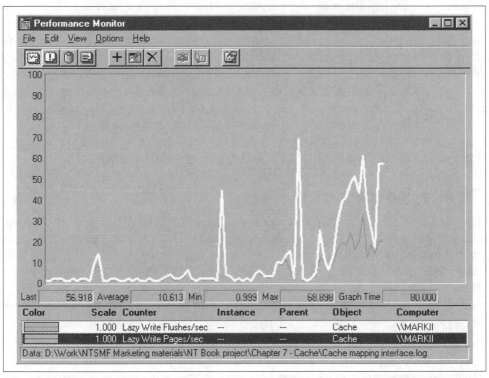

Figure 7-7. Two Cache object performance counters report on lazy write physical disk activity

Stolen mapped file pages. A third mechanism Windows 2000 uses to copy back changed pages to disk is the mapped page writer thread. During Balance Set Manager trimming, if Windows 2000 steals a page from the system cache (or a private address space page mapped to a file), the system checks to see if the page is *dirty*. A page becomes dirty when it is written into and remains dirty until the disk is updated. If a page is not dirty, it can be stolen and added immediately to the Standby list. If the page is dirty, the page cannot be used for any other purpose until the disk-resident copy is current.

The mapped page writer is a kernel thread with responsibility for sending changed file data to disk. There is more urgency associated with the mapped page writer than the lazy write thread because Windows 2000 has stolen a number of pages from the system working set that turn out to be mainly pages containing mapped file data from the cache, and the OS is unable to utilize them because they also contain updates. The mapped page writer is invoked on demand when the number of modified file pages in the system cache or associated with memory mapped files becomes too large.

Write-through caching

For the sake of data integrity, there are some applications that need to *write through* the cache to disk synchronously, specifically instructing the Cache Manager that certain dirty file pages in the cache be written to physical disk immediately. The standard Copy interface supports two different mechanisms to accomplish this. When a file is opened, the calling application program can specify that write-through semantics are to be used throughout for all write operations. Or, the application can open the file normally, but then issue a standard call to `fflush` (or its Win32 equivalent, FlushFileBuffers) to *commit* all dirty pages resident in the file cache associated with that file immediately. The number of explicitly requested file cache flushes, if any, are reported in the Data Flushes/sec and Data Flush Pages/sec counters.

The Mapping Interface

The standard file cache Copy interface has some obvious drawbacks in terms of memory efficiency. The Copy interface causes data to be copied to and from buffers in the application process virtual address space *and* the system cache. A more efficient approach would allow the application to access data in the system cache directly, passing a pointer to the file data residing in the cache back to the application. Windows 2000 supports two additional Cache Manager interfaces that return pointers to the calling application. These pointers reference file data residing in cache memory directly.

One problem with passing a pointer to the cache back to an application is that the Cache Manager no longer understands *how* file buffers are actually being used. Consequently, the Cache Manager cannot replace file segments that are referenced by pointers until those applications have signaled they are done with that specific portion of the file. Furthermore, the Cache Manager must lock the virtual memory areas pointed to by file segment pointers in real memory to prevent the Virtual Memory Manager from trimming those pages from the system working set. This ensures that the application using the file segment pointer is always pointing to the right file segment, but it does complicate the interface between the applications and the Cache Manager. Applications can take advantage of the more efficient Cache Manager interfaces, but you must develop extensive Windows 2000–specific code to do so.

Normal processes cannot access virtual addresses in the system cache range, so any application that wants to take advantage of the more efficient file cache interfaces has to be rewritten specifically for Windows 2000. Currently, the only applications that take advantage of these Cache Manager interfaces today are NTFS (the native Windows 2000 filesystem), the network Redirector, the Internet Information System (IIS), and the Windows 2000 file server service that implements file sharing on Windows 2000 workstations and servers. As we have seen, existing Win16 and Win32 applications do not need to be rewritten to enjoy the benefits of the Copy interface.

Both the Mapping interface and the MDL interface pass file cache pointers back to the calling application. The Mapping interface returns a *virtual address* pointer to the calling application, which allows it to access file data in the system directly. The MDL interface returns real addresses to the calling application. It is used by IIS and the file server service. We discuss the Mapping interface first.

The Windows 2000 Redirector uses the Cache Manager Mapping interface when a client application attempts to write or update a file stored on a remote machine. This allows Redirector to cache the remote file locally and to exercise more control over the manner in which dirty file pages are managed in local memory. This is part of the Common Internet File System (CIFS) file sharing protocol that Microsoft calls *op locking* or *opportunistic locking*.

The Mapping interface is also used by NTFS to manage file metadata structures associated with its Master File Directory, change log, and other filesystem files. (*Metadata* refers to the data the filesystem stores *about* the files it holds, e.g., their names, size, or last modified date.) Since *ntfs.sys* runs in privileged mode, it can access virtual addresses in the system cache directly.

Besides being more efficient, the Mapping interface provides a method for controlling the order and sequence of dirty page lazy write flushes. A request to *pin* a mapped page prevents that file page from being trimmed from the system cache. It instructs the Cache Manager and VMM to keep the referenced cache pages resident in memory until they are unpinned. While a page is pinned, the application using the Mapping interface must specify to the Cache Manager that the page has been changed. (Having a direct pointer to the file page in the system cache, the application is free to manipulate the data stored there directly without going through the Cache Manager interfaces.) Later, when an application like NTFS needs to commit filesystem changes to disk, it calls the Cache Manager to unpin the changed pages. Unpinning signals the lazy writer that dirty pages need to be flushed immediately. The Mapping interface also allows the application to mark a series of unpinned mapped pages that need to be written to disk together. NTFS uses the Mapping interface to cache filesystem metadata, taking advantage of this capability to ensure that certain physical disk write operations are executed synchronously. This is the mechanism NTFS uses to guarantee the integrity of the filesystem metadata stored on the physical disk media, while still reaping the performance benefits of the memory-resident file cache.

Several performance counters track the usage of the Mapping interface by the network Redirector and NTFS. Pin Reads/sec are calls to the Cache Manager to pin mapped data in the file cache. This is typically done prior to updating the information stored in the pinned page. Pinning normally occurs right after the unpinned page was flushed to disk so the page referenced is often still in the file cache. The Pin Read Hits % counter reports the percentage of pin reads that were satisfied from cache without having to access the physical disk. As Figure 7-8 illustrates, NTFS pinned reads are subject to extremely bursty behavior. The burst of activity illustrated was generated by emptying out the Recycle bin on our desktop machine. This initiates a flurry of NTFS filesystem metadata changes. If NTFS is going to work efficiently, the value of Pin Read Hits % should be close to 100%.

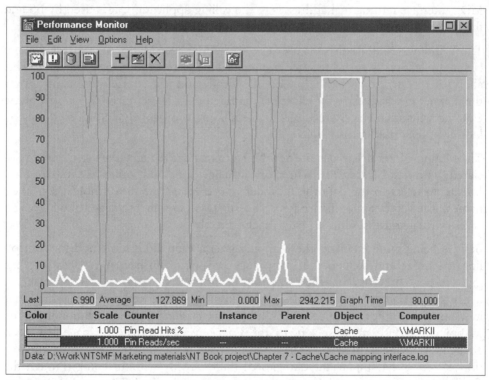

Figure 7-8. NTFS pinned reads are subject to "bursty" behavior

Be careful when interpreting the average values for the Pin Read Hits % counter as calculated by Microsoft's System Monitor. We discussed this problem back in Chapter 2. Instead of calculating an average hit % value based on the total number of hits compared to the total number of requests, System Monitor simply averages individual interval counter values. The average value for Pin Read Hits % (in light gray) that Perfmon reports in this case was 92.0% (not shown in this illustration). The actual average over the interval can be calculated by accessing the Report View or importing the chart data into Excel and computing a weighted average hit %, for example:

$$SUM(Pin\ Reads/sec \times Pin\ Read\ Hits\ \% \ / \ 100) \ / \ SUM(Pin\ Reads/sec)$$

The actual average hit % calculated using Excel in this case was 98.7%. (All the Cache object counters reporting file cache hits % are subject to similar problems due to Sysmon calculating an averages of averages, a well-known statistical no-no.)

Notice that the Pin Reads/sec counter in Figure 7-8 reports calls to the Cache Manager Mapping interface. These correspond to NTFS operations on file metadata buffered in cache memory—they do not represent either logical or physical disk operations. The Data Maps/sec and Data Map Pins/sec counters are similar. They also report the number of calls to the Mapping interface API, as shown in Figure 7-9. (Data Maps/sec is highlighted.) Having a direct pointer to the file cache data, NTFS is free to manipulate the data stored in cache as frequently as it needs to. Notice in Figure 7-9 that the scale for Data Maps/sec has been adjusted by a factor of 0.1. The maximum rate of Data Map requests reported was 1929 per second. The maximum value for Data Map pins was only 64 per second over the same interval. The Data Map Hits % counter is subject to the same averaging of averages reporting flaw just discussed.

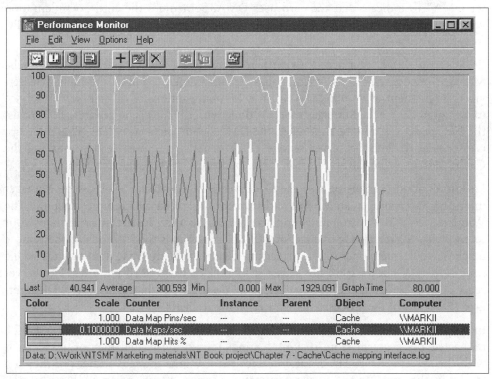

Figure 7-9. Data Maps/sec and Data Map Pins/sec report the number of calls to the Mapping interface API

MDL Interface

MDL stands for *Memory Descriptor List*, which refers to a set of one or more real address file cache pointers. Similar to the Mapping interface, the MDL interface is more efficient than the generic Copy interface because it stores file data in only one spot in memory. Any application that uses the MDL interface must be prepared to deal with all the complexities of managing real addresses.

This interface is used by both the Windows 2000 file server service and IIS to send real address cache pointers directly to a direct memory access (DMA) network interface card (NIC). Peripheral cards that support DMA can access PC memory directly without having to otherwise engage the CPU. The trick is that DMA cards can operate only on real addresses; using virtual addresses would require virtual-to-real address translation, which only the processor can do. To stay out of the CPU's way, DMA cards must operate exclusively on real memory locations.

Once a DMA device is passed a valid real address, it can read or write data at that real memory location without further intervention from the processor. DMA devices then raise an interrupt to indicate that the operation requested has completed. Nearly all NICs support DMA. You will sometimes see specifications like "Busmaster DMA" to indicate that the card uses DMA. Sometimes the card documentation won't specify DMA, but will otherwise indicate that it is able to read or write PC memory directly.

Because the MDL interface deals with real addresses, not virtual ones, the Cache Manager ensures that these cache pages remain in memory until the file server service marks them as complete. As in the Mapping interface, the file server service must signal the Cache Manager that it is done with the file cache pointer. To do this, the NIC generates an interrupt when the DMA operation is complete. This interrupt is processed by the file server service DPC, which is responsible for notifying the Cache Manager that the application is finished using the file segment pointer.

Let's look at an example of how the file server service uses the MDL Cache Manager interface. Say you open an MS Word document file stored on a remote machine. The Windows 2000 Redirector intercepts the file I/O request. Redirector translates your request into server management block (SMB) commands that it sends to the remote machine to request opening and reading the file. On the machine where the file resides, the Windows 2000 file server service fields these SMB requests. The Server service actually opens the file locally, enabling it for caching using the MDL interface. This part of the process is illustrated in Figure 7-10.

In response to specific Server file access requests, the MDL interface accesses the requested file segment from disk and brings it into the virtual memory associated with the system cache. The MDL interface then returns the real address of the data stored in the cache to the Server application. Server constructs an SMB reply message, which includes the real address pointer for use by the NIC. This request is

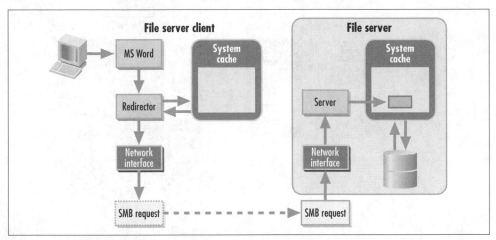

Figure 7-10. Caching using the MDL interface, part 1

passed down the network protocol stack to the NIC. Ultimately, the network device driver builds a request for the NIC that copies data directly from the cache buffer into packets that are returned over the wire to the sender.

Meanwhile, once the file is opened and caching is initiated, the Cache Manager on the file server begins to perform read-aheads automatically to stage the file in cache in anticipation of future requests. At the same time, the network Redirector also invokes the Cache Manager using the Copy interface as it begins processing SMB reply messages to return the data requested to the application. Figure 7-11 shows the file Server service replying to the client Redirector, which then copies the file data requested from the client cache into the application's file buffer. Notice that by the time the data requested is successfully passed back to MS Word, there are *three* copies of the data in memory: two on the client machine and one on the file server, as depicted. The MDL interface's more efficient use of memory is manifest only on the file server side, where just one copy of the file data is resident in memory.

Several Cache object performance counters measure MDL activity. MDL Reads/sec is the rate of file server (or IIS) reads from cache in reply to SMBs representing networked file requests. This counter is an excellent indicator of overall file server activity (see Figure 7-12). MDL Read Hits % is the percentage of MDL reads satisfied without having to access the physical disk. Again, Performance Monitor (and System Monitor) calculates an average of averages. Instead of the 37% MDL Read Hit % average that Perfmon reports (the lighter of the two gray lines), the overall hit ratio over the interval (recalculating the weighted average) was actually 68%. This calculated value allows you to measure the physical disk load associated with file server service requests that miss the cache. The file server service disk load corresponds to the MDL misses (1 – MDL Read Hits %) times the request rate (MDL Reads/sec). There is no current user of the MDL write interface, so no corresponding performance statistics

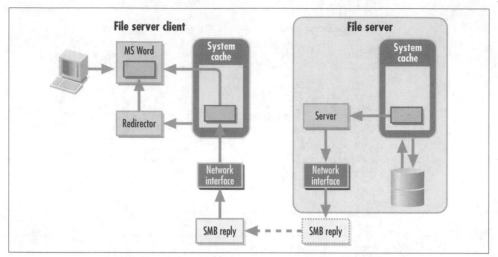

Figure 7-11. Caching using the MDL interface, part 2

are maintained. The MDL write interface was probably conceived for use by SCSI miniport drivers for disk and tapes, but never fully implemented.

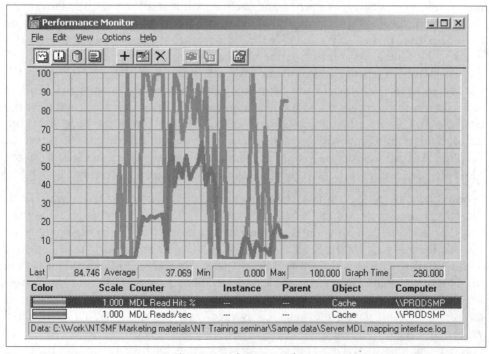

Figure 7-12. Monitoring MDL Read Hits % and MDL Reads/sec

Performance Monitoring Considerations

On Windows 2000 machines configured to run as file servers using NTFS, it is wise to monitor cache effectiveness across all three Cache Manager interfaces. Local applications running on a file server use the Copy interface. Network requests handled by the file Server service use the MDL interface. NTFS filesystem metadata is cached using the Mapping interface. As Figure 7-13 illustrates, there are a total of four Read Hit % counters worth tracking: Copy Read Hits %, Data Map Hits %, Pin Read Hit %, and MDL Read Hits %.

Unfortunately, calculating an overall cache read hit ratio for the Windows 2000 file cache is not easy. Calls to the Copy read interface and the MDL read interface correspond directly to logical disk and networked disk I/O requests, respectively. However, the Mapping interface counts calls that NTFS makes to the Cache Manager interface API, which relate to the status of a mapped data buffer. This count reflects more than just logical I/O requests. In constructing an overall weighted cache read hit %, a high rate of NTFS metadata Mapping interface requests would bias the average.

A reasonable alternative for monitoring cache effectiveness on a Windows 2000 file server is to calculate a combined average for logical disk and networked disk I/O requests, simply ignoring NTFS metadata requests to the Mapping interface. Given these difficult matters of interpretation, perhaps it is best to simply report the four hit ratio counters separately from our basic Windows 2000 performance reporting set, as shown in Figure 7-13.

Cache Tuning

About the only cache tuning action that can safely be conducted on most Windows 2000 machines is monitoring cache size and cache effectiveness, and adding memory to machines displaying signs of diminished cache effectiveness. In this section, we examine a series of file caching experiments that compare and contrast effective versus ineffective Windows 2000 file caching. These experiments were conducted using the Windows 2000 Resource Kit's Performance Probe program for generating artificial file I/O workloads. In the first scenario, we show how effective the Windows 2000 file cache can be when the cache size is adequate. In the second scenario, we observe the Windows 2000 Cache Manager under stress, attempting to manage a file access pattern that resists caching. Finally, we examine the impact of the one Cache Manager tuning parameter that is available for controlling the size of the Windows 2000 file cache. All tests were conducted originally on a Windows NT Server running Version 3.51 on a Pentium Pro 200 machine with 64 MB of RAM installed. Subsequently, we verified that the identical behavior occurs under both Windows NT 4.0 and Windows 2000. The tests were conducted on a standalone machine. The only other application running concurrently was Perfmon, which was logging performance monitor data to disk during the test runs.

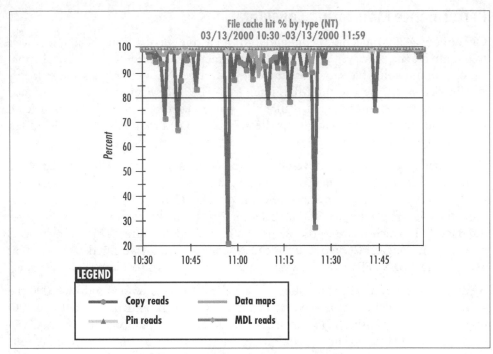

Figure 7-13. *It is best to report the four hit ratio counters separately*

Scenario 1: Effective Caching

In the first scenario, we ran the Probe program, available in the Windows NT Resource Kit, defining a 16 MB file to be accessed randomly. A read/write ratio of 1:3 was specified—there are three logical write operations occurring for each logical read request, all pointing to random 4K blocks within the file. The reason we used a logical I/O workload heavily skewed towards write activity is that we had initially planned to use the Probe program to test the speed of various hardware and software RAID configurations. RAID 5 performance, in particular, is very sensitive to a write-oriented workload. The set of benchmark runs reported here was initially conceived because we wanted to understand the Windows 2000 file cache loading effects first. As noted previously, cache effects make benchmarking notoriously difficult.

We were also motivated to test the very aggressive claims made in Russ Blake's original book *Optimizing Windows NT*, packaged as part of the Version 3.51 Resource Kit, advertising the NT file cache as "self-tuning." To test Blake's claims, we specified a file cache workload in Scenarios 2 and 3 that would defeat all but the most intelligent file caching algorithms. Needless to say, the Windows NT and 2000 file cache is not nearly as intelligent as Blake's book claims, although you can see for yourself how effective it can be under the right circumstances. Subsequent versions of the Resource Kit documentation, written after Blake retired from Microsoft, expunged his more extravagant suggestions that the Windows 2000 operating system was "self-tuning." By the way, when we found flaws in the Resource Kit's Probe program that made it difficult to interpret our disk benchmark results, we decided to switch and use the Intel Iometer disk I/O testing program instead. Some of the many disk performance tests we made using Iometer are reported in Chapters 8 and 10.

As the Perfmon report in Figure 7-14 illustrates, the Cache Manager is quite effective when the files being accessed fit nicely into the real memory available for caching. The Probe program uses the Fast Copy interface, which reports an average of 186.25 logical read requests per second during the test. This is the rate of read operations that the cache handled. Notice that these were all synchronous operations. The number of fast reads per second was almost identical. The Copy Read Hits % is reported as 99.9%. Pretty effective cache utilization.

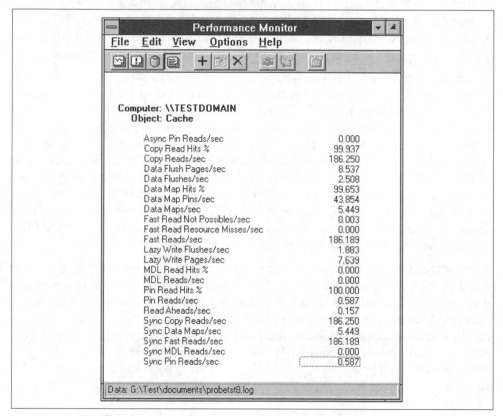

Figure 7-14. Overall cache statistics for Scenario 1

The lazy writer in this scenario operates at a leisurely pace of 1.883 flushes per second, writing 7.639 pages per second. Lazy write is using a burst size for writes of 7.639/1.883, or about four 4K pages at a time on average. The rate of data flushes is slightly higher because this counter includes lazy writes, but also counts pages flushed by the mapped file writer thread. Altogether, there are about 8.5 file pages being written through cache to disk per second. Since the test was set up to process 75% writes, if the Probe is generating almost 190 reads per second, it should be generating three times that number of writes, about 550 writes per second. Where did they all go? Windows 2000, in effect, absorbs these writes into memory. This shows how effective deferred write-back caching can be when an application overwrites the same file location locations repeatedly.

The Performance Probe is not the only application writing data to disk during the interval. Perfmon is writing data to its log file at the same time. In the 10-minute test, the Perfmon log grew to approximately 9 MB, so Perfmon is writing about 15 KB per second, too. Data Map Pins/sec is 43.854 per second. The *ntfs.sys* filesystem I/O drivers use the Data Map service to cache directories, the NTFS Master File Table, and other filesystem metadata. Windows 2000 pins an NTFS mapped file metadata page in cache in preparation for an update. As the Perfmon log file grows, NTFS filesystem changes reflecting the current size of the file must be written back to disk, too.

Figure 7-15 shows a Perfmon chart that displays a few of the important cache statistics from the test over time. The top line at the far left edge of the graph is the cache Copy Read Hits %. Within seconds, the file cache read hit ratio rises to almost 100%. (The scale is set to 200, so 100% cache hits is in the middle of the chart.) It takes a little bit of time at the start of the test to load the cache with data, which is evidence of a cache cold start. The Cache Bytes counter providing the total size of the system working set is also shown, highlighted as a white line. At the beginning of the test, Cache Bytes was 6 MB. The amount of memory the file cache consumes rises steadily over the course of the test, to about 13 MB by the end of the run. Since there is no other process running on the system making demands on memory, the file cache can acquire pretty much all the memory it wants. Because of the way the Copy interface works, the Probe process working set (not shown) expands, too.

Another point of interest is Lazy Write Pages/sec. This is the saw-toothed line in the lower portion of the screen in Figure 7-15. The peaks represent large bursts of lazy write activity triggered by a threshold at regular, predictable intervals. Lazy write is deferring I/Os to disk as long as possible. Eventually, the number of dirty pages in the file cache exceeds a threshold value, and the lazy write thread generates a spurt of activity. During peaks, more than 50 pages per second are written to disk. These spikes are followed by longer periods where the disk appears to idling along at a leisurely pace.

Scenario 2: Overrunning the Cache

Figure 7-16 shows data from a second test, identical to the first except that this time we used a 128 MB file that overflows available cache memory. In this test scenario, it is impossible to buffer the entire file in memory, so the random access pattern forces many more cache misses. In fact, the overall Copy Read Hits % is only about 48%.

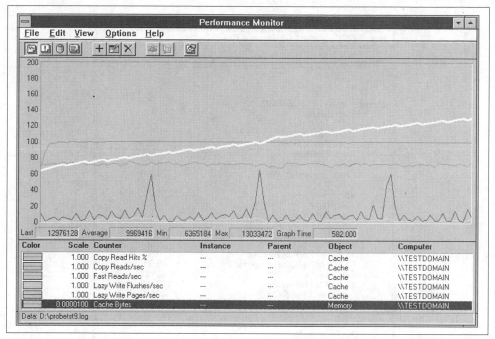

Figure 7-15. Performance Monitor displaying some important cache statistics

Because there are many more misses to process, the Performance Probe program is able to perform far fewer cached file I/O operations, slightly under 70 reads per second. Lazy write activity increases sharply to about 30 lazy writes per second, flushing about 50 I/Os per second from the cache to disk. Similar numbers of data flushes and data flush pages per second are also occurring.

Figure 7-17 shows the Copy Read Hits % over time, denoted by a narrow dotted line starting at near zero and increasing to about 50% after the first 30 seconds of the test. The dark, heavy line at the top of the screen is the number of Cache Bytes. It rises rapidly, only to level off at about 26 MB. This illustrates why it is not necessary to size the cache manually in Windows NT and 2000: the cache will grow depending on how much memory is available and how much it needs. The gray line in the lower half of the screen represents lazy write activity. Notice that there are bursts when the number of lazy writes exceeds 80 pages per second. The bursts are much more erratic than in the previous scenario, a sign that the operating system is having trouble managing in the face of this workload. This is not totally unexpected. Scenario 2 is accessing a file that is significantly larger than available RAM, a worst case for almost any kind of cache management.

Meanwhile, we are starting to accumulate some evidence about how intelligent the caching algorithms incorporated in Windows NT and 2000 are. In Figure 7-17, we changed the chart scale to make it possible to view the trend in the growth of the size of the cache (thick gray line at the top of the chart). We also track Available Bytes,

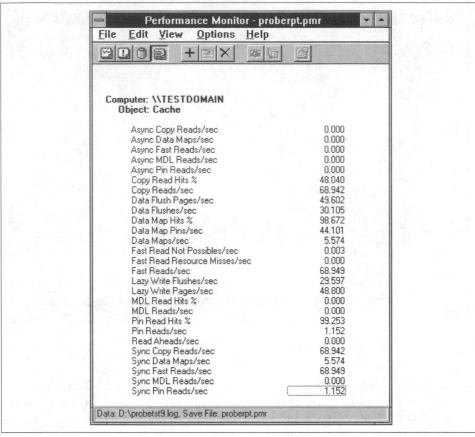

Figure 7-16. Overrunning the cache

highlighted in white. VMM allows the cache to grow rapidly up to the point where Available Bytes falls below 4 MB. With approximately 4 MB available, the system cache can no longer expand unrestrained. At this point, the system does not have many other applications from which to steal virtual memory pages, so evidently it begins to steal from the system cache. As the cache adds more pages to the system working set, they become subject to page trimming. Over time and in fits and starts, the file cache manages to pick up a few more pages at the expense of other processes, but overall its glory days are over. This system shows the classic symptoms of thrashing, but there is evidently no capability in the Cache Manager to detect that virtual memory thrashing is occurring and to take remedial action to minimize the damage.

Summarizing Scenario 2, this workload stresses the Windows NT and 2000 file cache, which expands to try to encompass the random disk I/O request pattern. The memory-resident file cache is managed like any other piece of real memory associated with the system working set. As free memory is absorbed (and the pool of Available Bytes is depleted), the memory allocated to the file cache becomes subject to

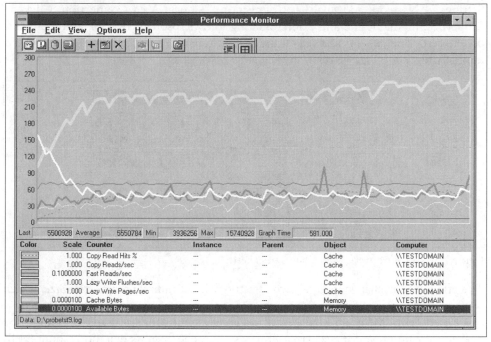

Figure 7-17. Cache statistics for Scenario 2

vigorous VMM page trimming. The random file references continue relentlessly, so finally something has to give. That something is the lazy write process, which grows noticeably more irregular and less efficient under stress.

Under the circumstances, we should not judge the performance of the Windows 2000 file cache too harshly. We deliberately selected a workload designed to defeat most caching schemes. Analyzing the test scenario measurements provides empirical evidence to support the following rule of thumb that should be incorporated into your daily performance monitoring regimen: any system that is observed consistently at or below 4 MB of Available Bytes *and* is paging heavily requires more RAM.

Scenario 3: Favoring the Cache

We performed one final experiment in this series, repeating the large file random access pattern of Scenario 2, but changing a performance parameter to favor system cache memory over application process working sets when it comes to page trimming. We changed a memory management parameter associated with file server optimization from its default value in Windows NT Server (Maximize Throughput for File Sharing) to Maximize Throughput for Network Applications. To access this parameter on a Windows NT Server, activate the Network applet from the Control Panel and access the Properties for Server under the Services tab, as illustrated in Figure 7-18. On Windows 2000 Server, you can find the same tuning knob from

Settings → Network and Dial Up Connections → Local Area Connection. Click on Properties, highlight File and Printer Sharing for Microsoft Networks, and then click on Properties again. To take effect, the system must be rebooted after the change is made. After rebooting, we reran the Scenario 2 workload.

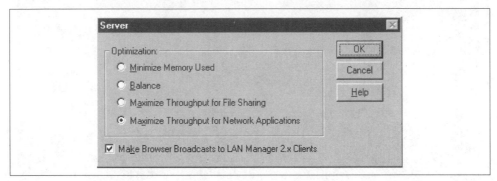

Figure 7-18. NT file server optimization parameters

The effect of this change is to set two registry-resident tuning parameters: Size, which is associated with the Server process address space, and LargeSystemCache, which is associated with Memory Management. LargeSystemCache is used to change the default maximum working set size of the system cache from its default of about 8 MB to a value equal to the size of main memory, minus 4 MB on Windows NT. It operates slightly differently under Windows 2000, as we explain shortly.

In Windows NT Server, clicking on the Maximize Throughput for Network Applications radio button sets LanmanServer Size to Large and LargeSystemCache to 1 from its default of 0, indicating that you want to run with a large system cache. The location of this parameter is shown in Figure 7-19, as the documentation is confusing. The *regentry.hlp* documentation file that comes with the NT Resource Kit explains that this setting "[e]stablishes a large system cache working set that can expand to physical memory minus 4 MB if needed. The system allows changed pages to remain in physical memory until the number of available pages drops to approximately 250." The *regentry.hlp* documentation file also suggests, "This setting is recommended for most computers running Windows NT Server on large networks." You might take exception to that advice when you see what happens in Scenario 3. The *regentry.hlp* documentation file also says that LargeSystemCache defaults to 1 on NT Server, which is incorrect. The value of LargeSystemCache is set to 0 (no large system cache) on both NT Server and Workstation.

Setting LargeSystemCache to 1 has somewhat less extreme behavior in Windows 2000. It sets the system cache maximum working set to 80% of the size of main memory, so that the file cache cannot overrun all the memory. (If you think reserving 20% of memory for other applications is a bit arbitrary, you are right. More on this subject later.) There is no trace of either the LanmanServer Size parameter or

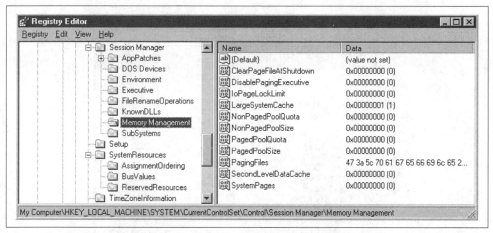

Figure 7-19. The location of the LargeSystemCache parameter in the Windows 2000 Registry

LargeSystemCache in the Windows 2000 Resource Kit documentation, but you can still find LargeSystemCache in its customary spot in the Registry. In Windows 2000, setting the Maximize Throughput for File Sharing radio button turns LargeSystem-Cache on. You still need to reboot to have this change take effect. (If you are confused about what radio button sets which option, as nearly everyone is, just check the Registry.)

We reran Scenario 2 to see what transpired after the change, and summarized the results in Figures 7-20 through 7-22. Figure 7-20 suggests that file cache performance improves slightly following the change. The Copy Read Hits % improves to 61%. Consequently, the read hit I/O rate improves to almost 74 I/Os per second. To put that number in perspective, that is an improvement of less than 10%. The rate of lazy write activity also decreases modestly. Flushes per second falls to about 21, and the number of pages flushed per second is reduced to just under 35.

Figure 7-21 shows the Copy Read Hits % trending upward over time. There is a spike about one minute into the test—the explanation for this anomaly is that after rebooting and rerunning the test, we discovered that we had not restarted MS Word. The spike in the Copy Read Hits % value corresponds to loading MS Word from disk. Besides MS Word, the Probe program, and Perfmon, there was no other activity on the system during the test. Outside that one blip, the trend is steadily up, although it levels off over time. The last measurement interval shows that the system reaches a read hit % of 69%, a distinct improvement over Figure 7-17.

Judging from just the Copy Read Hits % counter, it looks like the operating system is handling this workload better when LargeSystemCache is set to 1. However, the increase in I/O throughput is not as high as you would expect, given the improvement in the hit ratio. Figure 7-22 shows the cost at which this improvement is achieved. The heavy line trending upward to the top of the display is Cache Bytes. Previously, the Virtual Memory Manager refused to allow the cache to grow much

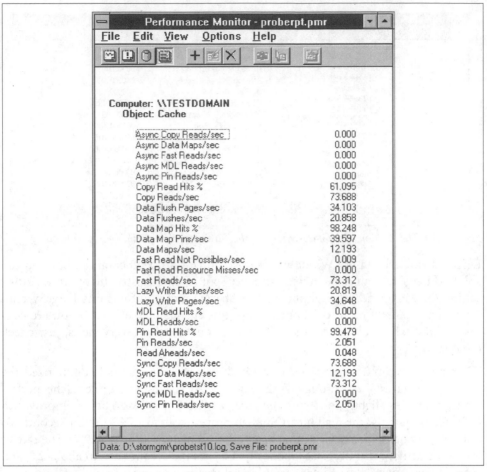

Figure 7-20. Setting the value of LargeSystemCache to 1 improves the cache hit ratio marginally

beyond a limit equal to about one half the total amount of real memory. Evidently, the parameter change relaxes that limit and allows the cache to grow and grow and grow. By the end of the 10-minute test run, the cache has increased in size to over 40 MB of the 64 MB total installed on the machine. These results show that the LargeSystem-Cache tuning knob allows the file cache to grow until it effectively takes over all of memory (minus 20% in Windows 2000) at the expense of any other applications.

We added one more detail to Figure 7-22. Highlighted in white is the Pages/sec counter, the system's hard paging rate. This is the total number of pages written to and read from disk. With file cache memory ballooning in size to over 40 MB, paging levels increase because there is so little memory left over. For the sake of comparison, the paging rate averaged 96 pages per second during this run, and only 45 pages per second during the previous run. During a peak interval, the total paging

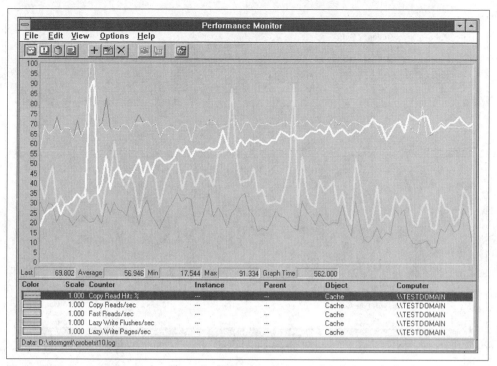

Figure 7-21. LargeSystemCache allows the file cache to grow at the expense of all other virtual address spaces

rate reached 235 pages per second, evidently an upper limit on what the disks in this configuration can deliver.

In this scenario, the system is subject to erratic spikes of paging activity, an additional element of instability and unpredictability. The additional paging load provides a clue to understanding why overall I/O throughput is not much improved in Scenario 3 when the LargeSystemCache parameter is changed. The cache hit ratio improves a bit, but I/Os that miss the cache have to contend with busier devices due to the extra paging, and therefore take longer.

The LargeSystemCache Tuning Knob

Now that you understand what the one tuning parameter available does, it seems appropriate to assess its usefulness. Under what circumstances should you change the default setting of LargeSystemCache? LargeSystemCache forces Windows 2000 to ignore the system working set where the file cache resides and look elsewhere when it needs to trim working sets. As described in the *regentry.hlp* documentation file, setting LargeSystemCache to 1 sets the system working set maximum in NT 4.0 to the size of RAM minus 4 MB—the designated target for the size of the Available Bytes pool. In Windows 2000, the system's maximum working set size is set to 80%

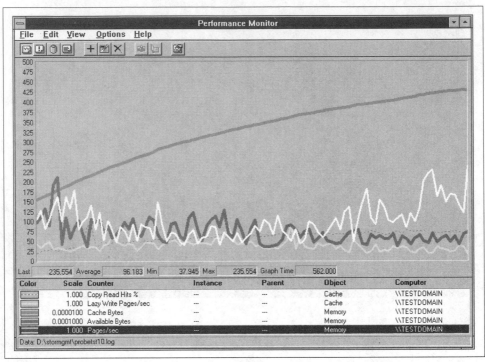

Figure 7-22. With LargeSystemCache set to 1, Pages/sec begins to spike

of the size of real memory. Under the default value, when LargeSystemCache is set to 0, the system working set maximum is set to approximately 8 MB in both Windows 2000 and Windows NT. When set to 1, LargeSystemCache preserves and protects the file cache, which is considered part of the system working set, from page trimming. Turning the LargeSystemCache on forces Windows 2000 to trim excess pages from other process working sets.

In the context of configuring a large Windows 2000 file server, setting LargeSystem-Cache to 1 may not be a bad idea. The *regentry.hlp* documentation file explains that both the Maximize Throughput for File Sharing and Maximize Throughput for Network Applications buttons set the value of the file server Size parameter to 3, which sets a large file server service working set. Presumably, the file Server service running in *services.exe* issues an appropriate call to SetProcessWorkingSetSize based on this Registry setting. In other words, the working set of the file Server service running in *services.exe* also must be protected from page trimming when the LargeSystemCache option is enabled. Remember that the file Server service uses the more efficient MDL Cache Manager Interface that stores file data in RAM only once. Meanwhile, the file Server service address space itself is also protected from excessive page trimming, while the file cache is allowed to expand until it fills the remainder of the system's memory.

The problem is any other applications running on the server. If you are trying to configure a consolidated Windows 2000 Server running more than file and print services and LargeSystemCache is set to 1, the new behavior in Windows 2000 is to preserve 20% of RAM for other applications (including the file Server service running inside *services.exe*). If you are not careful, Windows 2000 may trim back the working sets of other applications too much with the LargeSystemCache setting in effect. Some applications may become slow and unresponsive due to excessive page stealing directed at them. If file cache activity heats up, there may be a noticeable delay when desktop applications are swapped back into memory following a period of inactivity. Due to high paging rates, any application that suffers a hard page fault may encounter delays at the busy paging disk.

The fact that the file cache can map a maximum of 960 MB of RAM (or 512 MB in Windows NT) does establish an upper limit to the amount of memory the file cache will use, even when LargeSystemCache is set to 1. This limit suggests that when you configure a very large server with, say, 2 GB of RAM, setting the value of LargeSystemCache to 1 will not squeeze out other applications once the file cache grabs what it can. A final consideration is that server applications like MS SQL Server that make an explicit call to SetProcessWorkingSetSize to set their working set minimum and maximum are afforded a measure of protection from page trimming even when LargeSystemCache is set to 1.

This drastic behavior of the LargeSystemCache parameter was modified in Windows 2000. Instead of increasing the system working set maximum to the size of RAM minus 4 MB, turning on the LargeSystemCache in Windows 2000 sets the system working set maximum to 80% of available RAM. The intent of this change is to dampen the extreme behavior of this tuning knob, making it easier for a system running with a LargeSystemCache to run some *other* mission-critical applications inside the same box. Unfortunately, reserving 20% of the remaining RAM for other applications is a purely arbitrary partitioning of available memory resources. It is not clear why the Windows 2000 developers are not willing to accept the inevitable and provide a more flexible tuning knob to specify the desired size of the file cache.

No Minimum File Cache Setting

The corollary of not having a tuning knob to set a ceiling on the size of the file cache (or the system working set) is that there is no knob to establish a floor under the file cache either. Because of this, it is possible for memory contention due to other applications to shrink the size of the file cache. Figure 7-23 is a chart illustrating how other applications can drastically impact the size of the file cache. It shows a Windows 2000 Server running an application with a memory leak inside an infinite loop. The Paging File % Usage counter, charted on the right-hand Y axis, shows a steady increase in virtual memory allocations, with a dip at one point where Windows 2000 automatically extended the paging file to increase the system's Commit Limit. Finally, toward the end of the performance monitoring session, we used Task Manager to cancel the offending application. (It was one of those 3D graphics rendering applications where it takes so long to rotate a 3D image that you cannot be sure that is working correctly or looping uncontrollably. In this case, the app, which shall remain nameless, went haywire.) Canceling the application results in Windows 2000 being able to recover all the excess committed virtual memory that this application acquired.

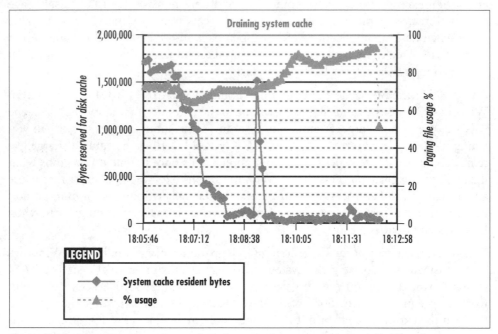

Figure 7-23. An application with an infinite loop can drain resources from the file cache

Notice the impact on System Cache Resident Bytes. The file cache size is a modest 2 MB to begin with, but when the memory leak loop occurs, the file cache is squeezed even further. The System Cache Resident Bytes is virtually at zero by the time we killed the looping process.

The implication of Figure 7-23 is that with no way to establish a minimum file cache size, there is no guarantee that any real memory will be available for the file cache when other applications are stressing real memory resources. It is no wonder that applications like MS SQL Server and Exchange, which rely on a memory-resident disk cache for performance, bypass the Cache Manager and develop their own virtual memory management routines under Windows 2000.[*]

---

[*] In the case of these two applications, another important factor in the decision to bypass built-in Cache Manager functions is that these rely on database management system (DBMS) objects (rows, columns, tables), which the OS does not understand. DBMS entities are not objects like files that the OS can cache.

The CacheSet Utility

For those who have a tin ear for Microsoft's "no knobs" mantra, you can always turn to Mark Russinovich and his trusty *http://www.sysinternals.com* shareware web site. At *http://www.sysinternals.com/cacheset.htm*, you can download Russinovich's Windows 2000 CacheSet utility, which provides a simple control for setting the minimum and maximum system working set size (see Figure 7-24). Unlike most of the other *http://www.sysinternals.com* freeware utilities, CacheSet has a command-line interface, which makes it suitable for use in automating parameter changes.

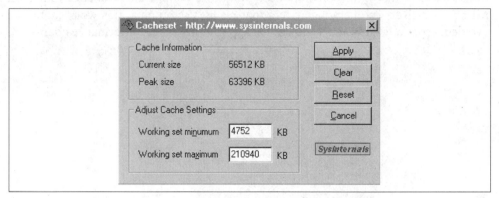

Figure 7-24. CacheSet's defaults for a 256 MB machine with LargeSystemCache enabled

Because CacheSet deals with the operating system, it cannot call SetProcessWorkingSetSize to set minimum and maximum working set size parameters. The CacheSet program that Russinovich wrote calls a Windows 2000 native API routine called NtQuerySystemInformation that resides in *NTDLL.DLL* to obtain information about the file cache settings (actually the system working set). It then calls NtSetSystemInformation to set the new sizing parameters. Of course, these minimum and maximum working set size parameters serve as guidelines for Windows 2000's Memory Manager; they are not definitive. When the system is under stress, which generally means having 1 MB or less of Available Bytes, the Memory Manager can and will shrink the system cache working set.

Using the CacheSet utility begs the question of how to set a minimum and maximum system working set to control the size of the file cache. The only method that works is trial and error, setting the file cache size minimum and maximum values and observing the cache hit ratio that results. The theoretical relationship between cache size and cache effectiveness postulated in Figure 7-1 suggests how to proceed. Iteratively, you can establish individual points on this theoretical curve, eventually filling in enough detail that you can extrapolate the rest. Keep in mind the normal variations in hourly or daily file server activity will add a good deal of noise to the tidy relationship hypothesized in Figure 7-1. Several measurements at different cache sizes that show great variation between the measured hit ratios strongly suggest

Region 1 of the theoretical curve. On the other hand, several measurements at different cache sizes that show little or no variation between the measured hit ratios suggest Region 3.

If the file access patterns are relatively consistent, and you eventually accumulate enough reliable measurements by changing the cache size parameters and measuring the cache hit ratios that result, you may be able to profile enough of the relationship between file cache size and cache effectiveness for your workload to make effective use of the CacheSet utility. Of course, this is exactly the sort of systems administrator tuning activity that Microsoft hopes its "no knobs" approach eliminates. But until Microsoft delivers an operating system that really is self-tuning, this work cannot be avoided, especially on systems and critical applications where performance counts.

## CHAPTER 8

Disk Subsystem Performance

The storage subsystem of Windows 2000 is comprised of a variety of technologies including high-speed cache memory, main memory, disk storage, and removable tape storage, all integrated to form a hierarchy. At the top of the hierarchy are technologies that provide very quick access but at a high cost per byte; at the bottom are technologies that provide very low cost per byte but slower response. The purpose of building this hierarchy is for the overall subsystem to achieve the access time of the technologies at the top of the hierarchy but at an overall cost per byte that is fairly low. The typical access patterns generated by users combined with carefully selected algorithms allow a relatively small amount of memory for cache and main memory to absorb the majority of the requests, thereby providing on the average a very short access time.

Until recently, disks were the storage medium at the lowest layer in the storage hierarchy. Now tape devices of all kinds have been added to the hierarchy to further decrease the average cost per byte. Windows 2000 introduced a service called *remote storage*. This service transparently migrates files, under the control of configuration parameters established by the system administrator, from disk to tape storage devices. It is called remote storage to differentiate it from the storage of files on disks, which is considered local storage. Remote storage provides a uniform interface to a variety of tape storage devices such as tape libraries or standalone tape drives.

Let us get back to the storage hierarchy. As shown in Figure 8-1, the hierarchy consists of a cache at the highest layer, a main memory layer, and disk storage at the next layer. The figure also shows the average access time for each device in the hierarchy, indicating how long it takes on average to access a unit of information from a particular storage medium.

Manufacturers of memory chips report the access times for cache memory and main memory in nanoseconds, whereas disk manufacturers report the access time for disks in milliseconds. Since most of us do not commonly use these units in everyday life, they are not very meaningful measures. Let us rescale the units such that the average

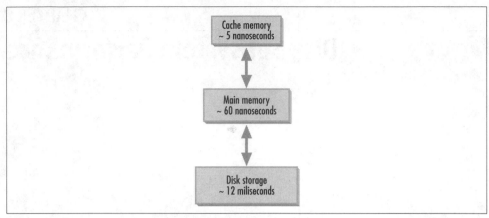

Figure 8-1. Storage hierarchy with average access times

access time of the cache is converted to one second (in other words, multiply everything by a factor of 200,000). In this way, we can better understand the difference in performance provided by each layer of this hierarchy.

Under our rescaled metrics, a miss at the cache will take 15 seconds to be serviced through main memory, since the average access time of main memory is 15 times that of the cache. Similarly, a miss in main memory will take almost 200,000 times as long to be serviced by the disk, which under our new scale implies a 40-day delay. This little rescaling game emphasizes our observation that disk storage is by far the slowest storage medium in the hierarchy. Consequently, any performance improvements made to the disk subsystem will have a tremendous impact on the performance of the overall system.

By now, you have probably noticed a theme that repeats throughout the whole book. We believe that if you understand the operation and functionality of a component of the system, then resolving a bottleneck associated with that component becomes a much easier task. So, following this theme, this chapter describes what takes place both at the hardware and software level in servicing a request to the disk subsystem. Initially, we describe briefly some of the aspects of the architecture of modern disks. There are a lot of details about the architecture of disks that we do not cover, mainly because of their added complexity and limited use in performance tuning.

The I/O Subsystem

The I/O Manager provides a set of interfaces, consistent across all physical and logical devices, that applications may use to retrieve data from or store data to. By making the interfaces consistent across all classes of physical devices, an application does not need to include separate code for each type of device. In addition to the interfaces for access to the devices, the I/O Manager also provides a number of services used by other components of the Executive or by device drivers to process the I/O requests. As the name implies, the I/O Manager simply supervises and provides an abstraction layer for drivers below it that work together to actually process the I/O requests. Figure 8-2 illustrates the relationship between user-mode applications, the I/O Manager, and the device drivers below it, all the way down to the physical devices.

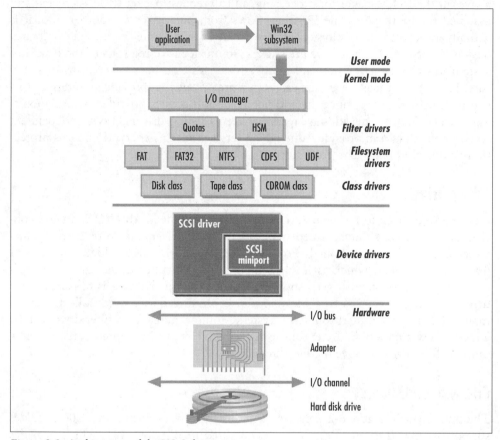

Figure 8-2. Architecture of the I/O Subsystem

You can see from the figure that lots of software components are hidden underneath the I/O Manager. The other subsystems of the operating system, such as the Memory Manager or the Cache Manager, can access those components only by using the interfaces provided by the I/O Manager, not directly. This design reduces the coupling between the components of the operating system, thereby reducing the overall complexity of it. Also, if changes need to be made in the future within the I/O subsystem, the other components will not be affected as long as the interfaces are preserved. Since we are focusing on the disk subsystem in this chapter, we include only the drivers related to disk access. The I/O Manager handles all I/O devices, so a complete picture would include the driver hierarchies for the other types of devices such as network drivers, display drivers, and multimedia drivers.

Before we look at the layers under the I/O Manager, we briefly talk about one more architectural issue. Windows 2000 uses the concept of *layers* in the design of drivers. Instead of using one monolithic driver in implementing the interface to a physical device, the driver support consists of many thin layers of drivers. When a request arrives at the I/O Manager for processing, an I/O request packet (IRP) is created and assigned to the request. The IRP then flows from one driver to another until it is actually processed by a physical device (many requests are processed by logical devices or drivers, but again we are sticking to our focus of requests to the disk subsystem in this chapter). There are many advantages to using a layered driver structure. First of all, it makes it much easier to write drivers that provide an interface to a specific physical device, since the additional support code is provided by other existing drivers. Second, by adding layers between existing drivers, ISVs (independent software vendors) can provide value-added services such as encryption, virus protection, and performance data collection.

Filter Drivers

Now let's get back to Figure 8-2. The first layer underneath the I/O Manager consists of filter drivers that intercept requests to other drivers and provide the value-added services just mentioned. For example, Windows 2000 added support for quota management, which is implemented through a filter driver that intercepts requests to a filesystem driver. Another example of a filter driver is diskperf. This driver intercepts requests to a filesystem or a physical device, and collects performance data for reporting through the System Monitor. In reality, a filter driver can be added below a filesystem driver, but to reduce the complexity of the figure, we show only the filter drivers above the filesystem drivers.

Filesystem Drivers

The next layer in Figure 8-2 consists of filesystem drivers. Windows 2000 provides support for five different filesystems as compared to Windows NT, which provides support for three. Those five filesystems are FAT (or FAT16), FAT32, NTFS, CDFS, and UDF. We have more to say about the first three filesystems in Chapter 9, since they are alternative choices for a disk filesystem and have different performance characteristics. Here, we briefly introduce each one of them. The FAT filesystem is very similar to the one available with the MS-DOS operating system, so it has been around for a while. It is still available in Windows 2000 merely to provide backward compatibility with previous versions of Windows. The FAT32 filesystem is the same as the filesystem available on the Windows 95, OSR2, and Windows 98 operating systems. The FAT32 filesystem provides support for smaller cluster sizes, resulting in a 20–30% increase in disk space efficiency, according to a technical report from Microsoft. We explain the reason for the increase in efficiency in detail in Chapter 9. The most suitable filesystem for most situations is the NTFS filesystem. NTFS was first introduced in the Windows NT operating system, but a number of features were added in the Windows 2000 version. It provides security, performance, and administrative features that are not available in the other two filesystems. The Compact Disk File System (CDFS) provides support for reading data from CD-ROMs that are formatted using the ISO 9660 specification. Finally, the Universal Disk Format (UDF) provides support for reading data from removable disk media, such as DVD, WORM, and CD-ROMs.

Class Drivers

Next in the hierarchy are class drivers. Physical devices that provide data to an operating system can be classified into classes of devices with similar characteristics. Class drivers implement similar functionality for all physical devices that belong to the same class and form the base classes that provide the common functionality and interfaces enhanced by derived classes. For example, hard disk drives, regardless of whether they are IDE or SCSI disks, provide a similar interface to an operating system. Figure 8-2 shows the Disk Class driver, which provides functionality that is common among SCSI and IDE disks, the Tape Class driver, and the CD-ROM Class driver. The Disk Class driver exports an interface to upper layers that makes a physical device appear as a logical device that provides a block-addressable space. The drivers above this layer are not aware of the host-bus adapter or the type of channel used to attach it to the server.

Mini-Drivers

The last layer of drivers before the hardware abstraction layer (HAL) consists of Mini-Drivers. A Mini-Driver exists within a wrapper and utilizes the services of that wrapper in implementing its functionality. The best example of a Mini-Driver is the SCSI Miniport driver shown in the figure. All SCSI adapter drivers need to construct a SCSI command data block, using the information provided in the IRP, and then submit that block to the SCSI adapter for processing. The process of submitting the request to the adapter is specific to the adapter used to attach the SCSI devices to the machine. The SCSI Port driver, which is the wrapper in this case, handles the common functionality, and the Miniport driver handles the adapter-specific functionality. This allows for reuse of the common functionality by multiple drivers and also makes the development of a driver for a SCSI adapter much easier, since most of the hard work is done by the SCSI Port driver. The SCSI Port and Miniport driver pair is just one example of a number of other driver pairs that use the same approach, such as the Video drivers and the network NDIS drivers. Despite the fact that Microsoft encourages vendors to write Miniport drivers, you can still find some monolithic drivers in the market.

At the same layer of the hierarchy is another set of drivers that interact directly with the hardware via the services of the HAL. This includes drivers for the various I/O buses, such as the PCI bus, or drivers for the serial and parallel ports.

The Hardware Layer

This brings us to the hardware layer. The data associated with a disk request does not flow directly between the hard drive and the server, but rather through a number of hardware devices. A read request from a hard drive to the server needs to pass through the I/O channel to which the hard drive is connected, the adapter that interfaces the I/O channel to the I/O bus, and finally the I/O bus itself. For an I/O channel, the dominant choices consist of IDE/EIDE, SCSI, and Fibre Channel. For the I/O bus, the primary choice is one of the two versions of the PCI bus, although the ISA and EISA buses are still supported on most motherboards. Finally, there is a great variety of hard drives with different features to choose from. In the next few sections, we discuss the architectural and performance characteristics of each of the available options for constructing the disk subsystem and the path between it and the server. We take a bottom-up approach, starting from the hard drive and working our way up to the I/O bus.

Disk Architecture

Figure 8-3 illustrates the architecture of a hard disk, which consists of a number of circular *platters* that rotate around a *spindle*. The number of platters can vary from one to about a dozen. Data is encoded and stored on both sides of each disk platter. Bits are stored on the platter magnetically. Originally, the presence of a magnetic field in a specific area of the disk represented a single bit of information with a value of 1, and the absence of a magnetic bit in the same area would be interpreted as a 0. Current technology detects the mere change in resistance caused by the presence of a magnetic field in one area, allowing manufacturers to cram more and more data on a magnetic disk. Recording densities in excess of an astonishing 2 billion bits per square inch can be achieved by using this technology—a number that will no doubt already be obsolete by the time you read these words.

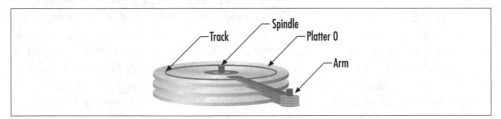

Figure 8-3. Hard disk architecture

Information is stored and retrieved from the platters using the recording and playback *heads* that are attached at the end of each of the arms. The smallest unit of data transferred to and from the disk is a *sector*. Almost always, the capacity of a sector is 512 bytes. All the sectors on a single platter at a fixed distance from the center of the platter form a *track*. Generally, data on the disk is addressed using a relative sector number, although specifically addressing sectors by their cylinder and track location may also be possible; a *cylinder* represents all the sectors that can be addressed without having to move the heads. A typical 3.5-inch disk today has about 1,500–3,000 cylinders. Head movement to a specific track location is known as a *seek*. These terms are defined in order to allow the information stored on the disk to be addressed and therefore located.

Typically, track numbers start from the outside of the first platter for track 0 and increase as you move towards the center. The same scheme continues on the bottom of the same platter and then on to the next platter. In order for the operating system to be able to retrieve a sector of information from the disk, each sector must be uniquely addressable. The disk logic translates a relative sector address into an operation aimed at a unique head, track, and sector. The head address locates the appropriate platter, the track specifies the radial distance of the sector, and finally the sector number identifies the specific sector within the track. The amount of time, t_{access}, it takes to service a disk request can, in a simplistic model, be broken into three individual components:

$$t_{access} = t_{seek} + t_{latency} + t_{transfer}$$

Initially, the head must be moved from its current cylinder to the cylinder that contains the requested sectors. This component is called *seek time* and is denoted by t_{seek}. When a sector from the same cylinder is requested, the seek time is zero. Next, the starting sector for the request must rotate under the heads, causing the *rotational latency* delay denoted as $t_{latency}$. The latency is directly related to the rotational speed of the disk. Let us assume that our disk rotates at 5,400 revolutions per minute. We can translate this into seconds by dividing by 60 to get 90 revolutions per second. This means that one revolution of the disk takes 1/90 seconds or 11.1 milliseconds. On the average, a disk will need to rotate half a revolution to get to the next sector. Most manufacturers use the time for half a disk revolution when they report average rotational latency.

The final component in our equation is the amount of time it takes the block to be transferred from the disk to the user. This is the *data transfer* delay, denoted as $t_{transfer}$. The transfer rate is related to the rotational speed of the disk and the track density. Every rotation of the disk transfers, at most, one track. So, for a disk with a track density of 100 KB per track and a rotational speed of 90 revolutions per second, up to 9,000 KB can be transferred in one second. Typical average values quoted by the manufacturers for these quantities for modern hard drives are 10 ms for seek time, 6 ms for latency, and 10 MB/sec for the data transfer rate. Assuming that an 8 KB block is requested, the actual transfer time is only 0.8 ms. In this example, the overall average access time is 16.8 ms, with seek and latency overhead contributing 96% of the overall transfer time. Figure 8-4 illustrates the breakdown of processing a request for an 8 KB block by a hard drive. If we were to provide a similar pie chart for the processing of a 16 KB block, the data transfer time would comprise 16% of the overall service time, with overhead contributing the other 84%.

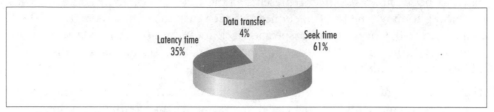

Figure 8-4. Breakdown of the service time of processing an 8 KB request by a hard drive

By understanding the mechanical delays in processing a request, we can use software techniques in one of two general approaches to improve the performance of the disk. One approach taken by engineers is to reduce the amount of time spent between requests in moving from one cylinder to another. Most applications tend to access files sequentially. Therefore, by keeping all the blocks that comprise the file close to each other, the overhead of moving from one block of a file to the next decreases (in Chapter 9 we see how the filesystem tries to cluster related blocks of date close together). The other approach is to increase the size of the request. By transferring more data every time we move the heads to a new location, we reduce the total head movement for transferring a file.

The average seek time is computed as the sum of all possible seek times (for all possible pairs of cylinder-to-cylinder distances) divided by the total number of such seek times. In reality, this value is not very useful for a number of reasons. First of all, the velocity at which the arm moves from one position to another depends on the distance traveled, but in a nonlinear way. For long distances, the arm accelerates to a maximum speed, travels at that speed for a certain amount of time, then decelerates until finally it settles at the desired location. For very small distances, the majority of the overall seek time is the settle time. Additionally, a cache within the disk may contain some of the data requested, removing the need for incurring the cost of an average seek and latency.

You should keep in mind that when disk manufacturers report transfer rates for their disks, they are only referring to the burst rate at which data is transferred from the disk's buffers to the system's memory. This data transfer rate cannot be attained in a realistic environment because the other two components (the seek and latency times) are left out of the calculation. In an actual transfer, the effective transfer rate observed by an application running on a Windows 2000 machine includes all the latencies and not just the transfer time.

One critical component that was left out of the previous equation is the disk queuing time, which is the amount of time that a request has to wait at the disk queue for other requests to be processed. We left it out because it is hard to predict the value of that component; it can range from zero to a very large value for the same disk with the same data stored in it, due to the intensity of the workload imposed on the disk, i.e., the number of requests submitted concurrently. Various analytical techniques are available for predicting the response time for a given workload, but the discussion of such techniques falls outside the scope of this book. The good news is that the System Monitor provides counters that allow us to measure the queuing time. The later section "System Monitor Counters" describes the appropriate counters and how to use them.

Disk performance has been a thorny problem for many years under all operating system platforms, and a number of optimization techniques have been applied to alleviate it. Many of these optimization tricks continue to be relevant to disk performance in the Windows NT/2000 environment. The next few sections describe some of those techniques.

Track Buffer

In earlier disk technologies, rotational latency affected performance considerably when the I/O subsystem was heavily utilized. In such technologies, once a request is received from the I/O bus by the disk, the bus is released while the request is serviced. After the heads move to the right cylinder, the disk controller waits for the requested sectors to rotate under the heads. By sensing the current position of the heads relative to the track underneath, the controller attempts to reserve access to the bus right before the requested sectors arrive under the head. If the bus cannot be reserved due to congestion, then the controller has to wait for an entire rotation before another attempt is made to reserve it. Figure 8-5 shows an example of this situation. The request is initially transferred over the bus. The heads are repositioned and when the data arrives under the heads, the disk controller attempts to reserve the bus, but the bus has been reserved by another device. The congestion at the bus causes the disk controller to wait for another rotation before it gets a chance to try again. This time the bus is free and the data is transferred.

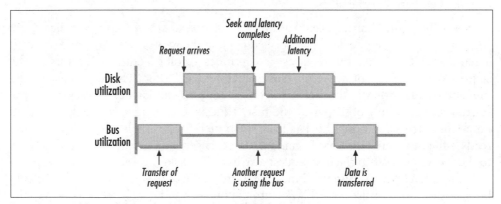

Figure 8-5. Additional delay due to congestion at the bus

To minimize the effect of rotational latency on the performance of a hard drive, a cache called the *track buffer* is now used. Now, as soon as the head is positioned at the correct track, the heads start reading the data passing under the head into the buffer. Since the data from the entire buffer is cached on the disk, the requested sectors can then be selected and sent to the operating system when the bus is available. Figure 8-6 shows an example of this situation. Here the data is transferred into the track buffer as soon as the data rotates under the heads. Although the bus is busy and the data cannot be transferred immediately to the host, as soon as the bus is free the data can be transferred without having to wait for another full rotation.

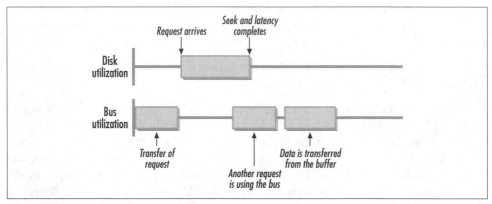

Figure 8-6. Using the track buffer reduces the delay

Prefetching Algorithm

Filesystems attempt to cluster related data together on the disk. Also, requests to the I/O subsystem are reorganized by some drivers into a new sequence based on their allocation on the disk platters. These two optimizations make the sequence of requests observed by the hard drive appear more sequential in nature than those actually generated by the users.

To speed up sequential requests, hard drives use a *read-ahead* or *prefetch algorithm*. This means that after the head has finished reading the requested sectors and detected a sequential pattern in the requests, it continues reading additional sectors in the sequence that have not yet been requested into the buffer. The advantage of the prefetching algorithm is that for contiguous requests, the latency of seeking to the starting block is only observed by the first requests; consecutive requests are served much quicker by retrieving the data from the buffer. For example, an application that reads a file in its entirety from beginning to end is generating sequential I/O requests to the filesystem. When the first request arrives at the disk, the arm is positioned properly through a seek operation and the disk starts reading not only the requested block, but also additional consecutive blocks into the prefetch buffer. The next request to the hard drive finds the data in the buffer and experiences a very fast response time. Therefore, the overall response time experienced by such an application is very low.

Multiple consecutive streams at the disk controller do not benefit as much, since two different streams compete for the same buffer. This implies that when the utilization of the disk increases, the benefit of the prefetch algorithm decreases as fewer requests are serviced right from the buffer.

Disk manufacturers have realized that the interleaved access to the disk buffer by multiple streams can decrease considerably the effect of the cache. If the entire buffer is used to prefetch data for one request, a single request from another location requires that the original contents of the buffer be purged. This may cause two or more applications to repeatedly compete with each other for the track buffer, resulting in neither of them getting the benefits of the buffer. To resolve this problem, drive vendors initially divided the single buffer into multiple segments, allowing multiple requests to be buffered concurrently into separate smaller segments. Quantum, for example, for some drives uses a four-segment buffer with a capacity of 64 KB in each segment. Three of the buffers are used for read requests, and the fourth for write requests. A miss from the disk cache causes a read from the disk and a prefetch of data into an entire segment. If the next read also causes a miss, only a segment needs to be overwritten with data as opposed to the entire cache. When a new segment is needed to prefetch a block of data, the segment to be purged is selected based on the utilization of the data in each segment. Using multiple segments allows multiple concurrent and sequential streams to benefit from the cache, although segmentation causes the effective cache of each stream to be smaller than in the nonsegmented case.

Modern drives take this design even further by providing *adaptive segmentation*. Instead of segmenting the cache into a fixed number, firmware within the hardware implements an algorithm that dynamically determines the most effective use of the available space on the disk. For example, consider the case where an application generates four read requests to a disk. The first three requests are for a 10 KB block and the fourth is for a 64 KB block. Figure 8-7 illustrates this example. In the fixed segmentation case, we have four segments of 64 KB capacity, three for read requests and one for write requests. After the first three requests arrive, the drive with fixed segmentation has all three read segments fully utilized although the buffer overall still has 226 KB of unused capacity (256 KB – 30 KB). This forces the drive to discard the first of the three 10 KB blocks in order to accommodate the 64 KB read request. In the adaptive segmentation case, the drive still has 226 KB of available space that it can use to load the 64 KB block, without having to discard that 10 KB block that may be requested again.

Typical buffer sizes for drives targeted towards file servers are between 2 and 4 MB, and between 512 KB and 2 MB for drives targeted towards workstations.

Zoned Bit Recording

Hard disks always rotate at a fixed angular velocity. The most common speed is 7200 revolutions per minute (rpm), although disks as fast as 10,000 rpm have recently

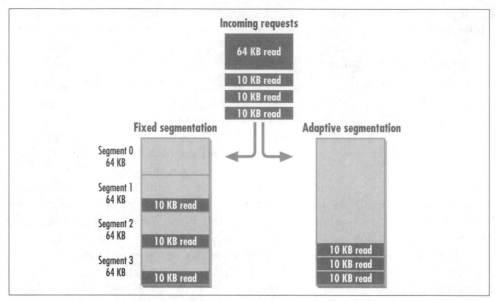

Figure 8-7. *A request sequence illustrating the advantage of adaptive segmentation*

become available on the market. The transfer rate of the disk is proportional to the linear velocity of the platter and can be expressed as:

$$TransRate = 2 \pi r \, AngVel \, Dens$$

where r is the distance of the head position from the center of the platter, *AngVel* is the angular velocity or rotational speed of the disk, and *Dens* is the density at which data is stored on the platter. The rotational speed of a disk is constant. This equation assumes that the density at which data is stored is also constant, implying that the further the head is from the center of the platter, the faster data travels underneath the head, since there is more recording area on the outside tracks than the inside tracks. Let us use an example to make this easier to understand. In Figure 8-8, the disk is rotating at 7200 rpm, and we look at two tracks, one at distance r1 from the center of the platter and another at distance r2. The length of the first track is 2πr1 and that of the second is 2πr2. The density of data stored on the platter is constant, given in terms of bits/inch. The total capacity of a single track is simply the product of the length of the track times the density. The data transfer rate at any track can then be expressed as the product of the rotational speed and the amount of data stored per track.

Since it is difficult to read and write data at different rates depending on the current cylinder at which the heads are located, the number of sectors per track is kept constant throughout the platter. This is accomplished by including sufficient spacing on the outside cylinders of the disk. The upper limit on the number of sectors per track, and therefore the overall capacity of the disk, is imposed by the inner cylinders.

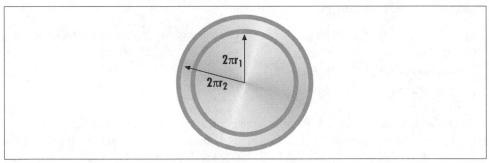

Figure 8-8. The length of a track is based on its distance from the center

Zoned bit or *multiple zone recording* is a new technology that uses up some of the space that is wasted on the longer outside tracks. The track density is kept constant throughout the disk platter. As you move from the inside tracks to the outside, there is additional space available on each track. As soon as that additional space is sufficient to store another sector, a new zone begins. This procedure divides the platter of the disk into zones with a constant number of sectors per zone, as shown in Figure 8-9. The number of zones varies from manufacturer to manufacturer, but is typically 20–50 zones per platter.

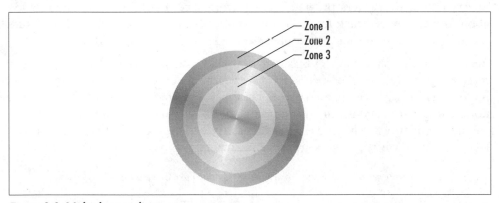

Figure 8-9. Multiple recording zones

Table 8-1 illustrates the effect of zoned bit recording by showing key characteristics of various hard drives on the market. For each drive, the table includes information on the model, the rotation speed, the minimum and maximum number of sectors per track, and the minimum and maximum transfer rate in MB/sec. As we can see in the table, there are substantial differences in the transfer rate as a result of the different sector density per track. For example, for the Maxtor DiamondMax, the transfer rate for the outer track is 60% higher than for the inner track, and for the Maxtor Crystal-Max, the transfer rate for the outer track is 50% higher than that for the inner track.

Table 8-1. Hard disk characteristics

Disk model	RPM	Sectors/track min/max	Transfer rate min/max
Seagate ST1120	5600	54/94	2.5/4.3
Maxtor DiamondMax 2160	5200	195/312	8.7/14
Maxtor CrystalMax 1080	4480	117/246	4.5/9

The transfer rates in Table 8-1 are internal rates: the rates at which data is transferred from the storage medium to the internal buffer. The rate at which the data is transferred to the operating system buffer is dependent on the bus used to attach the disk to the system. The following section on I/O buses provides more details on the transfer speeds of the various bus protocols.

Disks that do not use zoned bit recording have a fixed geometry, and that is the interface they export to the operating system. To preserve the same external interface, hard drives with zoned bit recording hide the variation in the geometry of the disk. The on-disk controller translates addresses to and from the operating system so that the disk appears to have a fixed number of sectors per track. Although not clearly stated in the specifications of a hard drive, the lower-numbered cylinders are arranged on the outside of the disk. For multiple zone recording drives, this means that partitions with lower-numbered cylinders provide better performance. For SCSI disks, information about the sectors per track for each zone can be obtained using the MODE SENSE command. Later in this chapter, we devote an entire section to the SCSI protocol.

Before we move on to the I/O buses that provide access to external devices to your motherboard, we take a look at a few drives currently on the market. Table 8-2 lists important performance characteristics for some of the more popular drives. This is not a comparison, and is only meant to familiarize you with the critical metrics you should consider before buying a drive. Some drives in the table are targeted at server-level machines, whereas others are targeted at workstations and desktop systems.

Table 8-2. Important performance characteristics of various hard drive models

	Internal transfer rate (MB/sec)	External transfer rate (MB/sec)	Average seek (msec)	Track-to-track seek (msec)	Average latency (msec)	Cache size (MB)	Spindle speed
Seagate Cheetah (ST318845)	395-492	160	3.9, 4.5	0.5, 0.7	2	4	15000
Seagate Barracuda	323	66.6	7.6	N/A	4.2	0.5	7200
Quantum Atlas IV	194-340	160	6.3	0.8	4.2	4	7200
Quantum Atlas V	151-257	160	6.9	0.8	4.2	2	7200
Quantum Atlas 10K	215-315	160	5.0	0.8	3.0	2	10000
IBM Ultrastar 72Z	280-473	160	5.3	0.6	3.0	16	10000
Maxtor DiamondMax Plus	345	66.7	< 9.0	1.0	4.2	2	7200

The internal transfer rate is the rate at which the drive can transfer data between the platters and the buffer. In some of the drives, the manufacturer reports a range. This is a result of the difference in transfer rates between the outside and inside tracks of the disk, which arises from zone bit recording. The external transfer rate is always reported as the theoretical transfer rate of the interface between the drive and the host. For the high-end drives, the 160 MB/sec is the bandwidth of the SCSI Ultra 160 interface, which we discuss later. This is not attainable by a single drive. The actual transfer rate will be closer to the value reported as the internal transfer rate for sequential workloads. Random workloads will of course have much lower transfer rates. For the Seagate Cheetah, there are two values for each of the seek statistics in the table because the manufacturer reported different seek values for read and write requests. Another thing to note is the relationship between the average latency and the spindle speed. As you would expect, the drives that spin faster have a lower latency value. Finally, notice the variability in the size of the buffers used by the drives. The high-end IBM drive has the largest buffer of the drives listed here, providing a capacity of 16 MB. Just a few years ago, that would have been a sufficient amount of memory to support a workstation machine.

The Windows 2000 Resource Kit includes a utility script called *drives.vbs* that lists all the physical drives attached to your machine. For each drive, it includes information about the manufacturer, the model, the geometry of the drive, and its capacity. In the case of a SCSI drive, it also includes the SCSI bus ID that the device is attached to, and the target ID of the device. Here is the output of running this script on my machine:

```
Microsoft (R) Windows Script Host Version 5.1 for Windows
Copyright (C) Microsoft Corporation 1996-1999. All rights reserved.

WDC WD205BA:   Disk drive
Status:              OK
Media Loaded:        Yes
Partitions:          2
System Name:         HERACLITOS
Manufacturer/Model: (Standard disk drives) WDC WD205BA
Size:                20,522,073,600
Total Cylinders:     2,495
Total Heads    :     255
Total Sectors:       40,082,175
Total Tracks:        636,225
Sectors Per Track:   63
Tracks Per Cylinder:255
Bytes Per Sector:    512
Name:                \\.\PHYSICALDRIVE0
Creation Class Name:Win32_DiskDrive

FUJITSU MAB3045SC SCSI Disk Device:   Disk drive
Status:              OK
Media Loaded:        Yes
Partitions:          1
```

```
System Name:        HERACLITOS
SCSIBus:            0
SCSILogicalUnit:    0
SCSIPort:           3
SCSITargetId:       3
Manufacturer/Model: (Standard disk drives) FUJITSU MAB3045SC SCSI Disk Device
Size:               4,548,579,840
Total Cylinders:    553
Total Heads    :    255
Total Sectors:      8,883,945
Total Tracks:       141,015
Sectors Per Track:  63
Tracks Per Cylinder:255
Bytes Per Sector:   512
Name:               \\.\PHYSICALDRIVE3
Creation Class Name:Win32_DiskDrive
```

A feature that has recently become available on drives is SMART (Self-Monitoring Analysis and Reporting Technology). It was originally developed by Compaq, but is now supported by many hard drive manufacturers, including Quantum, Seagate, and Conner. The firmware within the drive monitors drive activity and collects fault prediction and failure indication parameters. If it determines that a hard disk failure is imminent, it notifies the system through an alert, allowing the system administrator to either replace the drive or initiate a backup operation. Under Windows 2000 and Windows NT, the SMART error-reporting data is made available through the Desktop Management Interface or third-party utilities. Windows 2000 added support for SMART in Windows Management Instrumentation (WMI) through the addition of four new GUIDs: MSStorageDriver_FailurePredictStatus, MSStorageDriver_FailurePredictData, MSStorageDriver_FailurePredictEvent, and MSStorageDriver_FailurePredictFunction. A WMI agent can retrieve SMART data either through polling the drive periodically or through registering an event handler. Additional details regarding WMI support for SMART are available in the Windows 2000 DDK or in the WMI section of the Microsoft Platform SDK. Although the SMART feature is related to reliability rather than performance, it is good to be familiar with its existence.

I/O Buses

In this section, we talk about I/O buses and discuss the advantages and disadvantages of each of the available options. The I/O bus sits between the I/O devices, such as your disk, modem, and video card, and the system/memory bus. On your motherboard, the I/O bus makes itself visible through the expansion cards available on it, although your motherboard may have one or more I/O buses supporting the expansion cards that you see. The first standard I/O bus available in the PC industry was the ISA (Industry Standard Architecture) bus. For many years before that, cards were developed based on a loosely defined standard. As time went on, more and more problems surfaced as the bus clock speed kept being pushed further, so eventually the industry decided to firmly define the characteristics of the AT I/O bus interface. The result of this standardization effort was the ISA bus, which runs at 8.25 MHz and has a throughput of 1.5 Mbps to 5.0 Mbps. Given today's demanding applications and high-speed devices, this bus is considered too slow and is not present in high-end systems. On motherboards where it is available for backward compatibility, make sure that you use it only for slower devices where performance is not critical. For example, serial ports, modems, and sound cards can be supported at full capacity by an ISA bus slot. On the other hand, high-speed devices such as SCSI adapters and network adapters must be on a faster bus interface, such as a PCI bus. Even though the ISA bus has sufficient capacity to support a 10 Mbit/sec Ethernet card, that card requires a lot more CPU utilization than a PCI card. Since it is very hard to isolate the time it takes to transfer the data from the disk adapter to memory from measurements of the data transfer time, you have to make sure to configure your machine properly. Later in this section, we provide some guidelines you can use to avoid a bottleneck at the I/O bus while configuring your server.

VESA Local Bus

The video card was the first peripheral device to exceed the capacity of the ISA bus. Graphical operating systems such as Windows demanded high-speed graphics, and video cards quickly started hitting the limits of the ISA bus. The VESA Local Bus was invented to support such high-speed graphics cards. It is connected directly to the processor system bus, giving it a considerable performance advantage. The VESA local bus provided transfer rates of up to 133 MB/sec at the first specification and 160 MB/sec with Release 2.0. The direct connection to the CPU gave this particular bus architecture a performance advantage, but also had two important problems. Since under the VESA architecture the bus controller talked directly to the CPU, it had to be designed specifically for the CPU architecture it is used with. If the CPU was upgraded in the future, the VESA local bus had to be replaced as well, meaning that the whole motherboard had to be replaced. Also, due to its direct connection to the processor bus and the load-intensive nature of the cards that utilize it, the VESA bus generates considerable demands on the CPU. These problems caused the VESA bus to fall out of favor. It was quickly succeeded by the PCI bus, which became available shortly after the first release of the VESA Local Bus 1.0 specification.

PCI Bus

The most popular I/O bus today is the PCI bus. It first appeared on the market along with the introduction of Pentium-based machines. A very important architectural difference between the PCI bus and other I/O buses is that the PCI bus is detached from the processor's system bus. Figure 8-10 illustrates the relationship between the PCI bus and the processor's system bus. The PCI bus is attached to the rest of the system through a bridge. This feature makes the PCI bus processor-independent and allows computer manufacturers to provide multiple PCI buses on a single motherboard. In fact, some high-end servers available on the market, such as the NCR WorldMark 4380 multiprocessor, have up to 15 PCI slots spread across four PCI buses. The PCI bus at a clock rate of 33 MHz can provide a maximum transfer rate of 133 Mbytes/ sec with a 32-bit bus and 266 MB/sec with a 64-bit bus. The next-generation PCI bus, as defined in Version 2.2 of the specification, can operate at an enhanced clock speed of 66 MHz, providing a bandwidth of 266 MB/sec with the 32-bit bus and 532 MB/sec with the 64-bit bus. The 64-bit bus will become a more popular option for motherboards once 64-bit processor-based servers become dominant in the market. Other features include hot-plug capable PCI cards, as well as power management that complies with the ACPI and OnNow initiatives (look at *http://www.pcisig.com* for additional details).

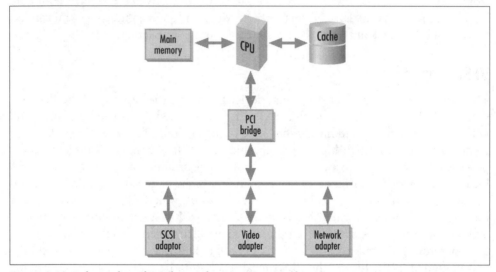

Figure 8-10. Relationship of PCI bus and processor system bus

There are two common configurations of motherboards with multiple PCI buses. One architecture uses peer buses, with each bus independently attached to the system bus through a PCI bridge. The second architecture has the second bus attached to the first bus through a bridge. This architecture is not as good as the first one, since the bandwidth is that of a single PCI bus even though the number of available slots increases. Before you purchase a motherboard for a server, you should review the technical specifications document that usually describes the architecture of the board.

Other advantages of the PCI bus include plug-and-play configuration and interrupt sharing. When the machine is powered on, the PCI bus takes control of the bus, interacts with the devices attached to it, and assigns them system resources. The configuration information is stored so that it can be accessed by the operating system. Once the operating system starts loading, it takes control of the PCI bus and retrieves the configuration information, making modifications to the resource allocations as necessary. The automatic assignment of resources to cards simplifies the configuration of a system and is less error-prone than configuring it manually.

The PCI bus allows for interrupt sharing but introduces an indirection layer between the interrupt mechanism used by the cards and the IRQs used by the CPU. The PCI bus and all the devices attached to it make use of INT lines. The PCI BIOS maintains a mapping of INT lines to interrupt requests (IRQs). This additional level of indirection and the fact that only one device is active on the bus at any given time gives PCI devices the ability to share one or more interrupts.

Configuration Tips

When you buy a server, make sure you configure enough bandwidth in the I/O bus to handle the cards and workload that your server is expected to support. As we mentioned, detecting a bottleneck at the bus is difficult using the metrics provided by Windows 2000, so you have to prevent the possibility of a bottleneck at the bus through proper configuration. For example, if your server's motherboard has a single 32-bit bus operating at 33 MHz, it is capable of handling 132 MB/sec of traffic. If you attach to this bus two Fibre Channel host bus adapters, which are capable of transferring 100 MB/sec each, you are bound to run into problems. A better configuration for this case would be to get a server with two peer PCI buses and plug one adapter into each. On motherboards with multiple PCI buses, make sure you allocate the cards evenly (in terms of the bandwidth of each card) across the two buses. The L440GX motherboard from Intel has four PCI slots on one 32-bit, 33 MHz bus, and two slots on a PCI peer 32-bit, 66 MHz bus. Read the technical specifications document for these boards to determine the allocation of PCI slots to the underlying buses.

Disk Interfaces

So far, we have discussed the architecture of disks and their impact on the performance of the I/O subsystem, as well as the I/O buses that are available. In order for the data to be processed by an application, it needs to be transferred from the disk device to the I/O bus over an interface. In this section, we describe in detail the two most popular interfaces for attaching disks to a Windows 2000 machine—the IDE and SCSI disk interfaces—and briefly discuss some of the more advanced interfaces that are starting to appear in the market.

The Device Manager snap-in in the Windows 2000 management console classifies the devices installed on a system by interface type. Figure 8-11 shows the main screen that the device manager presents, with the disk drives, IDE/ATAPI controllers, and SCSI and RAID controllers entries expanded in the tree view. Using this view, you can determine which devices are recognized by the system, how they are connected to the system, and you can change their advanced settings.

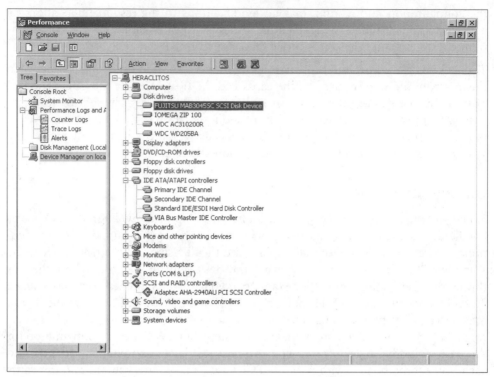

Figure 8-11. List of devices by interface type by the Device Manager snap-in

What Is an Interface?

Before looking into the operation and functionality of the IDE and SCSI disk interfaces, we first examine the services that must be provided by an interface. A hard disk consists of multiple components that ultimately provide persistent storage and transfer of data between a host and the disk device, as illustrated in Figure 8-12. The figure also shows the portion of the functionality that is not provided by the adapter attached to the disk by enclosing that functionality into a dotted box.

Starting from the device end and working towards the host, the first component comprises all the analog electronics that read and write bits of data from the disk platters. The next component is the data separator, whose job is to convert the analog signal into bits and to package the bits into bytes of data. The ST506 disk interface, one of the earliest interfaces used to attach disks to a PC host, was positioned between the analog electronics and data separator components. One advantage of this early approach was that different ST506 controllers could use different encoding schemes for writing data to the disk. The two common techniques used were modified frequency modulation (MFM) and run length limited (RLL). The disadvantage of placing the majority of the functionality on the adapter is that the adapter must

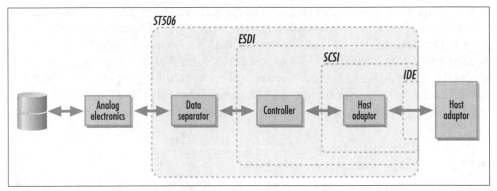

Figure 8-12. Disk-to-host interface components

have an intimate understanding of the geometry and operation of the disk drive. This implies that the same adapter cannot be used by the host to attach other types of storage devices to the system, such as tape drives and CD-ROM drives.

The next component is the controller, whose job is to organize and carry out operations on the storage device on behalf of the host. The ESDI interface moved closer to device independence by incorporating the data separator component as part of the controller that is embedded with the drive itself. Although the ESDI interface was designed to also support tape devices, no such tape driver was ever introduced into the market.

The next component is the host adapter. Its job is to provide the interface between the controller and the host's I/O bus. In the case of the SCSI bus, the host adapter component is part of the adapter, whereas in the case of the IDE interface, it is primarily incorporated into the embedded disk interface.

The IDE Interface

We begin this section by describing the IDE interface and the historical development of its specifications, including the programmed I/O (PIO) and direct memory access (DMA) modes that are available in each one. Devices use one of these two modes to transfer data between the device and the memory of the host. The simpler and earlier approach to data transfer is PIO. When a request arrives at the driver for either a read or a write operation, the data is transferred between the memory buffer on the host and the controller directly by the processor. This implies that during the processing of a PIO data transfer, the CPU is not available to do other processing on the system. The clear disadvantage of this approach is the resulting high CPU utilization.

DMA resolves this problem by delegating the actual transfer of the data to another chip, called the DMA controller. The DMA controller is programmed using the logical address of the buffer, the amount of data to transfer, and the direction of the transfer, and it autonomously performs the data transfer. This allows the CPU to perform other activities while the data transfer is taking place. There are two types of DMA devices: System DMA and Busmaster DMA. Traditionally, every PC was required to have a built-in DMA controller that was shared by all the devices that needed to do DMA transfers. Although a DMA controller is still available on every motherboard, only slow, ISA-bus devices still resort to it for support. With Busmaster DMA, the device itself provides a DMA controller that handles the transfers on its behalf. Now that we have a basic understanding of these two terms, we can continue with the history of IDE.

History

The IDE interface was introduced back in 1984. The original objective was to move some of the functionality provided by the ST506 controller to the disk drive itself. This would cause a minor increase in the cost of the drive but would reduce the cost of the AT adapter considerably. In 1994, the X3T9.2 working group of ANSI approved the standard for IDE under the official name ATA. The ATA-2 standard was approved in 1995 and offered a number of new features, including additional data transfer modes and synchronous transfers. We cover the various modes in detail shortly. Then came the ATA-3 standard, which was approved in 1996, providing some new commands and support for SMART (Self-Monitoring Analysis and Reporting Technology). The next release of the standard was ATA/ATAPI-4, which came in 1997. It introduced support for ATAPI devices and the packet interface, command queuing, and, most importantly, the Ultra DMA modes. The last approved standard as of this writing is the ATA/ATAPI-5, which was completed in 1999 and added support for Ultra DMA 4.

Today, IDE drives are popular among desktop machines or low-end servers due to the low cost of the drives. As we see in the next few sections, IDE generates high CPU utilization under most transfer modes, making it inappropriate for installations with heavy I/O workloads, such as file servers and web servers.

Topology

Each IDE channel can support two drives in a master-slave topology, as shown in Figure 8-13. The master drive has address 0, and the slave has address 1. The terms master and slave give the impression that one drive has higher priority than the other, but in reality this relationship affects the drives only when the system is started. Most motherboards now provide an embedded IDE channel, thereby increasing the number of slots available for other expansion purposes. Currently, it is more common to see motherboards with two separate IDE channels providing support for up to four drives. One of them is called the primary and the other the secondary channel, and in this case, the two are not the same performance-wise. The primary channel is connected directly to the PCI bus, which provides a 33 MHz clock speed, whereas the secondary is connected to the ISA bus, which only provides an 8 MHz clock speed. Therefore, it is always important to put the faster devices on the primary channel, and the slower devices, such as CD-ROM drives and tape drives, on the secondary channel. Mixing fast and slow devices causes the fast device to operate at the speed of the slower one.

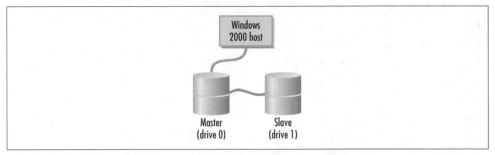

Figure 8-13. IDE drive configuration

A 40-pin cable is used to connect the drives to the adapter that is plugged into the PC host. The original IDE interface assumed that the adapter was attached to an ISA bus, but the interface was enhanced to incorporate PCI bus adapters. This change caused the prices of IDE and SCSI adapters to be comparable.

Commands and transfer modes

One of the design goals for the IDE standard was to hide the complexity of interfacing a drive from the host. This was accomplished by providing a set of high-level commands and a set of registers that the host must use to control the drive. The ATA interface views the disk as a set of sectors that can be addressed using either the cylinder, head, and sector numbers (the CHS mode) or a logical block address (the LBA mode). In LBA mode, the disk is treated as a sequence of blocks without requiring the host to have any knowledge of the disk's geometry. The mapping from the physical geometry of the disk to the LBA model is specified by the ATA in such a way that sequential access to blocks is always faster.

As we discussed already, data is transferred using either PIO or DMA. A number of modes are specified by the standard for each of the transfer types. The ATA-2 standard increased the number of modes to eight from four in ATA-1. The ATA-3 specification did not provide any additional data transfer modes. Before the release of the ATA-4 specification, disk manufacturers introduced the Ultra ATA protocol, which busted the maximum transfer rate to 33 MB/sec. The ATA-4 specification released in 1997 incorporated the Ultra ATA protocol as mode Ultra DMA 2. Again, the disk manufacturers moved further by introducing the Ultra ATA/66 protocol, which was standardized in the ATA-5 specification released in 1999. This latest specification introduced two more modes called Ultra DMA 3 (44.4 MB/sec) and Ultra DMA 4 (66 MB/sec). Due to the increase in electromagnetic interference in these two modes, you need a special 40-pin, 80-conductor cable to hook up the drive to your system.

Table 8-3 summarizes the characteristics of the various transfer modes.

Table 8-3. IDE transfer modes

Transfer mode type	Maximum transfer rate
PIO 0	3.3 MB/sec
PIO 1	5.2 MB/sec
PIO 2	8.3 MB/sec
PIO 3	11.1 MB/sec
PIO 4	16.6 MB/sec
DMA 0	4.2 MB/sec
DMA 1	13.3 MB/sec
DMA 2	16.6 MB/sec
Ultra DMA 2	33.3 MB/sec
Ultra DMA 3	44.4 MB/sec
Ultra DMA 4	66.6 MB/sec

Regardless of the mode, the commands that perform data transfers follow the same sequence of steps. The host initiates an operation by setting up registers with the address of the block or sequence of blocks that must be transferred, and then specifying the command or opcode corresponding to the operation that must take place. Commands include *Read Sectors*, *Seek*, and *Read Buffer*. As an example, for the *Read Sectors* command, the host specifies the starting sector address and the number of sequential sectors that must be read.

To utilize these high-speed modes, especially the Ultra ATA/66, your system needs to satisfy the following three criteria:

- The motherboard must have built-in support for Ultra ATA, or you can purchase an external Ultra ATA/66 controller.
- The hard drive must support these modes. Before you purchase a drive, review the technical specification available online at the drive manufacturer's site.
- To support the Ultra DMA modes 3 and 4, you need the new 40-pin, 80-conductor cable.

The only support required by the operating system itself is support at the driver level for DMA transfers. The IDE driver in Windows 2000, as well as later service pack releases of Windows NT, includes support for DMA transfers. You can use the Device Manager MMC snap-in to enable the use of DMA. To do this, select an IDE channel under the IDE ATA/ATAPI controllers entry and open the Properties page. Figure 8-14 shows the Advanced Settings tab that you can use to enable or disable the DMA transfer mode. You can select from the "PIO only" or "DMA if available" options. If you use the "DMA if available" option, it will use a DMA transfer mode when the drive and BIOS support it. The Current Transfer Mode edit box shows the transfer mode currently being used.

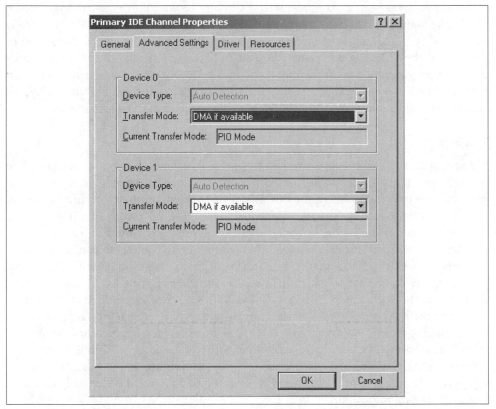

Figure 8-14. Device Manager Properties screen for enabling the use of DMA transfer mode

Tests at Microsoft Research that compared the performance of PIO versus DMA transfer modes on the same IDE disk revealed that the use of PIO mode transfer decreased the performance by 75% for unbuffered 64 KB reads, and increased CPU utilization by 50% across two processors.

The SCSI Bus

SCSI (pronounced *scuzzy*) is an acronym for *small computer system interface*. The first official specification was released by ANSI in 1986, and was referred to as the SCSI-1 standard or, more formally, as the ANSI X3.131-1986 standard. The second official release was made in 1994 as SCSI-2. A number of enhancements were introduced with this release, some of which are described in this section. The standardization group recently completed the SCSI-3 specification document. The main goal has consistently been to make the protocol as device-independent as possible so that a wide variety of peripherals can be supported. Accomplishing this goal requires that the commands supported by this standard do not make assumptions about the specific properties of the device.

Entire books have been written about the SCSI bus, so we won't go into a lot of detail about the signals used, cable requirements, and the protocol itself. We only cover aspects of SCSI that impact its performance. First, we talk about the organization of devices on the SCSI bus and their addressing. Then we describe the SCSI variations available on the market and their corresponding performance characteristics. We then briefly discuss the eight phases in the execution of a SCSI command, and finally, we talk about the options available for controlling the execution of the commands.

Topology

Devices and host adapters are attached to the SCSI bus in a daisy-chain fashion. The formal term for a single SCSI bus with some number of devices on it is a *SCSI domain*. The two endpoints of the bus must be properly terminated to prevent signal reflections that would overlay the signal and cause errors. Typically, the host adapter is attached to one endpoint, but that is not necessary. Most modern host adapters use automatic termination based on whether one or two of their connectors have cables attached to them. Figure 8-15 shows a SCSI bus with three devices and two host adapters connected to it. In this case, termination is provided by the two host adapters at the endpoints of the bus. SCSI-2 allows up to eight devices to be connected to the bus; wide SCSI increases this to sixteen devices. Each target is assigned an ID ranging from 0 to 7, or from 0 to 15. The SCSI target ID represents the address of the device on the bus, and also assigns a priority to the target within the bus. Later on we will see that this priority impacts only the arbitration of the bus. By connecting two host adapters to the same SCSI bus, the devices can be shared by the two hosts, as shown in the figure.

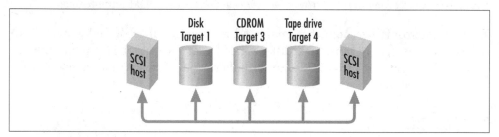

Figure 8-15. SCSI domain

The devices are attached to the bus function as initiators, targets, or both. An *initiator* sends out commands for execution by one of the targets. In a setup where a Windows 2000 server has a SCSI disk attached to it via a SCSI adapter, the host adapter is the initiator and the disk is the target when the Windows 2000 host sends a read request to the disk. A *target* consists of an ID, a target controller, and one or more logical units (LUNs). Each target can have up to eight logical units but must always provide logical unit zero. The single logical unit target is also the most common configuration of a SCSI device. Some tape libraries appear as a single target, with the robotic arm that does the tape mounting being one logical unit, and the one or more tape drives being other logical units. So, in the general sense, an initiator sends a command to be processed by one of the logical units within one of the targets.

SCSI devices can use one of two signaling conventions to communicate with each other. These two variations are not compatible with each other, so either one or the other will be present on a single bus. On *single-ended* buses, devices communicate using explicit voltage levels to represent a binary 1 or 0 value. On *differential buses,* devices detect the difference between pairs of wires to determine whether a 0 or a 1 is transmitted. This provides more noise immunity and longer cable lengths for the differential bus, but at a higher cost, so this is used for more expensive SCSI devices. More recently, the Ultra 2 specification introduced a new signaling technology, called low voltage differential (LVD), that reduces the cost of differential implementations. Most RAID storage servers, which require a high-bandwidth connection to the host, are differential SCSI devices, whereas server disks and tape drives are typically single-ended.

Standards and transfer modes

A variety of SCSI devices with varying bandwidth characteristics exist in the market. Table 8-4 summarizes the various options. SCSI-1 devices provide a maximum transfer rate of 3 MB/sec for asynchronous transfers and 5 MB/sec for synchronous transfer. In asynchronous transfers, the protocol requires an acknowledgment for each byte transferred, whereas in synchronous transfers, a target is allowed to send a certain number of bytes before waiting for acknowledgment. All commands, statuses, and messages are transmitted in asynchronous mode. Before a synchronous data transfer can occur between an initiator and a device, negotiation takes place where the target is interrogated for synchronous support. Most devices on the market today support synchronous transfers.

Table 8-4. SCSI variations

SCSI version	Bus width	Max. device support	Bandwidth
Synchronous SCSI-1	8	8	3 MB/sec
Asynchronous SCSI-1	8	8	5 MB/sec
Fast SCSI-2	8	8	10 MB/sec
Fast & Wide SCSI-2	16	16	20 MB/sec
Ultra SCSI or Fast 20	8	8	20 MB/sec
Wide Ultra SCSI	16	16	40 MB/sec
Ultra2 SCSI	8	8	40 MB/sec
Wide Ultra2 SCSI	16	16	80 MB/sec
Ultra3 SCSI or Ultra160	16	16	160 MB/sec
Ultra320	16	16	320 MB/sec

Wide SCSI increases the width of the bus to 16 bits, doubling the bandwidth. To support the additional data bits, wide SCSI uses a 68-pin cable in place of the normal 50-pin cable. Unlike single-ended versus differential devices, wide and non-wide SCSI devices can both be utilized on a single SCSI bus. Many host adapters provide both a 50-pin and a 68-pin connector so that both types of devices can be attached to the same bus, and custom-made cables are available for connecting wide and non-wide devices to each other. Fast-20, or Ultra SCSI as it is known in the industry, allows a bandwidth of 20 MB/sec for non-wide or 40 MB/sec for wide SCSI. It is important to remember that the increase in data transfer speed comes at the expense of the cable length. With up to four devices on an Ultra SCSI bus, the maximum cable length is 3 meters. Having more than four devices decreases the maximum cable length to 1.5 meters.

The next variation is Ultra2 SCSI. It is an enhancement to Ultra SCSI but provides a maximum transfer rate of 80 MB/sec by increasing the clock rate to 40 MHz. One subset of the Ultra2 specification includes the definition of the LVD I/O interface. This new signaling technology increases the cable length by increasing overall transmission reliability. Ultra2 is a high-performance, relatively low-cost solution targeted towards the workstation-level machine.

The latest version of the SCSI interface currently on the market is Ultra3 SCSI or Ultra160, as it is more commonly known. Ultra160 doubles the maximum transfer rate to 160 MB/sec by using both edges of the request/acknowledge signal to clock data. This is the same technique used in Ultra ATA/66. A number of disk manufacturers including Seagate, Quantum, and IBM have a wide variety of Ultra160 drives on the market, and appropriate host-bus adapters are available through Adapter and Mylex, among others. Although 160 MB/sec may seem sufficient, the SCSI Trade Association (*http://www.scsita.org*) is already defining the roadmap for further evolution of the SCSI standard. Based on historical data, they have determined that the hard disk drive media data rates double every 2.2 years. They also assume that the appropriate bus bandwidth must be four times the data rate of the hard drive. Based on these two requirements, they project that the SCSI interface should be able to provide a bandwidth of 260 MB/sec by 2002 and 360 MB/sec by 2003. The next version of the SCSI specification will be the Ultra320, followed in a couple of years by the Ultra640.

Commands

Let's now explore briefly the available SCSI commands and the phases of command execution. As mentioned, the most important goal of the SCSI bus has been to provide device-independence, and this is achieved by each command set. All supported devices are classified into device type groups based on their characteristics. The SCSI standard provides a small subset of commands that apply to all supported devices. Then, each device group is represented by a model of how the SCSI bus views the device and a command set that is specific to that device group.

Examples of devices types are *block devices*, such as disk drives and tape drives; *stream devices*, such as printers and communication devices; and *medium-changers*, such as tape and CD-ROM changers. A block device is viewed by the SCSI bus as a device that provides for the storage and retrieval of information to and from a sequence of logical blocks. A medium changer is viewed as consisting of one or more medium transport elements, which move media from one location to another; one or more storage elements, which provide storage for media while they are not used; and one or more data transfer elements, which perform the data transfer to and from the media.

The execution of a command on the SCSI bus is performed in eight distinct phases (Figure 8-16 shows a diagram):

1. Initially, the bus is free until one or more initiators try to acquire the bus.

2. In the arbitration state, the initiator with the highest SCSI ID will acquire the bus (wide SCSI allows 16 devices on a single bus, and there, the order of priority is the following sequence: 7,6,...0,15,14,...8). To take advantage of this priority scheme, faster devices should use higher-priority SCSI IDs than slower devices. When the bus is not heavily utilized, the possibility of two devices attempting to concurrently acquire the bus is very slim. As utilization increases, the priority arbitration scheme becomes more important.

3. In the selection phase, the winner of the arbitration specifies the target that it wants to communicate with.

4. In the message phase, the initiator and target exchange information about the protocol itself. For example, the negotiation of whether a synchronous data transfer can be supported takes place during the message phase.

5. Following the message phase, the initiator specifies the command that must be executed.

6. At this point, the target, depending on the command submitted, may receive data in the data phase or decide to disconnect and process the command while another initiator-target pair uses the bus. For example, when a read request is sent to a disk device, the controller may choose to disconnect while the heads are positioned properly and the requested data is read into the prefetch buffer. In servicing a request, a seek and a latency operation together may take up to 20 msec, so during that interval, another device can utilize the bus. The disconnection property of the SCSI bus increases its throughput, since the amount of time that the bus is idle is reduced.

7. The disconnect request takes place within a message phase.

8. The status phase is entered after the command has been either processed or ignored by the target. In this phase, the target returns an indication of success or error back to the initiator.

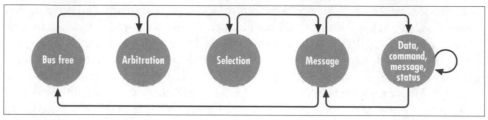

Figure 8-16. SCSI phase transition diagram

In summary, the SCSI interface provides better performance than the IDE bus due to its support for devices with higher bandwidth and more advanced features, support for more devices per channel, and lower utilization of the host's processor. This last advantage has to do with the number of interrupts generated per data transfer. However, the generality of the SCSI bus and its eight-phase command execution make it a protocol with high overhead. So typically, the applications and the operating system cannot observe the maximum bandwidth ratings for the various SCSI variations.

As the maximum transfer speeds of the SCSI interface have increased, the fraction of bandwidth wasted due to protocol overhead has increased as well. This is because commands, messages, and status are transferred through a narrow 8-bit bus at asynchronous data rates, regardless of the capabilities of the interface. So, as the time to transfer the data decreases with increasing data rates, the overhead of initiating the transfers remains constant. To resolve this issue, a new protocol has been introduced called *packetized* SCSI. With packetized SCSI using a single connection, a device can send data and status from multiple commands in a single packet. Not only does packetized SCSI provide the capability of combining multiple commands into one packet, it also allows the packets to be transferred at the maximum data rate of the interface. Packetized SCSI is part of a recent disk vendor specification called Ultra160+ and will definitely be part of the next official SCSI specification, which should be named Ultra320.

Tagged-command queuing

The SCSI-2 standard introduced a very important optimization feature called *tagged-command queuing*. This optimization allows a target device to accept multiple requests from an initiator by labeling each command with a different tag. This parallelism improves the performance of a target by overlapping the transfer of one command from the host to the target with the execution of another command. For example, while a read request is processed by a target, the initiator can send another command to the target. This way, as soon as the read request completes, the disk heads can start moving to service the second request. Without tagged-command queuing, a host adapter would have to wait for the target's response to the first request before sending a new one out. Another advantage of tagged-command queuing is that with multiple commands waiting in the queue for execution, the target can reorder the requests in such a way as to reduce their processing time.

Tests of the impact of tagged-command queuing on the performance of a single disk have shown that this feature provides the most improvement for workloads that consist of a small number of request streams for smaller blocks with some randomness. The response of a device to this kind of workload consists primarily of seek and latency overhead for placing the heads. By queuing up multiple requests at the device, it can reorder them to be processed more efficiently. When the workload consists of requests for large sequential blocks of data, the drive is pushing data to the server as fast as it can, so having multiple requests available does not give it much room for improvement.

As we will see in Chapter 10, tagged-command queuing is very important in disk arrays where multiple physical disks are used to form a single logical disk. When multiple requests are sent to the logical device, they can be processed concurrently by the underlying physical disks. This ability of the SCSI protocol to provide greater concurrency gives it an edge over the IDE interface. Even though the IDE may provide equal or even better performance than SCSI in environments with just one or two disks, the SCSI interface comes out on top in environments with a large number of disks and intensive workload.

Host adapter configuration

Most host adapters provide on-board, menu-driven utilities for setting up various options. Options such as negotiation of synchronous transfers, support for disconnection, negotiation of wide transfers, and support for tagged-command queuing can be enabled or disabled before the machine is booted. In a disk performance–hungry environment, it is important that all these features are enabled, since using them can result in a considerable increase in performance. In addition to settings on the host adapter, the Windows 2000 Registry can be used to configure some options of the SCSI miniport driver. A number of Registry value entries can be specified under the registry path HKEY_LOCAL_MACHINE\System\CurrentControlSet\Services.

All the options needed for high-performance support are set by default. If problems are observed with some older SCSI devices, the following Registry key values can be used to selectively disable some of those options:

DisableDisconnects (REG_DWORD)
> Setting this value disables support for disconnection of devices from the SCSI bus. It is advisable that you turn off disconnection on SCSI buses where there is only one SCSI device present. This reduces the overhead of the disconnect/reselection phases and thereby increases the throughput. Be sure to check with the specific host adapter vendor before disabling this feature, though. The Adaptec AIC-78XX series of adapters hang when disconnects are disabled.

DisableMultipleRequests (REG_DWORD)
> Setting this value prevents the SCSI miniport driver from sending multiple requests at a time to a SCSI target. As you can imagine, sending multiple

requests can provide for higher throughput since some devices can reorder the execution of the requests for better performance.

DisableSynchronousTransfer (REG_DWORD)

Setting this value prevents the SCSI miniport driver from negotiating for synchronous transfers with the target. This should be used only with very old SCSI-1 devices. Modern tape drives that support only asynchronous transfers simply reject the initiator's request for synchronous transfers, and no problems arise.

DisableTaggedQueuing (REG_DWORD)

Setting this value prevents the SCSI miniport driver from supporting tagged queuing on the host adapter. This option can be disabled if none of the devices on the SCSI bus supports tagged queuing.

In addition to the miniport driver entries, many host adapters have their own specific command-line options. As an example, here are the command-line options available on the Adaptec AIC-78XX adapter:

MAXIMUMSGLIST

This value determines the size of the scatter-gather list that is used for large I/O transfers. The range for this value is 1–255 and the default value is 7.

MAXTAGS

This value determines the size of the tagged-command queue list. The range is 1–255 and the default value is 128.

Figure 8-17 shows how to modify the Registry to set the values for these options. The Device *subkey* will cause the parameters to be set for all AIC78XX host adapters on your system. If you have multiple adapters connected to the system and you want changes to be applied to only one of them, change the Device subkey to DeviceX, where X is the index of the adapter (Device0 is the first, Device1 is the second, and so on).

On Windows 2000, the default behavior is to have the synchronous transfers and tagged-command queuing properties enabled for SCSI drives. You can inspect or modify the setting of these two parameters using the Device Manager MMC snap-in. Under the disk drives tree node, you can right-click any of the SCSI drives to bring up the Properties screen. Figure 8-18 shows the SCSI Properties tab. You can use the checkboxes to enable or disable either one of the two properties.

SCSI Versus IDE

Now that we have covered both the IDE/ATA and SCSI interfaces in detail, you are probably wondering which one you should choose for your server. Of course, there is no clear answer to this question; it depends on the machine you are configuring, the workloads you are expecting, and the amount of money you want to invest. If

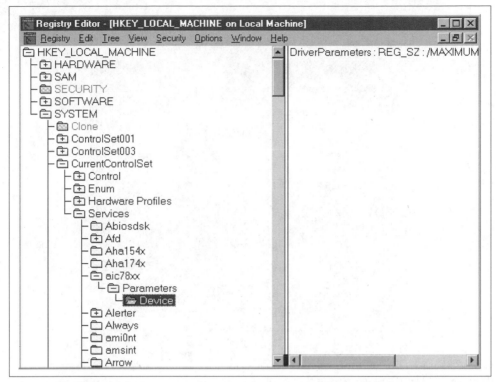

Figure 8-17. Changing the Registry parameters associated with Adaptec SCSI driver

you are configuring a mid- to high-end server with a large number of drives (more than four), SCSI is the clear choice for the following reasons:

- Most high-performance drives are only available with a SCSI or Fibre Channel interface, so if you were to choose IDE, you would be limited by the performance of the drives themselves.

- With the IDE interface, most motherboards provide two IDE channels for a maximum of four devices. You could configure more, but you would need additional adapter cards and careful configuration.

- The maximum transfer rate of the IDE interface is currently 66 MB/sec, as opposed to the 160 MB/sec available with Ultra 3 SCSI.

- When you combine a CD-ROM with a hard drive on an IDE interface, the performance of the drive is considerably affected due to the difference in protocols used. SCSI was designed from the beginning to be a device-independent protocol.

- Each IDE channel can have only 2 devices, whereas on a wide SCSI channel you can add up to 15 devices.

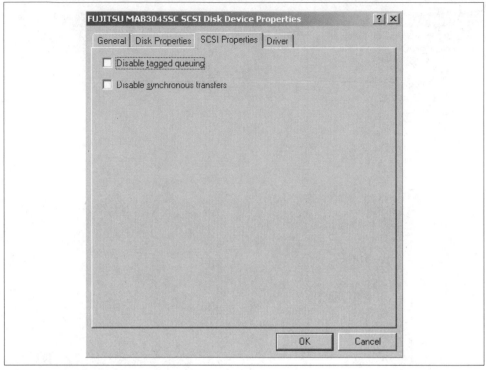

Figure 8-18. The SCSI Properties tab

If you are primarily concerned about cost and need only a few disk devices, then IDE is the clear winner for the following reasons:

- Both the drives and the adapters for the IDE interface are much cheaper. Almost every motherboard currently comes with two IDE/ATA channels, so for up to four drives you won't even need to purchase an adapter. Built-in SCSI adapters are available only on high-end, expensive motherboards, so you almost certainly would need to purchase an adapter.

- Since SCSI drives are targeted towards the high-end market, their advanced features and increased buffer memory tend to make them more expensive. Also, the market for SCSI drives is smaller than that for IDE devices, so the cost to manufacture them is higher.

A much more detailed comparison between the SCSI and IDE interfaces is available at the Storage Review site at *http://www.storagereview.com/guide/guide_ide_scsi.html*, along with a wealth of information relating to the storage subsystem.

Fibre Channel

One of the most recent developments to hit the market is the *fibre channel*. Unlike SCSI, which transfers data in parallel, the fibre channel interface allows devices to transfer data serially, much like in a network. Some of its advantages include high bandwidth, long cable lengths, a lot of flexibility in configuring its topology, and the ability to combine the data communications network with the storage interconnection channel.

Let us first familiarize ourselves with the terminology of the fibre channel. Each device connected to the channel is called a *node*, and is attached to the channel through a port. The fibre channel standard defines various port types with different capabilities. Here is a list of the port types:

N_Port

> N or Node ports are the simplest port types, and exist on all fibre channel storage devices. N ports can be used for point-to-point connections with another N port or for a connection to an F port on a switch.

F_Port

> F or Fabric ports are usually part of a fibre channel switch and are used to connect N ports to the switch fabric. (If you are not familiar with switch fabrics and arbitrated loops, be patient. We discuss the various fibre channel topologies in the next section.)

NL_Port

> NL or Node Loop ports are N ports that have the additional functionality to operate within an arbitrated loop.

FL_Port

> FL or Fabric Loop ports are usually part of a fibre channel switch and allow the switch to connect and communicate with other devices that are part of the loop.

The communications network that allows devices to talk to each other is called the *fabric*. Depending on whether copper, short-wave optical, or long-wave optical cabling is used to construct the fibre channel fabric, the nodes can be spread over a total distance of 30, 500, and 10,000 meters, respectively. The maximum bandwidth currently available for point-to-point or arbitrated loop topologies is 200 MB/sec, or 400 MB/sec in the full-duplex configuration. We talk about the available topologies in more detail next, and introduce an option that provides an even higher maximum bandwidth.

One considerable advantage of the fibre channel over the SCSI channel is the flexibility provided in putting together the fabric. The simplest configuration is the point-to-point link between a host and a storage device, such as a disk array using two N ports. Since the media is only used to connect two devices, only a subset of the fibre channel protocol is used for the point-to-point configuration. In a point-to-point link, the host and the device establish a connection over the dedicated link during initialization and have access to the full bandwidth offered over this link.

The next available option is the arbitrated loop that connects anywhere from 2 to 126 fibre channel devices to each other. This configuration looks a lot like a token ring or FDDI network. The arbitrated loop configuration is a low-cost option, since it does not require any additional equipment for forming the network. Despite the physical configuration of this topology in the form of a loop, devices attached to it still communicate to one another in a point-to-point manner. The fibre channel protocol allows the devices attached to the loop to obtain unique addresses and to compete for access to the loop via arbitration. During arbitration, a frame is passed around the nodes of the loop. After one rotation, the node with the highest priority will win the arbitration cycle. Until loop access is released again, all the nodes (except the initiator and target) simply forward the frames from the input port to the output port, forming a logical point-to-point connection between the initiator and the target nodes.

One disadvantage of the arbitrated loop topology is that all the devices are connected to a single channel and thereby have to share the available bandwidth. In environments with multiple high-performance drives or disk arrays and sequential workloads, it is possible for the channel to become the bottleneck. Another disadvantage of the early versions of this configuration was the lack of fault tolerance, since a single failed node could cause the entire channel to fail.

Much as Ethernet 10 base-2 networks were replaced with 10 base-T networks with the use of a hub, fibre channel hubs are available to convert the physical arbitrated loop topology to a star topology. Illustration A in Figure 8-19 shows the arbitrated loop topology, and Illustration B shows the star topology.

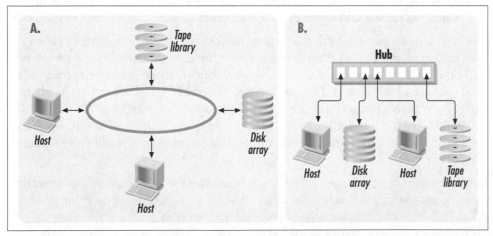

Figure 8-19. A: Arbitrated loop configuration; B: The star topology that uses a hub

Arbitrated loop hubs are typically available in 7-port and 12-port configurations that usually include an additional port for cascading two or more hubs. The hub provides bypass circuitry at each port to prevent dysfunctional nodes from impacting the other nodes in the loop. The fibre channel protocol provides support for arbitration of access to the shared loop as well as support for assignment of an address to each connected node during initialization of the loop.

The third and most popular (and most expensive) configuration is the switched topology that provides any-to-any connections between the nodes of the network. This is implemented using a crossbar architecture and provides the full bandwidth to each connection as long as no two hosts attempt to communicate with the same device at the same time. There are currently 8-, 16-, 32-, and 64-port switches available on the market. Switches use F ports to either connect to another switch on an F port or to connect to a device or host using an N port; or, they can support an FL port for attaching the switch onto an arbitrated loop network.

It should not come as a big surprise that the switch topology provides the best performance, in terms of throughput, of the three options. Although the maximum bandwidth on a point-to-point connection between a device and a host on a switched network is the same as that on an arbitrated loop, the switch can support multiple concurrent connections providing an aggregate throughput in the order of gigabytes. Although switch ports are more expensive than loop hub ports, they provide easy and almost unlimited expandability by simply allowing you to attach another switch to one of the available ports. The maximum number of switches on a single fabric is currently 239, and is imposed by the addressing scheme for ports in a switched fabric configuration.

To get started with a fibre channel network, you first need to equip your Windows 2000 storage servers with fibre channel adapters. These are available in both 32-bit and 64-bit PCI configurations from a number of vendors, including Qlogic and Emulex. If you have a considerable existing investment in parallel SCSI storage devices, there are FC-SCSI bridges or FC-SCSI routers (two different terms for the same thing) that you can use to attach them seamlessly into your fibre channel fabric. While designing your fibre channel network, you need to consider the workload that must be supported in terms of aggregate throughput, the total number of hosts and devices that will be attached to the network, and the maximum distance between any two devices.

Intelligent Input Output (I²O)

Another fairly recent development is the Intelligent Input Output or I²O initiative. The I²O initiative was started in January 1996 by a number of operating system and I/O peripheral manufacturers, and its objective was to develop a new standard and high-performance interface between the operating system and its peripherals. There are two primary goals of the I²O standard. The first is to reduce the overhead of having to develop and maintain drivers for each combination of operating system and device. The second is to reduce the overhead placed on the host CPU by I/O adapters through interrupt processing.

Currently, a vendor of network cards has to develop, test, and maintain a driver for each operating system and version that may be using a specific network card, and a system administrator of a Windows 2000 system needs to load a different driver for each host adapter supported by the system. This places a lot of demands on both the peripheral vendors and the administrators that maintain the servers. Figure 8-20 illustrates this situation where a separate driver needs to be developed, loaded, and maintained for each operating system and device pair.

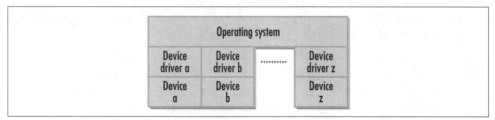

Figure 8-20. Interaction between the operating system and the device-specific device driver

The I²O standard solves this issue through the split-driver model. The split driver consists of two parts: the operating systems services module (OSM) and the hardware device module (HDM). The OSM is provided by and resides within the operating system. It is used for interfacing the I²O standard with the operating system and is therefore provided by the operating system vendor. Microsoft has already made I²O drivers available for both Windows NT and Windows 2000. Windows 2000 comes with I²O drivers, whereas you can download the drivers from Microsoft's web site (*http://www.microsoft.com/NTServer/nts/downloads/other/NTI2O*) for Windows NT.

The HDM is the device-dependent component and is provided by the peripheral vendor or an adapter that sits within the server, depending on the selected architecture. Using current terminology, you can think of the HDM as the network interface card–specific or SCSI adapter–specific software. The OSM communicates with the HDM layer through a transport layer and a messaging API that is open and standard. The key in this architecture is a message queue that provides the interface between request messages from the OSM and response messages from the HDM. When the operating system determines that it needs to retrieve some data from a peripheral device, a message is created and placed in the message queue. The HDM retrieves the message and translates it into a device-specific request that is then processed by the device. Eventually, the response is sent to the operating system by the HDM, again in the form of a message placed in the message queue. Figure 8-21 illustrates the interaction between the operating system and the devices under the I²O standard.

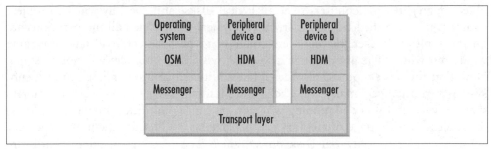

Figure 8-21. Interaction between the operating system and the I/O devices under the I²O standard

The second objective for the I²O initiative is to make this new interface as efficient as possible. High-speed devices such as disk controllers and high-speed network cards generate a load on the processor by frequently generating interrupts to get the CPU's attention. The I²O standard reduces this overhead by offloading the processing of I/O requests to powerful I/O processors that are specifically designed to handle I/O operations. One of the most popular I/O processors is the i960 RM/RN I/O processor by Intel, which provides either 64-bit or 32-bit PCI operations and multiple DMA controllers, and claims to provide a twofold to fourfold increase in bandwidth.

Although at the time of this writing the I²O standard is fairly new, there is already considerable support for it in the market. As mentioned, Microsoft has already released I²O–compatible drivers, and many vendors such as HP and Intel are providing peripherals such as RAID adapters and network interface cards that comply with the I²O standard. Given the benefits and potential of this new technology, it should not be long before it is widely available. If you are not familiar with RAID devices yet, Chapter 10 takes an in-depth look at their operation.

The next section describes the counters available through the System Monitor for analyzing the performance of the disk subsystem. Understanding the meaning of the counters is very important in being able to locate and solve performance problems at this subsystem. At the end of this chapter, we present a case study that uses these counters to analyze the results of some experiments.

System Monitor Counters

A number of objects provide performance metrics that are relevant for evaluating and monitoring the performance of the disk I/O subsystem. The Physical Disk object provides information about each physical disk attached to the system. The Logical Disk object provides information about each partition. When a physical disk has been partitioned into multiple logical disks, the metrics provided by the Physical Disk object are aggregates of the load imposed on all the partitions. There are instances for each available partition and an instance that summarizes the counters over all partitions. A number of counters appear under both the Physical and the Logical Disk object. Note in particular that the _Total instance from the Logical Disk object aggregates the counters over all logical disks, and the Physical Disk object counters measure the load on a particular physical disk. When all the partitions are on the same disk, then the counters common to both objects will have the same value. But when there are multiple disks, the two sets of counters will not be equal. Note that the System object provides a few additional counters related to disk subsystem performance. Finally, the Cache and Memory objects provide some counters that are very useful in determining whether the cause of a disk bottleneck is filesystem access or a shortage of memory. In this chapter, we discuss the most important counters under the Physical Disk object, since we are focusing on the hardware aspects of the I/O subsystem.

Measurement Methodology

Before we look at some of the counters available, it is important to understand how the System Monitor acquires these measurements. There is a filter driver called *diskperf.sys* that sits on top of the disk driver and collects disk performance data. The driver can be enabled and disabled using a command-line utility called *diskperf.exe*. The syntax for this utility is as follows:

```
diskperf [-Y[D|V] | -N[D|V]] [\\computername]
```

The -Y flag enables sampling of all disk performance–related counters, and -N disables it. The additional flags control the level of detail at which disk performance data is sampled. The D flag indicates that diskperf should sample performance data only for physical disks, whereas the V flag indicates that it should sample performance data only for logical disk and storage volumes (we cover storage volumes in Chapter 9). For example, to enable the performance counters for physical disks, you would type the command:

```
diskperf –yd
```

You would then need to reboot the system before the counters are enabled under the new settings.

Windows 2000 is by default configured to collect physical drive data. Notice that this is different from Windows NT, where the collection of disk performance metrics was disabled by default. Many years ago, Microsoft released a report indicating that disk performance data collection on a Windows NT machine running on a 386 processor incurred a 1.5% overhead on the performance of the system. Based on these measurements, Microsoft made the decision to disable disk performance data collection by default. Since such hardware is basically obsolete today, and the overhead of sampling the disk performance counters is negligible on Pentium-level processor machines, it now makes sense to enable these counters by default.

The source code for a version of the *diskperf.sys* filter driver is available with the Windows 2000 Driver Development Kit. By reviewing the code, you can get a good understanding of the meaning of the counters we cover in this chapter. Basically, the driver uses the following structure for collecting the counters for each device:

```
typedef struct _DISK_PERFORMANCE {
        LARGE_INTEGER BytesRead;
        LARGE_INTEGER BytesWritten;
        LARGE_INTEGER ReadTime;
        LARGE_INTEGER WriteTime;
        LARGE_INTEGER IdleTime;
        ULONG ReadCount;
        ULONG WriteCount;
        ULONG QueueDepth;
        ULONG SplitCount;
        LARGE_INTEGER QueryTime;
        ULONG   StorageDeviceNumber;
        WCHAR   StorageManagerName[8];
} DISK_PERFORMANCE, *PDISK_PERFORMANCE;
```

The QueueDepth variable keeps track of the number of outstanding requests at the device. It is incremented when a request arrives for processing by the disk driver and is decremented when the request comes back from the driver. The ReadCount and WriteCount variables maintain counts of read and write operations, and the Bytes-Read and BytesWritten variables maintain counts of bytes read and written. The interval of time from the instant that the last request was completely processed by the driver to the moment that the next request arrives (i.e., the duration of time that there are zero outstanding requests at the disk driver) is considered idle time. Finally, the SplitCount variable counts the number of requests that were split into one or more subrequests.

Counters

We now describe the following counters available under the Physical Disk object in the System Monitor:

% Disk Time, % Disk Read Time, % Disk Write Time
> The counter names and associated documentation suggest that these are utiliza-tion measures for the disk time, but this is not true. There is a problem with these counters. For a given sampling interval, the % Disk Read Time is calcu-lated as the ratio of the time that the device was busy processing read requests over the duration of the sampling interval. The % Disk Write Time is computed the same way but applies to write requests. The overall % Disk Time is com-puted as the sum of these other two measures. All three metrics are clamped at 100%, so if they exceed 100% they are still reported as 100%. These counters are able to exceed 100% due to concurrency at the physical device. For logical volumes, where more than one physical disk comprises the volume, it is possi-ble for the logical volume to be concurrently processing multiple requests using different physical devices. So by clamping these three metrics at 100%, we are losing information.

This measure is useful for evaluating the performance of individual disks, but you should not rely on it for evaluating RAID devices.

Avg. Disk Bytes/Transfer, Avg. Disk Bytes/Read, Avg. Disk Bytes/Write

The first counter reports on the average number of bytes transferred per disk request, and the other two break the information down into reads versus writes. These measures are useful in understanding the workload of a system. Transaction-oriented systems typically have smaller values for these metrics, whereas analytical types of environments, where data is processed sequentially and in large blocks, exhibit larger values. Larger values for these measures indicate a more efficient use of the disk. When the number of bytes transferred per request is small, the fraction of the response time taken up by latency is much greater.

Avg. Disk Queue Length, Avg. Disk Read Queue Length, Avg. Disk Write Queue Length

The first measure reports on the average number of requests that are currently queued or processed at a physical device, and the next two break out this number by reads and writes. They are calculated using the same approach as the corresponding % Disk Time counters, but the information is reported as a fraction rather than a percentage, so they are not capped at 100%. The advantage of these counters is that they can exceed 1.0 and are therefore accurate for heavily utilized and striped disks (more about this in Chapter 10).

Avg. Disk sec/Transfer, Avg. Disk sec/Read, Avg. Disk sec/Write

This set of counters measures the response time of a disk request. The first counter averages all requests, and the others average read and write requests. The response time for a request includes the total elapsed time from the instant the request is generated to the instant the response is passed back to a higher layer driver by the disk driver. On a lightly loaded system, these metrics are useful in understanding how fast your disk can process requests. When the load is heavy, you will experience queuing delays at either the disk, the system bus, or the I/O channel, depending on the configuration of the system. So as the load increases, these numbers will report large values but will not help you pinpoint the culprit. This metric makes more sense when it is considered in combination with a measure of the number of bytes transferred in an operation, such as the Avg. Disk Bytes/Transfer metric.

Current Disk Queue Length

This counter is a measure of the instantaneous size of the disk queue, and since it is not an average, it always has an integral value. This counter can be used to evaluate the level of load balancing across the available disks. If one disk has a consistently large number for this counter while the other disks jump between zero and one, that is a clear indication of a load imbalance. Usually when this occurs, the response time counters confirm the problem by indicating high response times for the overloaded disk. Any queue build-up is a sign of performance problems. On a heavily loaded system, you should rely more on the Average Disk Queue Length metric, since the Current metric is just a sample and may report incorrect information.

Disk Bytes/sec, Disk Read Bytes/sec, Disk Write Bytes/sec

These three counters provide information on the throughput of the system. A properly configured system can get close to the bandwidth of the slowest device in the service path, which may be the bus, the I/O interface, or the disk device. The culprit is usually the individual disk device, although you should not rule out the other two possibilities. A number of factors can affect these counters. Applications that consist primarily of sequential requests can attain higher values for these counters simply because the disk is spending less time moving the heads and more time transferring data. In addition, the average request size of the workload has an impact. Applications that transfer information in larger block sizes have higher throughput.

Disk Transfers/sec, Disk Reads/sec, Disk Writes/sec

These counters measure the total number of requests, read requests, and write requests that the device can process per second. Much like the previous set of counters, these also measure the throughput of the system. The difference is that this set does not consider the size of the request but treats all requests equally. This metric is normally used to determine the limits of a physical device when a well-defined workload is generated against a device. Keep in mind that the same system may complete twice as many 2 KB requests as 4 KB requests in one second, but the total amount of bytes transferred in both cases is the same.

% Idle Time

This is a new counter in Windows 2000 and indicates the percentage of time that the disk was idle during the sample interval. This counter is typically ignored, but in reality it is the best counter to use to determine the utilization of the device. If a device is idle 10% of the time, its utilization is 90% (or 100% − 10%).

Split I/O/sec

This counter reports the number of I/O requests per second that were split into multiple requests. A request is split into multiple requests either when the disk has been highly fragmented, when there are requests for large blocks while memory availability is scarce, or when a disk is actually a logical volume that consists of multiple physical devices.

Workload Studies

We have covered a lot of ground so far in this chapter. We talked about the wide variety of options available for configuring the physical I/O subsystem of your Windows 2000 or NT server. This included options for the system bus, the I/O interface, and the characteristics of the actual disks themselves. We then discussed the counters that the system provides for monitoring the performance of the disk subsystem and for detecting and resolving problematic situations.

In this section, we put some of this knowledge to work by taking it from the conceptual level to the real world. First we describe Iometer, a tool that you can use to generate a well-defined workload against your server. We use Iometer to experiment with some of the concepts we talked about this chapter, and put some of the counters we discussed to work. This will allow you a better understanding of what these counters really mean and how to use them to evaluate the performance of your I/O subsystem.

Intel's Iometer

We used the Intel Iometer tool to generate the workload for all the tests described in this chapter. It is a great tool for this type of testing, as it makes the task of changing the configuration parameters and running a test a very painless process. You can download the tool free from Intel's web site. Unlike some other Windows 2000– and NT Server–based benchmarking tools, Iometer explicitly bypasses the Cache Manager so you see measurements of logical or physical disks that are not distorted by the operating system's default I/O cache management. Using Iometer's graphical user interface, it is possible to change the size of the request, the fraction of reads versus writes, and the fraction of sequential versus random requests. Figure 8-22 shows the Access Specifications screen that you use to configure the workload.

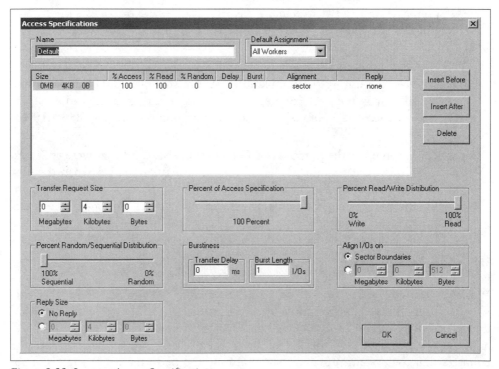

Figure 8-22. Iometer Access Specifications screen

In addition to its flexibility in configuring the workload, Iometer provides you with considerable flexibility in configuring the test itself. Figure 8-23 shows the Test Setup tab that you use to configure the test. Iometer includes a very detailed user's guide, so we won't go into the details of configuring each parameter that appears in the figure. Some test configuration parameters include the duration of the test, which can be specified in units of seconds, minutes, and hours, the ramp-up time before it starts to record the results, and the number of workers to spawn automatically for each manager. It also provides some automation parameters for running more complex tests. You can configure a test that uses an increasing number of workers as it progresses, a test that uses an increasing number of targets, or a test that increases the number of requests outstanding to each target.

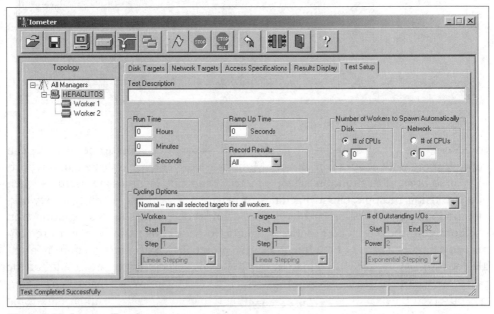

Figure 8-23. Iometer Test Setup parameters

Iometer provides its own built-in performance data collection facility that is primarily based on System Monitor data. Figure 8-24 shows the Results Display. It consists of a control at the top, which adjusts the update frequency, and six bars that present the selected metrics. You can select the specific metric that each bar reports by clicking on the button to the left of each bar. The title of the button is the selected metric.

The metrics are classified into seven categories: Operations per Second, Megabytes per Second, Average Latency, Maximum Latency, CPU, Network, and Errors. The metrics available within each category present the measured information at different granularities. For example, within the Operations per Second category, there are metrics for Total I/Os per Second, Read I/Os per Second, and Write I/Os per Second.

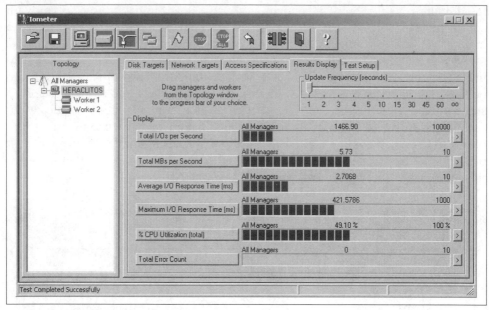

Figure 8-24. Iometer Results Display

In general, we prefer to use the System Monitor alongside Iometer because we can capture more data and use the System Monitor's more extensive logging and reporting capabilities. One situation where Iometer's reporting facilities are useful is when you are using multiple client machines to generate a workload against a network-attached storage subsystem such as a fibre channel disk array. In this situation, you can configure the workload generation agents (Iometer calls them Dynamos) to connect to a single instance of the Iometer GUI, so that you can control them from a single location. With such a configuration, Iometer presents aggregate results of the performance of the storage subsystem, which it calculates by summarizing the metrics observed by each of the clients generating requests. To collect similar data using the System Monitor, you would need to log information from each of the clients generating requests and then summarize them manually.

You can set up very elaborate testing scenarios using Iometer, but we suggest starting with simple test scenarios. A 100% random read scenario is a worst case for caching; a 100% write scenario eventually overruns the cache and stresses the back-end disks, too. An intermediate scenario mixing reads and writes is probably more representative of your real workload. Once you understand what is happening with a few simple tests, you can build more elaborate (and realistic) testing scenarios. For example, the Percent of Access Specification parameter allows you to construct a realistic and complex composite test workload. Iometer also allows you to save the contents of a test specification to disk, making it easy to replay that scenario later on a different configuration.

Sequential Versus Nonsequential Workloads

This case study investigates the difference in the performance of the disk subsystem between sequential and nonsequential (random) workloads. As you recall, disks can handle sequential I/O more efficiently for a number of reasons. Since the requests are sequential, we can take better advantage of the buffers that are built into the drives. Also, most drives are configured with a prefetch algorithm that should kick in when we generate sequential requests. Finally, when the requests to the disk are sequential, the disk does not have to spend a lot of time moving the heads around through long seeks and latencies.

As in all the workload studies we present, you should not concern yourself with the specific values we report or with the system configuration we use to arrive at these numbers. Our objective is to illustrate some of the concepts introduced in this chapter, to explore the real meaning of counters discussed, and to show you how to use those counters in a real environment.

Setting up and running this test using the Iometer tool is a breeze. We run the test using random read requests of various sizes. We chose the following request sizes: 512 bytes, 4 KB, 16 KB, and 32 KB. The small request size is rare in real environments, and represents a very transaction-oriented system with a large number of heterogeneous users. The largest request size represents an environment where applications process large amounts of data, such as data-warehousing and data-mining environments. The other two, especially the 4 KB request size, are typical. By running this benchmark using a variety of request sizes we can explore the entire performance spectrum of our disk subsystem.

For each test, we also log some counters using the System Monitor. For this experiment, we focus on monitoring the performance of a physical disk by collecting the following four counters:

- Average Disk Queue Length
- Average Disk sec/Transfer
- Disk Bytes/sec
- Disk Transfers/sec

Figure 8-25 shows the System Monitor screen while running the test with a 4 KB request size. The dark solid line corresponds to the Disk Transfers/sec counter, the dotted line to the Disk Bytes/sec, and the thick gray line to the Average Disk Queue Length. We don't show the Average Disk sec/Transfer counter in order to make the chart easier to read. During the first portion of the test, the workload consists entirely of random requests, while during the second portion it consists entirely of sequential requests. Clearly, the performance difference is tremendous. During the random portion, the disk can only process a bit more than 80 requests per second (watch the scaling of the metrics we used), whereas during the sequential portion, the request processing rate goes up to more than 1300 requests per second. This comparison emphasizes the importance of understanding the workload imposed on your system. When configuring a disk subsystem for an environment where the workload exhibits considerable randomness, you don't need to be as concerned with the bandwidth of the I/O bus and the adapter speed. Unless a large number of disks is used, the low effective throughput of the disks will not be able to consume even a 33 MHz, 32-bit PCI bus. Conversely, in an environment where the workload is very sequential in nature, you must pay more attention in configuring the I/O bus and channel.

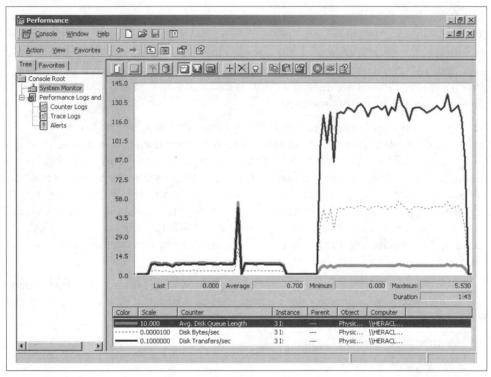

Figure 8-25. Key metrics in comparing the performance of sequential and random access

Table 8-5 summarizes the results of this test for the various request sizes. The I/O per second column corresponds to the Disk Transfers/sec counter, Latency to the Average Disk sec/Transfer counter, MB/sec to the Disk Bytes/sec counter, and QL to the Avg. Disk Queue Length counter. Notice the large difference between the latency numbers for the random and sequential tests. While running the random workload, the disk heads move constantly (you can actually hear this if you're sitting close to your disks), incurring expensive seek and latency delays. Even in the case where the disk is transferring only 512 bytes, the response time is still 11 ms, an effective transfer rate of only 0.04 MB/sec. With the exact same hardware configuration, this disk can transfer data at 7 MB/sec when the workload is sequential.

Table 8-5. Summary of results for random and sequential read requests

	Random requests				Sequential requests			
	I/O/sec	Latency	MB/sec	QL	I/O/sec	Latency	MB/sec	QL
512 B	89	11	0.045	0.90	3153	0.3	1.54	0.59
4 KB	83	12	0.33	0.91	1317	0.8	5.14	0.76
16 KB	69	14	1.1	0.91	425	2.3	6.64	0.84
32 KB	60	16	1.9	0.93	226	4.4	7.03	0.87

As you can see from the numbers, some of the optimizations that we talked about in this chapter kick in to provide considerable performance benefits for sequential workloads. The numbers for the random tests make clear that disks are inefficient in servicing random requests, where long mechanical delays are inevitably involved. The only way to improve the performance of the disk subsystem for random workloads is to configure a large filesystem cache (we talk about this in Chapter 9), which effectively reduces the number of requests that go to the slow disk device. Fortunately, real workloads are almost never purely random, and the randomness that does exist tends to have a relatively small working set.

Another component of the system that you should keep an eye on is the processor. In this next experiment, we run a workload and monitor the impact of disk I/O on the processor of the system. We again use Iometer to generate a 100% sequential workload of 4 KB read requests. The physical disk target in this case is connected to the system through an IDE interface. The driver is using PIO mode to perform the data transfers, so we expect the CPU utilization to be very high. While running the workload, we collect the % Processor Time, % Privileged Time, and % Interrupt Time counters from the Processor object to get a breakdown of the CPU utilization.

When a request is sent to the disk, the disk processes the request and interrupts the processor when the request is done. This implies a close relationship between CPU utilization due to disk I/O and interrupt activity. To look at the interrupt activity, we monitor the Interrupts/sec counter from the Physical Disk object.

Figure 8-26 shows the chosen performance counters while running this experiment. The thin line at the top of the chart is % Processor Time, the thick dark line is % Privileged Time, the dotted line is Disk Transfers per second, and the thin line at the bottom is % Interrupt Time. We did not include the % User Time counter to reduce the complexity of the chart, but it can be inferred from % Processor Time and % Privileged Time. As expected, the CPU is heavily utilized. Throughout the test, the CPU averages 92% utilization, with 87% of that taking place in privileged mode. The fact that most of the CPU time is consumed in privileged mode is not a good sign, since in general we prefer to use the CPU to support user processing.

A considerable portion of the privileged processor time is used in servicing interrupts. By looking at the Interrupts/sec counter of the Physical Disk object, we notice

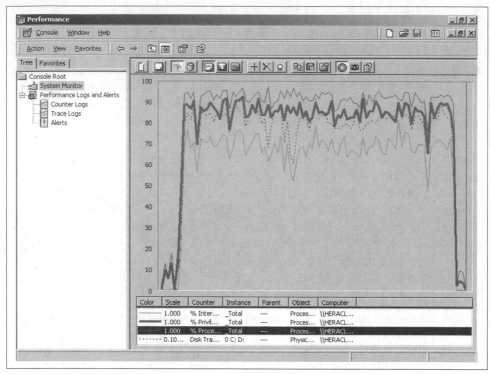

Figure 8-26. Reading sequential blocks from an IDE disk

that the system is processing an average of 910 interrupts per second while process-ing 800 reads per second. The system always generates at least 100 interrupts per second to service the clock, so if we subtract those 100 interrupts, we can infer that the disk is generating one interrupt per request. It is apparent that processing many disk I/O requests using PIO mode can lead to really high CPU utilization.

Let's now repeat this experiment using a similar disk that is connected to the system through a SCSI interface. Figure 8-27 shows the same counters as in the previous experiment. Notice the difference in the CPU utilization between the two cases. Now the CPU utilization is at 17% as opposed to 92%, though the great majority of this time is still spent in kernel mode. In addition to the lesser impact on CPU utiliza-tion, the disk can process around 1300 requests per second. So not only can this con-figuration process more disk throughput, but considerable CPU processing capacity is available for processing other tasks on the server. However, this simple test should not be considered a valid comparison between IDE and SCSI disk interfaces. The sys-tem on which we ran this test did not support DMA transfers over the IDE interface, so this put the IDE disk at a clear disadvantage. We are merely illustrating which of the counters are most useful, how to use them, and what to look for while evaluat-ing the performance of your disk subsystem.

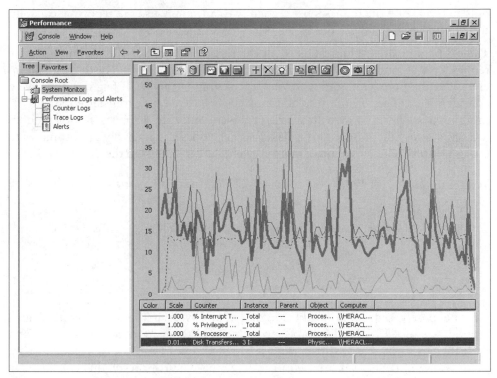

Figure 8-27. Reading sequential blocks from a SCSI Disk

In the next test, we investigate the effect of the Write Cache Enabled flag of the Device Manager. If you bring up the Device Manager, expand the Disk Drives node from the tree, and right-click on one of the drives on your system, you can bring up the Properties screen for that drive. The Disk Properties tab has a checkbox that can enable or disable the Write Cache Enabled (WCE) feature. When this feature is disabled, every write request to a disk must first be committed to the disk before an acknowledgment is sent back to the driver. By enabling this feature, you allow the disk to cache the request and send acknowledgment back immediately without actually writing the data to the disk. Obviously, this has some impact on the performance of write requests at the expense of increased risk for data corruption. If the system is shut down before the data has been flushed to the disk from the disk's buffer, the data is lost, even though the filesystem or application that generated the request has been left with the impression that the request completed successfully.

To determine if the risk is worth taking, let's run a couple of experiments to evaluate the impact of this flag on write requests. This time, we configure Iometer to generate write requests. We repeat the test while varying the request size between 4 KB, 16 KB, and 32 KB, and while also varying the nature of the workload from 100% sequential to 100% random. Since we want to look at the throughput of the disk only in terms of write requests per second, we can simply use the reporting capabilities of Iometer and not use the System Monitor for these tests.

Table 8-6 summarizes the results of all the tests by indicating the number of write requests per second processed by the system for each combination of the test parameters. For the purely random workload, the setting of the WCE flag did not have a considerable impact on the results. On the average, the disk transferred about 7% more requests per second with the flag enabled. Since the requests are for random locations across the surface of the disk, the cache does not get many opportunities to coalesce multiple requests into a more efficient, larger request to the disk.

Table 8-6. Impact of the Write Cache Enabled (WCE) flag on Write Requests/sec

	Random		Sequential	
	WCE Disabled	WCE Enabled	WCE Disabled	WCE Enabled
4 KB	64	69	101	1203
16 KB	57	60	90	416
32 KB	51	54	76	223

For the purely sequential workload, the results were impressive. For the small request size of 4 KB, the disk processed almost 12 times more requests per second with the WCE flag enabled than with it disabled. Even for the largest request size, there was still a threefold increase in throughput. The reason for this considerable increase in throughput is that since the requests are sequential, the disk can process them much more efficiently by combining multiple smaller requests into a single large request. The impact is much more pronounced for smaller requests because more of them can be combined into a single request to the disk.

Figure 8-28 graphically depicts the impact of the enabled WCE flag on the throughput of sequential write requests. However, despite the results of this experiment, we don't recommend that you enable the WCE flag. As we mentioned, the filesystem relies on the data to be safely stored in persistent storage to maintain consistency. A failure of the disk or controller can cause the data stored in the cache to be lost. This causes the filesystem to become inconsistent, a state that is highly undesirable.

The last experiment we conduct is related to the tagged-command queuing feature of the SCSI interface. To review, tagged-command queuing allows a controller to submit multiple requests to a single target device, without having to wait for completion of each request before submitting the subsequent one. Iometer has a configuration parameter, marked # of Outstanding I/Os per Target, which makes it very easy to evaluate the effect of tagged-command queuing on the performance of a disk device. The default value for this parameter is 1.

We will run multiple experiments, varying the value of the # of Outstanding I/Os per Target parameter while monitoring the number of I/O requests that the disk could process per second under each configuration. We repeat the test for both

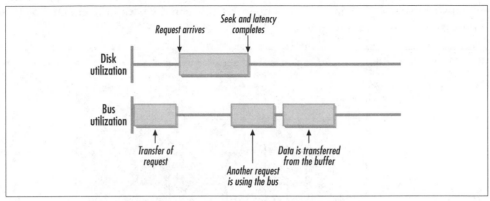

Figure 8-28. Impact of WCE flag on the throughput of sequential write requests

purely sequential and purely random workloads of 4 KB and 16 KB requests. Table 8-7 summarizes the results of these tests. The numbers along the top represent the Outstanding I/Os per Target parameter.

Table 8-7. Impact of tagged-command queuing on Read Requests/sec

	Random				Sequential			
	1	2	3	4	1	2	3	4
4 KB	79	89	101	109	1250	1682	1688	1389
16 KB	66	82	90	98	408	462	465	432

We can make a number of observations after analyzing the results. For both sequential and random workloads, the throughput of the disk increases as the number of concurrent requests submitted to the disk increases. For sequential requests, this trend stops and actually reverses after the number of outstanding requests exceeds three. As we know, disks are much more effective in processing sequential requests. So after a certain point, we are interfering with the processing of existing requests by submitting additional requests. The additional requests create congestion in the use of the bus for transferring data for previously submitted requests.

For random requests, the trend continues and we did not detect a reversal. Figure 8-29 depicts the increase in throughput as the number of outstanding requests to the disk increases. We repeated the test for even larger numbers of outstanding requests than we show in the figure. Although the rate of increase in throughput decreased as the number of outstanding requests increased past the value of six, we did not observe a configuration where the throughput decreased. Disks are not as efficient in processing random requests. The reason for these results is that by increasing the number of requests at the disk queue, the controller can better schedule the execution of the requests. Also, since the disk is spending relatively large amounts of time processing each individual request compared to the time it spends actually transferring the data, there is no interference in the use of the channel by the submission of additional requests.

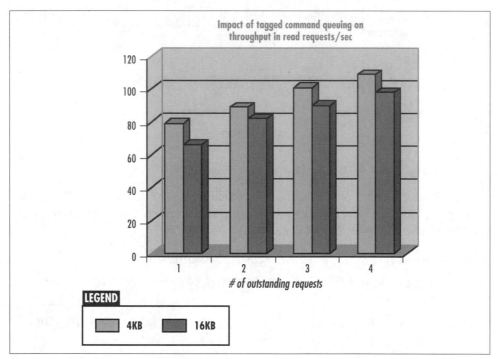

Figure 8-29. Impact of tagged-command queuing on the throughput in read requests per second

This sequence of experiments makes clear that understanding the characteristics of the disks that comprise your disk subsystem and the workload generated by your users is critical in being able to improve the performance of your system. You should now be familiar with some of the more useful counters that the system monitor provides for measuring and evaluating the performance of the disk subsystem. You should also feel comfortable using Iometer to benchmark your existing subsystem, defining its baseline performance and capacity.

## CHAPTER 9

Filesystem Performance

In Chapter 8, we discussed the actual hardware that forms the disk storage subsystem of your Windows NT and Windows 2000 servers, including the components in the path between the operating system and the physical disk devices. In this chapter, we continue talking about the disk subsystem, but the focus here is on the logical layers that the operating system places on top of the hardware.

We start by looking at how the operating system manages the storage available on each disk and discussing the two partitioning methods available in Windows 2000. At the same time, we introduce the terminology used to describe the logical partitions that these two methods create. Windows 2000 introduced the concept of a dynamic disk in addition to the concept of a basic disk, which is based on the partitioning scheme used in Windows NT and its ancestors. The introduction of this new storage management scheme comes with a whole new set of terms that allow us to differentiate partitions built on top of basic disks from those built on top of dynamic disks.

After covering the two storage management schemes, we move up the layers of the operating system to talk about the filesystems used to manage the storage of files. Windows 2000 provides three options in choosing a filesystem: the FAT filesystem, which has been with us for a long time; the FAT32 filesystem, which is introduced in the Windows NT line of operating systems for the first time with Windows 2000; and the NTFS filesystem, which is an enhanced version of the one available on Windows NT machines. We talk a little about the internal structure of these filesystems. By understanding the organization of each one of them, you can better understand the performance trade-offs between them.

All three filesystems are susceptible to fragmentation, in varying degrees. We describe what fragmentation is and what causes it, and then explore its impact on performance. We then mention a few tools available on the market for dealing with fragmentation. The amount of performance degradation that fragmentation can cause is surprising.

Storage Management

Storage management refers to the method that an operating system uses to manage the raw storage capacity provided by the hard drives. Most operating systems provide tools that allow the system administrator to partition the available disk space into multiple volumes that are easier to manage and can be assigned to the storage needs of particular logical groups. So there may be a partition for storing directories for each user, a partition for storing applications, and a partition dedicated to a database management system. In addition to these simple partitions, enterprise-level systems have additional requirements from their storage partitions such as high performance and reliability. Both Windows NT and Windows 2000 provide storage management support for disk arrays to satisfy such requirements. We describe the foundations for constructing advanced partitions in this chapter, and Chapter 10 provides complete coverage of the performance of disk arrays.

Windows 2000 provides two different methods for managing the available disk capacity. These two methods arise out of two different methods of partitioning a physical disk. Windows 2000 introduced the concepts of a basic and a dynamic disk. A basic disk is a new term that refers to a disk that has been partitioned using the scheme used in Windows NT and its predecessors. A dynamic disk is a disk formatted using the new partitioning scheme, which resolves some of the weaknesses of the basic disk scheme. Let's look at each one in a little more detail.

Basic Disks

The partitioning scheme used for basic disks is the same as that available in Windows NT and the later versions of the DOS operating system. The very first sector of the disk contains the *master boot record* (MBR) that itself consists of the master boot code, a disk signature, and the partition table. The master boot code is a small amount of executable code loaded by the BIOS when the system starts. The *disk signature* is a unique identifier for the disk assigned by the operating system. The *partition table* contains four entries that define the partitioning of the disk. Each entry is 16 bytes in length and contains information such as the beginning and end of each partition, its size in units of sectors, a boot indicator, and the partition type. Only one partition of a disk can have its boot indicator set to active. Each partition begins with the boot sector, followed by the data and free space that is allocated to that partition. The *boot sector* is a small piece of executable code, like the master boot code, but specific to the partition it is associated with.

When the system is started, the BIOS loads and executes the master boot code from the MBR. This code simply scans the partition table, locates the partition that has its boot indicator set to active, and loads and executes the boot code associated with the active partition. That boot code understands the filesystem format of the partition it is associated with, so it knows how to load and start the system using the system files on that partition.

Figure 9-1 shows a basic disk where three of the four partitions have been defined. This could be the system disk of a Windows 2000 machine, with the first partition being the active partition that boots the operating system, the second partition allocated to Windows 2000 for storing application executables and data, and the third partition allocated to Windows 98. All three partitions begin with a boot sector, but the actual code stored on the boot sector is specific to the filesystem used to format the partition.

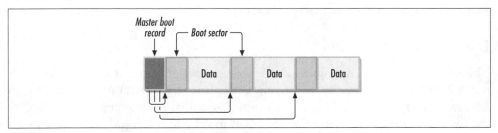

Figure 9-1. Layout of a basic disk with three primary partitions

Since there are four entries, each describing one partition, you might think that you are limited to a maximum of four partitions for a disk. Early versions of the DOS operating system had a similar partition table and indeed had this limitation. But DOS 5 introduced extended boot records and logical drives in order to remove this limitation. One of the four partitions in the MBR can be marked as an *extended partition* as opposed to a *primary partition*. An extended partition begins with an *extended boot record* (EBR), which is similar to an MBR but contains only two entries in its partition table. If you create an extended partition on your disk, you must also define at least one *logical drive*. The first entry in the partition table points to the boot sector of the first logical drive. If you have defined additional logical drives, the next entry in the table will point to the EBR of the next logical drive. The first entry in the partition table of this second EBR will point to the boot sector of the second logical drive, and the second entry will point to the next EBR if there is a third logical drive, or will be set to all zeros. This means that the logical drives will form a *linked list*.

Figure 9-2 shows an example of a basic disk with two primary partitions, an extended partition, and two logical drives. The first two entries of the partition table in the MBR point to primary partitions, and the third one points to the extended partition. The extended partition begins with an EBR with the first entry in its partition table pointing to the first logical drive, and the second entry pointing to the next EBR in the chain. The partition table of the second EBR points to the second logical drive, and the second entry is set to zeros.

The Windows 2000 CD includes a tool under *<CDDRIVE>:\Support\Tools* called DiskProbe. DiskProbe allows you to view and edit any sector on a basic disk at the byte level, including the MBR and the EBR. Since you have such direct access to the data on the disk, be extremely careful when using it: you could easily corrupt the disk.

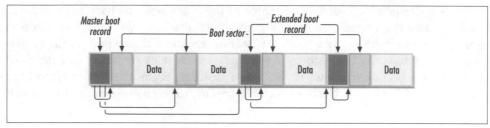

Figure 9-2. Example of the organization of a basic disk

Dynamic Disks

The second and preferred approach for storage management of disks under Windows 2000 is dynamic disks. A dynamic disk also maintains an MBR, but only for backward compatibility and safety reasons. The actual partitioning information for the disk is stored in a database that resides at the end of the disk. When you create a dynamic disk, the system allocates 1 MB at the end of the disk for storing this database. The database is replicated across all dynamic disks on your system for fault-tolerance purposes.

The Logical Disk Manager (LDM) subsystem, which consists of a number of executables, DLLs, and drivers that together manage the dynamic disks on a system, is also responsible for maintaining this database. The LDM is based on technology Microsoft has licensed from Veritas and is included as part of the Windows 2000 operating system. Since it is based on proprietary technology, no details are available about the organization of the database and the operation of the LDM other than the information included in two articles by Mark Russinovich that were published in the March and April 2000 issues of *Windows 2000 Magazine*. The database consists of four regions: the private header, the table of contents, the database records, and the transactional log. The private header is one sector in length and contains an ID of the disk on which the sector resides and the name of the disk group to which the disk belongs. The version of the Veritas software that is part of Windows 2000 places all the dynamic disks on a system in the same disk group, although the commercial version of the volume management software that you can purchase from Veritas supports multiple disk groups. The table of contents is 16 sectors in size and contains summary information about the database. The database consists of 128-byte records that provide information about the disks, partitions, and volumes that you have created on your system. On Windows NT, information about advanced volumes is stored in the Registry, whereas information about simple volumes is stored on the disk. The disadvantage of this approach is that if something were to happen to the Registry, you would not be able to recover the information from the disk. By integrating information for both simple and advanced volumes on a single replicated database, Windows 2000 storage management is able to resolve this weakness and provide fault-tolerance in cases where you have more than one dynamic disk on your system. The last region of the LDM database is the transactional log. Much like in a database management system, the log area is used to record changes to the metadata that are in the process of being committed, so that the consistency of the database can be maintained in case of a failure.

The Windows 2000 Resource Kit includes a tool called dmdiag.exe (Disk Manager Diagnostics) that dumps all the information about disk storage. The output that it generates includes information for both basic disks and dynamic disks. Another tool specific to dynamic disks is ldmdump, and is available for download from *http://www.sysinternals.com*. ldmdump dumps the contents of the LDM database from the disk and presents the information in a well-organized manner.

The presence of two different storage management mechanisms in Windows 2000 is transparent to the applications. Figure 9-3 shows a high-level view of the storage management organization in Windows 2000.

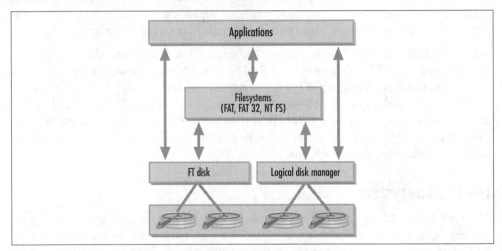

Figure 9-3. Storage management organization in Windows 2000

The figure portrays a system with four physical disks, two basic and two dynamic. The basic disks are managed by the FTDisk driver and the dynamic disks are managed by the DMIO driver (a component of the Logical Device Manager). In Windows NT, the FTDisk driver was only responsible for advanced volumes (we cover high-performance and fault-tolerant volumes in detail in Chapter 10). In Windows 2000, it takes responsibility for the handling of all requests to basic disks. When an application generates an I/O request, either to a file in the filesystem or to a raw partition, the request goes to the I/O Manager, where it is converted into an IRP (I/O request packet). The request is then forwarded either to the FTDisk or DMIO driver, depending on whether the target of the request is a basic or a dynamic disk, respectively. One major advantage of the new architecture of the storage management subsystem in Windows 2000 is that most changes made through the MMC plug-in take effect immediately, without requiring a reboot of the operating system.

By default, Windows 2000 will create basic disks unless you explicitly specify that you want to create a dynamic disk. It motivates users to move to dynamic disks by disallowing the construction of advanced volumes on basic disks. Despite this restriction, Windows 2000 still supports management of advanced volumes created on a Windows NT server.

Filesystems

Once a disk has been placed under the control of the operating system as either a basic or a dynamic disk, the next step is to create a filesystem structure on top of it. A filesystem consists of algorithms and data structures that manage the storage of files and directories on the disk, keep track of disk blocks that are available and disk blocks that have already been allocated to files. Some filesystems provide advanced features such as access control, disk quotas, and encryption. Different filesystems make different choices as to the data structures and algorithms that they use to perform their responsibilities so they exhibit different performance characteristics.

Windows 2000 provides three choices in selecting a filesystem: the FAT16, the FAT32, and the NTFS filesystem. The FAT16 and FAT32 filesystems are very similar in organization. Windows NT 4.0 provided two choices for a filesystem, as the FAT32 was introduced in Windows 2000 although it has been in the Windows 9x line of operating systems for a while. In this section, we describe the organization of these three filesystems from the performance point of view and indicate the advantages and disadvantages of each one.

The FAT Filesystem

The FAT (or FAT16) filesystem is a simple filesystem that has its origins in the good old days of the DOS operating system. When a disk partition is formatted using the FAT filesystem, the available space is divided into equally sized units called *clusters*. The size of the cluster in bytes is based on the total amount of space in the partition. Table 9-1 shows the cluster size in sectors based on the size of the partition.

Table 9-1. FAT16 cluster size for each partition size

Partition size	FAT type	Cluster size in sectors	Cluster size in bytes
0 MB – 15 MB	12-bit	8	4 KB
16 MB – 32 MB	16-bit	1	512
33 MB – 63 MB	16-bit	2	1 KB
64 MB – 127 MB	16-bit	4	2 KB
128 MB – 255 MB	16-bit	8	4 KB
256 MB – 511 MB	16-bit	16	8 KB
512 MB – 1023 MB	16-bit	32	16 KB
1024 MB – 2047 MB	16-bit	64	32 KB

Table 9-1. FAT16 cluster size for each partition size (continued)

Partition size	FAT type	Cluster size in sectors	Cluster size in bytes
2048 MB – 4095 MB	16-bit	128	64 KB
4096 MB – 8192 MB	16-bit	256	128 KB
8192 MB – 16384 MB	16-bit	512	256 KB

The cluster size is related to the partition size because the number of bits used to uniquely identify a cluster within the filesystem is kept constant at 16 bits. This means that the maximum number of clusters we can have is 2^{16} or 65,536, so as the size of the filesystem increases, so must the cluster size. If the cluster size were allowed to be too small for very large partitions, more than 2^{16} clusters would be needed to be able to address every single cluster. There is no magic in the information in Table 9-1. Take a 3 GB disk, for example. The disk consists of 12,582,912 sectors of 512 bytes each. With 16 bits, we can address 64 K clusters, which gives us 96 sectors in each cluster. Since the number of sectors per cluster must be a power of 2, we need to allocate 128 sectors per cluster, which is the value given in the table. Notice that for very small partitions, the tools available for formatting the disk automatically switch to a 12-bit cluster number instead of the normal 16 bits. This should not be an issue, since such small partitions are rarely used.

Windows 2000 added support for the FAT32 filesystem, which is very similar to that available with the Windows 95 and Windows 98 operating systems. The primary difference between the FAT16 and FAT32 filesystems is that in the FAT32 filesystem, the cluster is identified using a 32-bit number, instead of the 16-bit number used in the FAT16. This reduces the internal fragmentation problem, since for a given partition size the FAT32 filesystem uses a smaller cluster size than a FAT16 filesystem. Table 9-2 lists the cluster sizes that a FAT32 filesystem uses for various partition sizes. The maximum size partition that you can format using the FAT16 filesystem is 4 GB, and using the FAT32 filesystem is 32 GB. In the case of the FAT16 filesystem, the maximum is imposed by the 16-bit size of the cluster number, whereas for the FAT32 filesystem, the maximum is imposed by the Windows 2000 operating system itself. For partitions greater than 32 GB, the FAT filesystem is very inefficient, so by imposing this limitation, you are forced to make the right choice for large partitions. On the other hand, Windows 2000 will allow you to access a FAT32 partition larger than 32 GB that was created using the Windows 95 or Windows 98 operating system in a dual-boot environment.

Table 9-2. FAT32 cluster size for each partition size

Partition size	Cluster size in sectors	Cluster size in bytes
0 – 8 GB	8	4 KB
8 GB – 16 GB	16	8 KB
16 GB – 32 GB	32	16 KB
> 32 GB	64	32 KB

Information about the allocation status of each cluster is maintained in the file allocation table (FAT). The FAT filesystem used on Windows NT is also referred to as FAT16 because each entry in the FAT is 16 bits long. Figure 9-4 shows the overall structure of a partition formatted with the FAT filesystem.

Figure 9-4. Overall format of a FAT partition

The information in the FAT is critical; a bad sector within the FAT can cause all the contents of a file to be lost. To add to the reliability of the filesystem, two copies of the FAT are maintained (labeled FAT1 and FAT2 in the figure). Following the FAT tables is the root folder. For a given partition size, the beginning of the root folder can be computed directly. The root folder describes the files and folders in the root directory, and its size is fixed at 512 entries. The root folder is followed by clusters containing data for the files and other folders within the filesystem.

Let's look into the FAT filesystem structure in more detail. Each entry in the file allocation table is 16 bits long in the FAT16 filesystem and 32 bits long in the FAT32 filesystem, and contains information about the status of the cluster represented by the corresponding entry. The status information includes whether the cluster is used by a file or not, if it is a bad cluster, or if it is the last cluster in a file. If the cluster is being used by a file, then the value stored within the entry is the cluster number of the next cluster allocated to the file, or the two-byte sequence 0xffff if this is the last cluster in the file. This causes all the clusters of a file to form a chain. Given the first cluster allocated to a file, the rest of the clusters can be located by following the links in the file allocation table. Figure 9-5 illustrates the function of the file allocation table. There are three files shown in the figure: the first one occupies clusters 2, 3, 6, and 8, the second one occupies clusters 4 and 5, and the last one occupies cluster 7. To read the entire contents of the file, the filesystem code needs to follow the chain in the FAT to determine all the clusters that have been allocated to the file.

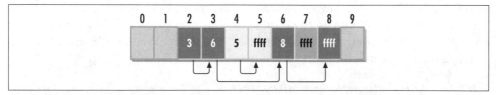

Figure 9-5. File allocation table (FAT)

Following the two copies of the FAT is the root directory or root folder. It consists of 512 entries describing the files and folders in the root of the partition. Each entry is 32 bytes long and includes the following information:

Name

Eleven bytes are allocated to the classical eight-plus-three character DOS file-name. To support long filenames, multiple entries are used.

Attribute byte

One byte specifies information about the entry. Two of the bits are reserved, and the other six are used as binary flags indicating whether the entry is archived, if it is a directory or a file, if it is a volume label or a normal directory entry, if it is a system or normal file, if it is hidden, and if it is read-only or read/write.

Creation time and date

Five bytes indicate the time and date the file was created.

Last access date

Two bytes indicate the date the file was last accessed.

Last modification time and date

Four bytes indicate the time and date the file was last modified.

First cluster

Two bytes identify the first cluster of the file. This is the head of the list for the file's allocation chain of clusters. The remaining information is stored in the FAT.

File size

Four bytes indicate the size of the file in bytes, implying that the maximum file size is 4 GB.

To support long filenames, FAT uses multiple directory entries. The first entry contains the eight-plus-three character filename with appropriate truncation and removal of spaces. Then, additional directory entries are used to store the long file-name. Thirteen bytes from each additional directory entry are used to store characters from the long filename. The long filename is stored using Unicode, so two bytes are used for each character. The attributes field of the additional entries is set to 0x0f, causing MS-DOS and OS/2 to ignore these entries.

The FAT filesystem has been around for many years, and its age is evident in its simplistic design. One of its disadvantages is that the pointers to the clusters allocated to each file may not be contiguous and may be spread over a large portion of the file allocation table. This occurs after the filesystem has been in use for a long time; the deletion and creation of files causes allocation of new clusters not to be contiguous. This is referred to as *fragmentation*. There are defragmentation tools available that reallocate clusters to files contiguously. Since the performance benefit of defragmentation can be significant, we dedicate an entire section to this topic later in this chapter. The obvious performance implication of fragmentation is an increase in the average response time of the filesystem. Reading a file requires following the cluster pointers in the file allocation table. When the file is fragmented, the FAT entries related to this file are not located close together, and following the pointers causes more disk head movement.

Another disadvantage of the FAT filesystem is high internal fragmentation. *Internal fragmentation* refers to the unused disk space within the last cluster allocated to a file that does not contain file data. In a 3 GB partition formatted with the FAT16 filesystem, the cluster size is 64 KB. When a 65 KB file is stored on this disk, two clusters are allocated but the second one has 63 KB of unused space. The amount of internal fragmentation depends on the partition size and also on the workload of the particular system. For systems where the average file size is very large, the percentage of internal fragmentation is much lower than a workload that consists of very small files. For example, a filesystem with a lot of HTML pages and email consists of small files, whereas one with many images and executables consists of large files.

To determine the total amount of internal fragmentation of a FAT filesystem, we wrote a program that walks through the entire directory structure of a partition and accumulates the internal fragmentation of each file. The application is based on the two Win32 functions FindFirstFile and FindNextFile. Both functions return a WIN32_FIND_DATA structure that includes the size of the file in nFileSizeHigh and nFileSizeLow. Given the total size of a partition, we can find the cluster size by looking at Table 9-1. We ran this application on a drive that included Microsoft Office and user directories, and determined that to store a total of 1,060,107,970 bytes of actual file data, an additional 597,100,862 bytes were wasted due to internal fragmentation. In other words, 36% of the bytes allocated from the partition were left unused: a pretty big price to pay for simplicity. That is where the NTFS filesystem comes in.

The NTFS Filesystem

The NTFS filesystem is a log-based filesystem that provides better reliability and recoverability than the FAT filesystems. NTFS is similar to the FAT filesystems in that the available space in the partition is divided into clusters that are the units of space allocation. Clusters are numbered sequentially from the beginning of the partition, forming a unique identifier for each cluster called the *logical cluster number*. As in the FAT filesystem, the cluster size depends on the size of the partition. Table 9-3 shows the relationship between the partition size and the cluster size in sectors. In the NTFS filesystem, clusters are numbered using logical cluster numbers that are 64-bit long values. Because such a large number of clusters can be addressed, we can still access partitions of 2^{73} bytes even if the cluster size is set to a single sector or 512 bytes. So unlike FAT partitions, where the cluster size varies based on partition size due to address space limitations, in the NTFS filesystem it varies to balance the trade-off between throughput (bytes transferred per I/O request) and internal fragmentation. When the cluster size is large, the number of bytes transferred per cluster request is high, so the throughput increases as the cluster size increases. As you remember from the previous chapter, disks are much more efficient in retrieving larger block sizes than smaller block sizes. At the same time, though, the amount of disk space wasted due to internal fragmentation also increases. On the other hand, when the cluster size is small, the amount of internal fragmentation is low but the throughput drops. NTFS has been around since NT was first released. As time has passed, disk drive prices have dropped and their capacities have increased to the point where it is unusual to encounter a partition less than 2 GB in size.

Table 9-3. Default cluster sizes for NTFS filesystem

Partition size	Cluster size in sectors	Cluster size in bytes
0 MB – 512 MB	1	512
512 MB – 1024 MB	2	1024
1025 MB – 2048 MB	4	2048
2049 MB and up	8	4096

When a partition is formatted with the NTFS filesystem, you can specify the cluster size if you do not want the default shown in Table 9-3. The format command has the /a:unitsize option, which allows you to select the cluster size. In addition to the default values, you may specify the additional cluster sizes of 8 KB, 16 KB, 32 KB, and 64 KB manually when creating the filesystem. The Disk Administrator application provides the same choices through a drop-down box. If performance is your primary concern and wasting some disk capacity due to internal fragmentation is not as much of an issue, you should consider formatting your NTFS partitions with a larger cluster size.

The NTFS filesystem stores all objects in the filesystem using a record, similar to the way a relational database stores information. Each record in the filesystem represents an entry that may be a file, a directory, or information about the filesystem itself. Each record consists of a number of fields or attributes. For a file object, the filename, security descriptor, and even the data are considered attributes of a record. The size of the file record is also selected based on the cluster size (shown in Table 9-3). All the records are stored within a single table called the *master file table* (MFT). The MFT is laid out similarly to a table in relational database terminology. Figure 9-6 shows the layout of a partition formatted with the NTFS filesystem.

Figure 9-6. NTFS partition format

The partition boot sector is similar to the one for the FAT filesystem, but it is longer and occupies the first 16 sectors. The boot sector consists of two sections. The first section contains the BIOS parameter block that stores information about the layout of the volume and the filesystem structures. The second section contains the boot code that loads the NT/2000 operating system when this NTFS partition is the active partition on the system disk.

Master file table

Next comes the master file table, which contains all the information necessary to retrieve files from an NTFS partition. There is a copy of the first four entries in the MFT at the end of the partition in Windows NT 4.0 and Windows 2000, or in the middle of the partition in Windows NT 3.51 or earlier. The copy includes only the first four records because they are essential for the recovery of the filesystem if there is a problem with the original copy. The rest of the partition is used to store data that cannot fit within the MFT. When an NTFS partition is formatted, the MFT is created, and the first 16 entries are reserved for storing information about the filesystem itself; these first entries are also referred to as the *system files*. Table 9-4 describes the purpose of each of the first 16 entries in the MFT.

Table 9-4. NTFS system files

Record #	Filename	Purpose
0	$Mft	Contains the master file table itself
1	$MftMirr	Holds the first four records of the MFT and is used in case the first sector of the MFT fails
2	$LogFile	Stores information about each transaction and commit timestamps to assist in quick recovery after the system has failed
3	$Volume	Stores information about the volume, including the name, and NTFS version number
4	$AttrDef	Maps each attribute name to its corresponding number and description
5	$.	Stores index for the root folder
6	$Bitmap	Contains a bitmap representation of cluster allocation information, used by NTFS to allocate clusters to files
7	$Boot	Contains the bootstrap information for the volume
8	$BadClus	Stores the location of all the bad clusters in the volume
9	$Secure	Contains unique security descriptors for all files within a volume
10	$Upcase	Converts lowercase characters to their corresponding Unicode uppercase characters
11–15		Reserved for future use

To prevent the MFT from becoming fragmented as the partition fills up, NTFS reserves a set of clusters after the MFT called the *MFT-Zone*. Clusters that are part of the MFT-Zone are allocated to files only when the partition is full. The rest of the MFT consists of records representing individual files or directories.

Attributes

Two types of attributes can describe a record: *resident* or *nonresident*. The contents of resident attributes are contained within the file record itself, and the contents of nonresident attributes are stored within the filesystem data section of the disk, as shown in Figure 9-6. Figure 9-7 shows the format of a typical resident record that represents a file. The *standard information* includes attributes of the file such as

---

access mode (read-only, read/write, etc.), timestamps describing creation and modification times, and link counts describing the number of directory entries that point to this file record.

Figure 9-7. NTFS resident record format

One of the attributes stored as part of a file is the short name of the file, also called the 8.3 filename. This makes filenames more readable for MS-DOS and 16-bit Windows applications. To determine the short filename, the filesystem driver must use additional CPU resources and, more importantly, must generate additional write requests to the disk. If you don't really need the short names, you can disable their generation by modifying the registry. All you need to do is change the setting of the Registry entry NtfsDisable8dot3name-Creation from the default value of 0 to 1. The registry key is HKEY_LOCAL_MACHINE\System\CurrentControlSet\Control\Filesystem.

Make sure that you do not have any legacy 16-bit Windows applications that need to make use of the short filenames before making this change.

The filename attribute is just what the name implies. A file record may include multiple such attributes when a file is known by multiple names. For example, both a file with a long and a short filename and a POSIX file with a hard link have multiple filename attribute entries in the record. The security descriptor includes the access control list for file protection information. For a more detailed description of the security descriptor, see *Inside Windows 2000* by David Solomon or the earlier edition by Helen Custer. Finally, the data attribute includes the data of the file. A file may have multiple data streams in Windows NT. The default data stream in a file is also called the unnamed stream. Additional streams may be associated with a file simply by adding additional data attributes within the same file record. Unlike the default stream, the additional data streams have names associated with them so that their contents can be selectively accessed. To read the default data stream of a file, the file is accessed through the filename, for example:

```
Filename.dat
```

To access another named stream within the file, a colon and the name of the data stream are appended to the name of the file. Here, data stream *otherstream* is accessed within file *Filename.dat*:

```
Filename.dat:otherstream
```

Data streams

File record sizes vary based on the size of the partition. A typical file record is 1 KB in size. For larger files and directories, there is not sufficient space in a single record to store the contents of the file. The data attribute can be and frequently is a nonresident attribute (another attribute that can be nonresident is the security descriptor for large access control lists). Figure 9-8 shows the format of a file record with a nonresident data attribute. Additional allocation blocks, called *runs* or *extents*, are used from the partition's data area to store the file's data. The file's file record entry in the MFT contains enough information to allow access to the runs. Each run allocated to the file is numbered sequentially using virtual cluster numbers. The data stream in the file's file record contains a sequence of virtual-to-logical cluster number mappings.

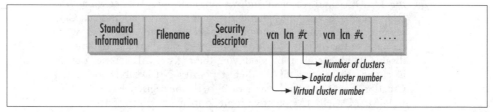

Figure 9-8. NTFS nonresident record format

The contents of each mapping are shown in Figure 9-9. Each entry contains the starting virtual cluster number for the entry, the corresponding starting logical cluster number, and the number of clusters that make up the run. Reading the contents of a file with a nonresident data stream requires that the file's file record is read first to get the list of VCN-to-LCN mappings, and the necessary clusters are read next. Initially when the partition is fairly unused, the logical clusters allocated to a file will likely be contiguous; therefore, reading the file will require little head movement. There is always head movement between the master file table, which is at the beginning of the partition, and the first logical cluster. As the partition fills up, allocation of logical clusters is less likely to be contiguous. Then the file is more fragmented, and additional head movement is necessary when retrieving different groups of logical clusters.

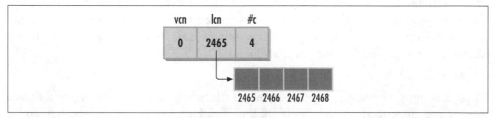

Figure 9-9. Virtual-to-logical cluster mapping

Directories are very similar to files in the attributes used to describe them; the difference is the contents of the data stream. For a directory, the data stream is a list of file references specifying the files or file folders in a particular directory. A file is referenced internally in the filesystem using a 64-bit value called the *file reference*, which is simply an index within the master file table that contains the file's file record.

Directories

The on-disk layout of directories varies depending on the directory's size. Figure 9-10 shows the two possible arrangements. A directory is simply a file where the contents of the data stream are filename-to-file reference pairs called *index entries*. When the directory is small, all the entries fit within the directory's file record, but after a certain point additional space is needed. At this point, NTFS uses a *b+ tree* index to store the entries. The b+ tree is an indexing algorithm, commonly used in databases, that performs well when part of the index is stored on secondary memory by reducing the number of I/O operations required when searching or updating information on the index. Searching for a specific entry in a very large directory arranged in a b+ tree takes *log(n)* time (where *n* is the number of entries in the directory). This just means that the amount of time it takes to locate an entry in the directory grows very slowly with respect to the size of the directory. The b+ tree index provides support for operations such as DIR, which are otherwise very time-consuming. Another advantage of using a b+ tree index is that the information is stored in alphabetic order, so listing the files in the directories alphabetically does not require additional sorting. NTFS was designed so that any of the file attributes could be indexed, but currently only the filename attribute index is supported.

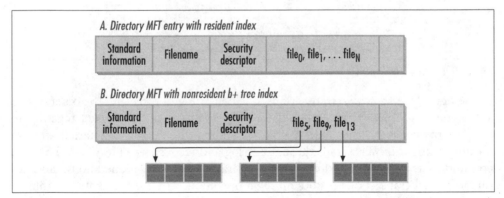

Figure 9-10. MFT directory record entry format

Filesystem transactions

Earlier we mentioned that NTFS provides very fast filesystem recovery after an unexpected system crash. It accomplishes this by borrowing again from relational database technology. NTFS uses a log and treats every operation that modifies the filesystem structure as a transaction. When a user generates a modification to the filesystem such as the creation of a new file in a directory, the filesystem treats this as a transaction possibly consisting of multiple suboperations (allocating space for the file in the MFT, modifying the directory, etc.). The transaction is first stored in the log, and then the modification is made on the filesystem through the cache. Finally, the transaction is *committed*. A committed transaction is one where the filesystem guarantees that, even if the system goes down before all the changes to the volume in the cache have been stored on the disk, the system can complete the operation and maintain the consistency of the filesystem the next time the system comes up. Using the information stored in the log, the filesystem also ensures that if any suboperations of a noncommitted transaction were performed on the volume on the disk, the filesystem can undo those operations.

The format of the log file is shown in Figure 9-11. It consists of the restart area and the logging area. The restart area is used to store information about the management of the log file, and the logging area is where the operations are appended. The logging area is treated as a circular buffer, which means that when the end of the logging area is reached, new records are written at the beginning. Periodically, NTFS writes a checkpoint record to the log file indicating that all transactions up to that point have been committed and the updates have been made on the disk. Checkpoint records are used by NTFS when the system is started to determine where in the log it should start recovery from and how far back to go. By treating the logging area as a circular buffer and by using checkpoint records, the logging area appears to be of infinite length.

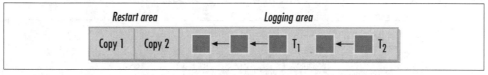

Figure 9-11. Log file format

In the figure, we show two transactions, one consisting of three and the other of two suboperations. All suboperations comprising a transaction are linked together to support the redo and the undo operations. When the system is restarted after an abrupt shutdown, NTFS reads through the log and recovers the filesystem. For each committed transaction, it does a *redo* operation of the suboperations, and for uncommitted transactions it does an *undo* operation. The redo operation is simply the execution of a suboperation, while the undo is the undoing of the effects of an incomplete operation.

Advanced filesystem features

NTFS includes a number of advanced features, some of which were introduced in Windows 2000. One of them is *Reparse Points*, a mechanism for adding extended functionality to the filesystem in processing selected files or directories. It works as follows. You first need to associate a reparse tag, which is assigned by Microsoft and is unique across independent software vendors (ISVs), with the file or directory whose functionality you want to extend. When the filesystem encounters the reparse tag while parsing the pathname of that file or directory, it forwards the request to an installable filesystem filter driver associated with that particular tag. Along with the request, the filesystem forwards up to 16 KB of data that can be associated with that file. The filesystem itself does not attempt to interpret this data; it is up to the filter driver to interpret it. This mechanism allows Microsoft or any ISV to extend the behavior of NTFS without requiring modification to the NTFS filesystem driver itself.

Microsoft has taken advantage of Reparse Point functionality to add a number of extensions to NTFS in the Windows 2000 release. One such extension is *Junctions*. Other operating systems, such as Unix, have provided symbolic link functionality in the filesystem for a long time. In Windows 2000, Junctions is basically support for symbolic links to directories. When you create a symbolic link to an empty directory, internally you are associating a reparse tag with that directory. When you list the contents of that directory by clicking on the directory icon through the Explorer, you cause the filesystem code to process this reparse tag. The associated filter driver intercepts the request and processes the associated reparse data, which includes the name of the directory that the symbolic link points to. Surprisingly, Windows 2000 does not itself include any tools for creating junctions. The Windows 2000 Resource Kit includes a program called linkd, or you can download the *Junction* utility from *http://sysinternals.com/misc.htm*. The Junction utility not only allows you to create symbolic links, but also to locate files and directories in your NTFS filesystem that are reparse points. Furthermore, you can also download the full source code for the utility if you want to get the inside scoop on how it works.

Another feature of NTFS based on Reparse Points is *Mount Points*. Windows NT and the other Windows operating systems always associate a drive letter with a partition or volume from the disk. Mount Points is a new feature that allows you to attach partitions to an empty directory of an already mounted partition. For example, you could create a directory named *Users* under *c:\Accounting* and then mount another volume to the *Users* directory. Users traversing the filesystem and listing the contents of the *Users* directory will not realize that they are actually crossing volumes when entering that directory. There are certain restrictions in using Mount Points. The host volume on which you are mounting additional volumes must be an NTFS volume, since Reparse Points, on which this feature is based, is part of NTFS. The mounted volume can be formatted with any of the following filesystems: FAT16, FAT32, NTFS, CDFS, and UDFS. One of the big advantages of Mount Points is that it removes the limitation of Windows NT and other Windows operating systems that a system can have a maximum of 26 mounted volumes. Using Mount Points, you can mount all your volumes on a single drive letter.

NTFS provides additional features that we won't delve into much, including support for hierarchical storage management through the remote storage service, compression, encryption, and support for sparse files. Using preconfigured criteria, NTFS can automatically migrate files that have not been accessed recently to remote storage, such as tape libraries or jukeboxes. If a file that has been migrated to tape storage is accessed by a user, the Reparse Points mechanism is used to bring back the file from tape to disk transparently to the user. Another NTFS feature that has been available since Windows NT 4.0 is file compression. You can mark a file, a directory, or a volume to use compression. The file will be compressed before being stored on the filesystem, and uncompressed while reading the data back into memory. You need to be careful with using compression, since it demands considerable CPU processing and degrades the performance of your filesystem considerably.

Windows 2000 supports encryption of files using *public key cryptography*. Microsoft has a very good white paper on their web site (*http://microsoft.com/windows2000/ techinfo/howitworks/security/encrypt.asp*) that describes EFS (Encrypting File System). Mark Russinovich (*www.sysinternals.com*) also published an excellent two-part article on EFS in the June and July issues of *Windows 2000 Magazine*.

The last feature of NTFS we mention is support for sparse files. This support is built using a new set of API calls that allows the operating system to efficiently store files that are potentially large but usually consume only a small portion of the maximum size. A typical example is a scientific application that needs to store a matrix that could be 1 GB in size but only has a few nonzero entries. Storing this matrix in a sparse file causes the size of the file to be close to that of a file that stored only the nonzero entries. The filesystem accomplishes this by maintaining a table that keeps track of sparse ranges in the file. So, instead of storing long sequences of zeros in the sparse file, the filesystem only adds some overhead to the file for an entry in the table that describes the sparse region.

Comparison of Filesystems

Now that you know a little bit about the design of each of the three filesystems available with Windows 2000, you are faced with the difficult decision of which one to select when formatting the new disk that you just added to your system. Here is a list of criteria that you can use to make the right choice:

- If for some reason you need to create a small partition (less than 512 MB), then the best choice in terms of performance is the FAT16 filesystem. It will impose the least overhead on the small available capacity of the partition and will have high performance.

- For partitions larger than 1 GB you should not use the FAT16 filesystem since it becomes inefficient as the partition size increases and a lot of space is wasted due to internal fragmentation. Your available choices are either FAT32 or NTFS.

- If security concerns are more critical to your environment than any other criterion, your only choice is the NTFS filesystem. NTFS provides security and encryption that are not available with the other two filesystems.

- For large partitions that are greater than 16 GB, the better choice in terms of performance and efficient use of the available capacity is the NTFS filesystem. The cluster size for the FAT32 filesystem for partitions of that size is at least 16 KB, and this introduces considerable internal fragmentation in most environments.

- Some of the advanced filesystem features in Windows 2000, such as Mount Points, Junctions, remote storage, compression, and sparse file support are only available with NTFS.

- In dual-boot environments where you need to share filesystems between Windows 2000 and a Windows 9x operating system, you should not use NTFS. Windows 9x operating systems do not have support for reading NTFS partitions. There is a driver you can purchase from *http://www.winternals.com* that provides access to NTFS partitions to Windows 98 and Windows 95, or you can download for free a read-only driver from *http://www.sysinternals.com*.

Defragmentation

Fragmentation is a term used to describe the degree of contiguousness in the clusters allocated to a file. When a filesystem is first created, there is plenty of space available on that partition. As users create new files or extend the size of existing ones, the filesystem is able to allocate contiguous clusters from its free list. As the filesystem fills up, it cannot satisfy requests for additional capacity using contiguous clusters and starts to use available clusters from any location on the surface of the disk. Figure 9-12 shows the allocation of two files on a partition. File A consists of 7 clusters, most of which are contiguous; File B consists of only four clusters, none of which are contiguous. When a user tries to read the entire contents of File A, the disk can retrieve the contents of that file very efficiently because they are located close to one another on the disk. If the user generates a similar read request against File B, the disk needs to seek around the surface of the disk in order to locate all the fragments that comprise the file, thus degrading the performance of the disk subsystem.

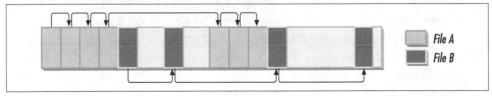

Figure 9-12. File B is more fragmented than File A

There is a rumor in the industry that partitions formatted with the NTFS filesystem do not get fragmented. Although NTFS uses more advanced algorithms in allocating clusters to files, it is not immune to fragmentation. It is true, though, that it develops fragmentation to a lesser degree than the other two filesystems due to its more sophisticated design. In addition to the fragmentation of files, NTFS is also liable to fragmentation of the MFT. When you create a new NTFS partition, the NTFS driver creates the MFT and allocates some extra space to allow it to expand. As you continue using the filesystem, especially on a busy server, NTFS reaches a point where the MFT runs out of space. At that point, NTFS allocates additional clusters, fragmenting the MFT. In addition to fragmentation of the entire MFT, it is also possible to develop MFT record fragmentation. NTFS uses a record size of 1 KB to store information about each file or directory in the filesystem. If you create a partition with a cluster size of 512 bytes, or if you have large files that require more than one MFT record to store their metadata, you are likely to experience fragmentation of the MFT records. This implies that before you retrieve the contents of the file, you need to perform at least two disk I/O requests to different locations of the disk simply to retrieve the MFT records that describe the contents of the file.

Before we describe some experiments that try to measure the impact of fragmentation on the performance of your filesystem, let's talk about a few more cases that require special treatment when it comes to fragmentation. Windows 2000 and Windows NT have a number of files that are considered system files. These files are hidden and must not be moved from their special locations on the disk. For example, the loader of the operating system itself, ntldr, is a system file, as is the multi-boot loader ntdetect. The defragmentation API that Windows 2000 provides recognizes those files and does not attempt to defragment them. Another issue that introduces complications is the treatment of paging files. As we discussed in Chapter 6, Windows 2000 uses paging files to persist pages from memory that are not actively used, so as to release some page frames for applications that need additional memory. Since the paging files need to be available constantly, Windows 2000 opens the paging files and holds a handle to them from the time it starts until it shuts down. The defragmentation API cannot work on the paging files because they are constantly locked by the operating system itself. So, paging file fragmentation can also degrade system performance. One way to get around this limitation is by following these steps:

1. Select System from the Control Panel, and on the Advanced tab, click Performance Options. Then click Change to open the Virtual Memory dialog box.

2. Create a new paging file to another drive and reduce the minimum and maximum sizes of the fragmented paging file to 0 bytes.

3. Reboot your computer and defragment the disk on which the fragmented paging file resided. This compacts the clusters that were previously allocated to the paging file.

4. Go back to the Virtual Memory dialog box and create the original paging file again. Then set the minimum and maximum sizes of the temporary paging file to 0 bytes.

5. Reboot your computer and you should be all set.

Until recently, the performance benefits of a defragmented partition were not quantified or analyzed properly. In October 1999, NSTL released the results of a well defined study of the impact of defragmentation on the performance of the disk sub-system. In order to define a test that was repeatable and applicable to partitions of varying sizes, they used an application called Fragger to create the fragmented dataset of files. The test was originally conducted on a combination of Windows NT 4.0 and 3.51 workstations and servers, but was later repeated against systems running Windows 2000, RC2 build 2128. We summarize their test configuration and results of the Windows 2000-based experiments.

NSTL wanted their system configuration to be as realistic as possible. They ran their tests on two separate configurations based on independent surveys of 6,000 NT system managers. Each configuration consisted of a server machine and a workstation machine. If you are interested in the details of the configuration of the server and workstation machine in each of the two configuration, we suggest that you read the full report.

For each configuration, NSTL first fragmented the data disk used by the various applications that generated the workload. They then ran their workload while collecting detailed measurements. After the first phase of the test was complete, they used Diskeeper 5.0 from Executive Software to defragment the data partitions; then, they repeated the generation of the workload and the measurement data collection and compared the results. The workload consisted of a variety of operations by Microsoft Excel 2000, SQL Server 7.0, Microsoft Outlook 2000, and Microsoft Exchange 5.5. In the first configuration, running the Excel and Outlook workloads on the workstation showed an increase in performance of 219.6% on the defragmented partition. The server running Exchange and SQL Server showed between 61.9% and 83.5% improvement. That is a significant improvement in performance and shows that it is well worth the effort of regularly defragmenting your filesystems. The leading defragmentation tools provide scheduling and network capabilities to simplify the process across a network of workstations and servers.

The NSTL report released in November 1999 also used the Diskeeper 5.0 software from Executive Software for defragmentation purposes. Symantec, the company that makes a competitive defragmentation utility called Norton SpeedDisk 5.0, requested that NSTL perform comparative testing between the two leading utilities in the market. As a result, NSTL released a third and final report in January 2000, which reported on a comparative study of these two defragmentation tools. Here are some of the conclusions, although we highly recommend that you read the full report:

> "SpeedDisk was more consistent at improving application performance than was Diskeeper. SpeedDisk improved the performance of all five of the applications used in the testing while Diskeeper improved the performance of three of the five applications."

> "SpeedDisk was more effective at improving the performance of the applications involved in the testing. SpeedDisk effected greater performance gains than Diskeeper for four of the five applications measured. The average performance gain effected by SpeedDisk, across all five applications, was 13.0 percent. The average performance gain effected by Diskeeper, across the five applications, was 1.7 percent."

"The SpeedDisk optimizations were much quicker than the Diskeeper optimizations. Diskeeper required an additional 9.25 hours to complete its optimizations on approximately 210,000 files on 19GB of disk space. Also, Diskeeper required twenty three hours of system downtime to perform its file defragmentations. SpeedDisk did not require any system downtime to perform its optimizations."

Norton SpeedDisk is actually more than a defragmentation tool; it also performs optimization of the files on the disk. It performs the following changes to the allocation of files on a volume:

- It places the most frequently accessed files on the outermost tracks of the disk, closest to the rest position of the head. This way, the heads can move quickly to the seek position of files that are accessed frequently. Since the MFT is located at the beginning of the volume, when you attempt to access a file, the heads go to the MFT and then to the file without wasting too much time on a seek operation.

- Files that are not accessed very frequently are placed closer to the center of the volume. This way, there is more space close to the beginning of the volume for storing the frequently accessed files.

- Files that are modified very frequently are placed close to available free space. This reduces fragmentation in the future, since these files will be able to expand with few, if any, additional fragments of space.

Windows 2000 provides the lite version of Diskeeper 5.0, which is accessible through the Computer Management MMC application. Figure 9-13 shows the main screen of the built-in defragmentation utility. Before you defragment a volume, you can run an analysis of it to determine whether defragmentation is needed.

After you analyze a volume, Diskeeper builds a report that you can view online, print, or save to a file. The following is a portion of a sample report of a fragmented volume. As you will notice, it reports separately on file fragmentation, paging file fragmentation, and MFT fragmentation in the case of a volume formatted with the NTFS filesystem.

```
Volume Root Disk (C:):
    Volume size                    = 10,001 MB
    Cluster size                   = 4 KB
    Used space                     = 3,648 MB
    Free space                     = 6,353 MB
    Percent free space             = 63 %
Volume fragmentation
    Total fragmentation            = 24 %
    File fragmentation             = 49 %
    Free space fragmentation       = 0 %
File fragmentation
    Total files                    = 28,887
    Average file size              = 157 KB
    Total fragmented files         = 994
    Total excess fragments         = 10,565
    Average fragments per file     = 1.36
```

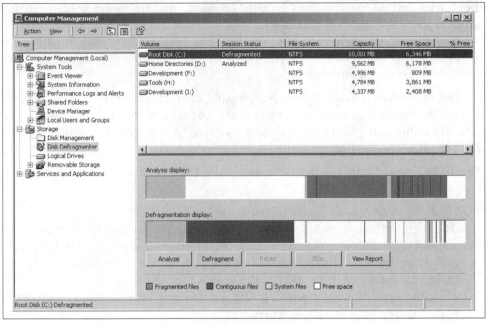

Figure 9-13. Sample display of the analysis of a fragmented volume

```
Pagefile fragmentation
    Pagefile size                  = 98,304 KB
    Total fragments                = 1
Directory fragmentation
    Total directories              = 1,810
    Fragmented directories         = 164
    Excess directory fragments     = 875
Master File Table (MFT) fragmentation
    Total MFT size                 = 43,987 KB
    MFT record count               = 30,759
    Percent MFT in use             = 69 %
    Total MFT fragments            = 2
```

The next section describes some of the counters available through the System Monitor for analyzing the performance of filesystems. They are almost identical to the ones covered in the previous chapter, but these apply only to the logical disk object.

System Monitor Counters

A number of objects provide performance metrics that are relevant for evaluating the performance of the logical disk subsystem. The Logical Disk object provides information about each partition. When a physical disk has been partitioned into multiple logical disks (partitions or volumes), the metrics provided by the Physical Disk object are aggregates of the load imposed on all the partitions. The System object provides a few additional counters related to disk subsystem performance. Finally, the Cache and Memory objects provide counters that are useful in determining whether the cause of a disk bottleneck is filesystem access or a shortage of memory. Some of these counters have been covered in their respective chapters in detail, but we include them here to remind you that they can help to resolve a performance problem with the disk subsystem.

By default, Windows 2000 collects performance counters only for the Physical Disk object. To enable collection of counters at the Logical Disk object you must use the `diskperf` command with either the –y or –yv flag. (We described the usage of the `diskperf` command in Chapter 8.)

The following counters are available under the Logical Disk object in the Performance Monitor:

% Disk Time, % Disk Read Time, % Disk Write Time
> These are utilization measures for the disk time, and indicate the percentage of elapsed time that the instance is busy servicing requests in general, read requests, and write requests. The % Disk Read Time and % Disk Write Time can be useful in characterizing the workload and in detecting the application that is generating the load. The corresponding Avg. Disk Queue Length counters are better in evaluating the utilization of a disk.

Avg. Disk Bytes/Transfer, Avg. Disk Bytes/Read, Avg. Disk Bytes/Write
> The first counter reports on the average number of bytes per disk request, and other two break the information down into reads versus writes. These measures are useful in understanding the workload of a system. Larger values for these measures indicate a more efficient use of the disk. When the number of bytes transferred per request is small, the fraction of the response time taken up by latency is much greater.

Avg. Disk Queue Length, Avg. Disk Read Queue Length, Avg. Disk Write Queue Length
> These measures report on the fraction of elapsed time that the disk is occupied servicing a request, a read request, or a write request. They are also utilization measures reporting the same information as the % Disk Time measures, but the information is reported as a fraction rather than a percentage. The advantage of these counters is that they can exceed 1.0 and are therefore more accurate for heavily utilized and striped disks.

Avg. Disk sec/Transfer, Avg. Disk sec/Read, Avg. Disk sec/Write
> This set of counters measure the response time of a disk request. The first counter averages all requests, whereas the second and third ones average read and write requests. The response time for a request includes the total elapsed time from the instant the request is generated to the instant the response is provided by the operating system. This measure makes more sense when considered in combination with a measure of the number of bytes transferred in an operation.

Current Disk Queue Length

This counter is a measure of the instantaneous size of the disk queue. Since it is not an average, it always has an integral value. This counter can be used to evaluate the level of load balancing across the available disks. If one disk has a consistently large number for this counter and the other disks are on and off between zero and one, that is a clear indication of a load imbalance. When this occurs, the response time counters usually confirm the problem by indicating high response times for the overloaded disk. Any queue build-up is a sign of performance problems. In Chapter 10 we see how striping provides perfect load-balancing across multiple disks.

Disk Bytes/sec, Disk Read Bytes/sec, Disk Write Bytes/sec

These counters provide information on the throughput of the system. A properly configured system can get close to the bandwidth of the disks. A number of factors affect these counters. Applications that consist primarily of sequential requests can attain higher values for these counters simply because the disk is spending less time in moving the heads and more time transferring data. In addition, the average request size of the workload has an impact: applications that transfer information in larger block sizes have higher throughput.

Disk Transfers/sec, Disk Reads/sec, Disk Writes/sec

These counters measure the total number of requests, read requests, and write requests processed per second. Like the previous set of counters, these also measure the throughput of the system. The difference is that this set does not consider the size of the request but treats all requests equally. For this reason, these counters should be interpreted only in combination with counters that take into consideration the size of the request. The same system may complete twice as many 2 KB requests than 4 KB requests in one second, but the total amount of bytes transferred in both cases is the same.

% Free Space

This is the fraction of the logical disk capacity that is still available. Its only relevance to performance is that when a disk is almost full, the cluster allocation algorithm is slower and fragmentation increases.

Free Megabytes

This is the amount of space that is still available on the partition in megabytes.

The following counters under the System object are also useful for disk performance monitoring:

% Total Interrupt Time

This counter measures the percentage of CPU time for all processors spent servicing interrupts averaged over all processors. For example, if one processor spent 60% of its time handling interrupts and the other processor spent 40%, the % Total Interrupt Time is 50 %.

File Control Bytes/sec

This counter measures the total number of bytes transferred for all filesystem operations that are not reads and writes. This includes bytes retrieved from the cache, so this is not necessarily load imposed on the disk.

File Control Operations/sec

This counter measures the total number of bytes transferred for all file control operations (operations that are not reads or writes) for all filesystems.

File Data Operations/sec, File Read Operations/sec, File Write Operations/sec

This counter measures the total number of operations per second, and the breakdown into reads or writes.

File Read Bytes/sec, File Write Bytes/sec

This counter measures the total number of bytes transferred per second due to read or write requests. Again, this includes bytes retrieved from the cache as well as from the disk.

Total Interrupts/sec

This counter measures the total number of interrupts generated per second. The clock generates at least 100 interrupts per second, so this value is always greater than 100. Other devices that generate interrupts are the mouse, the network interface card, and the disks.

The Memory object provides the following counters:

Page Reads/sec

This counter measures the number of requests to the I/O manager to retrieve pages of memory from the disk. Despite the name of this counter, it measures requests, not pages; a request can be for more than a single page.

Page Writes/sec

This counter measures the number of requests to the I/O manager to write pages of memory to the disk. Again, each request can be for more than a single page.

Pages Input/sec

This counter measures the number of pages read from the disk per second. Combining this counter with the Page Reads/sec counter can tell you how many pages are retrieved per request.

Pages Output/sec

This counter measures the number of pages written to the disk per second. Combining this counter with the Page Writes/sec counter can tell you how many pages are written per request.

Pages/sec

This counter measures the total number of pages read and written to the disk. This counter represents the sum of Pages Input/sec and Pages Output/sec. Using this counter along with the Disk Bytes/sec counter from the Physical Disk object, you can determine what portion of the data transferred to the disk is due to memory access, and what portion is due to filesystem access.

The Cache object provides the following counters:

Data Flush Pages/sec
> This counter measures the number of pages the cache has flushed to disk. Disk flushes occur as a result of either a direct flush request, a write-through request, or pages written out by the lazy writer thread.

Data Flushes/sec
> This counter measures the number of cache flush operations per second. Each flush operation may include multiple pages, so this counter is always lower than the Data Flush Pages/sec.

Lazy Writes/sec
> This counter measures the number of write operations to the disk by the cache manager's lazy writer thread.

Lazy Write Pages/sec
> This counter measures the number of pages written out by the cache manager's lazy writer thread per second.

Comparing Filesystem Performance

The case study presented here investigates the difference in the performance of disks based on the filesystem they are formatted with. To compare them, we simply create a number of volumes of varying sizes, format them with a filesystem, and generate a workload against them. The first question that arises is what kind of workload would bring out the differences between the filesystems. Your first reaction might be to use the Iometer tool from the previous chapter but unfortunately, it is not suitable for this test. Iometer either generates a workload against a physical disk or against a single file on a disk partition. It is meant to be used to compare the hardware components of the I/O subsystem, so it does not necessarily put the filesystem code to work.

Postmark

We chose to use the Postmark benchmark developed by Network Appliance. It is available from the web site for free and it includes the source code (*http://www. netapp.com/tech_library/3022.html*). It was developed primarily for Unix servers, but since it's written using standard C, it is very portable and compiles cleanly under the Win32 environment.

We decided to develop yet another benchmark because there is a lack of benchmarks that focus on typical application server workloads. Most servers currently provide services such as email, network news, and other applications that tend to deal with ephemeral files of small sizes. Postmark simulates heavy small-file loads for files that live for short amounts of time, such as temporary files.

When you run Postmark, it goes through three stages of execution. First it creates an initial number of random text files, which vary in size from a configurable lower bound to a configurable upper bound. In the next stage, it generates transactions against that pool of files, which are one of the following:

- Creating a new file
- Deleting an existing file
- Reading the entire contents of an existing file
- Appending to an existing file

The Postmark web site (*http://www.netapp.com/tech_library/3022.html*) includes a white paper that describes its operation in detail. You can also download the source code if you have questions about its operation or want to modify its behavior.

Unlike Iometer, Postmark runs and is configured through a command-line interface. One feature that is missing is support for reading and saving configuration files. Every time you start Postmark, you must manually specify the configuration of the test that you want to run. Here is the output from Postmark when you start it and inquire about its available command set:

```
PostMark v1.13 : 5/18/00
pm>help
set size - Sets low and high bounds of files
set number - Sets number of simultaneous files
set seed - Sets seed for random number generator
set transactions - Sets number of transactions
set location - Sets location of working files
set subdirectories - Sets number of subdirectories
set read - Sets read block size
set write - Sets write block size
set buffering - Sets usage of buffered I/O
set bias read - Sets the chance of choosing read over append
set bias create - Sets the chance of choosing create over delete
set report - Choose verbose or terse report format
run - Runs one iteration of benchmark
show - Displays current configuration
help - Prints out available commands
quit - Exit program
pm>
```

As you can see, there are a number of parameters you can modify. Some of the more useful ones include the number of files it creates, the number of transactions it generates, the location on the disk where it creates the files or subdirectories, and the block sizes it should use for read and write requests. The documentation does not mention the `subdirectories` parameter, since it was probably added after the documentation was written. This parameter specifies the number of subdirectories in which it will create files.

After you run a test, Postmark generates a report that summarizes the results during each of the three stages of the test. The first portion of the report consists of a header that summarizes the overall performance of your volume in terms of throughput and overall response time. Then it breaks up the results in terms of throughput for each transaction type. Here is a sample report:

```
Creating files...Done
Performing transactions.........Done
Deleting files...Done
Time:
        11 seconds total
        10 seconds of transactions (200 per second)
Files:
        1441 created (131 per second)
                Creation alone: 500 files (500 per second)
                Mixed with transactions: 941 files (94 per second)
        993 read (99 per second)
        1007 appended (100 per second)
        1441 deleted (131 per second)
                Deletion alone: 382 files (382 per second)
                Mixed with transactions: 1059 files (105 per second)
Data:
        30.69 megabytes read (2.79 megabytes per second)
        45.21 megabytes written (4.11 megabytes per second)
```

Test Results

The Postmark benchmark is suitable for testing the difference in performance between filesystems. Since it creates, deletes, and modifies lots of files during a test session, it effectively generates operations that modify the metadata as well as the data associated with each file. FAT and NTFS use different data structures and algorithms for maintaining such metadata and for allocating clusters to files. By running this benchmark, we should be able to evaluate the efficiency of each filesystem in performing these operations.

For the test configuration, we used two identical disks from a disk array (more on disk arrays in Chapter 10) and created three equal partitions on each disk. The partition sizes were 511 MB, 2 GB, and 10 GB. To ensure that the disks were treated equally by the disk array controller, we first ran a number of tests using Iometer and got the exact same numbers from both of them.

Then, we formatted one 511 MB partition with the FAT16 filesystem and the other with NTFS; one 2 GB partition with FAT16 and the other with NTFS; and one 10 GB partition with FAT32 and the other with NTFS. (For the 10 GB partition, we had to switch to FAT32 because Windows 2000 does not allow you to format partitions greater than 2 GB with the FAT16 filesystem.) For all six partitions, we used the default cluster size. Table 9-5 shows the cluster size in KB that we used for each combination of filesystem and partition size. Figure 9-14 shows the configuration of the volumes through Disk Management. We set the number of transactions to 10,000, the number of subdirectories to 100, the number of files to 500, and varied the file size between the sizes 4 KB, 64 KB, 128 KB, and 512 KB.

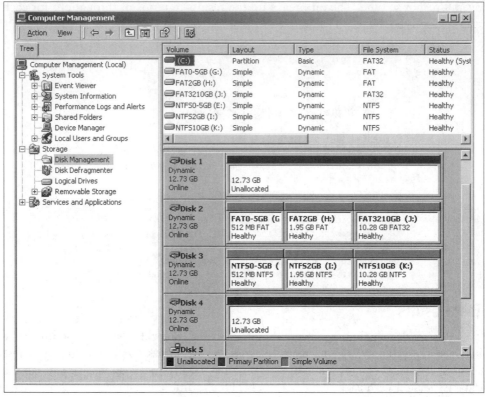

Figure 9-14. Configuration of the volumes for the filesystems test

Table 9-5. Cluster size (in KB) used for each partition and filesystem

	511 MB	2 GB	10 GB
FAT	8	32	8
NTFS	0.5	2	4

We summarize the results of the tests in Tables 9-6 and 9-7 for the FAT and NTFS volumes, respectively. The three major columns correspond to the three volume sizes that we run the tests against. For each volume and file size combination, we report four different results:

- CA is the number of create file operations per second when no other transactions are generated at the same time.

- CT is the number of create file operations per second when transactions are generated concurrently.

- DA is the number of delete file operations per second no other transactions are generated at the same time.

- DT is the number of delete file operations per second when transactions are generated concurrently.

Table 9-6. Summary of benchmark results for the FAT volumes

	0.5 GB				2 GB				10 GB			
File size	CA	CT	DA	DT	CA	CT	DA	DT	CA	CT	DA	DT
4 KB	500	763	348	775	500	763	348	775	500	827	348	839
64 KB	166	37	448	37	250	37	448	37	250	40	448	40
128 KB	71	22	320	22	83	23	320	23	83	22	320	23
512 KB	11	5	490	5	11	5	490	5	10	5	490	5

Table 9-7. Summary of benchmark results for the NTFS volumes

	0.5 GB				2 GB				10 GB			
File size	CA	CT	DA	DT	CA	CT	DA	DT	CA	CT	DA	DT
4 KB	500	300	348	305	500	310	348	314	500	225	348	229
64 KB	250	46	448	47	125	50	448	51	166	53	448	53
128 KB	71	24	320	25	71	23	320	23	71	26	320	26
512 KB	11	4	490	4	11	4	490	4	10	5	490	5

There are a number of observations we can make from the results of this test:

- All three filesystems are able to delete files at exactly the same rate, regardless of the file size, when deleting files is the only activity on the filesystem. It was surprising to see that the DA number for all three filesystems and file sizes were identical.

- For the small partition and small file size, the FAT filesystem provides better performance than NTFS. That is probably a function of the different cluster sizes used by the two filesystems. The FAT filesystem used an 8 KB cluster size, thereby requiring only a single cluster to accommodate the 4 KB file size, while NTFS used a 512 byte cluster size, requiring 8 clusters (notice that in this case NTFS had 0 internal fragmentation). One aspect of the two filesystems not covered in the tables is the effective use of space. In this case, the FAT filesystem wasted half of each cluster for internal fragmentation (4 KB file and an 8 KB cluster size) while the NTFS filesystem had 0% fragmentation (4 KB file and a 512 byte cluster size).

- For the two medium-sized file sizes, NTFS provides better performance across all partition sizes and for all metrics. Here is where the data structures used for maintaining cluster allocations to files really pays off. As you remember, the FAT filesystems store allocations using a linked list of clusters, whereas NTFS stores ranges of contiguous clusters as one table entry.

- For the large file size, all three filesystems provide about the same performance. Operations are bound by the speed of the disk device.

You may also want to run System Monitor while generating some of these workloads with Postmark. It was interesting to observe concurrently what the disk was requested to do while Postmark was submitting requests to the filesystem. Pay attention to counters such as Disk Reads/sec, Disk Writes/sec, Avg. Disk Bytes/Read, and Avg. Disk Bytes/Write.

Selecting a Filesystem

The following is a list of criteria that you can use in selecting a filesystem for your disk volumes.

- Windows 2000 recommends that you manage your disk storage devices using dynamic as opposed to basic disks. This bias will become even more obvious when we discuss disk arrays in the next chapter. The only disadvantages of dynamic disks are that you cannot use them for your system partition and that you cannot share volumes in dual-boot environments.

- The FAT16 filesystem wastes a lot of space on drives that are larger than 500 MB (which covers just about any drive on the market these days) and does not provide the security features available in the NTFS filesystem. The FAT32 filesystem does provide an alternative to FAT16 that allows you to share filesystems at additional cost in dual-boot environments, but still does not have some of the advanced features of the NTFS filesystem.

- For any heavy-duty file server environment where security is a concern, the only choice for a filesystem is NTFS. In addition to security, you get a wealth of features, some introduced in the Windows 2000 version, including Junctions, Mount Points, remote storage, encryption, compression, and quotas.

- Over time, filesystems become fragmented. There is not much you can do to avoid this (although recent versions of the leading defragmentation tools attempt to prevent fragmentation from occurring), but you should definitely implement a regular defragmentation policy on your network. A recent NSTL study made it clear that there are considerable performance benefits from keeping your volumes fragmentation-free.

- The System Monitor provides many counters that can help you identify a bottleneck at the disk subsystem. As suggested in the previous chapter, focus on the counters that give you information about utilization and about queuing of requests at the disk. The advantage of combining the monitoring of counters at the logical disk object with those at the physical disk object is that you can narrow down the performance issue to a specific volume if you have multiple volumes per physical disk.

- To benchmark the performance of your filesystem, try the Postmark utility. You can easily configure it to match your environment closely, and it can give you a good idea of what performance numbers to expect in a typical corporate environment.

## CHAPTER 10

Disk Array Performance

The rapid pace of improvements in the performance and density of semiconductor technology widens the gap between the performance of processors and secondary storage devices. According to the oft-quoted Amdahl's law, the performance of a computer system depends on the speed of its slowest serial component. In a modern computer system, this is often the physical disks. In addition, as applications get faster, they place even heavier demands on the secondary memory subsystem.

These concerns have caused academic and industry researchers to turn to the performance of the disk I/O subsystem. Parallel processing proved successful in advancing the performance of computer systems by using multiple processors concurrently to solve a single computing problem. The same principle applied to the disk I/O subsystem gave birth to *redundant arrays of inexpensive disks* (RAID). In general terms, a *disk array* refers to the partitioning of a request into smaller requests that are serviced in parallel by multiple disks, resulting in faster response times. The partitioning of the request into pieces is done by either the operating system or the controller hardware, depending on the specific configuration. In both cases, this partitioning is transparent to the user. Because this *disk striping* generates disk reliability issues, the disk industry has devised various ways to add redundant data to the data recording scheme to supply fault tolerance. Many of today's RAID disk products provide almost continuous data availability in the face of hard drive failures through the use of *disk mirroring*, *parity data* generation and recording, *hot sparing*, and *dynamic reconstruction* of data from a failed disk to a spare disk.

In this chapter, we review the various approaches to building RAID devices, along the way discussing the terminology to describe fault-tolerant disk arrays. We also address some of the very critical performance issues that arise from running RAID disks in the Windows 2000 environment.

Disk Striping

Predating the introduction of RAID, *striping* data across multiple disks was conceived as a way of introducing parallelism into secondary storage devices. With data striping, a collection of disks called a *disk array* forms (from the operating system's point of view) a single logical disk. A request for a block of data is striped across the physical disks, thereby reducing the number of bytes that need to be transferred by each disk. The number of bytes sent to a single disk is reduced by a factor equal to the number of physical disks. An additional advantage of striping is that the I/O load is evenly balanced across all the physical disks. Queuing delays are minimized across multiple disks when the I/O load is balanced across the disks.

One issue that detracts from the use of simple disk striping is reliability. Striping brings an increased exposure to disk failures. If data is striped across 10 disks, for example, *any* failure to one of the 10 disks in the array leads to a loss of access to all of the data. Take, for instance, a hard drive that the manufacturer estimates has a mean time between failures (MTBF) of 300,000 hours. That is equivalent to 34 years! (MTBF is the most commonly used statistical measure of the reliability of a disk component.) When 10 disks with this MTBF rating are combined to form a disk array, the MTBF of the logical disk is reduced by a factor of 10 to just 3.4 years. While striping can speed up disk access, it also significantly increases the exposure of data loss due to a hard disk failure.

Enter RAID

In a landmark paper on RAID, Patterson, Gibson, and Katz of the University of California at Berkeley suggested the reliability concerns with disk striping could be solved by adding redundant data used for automatic error correction to the array. They described five different approaches to building redundant disk arrays, which they named RAID Levels 1 through 5. The taxonomy of redundant disk arrays that Patterson et al developed has become the standard terminology for describing RAID disk architectures.

A decision to implement RAID disks is usually based on overriding disk reliability concerns. Hard drive failures are catastrophic events in the life of a Windows 2000 system administrator. Even with effective backup and recovery procedures, a hard drive failure leads to an extensive computer outage and a loss of service. There are also a number of performance issues associated with different RAID configuration choices. This chapter is mainly concerned with those performance issues. We try to provide a conceptual understanding of the cost/performance design trade-offs that are explicit at each RAID level, and the advantages and disadvantages of each option.

The material in this chapter is organized into three sections. The first section describes RAID Levels 1 through 5 in some detail. We also discuss RAID Level 0, as disk striping came to be known. The second section discusses hardware and software RAID options for the Windows 2000 and Windows NT platforms. Finally, the third section looks at the performance of disk array configurations, using the Intel Iometer benchmark program to generate test workloads that we evaluated on several different RAID configurations.

RAID Disk Organizations

Going back to the original Berkeley paper published in 1988 that first enumerated RAID Levels 1 through 5, the disk industry has struggled to come up with terminology to describe different disk array architectures. A broad-based effort by the RAID Advisory Board (RAB) resulted in some much-needed standardization of the terms involved. Disk vendors seeking to establish a competitive advantage for their products often deviate from standard usage. We try to relate proprietary architectures to more generally accepted terminology, but that is not always possible.

RAID Level 0

RAID Level 0 describes simple disk striping where no additional reliability data is added to the array. The RAID 0 designation became accepted after the Berkeley RAID group defined RAID Levels 1 through 5. RAID 0 is not really RAID because there is neither redundant data or fault tolerance. The Berkeley authors accepted this classification of striping as RAID 0 because of the primacy of striping in their original formulation.

Figure 10-1 shows the organization of data in a RAID 0 array. A single request is spread across multiple disks, allowing for parallel processing of each disk request. Because RAID 0 striping does not store any redundant error correction code data, it is the cheapest of the various disk array architectures. Striping data over multiple disks costs no more than writing that same data to individual disks. In contrast, each of the redundant disk array options described next increases the cost of disk storage.

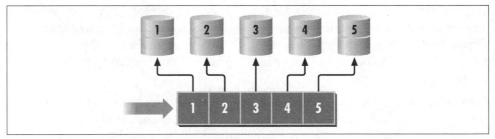

Figure 10-1. RAID Level 0 striping is a nonredundant disk array organization

Striping provides the best performance for write requests since no redundant information needs to be updated. In striping, each block written to the disk array is divided evenly among the disks comprising the array, creating a *striping unit* or *disk slice*. The striping unit or slice is the amount of contiguous data stored on each disk. We use the term *striping unit* consistently throughout the description of all RAID levels to refer to the amount of data read or written to a single disk in an array operation.

Performance considerations

RAID Level 0 arrays are commonly used in installations where performance and low cost have higher priority over reliability. But RAID 0 striping is not a panacea, as many seem to believe. It is important to understand that the performance gain in using striping is derived mainly from the ability to speed up data transfers. The overhead in setting up the transfer, namely the disk seek and latency, is not reduced at all by the striping of data over multiple disks. We will see that, depending on the implementation, striping can actually *increase* the amount of disk latency involved in an I/O request. Consequently, disk striping is a speedup technique that applies generally only to large block transfers.

For example, let us say that we have a four-way striped disk array with a stripe unit of 2 KB and a disk transfer rate of 8 MB/sec, as shown in Figure 10-2. With a request size of 8 KB, all four disks are active in servicing the requests, so we get the maximum possible concurrency. First, the disk heads need to be positioned to the appropriate disk sector on the corresponding disks. This involves both a seek and a latency, which typically take about 6 ms and 4 ms respectively. The actual data transfer of 2 KB from each disk takes only about 0.25 ms. Allowing for an additional SCSI overhead of about 0.5 ms, the response time of the entire request with striping is 10.75 ms. When the same request is issued to a single disk, the only difference is a slightly longer data transfer phase of about 1.00 ms. That implies that there is only a modest 7% improvement in the disk service time using striping. Figure 10-2 shows graphically that the improvement using a RAID 0 array is barely noticeable.

Now, let us repeat this example with a stripe unit size of 16 KB and a request size of 64 KB, assuming that the seek time and latency time is the same as before. The data transfer time for a 16 KB request takes 2 ms, for a total response time of 12.5 ms. A single disk takes 8 ms to transfer the entire 64 KB request for a total service time of 18.5 ms. This time, the reduction in the disk service time is better than 30%. Figure 10-3 illustrates the general principle that whenever data transfer is a sizable portion of overall disk service time, striping leads to a significant improvement in overall disk performance.

It should now be apparent that by increasing the stripe unit size, we improve the performance of the disk array. Why not just make the block size as big as possible? As usual, there is a trade-off. When the stripe unit size is large, smaller requests require only a few of the disks in the stripe set to service the request. To get the maximum theoretical benefit of striping, the stripe size and the number of disks in the set should be selected to match the workload on the specific system. This particular

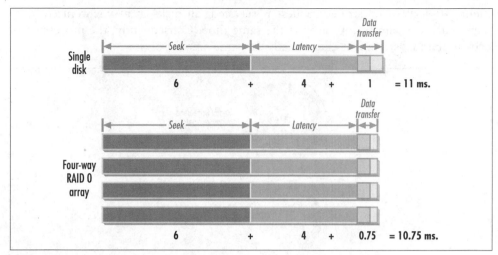

Figure 10-2. Improvement in response time for an 8 KB request using a 4-way RAID 0 array

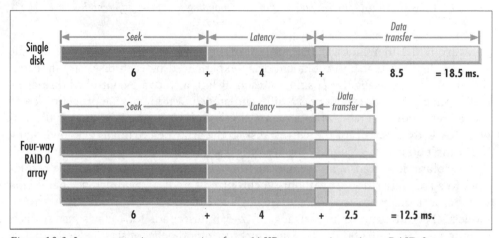

Figure 10-3. Improvement in response time for a 64 KB request using a 4-way RAID 0 array

trade-off, as well as suggestions for selecting the filesystem configuration parameters most suitable for striping, are discussed in more detail in later sections. In practice, the stripe size in Windows 2000 is a function of the filesystem, which may or may not lend itself to the performance improvements anticipated from disk striping.

Synchronized spindles

The overhead of positioning time (seek and latency) is not the only cause of reduced performance gain in striped arrays. A separate source is the requirement to synchronize the independent disks in the set. This synchronization delay is not a consideration in hardware RAID implementations that operate with *synchronized spindles*. This means that the platters and heads of each disk in the array move in unison. See

Figure 10-4. When a striped request is serviced, all disks in a synchronized array experience the same setup delay at the same time. Consequently, the processing of each individual stripe unit takes exactly the same amount of time.

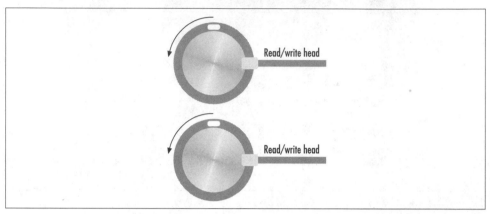

Figure 10-4. Synchronized spindles: positions of corresponding sectors on different disks are identical

Software RAID in Windows 2000, on the other hand, cannot make use of spindle sync, so the seek time and rotational delay experienced by each disk vary independently. Because the angular position of each disk in a software-controlled disk array is different, each disk experiences a different latency, waiting for the proper disk sector to spin under the read/write actuator. See Figure 10-5. The Windows 2000 software RAID drivers wait for the slowest disk in the array before finally acknowledging the completion of the request. The result is a *worst-case* latency approaching a full disk revolution, instead of an average latency, which is only a portion of one revolution. In a software stripe set without synchronized spindles, the difference between a worst-case latency and an average latency *increases* the service time of a striped request. The difference is in the range of 2–3 milliseconds for today's fastest disks spinning at 7,200–10,000 RPMs. This synchronization delay offsets the performance gains that can be achieved through striping for all but the largest I/O block requests.

Striped disk reliability

Of course, the major drawback of RAID 0 is reduced reliability. A single disk failure causes complete data loss. Increasing the reliability of the physical disk components in an array naturally addresses some of the reliability concerns. High-quality SCSI disks being built today have an estimated MTBF of 1,000,000 hours. This corresponds to about 114 years! These disks can probably be striped across three or four disks in an array and still provide an acceptable level of reliability in most Windows 2000 server environments. However, as we will see, RAID configurations can be very cost effective. The storage and maintenance of redundant error correction data protects from data loss if a hard drive fails. Given the serious consequences of a disk

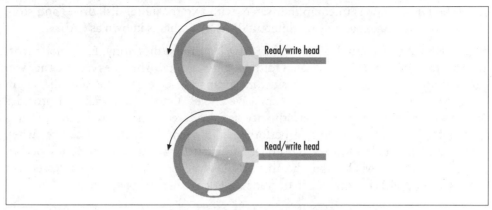

Figure 10-5. In most disk arrays, spindles rotate independently

crash on any important Windows 2000 server, no matter how unlikely the event, RAID's extra protection is reason enough to justify the incremental cost. The promise of nearly continuous data availability that RAID architectures provide is normally well worth the cost difference and decreased performance compared to both individual disks and striped disks.

RAID Level 1

RAID Level 1 is also frequently called *disk mirroring* or *disk shadowing*, and it was prevalent prior to the Berkeley RAID group hanging a new name on it. Disk mirroring has only one major drawback: cost. It requires twice as much disk capacity to mirror disks as it does to run them in native mode. On the plus side, disk mirroring is relatively easy to implement, and network operating systems going back to early versions of Novel Netware and IBM's OS2 all supported some form of server disk mirroring. Disk mirroring is frequently available as an application option, and database management systems like SQL Server can optionally mirror files at the database level or files like the transaction recovery log file, which is so critical to application availability. The advantage of application mirroring is that it can target just those files that are critical to application recovery. In general, hardware mirroring takes a broader approach to application availability by mirroring *everything* stored on disk, which is much more expensive.

Windows 2000 incorporates mirroring for several of its critical disk files, including NTFS file metadata entries and the Registry. In both of these applications, the data being mirrored is so critical to having a Windows 2000 system that initializes and runs correctly that it is worth storing this data in two different places on the hard drive—just in case. Of course, storing the same data in two places on a single disk is an example of a reliability scheme with a *single point of failure*. In the case of a hard drive failure, both copies of the data are inaccessible, so what have you gained? A much better solution is to equip the system with two (or more) disk drives and store the redundant data separately on different disks. And that is known as RAID 1.

Figure 10-6 shows the architecture of a RAID 1 mirrored disk array. Each block written to a mirrored array is duplicated for reliability reasons. This does require that you purchase *twice* as much physical disk storage capacity to achieve the same filesystem capacity, making RAID Level 1 an expensive choice. On the other hand, it provides an opportunity to improve performance for read requests (as we will see in a moment), and there is no loss of performance for write requests. Of course, when one of the disks fails, requests are serviced from the intact copy without any performance impact. We will see that the other RAID levels provide reliability at lesser cost than RAID Level 1, but operate in degraded mode when a disk has failed.

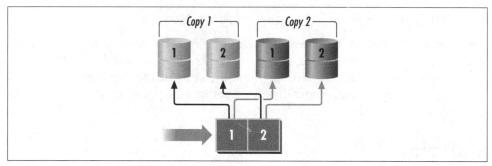

Figure 10-6. RAID Level 1 organization

The simplest organization for RAID Level 1 is to use two disks, each a mirror image of the other. Reads can be performed against either of the two disks. Most drivers that implement mirroring use a round-robin rule to load-balance read requests across the two disk copies. However, with unsynchronized spindles, it is possible to race the disks and accept the I/O with the best case latency. On writes, both disks must be updated to ensure they remain mirror images of each other. Again, without spindle sync, it is possible to race the disks and declare the write I/O sufficiently complete when the first disk operation completes successfully.

Remote mirroring

While people are accustomed to mirroring disks within the same physical location, that is not a requirement. A number of high-end vendors of RAID hardware offer *remote disk mirroring* across long distances for disaster recovery. Generally, high-speed fiber optic connections are used to configure disk mirroring between sites within a few kilometers of each other, and long distance phone lines are used for the long haul. Having a mirror image of your data maintained at a site several hundred miles away is fine if your primary site is knocked out because of a fire, hurricane, or earthquake, but it does not do you any good in recovering from a hardware disk crash at your primary site. The vendors that support remote mirroring must support multiple mirrors in that case—one additional copy of the data stored locally to support local recovery, and another copy stored at a hot site recovery center located some distance away.

RAID Level 0/1

The organization shown in Figure 10-6 is also called RAID Level 0/1 (or sometimes 1/0 or 1+0 or 10) because it combines elements of both RAID 0 striping and RAID 1 mirroring. We see that blocks are striped across multiple disks (RAID Level 0), and then each stripe unit is mirrored to a companion disk (RAID Level 1). This organization is popular because it combines the performance gains of RAID 0 with the reliability inherent in RAID 1 disk mirroring. The continuing drop in disk prices makes the RAID 0/1 organization especially viable today. If you can afford the extra hardware, RAID 0/1 is almost always an excellent choice. But keep in mind that the disk performance speedup that you can achieve using RAID 0/1 striping and mirroring remains a function of the block size. In the case of software RAID with unsynchronized spindles, the speedup in transfer is offset by the extra delay due to a worst-case latency. That is why the option is not available in Windows 2000 software RAID.

RAID Level 2

RAID Levels 2 through 5 are different approaches that add extended reliability to the disk array at a lower cost than RAID Level 1. RAID Level 2 uses error-correcting codes (ECC) for detecting and correcting disk errors in an array. See Figure 10-7. The specific error-correcting code used in RAID Level 2 is the *Hamming code* that is commonly used in memory chips. Given a four-bit sequence, for example, the Hamming code algorithm generates a seven-bit sequence that includes error-correcting information. The additional three bits are each computed using a parity computation over distinct overlapping subsets of the bits in the original sequence. In general, the number of ECC bit positions required in the Hamming code algorithm is proportional to the log of the length of the original sequence.

RAID Level 2 is of mainly academic interest for a number of reasons. First of all, Hamming codes by their nature require a significant number of disks to store the ECC data, making RAID 2 relatively expensive. The error detection capability in RAID 2, so important for determining which memory cell has failed, is not important in disk failure scenarios because components are engineered to report on faults. Having information on which disk has failed is unnecessary, since this is fairly easy to determine using other methods. So, since there are other techniques for detecting single-bit errors, RAID 2 schemes were not adopted by the disk industry. The lone exception is the massive RAID 2 disk subsystem developed by Thinking Machines, Inc., now defunct, for its massively parallel supercomputer called the Connection Machine back in the mid-1980s.

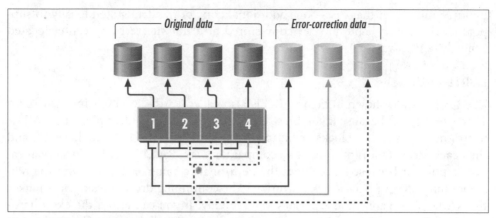

Figure 10-7. RAID Level 2 organization

RAID Level 3

RAID Level 3 introduces extended reliability with dynamic error correction at a lower cost than wholesale disk mirroring. Generally, the fact that a disk has failed is reliably reported by the disk electronics. Knowing which disk failed means that it is necessary only to be able to correct the error that occurred. RAID 3 uses a simple parity computation, usually implemented with the *Exclusive Or* (XOR) operator, to create redundant data that can be used in the case of a disk failure to reconstruct the data stored on the failed device. With RAID 3, we come to striping with parity—a characterization that applies to the rest of the RAID levels.

The XOR parity data computation has the property that the result of applying the operation on *n* bits can be used to determine the value of any one of those *n* bits by applying the operator on the *n – 1* bits and the parity result. Let us illustrate its application by an example. The truth table for the XOR operator is shown in Table 10-1.

Table 10-1. Exclusive OR truth table

p	q	p XOR q
0	0	0
0	1	1
1	0	1
1	1	0

Assembly language enthusiasts will notice that XOR is a lot like binary addition, except with no overflow or carry bit. The mathematical symbol for XOR is $\oplus$, a plus sign with a circle drawn around it. XOR shares with addition the associative and commutative properties. This means you can compute a string of XOR operations in any order without affecting the result. Suppose we have the two bit patterns 0010 and 1010. Using the truth table, we compute the parity bits as $0010 \oplus 1010 = 1000$.

Next, we store the two data bit patterns on two separate disks and the parity data on a third independent disk. Let's see what happens if the disk that contained the pattern 0010 dies. We can now apply the XOR operation again on the surviving bit patterns: $1010 \oplus 1000 = 0010$, which is the data we lost.

RAID Level 3 extends basic disk striping by adding an extra disk to store this bitwise parity information. RAID 3 is also called *bit-interleaved* or *byte-interleaved* organization because the interleaving usually takes place at the bit or byte level. The parity disk always contains the results of the XOR operation. Figure 10-8 shows a bit-interleaved RAID 3 disk array. Here, we want to store the single byte 01010010 across four data disks, with a fifth disk used to store the parity data. We call this a 4+1 RAID 3 array. RAID 3 interleaves data across the disks at the bit level. The byte is broken into two nibbles, and the XOR is computed for each.

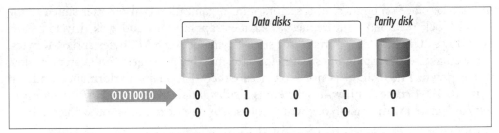

Figure 10-8. RAID Level 3 organization

Performance

A RAID Level 3 disk array comes very close to delivering performance equivalent to RAID 0/1 at a much lower cost. Because data is interleaved at such a fine granularity in RAID 3, the resulting disk I/O load is balanced across the disks in the array very evenly. Each write request places the same exact load on all the disks in the array. Read requests place a load only on the data disks, suggesting that RAID 3 disk arrays have the same performance as RAID 0 for reads. But RAID 3 exhibits a slight degradation for writes, because there is a parity computation and an additional concurrent write for each block of data that is written.

Reduced mode operation

When one of the disks in the RAID 3 parity group fails, the disk array is said to operate in *reduced mode*. This is identical to striping, and has the same reliability exposure until the failed disk can be replaced. When a single data disk fails, the performance characteristics of RAID 3 are the reverse of normal operation. Every write request during reduced mode is a little faster, since just $n - 1$ disks are involved (assuming unsynchronized spindles). On the other hand, every read request involves $n - 1$ disks just as in normal operation, but a parity computation must be performed before returning the data to the user, since the data from the failed disk must be recovered.

The bit or byte interleaving in RAID 3 is designed to maximize the performance benefits of disk striping by attaining the highest degree of parallelism. Like striping, these performance benefits accrue mainly for large block reads and writes. For small blocks, RAID 3 provides little performance benefit and, in the case of unsynchronized spindles, can actually result in slightly degraded performance.

RAID Level 4

RAID Level 4 is similar to RAID Level 3 except at the level where data and parity interleaving takes place. RAID Level 4 interleaves data at the level of the stripe unit. The size of the stripe unit may vary from a single sector (usually 512 or 1024 bytes) to multiple sectors, up to 64 KB blocks, for example. RAID 4 is designed to adapt to the way SCSI disks are built, which cannot be manipulated bit by bit anyway. Disk operations take place on physical disk sectors. This organization is also better suited to the small block read and write requests that most applications and disk drivers create. Windows 2000 NTFS supports sector sizes varying between 512 bytes and 64 K bytes. As we have seen, striping does not help with small block requests and can even slow them down. But RAID 4 is not a panacea either. The major performance trade-off with RAID 4 comes with writes. There is a substantial *RAID write performance penalty* associated with single-block write requests, as described in the following section.

So RAID 4 (and its cousin RAID 5) is best understood as an architecture for extended reliability that also happens to raise some critical performance issues. Unfortunately, these performance issues are subtle and not easily understood. Consider, for example, that using the physical sector size as the stripe unit in RAID 4 means that an individual read request usually involves a single physical disk. This means that RAID 4 performance on reads is no better than *Just a Bunch of Disks* (JBOD)—which is actually the terminology developed by RAID architects to describe something that is not RAID. In fact, RAID 4 organization effectively abandons any idea that disk I/Os will be speeded up through parallelism. However, there are circumstances where multiple concurrent read requests can at least be serviced in parallel from different disks in the array. Moreover, if write requests are large enough to span all the data disks in the array, RAID 4 performance similar to RAID 0 striping is possible. When a block of data is written that is equal to the number of data disks times the stripe unit size, the updated parity sector is computed just once, and both the data blocks and the parity can be written to the disks in parallel.

Figure 10-9 shows an example where there are four data disks, one parity disk, and the stripe unit size is 2 KB. Writing a 16 KB block on a RAID 4 volume with four data disks requires two phases. The 16 KB block is first broken into eight stripe units. In the first phase, stripe units 0–3 are written on the data disks, and their XOR is written on the parity disk. In the second phase, stripe units 4–7 are written on the data disks, and their XOR is written on the parity disk. Under these circumstances, RAID 4 performance is identical to RAID 3.

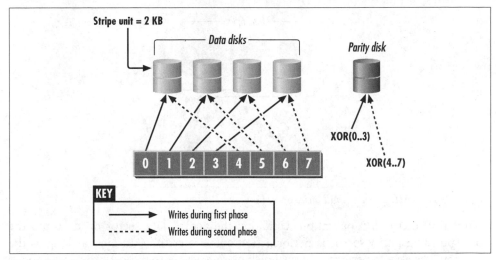

Figure 10-9. RAID Level 4 large write operation

RAID write performance penalty

Now let's consider the situation where the block written is smaller than the product of the stripe unit and the number of data disks. Modifying only the data disks affected would leave the disk array in an inconsistent state, as the corresponding parity block would no longer match the contents of the data stored across the full array stripe. For small writes, a RAID Level 4 array must execute a *Read-Modify-Write* operation to maintain the parity data. The original data sector and its corresponding parity sector must first be read into a work area. The new parity block is computed from the old data, the old parity, and the new data. Then the modified stripe unit and the modified parity block are both written back to their respective disks, as illustrated in Figure 10-10. The effect of the RAID write penalty is the transformation of a logical write operation into four physical disk operations: two reads and two writes. This significant performance penalty is, of course, subject to the rate at which small block writes occur. It is normally possible to schedule the two reads and two writes that must occur to run in parallel, which mitigates some of the performance impact of the penalty.

EMC Symmetrix

The popular EMC Symmetrix RAID-S implementation is the most familiar example of a commercial RAID 4 product. (EMC's proprietary RAID-S formulation is actually somewhat protean; depending on the actual configuration, it can also take on characteristics of a RAID 5 architecture.) Symmetrix makes use of a large battery-backed cache memory to mask the performance penalty associated with RAID 4 writes. The cache assists in several ways. The primary use of cache in the Symmetrix disk controller is to buffer writes in memory. As soon as write data is safely deposited in the Symmetrix's nonvolatile cache memory, the controller signals successful

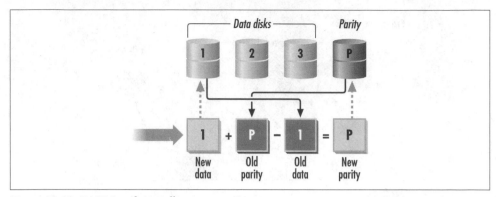

Figure 10-10. RAID Level 4 small write operation

completion of the I/O operation. Updating the actual data sector on disk and the corresponding parity sector is performed at some later time. In fact, as long as the Symmetrix is able to perform physical disk updates faster than host processes deposit them in cache memory, the EMC box is able to mask the RAID write performance penalty completely from the attached host application.

The large cache memory used in the Symmetrix can be useful in other ways. The RAID write penalty requires that the old data and parity sectors be read from disk first before the parity sector can be updated appropriately. The Symmetrix's large cache increases the probability that current copies of the old data and parity sectors can be found in cache and do not have to be fetched from disk. The Symmetrix implements a lazy write algorithm, similar to the cache manager in Windows 2000, that defers the actual disk updates. If you defer the update long enough and if the same disk data sector happens to be changed *again*, then the deferral is permanent and you have saved an expensive disk I/O.

So against almost all intuition, the EMC Symmetrix RAID-S implementation, with its large nonvolatile cache memory, manages to achieve extremely high performance levels. The Berkeley academicians responsible for the RAID taxonomy tended to disparage the performance of RAID 4 designs because the single parity disk, which is the focus of all update activity, can be a bottleneck. In EMC's formulation, this is rarely the case because of the lavish use of cache memory.

Figure 10-10 shows an example of the Read-Modify-Write cycle that takes place with small writes. If the write request is for a 4 KB block, only the stripe unit on the first disk is affected by the modification. The Read-Modify-Write cycle begins with a read of the corresponding stripe units from disks one and P. The new parity is computed in memory, and the modified data block and parity are written back to disks one and four respectively. This should stress the importance of configuring the stripe unit size of a RAID 4 disk array after the workload has been characterized. Otherwise, the performance degradation due to a workload dominated by small writes will be very noticeable.

RAID Level 5

There are two primary limitations with RAID Level 4. One is that for read requests, only $n - 1$ of the n disks are used to service the requests. The second is that for write requests, the parity disk can be a bottleneck since it is involved in every write. To deal with these two issues, RAID Level 5 rotates the parity stripe unit across all the disks. Figure 10-11 shows an example of a RAID 5 array where four disks are used for the data and the parity. Notice that the disk where the parity stripe is written changes on consecutive writes. Assuming that the stripe unit size is 2 KB, the first 6 KB block will occupy disks 1 through 3 and the parity stripe will occupy disk 4. The next data block will occupy disks 2 through 4, and the parity will occupy disk 1. The same pattern continues until it wraps around and then starts over again from the beginning.

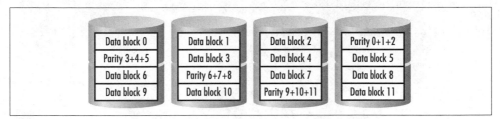

Figure 10-11. RAID Level 5 organization

Since the parity is stored on different disks, no single drive is occupied for all write requests. Also, all five disks are available to service small read requests concurrently, enhancing the potential parallelism of the disk array. The only disadvantage of the RAID 5 array is that it still suffers from the Read-Modify-Write cycle issue for small requests, just like RAID 4.

Because of its ability to service small reads, large reads, and large writes, RAID 5 is the most commonly used of the RAID levels. Another reason for the popularity of RAID 5 is the lower incremental cost of providing fault-tolerance features as compared to RAID 1 disk mirroring. For example, to build an 8 GB logical device with fault tolerance using 2 GB disks would require eight disks with a RAID 1 organization, as opposed to only five disks with RAID 5. Figure 10-12 summarizes these considerations for the various RAID levels discussed in this section. RAID 1 disk mirroring requires buying twice the amount of hardware as a simple, nonredundant disk configuration. In contrast, RAID 3–5 provide error recovery with only an incremental increase in the amount of disk capacity that needs to be configured.

In practice, disk capacity is only a paradoxically small part of the overall cost of a fault-tolerant disk array. In the case of a premium, high-performance product like the EMC Symmetrix, we doubt that hardware disk drives represent more than 10–15% of the total cost to manufacture the box. Other components, such as the battery-backed cache boards, the custom-engineered RAID disk controllers and interface

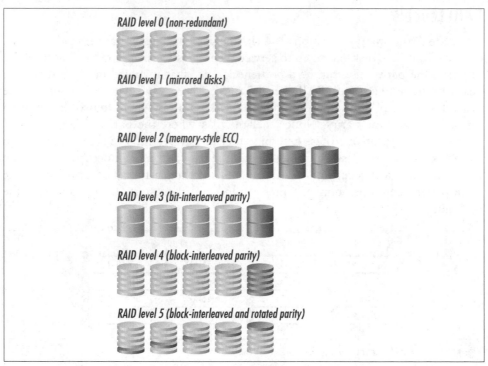

Figure 10-12. Data storage required in the different RAID organizations

boards, and the redundant AC and DC power supplies, are probably at least as costly. But the major cost factor in building a premium RAID disk product like the Symmetrix is the development of software to manage and control the disk array. In theory, developing a fault-tolerant disk controller looks pretty simple reading the academic literature on the subject. In practice, building software that can maintain data access in the face of the failure of any single component in one of these complex machines is very difficult and time-consuming. This is one area where the simplicity of RAID 1 and RAID 0/1 is a virtue, as they reduce the complexity of this task.

RAID Level 5 provides fault tolerance for arrays at a reduced cost, but it is far from an ideal solution. The Read-Modify-Write penalty is a very serious performance problem that is only partially alleviated using disk subsystem caching. For installations where a considerable fraction of the workload consists of write requests and where the average request size is small (workloads that are very common in databases and transaction processing environments), some amount of write caching is mandatory for RAID 5 arrays. And that means caching using battery-backed RAM. Most hardware-based disk arrays provide caching on board the controller to reduce the latency associated with the Read-Modify-Write cycle. The cache is battery-backed, so writes are acknowledged immediately by the hardware. This is described in more detail in the later section "Write caching."

Additional Fault-Tolerant Options

RAID architectures are fault tolerant of single disk hardware failures. This serves as the springboard for additional reliability enhancements that provide near continuous data availability. These additional features include hot spares, hot swap drives, automatic disk failure detection, and automatic reconstruction of the failed disk.

Hot spare refers to the ability to include an extra disk in the array that can automatically replace a failed drive. The hot spare drive is normally held in reserve until there is a device failure. Then, without any user intervention, the array goes into a rebuild mode where, using the redundant information in the RAID 1, 3, 4, or 5 configuration, the data that was stored on the failed drive is recreated on the hot spare. During the time that the failed drive is replaced by the hot spare, requests from users are still serviced continuously by the array, although performance suffers due to the background rebuilding process.

Figure 10-13 shows the automatic recovery of a RAID 1 array using a hot spare. When the controller detects that one of the two copies of the mirror have failed, the hot spare is allocated as a replacement, and the rebuilding process for the other copy of the mirror begins. During rebuilding, performance degrades since the surviving copy of the mirror must service requests from both the users as well as for the background copy operation to reconstitute the data on the hot spare.

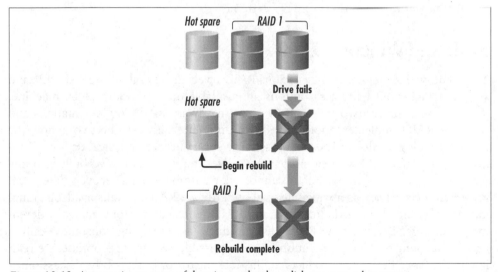

Figure 10-13. *Automatic recovery of data in a redundant disk array to a hot spare*

Support for a hot spare is a valuable option for any environment where fault tolerance is a priority. Normally, one or more spares are designated when the disk subsystem is configured, and these spares can be allocated dynamically to fill in for any disk drive failure that may occur within the RAID disk subsystem rack or cabinet.

During reconstruction, a redundant array with hot sparing must in effect support two concurrent I/O streams. The disk subsystem must service all externally generated requests to access or change data stored in the array. Internally, the disk array is regenerating the data (and parity) from the failed disk and writing it to a new disk. (The specifics of how this is accomplished vary based on the RAID organization.) Changes applied externally must also be applied internally to maintain the consistency of the data stored there, so things can get a bit tricky.

Many hard disks today incorporate some form of predictive failure monitoring that the RAID disk controller may support. Predictive failure monitoring involves the drive reporting the occurrence of certain events that tend to precede a complete failure of the disk reading and recording mechanism. A RAID controller that supports predictive failure analysis may take steps to replace a potentially failing disk drive component before an unrecoverable hard failure occurs. Failure of the drive to maintain proper head flying height over the spinning media, for instance, is an event that can be used to reliably predict an impending disk crash.

Hot swap refers to the property of a drive and drive enclosure that allows replacement of a failed disk with a new physical disk without first powering down the system. Many RAID enclosures and subsystems have this feature. You need to be careful with this option, however. If the failed drive is the one with the SCSI terminator, the requirement for terminating the SCSI bus may prevent swapping this drive without powering down the entire NT system.

RAID and Windows 2000

Now that we have discussed the various RAID levels in general, let's get specific and see what high-availability disk options are available on a Windows 2000 machine. We need to consider two types of solutions: hardware RAID implementations and software RAID implementations. The main difference between the two is how the request to a logical device is decomposed into subrequests to physical devices. Windows 2000 software RAID support is extensive, the most extensive built into any operating system we know. But it cannot offer automatic data recovery like hardware RAID can. There is a wide selection of hardware RAID options available, ranging from controller cards to separate RAID enclosures from many different manufacturers. Because new RAID disk products are emerging constantly, only a general account of the configuration issues is possible. Where appropriate, we refer in detail to specific vendor products to illustrate the major points of the discussion.

Hardware RAID

In general, the better hardware RAID solutions supply virtually continuous data availability, making worrying about outages due to disk failures a thing of the past. (Unfortunately, hardware disk failures cause a disappointingly small fraction of the "unplanned" system outages that occur.) Fault tolerance of a hardware RAID configuration is enhanced when the disks themselves are connected across multiple controller interfaces, and there is failover driver software to allow one controller to address the other's disks in the event of a controller failure. One advantage of hardware RAID is that it is independent of the operating system. When disks are locally attached, it is not as easy to move them to a new server when you are upgrading. Hardware implementations are also presumably more powerful, since the hardware controller deals with mapping logical requests into the appropriate RAID disk layout. Usually, the controller in a hardware RAID subsystem includes a fairly powerful processor that handles the computation of parity and the partitioning and distribution of the original request to the right physical disks. But, in practice, this is not a major factor for or against, since plenty of PCs are packed with power, too.

There is a wide range of options for hardware RAID on the Windows 2000 platform. Buying Guide surveys published in popular Windows 2000 trade publications typically identify more than 100 vendors of RAID disk products. These include internal RAID controllers, external RAID enclosures, and independent high/performance storage processors. In this section, we discuss some important features to look for when you are considering hardware RAID disk products for the Windows 2000 and NT platform.

Internal RAID controllers

One of the more economical hardware RAID alternatives involves RAID controller cards or chips that are installed inside your PC in place of your current SCSI adapter. RAID controller cards are available from the leading SCSI adapter card manufacturers such as Adaptec and Mylex, or they may be available directly from your server manufacturer. Plug in the controller card, install the accompanying configuration and driver software, and attach your disks to the card to set up a RAID configuration.

Figure 10-14 shows a typical architecture for a hardware RAID controller. Most RAID controller cards operate as PCI-to-SCSI or PCI-to-Ultra-SCSI bridges. They plug in to the PCI bus of the server and provide some form of SCSI backend connection to attach the disks to. The RAID controller in the figure operates as a PCI-to-SCSI bridge. Disks are attached to the controller through one or more backend SCSI channels. Although up to 15 disks can be connected to a single SCSI channel, configuring a full string of SCSI disks is not usually a good idea. Two or three fast SCSI drives attempting to transfer data concurrently are sufficient to saturate a single SCSI bus. If the controller provides two or more SCSI interfaces, data traffic between the disks and the controller can be distributed over multiple buses. This is necessary when larger arrays are implemented.

Each SCSI channel is managed by a SCSI processor in the form of an ASIC (application-specific integrated circuit) chip. The firmware that implements the various RAID levels is stored in the EEPROM and is loaded by the RAID ASIC when the system is

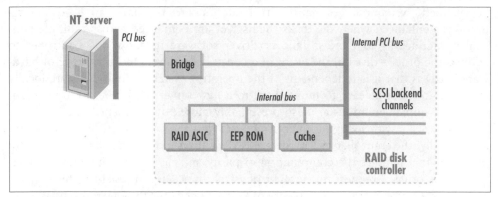

Figure 10-14. A hardware RAID controller card that operates as a PCI-to-SCSI bridge

started. When you purchase a controller card, software is provided that can be used to configure the controller as desired. The configuration is stored in NVRAM (non-volatile RAM) so that it is available to the controller when the system is started.

To increase the performance of the controller, some amount of cache memory is usually available as an option, typically between 32 MB and 128 MB. Both dynamic RAM and battery-backed memory may be available. Battery-backed RAM is especially important to mask the performance of RAID 5 writes, as discussed previously, and large amounts of dynamic cache memory can also speed up read processing. But remember that the Windows 2000 operating system itself caches files in dynamic memory, so configuring large amounts of controller cache memory should not be necessary.

Write caching

A number of controllers also allow the user to select the cache write policy—either write-through or write-back policies can be selected. *Write-through* caches write data to the disk immediately when a write operation arrives. Only after the data has been successfully stored on disk is acknowledgment sent to the operating system. Obviously this is the safest method, but it suffers from slowness, especially with a RAID 4 or 5 configuration, due to the additional physical I/O activity necessary because of the Read-Modify-Write sequence. The host acknowledgment is not sent until all four physical I/O operations necessary to update the data and parity sectors complete. The point of write-through caching is that some applications read back data that they recently wrote to disk. Indexes to large, dynamic databases function in this manner, as do some transaction processing applications that keep track of pending transactions in a scratch-pad disk file. Write-through caching is utterly safe. Although not visible to the average application, most SCSI disks incorporate write-through cache transparently at the very lowest level of the hardware.

The performance-oriented alternative is to use a deferred *write-back* caching policy, which plays it a bit looser in the area of data integrity. Write-back is also known as *lazy write* because disk updates are deferred until some later time, usually based on duration, inactivity at the physical disk, or a threshold value for deferred updates held in the cache. Write-back has a distinct performance advantage: once the data is copied to the cache on the controller, an acknowledgment is immediately sent to the operating system indicating that the operation is complete. Of course, this acknowledgment is a lie—the data involved may actually remain in the disk cache for a long time, depending on the specific implementation. The reason that writes to disk are deferred is to hide from the user the latency inherent in a physical disk operation. What makes it OK for a lazy write cache controller to lie to the application is reliable, battery-backed cache memory and performance.

Write-back caching using nonvolatile cache memory is especially important when a RAID 5 organization is used. The Read-Modify-Write penalty is masked from the Windows 2000 host computer, since the write operation does not have to wait until the four physical disk operations complete. Controllers that offer write-back as an option *must* provide battery backup for the cache memory. If there is a power failure, the controller, having lied to the operating system about what was actually written to disk, is responsible for any updated data pinned in the cache. It must ensure that this data can be retrieved from the cache and stored on disk safely when the system comes back up again.

Windows 2000 file cache

Windows 2000's built-in memory resident disk caching also uses deferred write-back or lazy write by default, which is certainly an endorsement for anyone who is squeamish about breaking the Ten Commandments in this fashion. (The official Microsoft 2000 documentation sometimes uses the term "lazy evaluation.") This means that Windows 2000 is subject to bursts of write I/O activity when there is a *lazy write flush,* and you must configure your caching disk controller to handle this type of bursty behavior. Two counters in the Cache object give an accurate picture of this behavior: Lazy Write Flushes/sec and Lazy Write Pages/sec. The ratio of Lazy Write Flushes/sec to Lazy Write Pages/sec gives you the average size of a write burst. You want to have enough battery-backed cache so that an entire write burst can always fit in cache memory. Remember, too, that RAID 4 or 5 doubles your cache requirements because there needs to be room for both data and parity sectors.

External RAID enclosures

A hardware RAID controller card attached to two or more physical disks is an adequate fault-tolerant disk solution for many smaller installations. When the amount of disk storage you need exceeds the number of hard drives you can install in your server internally, the next step is to consider an external disk array. An external RAID enclosure houses a set of disks and their controller or storage processor in a separate unit. Different vendors use different names to describe this type of hardware RAID architecture, so for lack of a common name we will refer to it simply as a

RAID storage processor or simply a *storage processor*. Storage processors typically attach to the host using one or more SCSI host adapters; some of the more expensive models sport faster fibre channel connections.

Unfortunately, some overlapping and confusing terminology arises with configurable RAID enclosures, which we address here. From the point of view of the RAID hardware controller, two or more *physical* disks are grouped into arrays of disks, which then represent a single *logical* disk. Using the manufacturer's configuration software, you decide how physical disks are grouped into logical disks. The confusion arises because the terms *logical disk* and *physical disk* used here mean something else entirely inside Windows 2000. The storage processor exposes a single logical SCSI address, called a logical unit number (LUN) for each disk array. When attached to your host computer, each logical disk that you have defined to the RAID hardware appears as a single *physical disk* from the standpoint of the Disk Management plug-in. Using Disk Management, you then create *logical disk* partitions on these physical disk representations, and ultimately format them to use either the FAT or NTFS filesystem. Whenever you come across the terms *logical disk* and *physical disk*, you have to identify the context—whether it is from the standpoint of the hardware disk controller or the Windows 2000 Disk Management plug-in—to understand what is being referred to.

Configuring external RAID controllers

Many of the hardware RAID solutions we have looked at provide a bewildering number of configuration options. Some RAID controllers offer a choice of RAID Levels 0, 1, 3, 5, and 0/1, for instance. In addition, it may be possible to select the number of disks in each array, set aside certain disks in reserve status to be used as hot spares, and select the size of the striping unit. As mentioned previously, the RAID level and the stripe unit size should be selected based on the workload characteristics. Hardware RAID controllers typically allow wide variation in the stripe unit size, typically between 8, 16, 32, or 64 KB.

The storage processor connects to the host using *frontend* SCSI (or fibre channel) interfaces. There are usually two or more backend SCSI paths that the physical disks are attached to. The storage processor is responsible for maintaining the mapping of physical disks on the backend into the logical array groups that you configured. For performance reasons, it is important to configure an array *across* SCSI buses. That way, if there is an array operation involving multiple disks, parallel requests do not have to run one at a time across a single, shared SCSI bus. As indicated here, configuring a full-featured external RAID controller for optimal performance can be a daunting prospect for even the most experienced performance analyst.

Performance considerations

It is important to build Windows 2000 logical disk stripe sets *across* LUNs because Windows 2000 disk drivers treat each LUN as a single physical disk. Common SCSI disk mini-driver behavior is to start only one disk I/O at a time to a LUN. Even though there is a whole set of disk drives configured for optimal parallelism behind each LUN, Windows 2000 normally only issues requests one at a time to each array of disks.

For example, Figure 10-15 shows a typical storage processor configuration. The NT host is connected to the storage server using two SCSI buses rated at a maximum transfer rate of 40 MB/sec each. The storage processor's controller module manages 16 SCSI drives that are evenly distributed over 4 internal SCSI buses. The storage controller maintains the configuration of the drives, routes the incoming requests to the appropriate internal bus and target, and provides caching for the data.

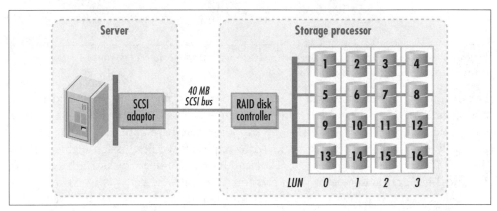

Figure 10-15. A storage processor configured with disk arrays arranged across internal SCSI buses

For maximum concurrency, configure drives 1, 5, 9, and 13 as a single RAID 5 disk array across internal SCSI buses. This arrangement is arguably superior to the more typical disk 1–4 RAID 5 configuration because each disk can be accessed independently. Disks 1 4 all share the same SCSI internal bus, which forces concurrent requests to serialize because only one disk at a time can be actively receiving commands or sending data over the shared bus. Using the Disk Management MMC plug-in, divide each physical disk representation that you see into three or four partitions. Create a stripe set across physical disks as illustrated in Figure 10-16.

To prevent the SCSI-to-SCSI bus that attaches the storage server to the Windows 2000 host from becoming the bottleneck, select the fastest available connection, perhaps a wide Ultra SCSI adapter with a 40 MB/sec maximum transfer rate. (In the final section of this chapter, we look in detail at the performance of an EMC CLARiiON series 2800 storage server. It uses a wide Ultra SCSI interface to the host. The machine we tested had dual internal controllers, which can each be connected to a server using two separate SCSI buses.)

One advantage of the storage processor approach to hardware RAID is support for many more physical disks. Having many disks housed nicely within a single enclosure provides flexibility in the logical disks (LUNs) that you can expose to the host.

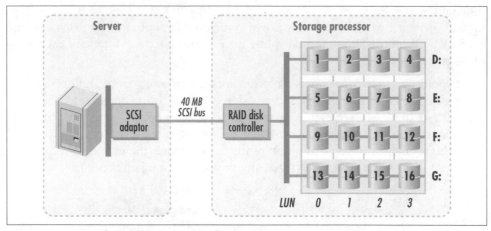

Figure 10-16. The storage processor in Figure 10-15 with stripe set logical volumes across disk array LUNs represented as physical disks

For example, the EMC CLARiiON 2800 supports just about any RAID and combination of RAID disk arrays that you can imagine. The storage enclosure we worked with holds up to 20 physical disks. To support a database application that consists primarily of small, random read and write requests, we first assign eight of those disks to form a 4+4 striped RAID 0/1 logical device. We select disks 1, 2, 5, 6, 9, 10, 13, and 14 to spread this stripe set across four internal SCSI data paths. Next, to support a Microsoft Windows 2000 Internet Information Server (IIS) web server that is dominated by read requests, we use another five disks to form a 4+1 RAID 5 logical device. Then four other disks are used to form a two-way striped RAID 0/1 logical device to support user directories and files. The three remaining disks are designated as hot spares. This way, if one of the disks of the three RAID arrays we configured fails, the EMC CLARiiON can reconstitute the data on the failed device to one of the hot spares.

Of all the different RAID combinations that a premium RAID disk product like the CLARiiON offers, why did we select this particular configuration? We try to distill the decision-making process into a few easy-to-apply configuration guidelines in the following section. To use these guidelines, you must be able to characterize your expected I/O workload in terms of reads, writes, and block sizes. Of course, we discussed how to use the diskperf performance statistics to do that in Chapter 2. One reason for stressing this area is that once you begin loading data into your disk array, configuration decisions made at the very outset are irrevocable. For most disk arrays, once they are loaded with data, the only way to change the RAID configuration without losing data is to back it up and then reload following the change.

Configuration guidelines

In general, when cost is no object, RAID 1 or RAID 0/1 provides the best overall performance. Since striping spreads the I/O load across multiple disks, RAID 0/1 has the best overall performance characteristics of any RAID option. However, if you know ahead of time that the proportion of writes to disk is low, you can fall back on a less expensive RAID 5 configuration. In addition, if there is adequate battery-backed cache memory in the configuration, you may be able to support a moderate amount of disk writes under RAID 5. But even with large amounts of cache, a heavy write-oriented workload is likely to cause performance problems under RAID 5.

You may also be able to define the size of the striping unit. Select a striping unit size that allocates a stripe across multiple physical disks to maximize parallelism. Here, we need to take notice of the filesystem allocation unit. Using FAT, the allocation unit is a function of the partition size, as noted in Tables 9-1 and 9-2. To maximize striping, select a stripe unit size that is equal to the allocation unit divided by the number of data disks:

Striping unit = filesystem allocation unit / # of data disks

For example, if a 32 KB FAT16 allocation unit is defined for a logical volume formatted across a 4+4 RAID 0/1 array, then an 8 KB striping unit ensures that each logical disk I/O request spans all four data disks in the array. Of course, in practice on a critical Windows 2000 server, you should be using NTFS instead of FAT. To ensure the maximum level of parallelism, select a striping unit that causes an NTFS allocation unit to span multiple disks. For example, if the 4+1 RAID 5 array defined previously was formatted with an NTFS partition size of 4096 bytes, a striping unit of 1024 bytes spreads logical I/Os across all the physical disks in the array. This also has the effect of ameliorating much of the impact of the RAID 5 write penalty because updates are always made to the entire array striping unit. The associated parity striping unit has to be changed only once each time an update is performed.

The objective here is to achieve alignment between the request size generated by the filesystem and the stripe size of the block stored on the disk. Studies of the performance of disk arrays with sequential workloads indicate that properly aligning the request size with the allocation size can result in performance improvements between 15% and 20%. The caches that are usually built into the disk arrays further complicate this matter, since they have their own alignment boundaries for their cache blocks. The situation would not be so bad if details on the architecture of these caches were widely available by the manufacturers of the RAID arrays, but unfortunately these details tend to be trade secrets that are hard to get a hold of.

When configuring a storage processor, it is critical to understand its internal architecture and configuration. Knowing the number of internal buses, their connectivity to the storage controllers, and their connectivity to the drives can have a considerable impact on the performance and fault tolerance of the logical volumes constructed. In

Figure 10-15, the storage processor has four internal SCSI buses. It is easy to create a 3+1 RAID Level 5 device using four drives on one of the buses, but that is the worst possible option. Requests to that logical device will be served by one or more physical disks from the same bus. For large requests, the bus will very likely get congested before the drives run out of throughput capacity. Furthermore, if the bus fails for any reason, the entire array will be unavailable and the fault tolerance provided by the parity drive will be useless. A much better approach is to build the array using four drives selected from four different controllers. This choice is fault tolerant of a single drive failure *and* a SCSI bus failure.

Storage processor manufacturers provide software for setting up and monitoring the hardware. In some cases, the software can detect a suboptimal configuration and inform the user. For example, the ArrayGUIde software that comes with the EMC CLARiiON storage processor detects when two or more disks are selected from the same internal bus when you are configuring a logical device. It pops up a message indicating that there is a better choice available. We take a closer look at the ArrayGUIde program in a moment.

SCSI command tag queuing

Cached RAID disk controllers like the CLARiiON and the Symmetrix rely on SCSI command tag queuing for performance. We discussed the rationale for SCSI command tag queuing at the device level in Chapter 8. Command tag queuing is absolutely crucial where RAID disk controllers are concerned. As we have seen, with RAID controllers the arrangement of disks in the array is transparent to Windows 2000 disk driver software. Whether the array is configured for mirroring, striping, or RAID 5 parity, it appears as a single SCSI LUN, which appears to the host as a single physical disk connection. The reality is that what looks like a single disk is actually an array of disks capable of many kinds of overlapped processing. Command tag queuing allows host SCSI driver software to issue multiple requests and let the controller figure out the best way to handle them. In the case of RAID 4 and 5, the underlying disk configuration can handle some requests in parallel. But unless the driver will actually issue multiple requests, no parallel processing will occur.

The Windows 2000 SCSI disk driver is enabled for command tag queuing by default. The SCSI miniport driver parameter DisabledTaggedQueuing has a default value of 1, which means that tagged queuing is not disabled. This is the right setting for almost any SCSI disk device or RAID controller. Depending on the make of your SCSI adapter, there may be additional SCSI miniport driver parameters that need to be specified. For instance, the Adaptec Ultra SCSI adapter we have been testing with has additional parameters named MaximumSGList and NumberOfRequests, which determine the maximum number of requests that the disk driver can have active concurrently. Examine the documentation that comes with your vendor's SCSI adapter card to find out what performance options are available.

Memory in the RAID disk controller is used to cache frequently used data and speed I/O requests. This caching function to speed up disk access (by avoiding it) is entirely transparent to host software. Command queuing allows for overlap in processing cache hits and misses, which require accessing the physical disks behind the controller. Cache that has battery backup is used to mask delays associated with writes. This is especially important when RAID 5 disk arrays are configured due to the well-known performance penalty that impacts RAID 5 writes. The idea is to send all pending requests to the controller and let the controller figure out the most effective way of processing them. Frontend cache hit processing can take place concurrently while background disk operations are running.

For these reasons, support for SCSI command queuing is critical with hardware RAID. Unfortunately, our experience in getting SCSI command tag queuing to work consistently under Windows NT has not been good, and we have learned to expect problems. At the slightest sign of a problem, the Microsoft SCSI driver disables SCSI command tag queuing to safeguard system integrity. This means that if the NT SCSI driver needs to reset the bus for any reason, it reverts to disabled command tag queuing. Knowledgeable SCSI programmers report that SCSI resets can happen quite frequently. One potential problem is when a device such as a tape drive or automated tape library that does not support command tag queuing is present on the same bus as devices that do. The NT SCSI driver has no detailed knowledge of the physical device that corresponds to a SCSI target or LUN. So if one device on the bus cannot support command tag queuing, then, erring on the safe side, NT disables command tag queuing entirely. For this reason, you should try to configure RAID controllers on their own dedicated SCSI bus to avoid problems of this sort. But given the limited number of IRQs available in the now-antiquated PC architecture, this is not always possible to do.

Therefore, we recommend using software RAID 0 striping on top of hardware RAID. This gives you the best of both worlds—the operational simplicity of recovering from disk failures with hardware RAID, and the performance boost from Windows 2000 software disk striping. In the next section, we discuss the Windows 2000 operating system's software support for RAID disk arrays.

Software RAID

Software RAID is a good, low-cost alternative that administrators responsible for smaller server configurations should consider. The software implementation available in Windows 2000 server involves using the built-in operating system support for some of the RAID levels inside Windows 2000. The advantage of the software implementation approach is lower cost, since there is no need to purchase a separate RAID controller. On the other hand, requiring the host to implement RAID imposes some additional load on the processor running the Windows 2000 system. Some of the overhead comes from the parity computation that must be made to support RAID 5 arrays, but most of it is due to the additional processing load from the I/O subsystem when RAID is configured. The operating system must keep track of both the request to the logical disk generated by applications and the resulting requests to the physical disks. Consider a software RAID configuration that uses disk mirroring. For each logical write operation, the operating system must issue two writes to separate physical disks and process the two I/O interrupts that result. In the case of RAID 5, the operating system must process interrupts for all four physical operations necessary to support the Read-Modify-Write sequence required for the data sector and the sector.

In this book, we use the term *software RAID* to refer to the support built into the Windows 2000 operating system Disk Administrator for constructing RAID logical volumes. This support is provided during runtime by the either the fault-tolerant disk driver *FtDisk.sys* for basic disks, or the *dmio.sys* driver for dynamic disks. Both these drivers sit between the I/O manager and the disk driver, as shown in Figure 10-17. Both provide the same RAID support, although with Windows 2000 you cannot create FtDisk-based RAID volumes. However, you can still use those volumes or delete them if you are upgrading from a Windows NT machine. Windows 2000 Professional provides support for spanned volumes and striped volumes. Windows 2000 Server provides support for fault-tolerant volumes through RAID 1 mirrored volumes and RAID 5 volumes.

With the introduction of dynamic disks in Windows 2000, the terminology used to describe advanced volumes changed. Table 10-2 below shows the translation of the terms from the Windows NT terminology to the Windows 2000 terminology.

Table 10-2. Translation between Windows NT and Windows 2000 terminology for RAID support

Windows NT term	Windows 2000 term	RAID level
Volume Set	Spanned Volume	N/A
Stripe Set	Striped Volume	RAID 0
Mirror Set	Mirrored Volume	RAID 1
Stripe Set with Parity	RAID-5 Volume	RAID 5

The two drivers *Ftdisk.sys* and *dmio.sys* maintain information about the organization of each logical volume you create. When a request arrives for processing, they route it to the appropriate physical disk or disks. By sitting in between the I/O manager and the hardware disk driver, the corresponding driver hides the physical organization of a volume from the rest of the operating system. In Windows NT, the fault-tolerant driver was started on your system only when you created a volume set, mirror set, or stripe set using the Disk Manager. Now it always runs as long as you have a basic disk configured on your system.

The new storage management support in Windows 2000 brought the great advantage that most changes to your storage management organization take place immediately, and you do not have to reboot your server. One of those changes that can be done on a live system is recovery from a failed disk that is part of a mirrored or RAID 5 volume. You might also consider installing an extra hard disk in your server that you can keep in reserve, so that you can recover from a hard drive disk failure that much faster. The ideal situation, we believe, is to use software striping on top of hardware RAID to take advantage of the easy recoverability of hardware RAID and the performance benefits of NT's software RAID support.

While the software RAID support in Windows NT is quite good, we do want to caution you that recovery from a disk failure is not quite as easy as in Windows 2000 or in hardware RAID. For one thing, reconstruction of the failed disk is manual, not automatic. Make sure you are least passably familiar with the fault-tolerant disk recovery procedures described in the NT Server Resource Kit before you commit yourself to this option. If your server supports hot swap disks, you may not be forced to shut down Windows NT when you take out the broken drive and replace it with a spare.

Spanned volumes

A spanned volume is a logical volume that results from the concatenation of multiple partitions, usually from multiple disks. Using the Disk Management MMC plug-in, you can combine multiple areas of unallocated disk space or existing volumes into a single logical volume that behaves like one big logical disk. *dmio.sys* hides the physical organization of the volume set, making it appear as a simple sequence of clusters to the disk driver layer above it. Figure 10-17 shows a volume set across three logical disk partitions on three separate physical disks. Notice that each partition in the volume set is a different size. When a logical request to read or write a particular disk cluster arrives, *dmio.sys* determines the actual cluster value based on the volume set grouping and the specific physical disk and offset where the cluster is stored.

After a spanned volume is created using Disk Management, either a FAT or an NTFS filesystem structure can be created on it. One advantage of using the NTFS filesystem with spanned volumes not mentioned earlier is that you can dynamically extend their capacity. For example, suppose you have a spanned volume, consisting of two partitions, that is formatted with NTFS. When the spanned volume is almost full, you can buy another drive and simply append another volume to the spanned volume, without having to reconstruct the filesystem from scratch or restart the machine (unless, of course, you had to add a new drive as opposed to using space on an existing one). If you had used FAT instead, the only option would be to back up and restore the filesystem after the spanned volume is extended.

One cautionary note with spanned volumes is that they have reliability considerations similar to striping. If any disk associated with a spanned volume fails, the logical volume is no longer usable, and it cannot be recovered because there is no fault tolerance.

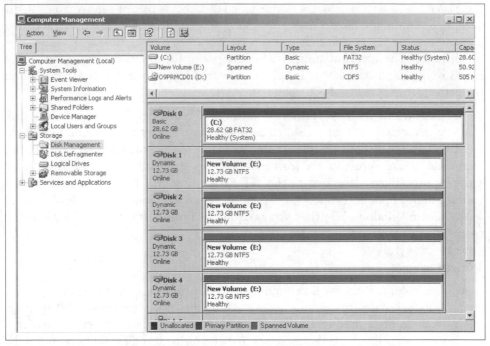

Figure 10-17. Using Disk Management MMC plug-in to define a spanned volume

Striped volumes

Both Windows 2000 Professional and Windows 2000 Server support striped volumes. These are equivalent to RAID 0 striping. Striped volumes are created with the Disk Management plug-in from equally sized areas of unallocated space. Although Windows 2000 sets the maximum number of physical disks you can use in constructing a striped volume to 32, in practice you should not need more than four. Striping works best with large blocks because it effectively transforms requests into parallel I/O. Both Windows NT and Windows 2000 use a stripe unit size of 64 KB. That means that when writing a large stream of data to a striped volume, transitions from one underlying physical disk to the next will take place every 64 KB of data.

NTFS under Windows NT had a maximum allocation size of 4 KB, which did not allow us to benefit from striped volumes as much. NTFS under Windows 2000 provides the following cluster sizes: 512 bytes, 1 KB, 2 KB, 4 KB, 8 KB, 16 KB, 32 KB, and 64 KB, so you have much more flexibility in configuring your volumes. Your objective here is to use the largest cluster size possible while trying to keep the amount of disk space wasted due to internal fragmentation to a minimum. The deciding factor is the average file size of your filesystems. For filesystems that consist primarily of small files, you have to keep the cluster size down towards 4 KB or you will waste a lot of disk space. For filesystems with larger files, you can increase the cluster size towards the maximum of 64 KB to get the most benefit from striping.

Figure 10-18 shows a sample striped volume, which has been assigned the letter E, that uses four physical disks. If you look at the size of drive E: from Explorer, it will indicate that it has a capacity of 51 GB (the combined size of the four underlying disks).

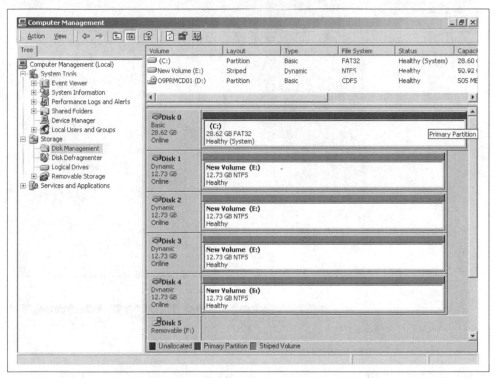

Figure 10-18. Using Disk Management MMC plug-in to define a striped volume

We have already discussed several areas where Windows 2000 resorts to prefetching—in resolving page faults, in caching sequential files, etc. Prefetching transforms individual I/O requests into bulk I/O requests that lend themselves to striping. Of course, this is where the recommendation to run a disk defragmentation program on a regular schedule is important, because disk fragmentation causes logically contiguous file requests to get scrambled around on your hard drives.

To see the difference in performance between spanned and striped volumes, we performed a quick experiment. We constructed two volumes of a total of 8 GB each in capacity. One volume was a striped volume across four disks and the other was a spanned volume across four disks. The spanned volume used an equal area of 2 GB from each disk. We then ran an Iometer workload of sequential read requests, with a request size of 8 KB, utilizing a maximum of 3 GB of the total disk space of each partition. We started the System Monitor and looked at the Disk Transfers/sec counter of the Physical Disk object for each of the four instances used to construct these test volumes. Figure 10-19 shows the results of the test for the striped volume and Figure 10-20 shows the results for the spanned volume.

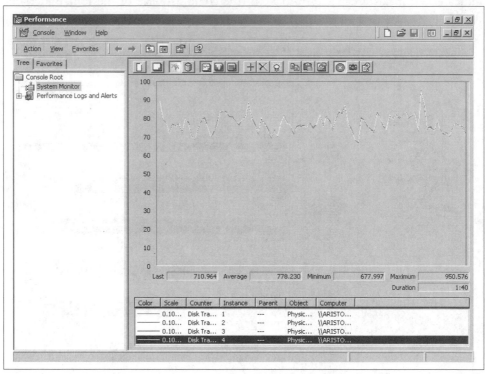

Figure 10-19. Disk Transfers/sec for each physical disk of a striped volume

The lines for each of the four disks overlap completely for the striped case, so you won't be able to tell from the figure which line corresponds to which disk. Since the stripe size is 64 KB and the request size is 8 KB, at the rate of 778 requests/sec it takes only a few milliseconds to go across all four disks and back again. The overall volume is able to process about 3100 requests/sec. For the spanned volume, notice that only one physical disk is active at a time. Since we ran the test against a 3 GB file in the spanned volume, the file should occupy either two or three disks, depending on its location. Since these are sequential requests, the Iometer benchmark simply walks itself across the file until it crosses over to the next physical disk. Around the middle of the figure, the Disk Transfers/sec for one disk goes to zero and the Disk Transfers/sec for another disk goes up. Another interesting observation you can make from this experiment is that a single disk is able to process a much greater number of requests per second than each of the four disks in the striped volume case. This is a result of more effective use of the track buffer on the disk and more effective use of prefetching, as well as less congestion at the controller. Still, the overall

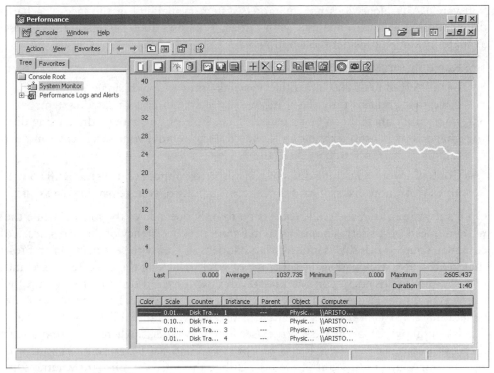

Figure 10-20. Disk Transfers/sec for each physical disk of a spanned volume

throughput of the spanned volume is 2600 requests/sec, as opposed to 3100 requests/sec for the striped volume.

Mirrored volumes

Windows 2000 software mirrored volumes are simple RAID 1 partitions of an equal size across two separate disks. If one disk fails, the surviving mirrored partition is said to be *orphaned*. The status of an orphan partition is indicated as Failed Redundancy in Disk Management. Using the Disk Manager, you can reestablish mirroring by assigning another unallocated area of the same size. The Disk Manager immediately initiates a copy operation to create a mirror image of the existing data on the new partition. During the copy operation, the status of the mirror set is marked Regenerating. During the striped volume regeneration process that we ran, the status of the damaged disk segment remained Regenerating until the entire process completed, when it was marked Healthy again. There was a big sigh of relief when Disk Management flashed the Healthy sign once more. During regeneration, your Windows 2000 server will function normally, although a little more slowly because of the background I/O process.

Software RAID alone does not guarantee system availability in the face of a hard drive failure. Overall, to maintain your critical Windows 2000 Servers in the highest availability status, consider these options:

- Run only server hardware that supports hot swap drives.

- Install Windows 2000 and other systems software on a single standalone C: drive that contains only the Windows 2000 system code, related systems software, and data that can be recreated. Then stockpile a spare C: drive using disk image copy backup technology so that you can rebuild your server environment rapidly in case of a primary disk failure.

- Configure your remaining disks to use mirrored volumes (2 disks) or RAID 5 volumes (3 or more disks). This assures recoverability of your remaining data disks.

On a software mirror, the read requests go to only one side of the mirror, while the write requests go to both sides so as to maintain the consistency of the two sides. To convince yourself that this is indeed what happens, it is easy to set up an Iometer test that generates a workload against the mirror while watching the Disk Reads/sec and Disk Writes/sec using System Monitor on the two physical disks that make up the mirrored volume. Figure 10-21 shows the results of such a test. The workload we are generating consists of 50/50 sequential reads and writes of 8 KB blocks. The dark line is a total overlap of the Disk Writes/sec for the two disks, whereas the thin line is the Disk Reads/sec. The Disk Reads/sec for the second physical disk in the mirror is zero throughout the duration of the test. Unlike the software mirrored volume support of Windows 2000, which sends all read requests to one side of the mirror, some hardware RAID implementations load-balance the read requests across the two sides of the mirror to accomplish better results. If your workload is dominated with large sequential requests, the non-load-balanced approach is better because it makes better use of the track buffers on the disk. For random workloads where the disk buffers have little if any effect, the load-balanced approach of some hardware RAID solutions will provide better results.

RAID 5 volumes

Defining a stripe set with parity provides RAID 5 support. You must have at least three equal-sized partitions defined on three separate disks to set up a stripe set with parity. A parity striping unit is rotated across the partitions involved, resulting in one logical volume with fault tolerance. Stripe sets with parity are supported only on Windows 2000 server versions. RAID 5 volumes tolerate single disk failures; you can replace the failed hard drive and then use Disk Management to recover the missing stripe. There are some limitations in recovering a RAID 5 volume. Disk Management must be able to gain exclusive control of the entire volume. That means if there is a paging file defined on the volume, then you must remove it before you can recover the striped volume. Plan your disk configuration accordingly.

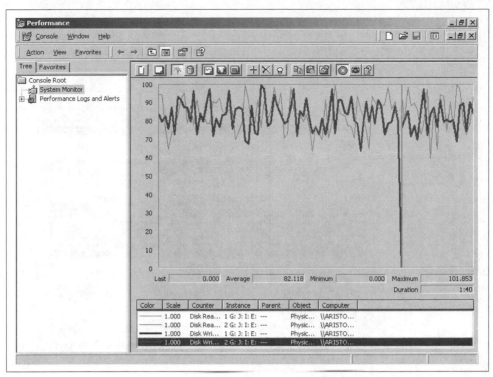

Figure 10-21. Disk Reads/sec and Disk Writes/sec on each of the two disks of a mirrored volume

Figure 10-22 illustrates using the Disk Management plug-in to set up a RAID 5 volume spread across four physical disks. With such a large volume, we have chosen to format it using NTFS. The stripe set consists of four 1 GB partitions, but the equivalent of one 1 GB partition is utilized for parity data. So the net capacity of the logical volume J: is just 3 GB. If performance is not an issue, you can always turn on NTFS compression to recover the disk space you lost to storage for parity data, although currently the cost per bit of disk storage has dropped tremendously.

Notice that the RAID 5 volume in Figure 10-22 has a Healthy status. Like a mirror set, if one of the disks is bad, the status will change to Fault Tolerance Failed. If you replace the failed drive, you can regenerate the data that was lost from the data and parity on the surviving drives in the stripe set. During regeneration of the lost data, the stripe set with parity is in *Regenerating* status. To assist in recovery, avoid defining a paging file on the RAID 5 volume.

From a performance standpoint, Windows 2000 RAID 5 volumes have a number of disadvantages. The major area of concern is the RAID 5 write penalty, which is a serious problem. Microsoft used to recommend that you do not place a paging file on a RAID 5 volume on Windows NT for performance reasons. It is not because of the quantity of write activity to paging files, which is normally low; it is the way that paging writes occur in big bunches, due to periodic dirty page lazy write flushes.

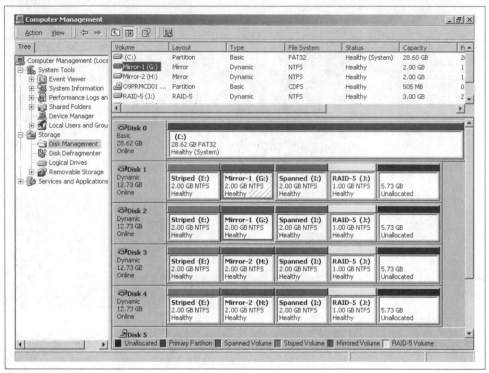

Figure 10-22. Using Disk Management MMC plug-in to define a RAID 5 volume

With software RAID, there is no controller-based disk caching to insulate the host from the RAID write penalty. A big bunch of lazy write flush disk requests takes a long time to process and monopolizes the disk for the duration of the operation. A request for a page to resolve a paging fault from the same paging file can be delayed significantly while that big batch of write requests to the paging file is being serviced. This is where the RAID 5 write penalty does play a role, because writes to the paging file take much longer than usual.

A second concern is the added CPU load from the *dmio.sys* driver that is responsible for extra processing on every operation. The extra load is palpable when parity computations are involved, again associated with a high volume of write operations. As PCs get faster and faster, obviously this becomes less and less significant. A final area of concern is that you are creating a single logical disk, which is a bit less efficient than having three or four disks to handle the workload concurrently. Spreading the disk I/O workload by hand, though, does not usually balance the workload as evenly as striping does automatically. This is probably an advantage of RAID 5 volumes, not a disadvantage.

Because writes are so critical to performance in a RAID 5 volume, it is a good idea to track the quantity of writes being performed. If the rate of write activity is very high, you are definitely better off using a mirrored set of drives instead. Figuring out exactly how the *dmio.sys* driver handles write requests by looking at the System Monitor gets complicated.

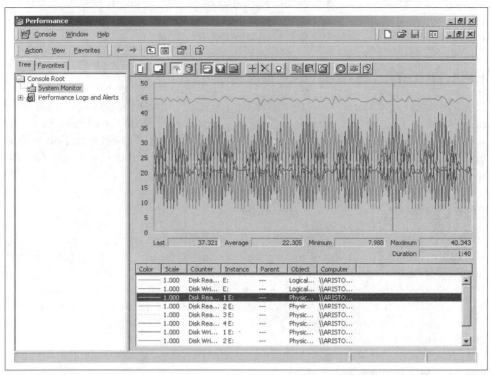

Figure 10-23. Disk Reads/sec and Disk Writes/sec on each of the four disks of a RAID-5 volume and on the logical volume itself

Figure 10-23 is a perfect example of these complications. When first looking at the graph, you may get the impression that you are looking at an oscilloscope that is attached to an analog device, but this is indeed the output of the System Monitor. In this experiment, we used Iometer to generate a 100% sequential writes workload with a request size of 8 KB against a RAID 5 volume that consists of 3+1, 1 GB ranges of disk space. This request size is relatively small compared with the stripe size of the RAID 5 volume, which is 64 KB. While generating this workload, we decided to use the System Monitor to observe the behavior of the software RAID 5 volume. We selected the Disk Reads/sec and Disk Writes/sec counters for the four physical disks (under the Physical Disk object) and for the single logical volume (under the Logical Disk object). The single thin line at the top of the graph is the Disk Writes/sec for the logical volume. The Disk Reads/sec for the logical volume was constantly at 0 throughout the duration of the test, as we expected because of the nature of the workload. The interesting part, although it should not come as a surprise after reading about the Read-Modify-Write cycle of RAID 5 earlier in the chapter, is that Disk Reads/sec for the physical disks is not zero. The oscillation is a result of the request size being relatively small compared to the stripe size, and the sequential nature of the requests. The performance of the RAID 5 volume in this worst-case scenario of a 100% write workload is disappointing. By running a 100% read workload against this same configuration, we got almost 50 times the throughput. This should be a good indication as to when and when not to use RAID 5.

Benchmark Testing

Configuration of disk arrays is almost never a straightforward process because there are so many options and parameters to consider. The most important decisions are whether to use hardware RAID or software RAID, which RAID organization to use, and the length of the stripe unit. It is important to understand the various trade-offs in performance, reliability, and cost that result.

EMC CLARiiON

In this section, we describe a number of experiments we conducted on the EMC CLARiiON disk array under Windows NT to explore the effects of the many configuration options. Note that these tests were run using a Windows NT server as opposed to a Windows 2000 server. Although the results may not be completely representative of what to expect with a Windows 2000 server, the exercise of running these tests and the amount of analysis we add to the results should be well worth the effort of reading through them.

Benchmarking methodology

The experiments evaluate the throughput of an external storage processor configured for RAID Level 0, RAID Level 5, and RAID Level 0/1 logical disks. To explore the advantages and disadvantages of each organization in detail, we applied three types of workloads:

- A workload of only reads
- A workload of only writes
- A mixed workload with a 65:35 read:write ratio.

A matrix showing the scope of our experiments is shown in Figure 10-24.

The extreme 100% read and 100% write cases illustrate RAID performance under theoretical best- or worst-case conditions. The mixed read/write workload is more typical of real workloads and, in fact, is quite representative of many commercial environments. The experiments were run with caching at the storage processor both enabled and disabled, allowing us to hone in on the critical importance of caching for each disk array organization. In this set of experiments, we used a mix of half

Test matrix	100% reads	Mixed read/write	100% writes
RAID 0 striping	✓	✓	✓
RAID 0/1 mirroring and striping	✓	✓	✓
RAID 5	✓	✓	✓

Figure 10-24. Test matrix of the combination of workloads run against the server

random, half sequential I/O activity. Since we were measuring disk subsystem throughput, we also investigated performance for a range of block sizes, from 512 bytes up to 512 kilobytes.

Reaching steady state

A critical Iometer configuration parameter to use when testing cached disk controllers is the Ramp Up Time. With a cached disk controller, some warm-up time is usually required to allow the working set to accumulate in memory. At the beginning when the cache is cold-started, read hit ratios tend to be artificially low. They rise steadily as the working set becomes established, and then level off. Normally, you should set the Ramp Up Time to run for a while before you begin measuring to mitigate these cache loading effects.

In general, in any benchmark or computer simulation, you want to wait until whatever initialization effects begin to settle down and the system reaches a *steady state* before keeping track of any measurements. Until these initialization effects dissipate, the benchmark is not repeatable, which of course is the whole idea of a benchmark to begin with.

The amount of time that you need to wait increases when the experiment has lots of randomly selected values or when caching is enabled. With Iometer, for example, when you set the workload to some proportion of random I/Os, the program invokes a random number generator. These need to generate a large number of values before the distribution of the requests generated begins to match the implied theoretical distribution. When you are running with a purely random read workload, on the other hand, you do not have to worry so much about cache loading effects. Random read activity spread across a wide enough area over the disk makes caching almost totally ineffective from beginning to end.

For writes, there is another cache loading effect. A lazy write disk cache can be viewed as having two asynchronous processes, as illustrated in Figure 10-25. Visualize a host process that deposits data in the cache. As soon as the data is copied to the battery-backed cache, the PC application is notified that the write was successful. Ultimately, the cache is responsible for flushing this data to disk. This is accomplished through a separate, asynchronous lazy write task that writes older data to disk. The host connects to the cache across a high-speed SCSI (or fibre channel) link. Destaging to disk involves performing time-consuming disk I/O. It is possible for a host process to pour write data into the cache at SCSI bus speeds faster than the controller can empty it to disk. When this happens, the cache begins to back up with data that has not yet been written to disk. Finally, when the cache becomes full, something has to give.

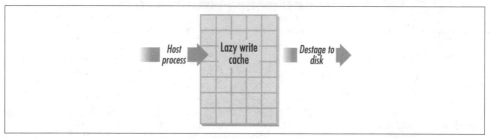

Figure 10-25. Lazy write caching is viewed as two separate processes

What normally gives is the ability to mask the disk latency. At this point, the host process can deposit new data in the cache only as fast as the controller can pull older data out of it. When benchmark testing a caching controller with deferred write-back (lazy write) caching, you will see this behavior as two distinct phases. In the first phase, the cache is not yet full and writes benefit fully. In the second phase, the cache is full and writes slow down to disk speed. It is certainly worth measuring performance in both stages, because Phase 2 is worst-case behavior. In real life, you may not be running any workloads that are write-intensive enough to ever get to Phase 2. How long Phase 1 lasts in a benchmark is a function of the cache size, the I/O rate and block size, and the difference between the throughput capability of the host process and the controller's destaging capability. We are almost always interested in Phase 2 worst-case performance, just in case.

The only way to determine precisely how long to set the Ramp Up Time in Iometer is by monitoring your tests. Watch the Iometer Results display while a test is running. If you see values like MB/sec or average response time varying greatly from one measurement interval to the next, you are not yet at steady state! In the EMC Symmetrix with an 4 GB cache memory and a write threshold of 80%, you can expect to wait a long time. Some storage processors have powerful internal processors and disks spread across multiple internal SCSI buses. You may never be able to drive a write load from your Windows 2000 system faster than it can destage data to disk. You will reach 100% processor utilization before you ever see Phase 2 behavior.

Hardware RAID configuration options

Our experiments were conducted using an EMC CLARiiON 2800 disk array storage system, which is one of the more popular RAID storage processors for Windows NT,

Windows 2000, and Unix systems. This particular unit contains 20 Seagate disk drives and two internal storage control processors, each powered by PowerPC 32-bit RISC processors. In addition, it is equipped with dual power supplies and a battery backup unit. Each storage processor consisted of a printed circuit board with four SIMM memory modules that provided a total of 64 MB of memory. Of this, 4 MB is used by the control processor itself for system buffers and the rest is available for read and write caching as configured by the user. The storage processor manages five internal SCSI-2 buses, each of which has four drives attached to it. An NT Server machine is attached to an individual storage processor array through a SCSI-2 adapter using a wide SCSI-2 differential bus. We only had one SCSI adapter to attach the CLARiiON to on our NT system, but dual SCSI connections are standard (and highly recommended for redundancy!).

In the CLARiiON benchmarks we report on here, we did not format or create a file-system on any of the logical volumes. Since we are interested only in the relative performance of the various RAID organizations, we want to avoid the additional overhead of maintaining a filesystem on the volume. In particular, we also bypass the file caching that NT normally performs on behalf of all disk I/O. We first run the three workloads against the disk array with caching at the storage processor turned off. Disabling caching will give us an idea of the performance of just the hardware itself. Then, enabling the cache and running the experiments again, we can clearly see the effect of controller cache on the various workloads.

This disk array was originally available through Data General, which provided the ArrayGUIde software for management and configuration of the disk arrays. Data General has since been acquired by EMC, and different software tools are available for this purpose. Figure 10-26 shows the Equipment View of the ArrayGUIde software. From here you can view the current configuration and change it by simply clicking on the corresponding component in the figure. The Cache button in the toolbar is used to enable or disable caching, as well as to set the amount of cache on the storage processors used for read requests and the battery-backed portion used to cache write requests. For high availability, the CLARiiON mirrors update data in both storage processor caches.

The Summary View, shown in Figure 10-27, is the screen for setting up array group logical disks. Each of the physical disks installed is represented by a rectangle in the center of the screen. Alphanumeric codes inside the disk icons identify the internal SCSI bus and unit number for each disk. Each of the five internal SCSI buses is identified by a letter (A–E), and each of the four disks on each bus is identified by a single digit (0–3). So, for example, disk B2 is the third disk on the second SCSI bus.

Icons on the right side of the Summary View represent the array group logical volumes that are exported to the host. Each one is assigned a numeric digit that corresponds to the SCSI LUN. The LUN is also displayed next to the physical disks that

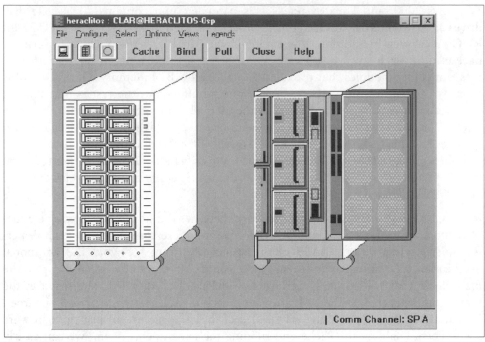

Figure 10-26. ArrayGUIde Equipment View

are members of the array group. A label on the array group icon shows which RAID organization you have selected. Configuring array group logical volumes is as simple as clicking on a number of available physical disks and assigning a specific RAID organization to them. For instance, Logical Volume 01 is a four-way striped RAID 0 array group consisting of physical disks A1, B1, C1, and D1. Notice that the disks were selected from different internal buses so that the load is evenly distributed among the buses. Volume 00 is a RAID 1/0 (Data General's terminology) striped and mirrored array across eight disks. Each LUN we defined in this fashion appears to Windows NT as a single large physical disk. In this set of experiments, we did not attempt to use software RAID on top of Data General's hardware RAID.

RAID Level 0 performance

We used the ArrayGUIde software to build a RAID Level 0 disk array using four disks. The stripe size was set to 64 sectors or 32 KB. Table 10-3 shows the resulting measurements. For each I/O block size, we report the transfer rate (counter Disk Bytes/sec from the Physical Disk object) and the response time per request (counter Avg. Disk sec/transfer from the Physical Disk object). The read workload consists of 100% read requests, the mixed consists of 65% read requests, and the write workload consists of 100% write requests.

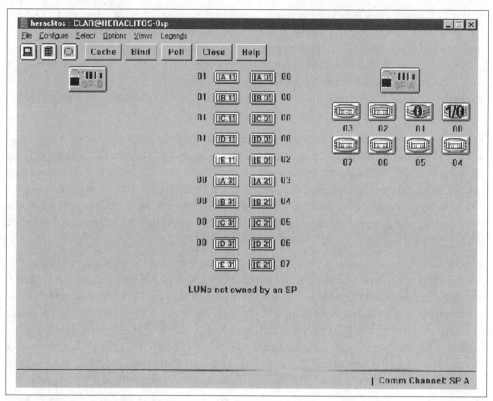

Figure 10-27. ArrayGUIde Summary View

Table 10-3. RAID 0 with no cache

Request Size	Reads		Mixed		Writes	
	MB/sec	msec	MB/sec	msec	MB/sec	msec
512	0.15	7	0.12	9	0.09	11
1 KB	0.30	7	0.23	9	0.18	11
2 KB	0.55	7	0.46	9	0.36	11
4 KB	1.01	8	0.84	10	0.69	12
8 KB	1.72	10	1.47	11	1.29	13
16 KB	2.67	12	2.42	13	2.25	15
32 KB	3.97	16	3.84	17	3.72	18
64 KB	6.92	19	6.57	20	6.14	21
128 KB	9.23	29	8.12	32	7.35	36
256 KB	11.61	45	9.74	54	7.97	66

Looking at these measurements, you will notice that while the disks in the CLARiiON are capable of high performance, there is little evidence of it here. Part of the problem is that NT sends only one SCSI read or write command at a time to the array. You are apt to be very disappointed in the I/O throughput from an expensive external RAID subsystem like the CLARiiON if you do not succeed in getting SCSI command tag queuing to run and do not implement software RAID support on top of hardware RAID to get more concurrent I/O traffic going. Just for comparison purposes, you might have noticed we were able to use Iometer to push 36 MB/sec to a single physical ATA disk using 32 K blocks in another experiment.

Transfer rates do increase dramatically as the size of the request grows. The disks used in this machine are rated at being able to transfer at 10–15 MB/sec, depending on which track the data is located on. But for the small block request sizes you expect from normal Windows NT applications, the transfer rate is very low. As we discussed previously, one reason is that for small request sizes, the overhead of the SCSI bus (eight phases for each command) is very high relative to the size of the data that is transferred.

We notice that as the fraction of write requests in the workload *increases*, the throughput *decreases*. Caching at the operating system level is disabled by Iometer, and we disabled caching at the storage processor in this first set of runs. So what we are seeing is native disk performance. Typically, disks are a little slower to write data than they are to read it. Seeking is more precise, for instance, so it takes a little longer. The extra time and care taken on writes is to ensure that the disk is later able to read back the data recorded there. Another reason that reads are a little faster than writes is the cache on board the disks. Since, on average, half of the requests are sequential, prefetching from the disk buffer on reads does reduce the response time for reads considerably.

The benefit of striping is not evident until we go from 32 KB to 64 KB. With the 32 KB striping units we defined, requests at 64 K and above finally get multiple disks going. You will notice a big increase in throughput with only a modest increase in average disk response time. The disks have a speed rated at between 10 and 15 MB/sec. Therefore, the data transfer component for a 64 K block is in the range of 4.4–6.5 ms. The 3 ms increase in disk response time between 32 KB and 64 KB can be accounted for almost completely by the longer time it takes to transfer the larger blocks. Beyond 64 KB, we are able to increase the throughput significantly, but at a significant cost in overall average disk response time.

Figure 10-28 shows these results. Reads outperform writes consistently across all block sizes, and there is a sharp increase in throughput when striping across multiple disks kicks in.

Now let's enable caching and see its effect on the performance of the RAID 0 array. See Table 10-4. The 100% read workload shows practically identical results, with response times about the same as before. The writes-only workload, on the other hand, shows considerable improvement in performance. The writes now hit the battery-backed cache on board the storage processor, which improves their apparent

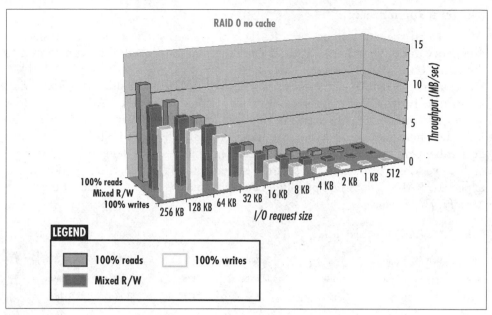

Figure 10-28. Throughput of a four-disk stripe set as a function of I/O block size

response time. The response time of small block write requests is especially good at 2 ms at 4 KB and just 8 ms at 32 KB. The mixed workload shows performance in between the other two workloads, as expected. As the request size increases, the small cache becomes less effective. That causes more write traffic to hit the disk, which is why the throughput of the writes workload ultimately levels off. Overall, though, throughput of writes is greatly enhanced with cache enabled. We analyze the impact of write caching in more detail when we review the RAID 5 results.

Table 10-4. RAID 0 with cache

Request size	Reads		Mixed		Writes	
	MB/sec	msec	MB/sec	msec	MB/sec	msec
512	0.15	7	0.16	7	0.59	2
1 KB	0.30	7	0.32	7	1.11	2
2 KB	0.55	8	0.61	8	1.99	2
4 KB	1.01	9	1.13	8	3.25	2
8 KB	1.53	11	1.87	10	4.90	3
16 KB	2.59	13	2.87	13	6.63	5
32 KB	4.29	15	4.13	19	8.04	8
64 KB	6.62	20	6.19	23	8.93	15
128 KB	9.12	29	7.67	36	9.56	27
256 KB	12.61	41	9.74	56	9.77	54

RAID Level 5 performance

We repeated the experiments on a RAID 5 array consisting of four data disks and one parity disk. We wanted a RAID 5 configuration that was directly comparable to the RAID 0 array used initially. Table 10-5 shows the results with caching disabled. First, we see that RAID 5 performs worse than RAID 0 on both reads and writes across the board. This supports our original contention that RAID 5 should be viewed as a reliability enhancement, not a performance one. The measurements do indicate where striping kicks in; again, between 32 KB and 64 KB blocks, there is noticeable performance improvement based on multiple disks being used. More generally, we observe that response time suffers most for the write workload. As expected, RAID 5 does not provide good performance for writes due to the Read-Modify-Write cycle.

Table 10-5. RAID 5 with no cache

Request size	Reads		Mixed		Writes	
	MB/sec	msec	MB/sec	msec	MB/sec	msec
512	0.09	11	0.09	11	0.06	16
1 KB	0.19	11	0.18	11	1.13	16
2 KB	0.36	11	0.35	12	0.24	17
4 KB	0.64	13	0.63	13	0.43	19
8 KB	1.09	15	1.08	15	0.70	24
16 KB	1.65	20	1.65	20	1.05	31
32 KB	3.02	21	3.11	21	2.15	31
64 KB	5.34	24	5.30	25	3.82	34
128 KB	6.28	42	6.34	42	4.14	63
256 KB	7.21	74	7.28	73	4.56	115

Now let's enable the cache and run the experiments again. The results are shown in Table 10-6. The most noticeable observation is that these results are virtually identical to the results from RAID 0 with cache, shown in Table 10-4. Talk about a repeatable benchmark! These results demonstrate the overriding importance of disk caching. The write-back cache successfully masks the write performance penalty so evident in the previous results. As with RAID 0 striping, despite the improvement brought on by caching, the throughput of the 100% writes workload does not reach that of the reads workload for large request sizes. For larger request sizes, the cache overflows, requiring more frequent lazy write cache flushes.

Table 10-6. RAID 5 with cache

Request size	Reads		Mixed		Writes	
	MB/sec	msec	MB/sec	msec	MB/sec	msec
512	0.15	7	0.16	7	0.59	2
1 KB	0.30	7	0.32	7	1.11	2
2 KB	0.55	8	0.61	8	1.99	2
4 KB	1.01	9	1.13	8	3.25	2
8 KB	1.53	11	1.87	10	4.90	3
16 KB	2.59	13	2.87	13	6.63	5
32 KB	4.29	15	4.13	19	8.04	8
64 KB	6.62	20	6.19	23	8.93	15
128 KB	9.12	29	7.67	36	9.56	27
256 KB	12.61	41	9.74	56	9.77	54

Figure 10-29 is a chart of the results from Table 10-6. The performance benefit of deferred write-back cache is very evident in this picture. For small block write requests, cache is extremely effective. It not only masks the RAID 5 write performance penalty, but it allows small block writes to outperform read requests. The benefit that the cache confers eventually tails off at high throughput levels when the cache overflows.

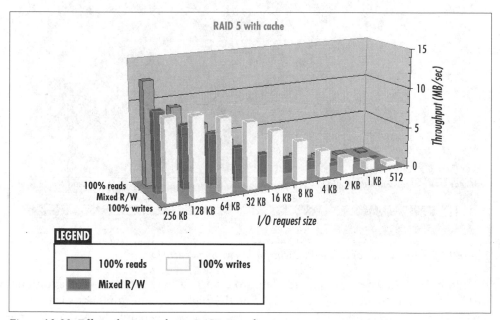

Figure 10-29. Effect of write cache on RAID 5 performance

The deferred write-back cache on the CLARiiON is managed based on low and high memory utilization thresholds, which are percentages of the total cache capacity. When the amount of deferred write data in the cache exceeds the high threshold, older data in the cache is flushed to the disk until the low threshold is reached. A lazy write cache flush unleashes a large burst of write activity to physical disk. The cache effectively masks this behavior from the host application—until there is a read miss that needs to access a physical disk while the flush is in progress. The interaction of lazy write cache flushes with ordinary reads is observed directly during mixed workloads. Figure 10-30 shows the Performance Monitor Avg. Disk sec/Transfer and Disk Bytes/sec counters while the mixed read/write workload is applied to the RAID 5 array. Periodically, there is a spike in the response time and a corresponding decrease in the throughput of the array. This is caused by the additional load imposed on the disks internally when the cache is flushed. Reducing the request size by half causes the length of time between the spikes to almost double, as predicted. Since the request size is half the previous one, it takes twice as long for the cache to reach its high threshold.

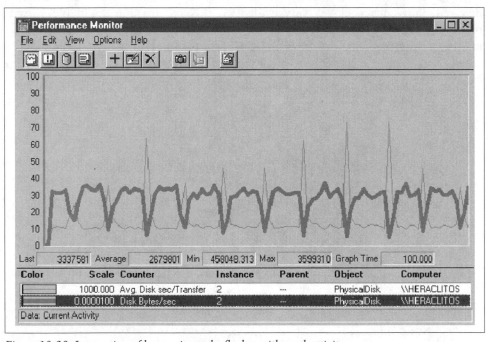

Figure 10-30. Interaction of lazy write cache flushes with read activity

In summary, RAID 5 arrays provide fault tolerance at very low cost (one additional disk). The main disadvantage of RAID 5 is the high response time associated with small write requests: the RAID 5 write performance penalty. Large nonvolatile caches allow you to avoid the performance penalty paid by small write requests—up to a point—but do add to the overall cost and complexity of a RAID subsystem.

RAID Level 0/1 performance

In this last set of benchmark tests, we repeated the experiments on a RAID 0/1 disk array with a total of eight disks. The stripe size is set to 32 KB, as before, and striping is done across four disks in the array, with mirroring to the other four disks. Table 10-7 shows the results with caching disabled. The performance of the reads and the mixed workload are almost identical with those of the RAID 0 disk array. Writes are a bit slower in the RAID 0/1 array due to the fact that for every write, two copies need to be made. The reduction in the performance is between 10% and 20%.

Table 10-7. RAID 0/1 with no cache

Request size	Reads		Mixed		Writes	
	MB/sec	msec	MB/sec	msec	MB/sec	msec
512	0.15	7	0.11	9	0.09	12
1 KB	0.30	7	0.23	9	0.17	12
2 KB	0.57	7	0.44	9	0.34	12
4 KB	1.03	8	0.80	10	0.64	13
8 KB	1.73	9	1.42	11	1.18	14
16 KB	2.64	12	2.34	14	2.01	16
32 KB	3.99	16	3.64	18	3.25	20
64 KB	6.42	20	5.97	22	5.30	25
128 KB	8.39	31	6.98	38	5.69	46
256 KB	10.32	51	8.35	60	6.30	83

Turning caching on has a similar effect on the RAID 0/1 array as it did in the previous instances. See Table 10-8. The 100% write workload experiences considerable improvement in performance. The improvement in write response time associated with disk striping kicking in between 32 KB and 64 KB is not as pronounced with RAID 0/1. A 64 KB request requires four separate disks—two data disks and two mirrored disks—to be active concurrently. It appears that that begins to stress the capacity of the EMC CLARiiON used in our test configuration.

Table 10-8. RAID 0/1 with cache

Request size	Reads		Mixed		Writes	
	MB/sec	msec	MB/sec	msec	MB/sec	msec
512	0.15	7	0.18	6	0.50	2
1 KB	0.29	7	0.31	6	0.87	2
2 KB	0.52	8	0.61	6	1.60	2
4 KB	0.92	9	1.06	7	2.84	3
8 KB	1.54	11	1.69	10	4.33	4
16 KB	2.54	13	1.65	13	5.92	5

Table 10-8. RAID 0/1 with cache (continued)

Request size	Reads		Mixed		Writes	
	MB/sec	msec	MB/sec	msec	MB/sec	msec
32 KB	4.14	16	2.73	19	7.24	9
64 KB	6.23	21	4.06	26	8.18	16
128 KB	8.30	33	5.69	36	8.77	30
256 KB	11.76	44	7.51	56	8.85	61

Comparing its performance against the other two organizations, we find that RAID 0/1 array falls somewhere in between RAID 0 (no redundancy) and RAID 5. Without cache, RAID 0/1 outperforms RAID 5. But with cache, RAID 0/1 striping and mirroring reaches the point where writes overrun the cache a little bit sooner than RAID 5. The throughput for the 100% write workload is slightly higher than the RAID 5 array, but slightly lower than the RAID 0 array. A RAID 0/1 array does not have a Read-Modify-Write performance penalty on writes, which explains why it is faster than the RAID 5 array. The fact that two copies of the data must be written translates into lower performance than the nonredundant RAID 0 array.

Disk Arrays Based on IDE Drives

Up until very recently, building a disk array on your Windows server implied that you had to use either a software- or hardware-based solution that utilized SCSI drives. Now there is an alternative to the SCSI approach. A couple of manufacturers, including 3ware and Promise Technology, have introduced hardware RAID controllers that utilize IDE drives. Clearly, the main benefit of such a solution is reduction in the cost of implementing a RAID storage system, although what immediately pops to mind is that you are trading off performance for cost. Actually, a number of studies by the manufacturers of these controllers and by independent parties such as Microsoft (*http://research.microsoft.com/scripts/pubs/view.asp?TR_ID=MSR-TR-2000-55*) are indicating that in many cases these controllers can actually provide equivalent if not better performance than the more expensive SCSI-based solutions.

You are probably wondering how is that possible. After all, the IDE interface has certain limitations, such as lack of support for tagged-command queuing and a two-device maximum per channel, that make it unsuitable for putting together multidisk storage system configurations. The secret lies in intelligence built into the controller using ASIC chips that resolves some of the limitations of the IDE interface and also of the SCSI channel. The folks at 3ware were kind enough to let us use and test their controller, so we focus this section on their product. Of course, our objective is simply to expose you to this new technology and share our experiences without endorsing one specific product.

3ware currently offers two product lines: the 5000 and 6000 series controllers. In each series, there are three models to choose from, depending on whether you want to attach two, four, or eight drives to the controller. The recently released 6000 series offers better performance, support for RAID 10 on the four- or eight-port version in addition to support for RAID 0 and RAID 1, and support for hot swaps and hot spares. In terms of performance, the manufacturer's literature claims that you can obtain more than 100 MB/sec of throughput for sustained reads and more than 84 MB/sec for sustained writes. The various RAID configurations can be set up with the very easy-to-use BIOS tool, or you have the alternative of configuring the drives on the controller as a JBOD (just a bunch of disks) and then using the software RAID support in Windows 2000 server for constructing RAID configurations.

IDE-based controllers are able to achieve impressive results at a low cost by resolving some of the limitations of their two predecessor interfaces, IDE and SCSI. Figure 10-31 shows a diagram of the architecture of the 3ware controller. Refer back to this figure as we go through each of the main features of this controller and describe how they are able to overcome the limitations of the other interfaces.

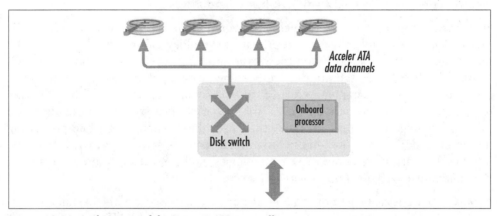

Figure 10-31. Architecture of the 3ware RAID controller

One limitation of the SCSI channel is its shared bus architecture. Whenever a shared medium is used in interconnecting devices, you need to introduce a mechanism for arbitrating access to that shared medium. For the SCSI channel, we described the various phases involved in executing a command and the resulting latency in the processing time of the command. Despite the continuous increases in the data transfer rate of the channel, which has reached a current maximum of 160 MB/sec, the latency remains the same, reducing the effective maximum transfer rate to a much lower value. But much as networking technology moved from a shared medium architecture to a switched architecture, the 3ware controller makes use of what they call DiskSwitch technology to bring switching to the IDE drive channel. Each IDE channel has a dedicated port to the controller called an AccelerATA data channel.

This ensures that as long as the drive is available to process a command, there is a channel available for transferring data in and out of the drive. The controller also includes an on-board processor that schedules requests against each of the data channels to ensure that the disks are processing requests at their full capacity without wasting time for arbitrating access to a shared bus. The on-board processor also offloads work from the server's CPU in supporting logical RAID configurations.

The use of a switch along with an on-board processor for the intelligent scheduling of requests resolves the lack of support for tagged-command queuing in the IDE interface. Since the IDE interface cannot queue up and optimize the processing of multiple requests, the proprietary controller manages this process. The requests are queued at the controller, which feeds them in an optimized order to each of the disks over their corresponding dedicated channel. You would think that all this intelligence at the controller must bring its price way up. But actually this controller does not have to provide the breadth of functionality of the SCSI interface, making it a lot cheaper than most SCSI RAID controllers. The SCSI interface is a general-purpose interface that works with hard drives, tape drives, tape libraries, and jukeboxes; this controller needs to deal only with IDE-based hard drives.

To further optimize the performance of mirrored organizations such as RAID 1 and RAID 10, the controller uses a proprietary technology called TwinStor. After the hardware is installed properly on the server and a mirrored organization is created using the BIOS utility, the firmware does some profiling of the disk drives to determine drive-specific parameters related to the layout of the disks. This includes parameters such as the amount of data stored on each track, zoning information, and head switching times. The scheduler then uses these parameters while processing requests to determine how to best assign read requests across the two sides of the mirror. To learn more about these technologies, you can get the white papers from the company's web site, *http://www.3ware.com*.

One last but critical benefit of this architecture is the low cost of the overall configuration. The controller itself costs a little less than most SCSI RAID controllers with similar functionality. The majority of the cost reduction, though, comes from the drives. The entire hard drive market consists of 85% IDE drive sales and 15% SCSI and fibre channel sales. The fact that the majority of the drives sold are IDE causes their production cost and thereby their price to be much lower than that of SCSI, even though the drive is the same. Many hard drive manufacturers are using the same head-disk assembly for both their SCSI and IDE drives and simply attach the appropriate disk controller.

To see the 3ware 6400 controller in action, we run a sequence of experiments with Iometer. The 6400 controller includes dedicated ports for four IDE drives. Since we wanted to keep the cost of our configuration down, we bought four Samsung SV1363 IDE drives for the bargain price of $75 each. By the time you read this, you can probably buy them a lot cheaper than that. This particular drive has a capacity of 13.6 GB, a spindle speed of 5400 RPM, an average seek time of 9.5 msec, a 66 MB Ultra DMA interface, and a 512 KB track buffer. There are better-performing IDE drives on the market, but our objective was to see what kind of performance we could obtain from a very low-cost configuration.

We ran a large number of experiments to try to understand the performance characteristics of the controller with these drives under different workloads. Our first test was against a RAID 0 configuration across four drives. We built the volume using the BIOS utility, making it visible to the Disk Management plug-in of Windows 2000 as a single logical drive. Unlike the software RAID available with Windows 2000, the hardware RAID configuration forces you to use the entire disks in forming the logical drive as opposed to using portions from each physical disk. This is common among hardware RAID controllers. Once Windows 2000 was up, we created a 2 GB volume on the logical disk using the NTFS filesystem with a 4 KB cluster size. We then ran various tests on the disk, using Iometer, for request sizes of 512 bytes, 4 KB, 16 KB, and 32 KB, for each of the four combinations of reads versus writes and sequential versus random requests. Table 10-9 summarizes the results of this test. In each column of results, we show two numbers: the first is the operations per second and the second is the data transfer rate in MB/sec. For the sequential workloads, the numbers are fairly high. The low numbers for random reads are the weak spot of any disk storage system configuration. As long as there are long mechanical delays involved in processing each request, you are bound by the speed of the disk. The random writes are better than reads because of the lazy write feature that you can optionally activate when configuring the striped volume.

Table 10-9. Benchmark results for the software RAID 0 configuration

	Reads		Writes	
	Sequential	Random	Sequential	Random
512	4850/2.4	112/0.05	4830/2.4	400/0.20
4 KB	2514/9.8	110/0.4	3520/14	380/1.5
16 KB	1116/17	100/1.57	1637/26	307/15
32 KB	637/20	92/2.9	1061/33	230/7

This table does not tell the full story, though. The one way of improving the effective processing rate of random read requests is through optimization of the request stream and through increased concurrency. This is made possible by the DiskSwitch technology in this particular controller, and this is where its true capabilities become evident. We used the Number of Outstanding I/Os property of Iometer to investigate the performance of the disk array in processing random reads as we increased the concurrency level. Figure 10-32 shows the results of the case where we are generating 8 KB random read requests against this volume. Clearly, the controller is able to improve the overall throughput considerably, even for random requests, when the workload is heavier. As you remember, the IDE interface does not allow multiple concurrent requests to be sent to a target device, but this controller is able to overcome this limitation through the switching architecture and the dedicated channel to each of the attached devices.

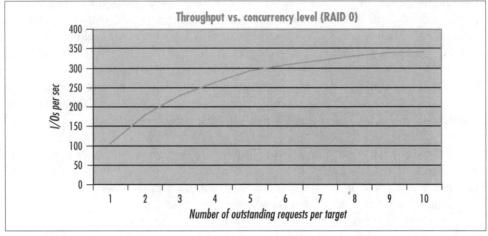

Figure 10-32. Throughput of a RAID 0 configuration in I/Os per second

To see if there was considerable difference between the software and the hardware RAID configuration, we broke up this volume and configured the four disks in a JBOD configuration. We then used the Windows 2000 support for RAID 0 and repeated our tests. We got almost identical results for all the tests, so we are not presenting the results here. We also monitored the CPU utilization to see if there was a difference between the hardware and software configuration, but again we did not detect one. Due to the use of DMA modes in the transfer of the data, the CPU utilization never exceeded 40%, even in the workloads for the small block sizes and with the Iometer software running on the server itself.

Next, we built a RAID 1 configuration using two disks and repeated the suite of experiments on this disk array. The results are shown in Table 10-10 and Figure 10-33. For the sequential reads and random reads workloads, the response of the mirrored configuration was very similar to that of the striped configuration. In the case of the random reads, the configuration was bound by the performance of the individual disks, so the configuration of the array had no impact. The performance of the mirrored configuration was slower for the sequential and especially for the random writes workloads. In the case of a write, the array needed to generate a write request against each side of the mirror, so the response of each write request was equal to the response of the disk that experienced the most latency in processing the individual requests.

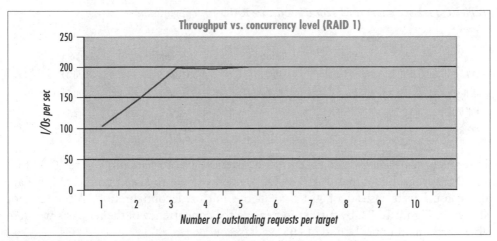

Figure 10-33. Throughput of a RAID 1 configuration in I/Os per second

Table 10-10. Benchmark results for the software RAID 1 configuration

	Reads		Writes	
	Sequential	Random	Sequential	Random
512	4868/2.4	104/0.05	3220/1.6	80/0.04
4 KB	3100/12.1	104/0.4	2846/11.1	80/0.32
16 KB	1389/21.7	97/1.5	1230/19	72/1.1
32 KB	700/22	91/2.8	682/21	68/2.1

As in the previous configuration, these tests allow us to evaluate the performance impact of the different RAID configurations, but these are not the numbers you will get in a realistic workload environment. The subsystem is able to perform better when there is more concurrency in the workload, as there would be if the array were hosting a transaction-oriented database server, for example.

The last configuration we tested was a RAID 10 configuration. The results are shown in Table 10-11. This configuration is not available through the software RAID support of Windows 2000, although you could implement it through a combination of hardware and software RAID by building two RAID 0 configurations at the hardware level and then mirroring the two resulting logical drives through the software RAID support. As RAID 10 is a combination of RAID 0 and RAID 1, it combines the benefits of each of the two RAID configurations. It provides better performance for random writes than the plain mirrored configuration, and provides the fault tolerance of RAID 0.

Table 10-11. Benchmark results for the software RAID 10 configuration

	Reads		Writes	
	Sequential	Random	Sequential	Random
512	4868/2.4	110/0.05	3150/1.5	182/0.09
4K B	2650/10.4	106/0.4	2580/10	166/0.65
16K B	1444/22.5	97/1.5	1207/19	133/2.1
32K B	924/29	90/2.8	669/21	104/3.2

In terms of scalability with respect to concurrency, we can see from Figure 10-34 that RAID 10 scales better than RAID 1. Of course, we have to keep in mind that we are using four disks instead of just two in the mirrored configuration. Although not shown in Figure 10-34, by further increasing the concurrency of the requests we were able to reach an upper bound of 465 reads/sec.

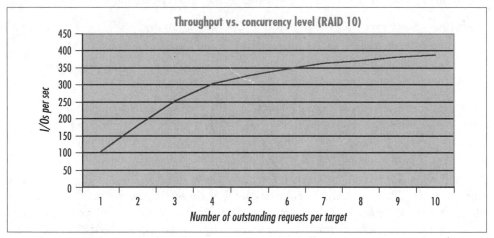

Figure 10-34. Throughput of a RAID 10 configuration in I/Os per second

In summary, we were pleased with the performance of this controller, keeping in mind the investment made in putting it together. In terms of maximum throughput, we reached an impressive 89 MB/sec using these drives. This result was obtained using a workload of sequential reads with large concurrency and a request size of 32 KB against a striped array across all four drives.

Selecting a RAID Configuration

Choosing among different RAID configurations requires an understanding of the explicit cost/performance trade-offs involved. Figure 10-35 compares the performance of striping (RAID 0), striping and mirroring (RAID 0/1), and striping with parity (RAID 5) on a mixed read/write workload that is 50% sequential and 50%

random. Four identical data disks were configured in each instance. RAID 0 disk striping improves disk performance, but generally only for very large blocks. To gain the benefits of disk striping, you must choose a stripe unit smaller than the size of the average I/O request. The stripe unit here was 32 KB. The most noticeable performance improvement occurs with 64 KB blocks that span two disks. Be sure to configure enough SCSI bandwidth to match the disk bandwidth of a striped disk array. Otherwise, the performance benefits fail to materialize. In this set of tests, internal SCSI bandwidth appeared to be a limiting factor above 64 KB blocks.

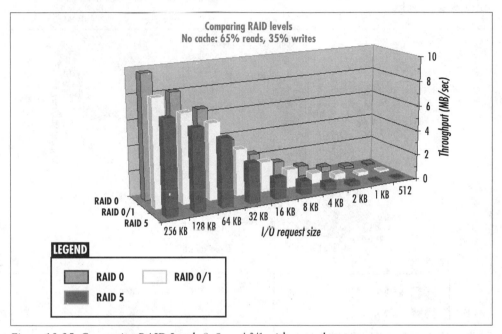

Figure 10-35. Comparing RAID Levels 0, 5, and 0/1 with no cache

RAID 0/1 has similar performance to RAID 0, but is expensive to configure, requiring twice as many physical disk storage devices. Disk mirroring does cause some loss of performance at high throughput levels because each write must be performed twice, ultimately creating contention for storage processor internal paths. RAID 5 suffers from a stiff performance penalty because of a Read-Modify-Write cycle that turns a single write request into four physical disk operations. But RAID 5 is less costly to configure. As long as the write activity rate is low, this can be a very acceptable cost/performance trade-off.

Nonvolatile cache memory emerges as having at least as big an impact on performance as the various RAID disk striping options. Figure 10-36 compares the performance of similarly configured RAID 0, RAID 0/1, and RAID 5 arrays on a battery-backed cached controller. With effective caching, the RAID 5 write performance penalty can be masked from the host entirely, as illustrated. The performances of the

RAID 0 stripe set and the RAID 5 array were indistinguishable. Again, the biggest gain from disk striping was evident with request sizes that spanned two disks. RAID 0/1 striping and mirroring tend to suffer at high throughput rates because all writes must be directed to two sets of disks. Sizing the cache is very important. Lazy write cache flushes occurring when the write cache fills tend to interfere with read operations that miss the cache, so it is important to have sufficient cache memory capable of handling large bursts of write activity. Windows 2000's paging and file cache lazy write threads generate this kind of bursty write activity and cause problems for an undersized cache.

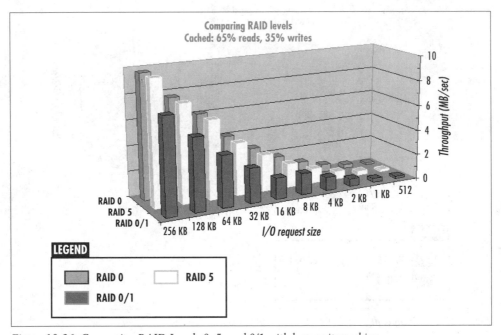

Figure 10-36. Comparing RAID Levels 0, 5, and 0/1 with lazy write caching

## CHAPTER 11

Introduction to Networking Technology

This chapter provides an overview of Windows 2000 networking with a particular emphasis on performance and capacity planning considerations. Network performance is an enormous topic, one that we could easily devote an entire book to. Our goal here is more modest. We introduce the most important networking concepts that affect performance, reviewing the basic technology associated with both local area networks (LANs) and wide area networks (WANs). We focus on the combination of networking technologies that are most common to Windows 2000 environments, which means we primarily discuss Ethernet, IP routing, and TCP. Because Windows 2000 networking services are built around the suite of networking protocols known as TCP/IP (commonly associated with the Internet), we are on familiar ground. Windows 2000 network performance concerns overlap considerably with the concerns of other computer systems that run the familiar TCP/IP environment.

We focus on the available metrics for measuring networking performance and the most commonly used utility programs available for Windows 2000. We concentrate on those network performance objects available using the System Monitor and introduce the use of the Network Monitor for analyzing individual packets. The Network Monitor is a software-based packet sniffer included in Microsoft's System Management Server suite of tools.

In this chapter, we illustrate basic networking concepts using familiar applications like Windows 2000 file sharing (Server and Redirector) and Microsoft's Internet Information System (IIS) and its web browser, Internet Explorer. These are networked applications that can be very sensitive to inadequate network planning. Hopefully, after reading this chapter, you will feel comfortable troubleshooting a performance problem involving these or other networked applications. The networking concepts that you need to understand to diagnose network performance problems are really quite basic. What complicates network performance is the complexity of the networks that computers are interconnected with. There is also a wide variety of networking gear, including routers, switches, links, and other equipment, that is required in large-scale networked applications. We attempt here to lay the groundwork for Chapter 12's in-depth look at IIS, which is at the heart of many complicated networked applications.

Networking Basics

Networking refers to data communication between two or more computers linked by some transmission medium. For the sake of simplicity, we concentrate on the more prevalent wired modes of digital data communication. Data communication technology is readily broken into *local area network* (LAN) technology, which is designed to link computers over limited distances, and *wide area network* (WAN) technology. LANs utilize inexpensive wire protocols suitable for peer-to-peer communication, making it possible to link many computers together cost-effectively. LAN technologies include the popular Ethernet 10BaseT and 100BaseT standards, as well as Gigabit Ethernet, FDDI, and Token Ring. WAN connections form the backbone of the World Wide Web, which literally interconnects millions of individual computers scattered around the globe. In contrast, WAN utilizes relatively expensive long distance lines normally provided by telephone companies and other common carriers to connect distant locations. Popular WAN technologies include Frame Relay, ISDN, DSL, T1, T3, and SONET, among others.

Local Area Networks (LANs)

There are many ways to link multiple computers together physically into a network so that they can communicate with each other. The most popular network topologies today feature ways to link all the computers in an organization and also tie them to public access networks so people can communicate with the outside world. An unavoidable consideration in wiring your computers together is that LAN technologies have built-in distance constraints that must be honored; after all, they are *local* area networks. The Ethernet protocol, for example, cannot be used to connect computers over distances greater than 1500 meters.

Wiring hubs

Ring configurations are the simplest network topology for a LAN segment. A ring is a simple loop where every computer, or *station,* on the ring is connected to two of its neighbors, as in the top illustration of Figure 11-1. Notice that every station can send data to or receive data from every other station by traversing the loop. However, LANs are rarely constructed by physically wiring computers together into a single interconnected strand as depicted here. Instead, individual connections are made from each station back to a wiring closet where a *hub* is installed. Hubs developed purely as a wiring convenience. They make it easy to ensure that the entire loop of wired connections stays within the uncompromising Ethernet distance spec.

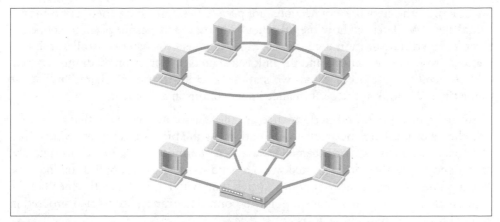

Figure 11-1. Networking topologies: a ring network (top) and a switched network (bottom)

Using a hub results in a *star* configuration whose behavior is logically the same as a ring configuration. Networking hubs are passive devices that simply propagate a signal received on one port to every other connected port. With the hub performing simple signal propagation, every station wired into the hub can communicate with every other station on the *segment*. Every connected station sees every packet, just as the stations on a ring do. From a performance standpoint, the capacity of the network segment is the capacity of any single point-to-point connection (10 Mb/sec, 100 Mb/sec, or 1 Gb/sec for 10 Mb Ethernet, 100 Mb Fast Ethernet, or Gigabit Ethernet, respectively).

Switched networks

More complex hub and spoke configurations are implemented using network *switches*. A switched network is wired identically to the hub configuration, but the difference is in the capability of the gear that the wire plugs into. Switches are intelligent devices that understand which stations are plugged into which ports on the switch. They create dedicated virtual circuits that send datagrams from one sending station directly to the receiving station. The performance implication of using a switched network is that there is dedicated link capacity between any two sending/receiving stations, meaning that it is possible to achieve higher transmission rates across the entire segment *if* multiple sender/receiver pairs are active. The lower illustration in Figure 11-1 depicts the logical topology that results from implementing a switched network. Multiple sender/receiver links capable of performing simultaneous transfers are shown. Notice that the maximum data transmission rates possible between any two stations are the same whether a switch or a hub is used. In both topologies, the underlying protocol (i.e., 100 Mb Ethernet) determines the data transmission rate.

In Ethernet, the network connections are *peer-to-peer*, meaning there is no master controller. (We later see how the Ethernet LAN protocols permit peers to cooperate over a shared transmission medium.) Because there is no master controller in Ethernet peer-to-peer connections and the link is a shared transmission medium, it is possible for *collisions* to occur when two stations attempt to use the shared link at the same time. We look at the performance impact of this in a moment.

Fault tolerance, price, and performance are the main considerations that determine the choice of local area network configuration. As the price of Ethernet switches has dropped, switched network segments have become more common. Unfortunately, many people are then disappointed when a bandwidth-hogging application like tape backup does not run any faster with a switch than with a hub. Since the speed of the underlying protocol is unchanged, point-to-point data transmissions that proceed in a serial fashion cannot run any faster.

Another caution is not to be confused about the terminology that is used to identify hubs and switches. Physically, hubs are wiring hubs that function logically as rings, where collisions occur whenever two stations attempt to send data concurrently. Switches create network segments that function logically as spoke and hub configurations, where multiple transmissions can be in progress simultaneously. Collisions occur in switched networks only when two (or more) stations A and B attempt to send data to the same station C concurrently.

Wide Area Networks (WANs)

Because of the built-in distance constraints, stations within an office or department or confined to one floor in a large office building are grouped into individual LAN *segments*. Multiple LAN segments are linked to other LANs using *bridges* or *gateways*. WAN technology, of course, is then used to interconnect autonomous network segments over longer distances than the Ethernet protocol can handle.

Point-to-point long-distance connections using circuits provided by common telecommunications carrier companies are used to link physically distinct network segments. A great variety of both wired and wireless connections is possible, distinguished mainly by relative cost and speed. See Table 11-1 for a look at representative circuits and their relative speeds. (LAN technologies are interspersed for comparison.) Internetworking technology using bridges and *routers* to link physically distinct LAN and WAN network segments is what makes a complex network like the Internet possible. Internet service providers (ISPs) of many different stripes connect private organizations to the public-access Internet. We discuss the IP router technology that is used at points where autonomous local networking segments intersect with outside long distance connections in more detail later in this chapter.

Table 11-1. *Absolute and relative speeds of networking connection technologies*

Circuit	Connection speed (bps)	Relative speed
Modem	28,800	0.5
Frame Relay	56,000	1
ISDN	128,000	2
DSL	640,000	12
T1/DS1	1,536,000	28
10 Mb Ethernet	10,000,000	180
16 Mb Token Ring	16,000,000	286
T3/DS3	44,736,000	800
OC1	51,844,000	925
100 Mb Fast Ethernet	100,000,000	1800
FDDI	100,000,000	1800
OC3	155,532,000	2800
ATM	155,532,000	2800
OC12	622,128,000	11,120
Gigabit Ethernet	1,000,000,000	18,000

The resulting network configuration within a large-scale organization with many physical locations is apt to be quite complex, making network capacity planning extremely complicated. Network planners responsible for large-scale networks use sophisticated simulation and modeling tools to plan for network expansion and growth. Network planning on this scale is beyond the scope of this chapter, but if you are interested in pursuing this topic further, the Bibliography references a number of technical books that discuss networking technology in great detail.

Packets

Data is transmitted over a communications line in a serial fashion, one bit at a time. Instead of simply sending individual bits between stations across the network, however, data communication is performed using groups of bits organized into distinct datagrams or *packets*. It is the function of the data communications hardware and software that you run to shape bit streams into standard, recognized packets. In this section, we discuss the overall shape of the packets being sent and received in Microsoft Windows 2000–based networks. We also introduce packet traces that are collected by a network sniffer. *Sniffers* are diagnostic tools that can be used to display the bit streams encoded into packet transmissions. They are often used to diagnose network performance problems, and they can also play a role in network capacity planning. The Network Monitor application that is included with Windows 2000 is a software-based sniffer. Later in this chapter, we look in more detail at some common types of packets that you can expect to find circulating on your network, and discuss using the Network Monitor to capture and examine network traffic.

At the heart of any packet is the *payload*, the information that we actually intend to transmit between two computers. Networking hardware and software inserts packet *headers* into the front of the data transmission payload to describe the data being transmitted. For instance, the packet header contains a tag that shows the type and format of the packet. It also contains the *source address* of the station transmitting the data and the *destination address* of the station intended to receive it. In addition, the packet header contains a length code that tells you how much data it contains; remember that the data appears as a continuous sequence of bits when coming across the wire. Using these packet header fields, we can calculate who is sending how much data to whom, and we can compare this to the capacity of the links connecting those stations to determine if network link capacity is adequate. Networking hardware and software also wraps packet headers and data with error detection and correction codes so that transmission errors across unreliable or noisy media can be detected and, in some cases, corrected.

Understanding the packet-oriented nature of data communication transmissions is very important. The various network *protocols* determine the format of data packets: how many bits in the header, the sequence of header fields, and how error correction code data is created and stored in the packet. Protocols simply represent standard bit formats that packets must conform to. Packets also must conform to some maximum size or maximum transmission unit (MTU). Transmitting blocks of data larger than the MTU is also problematic; large blocks must be broken into packets that will fit within the MTU. Consequently, packet disassembly and reassembly are necessary functions that must be performed by networking hardware and software. Packets representing pieces of larger blocks must contain instructions for their reassembly at the receiver. In routing, two packets from the same logical transmission might get sent along different routes and even arrive at their destination out of sequence. Receiving packets out of order naturally complicates the task of reassembling the transmission at the receiver.

Windows 2000 networking services

The networking services that Windows 2000 uses are based on prevailing industry standards, originally developed by a myriad of companies and supervised today by international standards bodies. From the beginning, Windows NT supported almost all the major networking protocols that had been developed. Microsoft's original goal was that machines running its upstart operating system software could be plugged easily into almost any existing network. Early versions of NT were concerned about coexisting with existing LANs and LAN protocols like NetBEUI, AppleTalk, IPX, and the Server Message Block (SMB) file and printer networking services that IBM and Microsoft originally developed jointly for OS2. The networking architecture built into NT and carried over to Windows 2000 allows Windows NT/2000 machines to service multiple networking protocols simultaneously. For example, a single Windows 2000 machine has no trouble communicating with a Macintosh computer running AppleTalk, a Novell NetWare server issuing IPX packets, and an MS-DOS machine running NetBEUI, all plugged into the same LAN segment. Even Windows 2000's harshest critics acknowledge that the operating system contains very robust networking support.

With the amazing success of the Internet, the Internet protocols have been adopted almost universally across the computer industry, and Windows 2000 is no exception. Windows 2000 is designed to operate with and is fully compliant with the bundle of networking standards associated with the Internet, including UDP, TCP, IP, ICMP, DNS, DHCP, HTML, RPC, and a bunch of other initials. Instead of this alphabet soup, the suite of Internet standard protocols is often simply called TCP/IP, the two components that play a central role. Reflecting the phenomenal growth of the Internet, Windows 2000 is the first version of NT where TCP/IP predominates. While Windows 2000 continues to support older, PC-oriented LAN protocols like NetBios, NetBEUI, AppleTalk, and IPX, the TCP/IP bundle of Internet protocols is now the native networking language of the operating system.

Meanwhile, the SMB standard for sharing files and printers has evolved into one of the two networked file and printing protocols that are almost universally accepted (NFS, the networked file system originally developed by Sun is the other). In this context, you may have heard about SAMBA (notice the S, M, and B), which is an open source software package that provides support for the SMB protocol in Unix, GNU, and Linux. SAMBA support is available to run on top of most Unix and Linux machines, allowing Unix machines to share files with Windows and Windows 2000 clients.

Protocol stack

It is customary to speak of networking hardware and software technology as a series of distinct, well-defined *layers*. The notion of building networking technology using layers of hardware and software began with a standardization process that originated in the early 1980s. When the ARPAnet, the predecessor of today's Internet, was created, it implemented four standard networking layers. These Internet protocol layers are almost uniformly accepted as standards today, and they form the basis of Microsoft Windows 2000's networking support. This layered architecture of the Internet is depicted in Figure 11-2. The Internet architecture defines both the functional layers and the specific interfaces that each layer supports for communicating between adjacent functional layers.

Media Access (MAC)
> The lowest-level layer is concerned with the physical transmission media and how the signal it carries is used to represent data bits. The MAC layer is also sometimes decomposed further into physical and data link layers. The various forms of Ethernet are the most common implementation of the MAC layer.

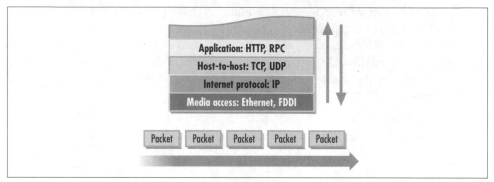

Figure 11-2. A conceptual view of the layered architecture of the Internet networking protocols

FDDI, ATM, Token Ring, SONET, and others also function at the MAC layer. The MAC layer must be consistent throughout any single network segment. *Protocol converters* are used to convert the signal in one protocol to another to bridge network segments that use different MAC protocols.

Internet Protocol (IP)

The IP layer is concerned with packet delivery. IP solves the problem of delivering packets across autonomous network segments. This is accomplished through technology known as *routing*, which delivers packets from neighbor to neighbor until the payload reaches its intended final destination. The IP layer also includes the Address Resolution Protocol (ARP), the Internet Control Message Protocol (ICMP), and the Border Gateway Protocol (BGP), which are involved in discovering and maintaining packet delivery routes.

Host-to-Host

The host-to-host layer is concerned with how machines that want to transmit data back and forth can communicate. The Internet protocols define two host-to-host implementations: the User Datagram Protocol (UDP) for transmission of simple messages, and the Transmission Control Program (TCP) for handling more complex transactions that require communication *sessions*.

Application

The Internet protocols include standard applications for transmitting mail (Simple Mail Transfer Protocol or SMTP), files (File Transfer Protocol or FTP), web browser hypertext files (Hypertext Transfer Protocol or HTTP), remote login (Telnet), and others. In addition, Windows 2000 supports additional networking applications that plug into TCP, including SMB, Remote Procedure Call (RPC), Distributed COM (DCOM), Lightweight Directory Access Protocol (LDAP), and others.

Processing of packets

As you can see, the layered architecture of the Internet protocols is much more than a conceptual abstraction. Next, let's look at the way that the layered architecture of networking services operates on individual packets. Consider a datagram originally created by an application layer like IIS, which supports HTTP for communicating with a web browser program. As created by IIS, this packet of information contains HTML format text, for example, to satisfy a specific HTTP GET request. (For the moment, let's not worry too much about the precise structure of this interaction; we deal with the HTTP protocol in much more detail in Chapter 12.)

IIS then passes the HTTP packet to the next appropriate lower layer, which in this case is TCP, for transmission to the requesting client program, which is a web browser program running on a remote computer. The TCP layer of software in Windows 2000 is responsible for certain control functions such as establishing and maintaining a data communications session between the IIS web server machine and the web browser client running Internet Explorer or Netscape Navigator. TCP is also responsible for *flow control*, which is concerned with how to ensure that the powerful routers at your ISP do not flood your much less capable client-side network with data.

The TCP layer, in turn, passes the datagram originally created by IIS to the IP layer, which is responsible for building packets of just the right size, consistent with the MTU of the next lowest layer. Finally, IP passes each packet to the MAC layer, which is actually responsible for placing bits on the wire. We see that each layer in the networking protocol stack operates in sequence on the packet. Each layer also contributes some of the packet header control information that is ultimately placed on the wire.

The protocol stack functions in reverse order at the receiving station. Each layer processes the packet based on the control information encapsulated in the packet header deposited by the corresponding layer at the sender. If the layer determines that the received packet contains a valid payload, the packet header data originally inserted by that corresponding layer at the sender station is stripped off. The remaining payload data is then passed up to the next highest layer in the stack for processing. In this fashion, the packet is processed at the receiving station by the MAC layer, the IP layer, and the TCP layer in sequence, until it is finally passed to the web browser application that originally requested the transmission and knows how to format HTML text to display on the screen.

Benefits of layering

Layering of the network protocols accomplishes two things. Decomposing the complex software that makes up the Internet protocols into different functional layers simplifies the job of making a complicated network like the Internet work. Each layer becomes responsible only for specific, well-defined, functional tasks.

Another benefit of the layering approach is greater flexibility. Where alternative implementations are available, layering affords data communications applications the flexibility of selecting just those services that are most appropriate. Using the Internet protocols, for example, applications can choose between two different implementations of the host-to-host layer. Many networking applications plug into Winsock, the Microsoft version of the TCP sockets interface standard. Persistent TCP connections are session-oriented, requiring complex and time-consuming hand-shaking, i.e., acknowledgments between the two computers that are sending data back and forth to each other. Meanwhile, the overhead of establishing and maintaining a TCP session can be avoided when you only need to send a simple message between one computer and another. In that case, the simpler, *connectionless* UDP protocol can be used instead. Both TCP and UDP occupy the same functional layer in the Internet networking architecture. TCP supplies a much richer set of services than UDP, but these services can be overkill for applications with very simple communications requirements. Different strokes for different folks.

Consider also the different physical link technologies available at the MAC layer, including Ethernet, Token Ring, FDDI, and ATM, to name just a few. It is possible to construct a network segment using any of these underlying physical connection technologies and still plug it into the Internet. Software at the IP layer is responsible for handing data to the MAC layer in an acceptable format. The IP layer in the Internet architecture effectively masks incompatibilities between various wire protocols like the different-sized MTUs used by Ethernet and ATM. That means higher-level layers need not be concerned with these lower-level implementation details. This is a pretty neat trick.

One reason for talking about the layered architecture of the Internet is that the layering is evident in individual packets that are processed across the network. When we capture the bytes transmitted between network nodes for measurement purposes, the packet header information that accompanies the data payload is also available. As illustrated in Figure 11-3, each successive layer adds a header to the data payload as the packet is processed by that layer. For example, the application layer protocol, such as Microsoft's SMB file sharing protocol, creates the packet and passes it to the next lower level. There, TCP adds additional control information onto the front of the SMB packet, as shown. TCP then passes the packet down to the next layer, where IP appends its control and routing information. Finally, the packet is passed to the MAC layer, where Ethernet adds additional control information.

As Figure 11-3 illustrates, each successive layer of networking software (and hardware) adds its control information to a header that is attached to the front of the packet. This is similar to the stack of control information that a computer program calling successive subroutines and functions creates when it executes. Consequently, this processing by the various networking hardware and software layers is often referred to as the *protocol stack* or sometimes the *TCP/IP stack*. When the packet is processed at the receiving host computer, the process is reversed. Each processing layer peels off its control information, then relays the packet to the next highest level receiving application in the stack.

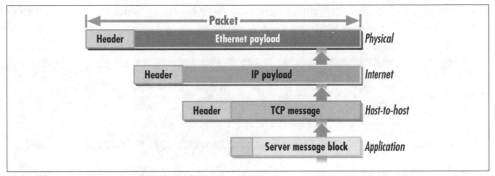

Figure 11-3. Each networking layer adds a header to the data payload as the packet is processed

The packet headers positioned in front of the data payload by the different layers of the protocol stack are the ultimate source of most network performance statistics. The headers contain length fields that tell you how big the packet is, and addressing fields that tell who sent the packet and who is intended to receive it. Different layers in the protocol stack use different addressing schemes: the MAC layer uses unique 48-bit network interface card (NIC) addresses embedded in the hardware, IP uses the familiar 32-bit hierarchical addresses that we associate with web browsing, and TCP headers reference the TCP socket interface ports associated with different applications. Each addressing scheme uniquely identifies the sender and receiver of each and every packet. Decoding the addressing scheme lets you determine who is sending what to whom. In the following sections, we describe the control information that each successive layer of the networking protocol stack adds to the data payload in some detail, as that information is relevant to performance analysis.

The protocol stack also has some distinct performance implications. For example, when it comes to connection-oriented data transmission acknowledgments (also known as ACKs) issued by TCP, acknowledgment packets contain only headers, with no other application data payload. When you consider that nearly every TCP packet transmission requires an explicit ACK, fully half of all the packets sent across typical TCP/IP sessions contain header information only. This requirement was relaxed in TCP's support for high-speed Gigabit Ethernet. Windows 2000 supports a new Selective Acknowledgment (SACK) feature in TCP/IP that is often used with Gigabit Ethernet hardware. We talk about this and other TCP session-oriented host-to-host functions later in this chapter.

Using packet sniffers

Network sniffer software like the Windows 2000 Network Monitor lets you capture and examine packet traces. Figure 11-4 shows a Detail screen from a Network Monitor capture session that allows you to look at the contents of individual data communication packets. Since the packet contains a complete trail of its origin, history, and ownership, you can drill down through successive layers of headers, as illustrated in Figure 11-4, to see who is sending what to whom.

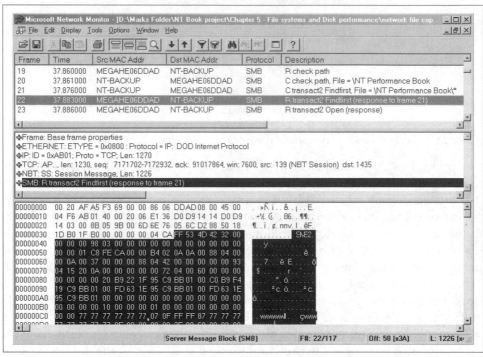

Figure 11-4. The Detail display of Network Monitor allows you to view the packet trace

The Detail display illustrated in Figure 11-4 features three scrollable windows for viewing the packet trace captured. The topmost panel shows the individual packets in the sequence in which they arrived at the machine where the Network Monitor is capturing data. In this example, packets captured at the machine, but not involved in a specific conversation between the two MAC addresses shown in the SRC (source) and DST (destination) fields, were filtered out to make the sequence of events easier to follow. Each packet shown in the upper window is marked with a sequence number and timestamp in microseconds relative to the start of the trace. The Protocol column indicates the highest-level protocol header that the Network Monitor software can interpret. The Description field column then interprets information from the packet header. Using the mouse, you highlight any packet in the list that you want to see in more detail, which drives the displays in the two lower windows.

The middle window shows the sequence of packet headers in the packet selected. We can see that the SMB application layer has called a lower-level service called NBT, which operates the named pipe communications channel that the SMB protocol uses. NBT stands for NetBIOS over TCP/IP, a Windows 2000 component that allows NetBIOS services to operate transparently over TCP/IP networks. NBT permits higher level OS networking services like user login and authentication, file and print sharing, and Registry access, originally developed to run with NetBIOS, to function consistently with TCP/IP. We see in this case that NBT passes the packet to TCP/IP. The TCP, IP, and Ethernet headers are shown with their important header fields interpreted. Using the mouse, you can click on any one of the layers that is displayed and decoded in the middle scrollable panel. As you navigate through the layers of the packet in the middle window, the Network Monitor highlights the appropriate portion of the packet in the binary and ASCII data display in the lower scrollable panel. In this example, the SMB application layer is selected. The Network Monitor understands this particular wire protocol, so the middle panel describes the function of the packet. Packet 22 is a response to a FindFirst SMB command issued in Packet 21 against a specific \NT *Performance Book* subdirectory on a remote computer. The binary display reveals all the data associated with this SMB response, including the names of the files in the directory being queried (in 16-bit Unicode format).

As Figure 11-4 illustrates, the Network Monitor display allows you to visualize the successive layering of the various protocol headers onto the data payload of a packet that is performed by each component of the protocol stack. Figure 11-4 shows a detailed view of a packet created in response to an SMB issued by the Windows 2000 Redirector while browsing a file directory on a networked drive. The SMB response packet is processed by TCP, IP, and Ethernet layers in succession prior to being transmitted. Notice that the Network Monitor records the time relative to the start of the trace when each packet was received at the machine capturing the packets. These timestamps can be used to determine the response time for this particular SMB transaction. With a little practice, you can become very skilled at using the Network Monitor and interpreting the streams of packets that it captures. Unfortunately, relating packet sequences to logical application transactions is often quite difficult, requiring detailed knowledge of the successive protocol layers.

The Network Monitor (or any other packet sniffer) can capture and display the raw data in any network packet, including the unencrypted passwords used in server login attempts sent over the network. Consequently, organizations control the usage of these monitoring tools very carefully. As you can see, packet traces are extremely detailed. Interpreting them requires a detailed understanding of the way network protocols work. Packet traces are primarily used to diagnose network problems of various kinds, but they can be useful in performance work, too. Because packet traces capture *all* network activity on a particular network segment, they can reveal details that more summarized network performance statistics can obscure. However, because of the amount of detailed data they capture, especially for busy networks, packet traces are usually not the tool of choice for network capacity planning. Network growth trends, for example, are much easier to visualize from higher-level summarized statistics obtained using the System Monitor that show overall data communication transmission rates.

In the following section, we examine the components of the Windows 2000 networking architecture. Then we consider what kinds of networking performance statistics matter and how to calculate them from network data packets.

Windows 2000 Networking Architecture

Figure 11-5 fills in a few additional details about the Windows 2000 TCP/IP architecture. This is a developer's view of the TCP/IP support Microsoft provides. The Network Device Interface Specification (NDIS) is an operating system software layer that resides below IP and corresponds roughly to the data link layer of the Internet protocol. Microsoft developed NDIS so that both Windows and Windows NT could use identical network adapter device driver software. This layer contains the so-called *miniport drivers* that are provided by your network adapter manufacturer for communicating directly to the hardware. In the early days of NT, the NDIS spec meant that Microsoft did not have to persuade NIC manufacturers to develop separate device drivers for the new OS. Manufacturers were assured that driver software developed for Windows according to NDIS specifications could run unmodified under NT. This approach proved so successful that ultimately Microsoft developed a common device driver specification called Windows Device Model (WDM) that is incorporated into current versions of both operating systems.

Above NDIS, Figure 11-5 shows the Transport Driver Interface (TDI) layer that provides a uniform set of interfaces to networking applications, transparent to lower-level TCP/IP, NetBEUI, and IPX/SPX interfaces. In addition to TCP/IP, Windows 2000 contains support for NetBEUI, IPX/SPX, AppleTalk, IrDA, and other networking protocols. The TCP/IP services implemented at this level conform to all industry standards. The NetBT component shown here is needed to convert networking services designed originally to run under NetBIOS to function without modification under TCP/IP. Various networking applications and application interfaces run in user mode above the TDI layer. These include the Microsoft version of the standard TCP sockets interface that many applications plug into. Support for other standard networking application services like RPC and DCOM is also available, as illustrated.

The Windows 2000 Network Monitor driver is a device driver named *NMnt.sys,* which resides in the NDIS layer of the protocol stack. When the Network Monitor driver is installed, you can use the Network Monitor application installed under Administrative Tools to capture packets being sent and received by this station. The Network Monitor driver also enables you to collect the Network Interface network performance object using the System Monitor. Unlike the Network Monitor agent available in Windows NT 4.0, the Windows 2000 Network Monitor driver does not place your network adapter into promiscuous mode. The Windows 2000 Network Monitor driver is a measurement layer that slides into the NDIS wrapper Microsoft provides, similar to the diskperf layer that can be inserted into the I/O Manager stack. While collecting network performance statistics in this fashion is much less

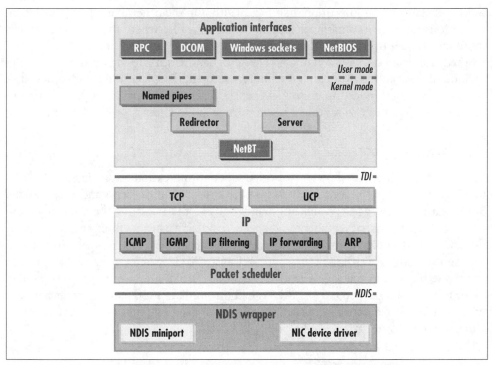

Figure 11-5. *The Windows 2000 networking architecture showing the NDIS, TDI, and application services layers*

intrusive than enabling promiscuous mode, the technique does have the disadvantage that only packets sent to or received by this machine are visible to NDIS. Because of the widespread use of switched networks, this is not much of a disadvantage. On a switched network, only packets that match the MAC address are sent to the network adapter anyway.

Bandwidth and Latency

Bandwidth and *latency* are the two most fundamental measures of network performance. Relating these concepts to the performance terms we use in this book, bandwidth is similar to network capacity as measured in bits (or sometimes bytes) per second, while latency is a measure of network response time. In this section, we look at how to measure network utilization, the most common measure of bandwidth. We also look at how to measure network response time and round trip time, the two most important measures of network latency.

Latency is primarily a function of distance, so it is especially important in wide area networking. Counterintuitively, perhaps, even when the bandwidth of a long-distance connection link is limited, network latency is usually a more important consideration in long-distance communication than bandwidth. On the other hand, bandwidth considerations tend to dominate performance in LAN traffic where the typical latency is minimal, frequently 10 µsecs (microseconds) or less. Of course, there are some networked applications where both latency and bandwidth are significant. Examples include almost any high-volume data-intensive operations like bulk file copies, disk backup, or digital video processing. When both are necessary for adequate performance, it is customary to represent network capacity as Latency × Bandwidth.

Bandwidth

Bandwidth refers to the data rate of the data communications transmission, usually measured in bits per second. It is the capacity of the link to send and receive data. Some authorities suggest visualizing bandwidth as the width of the data pipe connecting two stations, or as the rate bits per second arrive at the other end of the pipe. For instance, the top diagram in Figure 11-6 illustrates the rate at which bits travel through an Ethernet 10BaseT link clocked at 10 MHz where each wavelength can carry one bit of information. The 10BaseT link has a nominal bandwidth capability of 10 million bits per second (10 Mb). The bottom diagram illustrates what happens when you boost the capacity of the NICs, hubs, and/or switches on the Ethernet network segment to run at 100 million bits per second.

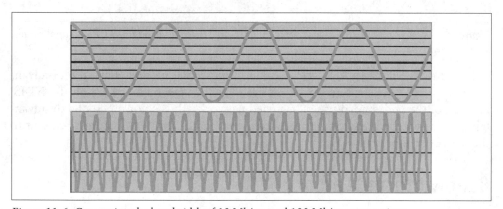

Figure 11-6. Comparing the bandwidth of 10 Mb/sec and 100 Mb/sec connections

Bandwidth describes the rate at which bits are sent across the link, but it tells you nothing about *how long* it takes to transmit those bits. Physically, each bit transmitted across the wire is part of a continuous wave form, as illustrated. The waveform cycles at 10 MHz for 10BaseT and at 100 MHz for 100BaseT. In the time it takes to send 1 bit using 10BaseT, you send 10 bits using the 100BaseT Fast Ethernet standard.

It is often more precise to speak of the *effective bandwidth* of a data communications link. Effective bandwidth attempts to factor in the many types of overhead that add additional bytes to the data payload you are attempting to move over the network. Consider what happens when you transfer a 10 MB (megabyte) file using Microsoft's

SMB network file-sharing protocol from one machine to another across a 10 Mb (megabit) Ethernet link. The first overhead to consider is the cost of redundant encoding of the bit stream performed at the MAC layer. Ethernet sends two error checking and correction bits along with every eight bits of data. This is known as 10/8 encoding and is a feature of most MAC layer implementations designed to improve the reliability of digital data transmissions. The use of 10/8 encoding results in a 10 Mb link having an effective data bandwidth of 1 MB: 10,000,000 bits per second ÷ 10 bits per byte = 1,000,000 bytes per second.

Of course, the 10/8 encoding scheme is not the only overhead of data communication that should be factored into any calculation of effective bandwidth. The 10 MB file that the SMB protocol transfers must be broken into data packets no larger than Ethernet's 1500 byte MTU. As illustrated in the SMB packet trace in Figure 11-4, each Ethernet packet also contains IP, TCP, NBT, and SMB headers for this application. The space in the packet that these protocol stack headers occupy further reduces effective bandwidth. There are other protocol-related overheads, discussed later, that further reduce effective bandwidth. Without attempting now to describe these additional overhead factors definitively, we suggest that the overhead of typical LAN technology probably reduces the effective bandwidth of a link to approximately 50% of its rated capacity. Try transferring this hypothetical 10 MB file across a typical 10 Mb Ethernet link: you will probably measure only about 500 KB/sec of throughput, which for planning purposes is the effective bandwidth of the link.

The most important measure of bandwidth utilization is line utilization. The measurement technique is straightforward. Using MAC layer length fields, accumulate the total number of bytes received from packets transferred across the link. Utilization is then calculated as:

Network Interface Utilization = Bytes Total/sec ÷ Current Bandwidth

where both fields are measured in bytes per second. In Windows 2000, in order to measure network utilization, you must first install the Network Monitor driver, the same component necessary to capture packets using the Network Monitor's packet sniffer function. When you collect the Network Interface object using System Monitor, the Network Monitor driver begins capturing packets. In creating a Network Monitor packet trace, entire packets are copied into a memory-resident buffer for later review and analysis. To create the Network Interface object that the System Monitor reports, it is only necessary for the Network Monitor driver to count both packets sent and received. By examining the packet headers, the Network Monitor driver can also calculate the number of bits sent and received. There is much less measurement overhead involved in this calculation compared to capturing a full packet trace. Only the packet headers are accessed and they do not need to be stored. Dividing the Bytes Total/sec counter by the current bandwidth yields the utilization of the link. Figure 11-7 illustrates using System Monitor to collect network interface utilization statistics.

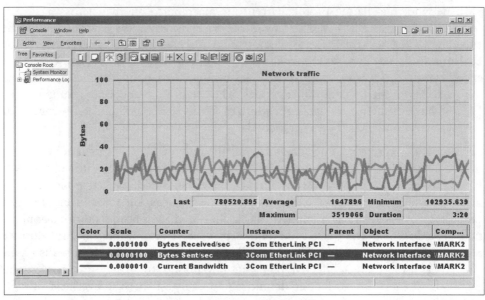

Figure 11-7. Using the System Monitor to track network utilization

As higher-bandwidth technologies (e.g., Gigabit Ethernet over 1 GB optical links) become available, a popular notion has arisen that these new technologies effectively resolve any legacy of network performance problems. This is an idea advanced by various computer industry pundits and trumpeted in the trade press. The principal function of this hyperbole appears to be to advance the business prospects of the companies involved in the manufacture and sale of these new products. Certainly, to the extent that there is a "bandwidth crisis" in networking today, higher-bandwidth technology will go a long way toward alleviating the condition. But keep in mind that bandwidth is a concern primarily in local area networking and even then only when large blocks of data must be moved from point to point. The long latency associated with long-distance data communications is a more pressing (and less tractable) performance problem for organizations attempting to do business on the Web, for example.

Latency

Latency refers to the delay in sending bits from one location to another. It is the length of time it takes to send a message across the link. Electronic signals travel at the speed of light, approximately 186,000 miles or 300,000 kilometers per second. The physical characteristics of transmission media do have a dampening effect on signal propagation delays, with a corresponding increase in latency. The effective speed of an electronic data transmission wire is only about 1/2 the speed of light, or 150,000 km/second. Optical fiber connections reach fully 2/3 the speed of light, or a latency of 200,000 km/second.

Knowing that it is physically impossible to exceed the speed of light (except in science fiction tales) and knowing just how fast light is, you might think that latency is not worth worrying about. Consider this. A message sent from a location in the eastern U.S. to a west-coast location across a single, continuous optical cable would traverse 5,000 km. At a top speed of 200,000 km/second, the latency for this data transmission is a not-insignificant 25 ms. For a rule-of-thumb calculation, allow for at least 5 ms of delay for every 1000 km separating two stations.

Of course, most long-distance transmissions do not cross simple, continuous point-to-point links. Over long distances, both electrical and optical signals attenuate and require amplification using so-called *repeaters* to reconstitute the signal and send it further on its way. These repeaters add additional latency to the transmission time. At various network junctions, additional processing is necessary to route packets to the next *hop* in the journey between sender and receiver. Processing time at links, including routers and repeaters and amplifiers of various forms, adds significant delays at every network hop. High-performance IP packet routers designed to move massive amounts of traffic along the Internet backbone, for example, might add 10 μsecs of delay. Slower routers like the ones installed on customer premises could add as much as 50 μsecs of additional latency to the transmission time. This yields a better estimate of long-distance data communication latency:

Distance / Signal Propagation Delay + (hop count × average router latency)

Since looking for ways to physically speed up long-distance communication is fruitless, organizations that promote the use of the Internet to sell goods and services electronically have had to approach data link performance issues from a different angle. Technology associated with web caching, for example, currently shows promise because it addresses the problem of long-distance delays. Elaborate web caching schemes split a central web site into multiple processing locations. Network latency is reduced because in a distributed web caching configuration, the web site physically closest to the customer processes the request. Processing web transactions across a distributed network of web servers is still problematic because it raises all the issues associated with maintaining cache integrity and maintaining data synchronization. Applications that need to run in that kind of distributed processing environment must be designed very carefully. They require a thorough understanding of the very serious performance and cache integrity issues that confront the developer.

Because determining network latency across a complex internetworking scheme is so important, the Internet protocols include facilities to measure network packet routing response time. The Internet Control Message Protocol (ICMP), a required component of the TCP/IP standard, supports an echo reply command that returns the response time for the request. ping is a simple command-line utility included with Windows 2000 that issues several ICMP echo reply commands and displays the resulting response time as reported by the destination node. A slightly more sophisticated tool called tracert decomposes the response time to a remote IP destination by calculating the time spent traversing each and every hop in the route. We discuss the use of ping, tracert, and other related utilities in the later section "IP Routing."

A related measure of latency is the *round trip time* (RTT). RTT is calculated as 2 × latency: the time it takes for a message to get to its destination and back. In typical client/server transactions, network RTT corresponds closely to the response time that the user of the application perceives. As discussed in Chapter 2, this perceived application response time is the most important performance metric of all, due to its relation to user satisfaction. Client/server networked applications aside, RTT is also important because the TCP/IP network protocol requires that acknowledgment messages be returned to the sender as part of session management. In Internet transmissions, for example, the receiver of a message is required to send an ACK packet back to the sender frequently. We discuss the details of the acknowledgments that TCP sessions require later. Due to the necessity of sending and receiving these ACK messages, RTT, not one-way latency, is the key performance metric for TCP transmissions.

Unfortunately, neither one-way latency nor back-and-forth RTT are measures available using the System Monitor counters. However, packet traces like the one shown in Figure 11-4 can be used to calculate RTT so long as you can identify related call and response packets. For example, in Figure 11-4, the Network Monitor identifies Frame 22 as the response packet issued to Frame 21's request for a file directory lookup. The Frame 21 Findfirst SMB transaction was issued at 37.876 seconds into the trace, and the response packet was received at 37.883 seconds, 7 ms later. Later in this chapter, we review additional packet traces, and you will be able to calculate the RTT for several types of TCP/IP transactions.

One obvious problem with using the Network Monitor packet traces is the amount of hand calculations necessary for any realistically sized network. As an alternative to working out RTT manually using Network Monitor packet traces, a number of third-party network monitor applications report this crucial metric systematically. A second concern is that RTT measurements derived from packet traces cannot easily be integrated with the rest of the performance statistics that the System Monitor provides for response time decomposition.

Next, we explore each of the major networking protocols in detail.

Media Access Layer

The media access (MAC) protocol layer corresponds to the lowest-level protocol in the protocol stack concerned with actually transmitting bits across some physical transmission medium. The MAC layer is often further decomposed into a physical Layer 1 (hardware) and a data link Layer 2 (software). There are a number of choices available for the MAC physical layer of data transmission, among them, Token Ring, FDDI, and various flavors of Ethernet, all of which we discuss to some degree. However, we do not discuss more exotic MAC protocols such as ATM and SONET that are rarely encountered on Windows 2000 machines. In this section, we explore the major architectural features of the MAC physical layer and compare and contrast various implementations. As always, we focus on those features that have the most impact on network performance.

Ethernet

The Ethernet standard represents by far the most popular choice for the data link layer. Ethernet's popularity is the result of several factors:

Simplicity
> The simple nature of Ethernet makes it very inexpensive to build hardware and software to support it, lowering the cost of all Ethernet components. Ethernet interface cards are quite inexpensive. In addition, the protocol does not require expensive wiring and cabling. It supports both coax (sometimes denoted as *thicknet)* and inexpensive twisted-pair wiring. The advantage of using coax is that Ethernet segments can be substantially longer, as Table 11-2 indicates.

Performance
> Ethernet networks are capable of transferring data at very high rates, equaling or exceeding the transmission speeds of alternatives.

Upward compatibility
> Ethernet performance can frequently be upgraded from 10 Mb to 100 Mb per second Fast Ethernet transfer rates without expensive and time-consuming rewiring. Note that upgrading to Gigabit Ethernet normally *does* require new wiring because it runs over fiber optical links instead of copper wire.

The combination of these factors makes Ethernet the clear cost/performance leader in physical link technology for most LANs. For most organizations, the choice is not whether or not to use Ethernet, but *which* Ethernet technology to implement. Table 11-2 compares the speeds and cable length restrictions of the different flavors of Ethernet currently available. The cost of Ethernet components varies widely from manufacturer to manufacturer, but you can expect generally to pay 2–4 times the cost of 10BaseT equipment for 100BaseT hubs, routers, and interface cards that run 10 times faster. Similarly, Gigabit Ethernet equipment is targeted at about 4 times the price of Fast Ethernet.

Table 11-2. Performance and wiring specifications for different varieties of Ethernet

	Ethernet 10BaseT	Fast Ethernet 100BaseT	Gigabit Ethernet 1000BaseX
Data rate	10 Mbps	100 Mbps	1000 Mbps
Category 5 unshielded twisted pair	100 m	100 m	
Shielded twisted pair/coax	500 m	100 m	25 m
Multimode fiber	2000 m	412 m	550 m
Single-mode fiber	25,000 m	20,000 m	5000 m

While it remains the most popular choice due to its distinct cost/performance advantages, Ethernet technology manifests a number of weaknesses that led many knowledgeable people to champion alternative approaches. Ethernet networks tend to get bogged down at relatively low utilization levels, which is a serious performance concern. Ethernet also lacks built-in support for dual pathing, which creates a concern about the reliability of the underlying network. (Note: high availability can be achieved with Ethernet simply by using more than one interface card, a practice known as *multihoming*.) There are many instances when performance and reliability concerns can justify the use of one of the popular alternatives to Ethernet.

Arbitration

The key to the simplicity of the Ethernet protocol is that it is purely peer-to-peer, requiring no master controller of any kind. Among other things, this makes an Ethernet network very easy to configure—you can just continue to extend the wire and add links, up to the physical limitations of the protocol in terms of the number of stations and the length of the wiring loop. (Thicknet, for example, is limited to 100 stations and a total cable length of 512 meters.) Unlike the SCSI protocol used to talk to a computer's disk, tape, and other peripherals, the Ethernet standard has no provision for time-consuming and complex bus arbitration. An Ethernet station that wants to send data to another session does not face any sort of arbitration. It simply waits until the transmission medium appears to be free for the duration of a 12-byte interframe gap and then starts transmitting data.

This simple approach to peer-to-peer communication works best on relatively lightly used network segments where stations looking to transmit data seldom encounter a busy link. The philosophy behind Ethernet suggests that it is not worth bothering about something that rarely happens anyway. Of course, the unhappy result of having no bus arbitration is that in busier network segments, multiple stations can and do try to access the same communications link at the same time. This leads to *collisions*, disrupted data transmissions that then must be retried.

CSMA/CD

Ethernet is only a nickname. Formally speaking, Ethernet belongs to the family of CSMA/CD protocols. CSMA/CD stands for Carrier Sense, Multiple Access with Collision Detection, which is shorthand for how the protocol functions. Carrier Sense refers to the fact that each station sees all the traffic on the wire. The basic topology supported is that of a ring where a packet is passed from station to station until it returns to the station where it originated, which then has the responsibility for taking the packet out of circulation. Ethernet also supports the star configurations using conventional hubs and switches. As indicated earlier in this chapter, Ethernet star configurations using passive hubs logically function identically to rings.

A station with data to transmit waits until the wire appears free before attempting to transmit. Each transmission begins with a characteristic preamble of alternating 0 and 1 bits of proscribed length. (The Network Monitor discards this preamble so it is not visible in the trace.) The preamble is followed by a one-byte start delimiter that contains the bit sequence 10101011, designed to distinguish the preamble from the beginning of the real data to be transmitted.

The station then continues with the transmission, always sending an entire packet or *frame* of information. Each Ethernet frame begins with the 48-bit destination address followed by the 48-bit source address. These 48-bit MAC addresses, also called *unicast* addresses, uniquely identify the Ethernet source and destination addresses; this is accomplished by giving every hardware manufacturer a distinct range of addresses that only it can use. Ethernet also supports *broadcast* addresses where the address field is set to binary ones to indicate that it should be processed by all LAN cards on the segment. Broadcast messages are used, for example, to pass configuration and control information around the network.

The length of the frame, including the header, is encoded in the frame header immediately following the addressing fields. For historical reasons, Ethernet frames were limited to no more than 1512 bytes (1518 bytes, if you include the required preamble and postamble bits) to keep any one station from monopolizing a shared data link for too long. Assuming that successive Ethernet, IP, and TCP headers occupy a minimum of 50 bytes, the data payload in an Ethernet packet is limited to about 1460 bytes. As the speed of Ethernet links has increased, the small frame size that the protocol supports has emerged as a serious performance limitation. For example, SMB access to remote files must conform to the Ethernet MTU, causing blocks of file data to get fragmented into multiple packets. This slows down network throughput considerably because each station must wait a predetermined interval before transmitting its next packet. Consequently, some Gigabit Ethernet implementations across 1 Gb/sec high-speed fiber optics links can utilize so-called *jumbo frames*. Since there is no standard jumbo frame size yet, Windows 2000 TCP/IP support includes a facility for discovering the MTU to use with a path dynamically. We discuss this option in more detail when we discuss various IP and TCP options.

Following the actual data payload, each Ethernet frame is delimited at the end by a frame check sequence, a 32-bit number calculated from the entire frame contents (excluding the preamble) as a cyclic redundancy check (CRC). A receiving station calculates its own version of the CRC as it takes data off the wire and compares it to the CRC embedded in the frame. If they do not match, it is an error condition and the frame is rejected.

Collision detection

When two (or more) stations have data to transmit and they both attempt to put data on the wire at the same time, an error condition called a *collision* is created.

What happens is that each station independently senses that the wire is free and begins transmitting its preamble, destination address, source address, other header fields, data payload, and CRC. If more than one station attempts to transmit data on the wire, the sequence of bits from two different frames become hopelessly intermixed. The sequence of bits received at the destination is disrupted, and, consequently, the frame is rejected.

A sending station detects that a collision has occurred because it receives a copy of the disrupted frame, which no longer matches the original. The frame must be long enough for the original station to detect the collision before it attempts to transmit its next packet. This key requirement in the protocol specification determines a minimum sized packet that must be issued. Transmissions smaller than the minimum size are automatically padded with zeros to reach the required length.

The latency (or transmission delay) for a maximum extent Ethernet segment determines the minimum packet size that can be sent across an Ethernet network. The IEEE 802.3 Ethernet standard 5-4-3 rule determines the maximum distance between any two stations on an Ethernet segment. There can be as many as five physical segments between two nodes, with up to four repeaters. The maximum length of a single segment using coax or shielded twisted-pair wiring is 512 meters. So the maximum total distance between two stations at the farthest ends of a maximum extent network can be 2560 meters. The propagation delay for a maximum extent network segment is 28.8 µsecs, according to the spec. The sending station must send data to the distant node and back in order to detect that a collision has occurred. The round trip time for the maximum extent network is 2 × 28.8 µsecs or 57.6 µsecs. The sending station must get a complete frame header, data payload, and CRC back in order to detect the collision. At a data rate of 10 Mb/sec, a station could expect to send 576 bits or 72 bytes in 57.6 µsecs. Requiring each station to send at least 72 bytes means that collisions can be detected across a maximum extent network. Ethernet pads messages smaller than 72 bytes with zeros to achieve the minimum length frames required.

Notice that Ethernet specifies a maximum extent latency of 28.8 µsecs or a maximum RTT of 57.6 µsecs. This maximum extent contains five 512 meter physical link segments. With wiring hubs, most Ethernet segments in use today do not approach anywhere near the maximum extent limits. With hubs, maximum distances in the range of 200–500 meters are typical. At the 512 meter limit of a single segment, Ethernet latency is close to 5 µsecs, and with shorter segments the latency is proportionally less. So you can see that with wiring hubs, Ethernet transmission latency is seldom a grave performance concern.

Switches help to minimize collisions on a busy network because stations receive only packets encoded with their source or destination address. Collisions can and still do occur on switched segments, however, and may even be prevalent when most network traffic tends to be directed at one or more Windows 2000 Servers configured on the segment. When there are two network clients that want to send data to the same server at the same time, a collision on the link to the server will occur.

Back-off and retry

The previous explanation indicates how collisions disrupt the flow of traffic across an Ethernet network segment. The data sender A intended to transmit is not received properly at the receiving station C. This causes an error condition that must be corrected. The frame must be re-sent!

Of course, sender station B, also trying to send data to C, also detects that a collision has occurred. If sender A and sender B *both* detect a collision and *both* try to resend data at the same time, it seems highly likely that the datagrams will collide again. In fact, this is exactly what happens on an Ethernet segment. Following a collision, Ethernet executes a well-known *exponential back-off and retry* algorithm to try to avoid potential future collisions. Each station waits a random period of time between 1 and 58 μsecs before resending data to recover from the collision. If a collision occurs the second time (the probability of another collision on the first retry remains high), each station doubles the potential delay interval and tries again. If a collision happens *again*, each station doubles the potential delay interval again, and so on until the transmission finally succeeds. As the potential interval between retries lengthens, one of the stations will gain enough of a staggered start that eventually its transmission will succeed.

To recap, the Ethernet protocol avoids the overhead of a shared bus arbitration scheme to resolve conflicts when more than one station needs access to the bus. The rationale is, "Let's keep things simple." This approach has much to commend it. As long as the network is not heavily utilized, there is little reason to worry about bus contention. This simple scheme works admirably when Ethernet line utilization remains under 20–40% busy; conflicts seldom arise when lines are lightly utilized.

When conflicts do arise, which they inevitably do on busier networks, Ethernet stations detect that the collisions have occurred and attempt to recover by retrying the transmissions until they succeed. Notice that each station executes the exponential back-off algorithm independently until the transmissions finally succeed. No master controller is ever required to intervene to bring order to the environment. (The problem with a master controller is that master controllers can fail!) No priority scheme is involved to bias the fairness with which the common transmission medium is shared. (The problem with priority schemes is that they often require manual adjustment due to unfairness and the potential for starvation.)

Performance monitoring

Unfortunately, Ethernet's simple and elegant approach does have a drawback: performance degradation occurs when lines are more heavily utilized. As network utilization increases above 20–30% busy with multiple stations attempting to transmit data on the segment, collisions begin to occur. When this happens, each station must retry the transmission, perhaps several times. Due to retries, utilization of the segment increases sharply, doubling from 30–35% busy to 60–70%. Figure 11-8 illustrates the bulge in utilization that can be expected on an Ethernet segment once collisions begin to occur. This characteristic bulge leads many authorities to recommend that you try to maintain the utilization of Ethernet segments below 30–40% busy.

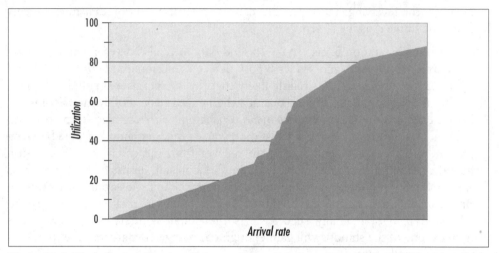

Figure 11-8. The bulge in utilization that occurs on an Ethernet segment due to collisions

Retry behavior causes Ethernet segments to degrade sharply under load. Latency increases and effective throughput decreases as the load on the network increases. In addition, the exponential back-off algorithm used in scheduling retries makes it very hard to drive effective utilization on an Ethernet segment to 100%. From the standpoint of performance monitoring, 30–40% utilization levels on the link are the effective saturation point, given the way Ethernet behaves. Remember, however, that the condition that causes collisions is contention for the transmission link. If the only activity on a segment consists of station A sending data to station B (and station B acknowledging receipt of that data with transmissions back to A) during an application like network backup, there is no contention on the segment. Under those circumstances, you can drive utilization of an Ethernet link to 100% without collisions.

Switched networks provide significant relief from performance problems related to Ethernet collisions, but they do not solve the problems completely. A switch provides a dedicated virtual circuit to and from every station on the segment. With a switch, station A can send data to B while station C sends data to D concurrently without a collision. However, collisions can still occur on a switched network if two stations both try to send data to a third station concurrently.

Unfortunately, there is no Network Monitor diagnostic or System Monitor counter that detects and tracks the collision rate on an Ethernet segment directly. Lacking direct measurement data, you must resort to assembling a case for collisions occurring more anecdotally. First, monitor the *effective* network utilization using the Network Interface Bytes Total/sec and Current Bandwidth counters. With these counters, you can calculate the effective utilization on an Ethernet segment, but you cannot measure the *actual* line utilization with collisions factored in. This is because detecting and recovering from collisions is a function of the network adapter card. The network adapter card masks this activity from the NDIS layer of software where the Network Monitor driver runs. Only packets sent and delivered successfully are visible to NDIS.

Even at relatively low effective utilization levels of 30–40%, it is reasonable to expect that Ethernet collisions are occurring with some frequency. Once you observe measurements of effective network utilization in this range consistently, you can use the Network Monitor capture facility to investigate conditions further. With the Network Monitor you can determine whether or not multiple stations are contributing to the network traffic aimed at this machine. If multiple sender/receiver pairs figure prominently in the packet traffic captured, it is reasonable to conclude that collisions are occurring. In that case, the actual line utilization is probably much busier than the effective utilization that you are able to measure with Microsoft's network monitoring software. You can confirm this hypothesis by installing a hardware-based sniffer to capture *all* the packets on the line and verify the rate of collisions directly.

The steps to relieve performance problems due to an overloaded Ethernet LAN segment are straightforward:

- If you are using a hub, consider upgrading to a switched network. This is the simplest and least disruptive hardware configuration change you can make to improve performance. However, switching hardware is not a guaranteed fix.

- If you are running 10 Mb Ethernet, consider upgrading to 100 Mb Fast Ethernet. Be advised that hardware that assists in the conversion from 10BaseT to 100BaseT using dual autosensing 10/100 ports will be clocked down to 10BaseT if *any* of the NIC cards on the segment continue to demand 10BaseT. Consequently, this is often a disruptive change since you need to swap out all your old 10 Mb cards to realize the performance benefit.

- If you are running 100 Mb Ethernet, consider upgrading to 1000BaseT Gigabit Ethernet. See the following discussion about this high-speed networking technology.

- If collisions are the result of multiple stations all trying to transmit to a shared file or application server, consider further segmenting the network and splitting the network traffic across multiple segments. The Windows 2000 DFS offers a number of opportunities to split a file server load across multiple machines, for example. In the case of an overloaded application server like an MS Exchange or Lotus Notes mail server, it may be possible to build a distributed cluster where transactions are distributed across multiple machines and (potentially) network segments.

Gigabit Ethernet

Gigabit Ethernet is an emerging standard for high-speed networking that maintains backward compatibility with older flavors of the venerable Ethernet specification. The revision of the IEEE specification that defines Gigabit Ethernet is known as 803.2z. The header structure of the frames that Gigabit Ethernet uses is identical to the format defined for 10BaseT and 100BaseT. Gigabit Ethernet is capable of very high performance, supporting data rates of 1 Gb/sec. Due to very strict distance limitations (refer back to Table 11-2), Gigabit Ethernet is usually installed with fiber optics links, which means a new wiring infrastructure is required. This alone is enough to slow down the adoption of this next generation in network technology. Due to the cost of the equipment and the rewiring involved, Gigabit Ethernet is today generally confined to high-speed backbones, although there are certainly applications where running Gigabit Ethernet to individual workstations is desirable. It seems clear that as prices for Gigabit Ethernet equipment continue to fall, the new technology will become more widespread.

The advent of 1 Gb/sec networking technology has exposed a number of latent performance issues in long-standing networking specifications, PC server architecture, and the TCP/IP protocol suite. There has been a concerted effort across the computer industry to address these concerns. We briefly discuss the challenges raised by high-speed networking and the steps taken to meet that challenge. Suffice to say at this point that you must configure Windows 2000 servers carefully in order to reap the full benefits of Gigabit Ethernet.

One of the most significant efforts is Microsoft's extensive reworking of the TCP/IP protocol stack for Windows 2000. Gigabit Ethernet performance on Windows NT Version 4.0 is marginal, but early experience with Gigabit Ethernet support in Windows 2000 shows substantial improvement. Based on the cumulative impact of the changes Microsoft has made in Windows 2000, Intel's initiatives to improve the PC server architecture, and various networking vendors' efforts in the area of jumbo frames, Gigabit Ethernet networking is an attractive option on current generation PC servers.

PC architecture considerations

Gigabit Ethernet technology uses essentially the same hardware, lasers, optics, and fiber links as the fibre channel specification for SCSI peripherals discussed in earlier chapters. For instance, both are based on identical lasers clocked at 1 GHz. In fact, at some point in the near future, it seems likely that these technologies will merge and one set of wires will be able to carry both SCSI and IP commands and traffic. Gigabit Ethernet shares many of the performance considerations of fibre channel. Most important is the need for Windows 2000 servers connected to a Gigabit Ethernet backbone to be equipped with high-speed internal PCI buses. Similar to fibre channel, the original PCI interface designed to run at 132 MB/sec saturates with the attachment of a single Gigabit Ethernet adaptor card. Servers configured with new flavors of the PCI 2.1 interface spec supporting speeds of two or four times the original PCI bus are a minimum requirement for supporting Gigabit Ethernet under either Windows NT or Windows 2000.

Advanced PC servers architected with multiple PCI buses are also desirable. If multiple high-speed PCI 2.1 buses are available, Gigabit Ethernet network traffic should be configured on one, and fibre channel SCSI cards configured on the other. Segregating network traffic on the PCI bus from SCSI traffic tends to reduce overall contention for the bus and the queuing delays that result. Mixing small network blocks, especially those associated with TCP ACKs, with (relatively) large block SCSI I/O operations yields a worst case for queuing. However, the necessity for segregating Gigabit Ethernet traffic from SCSI commands is reduced with the TCP/IP jumbo frame and selective acknowledgment support available in Windows 2000.

Jumbo frames

The Ethernet frame size of 1500 bytes, originally devised 20 years ago, is not a good match to the performance characteristics of high-bandwidth Gigabit Ethernet network backbones. Bulk traffic arriving in steady, intense patterns that is characteristic of network backbones tends to benefit from larger frame sizes. Consider the overhead and cost of turning 4 K, 8 K, and larger disk file blocks in routine SMB networked file operations into 1500 byte fragments. Besides the computational overhead of fragmenting file I/O blocks into smaller Ethernet-compliant packets and reassembling them on the receiver side, there is the cost of additional interrupt handling at both ends of the wire when small packets must be used.

This concern is hardly a new one. It was raised back when the 100 Mb/sec Fast Ethernet specification was being formalized. However, at that time, the desirability of maintaining full compatibility with the earlier 10BaseT 1518 byte frame size prevailed. Consequently, Fast Ethernet was designed to run over the same wiring infrastructure as first-generation Ethernet 10BaseT, and hubs, switches, and adapter cards built to support both 10BaseT and 100BaseT standards were built to permit intermixing equipment on the same network segments. These steps ease the conversion to the newer technology. On the other hand, enlarging the Ethernet frame size is a major break with the past, causing new equipment to be incompatible with the enormous installed base in 10BaseT. These considerations are not as important in converting to Gigabit Ethernet because maintaining complete upward compatibility is not the overriding concern. After all, new, dedicated wiring is required in most instances to convert to the new technology.

Figure 11-9, based on benchmark results reported by Alteon Systems, quantifies some of the performance advantages of using larger-sized frames with Gigabit Ethernet technology. Comparing throughput on a single 1 Gb link, increasing the frame size from the Ethernet standard 1518 bytes to a 9 KB frame, effective throughput across the link improves by 50%, while utilization of the server CPU drops precipitously because of the sharp reduction in the number of interrupts to be processed. Figure 11-9 suggests that one of the major benefits of so-called jumbo frames is a substantial reduction in the overhead of server-side interrupt processing. They reduce the server CPU requirements significantly, a very important consideration if you are thinking about installing Intel-based PCs on high-speed network backbones. When jumbo frames are combined with larger TCP window sizes and selective acknowledgments (two enhancements to the Windows 2000 TCP/IP stack discussed in more detail shortly), off-the-shelf PC server machines become viable and cost-effective networked file and web servers.

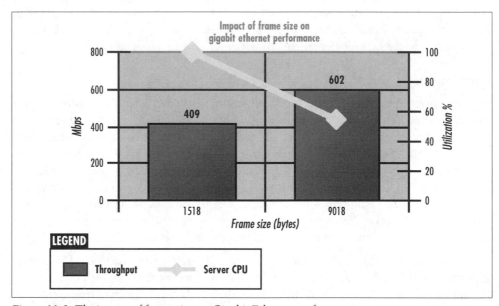

Figure 11-9. The impact of frame size on Gigabit Ethernet performance

Unfortunately, converting to jumbo frames for Gigabit Ethernet is still problematic, raising some serious conversion and vendor interoperability issues. For example, not all vendors' Gigabit Ethernet equipment supports jumbo frames. Moreover, jumbo frames cannot circulate freely on your network, but instead must be restricted somehow to those network segments that can specifically handle them. There are two basic ways to accomplish this: dedicated backbones that restrict the reach of jumbo frames, and the use of the 802.1Q frame tagging mechanism to create partitioned Virtual LANs (VLANs). Consult with your hardware vendor before deciding which of these options will work best in your environment.

Gigabit Ethernet hardware equipment from vendors like Alteon that are pioneering the use of jumbo frames may require additional customization for optimal performance. NDIS network miniport driver Registry settings for the Alteon ACENic, for example, include an option to turn on the use of jumbo frames, set the jumbo frame

MTU size, and allocate a sufficient number of memory buffers to support the desired data rate. No doubt you will have to experiment with some of these settings to optimize performance for your environment. For example, the jumbo frame size of 9018 bytes used in the benchmark reported in Figure 11-9 was chosen based on several relevant considerations. The 9000-byte payload in the jumbo frame is divisible evenly by the 1500-byte data payload of standard Ethernet frames. This allows a jumbo frame to be broken readily into standard Ethernet frames to bridge the Gigabit Ethernet VLAN. The 9 K payload also easily holds the 4 K and 8 K file I/O blocks frequently found in NTFS filesystem requests without fragmentation. This is a very important consideration in SMB networking. If you decide to use the larger size NTFS allocation units available in Windows 2000, you will probably need to adjust the jumbo frame size upwards accordingly.

Improved TCP/IP protocol stack

Several of the new features of the Windows 2000 TCP/IP protocol suite were included to provide superior performance with Gigabit Ethernet technology. These include Path Maximum Transmission Unit (PMTU) discovery, which is a feature of Windows 2000's IP support. Windows 2000 TCP enhancements that enhance Gigabit Ethernet performance include TCP scalable window sizes and support for selective acknowledgment. Because we have not yet discussed IP and TCP in depth, we defer discussion of those features for later when we can treat them in the proper context. Suffice to say that Microsoft has significantly enhanced its TCP/IP protocol stack with Gigabit Ethernet support in mind.

Token Ring

Token Ring networking architectures are a popular alternative to Ethernet and, in fact, have some distinct performance advantages over it. Two flavors of Token Ring networking are available: the original IBM Token Ring architecture, which is available at 4 and 16 Mb/sec data rates, and the Fiber Distributed Data Interchange (FDDI) protocol, which operates at 40 and 100 Mb/sec data rates. The IBM Token Ring is codified as the IEEE 802.5 standard and features a simple arbitration scheme that supports higher effective data rates than Ethernet over similar speed links. It is not unusual to be able to drive Token Ring network segments at 90% utilization without experiencing the type of performance degradation that Ethernet collisions cause. We explain this arbitration scheme in a moment.

The main obstacle to using Token Ring is that it is incompatible with the more commonly implemented Ethernet standard. Protocol converters are required to bridge Ethernet and Token Ring networks. In its early days, additional complexity associated with its arbitration scheme made Token Ring hardware more costly to build. Eventually, the much larger demand for Ethernet created a low-cost, high-volume commodity market for Ethernet components of all kinds, including NICs, hubs, and switches, giving Ethernet hardware a distinct price advantage. Moreover, outside of IBM there have never been many manufacturers of Token Ring hardware. Instead of an open standard, Token Ring was viewed as IBM proprietary technology even though IBM published the specification and standardized it. When IBM developed 16 Mb Token Ring, prospects for the standard improved because it had better performance characteristics than the then-current 10BaseT Ethernet standard. But the development of Fast Ethernet, which could run over existing wiring and coexist with 10BaseT hardware, doomed IBM Token Ring to being forever marginalized. Indeed, IBM is not even contemplating a next-generation Token Ring hardware implementation to compete with Fast Ethernet.

FDDI is quite similar to IBM Token Ring architecturally, with modifications suitable for use with fiber optical media and dual, redundant pathing. For several years, FDDI was the preferred choice for high-speed LAN backbones and was especially attractive in environments with high availability requirements. Today, with the low cost of 100 Mb Fast Ethernet components and availability of an even faster Gigabit Ethernet standard, the use of FDDI is on the decline. Due to the marginal status of both IBM Token Ring and FDDI, we treat them here only briefly.

Arbitration

Token Ring uses an arbitration scheme that features round robin "fair" scheduling, with a provision for multiple priority levels. Round robin scheduling is the most noteworthy feature that differentiates Token Ring networks from the CSMA/CD protocols. A special control frame called the token circulates continuously around the ring from station to station. Only a station holding the token can transmit data. That station waits until the data frame it transmitted makes the complete circuit around the ring back to its point of origin. The sender is then responsible for removing the data frame from circulation and passing the token to the next station on the ring. Because only the station holding the token can transmit data, there can never be a collision on the line.

Now let's look at how this token-passing scheme performs. Because Token Ring LANs have distance constraints similar to Ethernet, they also feature very low latency. On a lightly loaded ring, a station that needs to perform bulk transfers is delayed only slightly while it waits for the token to circulate around the ring. A priority mechanism can be used to let certain nodes hold the token longer, permitting more important stations to utilize proportionally more of the available bandwidth. If multiple stations need to transmit data, the token-passing mechanism ensures that use of the ring rotates fairly between the stations in a round robin fashion. Unlike Ethernet, multiple stations attempting to use the network segment can drive utilization close to 100% busy without degradation.

Still, Token Ring LANs can handle no more traffic than their specified bandwidth. 100 Mb Fast Ethernet, even with its inefficient mechanism for resolving line conflicts, achieves effective bandwidth of 30 Mb/sec under the worst collision scenarios. That is still greater throughput than a 16 Mb Token Ring segment offers.

The token-passing arbitration scheme does introduce some additional complexity to the protocol. For instance, a recovery mechanism is required to handle the case where the station holding the token dies. On every Token Ring, one station is designated as the Monitor, with responsibility for replacing the token on the ring if one does not appear within a designated interval. The Monitor station also removes a data packet that is in circulation from a station that has failed. Of course, having a designated Monitor means that there must be a suitable mechanism to recover from the failure of the Monitor node. While none of this arbitration-related logic is prohibitively complex, it does contribute to the manufacturing of Token Ring components being slightly more expensive than Ethernet.

FDDI Rings

FDDI uses a similar token-passing scheme. Its main distinguishing characteristics are its dual-ring topology for high availability and its use of fiber optical links for relatively long-distance connections at 100 Mb/sec. In normal operation, only the primary ring carries data; the other ring is idle. Traffic normally flows in one direction on one ring and the opposite direction on the other. When a station or link on the ring fails, the dual ring automatically wraps (doubles back on itself) into a single-ring configuration so that data can continue to be transmitted around the ring without degradation. A single FDDI segment can span 2 km, while the entire length of an FDDI ring can reach a perimeter of 200 km. The FDDI frame format is similar to Token Ring and it supports an MTU as large as 4500 bytes.

Internet Protocol Layer

The Internet Protocol (IP) layer, also known as Layer 3 (with the physical and data link layers associated with the MAC layer being Layers 1 and 2, respectively) is primarily concerned with delivering packets from one location to another. The technology that the Internet protocol implements is called *routing*. Routing is associated with a bundle of standards that include IP itself, ICMP, ARP, BGP, and others. Another important function of the IP layer is to make larger packets conform to the MTU of the underlying data link and physical layer protocol and transmission medium. In this section, we introduce the key aspects of IP routing technology that most impact network performance and capacity planning.

You will find that the basic technology used in IP routing is deceptively simple. What makes IP routing such a difficult topic from a performance perspective is the complicated, interconnected network infrastructures and superstructures that organizations have erected to manage masses of essentially unscheduled IP traffic. That the Internet works as well as it does is phenomenal, given the complexity of the underlying network of networks it supports. While there are many good books available on TCP/IP and how it works, there are not many places where a Windows 2000 system administrator can gain a good appreciation for the major performance and capacity issues facing organizations that rely on the Internet for mail, file transfer, e-commerce, and other data communications services.

IP Routing

Routing is the process by which packets are forwarded from one network segment to the next until they reach their final destination. These network segments can span organizations, regions, and countries, with the result that IP is used to interconnect a vast worldwide network of computers. IP is the set of routing standards that tie computers on both private intranets and the public Internet together so that they can send mail, messages, files, and other types of digital information back and forth.

Devices called *routers* serve as gateways, interconnecting different network segments. They implement Layer 3 packet forwarding. Routers are connected to one or more local LAN segments and then connect via WAN links to other routers located on external networks. It is worth noting that Windows 2000 machines can be configured to serve as routers by enabling the IP forwarding function. However, the more common practice is to use devices designed specifically to perform Layer 3 switching. Routers are basically responsible for forwarding packets addressed to some external network to the next hop in their journey. Routers also serve as gateways connecting separate and distinct network segments. They recognize packets that have arrived at the correct network and are intended for internal locations. They place these packets on the LAN, where they circulate until they reach the desired MAC address. Routers also initiate messages (encapsulated as packets, naturally) intended for other routers that are used to exchange information about route availability.

While IP is responsible for delivering packets from one address to another, you may be surprised to learn that IP does not guarantee delivery of those packets. Moreover, once a packet is entrusted to IP for delivery, there is no mechanism within IP to confirm the delivery of that packet as instructed. This idea may take a little getting used to.* IP was designed around a "best effort" service model that is both *unreliable* and *connectionless*. Before you get too disturbed about entrusting important network traffic to an unreliable packet delivery mechanism like IP, you can rest easy knowing that the host-to-host connection layer above IP is the component responsible for maintaining reliable, in-order delivery of packets. That component, of course, is TCP.

---

* It may be some solace to note that the U.S. Postal Service adopts a similar service model for ordinary first-class mail. The USPS does not guarantee delivery either, nor are you notified when mail is delivered to its intended recipient.

Being a best-effort service model, IP certainly works hard to deliver the packets entrusted to it. Using IP, if there is a serviceable route between two addresses on the Internet, no matter how convoluted, IP will find it and use it to deliver the goods. As you can probably imagine, route availability across a large system of interconnected public and private networks is subject to constant change. It is a good practice for every critical location on your private network to be accessible from more than one connection or path.

Determining which path to take is one of the responsibilities of Internet Protocol Layer 3 routers. Undoubtedly, some routes are better than others because they can deliver traffic faster, more reliably, or with less cost. Some routers implement the simple Routing Information Protocol (RIP), which selects routes primarily based on the number of hops involved. More powerful routers usually implement the more robust Open Shortest Path First (OSPF) protocol, which attempts to assess both route availability and performance in making decisions. The popularity of the public-access Internet has recently generated interest in having routers use policy-oriented Quality of Service (QoS) metrics to select among packets that arrive from different sources and different applications. An in-depth discussion comparing and contrasting these routing methods is beyond the scope of this book.

Routing tables

The dynamic aspects of routing create a big problem: how to store all that information about route availability and performance and keep it up to date. In local area networking, stations are organized into rings, a single, continuous circuit where every station can reach every other station. Delivering traffic in a LAN is simple. The sender creates a packet showing the destination address and places the packet on the wire. The packet circulates around the ring to every connected station. Eventually, it reaches the destination station, which makes a local copy of the packet. Meanwhile, the packet continues to circulate around the ring until it reaches the sender, which is then responsible for removing it from the transmission media.

Routing takes place in a much different environment. The Internet consists of thousands and thousands of separate autonomous network segments, interconnected in myriad ways. The route from your workstation to some location like *www.yahoo. com* is not predetermined. There is no way to know that such a route even exists.

IP solves the problem of storing information about route availability in an interesting way. The IP internetworking environment does not store a complete set of routing information in any one centralized location that might be either vulnerable to failure or become a performance bottleneck. Instead, information about route availability is distributed across the network, maintained in *routing tables* stored in individual routers. Routing tables list the network addresses an individual router knows how to deliver packets to. In addition, routers are programmed to send all packets that they do not know how to deliver to some default location for address resolution. The route command-line utility can be used to display the contents of a machine's routing table:

```
C:\>route print
=========================================================================
Interface List
0x1 ......................... MS TCP Loopback interface
0x2000002 ...00 00 86 38 39 5a ...... 3Com Megahertz LAN + 56K
=========================================================================
=========================================================================
Active Routes:
Network Destination Netmask Gateway Interface Metric
          0.0.0.0          0.0.0.0     24.10.211.1      24.10.211.47    1
       24.10.211.0    255.255.255.0    24.10.211.47     24.10.211.47    1
      24.10.211.47  255.255.255.255      127.0.0.1        127.0.0.1     1
    24.255.255.255  255.255.255.255    24.10.211.47     24.10.211.47    1
         127.0.0.0        255.0.0.0      127.0.0.1        127.0.0.1     1
     192.168.247.0    255.255.255.0   192.168.247.1    192.168.247.1    1
     192.168.247.1  255.255.255.255      127.0.0.1        127.0.0.1     1
     200.200.200.0    255.255.255.0   200.200.200.1    200.200.200.1    1
     200.200.200.1  255.255.255.255      127.0.0.1        127.0.0.1     1
         224.0.0.0        224.0.0.0   200.200.200.1    200.200.200.1    1
         224.0.0.0        224.0.0.0    24.10.211.47     24.10.211.47    1
         224.0.0.0        224.0.0.0   192.168.247.1    192.168.247.1    1
   255.255.255.255  255.255.255.255   192.168.247.1        0.0.0.0      1
=========================================================================
Persistent Routes:
 None
```

This sample routing table is for a Windows 2000 machine at address 24.10.211.47 serving as a router. This table marks addresses within the 24.10.211.0 Class C network range (with a subnet mask of 255.255.255.0) for local delivery. It also shows two external router connections at locations 200.200.200.1 and 192.168.247.1. Packets intended for IP addresses that this machine has no direct knowledge of are routed to the 192.168.247.1 interface by default.

The set of all IP addresses that an organization's routers manage directly defines the boundaries of an *autonomous system* (AS). Routers discover dynamically the IP addresses that can be reached within locally attached network segments using the Internet Control Message Protocol (ICMP). In a later section, we look at some ICMP facilities that are particularly useful in diagnosing IP routing problems. Routers also generate ICMP "Destination unreachable" error messages when they encounter packets they cannot deliver successfully.

For the Internet to work, routers in one autonomous system need to interchange routing information with the routers they are connected to in other autonomous systems. This is accomplished using the Border Gateway Protocol (BGP). Using BGP, routers exchange information with other routers about the IP addresses that they are of capable of delivering packets to.

As the status of links within some autonomous network configuration changes, the routers at the borders of the network communicate these changes to the routers they are attached to at other external networks. Routers use BGP messages to exchange this information. BGP is mainly something that the ISPs that manage the public-access IP network backbone that services the Internet community worry about. Naturally, ISP routers maintain extensive routing tables about the subnetworks the providers manage. We discuss some performance aspects of the routing performed on ISP premises later on.

One of the key ingredients that makes IP routing work across a vast network like the Internet is that each IP packet that routers operate on is self-contained. It contains all the information that Layer 3 switching devices need to decide where to deliver it and what kind of service it requires. The IP header, discussed in detail in a later section, contains the addresses of both the sender and the intended receiver. Another feature of IP is that routers operate on IP packets individually. It is quite possible for two packets sent by A and intended for B to be delivered following entirely different routes.

When a router receives a packet across an external link that is destined for delivery locally, the router is responsible for delivering that packet to the correct station on the LAN. That means the router sends this packet to the MAC layer interface, plugging in the correct destination address. (The router leaves the source address unchanged so that you can always tell where the packet originated.) The Address Resolution Protocol (ARP) is used to maintain a current list of local IP addresses and their associated MAC addresses.

Router performance

The fact that IP does not guarantee the delivery of packets does have some interesting performance consequences. When IP networks get congested, routers can either queue packets for later processing or they can drop the excess load. By design, most high-performance routers do the latter. They are capable of keeping only a very small queue of pending requests, usually no more than one or two. If additional requests to forward packets are received and the queue is full, most routers simply drop incoming packets. Dropping packets is OK in IP. After all, IP never guaranteed that it would deliver those packets in the first place. The protocol is only designed to make its "best effort" to deliver them.

There are several justifications for this strategy that are related directly to performance considerations. The original designers of the Internet included Dr. Leonard Kleinrock of UCLA, one of the pioneers in the application of queuing theory to the performance of digital computers and networks. Kleinrock understood that bottlenecks in the Internet infrastructure might be structural and persistent where some key component in the network was hopelessly undersized. In fact, given the range of organizations that can plug into the Internet, it is inevitable that some routes are not adequately sized. Therefore, the Internet packet delivery mechanism needs to be resilient in the face of persistent, mismatched component speeds.

The practical design issue, assuming that these mismatched capacity problems are structural, is, "What level of queuing should a router serving as the gateway between two networks attached to the Internet support?" Consider that queuing at an undersized component during peak loads would lead to queuing delays of exponential proportions whenever requests started to arrive faster than the router could service them. Furthermore, given the scope of the Internet, the queue length at an inadequately sized router would grow indefinitely. Whatever queue depth a bottlenecked router was designed to support could readily be exceeded at some point. When a router finally exhausts the buffer space it has available to queue incoming requests, it would be necessary to discard packets anyway. With this basic understanding of the fundamental problem in mind, it makes sense to discard packets before the queue of deferred requests grows large and begins to require extensive resources to manage.

Managing longer queue depths at routers also emerges as a disadvantage from another perspective. Having servers with the capability to manage large backlogs of queued requests leads to high variability in response times for these requests when the servers get overloaded and requests start to back up. This is a fundamental result in queuing theory. Having the ability to drop packets once the queue reaches a limit of just two or three active requests results in more deterministic response times for those packets that do get service. Having deterministic response times at routers reduces the overall queuing impact of an IP packet delivery request that is forced to traverse a complex network. So dropping requests at overloaded routers is good for the response time of the packets that make it through the network to their destination.

Routers have a specific processing capacity, rated in terms of packets/second. When packets arrive at a router faster than the router can deliver them, excess packets are dropped. Because most routers are designed to support only minimal levels of queuing, the response times of packets they deliver is very consistent, never subject to degradation when the network is busy. Obviously, you need to know when the rate of network traffic exceeds capacity because that is when routers begin dropping packets. Whenever this occurs, you should think immediately about replacing overloaded routers with faster units. Alternatively, you may need to add network capacity in the form of both additional routes and routers. When Level 3 routers are overloaded and begin to drop packets, the performance impact is significant. The impact is felt not at Level 3 where IP functions, but at the next highest level in the TCP/IP protocol stack, namely the TCP host-to-host functions responsible for in-order, reliable delivery of packets.

Performance statistics are available from most routers using either SNMP or RMON interfaces. Although Microsoft does supply an SNMP agent for Windows 2000, it does not provide an SNMP Manager application to poll routers and access their performance statistics. These statistics may be available to you if your organization runs an SNMP Manager application like the Tivoli Management Environment, CA-Unicenter, or HP OpenView. Most routers report the number of packets they process directly, the number of packets queued, and the number of packets dropped because the queue limit was exceeded. In addition, some routers return ICMP Source Quench messages when they reach saturation and need to begin dropping packets.

However, if you install the SNMP network service, you can access Windows 2000 internal IP statistics using System Monitor. These statistics count packets received and processed by the IP layer of software in the Windows 2000 TCP/IP protocol stack. These IP counters are mainly useful for network capacity planning—they keep track of the IP traffic generated by individual Windows 2000 servers running applications like IIS and Exchange. The counters of interest in this regard include Datagrams Received/sec, Datagrams Sent/sec, and the total Datagrams/sec. Some of the other IP counters are helpful mainly if you are using the IP forwarding function of Windows 2000 that allows your machine to serve as a router.

Obviously, dropping packets at a busy router has dire consequences for someone somewhere, namely the originator of the request that failed. While IP is not concerned about what happens to a few packets here and there, it is a concern at the next highest level in the protocol stack, the TCP host-to-host connection Layer 4. TCP will eventually notice that a packet is missing and attempt some form of error recovery, like trying to re-send the original packet. If TCP cannot recover from the error, it notifies the application that issued the request. This leads to the familiar "Request Timed Out" error message in your web browser that prods you to retry the entire request.

The structural problem of having an overloaded component on the internetwork somewhere also must be systematically addressed. In networking design, this is known as the problem of *flow control*, e.g., what to do about a powerful router at the core of the Internet backbone that is overloading some underpowered router installed on a customer's premises. Again, while flow control is not a concern at the IP level, TCP, as we will see shortly, does provide a robust flow control mechanism.

IP Addressing

An IP address uniquely identifies a specific node on a particular network in a standard way, independent of the underlying physical and data link networking technology. IP addresses are 32-bit numbers, usually displayed as a hierarchical series of four numeric bytes. The 32-bit address is divided into two separate components using a subnet mask. The first set of bits in the address is called the *network number* and is common for all addresses within the same autonomous network. The second set of bits is the *host number*, which uniquely identifies each station, router, gateway, or other device connected to the network. The subnet bit mask identifies how many bits are associated with each component.

With the popularity of the Internet, the 32-bit addressing range established by IP Version 4 is starting to shows signs of being exhausted. A newer version of IP, IPv6, has been proposed, which incorporates 128-bit addresses. The problem facing the industry now is how to phase in the new IP standard cost-effectively and without disrupting the networking services that millions of people have come to expect from the Internet. To date, no one has come up with a satisfactory resolution for this tricky problem.

There are two standard utilities that assist in the management of Internet protocol addresses. One is the Domain Name System (DNS), which allows you to access computers by name rather than by IP address. The other is the Dynamic Host Control Program (DHCP), which is used to assign IP addresses to computers dynamically.

DNS

Naturally, people usually refer to computers by name rather than by an obscure IP network address and host ID. The Internet provides a standardized Domain Name System that keeps track of computer naming *domains* and their corresponding IP network addresses. A domain is a name like *sales.microsoft.com* that is used to define a subset of all the computers in one department at Microsoft. The Internet DNS namespace database is distributed just like routing information. By distributing the dynamic management of the Domain Name System, an SMTP-compliant mail application like MS Exchange or Lotus Notes can reach the address of Microsoft's DNS server, first looking up the IP address for *microsoft.com* by contacting the DNS server at your ISP, and then requesting the address of the *sales.microsoft.com* subdomain from a Microsoft-managed DNS server.

Consequently, DNS also defines a protocol for one DNS server to query another DNS server to resolve a request for a domain name's address. Windows 2000 contains a native DNS server application. Normally, you would let your local DNS servers resolve the IP addresses of the computers attached to the local network, and point your DNS server to another DNS server located at your ISP to look up the IPO addresses of computers in external domains.

Earlier versions of Windows NT relied exclusively on WINS, the Windows Internet Name Service, which maps NetBIOS names into IP addresses. It is still necessary to run WINS if you have computers on your IP network running Windows NT 4.0. WINS performs comparable address lookup functions as DNS, but it is not 100% compatible with DNS.

The details of both DNS and WINS are beyond the scope of this book. Suffice to say that DNS and WINS provide a lookup function that enables TCP applications to translate domain names into IP addresses. For instance, if you want to contact *www.yahoo.com* from your web browser, IP calls the DNS server application to determine that the IP address of Yahoo's web site corresponds to 204.71.200.3.

DHCP

The Dynamic Host Control Program (DHCP) is a standard IP address management utility that centralizes and automates administration of local IP addresses, making managing a large, constantly changing IP-based network substantially easier. Windows 2000 Server contains DHCP.

Every node on an IP network must have a unique host ID. Keeping track of which IDs are in use across a large, distributed network subject to almost constant change can be very tedious. Clients can use DHCP to acquire an IP address and other standard configuration info—like the IP address of the nearest DNS server—automatically when they sign onto the network.

Usually, the IP addresses that DHCP clients acquire are not permanent. These addresses are *leased* by clients from a DHCP server for some temporary period, after which the client is forced to negotiate a new lease. Leasing IP addresses greatly facilitates making changes to the network. If you decide for some reason that you need to split one network into two, DHCP can be used to make all network clients negotiate new leases to acquire IP addresses in the range allocated by the new network. Permanent IP addresses called *reservations* can also be assigned using DHCP.

DHCP naturally defines several messages, which are used by clients to negotiate a lease for an IP address. A client with no current IP address issues a DHCP DISCOVER broadcast message to locate a DHCP server. A DHCP server application, listening to UDP port 67, responds with an OFFER message. The client normally replies with a REQUEST message accepting the IP address offered, which the DHCP server confirms with an ACK. Additional DHCP messages are defined to RELEASE an IP address previously defined, DECLINE a lease, etc.

IP Header Fields

The control information that IP places in its packet headers is shown in Figure 11-10. As noted earlier, the IP header contains all the information a Level 3 router needs to know to deliver the packet to its final destination. The source and destination address fields shown contain the unique 32-bit IP addresses discussed earlier. Notice that the packet addressing information is limited to the IP addresses themselves; the subnet mask is not part of the control information IP needs in the packet. Subnet masks are saved, stored, and used exclusively by Level 3 routers. Routers compare the destination address bits specified in the packet against the significant bits of the network ID (as determined by the subnet mask). If a match is detected, the packet is destined for a station on the local network segment that the router serves as a gateway for. If no match occurs, the router forwards the packet to its next intermediate destination. This is either a specific destination represented in the router's routing table, assuming the current router has specific knowledge (via BGP) of a route to the final destination, or a default router address to attempt delivery from there.

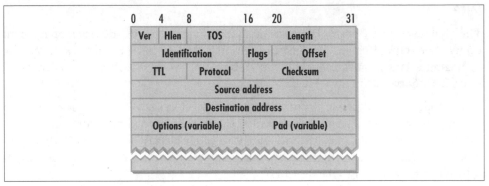

Figure 11-10. IP Version 4 packet header fields

The packet header illustrated in Figure 11-10 contains a number of other interesting fields that have performance ramifications. These IP header fields are described in more detail in the following sections.

Type of Service (TOS)

The Type of Service field can be used to specify the quality of service a packet delivered to a router should receive. The Type of Service that a TCP/IP application can request includes setting relative priority, which uses the first three bits of the TOS field. The three precedence bits are interpreted as follows:

Precedence bits	Interpretation
000	Routine
001	Priority
010	Immediate
011	Flash
100	Flash Override
101	Critical
110	Internetwork Control
111	Network Control

An application can also set a series of "hints" to suggest that the router select a route based on some combination of delay, throughput, reliability, and cost considerations. Four bits following the three precedence bits are used to request low delay, high throughput, high reliability, and low cost. The low-order bit in the TOS field is reserved. For example, a TOS value of '00110100'b (or 52^{10}) is a request for priority service and requests that routers select a route based on low delay and high reliability.

A TCP/IP Registry setting called DefaultTOS is available to establish a default TOS value. (Unless otherwise indicated, all TCP/IP parameters discussed in this chapter are located at HKLM\SYSTEM\CurrentControlSet\Services\Tcpip\Parameters.) If

DefaultTOS is not set, the Windows 2000 TOS value defaults to zero. DefaultTOS is one of many valid TCP/IP Registry settings not documented in the *Technical Reference to the Windows 2000 Registry* help file that ships with the Windows 2000 Resource Kit online documentation.

For many years, the Type of Service field in IP was neglected, and many routers provided only minimal support for the various "hints." Naturally, the hints have no impact when there is only one route to a destination.

Organizations struggling with difficult IP performance issues that result from mixing all sorts of traffic over a shared networking infrastructure have rekindled interest in IP Quality of Service (QoS) policies. The Windows 2000 QoS implementation includes the Resource Reservation Protocol (RSVP), a Layer 3 protocol to convey QoS policies to the network. With RSVP, Windows 2000 network administrators can reserve specific amounts of available bandwidth for specific applications. You can also specify a number of different classes of service, including Best Effort, Controlled Load, and Guaranteed service levels. Of course, you must also install routers that understand how to implement QoS policies on your network. For more information on RSVP QoS policies, read Chapter 9 in the Windows 2000 Server Resource Kit's *TCP/IP Core Networking Guide*.

Packet fragmentation and reassembly

Three header fields provide instructions used in packet fragmentation and reassembly. These are the Identification, Flags, and Offset fields that make up the second 32-bit word in the IP packet header. Messages handed to IP by UDP and TCP applications require fragmentation when they are longer than the MTU of the underlying MAC layer protocol. Routers also need to fragment packets they are forwarding when the MAC layer on the forwarded route supports a lower MTU value than the source route. The IP layer at the packet's destination is responsible for reassembling the message from a series of fragmented packets and returning data to the application in its original format.

The Identification field is a simple counter maintained by the sender and used by the receiver to determine the order in which the packet was originally sent. It is used to reassemble the original payload of a message that was fragmented into a series of packets. The Fragment Offset field is a 13-bit field set to indicate the relative byte position of the current data payload in the original message. In addition, three Flag bits are available, of which only the second two are currently used. When bit 2 in the Flag field is set to 0, routers are instructed never to fragment the message. This Don't Fragment flag is primarily used in ICMP control messages to determine the path MTU dynamically. The final Flag bit is set when the packet is the first or a middle fragment. It is set to 0 for the last fragment to mark it as the end of a sequence.

Time To Live (TTL)

The Time To Live (TTL) field is used to ensure that packets cannot circulate from router to router around the network forever. This is potentially a big problem in a network the size and scope of the Internet. Any arbitrarily large internetworking topology is bound to have loops that would allow a packet to circulate around and around, traversing the same gateway locations over and over again. As originally specified, the one-byte TTL field was designed to represent the number of seconds a packet could survive on the Internet before it was disregarded. Each IP router in the destination path was supposed to subtract the number of seconds that the packet resided at the router from the TTL header field and pass it on. But because packets tended to spend most of their time in transit *between* routers connected by long distance WAN links, the original scheme proved unworkable.

The TTL field was then reinterpreted to mean the number of path components on which a packet travels on the way to its destination. Today, each router that operates on a packet decrements the TTL field before sending it on its way. If at some point a router detects a packet with a TTL value of zero, that packet is discarded on the assumption that it is circulating in an infinite loop. The sender sets the initial value of the TTL field, which is interpreted as the maximum link count. Subtracting the final TTL value observed at the destination from the initial value yields the *hop count*, the number of links traversed before the packet reached its final destination. Obviously, this value can be extremely useful in determining why packet transmission took so long.

TTL is a one-byte field with a maximum possible link count of 255. Windows 2000 sets TTL to 128 by default. Since IP packets typically can span the globe in less than 20 hops, a TTL of 128 is generous. This default value can be overridden by setting the DefaultTTL TCP/IP parameter. Note: the Windows 2000 Resource Kit online documentation mistakenly reports that the TTL value still represents seconds. This is a common mistake.

Protocol

The Protocol is a one-byte field that identifies the upper layer protocol of the packet's payload data. Some common values of the Protocol field are shown here:

Protocol	Value
1	Internet Control Message Protocol (ICMP)
2	Internet Group Management Protocol (IGMP)
4	IP to IP encapsulation
6	Transmission Control Protocol (TCP)
8	Boundary Gateway Protocol (BGP)
17	User Datagram Protocol (UDP)
46	Resource Reservation Protocol (RSVP)

Now that we have discussed the important IP packet header fields, let's see how they figure in some important IP services.

ARP

For LANs, IP configures itself automatically. Every local IP node must run the Address Resolution Protocol (ARP) to discover the MAC addresses of other IP nodes connected to the network. This dynamic discovery function underlies the capability for stations to connect and disconnect to the network to support IP over dial-up lines or wireless LANs.

ARP runs continuously and is used to determine the 48-bit MAC address associated with a node's IP address. ARP initially issues a broadcast message to request the MAC address for a specific IP address. This broadcast message is processed by the ARP component on every connected node. The node that discovers a match between its IP address and the requested IP address responds by sending back its MAC address.

Once discovered, ARP entries are cached internally at each Windows 2000 network node. To prevent a condition called *network black hole*, where IP messages are sent to MAC addresses that no longer exist, ARP cache entries persist for only two minutes. Each time the ARP cache entry is referenced, the entry is given an additional two minute grace period, up to a maximum of ten minutes. After ten minutes of use, the ARP cache entry is flushed and ARP is forced to resolve the IP address again.

If you find that too many ARP broadcast messages are being issued, the Windows 2000 defaults can be modified. The ArpCacheLife parameter determines how long an entry can remain unreferenced in the cache before being flushed, while the Arp-CacheMinReferencedLife parameter determines how long a referenced entry can remain in cache in total. In addition, you can specify static ARP addresses that persist in cache using the ARP command-line utility. This is an effective technique to reduce the number of ARP broadcast messages that IP stations issue to stations with IP addresses that seldom change.

ICMP

The Internet Control Message Protocol (ICMP) is mainly involved in generating informational error messages on behalf of IP. While ICMP does not serve to make IP reliable, it certainly makes it easier to manage. In addition to its role in generating error messages, ICMP messages are used as the basis for several interesting utilities, including PMTU, ping, and tracert. These utilities are reviewed in the following sections.

PMTU

Not every segment that a packet traverses is going to run over the same MAC layer. The packet size chosen for one leg of the trip may not work on subsequent links. The IP layer is always capable of fragmenting a packet that is too large for the current

MAC protocol, but the overhead of constant fragmentation and reassembly is something that is better avoided. Sending uniformly small packets is not an answer either, because small packets waste bandwidth and increase message processing overhead. We saw this previously in our discussion of Gigabit Ethernet.

Path MTU (PMTU) discovery is an optional facility in Windows 2000 that attempts to discover the largest MTU common value that can be used across a path to minimize multiple fragmentation and reassemblies. The basic mechanism that ICMP uses is to send smaller and smaller control messages built with the Don't Fragment bit set until the transmission succeeds. The path MTU is found when no more ICMP Destination Unreachable–Fragmentation Needed error messages are returned. However, a possible problem with PMTU is that many routers are not programmed to return these error messages.

Path MTU discovery is disabled by default in Windows 2000. To enable Path MTU discovery, you must set the value of the EnablePMTUdiscovery TCP/IP parameter to 1. Without PMTU, Windows TCP/IP support will use an MTU of 576 bytes for all connections to computers outside the local subnet.

ping

ping is a standard command-line utility that utilizes ICMP messaging. The most common use of the ping command is simply to verify that one IP address can be reached from another. The ping command sends an ICMP type 0 Echo Reply message and expects a type 8 Echo Request message in reply. Figure 11-11 illustrates the output from the ping command using all default options. ping returns the RTT for the request and the TTL value for a one-way trip. (Note: ping sets TTL to a value of 255 initially.) By default, ping sends Echo Reply messages four times, so that you can see representative RTT and hop count values. Since different packets can arrive at the destination IP address through different routes, it is not unusual to observe variability in both measurements.

Figure 11-12 illustrates a more elaborate version of ping called FreePing, which is a useful diagnostic tool for monitoring network availability and performance. It is available for download from *http://www.tools4nt.com*. Using FreePing, you can poll a specified set of IP addresses continuously, as illustrated. The program also maintains statistics on both network availability and response time.

A more elaborate diagnostic tool is the tracert utility, which determines the complete path to the destination, router by router. Here is some typical output from the tracert command.

```
C:\tracert 204.71.200.3
Tracing route to unknown.yahoo.com [204.71.200.3]
over a maximum of 30 hops:
  1 <10 ms <10 ms <10 ms 208.217.20.1
  2 60 ms 60 ms 50 ms Falls-Church6.VA.Alter.Net [137.39.2.58]
  3 170 ms 60 ms 50 ms Hssi9-0-0.CR2.TC01.Alter.Net [137.39.100.34]
```

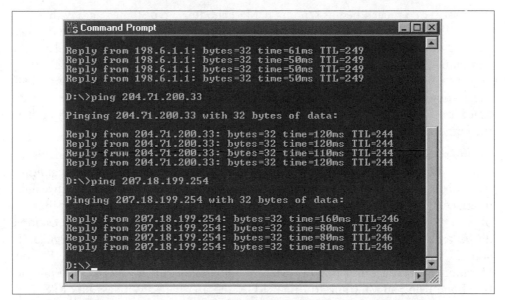

Figure 11-11. The ping utility for monitoring path availability

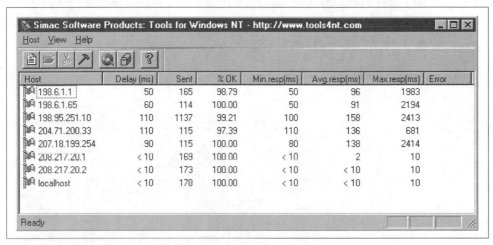

Figure 11-12. The FreePing utility for monitoring path availability

```
 4  50 ms  50 ms  50 ms 114.ATM10-0-0.XR1.TCO1.ALTER.NET [146.188.160.26]
 5  60 ms  60 ms  61 ms 193.ATM3-0.TR1.DCA1.ALTER.NET [146.188.161.166]
 6 110 ms 110 ms 110 ms 101.ATM6-0.TR1.SCL1.ALTER.NET [146.188.136.222]
 7 110 ms 120 ms 110 ms 199.ATM7-0.XR1.SFO4.ALTER.NET [146.188.146.69]
 8 110 ms 110 ms 130 ms 191.ATM1-0-0.GW1.SFO4.ALTER.NET [146.188.144.241]
 9 120 ms 120 ms 110 ms s6-0-1.br1.SNV.globalcenter.net [157.130.194.70]
10 120 ms 120 ms 120 ms fe1-0.cr1.SNV.globalcenter.net [206.251.5.12]
11 120 ms 120 ms 130 ms unknown.yahoo.com [204.71.200.3]
Trace complete.
```

The tracert command begins sending ICMP Echo Reply type 0 messages with a TTL of 1, then increments TTL until the message is successfully received at the destination. In this fashion, it traces at least one likely route of a packet and calculates the cumulative amount of time it took to reach each intermediate link. (This is why tracert sometimes reports that it takes less time to travel further along the route— the response times displayed represent different ICMP packets that were issued.) tracert also issues a DNS reverse query to determine the DNS name of each node in the path.

An interesting variant of the tracert utility is an inexpensive program called Visual-Route, which is available for downloading (at a moderate charge) from Fortel at *http://www.fortel.com*. VisualRoute, illustrated in Figure 11-13, wraps an attractive GUI interface around tracert, attempting to show the route a packet takes against the map of your choice. This is not an entirely foolproof technique, however. In the example illustrated, the packet originated in southwest Florida, not northern Virginia: IP address 39.200.111.193 is a customer premises router located in Naples, FL, not Herndon, VA. Notice also that this packet originates on PSInet, traverses the Internet backbone using an MCI link to Atlanta, GA and a Cable & Wireless link to Sunnyvale, CA on its way to *www.yahoo.com*. As you can see, the way a packet gets to its final destination is often quite interesting when the public-access Internet is involved.

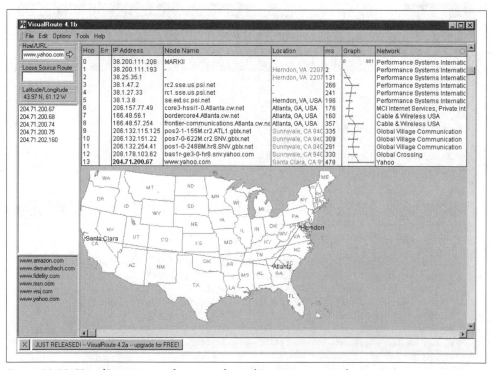

Figure 11-13. VisualRoute traces the route of a packet sent to www.yahoo.com

Note also that ping, tracert, and related diagnostic utilities tend to be conservative in measuring network response time because many routers process ICMP control messages at a lower priority than normal traffic.

The Internet Backbone

An organization poised to do business over the World Wide Web might be concerned that a typical packet that needs to travel from one end of the United States to another could take as long as 500 ms, judging from Figure 11-13. Companies hosting e-commerce web sites have told us that the order fulfillment rate declines in direct proportion to increases in measured RTT. When the network latency for delivery of a single packet is 0.5 seconds, it does not leave much room for error in fine-tuning the rest of your web application. According to Figure 11-13, that packet on its way from Florida to California appeared to spend a high percentage of its time in transit between routers separated by long distances. That is pretty much as expected, since network latency is a function of distance. But notice the difference between the RTT reported in Figure 11-13 for one ISP compared to the route traversed under a different ISP in the tracert output. How packets traverse public-access Internet routes evidently can make a big difference.

Packets destined for external network locations are inevitably routed by Internet backbone providers who maintain responsibility for moving bulk IP traffic between connections, usually over very high-bandwidth, long-distance links. The U.S. government originally selected a group of data communications carriers to interconnect Department of Defense sites and cooperating education and research organizations to build the original version of the Internet long before the commercial possibilities became evident. These carriers still provide the long-distance links that carry most Internet traffic that crosses autonomous system boundaries. Sooner or later, most packets directed at external locations wind up on this public-access Internet backbone.

It is useful to take a look at what one of these backbone networks looks like. Figure 11-14 shows the topology of the vBNS, the very high-performance Backbone Network Service operated by MCI Worldcom since 1995 on behalf of the National Science Foundation. Information about the performance of vBNS, one of the best-studied backbones, is available at *http://www.vbns.net*. vBNS is designed to interconnect five major supercomputing research centers in the United States, with additional links to other carrier networks, including Sprint in NY, Ameritech in Wisconsin, and IBM in North Carolina. vBNS consists of long-haul routes over predominately OC-12 lines (622 Mbps) that support IP data. The map shows an even higher bandwidth OCC-48 link (2.5 Gbps) to carry data between the San Francisco Bay Area and Southern California. Internet backbone providers have been installing lots of OCC-48 lines lately.

Internet backbone providers routinely report on the latency and throughput of their links. See *http://www.traffic.cw.net* for another typical view of network performance

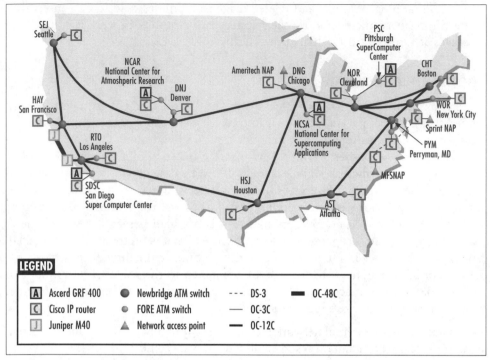

Figure 11-14. The topology of vBNS

from an Internet backbone carrier. In addition, a number of independent web sites produce regular Internet IP traffic reports designed for network administrators who want to monitor the public-access network. For example, at *http://www. internettrafficreport.com*, you can find regularly updated reports on router traffic, response time, and packet loss for the Internet backbone in the United States and around the world, as illustrated in Figure 11-15.

The performance of lines and routers associated with the Internet backbone is of more than academic interest to Windows 2000 system administrators responsible for the performance of applications like IIS, MS Exchange, and Lotus Notes, which rely on the Internet for long-distance packet delivery. The Internet backbone providers maintain extensive performance statistics on the IP packet traffic that crosses their networks. When you are diagnosing network performance problems, it can be extremely useful to access some of these performance statistics.

Depending on your provider, you may have access to detailed performance monitoring statistics detailing the throughput and response time of your provider's IP network. For example, Figure 11-16 shows the throughput for an IP boundary point on the Exodus backbone that connects to the Palo Alto Internet Exchange operated at Stanford University using a Gigabit Ethernet connection. The top line is the maximum data rate measured during the hour, while the bottom line is the hourly average.

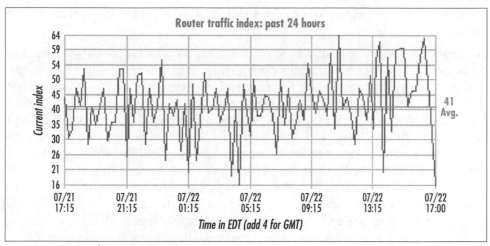

Figure 11-15. An Internet traffic report

Similar reports are available from AT&T, MCI Worldcom, Cable & Wireless, and other Internet backbone providers.

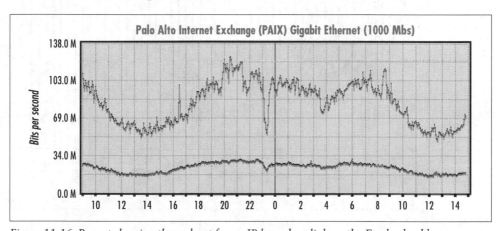

Figure 11-16. Report showing throughput for an IP boundary link on the Exodus backbone

The high-speed routers installed on the Internet backbone serve all comers. Packets associated with important commercial transactions traverse the same routes as messages sent between participants in an America Online chat room. A major concern is the potential of unanticipated *storms* of IP traffic overrunning the capacity of the public-access Internet. When the Melissa virus attack launched a storm of SMTP email over IP at sites infested with the virus in April 2000, some organizations were forced to close their networks to external IP traffic while they purged the virus from their systems. Many ISPs currently provide QoS guarantees to give preferred customers priority access to routes and bandwidth. Given that distance is a major factor in IP network latency, ISP web hosting services where the provider attaches your equipment directly to subnetworks connected to the high-speed backbone can be an attractive performance option.

In addition, a wide range of web site monitoring services are available. Some network performance vendors base their offerings on ping and tracert-like utilities that poll your network continuously. For example, the Keynote Business 40 Index monitors the response time of 40 major commercial web sites hosted in the U.S., including several powered by Windows NT 4.0/IIS. These include Microsoft (naturally), Dell, Compaq, and Intel. Web site service level reports gathered by Keynote are widely reported in the trade press, including *USA Today* and the *Wall Street Journal*. Figure 11-17 tracks the Keynote Business 40 Index over a period of several weeks. In addition, Keynote's Perspective software tool gathers web site performance statistics from a number of locations scattered around the U.S. and the world by actually connecting to the web site and running some of its applications. Of course, you can arrange for Keynote to begin monitoring your web site applications, too, for a fee.

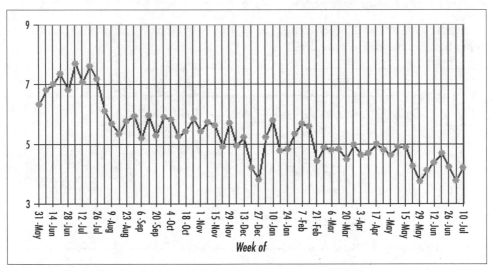

Figure 11-17. The Keynote Business 40 Index monitors a one-year period

Host-to-Host Connections

Layer 4 of the Internet Protocol suite provides host-to-host connection services. As the name implies, Layer 4 software runs on host computers exclusively. The Internet protocols provide two flavors of Layer 4 support: the lightweight User Datagram Protocol (UDP) and the more robust Transmission Control Protocol (TCP). TCP is the workhorse of the Internet, providing session management, error detection and recovery, and flow control. We review the facilities of UDP only briefly, concentrating instead on some of the key mechanisms in TCP that impact network performance. We will see that the way TCP works has a major impact on the response time and throughput of networked applications.

UDP

User Datagram Protocol (UDP) is a simple implementation of the Layer 4 host-to-host connection layer that provides an unreliable, connectionless service. UDP is a thin layer above IP that adds almost nothing to the services available in the underlying IP layer. For example, it performs no error recovery to speak of, nor does it introduce any additional performance considerations beyond those we have already discussed related to IP. Consequently, it is not necessary to devote much time and space to discussing UDP here.

UDP is used most appropriately by applications that communicate using simple messages that do not require reliable delivery. For instance, applications that perform their own error recovery may find that UDP provides a suitable set of host-to-host connection services. An application like ARP that performs periodic advertisements may also not require a reliable delivery mechanism.

Another candidate for UDP is an application that may have to service occasional messages from a prohibitively large number of host machines. DNS queries use the lightweight UDP protocol to avoid the overhead of session setup and breakdown between DNS servers and potentially large numbers of clients.

TCP

The Transmission Control Protocol (TCP) is the Layer 4 software that provides a reliable, peer-to-peer delivery service. TCP sets up point-to-point, connection-oriented *sessions* to guarantee in-order delivery of application transmission requests. TCP sessions are full duplex, capable of sending and receiving data between two locations concurrently. TCP sessions, or *connections*, are application-oriented. TCP will spawn separate sessions, for example, to communicate to a web server and an Internet Mail Connection hosted on the same computer. Port numbers uniquely identify applications that plug into TCP. Familiar Internet applications like HTTP, FTP, SMTP, and Telnet all plug into TCP sockets. Microsoft networking applications like DCOM, RPC, and the SMB server and redirector functions can also utilize TCP through the NBT interface that allows NetBEUI services to run over TCP/IP.

In the following sections, we review the way the TCP protocol works. We mainly discuss two important TCP performance options that are both related to round trip time (RTT). The combination of RTT and the size of the TCP sliding data window determines the throughput capability of a TCP connection. RTT also figures into TCP error recovery. If a sender fails to receive a timely acknowledgment that a packet was delivered successfully, TCP normally retransmits the datagram. The amount of time TCP waits for an acknowledgment is based on the connection RTT. But we also mention quite a number of other TCP configuration and tuning parameters that are available. As a word of caution, none of these TCP tuning parameters should ever be changed without first thoroughly analyzing your network traffic using the Network Monitor (or other sniffer product). Accordingly, we illustrate the discussion with Network Monitor trace samples.

The format of the TCP layer's packet header is illustrated in Figure 11-18. These fields and the way they are used are discussed in the next sections.

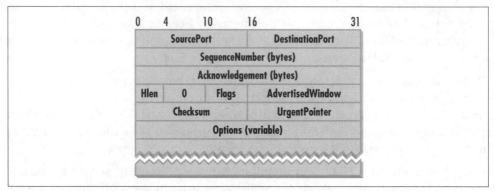

Figure 11-18. TCP packet header fields

Source and destination ports

TCP sessions are established by specific host applications, identified by a source and destination *port* associated with the Layer 5 application that initiated the request. Port number assignments in the range of 0–1023 are standardized. Some common TCP port assignments are listed here:

Port	Assignment
20	FTP data
21	FTP control
23	Telnet
25	SMTP
66	Oracle SQL*NET
70	Gopher
80	HTTP
111	SUN RPC
139	NetBIOS Session Service
160	SNMP Traps
161	SNMP
168	RSVP
179	BGP
389	LDAP
445	SMB

The complete set of official TCP port assignments are documented in RFC 1700, which is available from *ftp://ftp.isi.edu/in-notes/iana/assignments*. These reserved ports identify the application during the establishment of the connection. Once the connection is established, applications often use the TCP Sockets interface to acquire a dynamic port in the range of 1024–5000 to send messages and data back and forth over that connection.

Byte sequence numbers

The TCP packet header references two 32-bit sequence numbers that are byte offsets within the current *byte transmission stream*, the sequence of bits being sent between two peers engaged in a session. At the start of each TCP session as part of establishing the connection, the peers agree on initial byte sequence numbers for both ends of the full duplex connection. The SequenceNumber field in the header is the relative byte offset of the first data byte in the current transmission. This SequenceNumber field allows the receiver to slot an IP packet received out of order into the correct sequence. Because the sequence numbers are 32 bits wide, it is safe for TCP to assume that any packets received with identical sequence numbers are duplicates due to retransmission. Duplicates can safely be discarded by the receiver.

Acknowledgment

The Acknowledgment field acknowledges receipt of all bytes up to (but not including) the current byte offset. It is interpreted as the Next Byte a TCP peer expects to receive in this session. The receiver matches the Acknowledgment ID against the SequenceNumber field in the next message received. If the SequenceNumber is higher, the current message block is interpreted as being out of sequence. TCP accepts an out-of-sequence packet, but it leaves the Acknowledgment field of the ACK message returned unchanged. The Acknowledgment field is cumulative, specifically acknowledging receipt of *all* bytes from the Initial Sequence Number (ISN) + 1 to the current Acknowledgment byte number − 1. (A receiver can acknowledge an out-of-sequence packet only if the SACK is enabled.)

Header length

TCP headers can vary in length due to the inclusion of optional fields. To support optional length headers, the Header Length field points past the optional fields to the offset of the first actual data byte in the message. Many TCP Acknowledgment messages contain no information outside the header fields, so the Header Length can be zero.

Flags

The TCP header contains a Flag field that can be set according to the type of message intended. There is a SYN (synchronize) bit for establishing a session and a corresponding FIN bit for terminating one. An ACK flag signals that the Acknowledgment field in the header is valid. Another bit can be used to flag urgent data in the message. It signifies that the UrgentPointer field that points the end of the urgent data in the message payload is valid. There is also a Push indicator to signal that data in the message should be passed immediately to the application—something that needs to be done in Telnet, for instance, where data received is echoed at the terminal session. Finally, there is a Reset flag set for error conditions that forces a close of a session immediately.

Window

TCP also implements sender- and receiver-side flow control to avoid overloading components of the IP network. This is referred to as a sender-receiver *sliding window*, which we review in more detail in a moment. The size of the window determines the maximum amount of data a peer can transmit before receiving a specific acknowledgment from the receiver. Once the window is filled and no acknowledgment is forthcoming, the sender is forced to wait before sending any more data using that connection. The Window field is 16 bits wide, making 64 KB the largest possible window size. However, an optional Window Scale factor can be specified, which is used to scale up the AdvertisedWindow field to support larger windows. The combination of the two fields allows TCP to support a sliding data window up to 1 GB wide.

Options

Among the options that can appear in the TCP header are the Maximum Segment Size (MSS), Timestamps, Window Scale, Selective Acknowledgment (SACK), and the SACK-Permitted option. The Maximum Segment Size is normally the IP MTU minus the IP header and the TCP header (without options). The Window Scale and SACK options are discussed in context later on.

Timestamps are used in calculating the round trip time (RTT) of requests, which in turn is used to determine when to retransmit unacknowledged packets. What is meant by RTT in this context is the time it takes to send a TCP packet over the network, have it processed, and receive an Acknowledgment packet in reply from the destination. The TCP packet RTT includes all the time the packet spent in transit between the two locations *and* all the processing time at lower levels of the protocol stack at each node participating in the session. The RTT that TCP calculates is still not quite the end user response time because it ignores processing at the Layer 5 application layer initiating the transaction.

Now that we have covered the important TCP packet header fields, let's look in a little more detail at how the protocol works.

TCP sessions

TCP is session-oriented. A TCP session must be established prior to sending data between hosts. TCP sessions are established between two peers, both with equal capability to send and receive data and terminate the connection. The session-oriented behavior defined also insists that any data received from a sender must be acknowledged. TCP sessions are thus a *reliable* means for applications to exchange messages and data. A TCP session persists until it is finally closed by *both* peers.

Data sent over a TCP connection is sequenced, with acknowledgments required back from the receiver. An Acknowledgment (ACK) field in the packet header references the Next Byte location in the sequence of bytes that the receiver expects to receive. If no ACK is received within some RTT timeout value, a TCP sender assumes that the packet was lost in transmission or received in error. (Remember that IP can drop packets when routers are overloaded, and bits can get damaged in flight.) In either case, TCP automatically retransmits the lost data, unless the maximum number of retransmissions allowed is exceeded. This is known as Retransmission Timeout (RTO).

Meanwhile, at the receiver, duplicate segments are discarded and packets received out of order are restored to their original sequence. To support full duplex sessions in which the peers can transfer data independently, the TCP header contains both a byte sequence number uniquely identifying data in the outgoing message and an acknowledgment byte sequence number identifying any incoming data. Sending back data along with the ACK is known as *piggybacking*.

Session connections

Before any data can be transferred between two TCP peers, they first must establish a connection. In the setup phase of a connection, the two peers go through a handshaking process where they exchange information about each other. Because TCP cares about delivering data in the proper sequence, the hosts initiating a session need to establish a common sequence number to use when they want to begin transferring data. The peers also negotiate to set various options associated with the session, including establishing the size of the data transfer window, the use of selective acknowledgment (SACK), and the maximum segment size the parties can use to send data.

To initiate a connection, TCP Peer 1 sends a Synchronize SequenceNumber (SYN) message that contains a starting sequence number, a designated port number to send the reply to, and the various proposed option settings. This initial message is posted to a standard application port destination at the receiver's IP address, e.g., Port 80 for an HTTP session between a web browser and a web server. Then TCP Peer 2 acknowledges the original SYN message with a SYN-ACK, which returns the receiver's starting sequence number to identify the packets that it will initiate. Peer 2 also replies with its AdvertisedWindow size recommendation. Peer 1 naturally must acknowledge receipt of Peer 2's follow-up SYN-ACK. When TCP Peer 2 receives Peer 1's ACK message referencing its SYN-ACK message number and the agreed-upon AdvertisedWindow size, the session is established.

This sequence of messages used to establish a TCP connection is illustrated in the Network Monitor trace shown in Figure 11-19. Peer 1, attempting to establish the connection, sends sequence number 947003430 and the Windows 2000 default window of 16,384. The source HTTP number for this session is 0x046d or 1133. Because this is intended to establish an HTTP session, the connection message is sent to Port 80 at the destination, which is the *www.yahoo.com* IP address. Peer 2 replies with sequence number 169578969 and acknowledges the Peer 1 sequence number + 1. It also advertises a slightly higher window size at 17,520 bytes. Peer 1 responds with message 947003431, acknowledging 169578969 + 1 and accepting the larger advertised window. This finally establishes a session between the web browser on the local system and the *www.yahoo.com* web server.

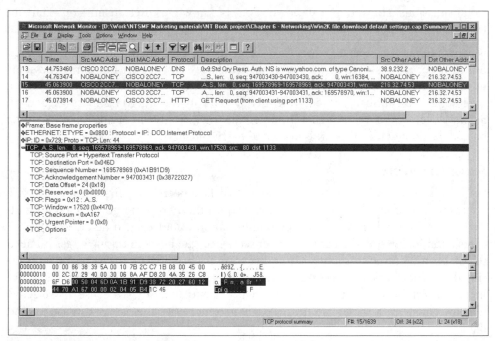

Figure 11-19. Two peers interchange three messages to establish a TCP session

Windows 2000 supplies one tuning parameter, called TcpMaxConnectRetransmissions, that is used to determine how many SYN messages can be retransmitted while trying to establish a connection. The default value is 2. The delay between retransmissions is determined by TcpInitialRTT, which defaults to three seconds. The retransmission timeout value is doubled following each failed connection attempt. Using the Windows 2000 default values for these parameters, TCP waits three seconds initially before timing out the original SYN message connection request, tries again six seconds later (Retry 1), then waits 12 seconds before sending Retry 2. If Retry 2 does not succeed, then TCP gives up, signaling the Layer 5 application requesting the session that the connection could not be established.

Once established, an application connection is maintained by the periodic exchange of data messages, which receivers must acknowledge. The TCP recipient explicitly acknowledges every byte of data received in the course of a session. TCP's acknowledgment mechanism is designed to be efficient. A single return message can acknowledge a sequence of messages, and, as noted previously, an acknowledgment message can also contain data being returned to the sender. If an acknowledgment message is not returned in a timely fashion, the sender automatically initiates error recovery. More on TCP retransmission behavior in a later section.

Because TCP connections are full duplex, an acknowledgment sent back to a sender can also contain a data payload. In practice, many TCP application sessions are one-sided, with one peer primarily sending data and the other primarily receiving it. (Consider most HTTP web browser requests or, for an even more extreme example, an FTP file transfer session.) When it has no data to send, the receiver returns simple acknowledgment messages containing TCP headers only, similar to those illustrated in Figure 11-19. As you can see, these are short messages that do not consume much in the way of network bandwidth. A high percentage of TCP messages are small, containing header fields only.

KeepAlive messages

Periodic exchange of KeepAlive messages indicates that both peers are still active. TCP KeepAlive messages are disabled by default in Windows 2000 on the assumption that the Layer 5 application will issue them; for example, Internet Explorer routinely does this anyway. The KeepAliveTime and KeepAliveInterval Registry parameters are available if you want to enable TCP KeepAlive messages for all TCP sessions by default, but this is normally not necessary.

Session termination

TCP connections also demand explicit termination by both peers, which must each send and receive finish messages (FINs) and explicit acknowledgments of the finish messages (FIN-ACKs) from the other peer. It takes a sequence of four messages back and forth to terminate a TCP connection correctly and completely.

Sliding window

While TCP session behavior requires peers to acknowledge the data they have received, TCP does not require an acknowledgment *immediately* following each send. A policy requiring an ACK for each send drastically limits the potential throughput of any remote connection that has to traverse a time-consuming WAN link, for example. Think about how long *www.yahoo.com* would have to wait between every send for a connection like the one shown back in Figure 11-13. On a link with an RTT of 100 ms, for example, requiring an ACK following each send would limit the rate of packet transmission to:

$$1 / RTT$$

or just 10 packets per second. Assuming an Ethernet segment on the route that limits the size of a single packet to 1500 bytes, that amounts to only 15 KB maximum throughput per connection, independent of the speed of the link. Accordingly, you can calculate the maximum throughput rate of a link as a simple function of packet size and RTT:

$$MaxThroughput = Packet\ Size\ / RTT$$

Figure 11-20 looks at the ramifications of this formula over a wide range of RTT values. This chart graphically displays the relationship between the theoretical maximum throughput and RTT for Ethernet 1500-byte packets and Gigabit Ethernet 9000-byte jumbo frames. On a low-latency LAN link where RTT is frequently less than 1 ms, waiting for TCP ACKs does not constrain performance, as you can see. With small values of RTT, Packet Size ÷ RTT exceeds the link capacity, so bandwidth rather than RTT is the main constraint. For 10BaseT, for instance, max throughput remains 1 MB/sec until RTT rises above 1 ms, which is simply inconceivable given the distance constraints on LAN technology. For 100BaseT, max throughput remains at 10 MB/sec until RTT rises above 100 μsecs. This is just as unlikely.

However, running at the bandwidth of Gigabit Ethernet, Figure 11-20 suggests that the small size of standard Ethernet packets can be a significant constraint on throughput if RTT rises above 20 μsecs. Figure 11-20 also illustrates the benefit of larger frames. With 9K jumbo frames, RTT does not become a constraint until it rises above 50 μsecs. RTT within 50 μsecs is well within reach of a properly configured Windows 2000 Server. Using jumbo frames with TCP on Windows 2000 requires several additional parameter settings (none of which are documented officially):

```
MaximumFrameSize = 9014          /* use jumbo frames
NumberOfReceiveBuffers = 100     /* use memory if you need it
NumberofTransmitBuffers = 100    /* ditto
MaxIRQperSec = 2500              /* interrupt coalescing
                                 /* and moderation
```

These parameters need to be set for any specific Gigabit Ethernet interface that supports jumbo frames. They need to be added to the HKLM\SYSTEM\CurrentControlSet\Services\Tcpip\Parameters\Interfaces\<interface-name> Registry key. You should consider setting a larger TcpWindowSize for Gigabit Ethernet interfaces, too.

At the opposite end of the spectrum, Figure 11-20 shows that when RTT exceeds 1 ms, bandwidth has little or no influence over network throughput, with 10BaseT, 100BaseT, and 1000BaseX all performing at the exact same level.

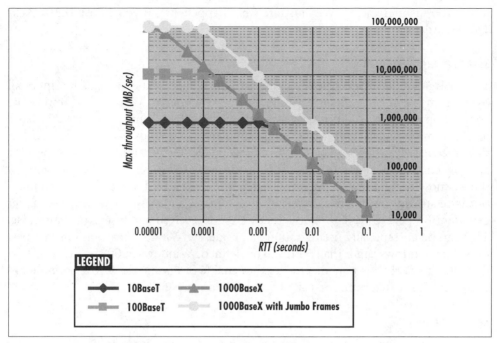

Figure 11-20. Maximum throughput related to RTT

Next, let's consider the impact on line utilization of a networking architecture that requires positive acknowledgment after every packet. On a network with an RTT of 10 ms, the theoretical maximum throughput for 10BaseT, 100BaseT, and 1000BaseX is an identical 150 KB/sec. That means that maximum line utilization is 15% for a 10BaseT link, an anemic 1.5% for 100BaseT, and a pitiful 0.15% for Gigabit Ethernet. So much for the bandwidth revolution solving all internetworking performance problems. The fact that a TCP session might not make good use of high-bandwidth links is a serious concern.

The sliding-window algorithm implemented in TCP specifically allows TCP/IP sessions to make better use of high-bandwidth links, especially over longer distances. The TCP windowing implementation allows a sender to send multiple messages without waiting for an acknowledgment. In the meantime, a receiver can defer sending an acknowledgment following every received packet and acknowledge multiple messages with a single acknowledgment. The TCP sliding window also serves as a flow control mechanism. To prevent a fast sender from overrunning a slow receiver, the sender can only send an AdvertisedWindow amount of unacknowledged data before it is forced to slow down and wait for an acknowledgment message.

In Windows 2000, TCP on the receiving end delays ACKs by default for 200 milliseconds (controlled by the TcpDelAckTicks parameter). If another packet from the sender is received during this delay interval, TCP can acknowledge both packets with a single reply message. You can manually adjust TcpDelAckTicks between 100–600 ms in 100 ms increments. We illustrate what happens when you adjust TcpDelAck-Ticks a little later.

Selective acknowledgment

The TCP Acknowledgment field is cumulative, explicitly acknowledging receipt of all bytes from the Initial Sequence Number (ISN) + 1 that was established during the connection setup up to the last Acknowledgement byte number. Using this basic mechanism, TCP can acknowledge only complete, contiguous byte sequences. *Selective acknowledgment* (SACK) is an optional TCP feature that allows a peer to acknowledge noncontiguous blocks. These are received blocks beyond the range of the Acknowledgment byte counter, which continues to mark the end of the contiguous byte stream that has been received successfully. With SACK enabled, the sender can identify specific message blocks that were not received and just retransmit those. This can be an especially useful option alongside the Window Scale option that permits data windows larger than 64 KB to be defined. Windows 2000 enables SACK by default. The SackOpts parameter is used to enable or disable the SACK option manually. SACK was not supported at all under Windows NT 4.0.

Send window

During connection setup, the peers negotiate a data window size that determines how much data can be outstanding at any time at either end of the connection, as illustrated back in Figure 11-19. Each TCP peer establishes a *send window* as a multiple of the receiver's MSS, the *maximum segment size* that is a function of the underlying Layer 1 protocol MTU. This is normally 17,520 bytes for Ethernet connections, which is 16 KB rounded up to accommodate twelve 1460-byte data segments (the Ethernet MSS). Previously under Windows NT 4.0, the window size for Ethernet segments was 8760 bytes, which allows room for six data segments. A sender is allowed to fill the send window before it is forced to stop and wait for an acknowledgment packet from the receiver. Large send windows allow TCP sessions to make better use of high-bandwidth, long-distance connections.

The TCP sender must ensure that there is no more than the receiver's advertised window amount of data outstanding on the session at any time. Based on the last acknowledgment received, a sender calculates the amount of data active on the current session by subtracting the LastByteAcked number from the sequence number of the next byte it is ready to send. So long as this value is less than (or *inside*) the AdvertisedWindow, the sender can continue to send the next block of data. The sender ensures that the bytes sent in the next message do not fall *outside* the advertised window. Then, as acknowledgments are received, the send window *slides* forward on the transmission byte stream, as illustrated in Figure 11-21.

Meanwhile, the LastByteReceived acknowledgment that the sender receives defines a sliding window over the receive window. For instance, if the application layer is slow

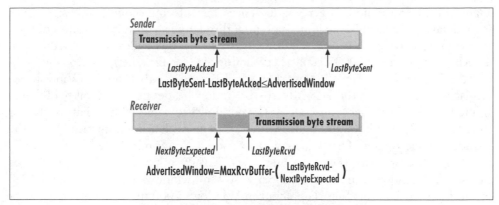

Figure 11-21. Calculating the current advertised window of the sender and receiver

to respond, the receiver will close the advertised window in its ACK message by the amount of data that remains unprocessed in its receive buffer.

Back on the sender's side, if the number of unacknowledged bytes ever equals the advertised window, the sender must delay sending more data. On the receiver's side, any data received that is outside the advertised window is rejected.

Figure 11-22 shows the normal traffic pattern between a sender and receiver in a TCP session over a link with long latency. The sender fills the link's advertised window, issuing multiple sends before it is forced to pause until an acknowledgment is returned. In this illustration, four sends fill the advertised window. The sender then waits until it receives a positive acknowledgment packet from the receiver. Clearly, how long the sender must wait is still a function of the RTT for a send message to get to the receiver and for the receiver to send an acknowledgment back. However, the ability to fill the window to capacity before stopping improves potential utilization on the link by a factor of Window Size / Packet Size. Accordingly, this changes the max throughput equation shown earlier to:

MaxThroughput = Window Size / RTT

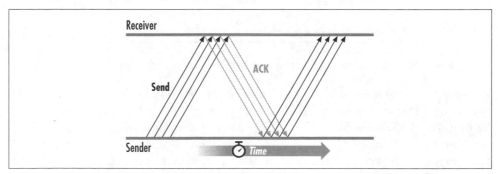

Figure 11-22. The normal traffic pattern between a sender and receiver

Figure 11-23 shows how larger window sizes benefit connections with significant RTT delays. It calculates maximum potential throughput with varying values of RTT for window sizes of 8 KB (the Windows NT default TcpWindowSize for Ethernet), 17 KB (the Windows 2000 default TcpWindowSize for Ethernet), 64 KB (the Windows NT maximum TcpWindowSize), 256 KB, and 1 MB. The TcpWindowSize Registry parameter sets the TCP AdvertisedWindow header field, a 16-bit field that is limited to 64 KB. When you code a TcpWindowSize value higher than 64 KB or '0x0000FFFF', Windows 2000 documentation reports that it automatically sets the Window Scale option. That allows you to code a TcpWindowSize value of up to '0x3FFFC000' or 1 GB. (Due to a bug in its TCP/IP support, Windows 2000 does not set the Window Scale option properly, so send window sizes larger than 64 KB are not advertised. This bug is apparent in Windows 2000 up through Service Pack 1. Fortunately, Figure 11-23 illustrates that very large TCP windows provide diminishing returns.)

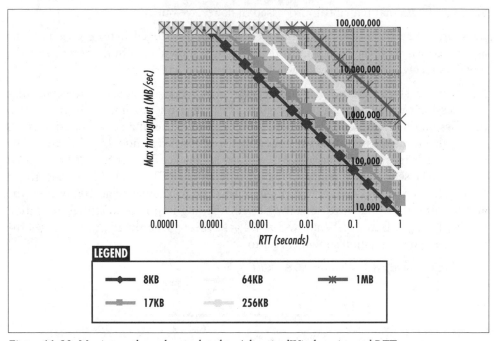

Figure 11-23. Maximum throughput related to AdvertisedWindow size and RTT

As Figure 11-23 illustrates, Windows 2000 default TCPWindowSize values are probably adequate for most localized LAN traffic, even when Gigabit Ethernet is installed. Setting the TCPWindowSize to some large number does not guarantee that your session can take advantage of a large send window. For instance, if the other peer cannot support windows larger than 64 KB, your TCP session is forced to accept a lower value for the other half of the full duplex session. This is a problem when you are accessing Windows NT servers from a Windows 2000 client, for example. Windows

NT 4.0 does not support TCPWindowSize values larger than 64 KB. Another problem over very slow WAN connections is that the TcpDelAckTicks timer will kick in and fire off an ACK well before the receive window is full.

We now analyze a packet trace where we coded large values for both TCPWindowSize and TcpDelAckTicks to see what difference these parameters made using Internet Explorer to download a file from a remote web site. First, let's look at a normal IE connection made with standard Windows 2000 TCP/IP defaults. Figure 11-24 shows a packet trace using a connection with a standard 16 KB send window defined. Following a DNS query to look up the address of *www.microsoft.com*, the local TCP peer establishes a session with 207.46.131.137, one of the cluster of IIS web servers that Microsoft uses to power its web site. The initial SYN packet (Frame 560) sends SequenceNumber 9918832386 and advertises a ReceiveWindow of 16384, the Windows 2000 default. In Figure 11-25, 207.46.131.137 acknowledges with 9918832387, the expected SequenceNumber of the next packet, advertises a SendWindow of 17520, which implies an Ethernet backbone on the Microsoft network, and sends SequenceNumber 3754921143. When the local session ACKs back (Frame 562), the connection is established. Subsequently, the local session sends an HTTP GET request to begin retrieving the *www.microsoft.com* home page.

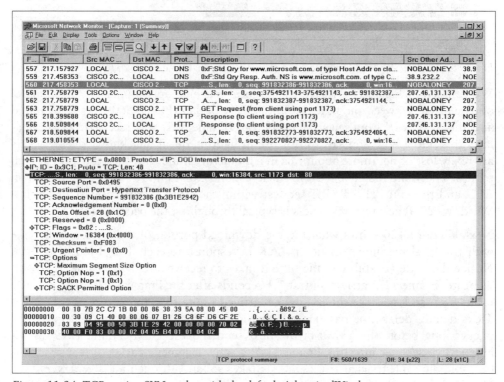

Figure 11-24. TCP session SYN packet with the default AdvertisedWindow

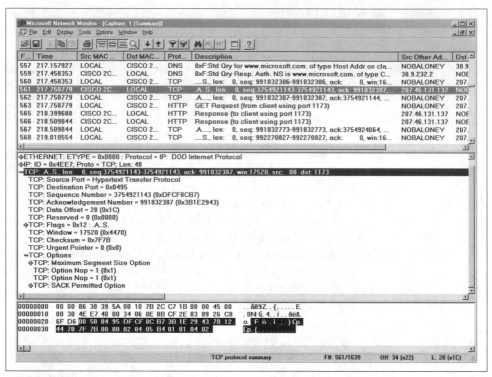

Figure 11-25. The SYN-ACK reply packet negotiates a send window of 17520 bytes

We can see in Figure 11-24 that on the local machine approximately 300 milliseconds elapsed between the time the initial SYN packet (Frame 560) was transmitted and the SYN-ACK from *www.microsoft.com* (Frame 561) was received. TCP calculates this initial RTT and saves it for use in figuring out if unacknowledged packets are really lost or not (more about this in a moment). Notice how fast the local system replies. The Windows 2000 TCP/IP stack responds to Frame 561 with two frames, an ACK and the initial HTTP GET request within the same microsecond. This level of Windows 2000 host responsiveness is typical throughout the packet trace.

Next, Figure 11-26 shows what the file download portion of the session looks like with the local machine sending an ACK in response to each TCP 1460 byte send. Notice the wide variability in the time it takes to receive a reply from the Microsoft web site. Frame 1277 arrives almost 1.1 seconds after the Frame 1276 ACK. Because it has been so long since the last packet arrived (more than the 200 ms TcpDelAck-Ticks default delay time has elapsed), the local system acknowledges receipt of the packet long before the arrival of the next send request. Next, Frame 1279 arrives almost five seconds after the Frame 1278 acknowledgment packet. Because in this example the route to *www.microsoft.com* takes so long, throughput is very, very low. No doubt, TCP has a difficult time determining whether packet delivery is just delayed or packets are being lost somewhere along the congested Internet route.

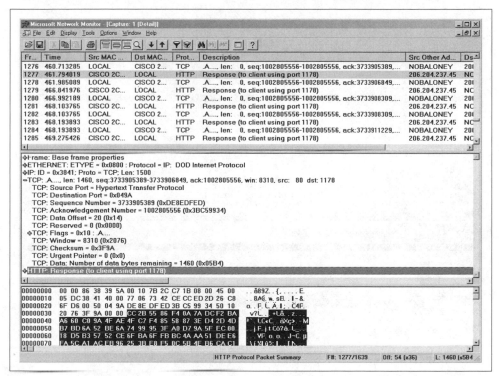

Figure 11-26. An HTTP file download using Windows 2000 standard TCP defaults

With different TCP parameter settings, Figure 11-27 shows modest improvement, a somewhat lower rate of ACK packets being sent during the file download phase of the session. For this TCP connection, we adjusted the value of TcpDelAckTicks upwards to 600 ms. The longer delay between ACKs sometimes allows the Microsoft web site to send two packets before triggering the ACK, as illustrated. Throughput on the link effectively doubles, although in this case it is a matter of improving from anemic to merely poor. Again, this is an optimization to consider for busy IIS servers, Exchange servers supporting Internet mail connections or other external links, and Windows 2000 servers attached to high-speed Gigabit Ethernet backbones.

Sliding window in action

Figure 11-28 illustrates the performance improvement possible when both Windows 2000 peers support large values for AdvertisedWindow. This packet trace shows an SMB file transfer in progress (using NBT) between a Windows 2000 server (local system 38.200.111.214) and a Windows 2000 client (IP address 38.200.111.203) over an Ethernet 10BaseT backbone. We coded a TcpWindowSize value in excess of 64 KB (0xFFFF) on both computers, but the actual negotiated send window was 64 KB. During bulk data transfers, the Windows 2000 client continued to advertise a receive window of 17520 bytes, the Ethernet default.

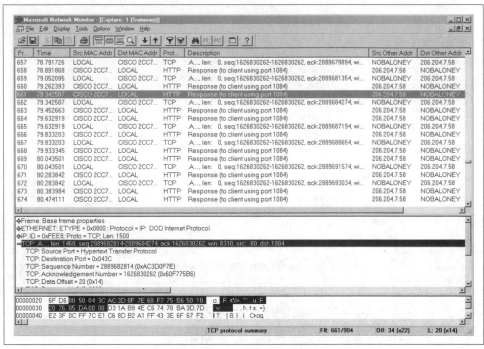

Figure 11-27. A higher value of TcpDelAckTicks shows some improvement

The packet trace fragment we look at begins at Frame 171, which is an ACK from 38. 200.111.203 to 38.200.111.214 showing receipt of all bytes up to 407987528 and an AdvertisedWindow of 17520 bytes. 38.200.111.214 follows the SMB write confirmation in Frame 172 received about 10 ms later with a series of sends designed to fill the receiver's AdvertisedWindow. The 38.200.111.214 file server issues another SMB write command for 0xf000 (61440) bytes, followed by Frames 174–184, which are successive NBT transfers of 1448 data bytes. Notice that Frames 174–184 are all issued within the same microsecond precisely at 0.270384 seconds into the trace. In all, 38.200.111.214 sends 12 Ethernet packets in a row, enough to fill 38.200.111. 203's receive window.

At Frame 185, a single ACK packet is received from 38.200.111.203, acknowledging receipt of a contiguous set of bytes from 407987528 to 407990423, or a total of 2896 bytes spanning two NBT frames. Frame 185 again advertises a 17520-byte receive window. Obviously, there is more data outstanding in the receive window, but 38. 200.111.214 does not have to slow down yet because the AdvertisedWindow is not quite full. 38.200.111.214 immediately sends two more NBT file packets, but at this point it calculates 38.200.111.203's receive window is full. Now TCP on 38.200.111. 214 is forced to wait for an ACK from 38.200.111.203, which finally arrives at Frame 188 acknowledging another 2896 bytes.

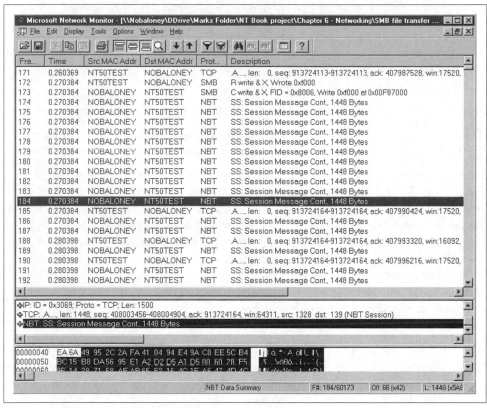

Figure 11-28. Improved performance with the TCP sliding window

The TCP sliding window mechanism allows the NOBALONEY file server to fill a 17520-byte window with data, but forces it to slow down while a slower client machine processes the data that is being sent.

Adaptive retransmission

The final topic in the performance of the TCP protocol that we will review is the adaptive retransmission mechanism. This calculates a retransmission timeout (RTO) value that governs the error recovery behavior of each TCP session. The only means of error recovery available in TCP is for a sender to retransmit datagrams that were not received correctly, either due to data transmission errors or IP packet loss. The sender compares the acknowledgment sequence number against the sequence number of the next packet in the transmission stream. If the acknowledgment sequence number is less than the sender's current sequence number, then at least one packet is missing. The sender cannot tell what happened to the packet, only that no acknowledgment has been received. Eventually, enough time will elapse since the original transmission to assume that something probably has gone wrong.

Here are some things that could have happened to the unacknowledged packet:

- A router or NIC card detected a damaged packet and dropped it.
- A router was forced to drop a perfectly good packet on its way to its destination because of capacity constraints.
- The ACK packet was damaged in transit and dropped.
- An overloaded router dropped the ACK packet due to network congestion.

TCP's only recourse is to resend the unacknowledged packet, after waiting a long enough period to determine that an ACK is not forthcoming.

How long should a TCP peer wait before resending an unacknowledged packet? First, consider the case of a retransmission timeout value that is too small. If the retransmission timeout is too small, TCP sessions send unnecessary duplicate data transmissions, since if the TCP session had waited a little longer for ACK messages, these retransmissions would have been avoided. Retransmitting a packet unnecessarily wastes network bandwidth. Suppose there are transmission failures due an overloaded Layer 3 router that is forced to drop packets. If the route is overloaded, TCP senders need to be extra careful about retransmissions, as we do not want to further overload any saturated components. This is something the designers of TCP were especially concerned about.

On the other hand, consider the case of a retransmission value that is too big. Now the TCP session waits too long before retransmission. If, in fact, packets are being dropped before they reach the intended destination, waiting too long unnecessarily slows down the intended peer-to-peer interaction.

Considering that we need a retransmission timeout value that is just right, having a single retransmission timeout value governing all TCP sessions at a host computer is not a good idea. Compare one session between Peer A and Peer B over a low-latency LAN connection to another session between Peer A and Peer C separated by a high-latency WAN link. If an acknowledgment is not received within 300–1000 μsecs for two peers on a local LAN connection, something is probably wrong. On the other hand, if my host computer is in a session with *www.yahoo.com* across a connection that is routed cross-country, then it might make sense to wait several seconds before assuming the packet needs to be retransmitted. The best approach is for TCP to calculate retransmission timeout values individually on a session-by-session basis, based on experience.

Consequently, TCP's error retransmission behavior is based on the RTT of the session. TCP establishes the RTT of the session at the outset using the TcpInitialRTT parameter that governs reconnect transmissions. By default, TcpInitialRTT is set to three seconds. You may remember from the previous discussion of TcpInitialRTT and TcpMaxConnectRetransmissions that there is an exponential backoff component to retransmissions where the retransmission delay based initially on TcpInitialRTT is doubled for each retransmission attempt. Once a SYN-ACK packet is returned and a session is established, TCP can calculate the RTT of the actual connection and use that value to determine a good retransmission timeout value.

So initially, RTO is based on the amount of elapsed time between sending the initial SYN packet and receiving a SYN-ACK packet in reply. During the course of a session, TCP makes additional measurements of the actual RTT. By default, TCP samples values of RTT once per send window, rather than for every packet sent and acknowledged. This is partly due to the desire to save the overhead of figuring out which ACK packet corresponds to which send time; this gets a little complicated with ACK packets able to acknowledge multiple send messages. For relatively small send windows, this sampling technique is adequate.

Timestamps option

For larger send windows, the rate of sampling RTT values may be too small to adequately assess current network conditions, which can change rapidly. Alternatively, Windows 2000 supports the new RFC 1323 TCP timestamps option, which makes it easy for TCP to calculate RTT for each and every packet. When the timestamps option is set, a TCP sender plugs into the header a current four-byte timestamp field. The receiver then echoes this timestamp value back in the ACK packet that acknowledges receipt of the original send. Since TCP sessions are full duplex and the receiver may be piggybacking data on the ACK, the receiver plugs its own timestamp into the ACK packet, too. The sender looks in the ACK packet for its original time stamp, which is then subtracted from the current time to calculate RTT. When the timestamps option is specified, TCP can calculate the RTT associated with every send-ACK sequence in the data transmission stream.

In Windows 2000, timestamps are enabled by default. If, for some reason, you want to turn timestamps off, you can set the Tcp1323Opts Registry flag to either 0 (00) or 2 (10). When a connection is established with a TCP peer that does not support RFC 1323 options (any Windows NT 4.0 host, for example), no timestamps will be exchanged and the method for calculating RTT will revert to sampling.

Calculating Retransmission Timeout (RTO)

As indicated, TCP bases RTO on the actual RTT calculated for the session. The actual RTO calculation in Windows 2000 TCP/IP uses a weighted smoothing formula as recommended in RFC 1122, which draws heavily on the work of Van Jacobson and Michael J. Karels in a well-known article called "Congestion Avoidance and Control" published in 1988. In the early days of the experimental ARPAnet, Jacobson and Karels noted that retransmission behavior would exacerbate a transient capacity problem and lead to a devastating condition known as *congestion collapse*. (For interested readers, Peterson and Davie's *Computer Networks* provides an excellent introduction to this topic.) One of their contributions was a new formula for calculating RTO that would be more responsive to current network conditions. The

Jacobson/Karels formula factors in the current RTT and the variance between the current RTT and the mean RTT. Their insight was to calculate an RTO value that would respond quickly to sudden changes in network performance.

TCP will retransmit an unacknowledged packet once the current RTO timeout value is exceeded. The TcpMaxDataRetransmissions Registry parameter determines the number of times TCP attempts to retransmit a packet before it decides to abandon the session altogether. The default value of TcpMaxDataRetransmissions is 5. After each unsuccessful retransmission, TCP doubles the RTO value used. This use of exponential backoff parallels Ethernet's collision avoidance mechanism: once retransmission needs to occur, it is good for TCP to extend the delay time between retransmissions to avoid making a congested network situation even worse.

Karn's algorithm

A problem arises in calculating RTT for a successfully retransmitted packet. If time-stamps are not in use, TCP cannot tell whether the ACK received is for the initial packet or for the retransmitted packet. Karn's simple solution to this problem was to ignore RTT samples measured for a retransmitted packet. Windows 2000 implements Karn's algorithm, ignoring RTT values for any retransmitted packets. However, if timestamps are used, the echoed timestamp identifies unambiguously which packet transmission is being acknowledged.

Fast retransmit

Suppose a TCP receiver receives a packet out of sequence; that is, the packet received contains a SequenceNumber that is higher than the expected sequence number. The implication is that there is a missing packet somewhere in the sequence. Hopefully, this packet is on its way via a slower route and will arrive shortly. Or perhaps the missing packet was dropped by a router in flight somewhere along the route. (Remember that IP is not a reliable delivery service.)

Fast retransmit is a mechanism for a receiver that has received a packet out of sequence to inform the sender, so that the missing packet can be retransmitted without waiting for the RTO value to expire. This is a bit tricky, because if the packet is on its way via a slower route, retransmitting it is a waste of network bandwidth. On the other hand, forcing the receiver to wait for the RTO value to expire may engender an unnecessarily long wait, especially as additional packets from the same session start to pile up at the receiver's end.

The receiver, of course, cannot acknowledge a packet it has not received. What the receiver does upon receipt of an out-of-order packet is send an ACK showing the still-current high-water mark of the contiguous byte stream it has received. In other words, the receiver sends a duplicate ACK. This shows the sender that the connection is alive and packets are getting through, although it does not specify precisely which packets arrived. When these duplicate ACKs pile up at the sender, the sender responds by retransmitting unacknowledged packets whether or not RTO triggers the event. (If SACK is enabled, the sender can more easily identify missing packets in the byte transmission stream and just retransmit those. Without SACK, the sender has to start retransmitting all unacknowledged packets.)

A Registry parameter called TcpMaxDupAcks determines how many duplicate ACK packets a sender must receive before retransmitting unacknowledged packets. Valid values for TcpMaxDupAcks are 1, 2, and 3. Windows 2000 sets TcpMaxDupAcks to 2 by default, which is a bit more aggressive than the RFC-2581 recommendation of 3. The Windows 2000 value reflects a more current sense of the reliability of the Internet.

CongestionWindow

Although the AdvertisedWindow is probably the main mechanism used in flow control, TCP does not rely solely on it. In addition, TCP also defines something called a CongestionWindow, which overrides the receivers AdvertisedWindow settings. The CongestionWindow allows TCP to cope better with current network conditions. At the outset of a connection, TCP does not attempt to ram a full AdvertisedWindow's worth of data down the network route to the destination. Instead, TCP ramps up the rate of data transmission gradually. If TCP transmissions are able to flow freely through the network from sender host to receiver host, the size of the CongestionWindow eventually reaches the AdvertisedWindow value.

TCP also reacts swiftly to signs of network performance constraints to shrink the CongestionWindow and reduce the network load quickly. There are two signs of network congestion that TCP reacts to: first, a ReceiveWindow full condition that indicates the sender is transmitting data at the limit of the receiver's capacity to process it, and second, any data packet loss requiring a data retransmission. If either of these events signaling congestion somewhere on the network occurs, then TCP reduces the rate of data transmission sharply.

Slow Start

TCP does not attempt to fill the receiver's AdvertisedWindow immediately following the establishment of a new connection. What can easily happen if the network connection cannot handle a full load of an AdvertisedWindow's worth of bytes is that the receiver is swamped and the sender is likely to have to retransmit many frames anyway. Slow Start is used to allow a TCP connection to try and gauge the performance of a connection first before flooding it with data.

With Slow Start, the sender tries to ramp up its rate of data transmission gradually until it receives an event notification indicating the connection is saturated. Using Slow Start at the beginning of a connection, the sender opens the CongestionWindow gradually. The sender begins by sending a single data packet and waiting for an ACK in reply. Following the ACK, the sender next tries sending two packets and waits for the return ACK message. The sender proceeds to try sending 4, 8, 16, etc., packets, doubling the amount of data until the full AdvertisedWindow value is reached.

Additive Increase/Multiplicative Decrease

If a ReceiveWindow full condition is encountered, the TCP sender deactivates Slow Start and activates a different congestion control mechanism called Additive Increase/Multiplicative Decrease to reduce the size of the CongestionWindow and slow down the rate of data transmission. As the name implies, Additive Increase/Multiplicative Decrease reduces the current CongestionWindow by a factor of two. If that reduced transmission rate does not saturate the ReceiveWindow, then TCP starts increasing the number of packets transmitted in a burst one at a time, up to a limit of the AdvertisedWindow value, or until another ReceiveWindow full condition occurs.

If the sender is ever forced to wait for a retransmission timeout to occur and resend lost data, the status of the connection returns to Slow Start mode. Again, the basic assumption is that a congested router being forced to drop packets is the root cause of the packet loss. The TCP congestion control mechanism kicks in to reduce the rate of packet transmission to try to reduce the load on some saturated component somewhere in the route.

While waiting for the RTO timer to go off, the connection is essentially dead, with the sender paused waiting for an ACK that never comes. With no data being transmitted, the status of the connection is similar to the initial state because there are no bytes en route to the destination. Returning to Slow Start mode means the sender begins by sending one packet and waiting for a reply. Initially, this is the lost packet that is retransmitted. When the ACK is received for the retransmitted data, the sender in Slow Start mode starts doubling the rate of data transmission again. This time, however, unlike at the initial session connection, TCP has the benefit of some experience with this connection. The last value of the CongestionWindow is used as an upper limit for ramping up the connection again. If the sender is able to reach the full CongestionWindow, the connection then switches into Additive Increase/Multiplicative Decrease mode and attempts to reach the full AdvertisedWindow adding one packet at time.

The TCP congestion control mechanism tends to trigger overloading of the network, then reacts to the condition it caused. The effect of Slow Start and Additive Increase/Multiplicative Decrease is that TCP gradually ramps up a session until it is noticeably sending too much data over a connection. TCP then reacts by drastically reducing the traffic being generated. A public network the size of the Internet becoming overloaded is the result of literally millions of active TCP connections functioning independently of each other. The load on the network is a function of all these independent TCP connections, so it is very dynamic. The best TCP can do is to react to signs of congestion and try to choke off network flows once congestion occurs. This makes network capacity planning even more important, because otherwise congestion is an inevitable byproduct of the way TCP works.

Congestion control in action

TCP reacts to signs of network components becoming overloaded by acting to reduce traffic flows. If network bottlenecks exist, TCP connections are characteristically bursty as a result of these reactive congestion control mechanisms. Refer back to Figure 11-28, which illustrates the kind of bursty packet transmission behavior that is typical of TCP due to the congestion control mechanisms described. This packet trace shows an SMB file transfer in progress (using NBT) between a Windows 2000 Server (local system 38.200.111.214) and a Windows 2000 client at IP address 38.200.111.203 over an Ethernet 10BaseT backbone. During this bulk data transfer operation the Windows 2000 client advertised a ReceiveWindow of 17520 bytes, the Ethernet default, to the Windows 2000 Server.

The packet trace fragment we will look at begins at Frame 171, which is an ACK from 38.200.111.203 to 38.200.111.214 showing receipt of all bytes up to 407987528 and an AdvertisedWindow of 17520 bytes. 38.200.111.214 follows the SMB write confirmation in Frame 172 received about 10 ms later with a series of sends designed to fill the receiver's AdvertisedWindow. (We can speculate that this delay is likely due to having to read the disk.) The 38.200.111.214 File Server issues another SMB write command for 0xf000 (61440) bytes, followed by Frames 174-184, which are successive NBT transfers of 1448 data bytes. Notice that Frames 174-184 are all issued within the same microsecond, precisely at 0.270384 seconds into the trace. In all, 38.200.111.214 sends 12 Ethernet packets in a row, enough to fill 38. 200.111.203's ReceiveWindow. At this point in the connection, we can conclude that the CongestionWindow equals the full AdvertisedWindow. At Frame 185, a single ACK packet is received from 38.200.111.203, acknowledging receipt of a contiguous set of bytes from 407987528 to 407990423, or a total of 2896 bytes spanning two NBT frames. Frame 185 again advertises a 17520 byte ReceiveWindow. Obviously, there is more data outstanding in the ReceiveWindow, but 38.200.111.214 does not have to slow down completely since the AdvertisedWindow is not quite full. 38.200.111.214 immediately sends two more NBT file packets, at which point TCP calculates that 38.200.111.203's ReceiveWindow is full, forcing the sender to stop and wait. Now TCP on 38.200.111.214 is forced to wait for an ACK from 38. 200.111.203, which finally arrives at Frame 188, acknowledging another 2896 bytes and simultaneously reducing the size of the AdvertisedWindow to 16092 bytes. Because of the ReceiveFull condition, the sender reduces the CongestionWindow to half the value of the original 17520 AdvertisedWindow. However, since the sender calculates a current ReceiveWindow of 1448 bytes that is even less, the sender can only follow up with one more packet (Frame 189).

In summary, although TCP's congestion control mechanisms have proved effective in avoiding the severe congestion collapse conditions that characterized the early Internet, they still tend to cause congestion rather than seek to avoid it by understanding the capacity limits of the route. You will probably find that TCP connections tend to function in the fashion illustrated in Figure 11-28, first overloading a destination and then backing off the rate of data transmission abruptly. When network components are saturated, TCP data transmission rates tend to become very bursty, which introduces more extreme queuing at routers. This is the impetus behind the Quality of Service (QoS) initiatives from the major network equipment manufacturers and Internet backbone and service providers to manage router queues according to customer specifications.

## CHAPTER 12

Internet Information Server Performance

No other technology has experienced growth like that experienced by the Web. A few simple web sites started to appear back in 1993, and by early 1994 there were fewer than 1000 web sites on the Internet. According to surveys by Netcraft, Nielsen Media Research, and CommerceNet, in December of 1999 there were at least 9.5 million web servers on the Internet, 120 million web users, and 60 million web shoppers. In a statement explaining the high Internet valuations, William W. Priest, the chief executive officer of Credit Suisse Asset management, referenced a chart produced by the Dallas Fed. "It looked at inventions and the amount of time they took to reach 25 percent of the population," says Priest. "Nothing reached that level faster than the Internet. It took the Internet about 7 years to reach 25 percent of the population, whereas for some of the biggest inventions in the past it took about 30 years."

Furthermore, the Internet model of information distribution has entered every organization in the form of an intranet. More and more companies and institutions are using intranets for distributing information across the organization and enhancing collaboration among divisions. This tremendous growth of the Internet and intranets has made the web server a critical application for almost every organization. At the same time, workloads imposed on web servers tend to be bursty and hard to characterize, making tuning of those servers more difficult than it is for other servers.

Microsoft's Internet Information Server (IIS) is at this point the second most popular web server; Apache is the most popular primarily due to its cost (free) and its availability on multiple platforms (Apache is available for various Unix versions and Windows 2000/NT). IIS can support multiple web sites on a single server and, as an applications server, provides a number of alternative technologies for the generation of dynamic content. Over time, Microsoft has improved the performance of the web server through a number of features, and had made available a number of registry variables and tuning knobs for configuration of those features.

In this chapter, we take a close look at how to tune the performance of IIS. We focus first on how web servers and IIS in particular work, and then look into sources of information for understanding the workload imposed on the server and for monitoring the performance of the server. After that, we go through each critical operating system resource, analyzing how IIS utilizes that resource, how to detect problems at each resource, and what you can do to resolve the problem. Throughout, we use the Web Capacity Analysis Tool (WCAT) from Microsoft to generate various workloads on the web server, and Performance Monitor to illustrate the effect of the workload on each resource. We also include a section on benchmarking tools for IIS.

Web Server Architecture

Before delving into the specifics of how to evaluate the performance of Internet Information Server, detect and resolve bottlenecks, and perform capacity planning, we need to invest some time in understanding the function of a web server in general, and IIS more specifically. The best way to understand the operation of a web server is by tracing how it processes a request from a web browser. In this section, we trace every step of how a web server processes both static and dynamic requests.

The World Wide Web is based on client-server architecture where browsers are clients generating requests for content, and web servers are content providers. Due to its global scale and rapid growth, the Web is probably the most complicated client-server system in existence. The conversation between the client and the server takes place using the Hypertext Transfer Protocol (HTTP). HTTP is a simple protocol based on a simple request/reply exchange of messages. It currently runs on top of the TCP transport protocol of the TCP/IP protocol stack, although that is not a requirement. The HTTP protocol itself requires only that a reliable transport protocol is used to carry the messages from the client to the server and vice versa.

Clients submit requests to a web server by typing the name of the requested resource directly or by selecting a link on a web page. The name of the resource is specified in a standardized format, forming what is known as the uniform resource identifier (URI) or the more widely known uniform resource locator (URL). A URI is a string used to uniquely identify a resource universally, whereas a URL is a type of URI that names a resource within the Internet by combining the scheme used to obtain the resource (for example, the HTTP protocol), the location, and the resource's name. The URI specifies the server that should provide the resource, the protocol to use to obtain the resource, and the port at which the server is listening for requests. The protocol may be HTTP, FTP, gopher, or many others. In this chapter, we focus on the HTTP protocol because it is the most commonly used protocol for retrieving resources from the web server.

Once the browser receives the request, it must format it using the appropriate protocol format and submit it to the server for processing. When you explicitly enter a URL on the browser, it generates a GET method. When the request is embedded within an HTML page, the generated method can be a GET, PUT, or POST. We won't go into the details of how each method is processed by the server, but you can find this type of information in the HTTP protocol specification or a good HTML book such as Musciano and Kennedy's *HTML: The Definitive Guide* (O'Reilly).

Once the request is formatted properly, the browser completes the request by establishing a TCP connection with the web server at the address and port specified in the URI and passing the request. The server processes the request, sends the reply back in the form of an HTTP response, and closes the connection.

IIS is described as an *application server* to stress the fact that it provides additional facilities over the traditional web server. Its architecture is shown in Figure 12-1. In addition to static content, it supports the execution of Internet or intranet applications through ISAPI extensions, CGI scripts, and built-in scripting languages such as Active Server Pages, Server-Side Include scripts, and IDC scripts. An application server consumes resources differently in providing static and dynamic content. In processing a request for a static page, the server needs to access the disk to retrieve the file corresponding to the request. So a request for a URL by the browser is translated into a filesystem access by the server. As with all filesystem accesses, the file cache enhances the performance of the server by caching frequently accessed files in main memory. This implies that servers that provide primarily static content will require more attention from the performance analyst at the I/O subsystem, since that is the critical resource. In servicing a request for dynamic content, the server may need to execute a new process or call a function in order to generate the content to be sent back to the client. This implies that servicing a dynamic content request requires more involvement of the CPU.

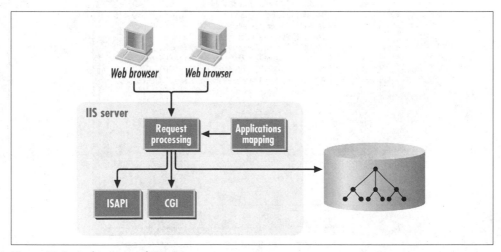

Figure 12-1. Architecture of IIS

At this point, you are probably wondering how the server knows how to process a request. When an HTTP request arrives at the server, IIS uses the extension of the requested filename to determine how to route the request. The configurable table of extension-to-application pairs, called the *application mappings*, defines how an extension is mapped into an application. The server matches the filename extension against the application mappings to determine whether to forward the request to an ISAPI extension, a CGI script, or, in the case of a simple HTML page, to the document tree, as shown in Figure 12-2. The application mappings can be displayed or modified by bringing up the Properties of the server from the Internet Services Manager, selecting the Home Directory tab from the WWW Server Master Properties window, and clicking on the Configuration button. From Figure 12-2, we can see that the requests with a known extension are processed by one of the six different DLLs (dynamic link libraries). In IIS Version 4.0, the column that is now named Verbs was named Exclusions. *Verbs* is another term used to refer to HTTP methods such as GET, HEAD, and POST. In IIS 4.0, when adding a new application mapping, you had to specify the methods that should *not* invoke the executable; in IIS 5.0, you specify the verbs or methods that *should* invoke the executable. So be careful, since the same field is used to accomplish the opposite end result.

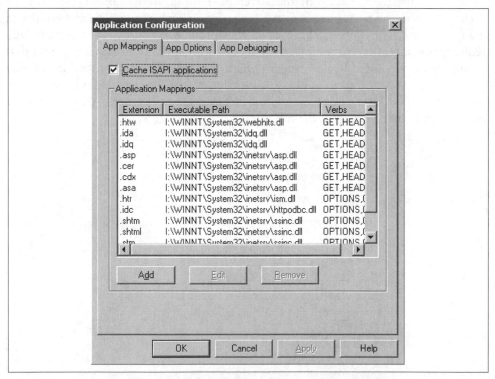

Figure 12-2. Application Mappings dialog

Let's digress briefly to discuss the difference between the user's and the server's view of requests to the web server. A user generates a single request to the web server when he enters the URL for an HTML page at a browser and presses Enter to retrieve its contents. Most of the time, a single HTML page contains multiple images within it to spice up the content. These are called *inline images*. When the request for the HTML page arrives at the server, IIS simply retrieves the file from the disk or filesystem cache and returns the file to the client. At that point, the browser parses the HTML file and determines that there are a number of inline images embedded within the document. The browser then generates additional requests to the server to obtain the inline images. Even though the user of the browser generated one initial request, the server has to process multiple requests to provide all the content that comprises that single HTML page. As a result of those additional requests for inline images, the server needs to create multiple entries in its log file, one for each of the individual requests submitted by the browser. This subtle difference between the user's and the server's perception of requests can help you better understand the contents of the IIS log file.

Let's summarize what we have discussed so far about the functionality of IIS by looking at Figure 12-3 and tracing a GET request. The request is initiated when a user enters a URL at the browser. The browser formats the URL requested using the HTTP protocol standard and sends the request to the server. Before the actual request can be transferred to the server, lower layers of the protocol stack must determine the IP address of the web server and establish a TCP connection with it. Once the connection is established, the request is transferred to the server, which then parses the request. IIS determines how to process the request based on its current configuration and on the request type. For static content, IIS locates the resource either on the disk or on the filesystem cache depending on whether the same resource has been recently accessed. For dynamic content, IIS either invokes functions within some DLL or spawns an external process to process the request. (Later, we discuss in more detail the various configuration options available for running applications through IIS.) In all cases, if the processing of the request is successful, the response is sent back to the client over the existing connection; otherwise, an error message is generated and sent back.

In tracing a simple GET request, it becomes clear that IIS, in processing requests submitted by clients, has to consume units of every underlying resource available on your system. When the connection is established, some memory is consumed to set up the operating system–level data structures for maintaining information about the connection. Network resources are consumed in setting up the connection and transferring the request and the response between the client and the server. In processing the request, the inetinfo process must use up some CPU and disk time. For a CGI request, an additional process is created and executed to generate the content that forms the response to be returned to the client. Since IIS requires a variety of resources in doing its job, scarcity of any of those resources can cause its performance to suffer.

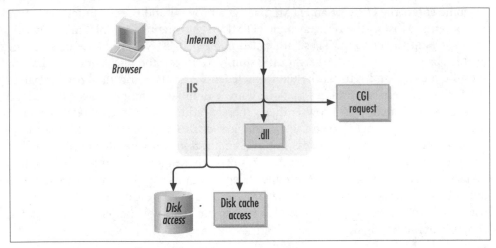

Figure 12-3. Processing of browser request

The rest of this chapter is dedicated to looking in more detail at how each underlying system resource is used by IIS, how to detect bottlenecks in those resources, and how to plan the capacity of your system so that satisfactory service levels are observed by your users. The following sections cover sources of information related to IIS performance that will assist in your goal of analyzing IIS performance issues and detecting bottlenecks. We also include a section on benchmarking tools that can be very useful in capacity planning for your server as well as for experimenting with new configuration settings. Throughout the rest of the chapter, we use the WCAT (Web Capacity Analysis Tool) tool from Microsoft extensively in analyzing the performance of IIS. The architecture and configuration of WCAT is described in detail in the section "Web Server Benchmarks."

Sources of Information

A number of sources of information can assist you in tuning and performing capacity planning of IIS. As usual, the System Monitor has lots of metrics, some specific to IIS, and some of other resources that are critical in a high-performance IIS configuration. The log files generated by the server also provide valuable input on the workload imposed on your system. Another source of information is the IIS Metabase. Although the information stored in the Metabase is not directly related to performance, it contains crucial configuration parameters for IIS that can be used for tuning purposes. These sources provide loads of information for understanding the workload and the operation of your application server. If you understand the characteristics of the requests processed by IIS and know how the response time is allocated across the resources utilized in processing a request, you have won half the battle of tuning the server's performance and in planning its capacity.

System Monitor Metrics

IIS uses all the underlying resources of the server in providing its service. Therefore, to understand its performance you need to look at a variety of objects, such as the Processor object and the Physical Disk object. Later, as we evaluate the impact of IIS on basic system resources, we point you toward counters from other objects that become relevant. Here, we describe only the Performance objects made available to the System Monitor after IIS 5.0 is installed and that are thereby specific to IIS and its bundled applications (web service, FTP service, SMTP service, and NNTP service).

Those four performance objects are:

- The Active Server Pages object
- The Internet Information Services Global object
- The FTP Service object
- The Web Service object

Version 2.0 of IIS provided the Gopher Service and HTTP Service objects. Since the gopher protocol is pretty much obsolete now, the Gopher object is not available after Version 4.0. The HTTP Service object is basically the same as the Web Service object, although a few counters have changed.

A description of most of the counters for these objects is available in the IIS 5.0 online documentation, accessible after a default installation of IIS 5.0 through the URL *http://localhost/iishelp*. The description of the counters can be found under Administration → Administrator's Reference → Counters Reference. A brief description of each counter can be found in the Windows 2000 Resource Kit installation directory in the file *counters.chm*. If you are running IIS on Windows NT, you can access similar information within *IIS Resource Kit\Chapter Samples\Counters\ Counters.hlp,* as well as in the Windows 4.0 Option Pack documentation, under the "Performance Monitoring" section.

The Active Server Pages (ASP) object provides counters covering all aspects of applications that make use of the ASP scripting language. It includes information on any errors generated (whether they were generated by the preprocessor, the compiler, or at runtime), information about the performance of the application, such as the throughput in ASP requests per second and response time, and information on sessions and transactions. We examine how to tune ASP applications later in this chapter, and describe the use of some of these metrics at that time. Right now, let's just look at some of the more important counters available through the ASP object:

Memory Allocated
> ASP runs as a DLL that gets loaded when an ASP file is requested by a user. It allocates memory to run each script as well as to maintain state information. This counter reports on the total amount of memory allocated to ASP and can help narrow down a memory shortage problem.

Request Bytes In Total

The total number of bytes of data received due to ASP requests.

Request Bytes Out Total

The total number of bytes of data sent to users due to ASP requests. This counter does not include HTTP header information.

Requests Executing

The number of ASP requests currently being processed by a worker thread.

Requests Queued

The number of ASP requests currently in the queue waiting to be processed by a worker thread.

Requests/sec

The throughput of ASP requests that the server can process. When the intensity of the workload exceeds the maximum rate at which your server can process ASP requests, additional requests will either be queued or rejected, and the performance will degrade.

Request Execution Time

The amount of time in milliseconds that it took to execute the most recent ASP request. This is only running time; you must also consider the queuing time to get an idea of the response time observed by the client.

Request Wait Time

The amount of time in milliseconds that the most recent request spent waiting in the queue for processing by a worker thread. This is one of the most important counters to look at in determining whether your ASP application or IIS server is in need of tuning.

Requests Queued

The number of ASP requests currently waiting in the queue for service. A web server that has sufficient capacity should always have zero for this metric. When you start to consistently see a small integer in this counter, your server is running out of capacity.

You may have noticed that the Request Execution Time and Request Wait Time counters report information about only the very last request processed. The fact that the metrics relate only to the last request makes these counters fairly useless. It is possible that the last request processed was a really simple one compared to the rest of the ASP scripts on the site. The values reported by these two metrics in this case would underestimate the response time of a typical request. On the other hand, it is possible that the last ASP request was very resource-intensive. The values reported in this case would overestimate the response time of a typical request. What would be more useful is the *average* response time of an ASP request. Here is where Little's Law comes to the rescue. If you remember from Chapter 1, Little's Law establishes the following relationship between the average number of jobs in the system, $\bar{n}$, the arrival rate of jobs, λ, and the average time spent in the system, $\bar{R}$:

$$\bar{n} = \lambda \times \bar{R}$$

In this case, we have the average number of jobs in the system, which is given by adding the values of the counters Requests Executing and Requests Queued. We also have the arrival rate of jobs, which is given by the counter Requests/sec. By rearranging the previous equation, we can compute the average time spent in the system as follows:

$$\bar{R} = \frac{(RequestsExecuting + RequestsQueued)}{RequestsPerSecond}$$

The best way to accomplish this is to export the raw data from the System Monitor into a comma-separated flat file that can be imported into Excel.

The Internet Information Services Global object includes counters that are related to both the HTTP and FTP services. The counters in this object focus on the status of the IIS object cache and on the effect of the bandwidth throttling feature. The IIS cache is used and maintained by IIS for improving the performance of the server by maintaining in memory frequently accessed objects that are relatively costly to obtain every time. (We discuss the IIS object cache when we talk about the effect of IIS on server memory in the section "Managing the Memory," and we discuss the bandwidth throttling feature in "Managing the CPU.") The counters provided for reporting on the effectiveness of the object cache in IIS 5.0 are different from those available under Version 4.0. In Version 4.0, the counters provided information at a summary level, whereas in Version 5.0, the counters report on the effectiveness of each component of the object cache. The object cache consists of three components that cache file handles, URI information blocks, and BLOBs (binary large objects). IIS 5.0 provides cache effectiveness metrics for each of these three components separately. Here are the most critical counters:

File Cache Hits

> The total number of requests for file handle objects resolved through an access to the IIS object cache. This is a measure of the effectiveness of the object cache in caching file handles. There is some tuning available of this cache that can help improve this metric if it seems low.

File Cache Hits %

> The fraction of all the requests resolved through an access to the IIS object cache. Combined with the number of hits, this measure can tell us how effective the object cache is in caching file handles.

File Cache Flushes

> The total number of times that the file cache has been flushed since the IIS server was started.

Total Allowed Async I/O Requests

The total number of I/O requests for all services that were permitted by the server since it started. This counter and all the others under this object that include "Async I/O" in the counter name are available only if bandwidth throttling is enabled.

Total Blocked Async I/O Requests

The total number of I/O requests for all services that were blocked by the server since it started. Requests are blocked when the maximum bandwidth setting has been reached, and they are placed in a queue until more bandwidth is available.

Total Rejected Async I/O Requests

The total number of I/O requests for all services that were rejected by the server since it started. Requests are rejected when the maximum bandwidth is reached and the queue of blocked requests is filled. This and the previous two counters describe the effectiveness of the bandwidth-throttling feature.

The Web Service and FTP Service objects provide most of the counters useful in bottleneck detection and performance management of an IIS server. They include counters that describe the operation of the corresponding service from the performance perspective. Here is a list of some of the more useful counters:

Bytes Received/sec

The total number of bytes that have been either received or sent by all services, including bytes transferred by HTTP and FTP. It is very useful in understanding the network bandwidth requirements of the web server and in evaluating the available capacity. Other counters break up this total into received and sent bytes.

CGI Requests/sec

The rate of incoming CGI requests to the server. This is another counter that can help in understanding the workload mix of this server. For example, when the CPU is heavily utilized and this counter is high, it may be time to rewrite these scripts using more efficient methods.

Connection Attempts/sec

The total number of requests for connections received by the server. This counter provides information regarding the intensity of the workload imposed on your server. One approach to improving the performance of a very busy server is limiting the number of simultaneous connections that it allows. Using this counter, you can determine whether such an approach would help. This and some other counters from this object disregard the instance that you select from the Performance Monitor, so be careful in interpreting their meaning.

Files/sec

The total number of files received or sent by this server. This counter defines the throughput of the server at the granularity of a file. It is valuable in understanding how much work the web server can do for you, but the number of files transferred will depend on the kind of content that you are providing.

ISAPI Extension Requests/sec

The total number of requests for dynamic content generated using ISAPI extensions. If you have a server that provides dynamic content using different approaches (such as some CGI and some ISAPI scripts), this counter can help you break down the traffic on your server into categories by application type.

Total Method Requests/sec

The total number of HTTP requests to your site, such as GET, PUT, POST, etc. Other counters in this object break down the requests by method type.

IIS Logs

Another very useful source of information for your web site are the logs generated by IIS. Logging can be activated and deactivated for each site managed by your IIS server. Its logging is very flexible in that you can choose the log format based on the type of analysis you plan to do. For web sites, you have four different choices for the log format; for FTP sites, you have three choices. One of the available choices for both types of sites is logging into an SQL Server database. This is a powerful option in that it makes analysis of the data as simple as executing an SQL query against a database. The disadvantage of this option is that you must have SQL Server running, which is definitely a resource-intensive application. In addition to providing a wealth of log formats to choose from, IIS provides log file management, thereby reducing the effort required by the systems administrator in maintaining them.

Activating logging can be done through the Internet Service Manager. Simply select from the list of sites in the Microsoft Management Console and click on the Properties button. This brings up the window shown in Figure 12-4. From this window you can enable logging, specify the desired log format from the available drop-down list, and configure log file management and fields to log for the extended log format.

When you activate logging, you must also choose one of the available log formats. The four options for a web site are:

- NCSA Common Log Format
- Microsoft IIS Log Format
- W3C Extended Log Format
- ODBC Log Format

The three options for an FTP site are:

- Microsoft IIS Log Format
- W3C Extended Log Format
- ODBC Log Format

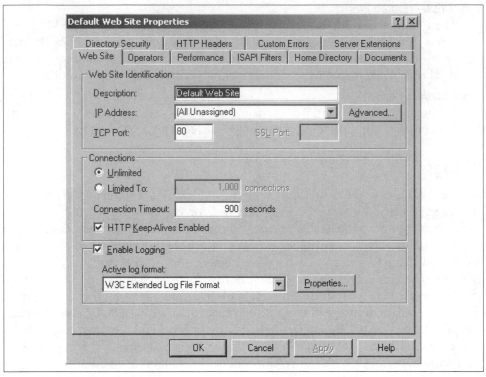

Figure 12-4. Enabling logging on a site

NCSA Common Log Format

The simplest option is the NCSA Common Log Format (CLF), the standard format used by the National Center for Supercomputing Applications (NCSA) server. Each request to the server generates one line or record in the log. The record includes the client's hostname, the client's username, the date and time of the request, the request type, the name of the requested resource, the standard HTTP status code, and the number of bytes transferred by the server. The fields in each record are separated by spaces. Notice in the following line from a log of the NCSA Common Log Format that spaces are also used within the fields, making it difficult to parse the log file:

```
127.0.0.1 - EPICUROS\Administrator [2/Dec/1998:08:29:27 -0500] "GET /blank.htm HTTP/
1.1" 200 304
```

This line tells us that this was a GET request generated at 8:29:27 on December 2, 1998 from the host 127.0.0.1 (*localhost*) for the resource *blank.htm*. This request was successfully processed by the server (status code 200), which received 304 bytes.

Microsoft IIS Log Format

The Microsoft IIS Log Format adds more information than the NCSA format and uses a comma as the field separator. This second feature makes the parsing of the log file easier. In addition to the information you get from the NCSA CLF formatted file, you get the elapsed time for the request and the number of bytes transferred by the server. Here is an example of a request as recorded in the log file:

```
135.100.0.1, -, 8/13/99, 17:00:45, W3SVC1, EPICUROS, 135.100.0.2, 260, 271, 4324,
200, 0, GET, /perfsize/file4K.txt, -,
```

This entry tells us that an unknown user ("-") on the machine with the IP address 135.100.0.1 generated a GET request for resource *iistat.asp* on 8/13/99 at 9:13:46 against the web service W3SVC1, which is running on machine EPICUROS (with IP address 135.100.0.2). The request, consisting of 271 bytes, took 260 milliseconds to be processed by the server, which responded by sending back 4,324 bytes. Both the HTTP standard status and the Win32 status reported success by returning codes 200 and 0, respectively.

W3C Extended Log Format

The World Wide Web Consortium Extended Log Format (ELF) was proposed by the W3C in an effort to resolve a number of issues in the NCSA CLF and many of the other proprietary formats. One of the problems with most log formats is that they are fixed field formats. They do not provide the means for the server administrator to decide what fields should be recorded about each transaction processed by the server. The administrator at one site may not want to record certain fields due to security reasons; the administrator at another site may need to store every piece of information available in an effort to resolve a performance concern. Another issue is the ambiguity that arises when parsing a log file where the delimiter character between fields of the log file is also used as a valid character within one of the recorded fields. An example of this issue is the space character in the CLF format, where the space is also used within the date/time field.

The proposed ELF format resolves both those issues. We take a look at the ELF format here, but the detailed format specification can be found at *http://www.w3.org/pub/WWW/TR/WD-logfile.html*. Since the number of fields logged on each record under this format varies based on the configuration of the site, each record must include a header providing a list of field identifiers, among other information. A field identifier can be in one of the following three forms: *identifier*, *prefix-identifier*, and *prefix(header)*. The *prefix* is used to indicate the parties involved in the generation of the field. For example, the prefix *c* indicates the client, *s* indicates the server, *cs* indicates client to server, and *sc* indicates server to client. The second and third forms of the field identifier are used for fields that do not uniquely identify the information without specifically indicating the prefix. For example, to record the IP address of the client, the field identifier is *c-ip*, and to record the HTTP method sent from the client to the server, the identifier is *cs-method*. For a list of all the available fields and their meanings, you can look at the online help for IIS under Administration → Administrator's Reference → Logging Properties Reference. Here is an example of the first few records from an ELF-formatted log file:

```
#Software: Microsoft Internet Information Server 5.0
#Version: 1.0
#Date: 1999-12-24 17:00:50
#Fields: time c-ip s-sitename s-computername s-ip cs-method cs-uri-stem cs-uri-query
sc-status sc-win32-status s-port
17:00:50 127.0.0.1 W3SVC1 YIANNIS 127.0.0.1 GET /iisHelp/iis/misc/default.asp - 200 0
80
```

In IIS, you can configure which fields get logged through the Microsoft Management Console. First select the web site that you want to configure, and from the web site properties screen select Properties → Web Site → W3C Extended Log File Format → Properties. When you select the Extended Properties tab, you should see a screen as in Figure 12-5.

Figure 12-5. Log field selection screen for the W3C Extended Log Format

The log field selection screen is a little bit different if you are running IIS 4.0. The reason for the difference is the introduction of process accounting related fields into the W3C Extended Log Format in IIS 5.0. Process accounting is itself a new feature of Windows 2000, along with support for the job kernel object. (The job object is described in detail in Chapter 3.) Process accounting can be activated at the web site level and applies only to sites running outside the *inetinfo.exe* process itself. We explain what it means for a web site to run outside the *inetinfo.exe* process in a little while, when we discuss the various process isolation options. In addition to recording information about the requests that the IIS server is processing, process accounting allows you to collect event logging information and performance statistics about the consumption of CPU resources by the web site.

The process accounting information is logged into the same file as the other information, but the two sets of data are in separate blocks. Information about an interactive request to the server appears as a single line of data. Whenever a process accounting event occurs, such as the event that the site was stopped, a header is written in the log file that describes the event, and one or more lines are added that pertain to that event. If a new HTTP request arrives at the server right after an event is logged, a new header will be added, which describes the format of the HTTP request entry followed by the entry itself. As you can see, the introduction of process accounting information complicates the parsing of the log file.

You can activate the logging of process accounting information simply by clicking the checkbox for Process Accounting in the field selection screen; you may then select any of the available metrics individually. Here is an example of a log file with process accounting information:

```
#Software: Microsoft Internet Information Services 5.0
#Version: 1.0
#Date: 2000-02-29 04:15:32
#SubComponent: Process Accounting
#Fields: date time s-event s-process-type s-user-time s-kernel-time s-page-faults s-
total-procs s-active-procs s-stopped-procs
2000-02-29 04:15:32 Periodic-Log All 00.005% 00.002% 14377 2 2 0
#Software: Microsoft Internet Information Services 5.0
#Version: 1.0
#Date: 2000-02-29 04:15:35
#Fields: date time c-ip cs-username s-ip s-port cs-method cs-uri-stem cs-uri-query
sc-status cs(User-Agent)
2000-02-29 04:15:35 127.0.0.1 SYSNET\Administrator 127.0.0.1 80 GET /iisadmin/iihd.
asp - 200 Mozilla/4.0+(compatible;+MSIE+5.01;+Windows+NT+5.0)
2000-02-29 04:15:36 127.0.0.1 SYSNET\Administrator 127.0.0.1 80 GET /iisadmin/images/
cube.gif - 200 Mozilla/4.0+(compatible;+MSIE+5.01;+Windows+NT+5.0)
```

Table 12-1 lists the available metrics.

Table 12-1. Metrics available through process accounting for logging

Field	Appears as	Description
Process Type	s-proc-type	The type of process that triggered the event. Takes the value CGI, Application, or All.
Process Event	s-event	The name of the event that was triggered.
Total User Time	s-user-time	The total amount of user-mode CPU time in seconds that the site used during the current interval.

Table 12-1. *Metrics available through process accounting for logging (continued)*

Field	Appears as	Description
Total Kernel Time	s-kernel-time	The total amount of privileged-mode CPU time in seconds that the site used during the current interval.
Total Page Faults	s-page-faults	The total number of page faults generated by this web site.
Total Processes	s-total-procs	The total number of CGI and out-of-process applications that were created during the current interval.
Active Processes	s-active-procs	The total number of CGI and out-of-process applications that were running when this entry was added to the log.
Total Terminated Processes	s-stopped-procs	The total number of CGI and out-of-process applications that were terminated due to process throttling during the current interval.

ODBC Log Format

The next option for a log format is to tell IIS to log every request as a record in an ODBC data source. Typically, users use either a Microsoft Access or a Microsoft SQL Server database as the data source, although any ODBC-compliant database will work. The main advantage of this option is that there is no need to parse the file in order to analyze the log contents, nor do you have to deal with log file management issues. The obvious disadvantage is that you need to keep a database around for logging the information. This introduces database maintenance and management issues.

To set up ODBC logging, you must first prepare the database by creating a table in which to store the log contents, define the ODBC system data source, and then set up IIS to use the data source. To simplify the first step, IIS comes with an SQL script for creating the inetlog table. The name of the script file is *logtemp.sql* and it is located by default in the *\winnt\system32\inetsrv* directory. The definition of the table is shown in Table 12-2. Although the format is fixed, the table includes most of the fields included in the W3C ELF format.

Table 12-2. *Definition of the inetlog table that is used to store the logged records*

Field	Description	Data type
ClientHost	Name of the host that generated the request	varchar(255)
Username	Username that generated the request	varchar(255)
LogTime	Date and time at which the request was completed	Datetime
Service	Type of service that processed the request	varchar(255)
Machine	Name of the server that processed the request	varchar(255)
ServerIP	IP address of the server that processed the request	varchar(50)
ProcessingTime	Amount of time that it took to process the request	Int
BytesRecvd	Number of bytes received by the server	Int
BytesSent	Number of bytes sent out by the server	Int
ServiceStatus	Standard HTTP server status response	Int

Table 12-2. Definition of the inetlog table that is used to store the logged records (continued)

Field	Description	Data type
Win32Status	Windows-specific status response	Int
Operation	Name of the HTTP method	varchar(255)
Target	Name of the resource that was requested	varchar(255)
Parameters	List of parameters that were passed to the resource	varchar(255)

As already mentioned, the primary advantage of using the ODBC format for storing the web server logs is that the information is immediately available without any need for parsing. By adding the log records in the database, we can now use SQL queries to analyze the information in the logs. To obtain interesting statistics, a task that would normally require parsing and searching through the log file, we can now simply construct the appropriate SQL query and just watch the statistics scroll across the screen. For example, let's say we want to know the average file size of all requests processed by the web server today. The following select statement will return that number:

```
select avg(BytesSent) from inetlog where LogTime=today
```

Or, as another example, say we want to know how many GET requests generated by each client today were successfully processed by the server. Here is the query:

```
Select count(*), ClientHost from inetlog
where LogTime=today and ServiceStatus=200
```

Except when logging to an ODBC data source, IIS writes the logged requests in batches to reduce the amount of disk traffic generated. The default batch size is 64 KB. The batch size can be configured using the Registry entry HKLM\CurrentControlSet\Services\InetInfo\Parameters\LogFileBatchSize. This is a REG_DWORD, with a range of 0–0xFFFFFFFF, specified in bytes. Increasing the value of the batch size reduces the amount of disk traffic generated, but also prevents the log file from being updated as frequently.

On a per-service basis, you can also control whether logging should be done for anonymous, nonanonymous, or both types of connections. The Registry entries are LogAnonymous and LogNonAnonymous under the key HKLM\CurrentControlSet\Services\<ServiceName>\Parameters. The <ServiceName> is either MSFTPSVC for the FTP service, or W3SVC for the HTTP service. Both entries are REG_DWORDs, with a range of 0 or 1, where 0 means logging is off and 1 means logging is on. By default, logging for both types of connections is activated.

Now that we have covered all possible log file formats available through IIS for a web site, let's turn our attention to the management of those log files. Management of log files is a tedious task that is usually automated through scripting. The administrator of a typical web server needs to stop the server, move the current log file to a location with sufficient storage capacity, and restart the server. IIS provides automated management of the log files with a number of options to accommodate sites with different hit rates. When setting the log format for a specific site, you can also set the location of the log file as well as the frequency at which the log file is closed and replaced with a new one. There are five options in specifying the frequency: *daily*, *weekly*, *monthly*, *unlimited file size*, and *specified file size*. The first three specify that a new log file should be created at the beginning of each daily, weekly, or monthly cycle. If your site is only lightly used, monthly should be sufficient, whereas for very busy sites a daily setting may be necessary. The files are named using a two-letter prefix to identify the log file format, followed by the year, month, and day on which logging to this file was started. The other two options use file size to specify when a new log file should be created. With the specified file size option, you indicate that logging to a new file should begin when the log file has reached a certain size. The unlimited file size option indicates that logging always takes place in a certain file, which basically disables the automated log file management capabilities of IIS.

The IIS Metabase

Yet another source of information is the Metabase. The Metabase is a hierarchically structured binary format for storing configuration information about IIS. You may be wondering why the architects of IIS came up with yet another configuration file format and did not stick with the Registry. The answer has to do with efficiency. IIS has two unique requirements from a system that stores its configuration information:

Fast access to a key/value pair
> IIS must be able to respond to HTTP requests as fast as possible and its performance should not be impacted considerably by the need to retrieve configuration data during the processing of a request.

Ability to store information at multiple levels
> IIS can support hundreds of web sites running on a single server. Many or even all of the sites may have the exact same configuration information. So, IIS must be able to define default values for all parameters at a higher level that are inherited by default by all lower levels, thereby making the storage of this information much less redundant.

The Metabase looks a lot like the Registry, but addresses these two requirements. The data is stored in a binary file, *metabase.bin*, which is located at *%SystemRoot%\system32\inetsrv*. Much like the Registry, each node in the hierarchy is a key that contains properties and other subkeys. To provide efficient access to the data, each key has an associated numeric ID that is used in locating the entry.

To support the second requirement, the Metabase provides a hierarchical structure for storing the configuration information of IIS at different levels, with the option of inheriting any parameter at a lower level that is defined at a higher level. Figure 12-6 shows a partial view of the tree hierarchy maintained by the Metabase. Note that the names are not those found within the Metabase, but are used to make it easier to understand conceptually what the tree looks like. At the top level, you define parameters that apply to the entire machine. This includes all web sites, FTP sites, and all the subtrees of the top-level key. As you move down the tree, you specify parameters that apply to more specific portions of the IIS server. For example, the second branch below the top-level key is the Web Service (W3SVC is the key name used in the Metabase). Parameters at that level apply to all the web sites on the machine. Below that, any parameters specified at the Web Service *n* level apply to a specific web site, and below that any parameters specified at the Web Service apply to a specific virtual directory.

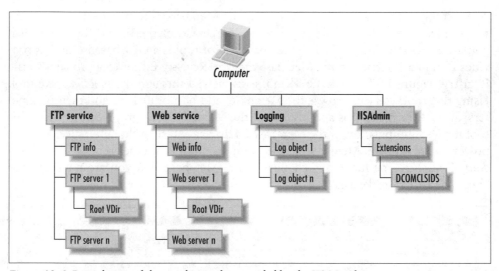

Figure 12-6. Partial view of the tree hierarchy provided by the IIS Metabase

Again, the advantage of storing configuration information this way is the reduction of redundant information. If a common set of parameters apply to all the web sites supported on a particular machine, those parameters only need to be defined once at the Web Service level. At the same time, if a specific site needs to be configured differently from the others, then you can simply override one or more of the inherited parameters by defining those parameters at the level of the particular web site. For example, the parameter MaxConnections specifies the maximum number of connections that the server will accept. It is defined by default at the Web Service level and applies to all the web sites you create. If you change this parameter through the Internet Service Manager for a particular web site, you are actually specifying a nondefault value for this parameter at the Web Service *n* level.

There are three ways to configure the Metabase. The simplest way is through the Internet Service Manager. Most of the configuration parameters you specify when you create a site are stored in the Metabase in a transparent way to the user. The advantage of this approach is that the Internet Service Manager validates the value used to ensure that the Metabase does not get corrupted. The second way is to use the IIS Admin objects through a scripting language. IIS provides a set of DCOM automation components that you can use through VBScript or JScript to manipulate the Metabase. You can find sample scripts in the directory *%SystemRoot%\Inetpub\AdminScripts*, and documentation for the scripting API at the *http://localhost/iishelp* site that is installed by default along with IIS. In particular, the *adsutil.vbs* script allows you to perform a number of administration tasks on an IIS server through the command line. For example, the following command sets the CGITimeout value for the first web site to 5 minutes (300 seconds):

```
C:\Inetpub\AdminScripts>cscript adsutil.vbs set W3SVC/1/Root/CGITimeout 300
```

The last approach available for configuring the Metabase is to use the Metabase Editor tool from the Windows 2000 Server Resource Kit, or the IIS 4.0 Resource Kit if you are using Windows NT. The Metabase Editor tool is a GUI-based tool that provides a similar interface to the Metabase that the Registry Editor tool provides to the Registry. Figure 12-7 shows the Metabase as viewed through the *metabase.exe* tool. Using this tool, you can browse the Metabase, add or modify keys and their parameters, and perform backups and restores of the Metabase. The graphical nature of this tool makes manipulation of the Metabase a fairly easy task, although it gives you the power to corrupt the Metabase to the point where the Internet service won't even start. So before you make any changes to the Metabase that you are not very sure about, be sure to make a backup of the data first.

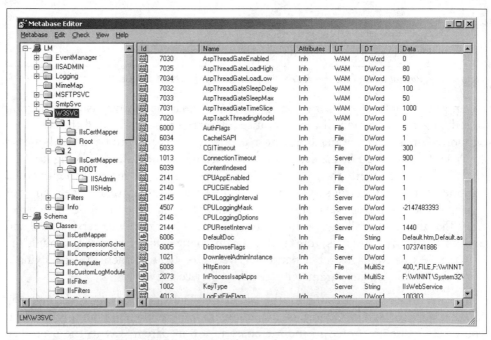

Figure 12-7. The Metabase as viewed through the metabase.exe tool

The Metabase maintains almost all the critical parameters that can be used to tune the performance of your IIS server. We list some of the more useful properties here to give you a taste of what is available, but throughout the rest of the chapter we mention a number of additional Metabase properties as we come across the relevant context. The complete set of Metabase properties is described in the IIS help web site, *http://localhost/iishelp*.

AspBufferingOn
> Specifies whether output generated by an ASP script will be buffered

CGITimeout
> Number of seconds that the server will wait for a CGI script to complete execution

CPULoggingInterval
> Number of minutes between the writing of samples of process accounting information in the log

MaxBandwidth
> The maximum amount of bandwidth allocated to IIS

Web Server Benchmarks

In understanding the performance of your web server and for evaluating the effect of hardware and software configuration options, having a good benchmarking tool is essential. In this section, we describe a number of benchmarking tools that are available for free or for a low cost. We especially concentrate on the Web Capacity Analysis Tool from Microsoft, which we use extensively in the rest of this chapter to illustrate various concepts.

SPECweb96/SPECweb99

The SPECweb96 is a standardized benchmark for web servers developed by SPEC (Standard Performance Evaluation Corporation). SPEC capitalized on its established expertise in the benchmarking field in developing this benchmark. The objective in the design of this tool was to provide a well-defined workload and environment for testing the performance of web servers so that their relative performance could be compared using a single metric.

The architecture of the SPECweb96 benchmark consists of a prime client and a number of worker clients that generate requests against a web server. In the Unix version, when the program is launched, multiple client processes are created for generating the requests, and the original process becomes the prime, which coordinates the operation of the workers and collects statistics from the test. The Windows NT version is very similar but uses a single multithreaded process instead of multiple processes.

The workload of the benchmark was derived by analyzing logs from several servers. Some of the logs came from the NCSA site, the home pages of Hewlett-Packard and HAL Computers, and from a small site that supports multiple users. The logs were retrieved from a variety of servers to create a workload that was representative of typical user access patterns as observed by the web server of an ISP. A number of observations resulted from the study of these logs. Most of the requests are for files of small size, typically between 1 KB and 10 KB. The frequency of access to files of larger size quickly drops off as the file size increases.

These observations are reflected in the file mix of the SPECweb96 benchmark. The overall set of files consists of four classes of files with the characteristics shown in Table 12-3. Each class consists of nine files, for a total of 36 files. When generating a request, a client first determines the class of the request by generating a random number and choosing the class using the distribution shown in the table. Requests for files within the class are made using a Poisson distribution. The single parameter that defines the Poisson distribution is set to the midpoint of the file range for the class.

Table 12-3. SPECWeb96 workload characteristics

Class	File size range	Frequency of access
Class 0	0 – 1 KB	35%
Class 1	1 KB – 10 KB	50%
Class 2	10 KB – 100 KB	14%
Class 3	100 KB – 1 MB	1%

The designers of the workload tried to model the workload observed at an ISP where multiple user directories are hosted. The basic file set of 36 files is replicated across multiple directories. The number of directories and thereby the total amount of content support is dependent on the expected throughput of the server. The simple rule that relates the expected throughput rate to the size of the fileset says that the size of the fileset doubles as the size of the throughput of the server quadruples. The rationale behind this rule is that a server that can provide the same throughput as two other servers should also be able to support the content of those other servers. When running the SPECweb96 benchmark, the workload's intensity increases until the maximum throughput for the server is determined.

SPECweb96 was meant to be an early release of a benchmark that would continuously evolve to track the change of the workload observed on the Internet by popular web servers. In the fall of 1999, SPEC released a new version of the benchmark, SPECweb99 (see *http://www.spec.org/osg/web99/docs/whitepaper.html*). This version includes a number of changes that make it a more appropriate benchmark for most web sites.

One important change is the redefinition of the performance metric. The SPEC benchmarks produce a single metric that can be used to compare different configurations or web servers. In SPECweb96, that metric was the number of HTTP requests that the test system can process per second, whereas in SPECweb99 the metric is the total number of concurrent connections that can be supported at a given maximum bit rate with a maximum segment size. Needless to say, these two metrics should not be compared to one another.

Another major change in SPECweb99 is the workload processed by the server. The new workload consists of five different components:

Static Workload

> This is very similar in nature to the workload definition of SPECweb96, except that a Zipf distribution is used to determine the access probability to each directory. Seventy percent of all requests are for the static component of the overall workload.

Standard Dynamic GET

> This component simulates the use of dynamic scripts to generate ads on web pages. It comprises 12.45% of the overall workload.

Standard Dynamic CGI GET

> This component is identical to the previous one, except that it must be implemented using the CGI approach. This requires that a new process is created to process each request, as opposed to using a pool of processes or threads to accomplish the same task. It comprises 0.15% of the overall workload.

Dynamic GET with ad rotation

> This component simulates the dynamic generation of ad rotation with support for customer profile–based generation of the ads. Cookies are used with each request as the key for retrieving customer profile information from a database. It comprises 12.6% of the overall workload.

Dynamic POST

> This component simulates the registration of a user at an ISP site. The posted information is written to a file.

One more enhancement to the benchmark is the support for both the HTTP/1.0 and HTTP/1.1 protocols. Seventy percent of all requests are generated over either an HTTP/1.1 persistent connection, or an HTTP/1.0 connection with keep-alive headers; the rest are generated over an HTTP/1.0 connection without keep-alive headers. The difference between these two options and how they impact the performance of a web server is discussed in more detail in the section "HTTP/1.1 versus HTTP/1.0."

Web Capacity Analysis Tool (WCAT)

The Web Capacity Analysis Tool or WCAT is a load generator tool for web servers and more specifically for IIS. It is developed by Microsoft and is available in the IIS Resource Kit CD and the Windows 2000 Server Resource Kit; it is also available to MSDN Professional and Universal subscribers. The software includes a large set of prepared workloads that you can run against a web server. The workloads range from a simple workload for simple HTML files, to workloads with some fraction of requests for dynamic content such as CGI or ISAPI requests, to more complex workloads that test the overhead of SSL and the benefits of the HTTP keep-alive protocol. In addition to the predefined workloads, it gives you the ability to create your own workloads, so you can configure WCAT to generate a workload that is representative of your own. One weakness shared by all benchmarks is that their workloads are not representative in many cases of the true workload of the system under test. This causes the results of those benchmarks to be of little value in many cases.

Architecture

Let's begin by looking at the architecture of WCAT. There are three components to WCAT: the server, the client, and the controller (see Figure 12-8). The server is the machine being tested. Although WCAT was designed to test servers running NT server and IIS, it can also be used to test other web servers. When WCAT is installed on the server, a set of files is copied to the root directory of your server (typically to *inetpub\wwwroot*). These files form the content of the predefined tests.

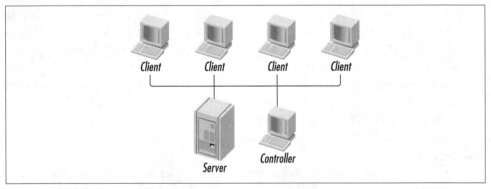

Figure 12-8. WCAT test architecture

The client component of WCAT can be installed on any number of machines based on the capacity of your web server and the amount of traffic that you want to generate. The installation of the WCAT client on a machine consists of the executable called *wcclient.exe* and a couple of batch files that are used for starting and configuring the client. The client is a multithreaded application that spawns a number of threads, as specified in the configuration file, for generating requests against the server. Using the WCAT terminology, each thread implements a *virtual client*. This design allows you to generate a large number of requests even if you have just a couple of machines that you use for testing purposes.

The controller is the most critical component of WCAT. It consists of an executable, *wcctl*, some batch files that are used for starting and configuring the controller, and a large number of scripts that define the behavior of WCAT. All the information regarding the parameters of a test are stored as configuration files under the web controller directory (the default is *webctrl\scripts*). When the controller is started, it reads the configuration information, instructs the clients on what requests to generate, and, if configured to do so, collects performance statistics from the server.

The controller treats the duration of the test as consisting of the warmup time, the execution time, and the cooldown time. During warmup and cooldown, the clients do not collect statistics in order to remove the transient effects of starting and ending a test. When the test completes, the controller accumulates all the statistics collected by the clients and generates a summary report for the test. It is possible to have the client, controller, and server all running on the same machine, but that is not recommended because the overhead of the client and controller will impact the accuracy of your measurements. For simple tests you can run the controller and client on the same machine, but for heavier tests you will need additional clients.

Workload

WCAT comes with a large number of predefined tests. Although it allows you to define your own customized tests, the predefined ones should be sufficient for basic benchmarking of an IIS server. The Users Guide breaks up all the tests into four groups: basic tests, CGI and ISAPI tests, HTTP keep-alive tests, and SSL tests. The basic tests only generate requests for static content of varying size. CGI and ISAPI tests mix requests for static content with some defined fraction of requests for dynamic content. There are tests that focus on ISAPI performance and tests that focus on CGI performance, but no tests combine the two types of dynamic content. HTTP keep-alive tests are modified versions of the basic tests and the CGI and ISAPI tests that activate the keep-alive feature. If you are testing a server used in an intranet environment where all your clients are using keep-alive, these tests would be appropriate. The SSL tests are modified versions of the first two types of tests that use the Secure Socket Layer encryption protocol. The SSL protocol imposes a considerable load on your server, so it is wise to use these tests to evaluate its impact if you are planning to use it on your site.

Each test is defined using three files: the configuration file, the script file, and the distribution file. The configuration file contains general information about the test, such as its duration, the length of the warmup and cooldown times, the think time, and the number of clients involved in the test. The controller does not start the test until the number of clients specified in the configuration file have contacted the controller for configuration information. If more clients attempt to participate in the test than specified in the configuration file, the controller simply ignores their requests.

Here is the configuration file for the *CGI25* test (*cgi25.cfg*):

```
# ########################################################################
#
#    Configuration for WCAT 3.1
#
# ########################################################################
```

```
# unused parameters will have their default values
ThinkTime:              0m        # max think time before next fetch.
MaxRecvBuffer           128K      # suggested max receive buffer in bytes 64K

CooldownTime            30s
WarmupTime              30s

NumClientMachines:      1         # given by user
NumClientThreads:       5         # given by user
Duration:               5m        # given by user
```

The script file defines the exact set of transactions that comprise the test and the characteristics of those transactions. In the script file, you define the different classes of requests that the clients will be generating. You may define multiple transactions as belonging to the same class. In such cases, the controller presents the client with a set of transactions to choose from in generating a request from that class. The controller collects statistics at the overall level and class level, but not at the individual transaction level. So, from the statistics point of view, all transactions from the same class are treated as having a similar impact on the server. Putting requests with considerably different demands on the server in the same class will cause your statistics for that class to have a large variance, making the average practically meaningless.

Here are portions of the script file for the *CGI25* test (*cgi25.scr*). We removed some of the transactions for the sake of clarity.

```
NEW TRANSACTION
  classId = 1
  NEW REQUEST HTTP
  RequestHeader = "Accept: image/gif, image/x-xbitmap, image/jpeg, image/pjpeg,
*/*\r\n"
  RequestHeader = "Accept-Language: en\r\n"
  RequestHeader = "Host: WCAT\r\n"
  RequestHeader = "UA-pixels: 1024x768\r\n"
  RequestHeader = "UA-color: color8\r\n"
  RequestHeader = "UA-OS: Windows NT\r\n"
  RequestHeader = "UA-CPU: x86\r\n"
  RequestHeader = "User-Agent: Mozilla/2.0 (compatible; MSIE 3.0; AK; Windows NT)
\r\n"
  Verb = "GET"
  URL = "/perfsize/file512.txt"
NEW TRANSACTION
  classId = 2
  NEW REQUEST HTTP
  RequestHeader = "Accept: image/gif, image/x-xbitmap, image/jpeg, image/pjpeg,
*/*\r\n"
  RequestHeader = "Accept-Language: en\r\n"
  RequestHeader = "Host: WCAT\r\n"
  RequestHeader = "UA-pixels: 1024x768\r\n"
  RequestHeader = "UA-color: color8\r\n"
  RequestHeader = "UA-OS: Windows NT\r\n"
  RequestHeader = "UA-CPU: x86\r\n"
```

```
    RequestHeader = "User-Agent: Mozilla/2.0 (compatible; MSIE 3.0; AK; Windows NT)
\r\n"
    Verb = "GET"
    URL = "/perfsize/file1K.txt"


# Simple & Minimal CGI Query
NEW TRANSACTION
    classId = 201
    NEW REQUEST HTTP
    RequestHeader = "Accept: image/gif, image/x-xbitmap, image/jpeg, image/pjpeg,
*/*\r\n"
    RequestHeader = "Accept-Language: en\r\n"
    RequestHeader = "Host: WCAT\r\n"
    RequestHeader = "UA-pixels: 1024x768\r\n"
    RequestHeader = "UA-color: color8\r\n"
    RequestHeader = "UA-OS: Windows NT\r\n"
    RequestHeader = "UA-CPU: x86\r\n"
    RequestHeader = "User-Agent: Mozilla/2.0 (compatible; MSIE 3.0; AK; Windows NT)
\r\n"
    Verb = "GET"
    URL = "/scripts/wscgi.exe?"
```

Each transaction is preceded with the New Transaction keyword, and each request within that class is preceded with the New Request HTTP keyword. The first two transactions shown in the previous file are for plain files and the third one is a CGI request. The required commands within each HTTP request are the *Verb*, which identifies the method to be used in submitting the request (GET, POST, etc.), and the *URL*, which identifies the resource to be requested. There are many additional commands that you can use in defining your workload, such as deciding whether to use the Keep-Alive protocol or the SSL protocol. The commands are explained in detail in the WCAT Users Guide.

Each configuration file has a header of comments that propose a convention in naming class IDs. According to that convention, class IDs between 1–10 should be used for plain text files, 101–110 for CGI requests, 201–210 for ISAPI requests, and 301–310 for POST method requests. Despite this, the *cgi25.scr* file uses class ID 201 for a CGI request. I guess rules are made to be broken.

The last required file is the distribution file. This file defines the percentages of each request class of the overall workload. It lists pairs of values where each pair consists of the class ID from the script file and a percentage. The sum of the percentages must equal 100 for a properly defined distribution file. The distribution file for the *CGI25* test (*cgi25.dst*) is shown here:

```
#
# Format of Script Specification:
#
# ClassId Distribution Factor(0 to 100)
#
```

```
# Sum of all distribution factors should be strictly 100 and
# each factor is an integer only
#
11 6 # 256 bytes = 7.64%
1 7 # 512 bytes = 9.44%
2 6 # 1K = 7.95%
3 12 # 2K = 16.77%
15 9 # 3K = 11.68%
4 5 # 4K = 7.28%
16 8 # 6K = 9.86%
5 4 # 8K = 5.47%
6 8 # 16K = 10.40%
7 5 # 32K = 6.69%
8 3 # 64K = 4.26%
10 2 # 256K = Remaining ( big range. choose one file out of this)
201 25 # CGI test
```

Notice that the syntax for this file requires that the fraction allocated to each class be an integer. You may ignore the percentages shown as comments at the right column of this file. All the distribution entries in this file, except for the CGI entry, were copied from another distribution file, so these fractions correspond to a distribution without the 25 CGI requests. Perhaps in a later release of WCAT, the configuration files will be cleaned up to contain accurate comments.

There is one more configuration file for WCAT, but it's optional. It can be used if you want to collect performance metrics from the server using Perfmon while the benchmark is running. This configuration file has an extension of *.pfc* and lists all the performance counters that you want collected during the duration of the test. You need to let WCAT know to collect performance data by passing the -p option when starting the controller. WCAT will then collect the metrics included in the performance metrics file throughout the duration of the test.

Here is the *server.pfc* file provided with WCAT:

```
#
# Counters for NT server
#
# For Microsoft Internet Information Server, the process name is: :
# inetinfo.exe
#
#
System\% Total Processor Time
Processor(0)\DPC Rate
Processor(0)\Interrupts/sec
Processor(0)\DPCs Queued/sec
Process(inetinfo)\% Processor Time
Process(inetinfo)\% Privileged Time
Process(inetinfo)\% User Time
System\Context Switches/sec
System\System Calls/sec
Process(inetinfo)\Thread Count
```

Basically, this file consists of a list of objects and counters that you want collected at the server. Data is collected at the fixed interval of 10 seconds, so prepare for a lot of data to be collected if you run the test for a long time.

Running a test

The typical sequence for starting a WCAT test is as follows. First, prepare and modify the scripts if you are not using the planned scripts that come with the server. Once that is complete, start the clients. Starting the clients first allows you to synchronize them to all start at the same time. This is the reason why the controller will not start the test until it has received a request from as many clients as are specified in the configuration file. The *wcclient.exe* application simply checks every 10 seconds to see if it can connect to the controller so that it can receive its instructions.

The next step is to start the controller. You do that by going to the directory where it was installed and typing run *test*, where *test* is the name of the test to run. The controller looks for the configuration files *test.cfg*, *test.scr*, and *test.dst* in the scripts directory to obtain the configuration information for the test. The controller then accepts requests from the clients until the number of clients that have connected is equal to the number specified in the configuration file. At that point, it sends instructions to all the clients and the test begins.

After the test completes, the clients send back to the controller the performance data they collected during the test. The results are summarized and stored in the *test.log* file. A considerable amount of information is stored in this log file, ranging from information about the IP address of the server that was tested to the number of errors detected. The file consists of two sections. The first contains summary information about the test, and the second breaks down some of the statistics by class. The most useful statistics are the total responses/second, which is the throughput measure of the server, and the average response time, which is the response time measure.

If you specify that the Performance Monitor should run during the test, the controller adds another section to the log file with the performance data collected by Perfmon.

Developing a custom test

In developing a customized test for your site, you need to create a set of configuration files that represent the workload that you want executed by the clients. Typically, this workload should be as representative of the workload imposed on your machine by real users as possible. Here is a simple framework for coming up with a representative workload of your server:

1. Analyze the log files and determine the small subset of the files that are retrieved most often. In most cases, a very small fraction of the files accounts for a very large fraction of the requests. If you concentrate on those files, you will capture the behavior of your server fairly accurately.

2. Group files of related characteristics together into the same class. For example, simple HTML files with the same size can be grouped into one class. The purpose of this step is to reduce the total number of transactions that need to be defined as much as possible without hindering the accuracy of the measurements. In general, 10 classes should be more than enough to accurately model the workload of your web server. Of course, this depends on the complexity of your site.

Why do we need classes ?

You may be wondering why there is a need to break the various files into groups. It would be much simpler, from the perspective of setting up the test, to put all the files into one class and just concentrate on the performance metrics reported by WCAT at the summary level. The disadvantage of this approach is that you will miss the effects on the server of different parts of your application. By using one class, the statistics provide overall information on the performance of the server and at the same time average out the effects of different types of content provided by the server. For example, let's say we put both CGI scripts and plain HTML pages into the same class. The reported response time and throughput will be an average of all the requests and will not give us the corresponding metrics for the CGI scripts and the HTML pages separately. This implies that if we are not happy with the performance of the server, we will not know whether to concentrate on improving the scripts or on enhancing the capacity of the server.

3. Create the script file by inserting a new transaction for each class determined from the previous step. For cases where multiple files were grouped into the same class, you can include multiple New request HTTP entries within the same class.

4. Create the distribution file by specifying the percentages for each request class. These should come from the analysis of the most popular requests in Step 1. Just make sure that you use integers to specify the percentages and that the sum of the percentages add up to 100.

5. Create the configuration file. The critical parameter here is the number of clients involved in the test and the number of threads created at each client. If your goal is to determine the maximum capacity of your server, you need to choose these parameters so that they cause your server to reach saturation. Start with low values and repeat the test until one of the critical system resources is saturated. If you make the number of virtual clients or threads very large initially, you may cause the client to saturate, so pay attention to what the clients are doing during the test.

In summary, WCAT is an excellent tool for evaluating the performance of a web server. It comes with a large number of predefined workloads, including tests for the keep-alive protocol, the SSL protocol, and CGI and ISAPI resources. Such tests are not found in other benchmark programs. WCAT also allows you to define your own customized tests that model more accurately the workload imposed on your site.

When using WCAT to determine the maximum number of requests that your server can support at a reasonable service level, you must carefully select the number of clients and threads used in running the test. The procedure for coming up with these values is an iterative one, where you change the parameters, run the test, look at the results, and repeat until you have determined the saturation level for your server. It's easier to understand the process by looking at a typical throughput curve. Imagine a plot of requests per second, which we can read from the log after running the test, against the number of interactive users. In this case, the number of interactive users is the product of the number of clients and the number of virtual clients (or threads) per client.

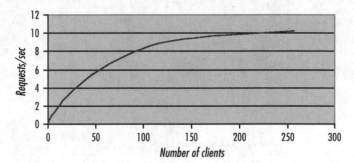

Notice that the throughput, which is measured in requests per second, increases up to a maximum value as the number of interactive clients increases, and then remains almost flat. Looking at the plot, we can see that this server can support up to 150 users before saturating. So we can start the iteration by picking a fairly small number and increasing it continuously, keeping track of the requests per second processed by the server. In general, plotting the throughput attained after every test against the number of clients is the easiest way to determine the saturation point.

Make sure that you choose a reasonable value in the beginning. If we had started the test using 200 clients and then increasing it slowly, we would get a very flat curve since we would be in saturation from the beginning. You would know that the server was saturated, but you would not know the number at which it reached saturation.

Web Application Stress

This tool is a more recent addition to the IIS toolset that is made available by Microsoft through the Windows 2000 Server Resource Kit. You can currently get the Web Application Stress (WAS) tool, which is also known as Homer, from *http://webtool.rte.microsoft.com*, but the site includes a disclaimer indicating that availability of the tool from this site may terminate at any time. WAS provides many of the features available with WCAT but is more user-friendly, being a GUI-type application. Figure 12-9 shows the main screen of the tool.

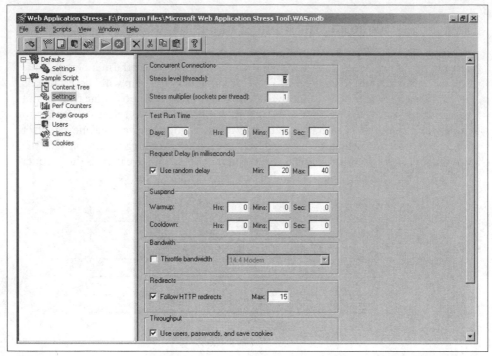

Figure 12-9. Main screen of the Web Application Stress tool

When you first start the application you have access to a predefined script called *Sample Script*. This defines the characteristics of a predefined workload that can be used to stress-test your server. The set of files and scripts processed by the sample script are included in the installation of WAS. You can create other scripts yourself that better reflect the workload experienced by your server. You can automatically create a script by either importing an IIS log file or by recording a browsing session of a web site; these are powerful capabilities, and a lot easier than manually creating configuration files as you would do in WCAT.

A script in WAS is defined through a number of components that appear graphically as nodes in a tree control, as shown in Figure 12-9.

Root

Through this component, you define the sequences of requests that will be used during stress testing. For each request you specify the HTTP verb (GET, POST, etc.) used in the request, any parameters that should be passed on the query string, header options, and a delay that behaves as sleep time.

Content tree

This component allows you to specify the HTML pages and scripts that this workload will use. You do that by first pointing the tool to either a physical directory where the files are stored or a virtual directory that is defined through IIS. You can then select each file that will comprise the workload.

Settings

This allows you to configure myriad options that define the runtime behavior of the stress test. Some of the options that you can configure include the runtime of the test, the warmup and cooldown time, inter-arrival time between requests, and bandwidth throttling.

Perf Counters

This component allows you to optionally define a list of performance counters that you would like to have collected from the server while the load is being generated. This is useful in helping determine which system resource limits the throughput measured by WAS. You can then make modifications on the configuration of this resource and rerun the test.

Page Groups

The requests are combined into page groups. Through this component, you can define what percentage each page group makes up the overall workload.

Users

To provide support for more realistic workloads, WAS allows you to define a set of user names and passwords, which are then used randomly during the execution of a workload in parameterized scripts.

Clients

Through this component, you specify the set of client hosts that will take part in the stress test. Each client must have the same version of WAS installed, and the WebTool service must be running.

Cookies

Through this component, you can associate a cookie with each one of the users that have been defined.

Overall, WAS is a very powerful tool for stress-testing web servers, and certainly the price is right. Early builds of this tool had reliability problems when running against large sites, but recent versions seem to be much more reliable. You can find additional information for WAS at its web site, *http://webtool.rte.microsoft.com*.

WebBench

WebBench is a licensed benchmark available from Ziff-Davis. Its most current version at the time of this writing is 3.0, and it can be downloaded from *http://www. qadownloads.com/Tools/more2.html*. It comes with a set of test suites for testing the performance of the server in providing both static and dynamic content. It also allows you to create your own custom tests.

The architecture of WebBench is similar to that of the other benchmark programs in that it uses the client/controller/server concept. One portion of the benchmark runs on the controller machine and is responsible for starting, monitoring, and terminating the test. The client executables run on multiple machines and generate the requests under the supervision of the controller. When the test completes, the clients report the measurements to the controller, which summarizes the information in the form of Excel worksheets.

WebBench provides a number of test suites for both static and dynamic content. The dynamic content portions come in a variety of formats so that you can test the performance of your server with different types of applications. Currently the benchmark includes dynamic content in the form of CGI executables, Internet Server API (ISAPI), Netscape Server API (NSAPI), and an IntranetWare local-CGI Netware Loadable Module (NLM).

After running the test, the controller provides a report primarily focusing on two measures of performance: requests per second and bytes per second. Notice that both are measures of throughput at different granularity levels.

Webstone

Webstone is one of the first benchmarks dedicated to testing the performance of web servers. It was originally developed at Silicon Graphics, but more recently Mindcraft acquired the rights to it. You can download the latest version from *http://www. mindcraft.com.*

Its architecture is similar to that of WCAT, although the terminology used is different. The workload is generated by one or more clients that run under the control of the WebMaster. Each client runs on a different machine and spawns a user-defined number of WebChildren (similar to the virtual clients of WCAT). The configuration file is read by the WebMaster, which then spawns the WebChildren at the various clients and initiates the test by sending the test instructions to the clients. It allows for a fairly large number of configuration parameters for the test, including the duration of the test, the number of WebChildren, and the number of clients.

The workload is defined using requests for pages. Each page can then consist of up to 50 files. This is done so that the clients can model the behavior of inline images. A client sends a request to the server by requesting, in sequence, each of the files that comprise the page. A new connection is created for each file by the clients as in the HTTP/1.0 protocol. At this point, there is no support for the keep-alive protocol in WebStone.

The original version of WebStone included four different workloads. These are the *general modem mix*, which consists of small files with very few inline images; the *general mix*, which is similar to the general modem mix with slightly larger files; the *media rich mix*, which consists of pages with multimedia content such as images, movie files, and sound clips; and the *general and media rich mix*, which is a combination of the other workloads. Given the workloads observed at most web sites today, all four of these workloads are inadequate for any kind of capacity planning. Version 2.0.1 of WebStone, also from Silicon Graphics, provided support for CGI requests.

Release 2.5, from Mindcraft, added support for an additional CGI-based workload and an ISAPI-based workload, making WebStone a much more useful benchmarking tool for web servers.

Performance Management

At the beginning of this chapter, we took a detailed look at the processing of an HTTP GET request by IIS, and saw that IIS makes use of most of the underlying resources of the system in processing that request. Now, to gain a better understanding of how to monitor the impact of IIS on those resources, detect bottlenecks, and perform capacity planning of the server, we look closely at how IIS utilizes those underlying resources. For each major resource—the CPU, memory, disk subsystem, and network—we look at how the resource is utilized by IIS, sources that provide us with information on how the resource is utilized, and methods of dealing with a potential bottleneck at that resource.

Managing the CPU

In Chapter 3, we took an in-depth look at how the processor is utilized by the Windows 2000 operating system and the applications running on it, how you can monitor that utilization, and what you can do to improve the performance of a system with a CPU bottleneck. Here, we look at how IIS utilizes the CPU in servicing its requests.

Connection requests

IIS is basically a passive application that waits for requests from its clients to put it to work. A request arrives over the network when a client submits an HTTP request for a resource. At that point, a TCP connection is established between the client and the server so that the request and response can flow between them. So for every connection request that arrives over the network, the CPU needs to process the packet of information, moving it up through the layers of the network protocol until it reaches the application layer where the information is passed to IIS. This implies that the CPU is utilized by IIS indirectly in processing all the packets that arrive over the network that have IIS as the ultimate destination.

What we want to understand, then, is the relationship between the CPU utilization and the connection requests that arrive over the network for service by IIS. Let's use our friend the Performance Monitor to help us understand this relationship. We want on one hand to monitor the CPU utilization, which we can get using the counters Processor % Privileged Time and Processor % User Time, and on the other hand to monitor the connection requests, which we can get using the counter Web Service Current Connections. To see how the CPU utilization increases as the hit rate increases, we use WCAT to generate a workload with increasing intensity over time.

We create a small batch file that uses the *filmx200* workload but runs the test multiple times, starting initially with 10 threads and each time increasing the number of client threads by 10.

Figure 12-10 shows the measurements we observe with Performance Monitor.

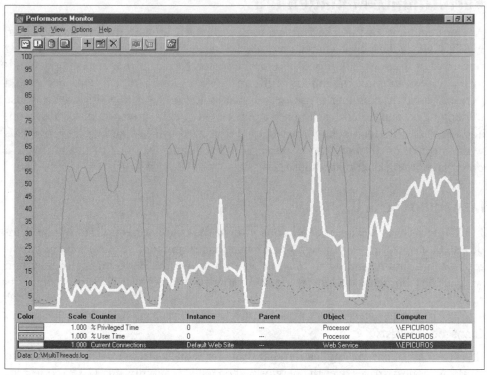

Figure 12-10. Perfmon showing the relationship between connection requests and CPU utilization

The thin line at the top is the % Privileged Time, the thin dotted line is the % User Time, and the thick white line is the Current Connections. As we expected, the chart makes it clear that as the intensity of the workload increases, the CPU utilization increases as well. Notice that most of the CPU time is spent in privileged mode. This can be explained by considering the workload being processed. The *filmx200* workload consists entirely of static content, the majority of which is relatively small files that are less than 16 KB (the *filmx200.dst* file gives us all this information). For each request, IIS only has to parse the HTTP request, locate the file, and send it out. The reading of the file and the writing of the data out to the network is also done by the operating system in privileged mode. The *Inetinfo.exe* process (the executable image of IIS) makes use of the AcceptEx( ) and TransmitFile( ) API calls, which are Microsoft-specific extensions to the Windows Sockets 2 API, in processing requests. The AcceptEx( ) function accepts a new connection, returns the local and remote address, and receives the first block of data sent by the client, all in one system call.

This reduces the number of context switches needed to perform these operations using API calls. Given that HTTP requests are typically of small size, the whole packet of data can be read into a memory buffer with one call. The TransmitFile( ) call transmits a file over a socket through the filesystem cache. Normally, you would need to allocate a buffer and then read and transmit the contents of the file block by block, copying each block to the buffer before writing it out to the socket. This new API call avoids both the copying of the data into a local buffer and the context switches needed for transferring each block. Both of these API calls do all the work in kernel or privileged mode, which is why we see the CPU spending so much time in that mode.

 The use of the AcceptEx( ) API call in place of Accept( ) can be enabled and disabled through an entry in the Registry. The parameter UseAcceptEx under the key HKLM\SYSTEM\CurrentControlSet\Services\InetInfo is used to control the activation of this feature. By default, with a value of 1, this feature is activated, whereas setting the parameter to 0 deactivates it. We do not recommend turning this feature off because it provides a considerable performance improvement in the processing of HTTP requests. The AcceptEx( ) API call requires that the caller already has a connection that is open and that is not bound or connected before making the call. To ensure that there are always open connections available before making a call, IIS maintains a pool of them. The desired number of connections in the pool is controlled by the parameter AcceptExOutstanding under the same key as the previous parameter. When the number of available open connections falls below this parameter, the server opens additional sockets to restore the size of the pool to the desired value. The default value of this parameter is 40. On a high-demand server with plenty of memory available, it makes sense to increase this value even more; on a lightly loaded server, it makes sense to reduce it so as to increase available memory.

The occasional spikes in the number of connections can be explained by the distribution of the workload. 97% of the requests are for files that are less than 64 KB, but the small percentage left is for a 256 KB file, a 512 KB file, and a 1 MB file. When one of those large files is requested, there is a queuing effect on the connections that causes them to accumulate while that large file is transferred to the client.

It should now be clear that the intensity of the workload has a direct impact on the CPU utilization. An increase in the number of client connections causes an increase in the CPU utilization. To detect whether the CPU is the bottleneck on your server, use the techniques discussed in Chapter 3; however, for sites that provide static content, this is usually not the case. Usually the bandwidth of the network link or the bandwidth of the disk subsystem is fully consumed first. In cases where there is ample disk and network bandwidth, the CPU may reach 100% utilization. The two most important counters to look at are Processor % Processor Time and System Processor Queue Length. If over a sufficiently long interval of time the CPU utilization is close to 100% and the queue length is constantly a small positive number, then the CPU is most likely the bottleneck, if you have also excluded a memory shortage.

 To process requests for static content, IIS creates a default of four threads per processor. There is some dynamic behavior as to the lifetime of these threads and the creation of additional threads when the workload increases, but there is no documentation of the exact algorithm anywhere. The number of threads created per processor is defined through the registry entry MaxPoolThreads under the key HKLM\SYSTEM\CurrentControlSet\Services\InetInfo\Parameters.

Make sure that you test any configuration change you make to this value; by making it too large, you can easily overwhelm the CPU. Documentation from Microsoft recommends that you never increase this value beyond 20 threads per processor. The ThreadTimeout value specifies the amount of time that I/O processing threads should be kept around if there have been no I/O requests in ThreadTimeout seconds. The default value is 24 hours (or $24 \times 60 \times 60$ seconds). Consider modifying this value if IIS is lightly used on your server, your memory capacity is highly utilized, and there are other more critical applications running on the same server.

Limiting concurrent connections

Since the large number of connection requests is the cause of the congestion, limiting the number of connections we admit in the system should resolve this problem. IIS allows you to do exactly that, but it is a common misconception that limiting the number of connections admitted will reduce the CPU utilization. Let's see why this approach does not always work. Our good friend the Performance Monitor will come to the rescue again. For each site, you can limit the number of requests allowed to connect to the system concurrently by accessing the Properties window for the particular site and selecting the Web Site tab, shown in Figure 12-11.

In this experiment, we use WCAT with the *filmx200* workload to generate the requests on the web server. We monitor the CPU utilization using the counter Processor % Processor Time, and the connections using the counters Web Service Current Connections and Web Service Connection Attempts/sec. The first time we start WCAT, we set the connection policy to unlimited, and the second time we limit the number of connections. We can analyze the effect of this configuration change on the clients by looking at the logs generated by WCAT after the test. The average response time, which is reported as Avg Response Time in the WCAT log, dropped by more than 50% in the second case, but the throughput, which is reported as Rate of Pages Read, was reduced considerably. These results should not be surprising.

Let's see how the server is doing. Figure 12-12 shows a chart of the selected counters during the duration of the two tests.

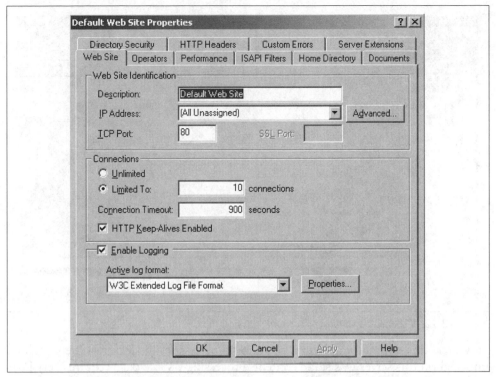

Figure 12-11. Limiting the number of concurrent connections to a web site

By looking at the % Processor Time curve, which is the thin, solid line, we can see where the first experiment ends (unlimited connections) and the second starts (limited connections). The small spike in the % Processor Time curve in the middle was caused when we changed the connection policy for the site before starting the next experiment. As expected, limiting the number of concurrent connections caused the Current Connections to drop considerably. What is surprising, though, is the behavior of the % Processor Time. The utilization of the CPU increases when the connections are limited. The reason for this unexpected result is that the policy of limiting the number of concurrent connections is enforced at the application layer. The connection request arrives over the network and the CPU picks it up, moves it through the network layers, and delivers it to IIS. At that point, based on the current number of connections, IIS decides whether to accept the connection or not. Now, since the server slows down its processing of incoming requests, requests start to accumulate, as illustrated by the increase of Connection Attempts/sec during the second experiment. So to summarize, limiting the number of concurrent connections affects how much work is done by IIS, but does not affect the overhead imposed on the system for processing the incoming request.

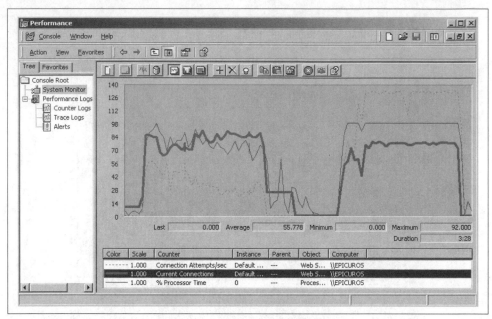

Figure 12-12. The effects of limiting the connections on the CPU utilization

However, this does not imply that you should never use this feature. The workload imposed on this server was static content. Processing a static page requires very little CPU involvement after a request has been delivered to IIS. In the case of dynamic content, this feature becomes much more important. For a site where generating dynamic content involves the execution of a CGI script, the CPU utilization in the generation of the dynamic content far exceeds the CPU utilization in delivering the request to IIS. Later on, the section "Dynamic content generation" takes a more careful look at dynamic content generation and its performance implication.

Interrupt processing

Another factor affecting CPU utilization that is related to the intensity of connection requests is *interrupt processing*. Devices generate interrupts when they need the immediate attention of the CPU. Figure 12-13 illustrates how interrupts are generated when an HTTP request arrives over the network for processing by IIS:

1. When the packet arrives over the network, it is temporarily buffered within the network interface card (NIC).

2. Eventually, the NIC interrupts the processor, and the interrupt service routine (ISR) for the particular network card runs to process the request. The ISR, since it runs at very high priority, simply acknowledges receipt of the data and schedules the deferred procedure call (DPC) to complete the processing of the request.

3. The DPC routine copies the received packet from the NIC's buffer to main memory and informs the TCP/IP protocol stack in the kernel that a packet has arrived.

4. Eventually, the packet that includes the HTTP request reaches IIS. IIS parses the request and determines that this is a GET request for a file in its tree.

5. Assuming that this HTML page has not been accessed recently, IIS must retrieve the file from the disk. It sends a request to the disk, through the filesystem code, to have the file transferred over the socket (using the `TransmitFile` API call).

6. The disk transfers the file's data blocks to the filesystem cache.

7. During the data transfer, the disk generates one or more interrupts to the CPU depending on the I/O bus used to connect the disk to the system (see Chapter 8).

8. The data is transferred directly from the filesystem cache to the NIC after being processed by the TCP/IP protocol stack code. Depending on the size of the file, one or more packets may be transferred to the client.

9. The NIC sends the data out to the client packet by packet.

10. The NIC generates an interrupt to indicate that the packet has been transferred.

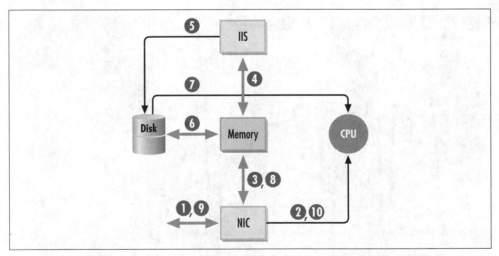

Figure 12-13. Interrupt generation by the NIC and disk devices in processing an HTTP request

In summary, both the network cards and the disks generate interrupts as a result of incoming requests to IIS. A larger portion of the CPU time is always consumed in processing the requests themselves rather than processing the interrupts. However, looking at CPU utilization due to interrupts and the rate at which interrupts are generated can tell you whether your server can handle the intensity of the current workload. Also, if we know that a considerable fraction of the CPU is consumed due to interrupts, there are a couple of things we can do to alleviate some of the CPU load. The Performance Monitor counters to pay close attention to are Processor % Interrupt Time, Processor % DPC Time, Processor Interrupts/sec, and Processor DPC Rate. Keep in mind that both ISRs and DPCs run within the context of whichever process happens to be running when the interrupt occurs. Since the processing that takes place within the ISR and the DPC may be totally unrelated to the process whose context is loaded at the time, it would not be fair to charge the time taken by the ISRs and DPCs to that process. So both % Interrupt Time and % DPC Time are just components of the overall % Privileged Time of the processor object. On a server with multiple processors, it is important to monitor the utilization of each CPU due to interrupts to ensure proper distribution of the interrupts across all processors.

Figure 12-14 shows a chart of these counters along with Web Service: Total Method Requests/sec while a heavy load is generated against the server by WCAT. The Web Service: Total Method Requests/sec counter was selected so that we can see the correlation between the HTTP requests and the overall interrupt processing time (both ISR and DPC processing time). Clearly, as the load on the IIS server grows, so does the CPU time dedicated to processing interrupts. As expected, the amount of time dedicated to DPCs is much greater than the amount of time dedicated to ISRs.

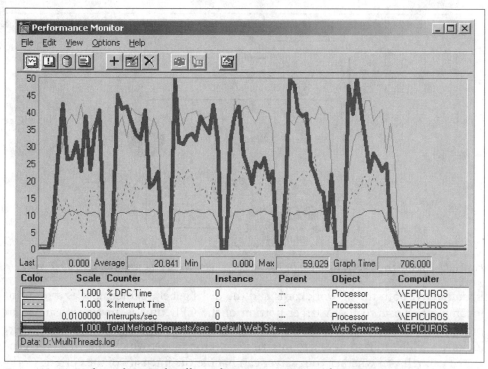

Figure 12-14. Perfmon showing the effects of interrupts on CPU utilization

Suppose you use Performance Monitor and determine that the CPU utilization due to interrupts is very high. What can you do to improve the performance of the system? The cheapest solution on a single-processor system is to buy a network card that supports *interrupt moderation*, a feature present in the device drivers of many modern network cards. Instead of generating an interrupt for every packet that arrives at the NIC, the interrupts are buffered and presented to the server in a batch. There are two variations of interrupt moderation: fixed and dynamic. With *fixed* interrupt moderation, the number of packets received before an interrupt is generated is fixed, whereas with *dynamic* interrupt moderation, the card adjusts the batch size based on the intensity of the traffic. When traffic is heavy, the batch size increases, whereas with lighter traffic the batch size decreases. On network cards with both variations available, there are Registry entries that allow you to choose which one is used. By activating interrupt moderation, you can reduce CPU utilization considerably.

On servers with multiple processors, interrupts from the first NIC are assigned to the highest-numbered processor first and the interrupts from each additional NIC are assigned to the next processor in descending order. One problem we have discovered in practice is that most installations use a single network card. In that case, both the ISR and DPC are scheduled to run on a single processor, causing a heavy load on that particular processor. It is easy to detect this imbalance by monitoring and charting the counters shown in Figure 12-14 for each processor on the server. A solution that works very well in this case is to add additional NICs, ideally one per processor. Windows NT supports the assignment of multiple NICs to the same logical network, making it easy to distribute the workload from a single network across multiple NICs. By adding multiple NICs on the server, the interrupts are distributed across the processors by the HAL, causing more even loading of the processors. Chapter 5 describes interrupt distribution in more detail.

HTTP/1.1 versus HTTP/1.0

Before we talk about dynamic content generation technologies and their effects on performance, let's briefly take a look at the differences between the HTTP/1.0 and HTTP/1.1 protocols. In HTTP/1.0, every request generated by the browser requires that a TCP connection be established between the browser and the server. Once the server processes the request and sends back a reply, the connection is closed, regardless of whether additional requests need to be made to the same server. So to transfer an HTML page with multiple inline images from the server, multiple connections need to be opened and closed. The following describes the exchange of packets between the browser and the server in just opening and closing a single connection:

1. Client sends a segment (i.e., a packet at the transport layer) that includes the port number to which the client wants to connect.

2. Server responds with an acknowledgment.

3. Client responds also with an acknowledgment.

This exchange ensures that both sides are aware that the connection has been established. The termination of the connection requires the following four segments to be exchanged:

4. Client sends a FIN to indicate that it wants the connection closed.

5. Server responds by acknowledging the FIN.

6. Server sends a FIN to indicate that it wants the other side of the connection closed.

7. Client acknowledges the FIN.

These steps are illustrated in Figure 12-15.

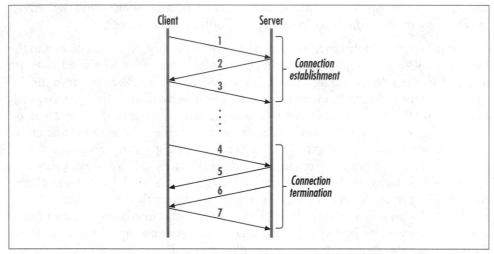

Figure 12-15. Message exchange between client and server in establishing and terminating a TCP connection

It may seem that there is redundancy in the number of messages needed to terminate a connection, but that is not true. TCP supports a full-duplex connection that can be half-closed. That means that one side of the connection may close while the other can still be used for the transfer of data. So, to establish and bring down a TCP connection, a total of seven messages need to be exchanged between the client and the server. Shortly after HTTP/1.0 was deployed, people realized that it wasted resources to repeatedly establish and terminate connections between a client and a web server in order to transfer multiple resources. The HTTP/1.1 version of the protocol resolves this inefficiency by using persistent connections and pipelining of requests. By using a persistent connection, the client and server can exchange a number of request/reply transactions without having to terminate and re-establish connections over and over again. This enhancement has a number of advantages:

- Reduces the number of packets exchanged between the client and server over the Internet/intranet

---

- Reduces the load on the server in having to process additional connection establishment and termination requests
- Reduces the number of TCP data structures that need to be used in maintaining information on the server about the connections with a single client

For HTTP/1.1, connections are assumed to be persistent. This implies that both the server and the client must explicitly specify that the connection must be closed after a request by including the appropriate header as part of the HTTP request. IIS supports both HTTP/1.0 and HTTP/1.1 protocols and chooses the appropriate protocol as specified by the request.

 The server maintains a persistent connection when there is no activity for 900 seconds, by default (it was 600 for IIS 4.0); after that, the server closes the connection. This amount of time is controlled by the Metabase variable ConnectionTimeout, which is inheritable, or the Registry entry ConnectionTimeOut under the key \HKLM\SYSTEM\CurrentControlSet\Services\W3SVC\Parameters. By closing connections sooner, more memory is made available. The Metabase entry applies to both the web and FTP services, and is the preferred approach for configuring your IIS 5.0 installation.

A client that supports persistent connections may also pipeline multiple requests to the server, i.e., send multiple requests to the server without having to wait for a reply first. By pipelining the requests, the effective throughput of the connection increases. A recent study of the use of persistent connections and pipelining by popular browsers discovered that neither Netscape Navigator nor Internet Explorer make use of pipelining over persistent connections. Support for this feature will probably be available through those browsers in the future.

Dynamic content generation

Soon after web sites started to appear on the Internet, it became obvious that simply presenting static content is not very interesting. To fully utilize the Web, it is necessary to interact with users by getting input on what they are looking for and providing customized content in response to that input. A web site for a retail store that accepts and processes orders is a lot more beneficial to the business owner and the customer than one that simply presents a list of the products available at the store.

The first technology that became available for dynamic content generation was the Common Gateway Interface (CGI). CGI was a standard proposed by NCSA for specifying how a script can be invoked in response to an HTTP request and how parameters should be passed back and forth between the server and the script. The term *script* is misleading here in that it implies that a scripting language, such as Perl, should be used for writing it. In fact, a script can be written in any programming language (C, C++, Perl, etc.) as long as the generated program is an executable. Information is passed from IIS to the CGI script using environment variables or the standard input, depending on the HTTP method used to submit the query to the server.

When a request arrives for a CGI script, IIS must determine whether the user has the right to execute that script. If the user has the proper permissions, IIS creates a new process and executes the CGI script in the address space of the new process. If another request arrives shortly for the same CGI script, a new process must be created to handle this new request. As you have probably guessed, CGI scripts impose a considerable load on the server. However, an advantage of CGI scripts is that, because they run in their own address space, IIS is not affected if the script is badly written and crashes.

Once CGI scripts became common across the Internet, webmasters started to realize that CGI scripts consume a lot of resources. The CGI processing model of using a separate process to service each request consumes a considerable amount of both processor and memory resources. The next technology that appeared for generating dynamic content was the Internet Server API (ISAPI). ISAPI is a standard for developing DLLs that are loaded in response to an HTTP request. An ISAPI DLL is loaded in the address space of IIS itself. For IIS to be able to load an ISAPI DLL, the DLL must expose the `GetExtensionVersion` and `HttpExtensionProc` functions. The `GetExtensionVersion` function is called only once when the DLL is first loaded into memory and it is used by IIS to get information about the DLL. The `HttpExtensionProc` function is called for every HTTP request directed to the DLL and is the main routine for all processing within the DLL. Information is passed back between the ISAPI DLL and IIS using the Extension Control Block (ECB) data structure that is passed to the `HttpExtensionProc` function by IIS.

Figure 12-16 illustrates the main difference, from the performance point of view, between processing CGI and DLL requests. To process a CGI request, IIS creates a new process that requires both CPU and memory resources. To process a DLL request, IIS simply calls a routine that will be in its address space after the DLL is loaded. Loading the DLL happens after the first request for that DLL, and the default behavior is for IIS to cache the DLL in memory. If performance is critical in developing a web application, using ISAPI is the best choice; no other approaches can provide the performance of ISAPI.

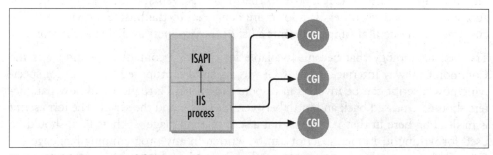

Figure 12-16. Processing CGI requests versus processing ISAPI DLLs

To get a better feel for the performance implications of using CGI over ISAPI, let's use WCAT to generate a CGI workload and an ISAPI workload, and then use Performance Monitor to measure the impact. For a CGI workload, we use the *cgi75* scripts, and for an ISAPI workload, we use the *isapi75*. For the CGI test, we want to see the amount of CPU utilization and the intensity of the workload, so we choose the counters Processor % Processor Utilization and Web Service CGI Requests/sec. Figure 12-17 shows the chart for these counters during the generation of the CGI workload.

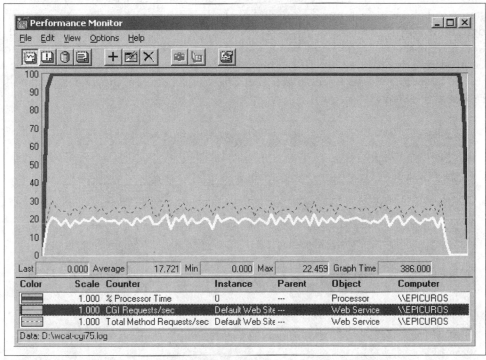

Figure 12-17. CPU utilization during generation of a CGI workload

Clearly, the CPU is 100% utilized during this test. One important note here is the monitoring of the CPU utilization due to CGI requests. Since IIS creates a new process to process each CGI request, the CPU time consumed by that CGI request is not added to the *inetinfo.exe* process. Also, monitoring the CPU utilization through the process object of the CGI script is difficult, since CGI processes can be created and destroyed during a single sampling period of the Performance Monitor. So, the best way to monitor CPU utilization is by looking at the Processor object. If you have processes other than IIS running on the server that may be consuming considerable CPU resources, you need to compensate for them in your measurements of CPU utilization due to IIS.

Let's now run the second test that generates an ISAPI workload. This time, we monitor the CPU utilization versus the Web Service: ISAPI Extension Requests/sec counter. The impact on the utilization of the CPU is considerable, as shown in Figure 12-18. The average CPU utilization during the duration of the test is only 50%, as compared to 100% during the previous test. These tests make it clear that it really pays to convert CGI scripts to ISAPI scripts if the utilization of the CPU is high. To reduce the cost of this conversion, it is worthwhile to examine the logs of the web server to determine which scripts are the most commonly used and convert only those. To further focus the effort, it is usually fairly easy to modify each CGI script to include timestamps before and after processing the request. You can then determine which CGI scripts to modify by selecting the ones with the highest product of requests per second and average response time. The requests per second can be measured by analyzing the IIS log files, and the average response time can be computed by taking the averages of all the differences between the two timestamps recorded for each CGI script.

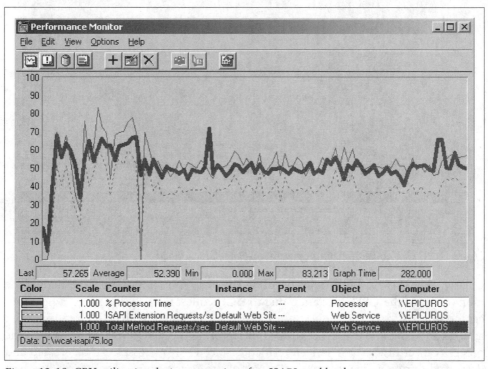

Figure 12-18. CPU utilization during generation of an ISAPI workload

The third approach we cover for developing dynamic content for IIS is Active Server Pages (ASP). If ISAPI provides such high performance, why do we need another approach? ISAPI provides a very low-level API for writing scripts, making the development of a web application a time-consuming and error-prone process. You can think of ASP as a solution that in terms of performance sits between CGI and ISAPI. ASP scripts are written in a high-level scripting language, making development of scripts easier than using ISAPI. You can choose to write your scripts in either JScript or VBScript, depending on your background: JScript is similar to Java, and VBScript is similar to Visual Basic.

When an HTTP request arrives for an ASP script (the resource has the extension *.asp*), IIS forwards the request to the *asp.dll* DLL. The DLL then reads the requested resource from the disk, interprets the script, and sends a request back to the client. Since ASP requests are processed through a DLL, there is no need to create a new process for each request, but the script needs to be interpreted. In addition to providing a high-level language for the development of scripts, ASP makes script development easier by providing a number of objects whose services can be used within the script. Examples of such objects are the Request object, which provides information about the HTTP request; the Response object, which is used to prepare the response to the client; the Server object, which provides access to utility functions for URL and HTML encoding; and the Session object, which provides a session scope for the script. In addition to the objects made available by ASP, you can create your own COM (Component Object Model) objects to provide custom business logic and make them accessible through ASP scripts. This capability makes ASP very extensible.

Another major advantage of ASP is that it provides access to any ODBC-compliant database through the ActiveX Data Objects (ADO). The API for accessing data from an ODBC database is similar to the ODBC API but even easier to use. Since most web sites need to access information stored in a relational database and make it accessible through a web site, ASP has become the most popular dynamic content generation technique for IIS.

Application isolation

The introduction of more powerful and easy-to-use dynamic content generation techniques brought problems of its own to the web server arena. As mentioned in the previous section, early versions of IIS provided support for ISAPI scripts to improve the performance of the dynamic content generation. When the first request arrived for one of these scripts, the DLL was loaded into the memory space of the *inetinfo.exe* process. This provided faster performance since a new process did not have to be created to process the script. The downside of this approach, though, was that if the script had bugs that caused it to crash during execution, the IIS server itself crashed as well, since it hosted the execution of the faulty DLL. Also, once a DLL was loaded into the *inetinfo.exe* process, there was no way to unload it without shutting down the IIS server process. In addition to the runtime issues, this lack of fault tolerance caused development of ISAPI modules to be time-consuming, as the server had to be constantly restarted every time it crashed during debugging sessions.

To resolve this problem, IIS 4.0 introduced *application isolation.* Through the Internet Service Manager, you could configure each application to start in an isolated process, causing IIS to create a new MTS process (*mtx.exe*) to host the application. This option provides the high performance of a loaded DLL with added safety for the IIS server executable. If the DLL has bugs and crashes, it affects only the application itself, not the server. Furthermore, if you want to unload the DLL, you simply need to stop the application instead of bringing down the server.

This new solution is not perfect either. If you try to isolate all the applications in a site, you cause IIS to create one separate instance of the MTS process for each application. The disadvantage of this solution is that you are consuming valuable system memory for each application you run, in effect trading memory for performance and safety.

IIS 5.0 provides a solution to this problem by introducing the *Pooled Process* option. When you choose application isolation mode in IIS 5.0, you have two options: high (isolated) or medium (pooled). High is the same as the application isolation option available in IIS 4.0, in which the application runs in a separate process. The name of the isolated process executable is *dllhost.exe* instead of *mtx.exe*. The medium option creates a separate instance of the *dllhost.exe* executable that is used to host all applications that are configured with the medium application isolation option. This combines the benefits of all the approaches in that the performance is high, the IIS server is safe from the applications it supports, and memory is conserved. The recommended configuration approach is to use the pooled process option for all applications except very critical ones. This way, you minimize the number of external processes running while at the same time protecting the critical applications from the less critical ones.

Process throttling

The option to throttle processes is new in IIS 5.0. *Process throttling* allows you to place a limit on how much CPU time a web site running in high isolation mode can consume. This way, if your server is hosting a number of web sites, you can control how the CPU resources are shared among the sites. It is hard to figure out what values to use for these percentages initially, so it is best to first activate process accounting on each site where you want to consider enabling process throttling. After monitoring the CPU consumption by each site in the log file, you can make more accurate estimates of how to allocate the available CPU resources.

Figure 12-19 shows the Performance Properties dialog for the Default Web Site. You can enable process throttling on a web site by simply clicking on the appropriate checkbox. You then select the percentage of the CPU resources that you want to allocate to the site. The limits are checked and enforced on each site periodically, based on the CPULoggingInterval entry specified in the Metabase for the particular site. Unfortunately, there is no way to change the value of this interval through the GUI

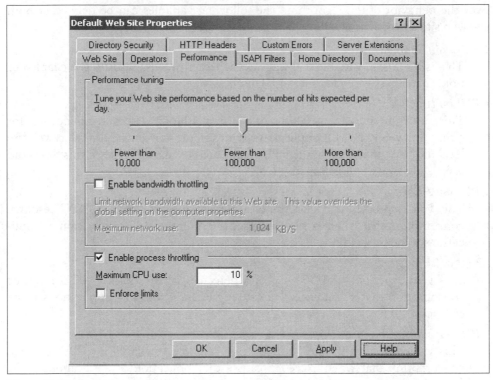

Figure 12-19. Dialog for configuring performance-related parameters

of the Internet Services Manager. There are three levels of consequences imposed on the web site applications if the threshold is exceeded. If you don't check the "Enforce limits" checkbox, only the first level of consequences applies. The three levels are as follows:

Level 1

IIS writes an event in the Windows 2000 event log if the threshold is exceeded in the current time interval.

Level 2

If the CPU consumption exceeds 150% of the specified limit, an event is written in the event log, and all the out-of-process applications on that web site have their CPU priority set to idle. This restricts them from accumulating additional CPU time unless there is no contention for the CPU by other processes.

Level 3

If the CPU consumption exceeds 200% of the specified limit, an event is written in the event log, and all the out-of-process applications on that web site are stopped.

Process throttling is controlled through a number of Metabase variables. The GUI sets these variables accordingly, but modifying them directly gives you finer control over the behavior of the algorithm. The following variables can be defined at both the web site and virtual directory level of the Metabase hierarchy:

CPULimitsEnabled
> This is a Boolean variable that indicates whether process throttling is enabled or not. The value of 1 enables it, and 0 disables it.

CPULimitLogEvent
> This value specifies in 1/1000ths of a percent the CPU resource allocation for either the web site or the application. For example, a value of 10,000 at web site level indicates that 10% of the CPU is allocated to that web site. If this threshold is exceeded, an event is logged.

CPULimitPriority
> This value specifies in 1/1000ths of a percent the threshold on CPU resource consumption that when exceeded causes the priority of the application or applications to be set to idle.

CPULimitProcStop
> This value specifies in 1/1000ths of a percent the threshold on CPU resource consumption that when exceeded causes the application or applications to be stopped.

CPULimitPause
> This value specifies in 1/1000ths of a percent the threshold on CPU resource consumption that when exceeded causes the application or applications to be paused.

CPUCGIEnabled
> This value indicates whether process accounting should be performed for CGI applications.

CPUAppEnabled
> This value indicates whether process accounting and process throttling should be performed for ISAPI and ASP applications.

As you can see, by modifying the Metabase directly you have complete control over how the process throttling algorithm operates. For example, say that you want to impose process throttling on ISAPI and ASP applications such that if more than 50% of the CPU is consumed during a one-hour period, the applications should be paused but no event should be logged. You would set CPULimitsEnabled and CPUAppEnabled to 1 to indicate that you want to enable process throttling for ISAPI and ASP applications, and then set CPULimitPause to 50,000 since you want to pause the application only after the 50% threshold is exceeded. Finally, you set the enforcement interval to 60 minutes by setting CPULoggingInterval to 60.

We should note one disadvantage of the medium application isolation option. All applications that run in the pooled process cannot have process accounting or process throttling activated, since both are made possible by the introduction of the job object into the Windows 2000 kernel. The IIS process itself and the pooled application process are executing within one job, and every web site has its own job object that includes all out-of-process applications in that web site. If IIS allowed you to impose process throttling at the job object, you would be able to terminate the IIS process. This, of course, would be undesirable.

ASP request queueing

One very effective tuning procedure for improving the performance of an IIS 4.0 server that supports an ASP application is to monitor and tune the ASP thread pool and request queue. This is not as critical in IIS 5.0, since the tuning process is semi-automated within IIS. Before we talk about IIS 5.0, let's review what to do on an IIS 4.0 server.

When a request for an ASP script arrives at IIS, it is assigned to the next thread from the ASP thread pool. If no threads are available, the requests are placed in the ASP request queue and processed in FIFO order. The ProcessorThreadMax Registry key under HKLM\SYSTEM\CurrentControlSet\Services\W3SVC\ASP\Parameters defines the number of ASP threads per processor that IIS will start. The default value is 10, and Microsoft strongly suggests that you not increase it above 20.

During light or regular loading conditions, your server is able to process the workload while maintaining the request queue at small values. The queue may increase above zero but will clear fairly fast. Under very intense workloads or when the ASP scripts perform database access, it is possible and fairly common to exhibit considerable congestion at the ASP request queue. You can monitor the size of the queue by logging the counter Active Server Pages: Requests Queued. Long queues can cause unacceptable response times; most often a user will press the stop button on the browser before the request even reaches the front of the queue, making the processing of the request a waste of resources. Worse yet, when the queue length exceeds a certain threshold specified by the RequestQueueMax Registry key, the response "System Too Busy" is sent back to the client.

Say that you logged the counter Active Server Pages: Requests Queued and detected a large queue length. If, at the same time, the % Processor Utilization for the CPU is less than 50–60%, that implies that there is blocking within the ASP code or at the database backend. Besides improving the scripting code or the database configuration, you also have the option of increasing the ProcessorThreadMax value. The measurements tell you that the available threads are blocked waiting for the scripts to complete execution, and the CPU is being lightly utilized otherwise. By increasing the number of threads in the ASP pool, you increase the concurrency level, making it less likely for a queue of requests to accumulate. On the other hand, if the CPU is heavily utilized, you may want to reduce the size of the ASP pool to decrease the concurrency level.

Unfortunately, workloads on the Web change so dynamically that any optimal, static configuration you implement for these two Registry values today may become unsuitable as time goes by. IIS 5.0 resolves this problem by providing automated tuning of these values through a process called *ASP thread gating*. Basically, IIS monitors CPU utilization and dynamically adjusts the size of the ASP thread pool to keep the utilization between a high and a low threshold. To our knowledge, how the number of threads is adjusted is not documented anywhere. The algorithm is controlled by Metabase variables that can be defined as low in the hierarchy as the web site level for in-process and pooled applications, or as low as the application level for out-of-process applications. The Metabase variables are:

AspThreadGateEnabled
  Boolean variable that enables or disables ASP thread gating. A value of 1 enables it, and 0 disables it.

AspThreadGateLow
  The maximum CPU percent utilization below which still indicates a low utilization of the CPU resources. The default value is 75%.

AspThreadGateHigh
  The minimum CPU percent utilization above which indicates a high utilization of the CPU resources. The default value is 90%.

AspThreadGateTimeSlice
  This value is specified in milliseconds and indicates how frequently IIS checks the CPU utilization against the gates defined. The default value is 1000 milliseconds.

AspThreadGateSleepDelay
  This value is specified in milliseconds and indicates how long to defer a request before checking the thread-gating algorithm again. This is used to prevent starvation of requests. The default value is 100 milliseconds.

AspThreadGateSleepMax
  The maximum number of times that a request is deferred while IIS performs thread gating. This is used to prevent starvation of requests. The default value is 50 times.

AspProcessorThreadMax
  The maximum number of threads that IIS creates under any loading condition per processor. The default value is 25 threads.

The IIS 5.0 Resource Guide indicates that the default values were chosen to be optimal for most web server configurations, and suggests that you do not modify the defaults. However, if you understand what these variables do and you follow the proper methodology in changing their values and observing the effect of the change, you may be able to find a much more suitable configuration for your environment.

To prevent the server from consuming resources unnecessarily under the scenario we discussed previously, IIS 5.0 introduces one more Metabase variable called AspQueue-ConnectionTestTime. If an ASP request has been queued for longer than the value of this variable in seconds, IIS checks whether the browser is still connected before sending this request for processing by a thread. The test is performed when the request becomes eligible for execution by an ASP thread. The default value is 3 seconds.

Managing the Memory

We now move to the next critical resource of a server, the memory. As in the previous section, we first try to understand how IIS makes use of memory. While looking at each component of memory utilization, we also cover sources of information for quantifying the utilization of memory by each component. After we show how memory is utilized and how to detect and isolate a memory bottleneck due to IIS, we discuss techniques for resolving or alleviating the bottleneck.

So, how does IIS utilize system memory? First of all, the services that comprise IIS must be loaded in memory. According to the IIS Resource Kit, with all the services resident in main memory, IIS requires 2.5 MB of memory. The actual memory requirements can vary, though, since the working set of the process can be paged in and out of memory as needed. The working set size, and therefore the physical memory requirements of IIS at your site, depends on how many features of IIS are used and on the amount of physical memory available. To find out the memory requirements of IIS at your installation, use the Performance Monitor to look at the counters Process Working Set, Process Pool Paged Bytes, and Process Pool Nonpaged Bytes for the *inetinfo.exe* instance. The text, data, and heap portions of the *inetinfo.exe* process that are resident in memory together account for the process's working set. Data structures maintained within the operating system for the pool of threads, which do most of the work for IIS, account for the paged pool and non-paged pool bytes. For a quick check of the working set size, you can also use the Task Manager to look at the memory usage of the *inetinfo.exe* process under the Processes tab.

To process each request, IIS creates and maintains some internal data structures with information about the request and its status. Each request requires about 10 KB of data of the working set. When processing of the request completes, that memory is released. Therefore, the total amount of memory consumed depends on the number of simultaneous connections processed by the server. For servers that process hundreds of requests, the memory demands can add up, so careful monitoring of the memory requirements is imperative.

The IIS object cache

Another considerable portion of the IIS working set is the IIS object cache. IIS constantly receives requests for files that need to be retrieved from the disk (or from the filesystem cache) and sent to the client. To retrieve the file from the disk, IIS needs to obtain a handle for the file from the filesystem. The filesystem must locate the data structures that represent the file within the operating system and send a handle back to IIS that can be used for future API calls against that resource. Translating a resource name into a handle is a time-consuming operation, and since users normally request a small subset of the more popular content on the site, IIS caches these handles. The IIS object cache is used for caching such file handles, directory listings, and other binary large objects (BLOBs) that IIS needs access to in processing incoming requests.

The IIS object cache is part of the working set of the *inetinfo.exe* process image, but IIS includes counters for looking at the cache in detail. The Performance Monitor counters for the IIS object cache fall in two categories: counters that describe the effectiveness of the cache and counters that describe the contents of the cache. Starting with IIS 2.0, a third category described the size of the cache, but those counters were discontinued as of IIS 4.0. The size of the object cache can be configured through the Registry key MemoryCacheSize. This is a REG_DWORD key under HKLM\SYSTEM\CurrentControlSet\Services\InetInfo\Parameters, and its value can range from 0 – 0xffffffff. The default value is 3072000, or 3 MB of memory.

The Internet Information Services Global: Cache Size and Internet Information Services Global: Cache Used counters indicate the total size of the cache and the portion that is currently used. Unfortunately, these counters are not available after IIS 4.0. This may imply that the size of the object cache is now dynamically managed by IIS, but this is not documented anywhere as far as we know. The documentation of the object cache in the IIS 5.0 Resource Guide, which comes with the Windows 2000 Server Resource Kit, seems to be out of date: it covers counters that are no longer available and ignores some counters that are available.

Since the object cache is part of the working set, we are monitoring the object cache size by monitoring the working set size for the *inetinfo.exe* process image. Table 12-4 lists all the counters that relate to the object cache and some of the counters available through the Internet Information Services Global object.

Table 12-4. Performance Monitor counters related to the IIS object cache

Counter	Description
BLOB Cache Hits	Number of successful lookups in the object cache for binary large objects.
Current BLOBs Cached	Number of binary large objects currently in the object cache for both the WWW and FTP services.
File Cache Hits	Number of successful lookups in the object cache for open file handles.
Current File Cache Memory Usage	Number of bytes currently used for caching open file handles.
Total BLOBs Cached	Total number of binary large objects ever added to the cache.
Total Files Cached	Total number of open file handles ever added to the cache.
Total URIs Cached	Total number of URI information blocks ever added to the cache.
URI Cache Hits	Number of successful lookups in the cache for URI information blocks.
Cache Flushes	Number of times that an object was removed from the cache because of a timeout or because of a change (IIS 4.0).

Table 12-4. Performance Monitor counters related to the IIS object cache (continued)

Counter	Description
Cache Hits	Total number of hits in the cache since the services were started (IIS 4.0).
Cache Hits %	Fraction of the requests that were serviced from the cache (IIS 4.0).
Cache Misses	Total number of misses in the cache since the services were started (IIS 4.0).
Cached File Handles	Total number of file handles that are stored in the cache (IIS 4.0).
Directory Listings	Total number of directory listings that are stored in the cache (IIS 4.0).
Objects	Total number of objects that are stored in the cache. This number is equal to: file handles + directory listings + other objects (IIS 4.0).

When an object is first added to the cache, a time-to-live value (TTL) is associated with that object. Every time the object is accessed, its TTL value is reset; if the object is not accessed for a while, the TTL eventually expires. An *object cache scavenger* thread runs periodically and removes from the cache objects whose TTLs have expired or objects that have changed since they were cached. The Cache Flushes counter reports on the total number of objects removed from the cache by the object cache scavenger.

The TTL value for an object in the cache is controlled by a Registry key. The Object-CacheTTL key specifies the number of seconds that an object will reside in the cache before it is removed by the object cache scavenger. The default value is 30 seconds. This key can be added under HKEY_LOCAL_MACHINE\System\CurrentControlSet\Services\Inetinfo\Parameters if you want to change the default value. If you have sufficient memory, you may want to tune the TTL value. First, monitor the Cache Flushes and Cache Hits % counters over a period of a few days. This period actually depends on the traffic at your site. (On heavily loaded sites a shorter interval is sufficient, whereas on lightly loaded sites you need a longer interval.) Then increase the TTL value and repeat the measurements. If the Cache Flushes counter shows a decrease and the Cache Hits % counter shows an increase, performance has improved, and you may want to continue increasing the value. If there is no change in these counters, you should return the TTL value to where it was.

IIS 5.0 breaks down the cache effectiveness metrics by BLOBs, files, and URIs, whereas IIS 4.0 breaks them down by files, directory listings, and BLOBs. The Cache Hits % counter in IIS 4.0 shows the overall effectiveness of the cache. A good value for the hit ratio depends on the content of each site. For sites that provide primarily static content it is not unusual to see hit ratios close to 90%, and for sites with more dynamic content 60–70% is more common. The Cache Hits and Cache Misses counters provide useful information, but since they are cumulative from the point that IIS services are started, they tend to be hard to read through Performance Monitor and can be misleading. Since you have no control over the size of the IIS object cache in Version 4.0 of IIS, the only way to tune the effectiveness of the cache is by tuning the TTL value. The cache loses its effectiveness if it is paged out. Since it is part of the working set of IIS, the cache can get paged out when there is a shortage of memory in the system. It is important to try and maintain the working set for IIS in physical memory. The Cached File Handles counter indicates the current number of file objects in the cache, and the Directory Listings counter indicates the number of directory listings in the cache. Directory listings are generated by the FTP service in response to a `dir` or `ls` command from an FTP client. The Objects counter indicates the total number of objects that are currently saved in the cache. This includes all file handle objects, directory listing objects, and other objects such as Internet Database Connector queries and responses.

Figure 12-20 illustrates some of these counters as we generate a varying load on IIS with WCAT. The thin white line at the bottom is the Total Method Requests/sec counter that shows the intensity of the workload. While collecting these measurements, we were running consecutive WCAT workloads, increasing the number of threads each time. The Cached File Handles and Objects counters increase quickly at the beginning of each test while the cache warms up, remain fairly constant throughout the duration of each test, and drop down in the interval before the next test is started. This drop at the end of each test is a result of the object cache scavenger removing objects from the cache whose TTL has expired.

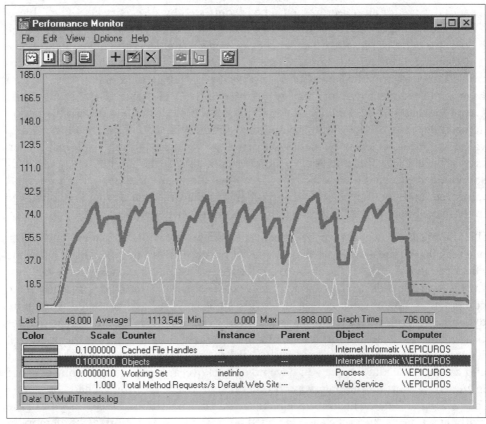

Figure 12-20. Performance Monitor chart that illustrates the IIS object cache counters

Paged and non-paged pool

Another component of memory utilization that increases as the load on the server increases is the allocation of control blocks to maintain state information for each connection. Every connection request to IIS (or to any application that uses TCP) causes the TCP layer within the operating system to allocate a transmission control block (TCB) and add it to a hash table. When the connection terminates, the TCB is kept for a small amount of time for security reasons and then it is either allocated to another connection request or released, depending on the intensity of the workload. This block of memory is allocated out of the non-paged memory pool so it is always resident in memory. Each connection requires only 10 KB of memory from the non-paged pool, but as the number of concurrent connections increases, this component can add up to overall memory requirements for IIS. You can monitor this component by determining the total number of concurrent connections and multiplying that number by 10 KB. The total number of connections is the sum of values of the Performance Monitor counters Web Service: Current Connections _Total, FTP Service: Current Connections _Total, SMTP Service: Inbound Connections Current _Total, SMTP Service: Outbound Connections Current _Total, and NNTP Service: Current Connections _Total. If you are using only a subset of the services, just consider the appropriate counters for the current number of connections.

IIS 5.0 introduced another optimization feature that conserves memory consumption through socket pooling. IIS can support multiple web sites on one server. There are three ways you can differentiate one site from another:

Port number
> You can assign each web site to a different port number. The default port number is 80, but you can use any available port. This requires users to append the appropriate port number to their requests, such as *http://127.0.0.1:4999* to gain access to a site at port 4999.

Multiple IP addresses
> You can assign a unique IP address to each site. Windows NT and Windows 2000 allow you to bind multiple IP addresses to the same network card. This approach is better for the users, since they do not need to remember arcane port numbers.

Host header names
> You can assign a unique host header to each web site. When a browser submits a request to the web site, the hostname is included in the host headers. IIS routes the request to the appropriate site based on the name specified at the host header. To accomplish this, add all the names to your name resolution scheme and map them to the same IP address. This approach has a number of limitations, including lack of support for SSL and for older browsers that do not understand host headers.

For installations using the second approach, IIS 4.0 needs to create multiple sockets for web sites even if they have the same port number. In IIS 5.0, multiple sites can share a socket as long as the port number they use is the same. Each socket consumes a considerable chunk of the limited amount of non-paged pool available on your server. By allowing multiple sites to share the socket, an IIS 5.0 server can host a much greater number of sites than an IIS 4.0 server. One drawback of socket pooling is that the bandwidth-throttling mechanism applies to all sites that share a socket, as opposed to an individual site. You can enable and disable socket pooling by modifying the Metabase variable DisableSocketPooling. By default, the variable is FALSE, which enables socket pooling.

The file cache

We have talked about the IIS object cache and how it caches the most recently accessed handles for IIS. But where do the actual contents of the files that the clients request get cached? That is the responsibility of the Cache Manager. When the IIS server retrieves the contents of the file from the filesystem, the filesystem driver interacts with the Cache Manager to arrange for caching of the file data. (Chapter 8 describes the operation of the filesystem cache in detail.) In summary, NT treats the cache as a working set that has a certain number of pages allocated to it based on the available memory and configuration of the system. When an application requests data from a file, the request is forwarded from the filesystem driver to the Cache Manager. If the file has not been accessed for a while and its data does not currently reside in the cache, the Cache Manager maps the file into a portion of the system virtual address space that has been allocated to the Cache Manager. The access to the file's data by the application is then converted into an access to a virtual address, and the data is brought into main memory through page faults that are handled like any other page fault by the Memory Manager. In earlier operating systems, the filesystem cache was treated as a buffering mechanism separate from the caching mechanism provided by the memory management. This required that a fixed portion of physical memory was allocated to the filesystem cache, and the rest was allocated to memory management. The problem with a fixed and static allocation is that it is difficult to adjust to changes in the workload. The integration of the filesystem cache with the memory management cache resolves this problem, since memory is allocated dynamically based on the demands placed on these two subsystems by the applications.

The Cache Manager at the Executive level within the NT operating system provides four mechanisms for access to its services: the Copy, the Memory Descriptor List (MDL), the Pin, and the Data Map mechanisms. Here we discuss only the MDL mechanism, since IIS makes heavy use of it. Refer to Chapter 7 or Rajeev Nagar's *Windows NT File System Internals: A Developer's Guide* (O'Reilly) for a more detailed description of these four mechanisms. The MDL mechanism allows device drivers to transfer data between the cache and the device using direct memory access (DMA), which is the most efficient means to transfer the data.

Earlier in this chapter, we discussed the TransmitFile( ) Win32 API call that allows for the transfer of a file between the filesystem and a connected socket. In response to a request by a web browser for static web content, IIS needs to locate the file on the filesystem and transfer its contents over the network. The traditional socket interface requires that data is copied from user buffers to the network. When data comes from a file in the filesystem and is sent over the network without any modification, the traditional interface creates a redundant copy: the data is copied from the filesystem to the cache within the operating system. It is then copied from the cache to buffers within the application process's address space, and from there to the network interface card (NIC). The TransmitFile( ) Win32 extension API call avoids this unnecessary copying of the data from the cache into the user address space. In this case, the data goes from the disk device into the cache and then is directly transferred to the NIC. To transfer the data in and out of the cache in the most efficient manner, the MDL interface is used.

To see that IIS is a heavy user of the MDL interface, monitor the Cache Manager mechanisms using the Performance Monitor. The counters Copy Reads/sec, MDL Reads/sec, Pin Reads/sec, and Data Maps/sec of the Cache object indicate the number of reads through each of the Copy, MDL, Pin, and Data Map mechanisms. You can monitor the Cache object while IIS is running, using frequent samples over a period of time, and then plotting the results.

Figure 12-21 shows the values of these four counters while WCAT is generating a workload that consists entirely of static content. The solid line at the upper part of the graph is the MDL Reads/sec, the dotted line is the Data Maps/sec, the solid line at the lower part of the graph with the occasional spikes is the Copy Reads/sec, and the heavy line is the Pin Reads/sec. Clearly, the use of the MDL Reads/sec interface far exceeds the use of any of the other interfaces.

Memory utilization by CGI and ASP scripts

Another somewhat hidden component of memory utilization by IIS is memory consumption by CGI scripts. Earlier in this chapter, we noted that the primary difference between CGI scripts and ISAPI or ASP scripts is that CGI scripts run within their own address space, and the others use the address space of IIS (unless a higher application isolation setting has been used). So for every request that requires the invocation of a CGI script, a new process must be created and executed to generate the content. This requires memory from both the system paged and non-paged pools as well as memory for the process working set. Since CGI scripts tend to execute for a short amount of time, they come and go fairly quickly, making them difficult to monitor using the Performance Monitor. The easiest way to keep track of them is by monitoring overall memory utilization and hard page fault generation.

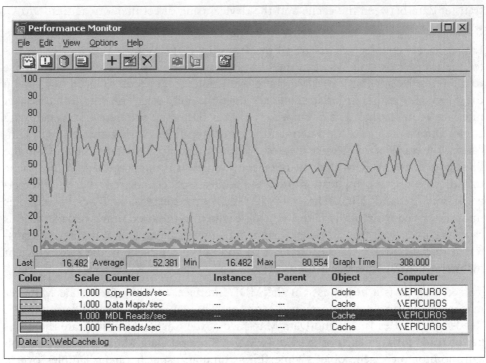

Figure 12-21. Performance Monitor illustrating various Cache Manager interfaces

One last component of memory utilization that causes a lot of problems with IIS 4.0 is the consumption of memory by the ASP file cache. ASP scripts are written in an interpreted language that needs to be parsed and interpreted before the script is executed. To improve the performance of IIS in processing ASP scripts, the designers included a cache of precompiled scripts. The AspScriptFileCacheSize Metabase variable controls the size of this cache. In IIS 4.0, the default value is −1, which implies that the cache size is infinite; this causes IIS on heavily used installations to run out of memory and generate "Server Too Busy" errors. This difficult-to-diagnose problem was corrected in IIS 4.0 Service Pack 6 and IIS 5.0. Service Pack 6 modifies IIS to flush the cache when it receives an "Out of Memory" error so that it can continue working properly after that. In IIS 5.0, the default value for AspScriptFileCacheSize is set to 256 instead of −1.

Monitoring memory utilization

Let's now talk about how to monitor the overall memory utilization of IIS and how to configure the server in terms of memory for maximizing its performance. The integration of the Memory Manager with the filesystem cache (Cache Manager) simplifies monitoring the utilization of memory resources. Both an access to a block of a file and an access to a memory page that does not reside in physical memory will result in a page fault. To increase the throughput of the server you need to minimize the number of requests that will result in a disk access.

The following counters will help you monitor the current utilization of the memory subsystem. The Memory: Cache Bytes counter indicates the current size of the cache. Keep in mind that the cache grows dynamically based on the demand for filesystem data, the availability of physical memory, and an upper limit that is defined based on the system architecture. The Memory: Cache Faults/sec counter indicates the number of requests for data that are not immediately satisfied by the Cache Manager. It is possible that some of these faults will be resolved by locating the data in some other location in virtual memory, so this counter is not sufficient for concluding that memory utilization is high. Similarly, the Memory: Page Faults/sec counter indicates the number of page accesses to invalid pages in a virtual address space. Again, these faults may also be resolved by locating the data somewhere else in memory. The Memory: Page Reads/sec and Memory: Pages Input/sec counters indicate the number of reads for pages from a disk device, and the number of pages read from a disk device, respectively, in response to a page fault.

If after monitoring these counters for a certain period of time we find that the number of hard page faults is consistently high, we can safely conclude that the system does not have enough physical memory to satisfy the workload imposed on it. We can further narrow down the problem by comparing the Page Faults/sec counter with the Cache Faults/sec counter. If Cache Faults/sec is high, it implies that the size of the cache is not sufficient to support the static content that the users are retrieving from the system. If the Page Faults/sec value is high, there is not enough memory to support the working sets of the processes running on the server. The Process: Page Faults/sec inetinfo and Process: Working Set inetinfo counters give a clearer picture of the demands of IIS. If you find that Memory: Page Faults/sec is much higher than Process: Page Faults/sec inetinfo, either another application on the server is generating the page faults, or IIS is indirectly demanding a lot of memory by spawning many CGI scripts. An inspection of the Web Service: CGI Requests/sec counter will help you answer this question. If you do find that a large number of CGI requests is the culprit, consider implementing some of those scripts using a more memory-efficient approach, such as ISAPI or ASP.

Let's look at an example of how to diagnose a memory problem on a heavily loaded server. We again use WCAT to generate a very intense workload for static content against an IIS server with a modest amount of memory. Figure 12-22 presents the counters Cache Bytes, Cache Faults/sec, Page Faults/sec, and Pages Input/sec. We did not include all the counters described in the previous paragraph to make the figure more readable, but in reality you will need to collect and analyze all of the counters. The gray line at the top of the figure is the Cache Bytes counter. The cache is growing dynamically to accommodate more and more files as requests arrive from the clients. Eventually the cache reaches a critical size where the Memory Manager intervenes and starts to trim the working set of the cache. The other three counters seem to have approximately the same values. The similarity of the Cache Faults/sec and the Page Faults/sec implies that the page faults are generated in response to accesses to the file cache. The fact that the Pages Input/sec is also high implies that there is not enough memory to accommodate the working set of the file cache, resulting in too many accesses to the disk.

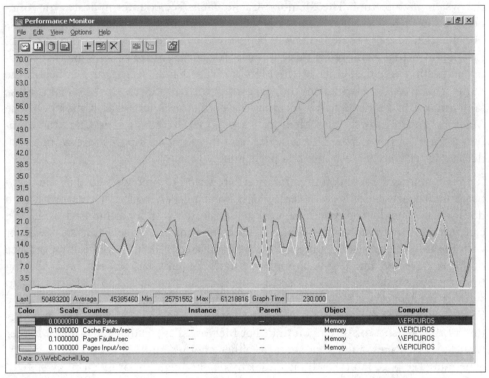

Figure 12-22. Performance Monitor illustrating memory utilization on a heavily loaded IIS server

To plan the memory capacity of your IIS, you need to consider and estimate the memory demands of each of the components discussed. You must provide enough physical memory for the working set of the inetinfo process itself to prevent page faults generated by IIS. You can estimate the memory demands of the system for setting up and maintaining connections, which requires that you estimate the number of concurrent requests. You must provide sufficient memory for the IIS object cache to provide a hit ratio of at least 80%. Remember that the IIS object cache is part of the working set of the IIS process. Finally, you ideally need to provide enough memory to maintain the majority of the most accessed files on your web site in the file cache. By analyzing the logs of your server, you can determine which files comprise 70–90% of the requests as well as their total size.

Managing the Disk

Understanding the utilization of the disk subsystem by IIS and configuring this subsystem appropriately is fairly straightforward. You can think of IIS as a special-purpose file server. Requests for static and dynamic content initially result in an access to the disk subsystem. Frequently accessed resources are stored in the cache by the Cache Manager. There are two approaches to improving the performance of your IIS server with respect to the disk subsystem. The first approach is to minimize the number of accesses to the disk subsystem by caching the most frequently accessed files into main memory. The second approach is to increase the bandwidth of the disk subsystem.

The first approach requires a good understanding of the memory subsystem. Many analyses of web server log files both at academic and industry sites have arrived at the conclusion that a very large percentage of the requests are for a small percentage of the files. As described in the previous section, you can determine both popular subset and its total size in bytes by analyzing the log files of the IIS server. This should be a good indicator of the ideal amount of memory you should provide on your server.

You can detect a bottleneck at the disk subsystem due to IIS by combining the memory-related counters in the previous section with some of the counters from the Physical Disk object. Figure 12-23 was generated using the same dataset as the one used for Figure 12-22, but we have added the Physical Disk Current Disk Queue Length counter, which is a measure of the congestion at the disk that contains the IIS server's content. Clearly, the disk is overutilized as a result of all the faults in the cache.

For very large sites with enormous amounts of content, it is unrealistic to expect a large portion of the most requested files to be always present in the cache. In those cases, the solution for improving the performance of the disk subsystem lies in the second approach of increasing the throughput of the disk subsystem. Most of the suggestions discussed in Chapter 10 apply here.

If you discover that the disk on which the web server's content is stored is heavily utilized, as in Figure 12-23, try to distribute the workload to reduce the utilization. If other applications are generating a workload against that same disk, move those applications or the content to another disk. It is not uncommon to find both SQL Server and IIS installed on the same disk. Make sure that the web server's content is on a physical disk that does not have a paging file assigned to it. This ensures that the servicing of hard page faults does not interfere with disk access for the retrieval of files. Also, if you are logging IIS traffic to a file, make sure that the log file is on a different physical disk than the content.

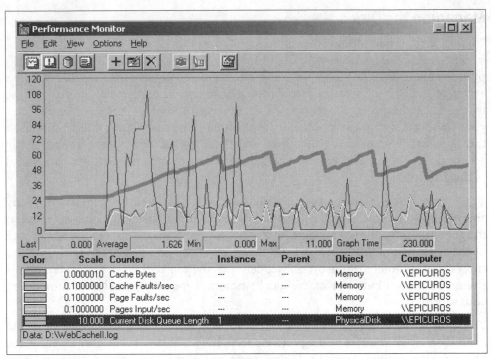

Figure 12-23. The high disk utilization results from an insufficient physical memory configuration

The next step in enhancing the throughput of the disk subsystem is the use of a RAID subsystem. Chapter 10 discussed in detail the various organizations of RAID arrays and described the pros and cons of each. The most appropriate RAID organization for supporting an IIS server is a RAID Level 5 array. RAID Level 5 provides fault tolerance at low cost, since only one additional disk is used for storing redundant data. The disadvantage of the RAID Level 5 organization is the Read-Modify-Write penalty that occurs with small writes. This becomes much less of an issue when supporting IIS, because the workload on the disk subsystem is dominated by read requests.

Managing the Network

Like the disk subsystem, monitoring the utilization of the network subsystem and planning its capacity are not complicated tasks. IIS delivers its content to the clients over the network. No matter how efficiently the server processes the requests, if the network technology does not have sufficient capacity to handle the load, the clients will observe long latencies. Therefore, tuning and capacity planning of the network is critical.

Within the context of IIS, the network subsystem consists of all the components starting from the network interface card (NIC) and extending to the users of the server. In the case of an intranet, you usually have some control or at least an understanding of the path that the traffic must traverse between the clients and your server. In the case of an extranet or Internet server, your control only extends to the ISP that you select to connect you to the rest of the Internet.

A wide variety of technologies can be used to set up a connection between your server and its clients. The most important characteristic of a network technology is its bandwidth, defined as the maximum transfer rate of the network technology. The cheapest network technology available is the modem, with bandwidths ranging today from 28.8 kb/sec to 56 kb/sec. The next step up is ISDN technology, which is based on digital modems. The typical rate for ISDN is 128 kb/sec; the cost is fairly low although its availability is limited. Next comes cable modem technology, with bandwidths of 1.5 Mb/sec downstream and 192 kb/sec upstream. Cable modem technology is an attractive option for a low-traffic web server. For sites with higher traffic demands, the next available options are a fraction of a T1 line or a T1 or T3 line. The bandwidth of a T1 line is 1.544 Mb/sec, and that of the T3 line is 45 Mb/sec. Although the cost of a T1 or fractional T1 is much higher than that of a cable modem, these are dedicated digital connections, while the cable line is shared by the community. Other high-speed technologies available are Frame Relay and ATM with bandwidths in the neighborhood of 155 Mb/sec.

The bandwidth of the network technology should only be considered an upper bound on the effective transfer rate of your network; a number of factors make the actual transfer rate observed by IIS to be lower than that upper bound. First of all, the data must cross a number of network layers as it travels from the application layer down to the NIC to be transported to the client. Each of those layers insert headers that add overhead to the traffic that must be sent to the client. In addition, certain network technologies have inherent overhead that is part of the peer-to-peer protocol. For example, Ethernet networking uses a backoff mechanism in handling collisions when multiple hosts attempt to access the network at the same time. When a collision occurs, the parties involved release the network for a randomly selected amount of time and try to retransmit their packet after that time. Because of this behavior, Ethernet's effective bandwidth starts to decline when the network reaches a utilization of 40% or more due to the large number of collisions.

To illustrate the effect of network layer overhead on the effective transfer rate observed by IIS, we conducted a simple experiment using WCAT to generate traffic against a web server. During this experiment, we measured the transfer rate as observed by IIS using the counter Web Service Bytes Total/sec, and the transfer rate as observed by the network interface using the counter Network Interface Bytes Total/sec. By measuring the transfer rate in bytes at the two different extremes, we capture all the overhead introduced by the headers of all the network layers between the application and data link layer.

Figure 12-24 illustrates the values of the two counters over the duration of the test. The thin line is the effective transfer rate observed by IIS and the heavy line is the transfer rate observed by the network interface. When first looking at the figure, you wonder how it is possible for IIS to exhibit a higher transfer rate than what the network interface sees. In reality, the effective transfer rate measured by IIS has a more bursty behavior than that measured by the network interface. When a request for a file is serviced by IIS, the file as a unit is transferred to the client and at that instant the outgoing transfer rate is very high. Between requests, there is not much to transfer, so the transfer rate drops. This effect causes the Web Service object counter to exhibit large fluctuation. As the file's data travels from the application layer down to the network interface, the large block of data is partitioned into segments, datagrams, and packets. Also, to accommodate spikes in traffic, the network interface layer provides buffering of the data. These two activities cause the transfer rate at the network interface to exhibit a much smaller variation.

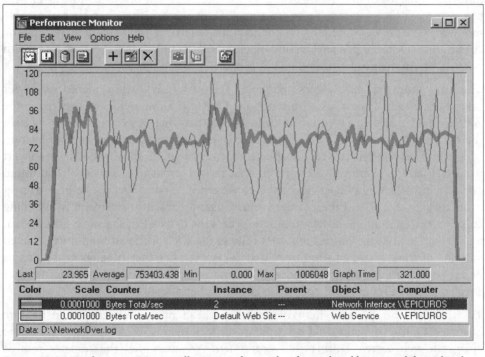

Figure 12-24. Performance Monitor illustrating the overhead introduced by network layer headers

To get back to the topic of network layer overhead, we can compare the average transfer rate at the two endpoints as measured during the test by the Performance

Monitor. The average transfer rate at the network interface layer is 753.4 KB/sec while at the application layer it is 713.0 KB/sec. Given that there is no other activity over this network for the duration of the test, this result implies that the network interface is transferring 40 KB/sec of overhead traffic, or that 5% of the bandwidth is consumed by overhead traffic. In this test, the majority of the requests are for large files so the overhead is relatively small. In cases where the workload consists primarily of requests for small files, the overhead can be a much greater percentage of the overall traffic.

At this point, we know the capacity of each of the available network technologies for connecting the web server to the clients. The next step is to figure out the bandwidth requirements of your server so that you can choose the appropriate technology or figure out if your current one is sufficient. If your server is already connected to the network, the most accurate approach for determining the bandwidth requirements is to measure them using the Performance Monitor. Each of the services that IIS provides has its own counter to measure the consumption of bandwidth. Those counters are Web Service Bytes Total/sec, FTP Service Bytes Total/sec, NNTP Server Bytes Total/sec, and SMTP Server Bytes Total/sec. Summing the values of these counters gives you the total bandwidth demand of your server. You should compute this demand during periods of the day when traffic is heaviest. The workload on web servers grows as the number of users increases, the exposure of the company increases, and so on. To determine the growth rate of the demand on your network and be able to predict ahead of time when the existing capacity will be insufficient to accommodate the demand, you need to use a *workload forecasting technique*. This allows you to develop a model of the growth of the workload using previous measurements. You can then use this model to predict the size of the workload in the future. There is a brief discussion of workload forecasting techniques in the sidebar "Workload Forecasting." For a more extensive discussion, you can look at *Forecasting and Time Series Analysis* by Montgomery et. al. (McGraw Hill) or Menasce and Almeida's *Capacity Planning for Web Performance: Metrics, Models, & Methods* (Prentice Hall).

What if you haven't yet released the web server to your clients? How do you determine the necessary capacity of the network? In this case, you will have to estimate the requirements based on business projections and benchmarking. Using business projections, you can derive estimates on how many of each type of transaction to expect. You can then design representative configuration files for WCAT and generate an artificial workload against your server. This procedure will give you a workload that is fairly representative of what you can ultimately expect.

Performance monitor counters

So far, we have introduced only a few of the counters available for monitoring the network traffic on your server. There are counters to describe the traffic as it flows through each layer of the TCP/IP suite; each layer uses units of throughput for the counters that are appropriate for that specific layer. Unfortunately, since the relationship between the units of two layers is not straightforward, it is not easy to figure out exactly what is going on with the traffic as it flows through each layer. Here is a list of the counters that describe the traffic going through each layer of the TCP/IP suite. We have left out other protocols, such as UDP, that are part of the TCP/IP suite and are utilized in processing web server traffic. Note that the TCP, UDP, IP, and Network Interface Performance Monitor objects are available only if SNMP service is installed on your system. You can install it by going to Control Panel → Network → Services, pressing the Add button, and selecting the SNMP Service.

Web Service: Bytes sent/sec, Bytes received/sec, Bytes Total/sec
> These counters indicate the number of bytes sent, bytes received, and total bytes transferred by the web service per second. Each of the other services, such as the FTP service, provides equivalent counters. These are measures of throughput at the application level. Notice that due to buffering, it is possible for these values to exceed the capacity of the network interfaces. If that condition persists over long periods, it may indicate that the demand exceeds the available capacity.

TCP: TCP Segments sent/sec, TCP Segments received/sec, TCP Segments/sec
> When a stream is passed from the application layer to the transport layer to be sent to the client using the TCP protocol, the TCP layer partitions the stream into segments. In the other direction, data passed from the network layer up to the TCP layer may be in the form of one or more segments. It is the responsibility of the TCP layer to piece them together into the original stream before passing the data up to the application layer. These counters indicate the throughput through the TCP layer using units of segments. The size of the segment is determined based on the two peers when they set up the connection, the minimum capacity of the intervening network, and congestion on the network. This makes it difficult to understand the relationship between bytes transferred at the application layer and segments transferred at the transport layer. TCP provides reliability through retransmission of segments, but further complicates the relationship between the two layers.

IP: IP Datagrams sent/sec, IP Datagrams received/sec, IP Datagrams/sec
> IP transfers data in units of datagrams, treating each datagram as an independent unit of data. It is up to the TCP layer to handle the reconstruction of streams from individual datagrams. If transport layer protocols other than TCP are not actively used on your system, the relationship between the transfer rate in segments and datagrams should be 1 to 1.

Network Interface: Bytes sent/sec, Bytes received/sec, Bytes Total/sec
> These counters indicate the number of bytes transferred at the data link layer. This includes traffic from all upper layers, so the fraction of this traffic attributed to IIS depends on the other applications and servers running on your system.

These counters describe the flow of data through the four layers of the TCP/IP suite. By following the traffic through the network layers, you can get a good idea of which applications are using the network and how much of the network is utilized by each one. For example, say that you have determined that your network interface is heavily utilized. By looking at the traffic at progressively higher layers, you can determine how the traffic is distributed across the protocols and applications, and figure out which application is the cause of the overload. The following counters can detect heavy utilization conditions and network problems:

Network Interface: Current Bandwidth
> This counter indicates the rated bandwidth of the network interface. This is the upper bound on the transfer rate of the network interface in bits/sec. This counter has a fixed value and never changes. By transforming this value to bytes/sec (dividing by 8), and then dividing the Bytes Total/sec by that, you can get an indication of the utilization of the network interface.

Network Interface: Output Queue Length
> This counter indicates the instantaneous value of the size of the output queue for the network interface. When the network is busy or there is incoming traffic, outgoing packets are placed temporarily on a queue. When this value is consistently high over long measurement periods, it is an indication that the network interface is overutilized.

Network Segment: % Network Utilization
> This counter indicates the utilization of the network segment as a whole. The value of this counter along with the utilization of this particular interface gives you an indication of whether this server is the source of the workload or whether the segment is overloaded with other servers and clients.

IP: Datagrams Outgoing Discarded, Received Discarded
> These counters represent the count of packets that were correctly received but could not be correctly passed to their destination layers due to congestion issues. For outgoing packets, the congestion is at the network interface layer, whereas for received packets the congestion is at the transport layer. When values for these counters are consistently not 0, it is an indication of congestion problems.

TCP: Connections Established, Connection Failures
> The first counter indicates the current number of TCP connections established, and the second counter indicates the number of TCP connections that failed to be established since the machine was started. When the number of failures grows quickly, there may be congestion problems. Note that the Connection Failures counter counts the failures since the time the machine was started, so to determine the failures during a small period of time, you have to subtract the minimum value from the maximum value for the period.

Once you have determined that the network is a bottleneck, you can apply the techniques for resolving this bottleneck described in Chapter 11.

Workload Forecasting

The most common techniques for workload forecasting are based on *time-series analysis*, which is the investigation of a collection of observations made sequentially in time for prediction, description, and control. This sidebar describes two of the simpler but more commonly used time-series methods that have been applied to workload forecasting. The first is a simple technique called moving-averages. Under this approach, the forecast value for the next sample is the average of a number of previous observations. The number of previous observations that should be used for the forecast is determined based on the specific workload such that a measure of the error of the prediction is minimized. The second technique is *exponential smoothing*. It is similar in that it forecasts the next value in the sequence based on a set of previous observations, but this algorithm uses different weights in computing this average.

One of the simplest workload forecasting techniques is *moving averages*. The forecasting decision is made based on a mean of the previous observations. To describe the moving-average approach, we consider two models of the data. The simplest is the *constant process* model, where the variable to be predicted x_t can be expressed as $x_t = b + \varepsilon_t$ where b is the unknown parameter and ε_t represents the noise in the measurements. Given N past observations, x_{t-N+1} through x_t, we can predict the value $\hat{x}_{t+1}$ at the next forecasting period as:

$$\hat{x}_{t+1} = \frac{1}{N} \cdot \sum_{i=t-N+1}^{t} x_i$$

So if we are using as measurements the maximum rate at which traffic was transferred by our web server in each of the past N weeks, the model can predict next week's demand very accurately. For example, let us say that we want to predict the average number of GET requests that will be imposed on the server tomorrow given the measurements from the past 100 days. The following figure shows a plot of the measurements of the past 100 days. Applying the moving average algorithm, we find that the predicted number of requests tomorrow will be 13,050. The same approach can be repeated tomorrow by replacing the oldest measurement with tomorrow's measured value to get an updated forecast.

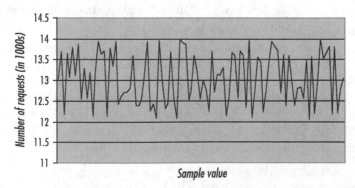

—continued—

A better model for a situation with a clear growth trend is $x_t = b_1 + b_2 t + \varepsilon_t$. The only difference between this model and the constant model is the additional additive trend term $b_2 t$. The unknown parameters can be computed as follows:

$$b_1 = 2M_t - M_t^2 - b_2 t, \quad b_2 = \frac{2}{N-1} \cdot (M_t - M_t^2)$$

where M_t denotes the moving average as in the constant model and M_t^2 is a symbol used to denote the *double moving average*. The double moving average is simply the moving average computed using the results from the moving average technique applied to the initial time series as input data. If we plug the equations for b_1 and b_2 into the equation for $\hat{x}_t$, we get $\hat{x}_t = 2M_t - M_t^2$, which is the forecasting equation. Notice that with this approach, to make a decision using $N=5$ requires that we have at least 10 data points.

The next technique is *exponential smoothing*. Again, we consider the constant model case and the trend model case. For the constant model case at instant t we have the current measured value x_t and the predicted value for this period $\hat{x}_t$. The predicted value for the next forecasting period should be obtained using the predicted value for this period and a slight update value that should be based on the error between the latest measurement and the predicted value. In other words, the next forecast value should be $\hat{x}_{t+1} = \hat{x}_t + \alpha(x_t - \hat{x}_t)$, which can also be written as $\hat{x}_{t+1} = \alpha x_t + (1-\alpha)\hat{x}_t$. This operation is called *simple exponential smoothing*. The fraction α in the equation is called the *smoothing constant*. The value of the smoothing constant should be chosen after experimenting with the measured data to determine the optimal value for the particular dataset. Various values should be used for forecasting known values. The value of the smoothing constant that gives the lowest error should be selected for forecasting future values. When the value of the smoothing constant is small, the predictor responds quickly to fluctuations in the time series, whereas larger values cause slower response.

If the network technology has sufficient bandwidth available but the NIC has already reached its maximum capacity, it's time to change the NIC. The latest NICs from most manufacturers have advanced features that enhance their performance, including multitasking at the hardware level to improve the transfer rate of the card, separate buffers for incoming and outgoing packets, and full-duplex operation. There are also NICs available with two or four channels on the same card, almost doubling the transfer rate of the card without taking up additional slots on your motherboard. NICs with multiple channels come with drivers that make the two channels behave as a single channel, but with much greater capacity. You can also purchase additional cards, which can be configured such that they have a single logical address on your network. The advantage of this approach when you have multiple CPUs on your server is that the interrupts are distributed across the CPUs, balancing the load. Another feature that you should look for is interrupt moderation, which was discussed in detail earlier in this chapter.

Load Balancing and Server Clustering

When you are finally convinced that your IIS server has reached its maximum capacity in servicing requests and have squeezed every ounce of performance out of each of the subsystems, there is yet another way to improve performance. Just like using a multiprocessor when your CPU subsystem is overworked or a RAID device when your disk subsystem is the bottleneck, you can use multiple physical machines to support a single logical web server. There are a number of ways to do this, ranging from a simple, low-cost solution such as round-robin DNS to a more sophisticated solution such as the Windows Load Balancing Service (WLBS). In addition to the performance benefits, using multiple physical servers provides enhanced fault tolerance. In this section, we describe three alternatives that are available for combining the processing power of multiple servers to provide a single, logical, high-performance web server.

The first option is the use of round-robin Domain Name System (DNS) for load distribution across multiple servers. The DNS server is a hierarchical and distributed database that provides both forward and reverse mapping of hostnames to IP addresses. For details on how to set up DNS and how it works, look at *DNS on Windows NT* by Paul Albitz, Matt Larson, and Cricket Liu, or *DNS and BIND*, by Paul Albitz and Cricket Liu (both from O'Reilly).

When the IIS server is installed and configured, A and PTR records are added to the DNS server. This allows the primary server for the domain to resolve requests for the IP address of the IIS server given the hostname. Since it has become a convention to use the hostname *www* for the web server of an organization, an alias is usually added to the DNS server using a CNAME record. For example, if you use nslookup to determine the IP address for server *www.oreilly.com*, the server returns the IP address of the server along with the name of the server, *helio.ora.com*. In this case, *www.oreilly.com* is an alias for the server *helio.ora.com*.

To add multiple physical hosts in support of the web server, simply replicate the content across those machines and make the *www* hostname an alias for all the physical server hostnames. So if servers *srvr1.company.com*, *srvr2.company.com*, and *srvr3.company.com* all support the web server for *www.company.com*, *www.company.com* should be an alias for all three hostnames *srvr1*, *srvr2*, and *srvr3*. When a client request arrives at the DNS server to resolve the hostname *www.company.com*, the DNS server returns a list of all three IP addresses back to the client, and the client sends its request to the first IP address in the list. The next time the server is queried for *www.company.com*, it sends the same list out to the client but the order is changed in a round-robin fashion. This causes the second request to go to a different server since the client again selects the first IP address in the list. To see an example of this in practice, use nslookup to resolve the IP address for *www.microsoft.com*. We executed the nslookup command twice in sequence; on the first run, the DNS server returned the list 207.46.131.13, 207.46.131.15, 207.46.131.137, 207.46.130.14, 207. 46.130.149, 207.46.130.150, and on the second run it returned the list 207.46.131. 13, 207.46.131.15, 207.46.131.137, 207.46.130.14, 207.46.130.149, 207.46.130. 150. As you can see, in both cases the same list is returned, but the order of the addresses varies.

This simple load-balancing approach works well but has its disadvantages. First of all, it does not work well when a server goes down. Since the mapping of the alias to the collection of servers is static, the DNS server is not aware of the availability of all the servers in the collection. When a server goes down, the DNS server periodically continues resolving the alias to the server that failed, thereby causing some of the client requests to fail. This problem persists until the system administrator updates the DNS server to prevent requests from going to the failed server, or until the server eventually becomes available. Another problem with this approach is that it does not ensure that the load is balanced across all servers. The DNS server evenly distributes the requests across the collection of servers regardless of the capabilities of each server. For example, in the case of a two-machine server, if one server is a Pentium machine and the other a multiprocessor Pentium II machine, both will service an equal number of requests despite the considerable capacity available in the second machine.

The second alternative to balancing the load across a number of physical servers is the use of a hardware solution such as the LocalDirector by Cisco Systems. The LocalDirector is a network appliance that includes a real-time, embedded operating system, which sits between the farm of web servers and the incoming traffic from the clients, as shown in Figure 12-25. The clients view the server farm as a virtual IP address. The LocalDirector maps that virtual address to one or more real IP addresses. When a virtual address is mapped to multiple real IP addresses, the Local-Director load-balances the traffic evenly among them by modifying the incoming packets and forwarding them accordingly. It can load-balance any type of TCP/IP traffic, although it is targeted toward Internet servers for HTTP and FTP traffic.

One advantage of the LocalDirector is that it solves the problem of round-robin DNS, where requests are forwarded to servers that are unavailable because of the static mapping. The LocalDirector keeps track of the status of all the servers connected to it. If a server goes down, the LocalDirector automatically removes it from any mappings that it belongs to. As soon as the server comes up again, the mapping is enabled immediately without intervention from a network administrator. Servers can also be added or removed from the farm while the system is running simply by changing the configuration of the LocalDirector.

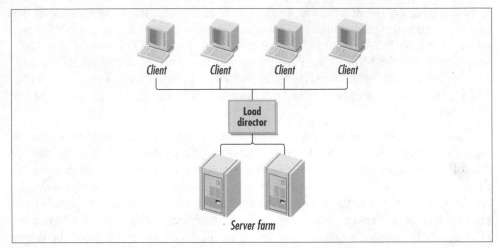

Figure 12-25. The LocalDirector web server load-balancing solution

An additional advantage of this solution is the ability to include port numbers in the virtual-to-real address map. Suppose you want to use two physical servers for processing HTTP traffic and two servers for processing FTP traffic. The default application port for HTTP traffic is port 80, and for FTP traffic, port 21. Figure 12-26 shows the configuration that can be used with LocalDirector to establish this mapping. Requests for port 80 are load-balanced across the two HTTP servers at addresses 192.168.1.1 and 192.168.1.2, and requests for port 21 are load-balanced across the two FTP servers at addresses 192.168.1.3 and 192.168.1.4. This ability to use ports in the mapping provides some security filtering of the traffic. It is possible to set up LocalDirector so that traffic for ports other than those explicitly included in the mapping is rejected.

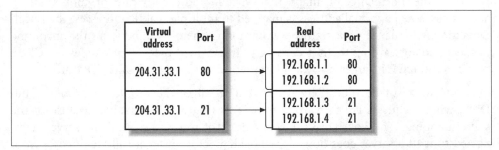

Figure 12-26. The mapping of virtual addresses to real addresses can include the port number

Yet another advantage of this solution is its failover capability. For installations where the servers must be up and running 24 hours a day, 7 days a week, two Local-Director units can be used in a failover configuration. A cable connects the two units and indicates that one should be in active mode and the other in standby mode. If one of the units fails, the other automatically switches into active mode and starts processing the incoming traffic.

The last approach we introduce here is a pure software solution. This solution was originally developed by Valence Research under the name Conroy Cluster, but it was acquired by Microsoft Corporation in August 1998 and is now available as part of the Windows NT Enterprise Server installation under the name Windows NT Load Balancing Service (WLBS). WLBS installs itself as a networking driver that logically sits between the TCP/IP driver and the NIC. It is installed on every machine that will be part of the cluster, and requires a dedicated hostname and IP address for the cluster itself.

When a request arrives for service at the virtual IP address assigned to the cluster, all physical servers pick up the request. All the hosts in the server farm use a distributed algorithm to determine which one will service the request. This determination is made based on a mapping established by the cluster upon initialization. The mapping changes only when the status of the cluster changes, which occurs when servers enter or leave the cluster. When the status of the cluster changes, all the servers in the farm reestablish the mapping or filtering through a process called *convergence*. The servers that comprise the cluster can exchange information in two different ways based on the configuration. The preferred way to exchange configuration information is through a multicast MAC address that is added to each NIC during installation. The other approach is to use a second NIC on each server for exchanging cluster information while the primary NIC is used for servicing traffic.

Like the LocalDirector solution, WLBS can automatically detect the failure of a server in the cluster and redefine the cluster configuration to prevent requests from being forwarded to servers that are not available. This process is automatic and transparent to the clients and typically takes about 10 seconds to complete from the instant that the server goes down. With WLBS, the load balancing is performed by the servers that actually process the traffic, so there is no need for retransmission of requests to the actual server as in the hardware-based solution. On the other hand, all hosts in the cluster listen in on the traffic and perform some processing on each packet that arrives.

There is one problem that arises from server clustering. As you know, HTTP is a stateless protocol. Every response from the server is a result of the current request and no previous information. Unfortunately, for applications such as electronic commerce it became critical for servers to maintain state. For example, when shopping at an online bookstore, the server needs to keep track of your shopping basket. ASP provides a session object that allows web applications to maintain state. The problem is that the state is maintained on the server that processed the latest request, so if the load-balancing solution forwards the subsequent request to another server, the current state of the client is lost. One solution to this problem is to transport state information back and forth between the client and server, hiding the data within hidden fields. Another solution that is more appropriate for sophisticated web applications is to save the state in the backend, such as a database, that is shared by all the servers in the farm. This is illustrated in Figure 12-27.

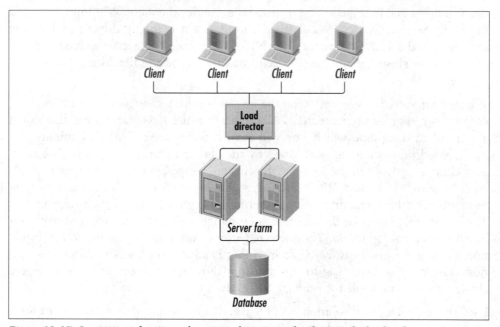

Figure 12-27. Servers in a farm can share state by using a database at the backend

Bibliography

This bibliography includes references to additional readings related to each chapter in this book. Some of the references are to web pages that were available at the time that we wrote this book. If you find that some of them are no longer available, please let us know.

Performance Management

Edward D. Lazowska, John Zahorjan, G. Scott Graham, and Kenneth C. Sevcik, *Quantitative System Performance: Computer System Analysis Using Queueing Network Models*, Prentice Hall, 1984.

A. Menascé Daniel, Virgilio A. F. Almeida, Larry W. Dowdy, *Capacity Planning and Performance Modeling: From Mainframes to Client-Server Systems*, Prentice Hall, 1994.

Computer Measurement Group. CMG is a nonprofit, worldwide organization of data processing professionals committed to the measurement and management of computer systems. More information is available from their web site at *http://www.cmg.org*.

Measurement Methodology

Microsoft Corporation, "Windows Management Instrumentation: Background and Overview," *http://eu.microsoft.com/windows2000/techinfo/howitworks/management/wmioverview.asp*, November 17, 1999.

Desktop Management Task Force (DMTF), "Web-Based Enterprise Management," *http://www.dmtf.org/download/spec/wbem.pdf*.

David A. Solomon and Mark E. Russinovich, *Inside Microsoft Windows 2000*, Third Edition, Chapter 5 on Management Mechanisms, Microsoft Press, 2000.

Jeffrey Richter and Jason D. Clark, *Programming Server-Side Applications for Microsoft Windows 2000*, Chapter 7 on Performance Monitoring and Chapter 8 on Windows Management Instrumentation, Microsoft Press, 2000.

Stan Dylnicki, "Monitoring 2000+ Windows NT in a WAN/LAN Environment," Proceedings of CMG2000, Computer Measurement Group, Turnersville, NJ.

Processor Performance

John L. Hennessy and David A. Patterson, *Computer Architecture: A Quantitative Approach*, Second Edition, Chapters 2–5, Morgan Kaufmann Publishers, 1996.

Tom Shanley, *Protected Mode Software Architecture*, MindShare Inc., 1996.

David A. Solomon and Mark E. Russinovich, *Inside Microsoft Windows 2000*, Third Edition, Chapters 3 and 6, Microsoft Press, 2000.

Jeffrey Richter, *Programming Applications for Microsoft Windows*, Fourth Edition, Chapters 4–12, Microsoft Press, 1999.

Roger Penrose, *The Emperor's New Mind: Concerning Computers, Minds, and the Laws of Physics*, Penguin, 1991.

http://www.aip.org/history/heisenberg. Historical information on Werner Heisenberg and the Uncertainty Principle.

http://www.sysinternals.com/ntw2k/freeware/frob.shtml. Site where you can download the Frob utility and other related system utilities.

Optimizing Application Performance

Connie U. Smith, *Performance Engineering of Software Systems*, Addison Wesley, 1990.

Chris Loosley and Frank Douglas, *High-Performance Client Server*, John Wiley & Sons, 1997.

http://www.rational.com/products/quantify_nt/index.jsp. Information on the Rational Quantify profiler.

http://developer.intel.com/software/products/vtune/index.htm. Information on Intel's Vtune Performance Analyzer tool.

http://developer.intel.com/design/ia-64/index.htm. Information on the Itanium IA-64 architecture.

Multiprocessing

John L. Hennessy and David A. Patterson, *Computer Architecture: A Quantitative Approach*, Second Edition, Chapter 8 on Multiprocessors, Morgan Kaufmann Publishers, 1996.

Intel, *The IA-32 Intel Architecture Software Developer's Manual, Volume 3: System Programming Guide*, available from *http://developer.intel.com/design/pentium4/ manuals/245472.htm*.

http://www.sysinternals.com/ntw2k/freeware/cpumon.shtml. Site where you can download the CPUMon utility and other related system utilities.

Memory Management and Paging

John L. Hennessy and David A. Patterson, *Computer Architecture: A Quantitative Approach*, Second Edition, Chapter 5 on Memory Hierarchy Design, Morgan Kaufmann Publishers, 1996.

David A. Solomon and Mark E. Russinovich, *Inside Microsoft Windows 2000*, Third Edition, Chapter 7 on Memory Management, Microsoft Press, 2000.

Jeffrey Richter, *Programming Applications for Microsoft Windows*, Fourth Edition, Chapters 13–15, Microsoft Press, 1999.

Microsoft Corporation, "Address Windowing Extensions and Windows 2000 Data-Center Server," available from *http://www.microsoft.com/hwdev/ntdrivers/awe.htm*, March 1999.

File Cache Performance and Tuning

John L. Hennessy and David A. Patterson, *Computer Architecture: A Quantitative Approach*, Second Edition, Chapter 5 on Memory Hierarchy Design, Morgan Kaufmann Publishers, 1996.

David A. Solomon and Mark E. Russinovich, *Inside Microsoft Windows 2000*, Third Edition, Chapter 11 on the Cache Manager, Microsoft Press, 2000.

Peter Viscarola and W. Anthony Mason, *Windows NT Device Driver Development*, MacMillan Technical Publishing, 1999.

http://www.sysinternals.com/ntw2k/source/cacheset.shtml. Site where you can download the CacheSet utility and other related system utilities.

Disk Subsystem Performance

Microsoft Corporation, "Enterprise Class Storage in Windows 2000," white paper, 1999.

Quantum Corporation, "Hard Drives and Computer System Performance," white paper, *http://www.quantum.com/src/whitepapers/wp_hddperformance1.htm*.

Rodney Van Meter, "Observing the Effects of Multi-Zone Disks," Proceedings of the Usenix 1997 Technical Conference, Anaheim, CA, January 1997. Postscript version available at *http://www.isi.edu/netstation/zcav/*.

Rajeev Nagar, *Windows NT File System Internals: A Developer's Guide*, O'Reilly & Associates, 1997.

Peter Viscarola and W. Anthony Mason, *Windows NT Device Driver Development*, MacMillan Technical Publishing, 1999.

Leonard Chung and Jim Gray, "Windows 2000 Disk I/O Performance," Technical Report MS-TR-2000-55, Microsoft Research, Advanced Technology Division, Redmond, Washington, 2000.

Ravi Chalaka and Dave Schwaderer, "Ultra2 SCSI: I/O Power for Mainstream Computing," *http://www.adapter.com/technology/whitepapers/ultra2scsi.html*, Adaptec, Inc., 1999.

Sean Daily, *Optimizing Windows NT*, IDG Books Worldwide, Inc., 1998.

Friedhelm Schmidt, *The SCSI Bus & IDE Interface Protocols, Applications, & Programming*, Second Edition, Addison Wesley, 1997.

Randy Kerns, "SCSI Command Tag Queuing and Cached Disk Performance," Demand Technology's Storage Management newsletter, Volume 6, Number 11, November 1998.

Brian L. Wong, "The Ubiquitous SCSI: What Is It?," Proceedings of the Computer Measurement Group Conference, 1998.

Ted McGavin, "Fibre Channel: The Third Age of Disk Connectivity," Proceedings of the Computer Measurement Group, December 1998.

Paul Massiglia, "Fibre Channel, Storage Area Networks, and Disk Array Systems: How Fibre Channel will Affect the Future of Disk Array Systems," *http://www. fibrechannel.com*.

Tom Clark, "Designing Storage Networks with Fibre Channel Switches, Switching Hubs and Hubs," white paper from Vixel Corporation, August 1999.

Ezio Valdevit, "Cascading in Fibre Channel: How to Build a Multi-Switch Fabric," white paper from Brocade Communications Corporation, 1999.

Marc Farley, *Building Storage Networks*, Osborne/McGraw-Hill, 2000.

Staffan Bo Strand, "Storage Area Networks and SANTK," Masters of Science Thesis at the University of Minnesota, April 2001.

Filesystem Performance

Mark Russinovich, "Inside Storage Management, Part 1," Windows 2000 Magazine, *http://www.win2000mag.com/Articles/Index.cfm?ArticleID=8127*, March 2000.

Mark Russinovich, "Inside Storage Management, Part 2," Windows 2000 Magazine, *http://www.win2000mag.com/Articles/Index.cfm?ArticleID=8303*, April 2000.

David A. Solomon and Mark E. Russinovich, *Inside Microsoft Windows 2000*, Third Edition, Chapter 9 on the I/O System and Chapter 10 on Storage Management, Microsoft Press, 2000.

Uresh Vahalia, *"UNIX Internals: The New Frontiers,"* Prentice Hall, 1996. Although not related to Windows 2000, Chapters 8–11 have in-depth coverage of filesystem design issues.

Mark Russinovich, "Inside Win2K NTFS, Part 1," Windows 2000 Magazine, *http://www.win2000mag.com/Articles/Index.cfm?ArticleID=15719*, November 2000.

Mark Russinovich, "Inside Win2K NTFS, Part 2," Windows 2000 Magazine, *http://www.win2000mag.com/Articles/Index.cfm?ArticleID=15900*, Winter 2000.

Microsoft Corporation, "Encrypting File System for Windows 2000," *http://microsoft.com/windows2000/techinfo/howitworks/security/encrypt.asp*.

Steve Widen and Chris Chris, "Disk Defragmentation for Windows NT/2000," IDC white paper.

NSTL Final Report, "Defragmentation Performance Testing," November 1999.

NSTL Final Report, "Performance Comparison: SpeedDisk 5.0 (Symantec Corporation) and Diskeeper 5.0 (Executive Software)," January 2000.

Disk Array Performance

Kenneth Salem and Hector Garcia-Molina, "Disk Striping," Proceedings of the Second International Conference on Data Engineering, pp. 336–342, 1986.

Mark Friedman, "RAID keeps on going and going," IEEE Spectrum, April 1996.

David A. Patterson, Garth Gibson, and Randy H. Katz, "A Case for Redundant Arrays of Inexpensive Disks (RAID)," International Conference on Management of Data (SIGMOD), pp. 109–116, June 1988.

Peter M. Chen and David A. Patterson, "Maximizing Performance in a Striped Disk Array," Proceedings of the 1990 International Symposium on Computer Architecture, pp. 322–331, May 1990.

Richard W. Hamming, *Coding and Information Theory*, Second Edition, Prentice Hall, 1986.

Odysseas I. Pentakalos, Daniel Menasce, Milt Halem, and Yelena Yesha, "Analytical Performance Modeling of Hierarchical Mass Storage Systems," IEEE Transactions on Computers, Vol. 46, No. 10, October 1997, pp. 1103–1118.

Brian L. Wong, *Configuration and Capacity Planning for Solaris Servers,* SUN Microsystems Press, 1997.

Erik Riedel, "A Performance Study of Sequential I/O on Windows NT 4," Proceedings of the 2nd USENIX Windows NT Symposium, Seattle, WA, August 1998.

3ware, "The 3ware DiskSwitch Architecture: Switched I/O for Performance Computing," September 1999.

Robert Horst, "TwinStor Technology: A Compelling Case for Multiple Drives in PCs, Servers, and Workstations," August 1999.

Networking Technology

David A. Solomon and Mark E. Russinovich, *Inside Microsoft Windows 2000*, Third Edition, Chapter 13 on Networking, Microsoft Press, 2000.

William Boswell, *Inside Windows 2000 Server*, New Riders Publishing, 2000.

Larry L. Peterson and Bruce S. Davie, *Computer Networks: A Systems Approach*, Second Edition, Morgan Kaufmann Publishers, 2000.

Microsoft Corporation, *Microsoft Windows 2000 Server: TCP/IP Core Networking Guide*, Microsoft Press, 2000.

Internet Information Server Performance

T. Berners-Lee, R. Fielding, H. Frystyk, "RFC 1945 Hypertext Transfer Protocol – HTTP 1.0," Network Working Group, May 1996.

R. Fielding, J. Gettys, J. Mogul, H. Frystyk, T. Berners-Lee, "RFC 2068 Hypertext Transfer Protocol – HTTP 1.1," Network Working Group, January 1997.

T. Berners-Lee, R. Fielding, L. Masinter, "RFC 2396 Uniform Resource Identifiers (URI): Generic Syntax," Network Working Group, August 1998.

Chuck Musciano and Bill Kennedy, *HTML: The Definitive Guide*, Third Edition, O'Reilly & Associates, August 1998.

Phillip Hallam-Baker and Brian Behlendorf, "Extended Log File Format," W3C Working Draft, 1996.

Microsoft Corporation, "Users Guide: Microsoft Web Capacity Analysis Tool," Version 4.13, 1997.

SPECweb99 Release 1.01, November 8, 1999, *http://www.spec.org/osg/web99/docs/whitepaper.html*.

Mindcraft, "WebStone Users Guide," *http://www.mindcraft.com/webstone/ws201-descr.html*, December 1998.

Gene Tren and Mark Sake, *WebSTONE: The First Generation in HTTP Server Benchmarking*, Silicon Graphics, February 1995.

Venkata N. Padmanabhan and Jeffrey C. Mogul, "Improving HTTP Latency," Computer Networks and ISDN Systems, Vol. 28, pp. 25–35, December 1995.

Simon E. Spero, "Analysis of HTTP Performance Problems," *http://sunsite.unc.edu/mdma-release/http-prob.html*.

Joe Touch, John Heidemann, Katia Obraczka, "Analysis of HTTP Performance," *http://www.isi.edu/touch/pubs/http-perf96/index.html*, USC/Information Sciences Institute, August 1996.

Microsoft Windows 2000 Server, "Internet Information Services 5.0 Technical Overview," December 1999.

Philippe Joubert, Robert B. King, Rich Neves, Mark Russinovich, John M. Tracey, "High Performance Memory-Based Web Servers: Kernel and User-Mode Performance," IBM T.J. Watson Research Center, available from *http://www.sysinternals.com/files/webserver.pdf*.

M. Arlitt and C. Williamson, "Web Server Workload Characterization: The Search for Invariants," Proceedings of the 1996 SIGMETRICS Conference on Measurement & Modeling of Computer Systems, Philadelphia, PA, May 1996, pp. 126–137.

M. Crovella and A. Bestavros, "Self-Similarity in World Wide Web Traffic: Evidence and Possible Causes," Proceedings of the 1996 SIGMETRICS Conference on Measurement & Modeling of Computer Systems, Philadelphia, PA, May 1996, pp. 160–169.

Stephen Lee Manley, "An Analysis of Issues Facing World Wide Web Servers," Harvard College, Cambridge, Massachusetts, April 7, 1997.

M. Arlitt and T. Jin, "Workload Characterization of the 1998 World Cup Web Site," Hewlett-Packard Laboratories, September 23, 1999.

Douglas C. Montgomery, Lynwood A. Johnson, and John S. Gardiner, *Forecasting and Time Series Analysis*, McGraw Hill, 1991.

Daniel Menasce and Virgilio A. F. Almeida, *Capacity Planning for Web Performance: Metrics, Models, & Methods*, Prentice Hall, 1998.

Paul Albitz, Matt Larson, and Cricket Liu, *DNS on Windows NT*, O'Reilly & Associates, October 1998.

Paul Albitz and Cricket Liu, *DNS and BIND*, Third Edition, O'Reilly & Associates, September 1998.

Cisco Systems, "Scaling the Internet Web Servers," white paper, *http://www.cisco.com/warp/public/cc/pd/cxsr/400/tech/scale_wp.htm*, 1998.

Cisco Systems, "Local Director," white paper, *http://www.cisco.com/univercd/cc/td/doc/product/iaabu/locadir/ld20ms/ldicgd/ld3_ch1.htm*, 1998.

Cisco Systems, "Local Director Failover," white paper, *http://www.cisco.com/warp/public/cc/pd/cxsr/400/tech/locdf_wp.htm*, 1998.

Microsoft Corporation, "Microsoft Windows NT Load Balancing Service Technical Overview," *http://www.microsoft.com/ntserver/ntserverenterprise/techdetails/prodarch/Wlbs.asp*, January 1999.

Sunbelt Software, "Clustering for Win NT Web Servers," *http://www.sunbeltsoftware.com/convoy.html*, January 1999.

Microsoft Corporation, "Deployment Notes for Windows NT Load Balancing Service (WLBS)," *http://www.microsoft.com/ntserver/ntserverenterprise/deployment/planguide/WlbsDeploy.asp*, January 1999.

Index

We'd like to hear your suggestions for improving our indexes. Send email to *index@oreilly.com*.

ISAPI Extension Requests/sec counter, 591
ISAPI (Internet Server API)
  DLLs, 626, 629
  dynamic content and, 626
  extensions, IIS and, 583
ISDN technology, 647
ISPs (Internet service providers), 508
ISRs (interrupt service routines), 138
  CPU usage and, 126
ISVs (independent software vendors), 364

J

JBOD (Just a Bunch of Disks), 458
Job Object Detail counters, 177
Job objects, resource limit setting, 176
jumbo frames, Gigabit Ethernet, 527, 533
Junctions extension, Reparse Point, 431

K

Karn's algorithm, retransmission, 576
KeepAlive messages, TCP, 563
kernel
  event tracing, 44
  objects, counting, 67
  threads, total number of, 168
kernel-mode thread synchronization
      objects, 162
Kleinrock, Dr. Leonard, 541

L

LANs (local area networks), 505, 506
  ring configuration, 506
  star configuration, 507
  stations, 506
  switches, 507
  troubleshooting, 531
  wiring hubs, 506
LargeSystemCache Registry setting, 309, 352
  operation of, 355–357
last access date entry, root folder, 423
last modification time and date entry, root
      folder, 423
latency, 7, 522–524
  extent, Ethernet, 528
  masking, benchmark testing and, 486
  repeaters, 523
  RTT, 524
layers, 511
  Application layer, 512
  benefits, 513
  Host-to-Host, 512, 556–577

I/O Manager, 364
  class drivers, 365
  filesystem drivers, 364
  filter drivers, 364
  hardware layer, 366
  Mini-Drivers, 365
  IP (Internet Protocol), 512, 537–556
  MAC (Media Access), 511, 524–537
lazy write caching, 324, 335
  disk idle writes, 336
  physical disk updates, 335
  stolen mapped file pages, 337
  threshold-triggered flushes, 336
lazy write disk caching, benchmark testing
      and, 485
Lazy Write Flushes, hardware RAID
      and, 467
Lazy Write Pages/sec counter, 441
lazy writes, hardware RAID, 467
Lazy Writes/sec counter, 441
LBA (logical block address) mode, 383
LDM (Logical Disk Manager), 418
ldmdump tool, dynamic disks, 419
leaks (memory), detecting, 312
leasing IP addresses, 545
linear scalability, multiprocessing, 223–225
linked lists, logical drives, 417
Little's Law, 13–15
  thread pooling and, 248
load balancing, 654–658
  LocalDirector and, 655
local area networks (see LANs)
LocalDirector, load balancing and, 655
locality of reference (paging file access), 278
LOCK prefix, 220
  serializing locked instructions, 226
locking
  database scalability and, 34
  multiprocessing, 218
log files, System Monitor, 61
logical cluster number, 424
Logical Disk Avg. Disk Queue Length
      counter, calculation for, 15
Logical Disk object, 399
  % Free Space counter, 81
  counters, 438
  diskperf command and, 438
  Performance Monitor, partition
      information, 437–441
logical disks
  Disk Management, 468
  instance names, 73

workload
  balanced systems and, 28
  benchmark development and, 31
  benchmark engineering, 32
  scalability issues and, 34
  WCAT, 605–609
workload characterization (benchmark
      testing), 33, 46
workload forecasting technique, network
      management and, 649
workload studies, hard disks, 403–414
write caching, hardware RAID and, 466
write performance penalty, RAID Level
      4, 459

write-back caching, hardware RAID, 466
write-through caches, 338
  hardware RAID and, 466

X

X axis (System Monitor), 62
XOR (Exclusive Or) operator, 456

Z

Zero List (pages), 296
zoned bit recording, hard disk, 371–376

About the Authors

Mark Friedman began his career in 1977 as a programmer for the DuPont Corporation and has been in the computer field ever since. He has a Master's degree in Computer Science from Temple University and is the founder and president of Demand Technology Software. He has written numerous technical articles, conducts training seminars in Windows performance, and publishes a monthly newsletter. Currently, he is working on the design and development of professional software tools for Windows performance management.

Odysseas Pentakalos is Vice President of SYSNET International, Inc., where he focuses on performance management of computer systems and on the architecture, design, and development of large distributed systems that utilize Java and J2EE technologies. His clients have included major government agencies and corporations such as NASA Goddard Space Flight Center, the Army Research Lab, Sun Microsystems, Concert Communications, KPMG, and Northrop Grumman IT. He holds a Ph.D. in Computer Science with a specialization in performance management of computer systems. He has published dozens of papers in conference proceedings and journals and is a frequent speaker at industry conferences. Odysseas can be reached at *odysseas@sysnetint.com*.

Colophon

Our look is the result of reader comments, our own experimentation, and feedback from distribution channels. Distinctive covers complement our distinctive approach to technical topics, breathing personality and life into potentially dry subjects.

The animal on the cover of *Windows 2000 Performance Guide* is a stickleback fish. Sticklebacks are small, elongated fish that reach a maximum length of about six inches and are characterized by a row of spines on the back and a soft-rayed dorsal fin. They have no scales, but are instead protected by hard armor plates on the sides of their bodies. An extremely common fish, sticklebacks live in the temperate regions of the Northern Hemisphere. They can live in either fresh or salt water, and some species inhabit both. During the springtime breeding season, the male stickleback becomes bright red in color. Using mucus secretions from his own kidneys as glue, he builds a nest of plants and coaxes a female (or females) to lay her eggs there, following behind her to fertilize them. When the nest is full, the male becomes the sole guardian of the eggs and young, defending the nest from any intruders.

There are about 12 species of stickleback fish. One of the most common is the three-spined stickleback (*Gasterosteus aculeatus*), which inhabits both fresh and salt water almost everywhere in the Northern Hemisphere. The sea (or 15-spined) stickleback (*Spinachia spinachia*) is found off the coasts of Europe. Other species include the four-spined, nine-spined, and brook sticklebacks.

Emily Quill was the production editor and copyeditor for *Windows 2000 Performance Guide*. Sue Willing, Colleen Gorman, Matt Hutchinson, and Mary Anne Mayo provided quality control. Tom Dinse wrote the index. Derek DiMatteo and Philip Dangler provided production assistance.

Ellie Volckhausen designed the cover of this book, based on a series design by Edie Freedman. The cover image is a 19th-century engraving from the Dover Pictorial Archive. Emma Colby produced the cover layout with QuarkXPress 4.1 using Adobe's ITC Garamond font.

David Futato designed the interior layout. Neil Walls converted the files from Microsoft Word to FrameMaker 5.5.6 using tools created by Mike Sierra. The text font is Linotype Birka; the heading font is Adobe Myriad Condensed; and the code font is LucasFont's TheSans Mono Condensed. The illustrations that appear in the book were produced by Robert Romano and Jessamyn Read using Macromedia Free-Hand 9 and Adobe Photoshop 6. The tip and warning icons were drawn by Christopher Bing. This colophon was written by Emily Quill.

Whenever possible, our books use a durable and flexible lay-flat binding.

How to stay in touch with O'Reilly

1. Visit Our Award-Winning Web Site

http://www.oreilly.com/

★ "Top 100 Sites on the Web" —PC Magazine
★ "Top 5% Web sites" —Point Communications
★ "3-Star site" —The McKinley Group

Our web site contains a library of comprehensive product information (including book excerpts and tables of contents), downloadable software, background articles, interviews with technology leaders, links to relevant sites, book cover art, and more. File us in your Bookmarks or Hotlist!

2. Join Our Email Mailing Lists

New Product Releases

To receive automatic email with brief descriptions of all new O'Reilly products as they are released, send email to:
ora-news-subscribe@lists.oreilly.com
Put the following information in the first line of your message (not in the Subject field):
subscribe ora-news

O'Reilly Events

If you'd also like us to send information about trade show events, special promotions, and other O'Reilly events, send email to:
ora-news-subscribe@lists.oreilly.com
Put the following information in the first line of your message (not in the Subject field):
subscribe ora-events

3. Get Examples from Our Books via FTP

There are two ways to access an archive of example files from our books:

Regular FTP

• ftp to:
  ftp.oreilly.com
  (login: anonymous
  password: your email address)
• Point your web browser to:
  ftp://ftp.oreilly.com/

FTPMAIL

• Send an email message to:
  ftpmail@online.oreilly.com
  (Write "help" in the message body)

4. Contact Us via Email

order@oreilly.com
To place a book or software order online. Good for North American and international customers.

subscriptions@oreilly.com
To place an order for any of our newsletters or periodicals.

books@oreilly.com
General questions about any of our books.

cs@oreilly.com
For answers to problems regarding your order or our products.

booktech@oreilly.com
For book content technical questions or corrections.

proposals@oreilly.com
To submit new book or software proposals to our editors and product managers.

international@oreilly.com
For information about our international distributors or translation queries. For a list of our distributors outside of North America check out:
http://www.oreilly.com/distributors.html

5. Work with Us

Check out our website for current employment opportunites:
http://jobs.oreilly.com/

O'Reilly & Associates, Inc.
1005 Gravenstein Hwy North
Sebastopol, CA 95472 USA
TEL 707-829-0515 or 800-998-9938
    (6am to 5pm PST)
FAX 707-829-0104

International Distributors

http://international.oreilly.com/distributors.html • *international@oreilly.com*

UK, EUROPE, MIDDLE EAST, AND AFRICA (EXCEPT FRANCE, GERMANY, AUSTRIA, SWITZERLAND, LUXEMBOURG, AND LIECHTENSTEIN)

INQUIRIES
O'Reilly UK Limited
4 Castle Street
Farnham
Surrey, GU9 7HS
United Kingdom
Telephone: 44-1252-711776
Fax: 44-1252-734211
Email: information@oreilly.co.uk

ORDERS
Wiley Distribution Services Ltd.
1 Oldlands Way
Bognor Regis
West Sussex PO22 9SA
United Kingdom
Telephone: 44-1243-843294
UK Freephone: 0800-243207
Fax: 44-1243-843302 (Europe/EU orders)
or 44-1243-843274 (Middle East/Africa)
Email: cs-books@wiley.co.uk

FRANCE

INQUIRIES & ORDERS
Éditions O'Reilly
18 rue Séguier
75006 Paris, France
Tel: 33-1-40-51-71-89
Fax: 33-1-40-51-72-26
Email: france@oreilly.fr

GERMANY, SWITZERLAND, AUSTRIA, LUXEMBOURG, AND LIECHTENSTEIN

INQUIRIES & ORDERS
O'Reilly Verlag
Balthasarstr. 81
D-50670 Köln, Germany
Telephone: 49-221-973160-91
Fax: 49-221-973160-8
Email: anfragen@oreilly.de (inquiries)
Email: order@oreilly.de (orders)

CANADA

(FRENCH LANGUAGE BOOKS)
Les Éditions Flammarion ltée
375, Avenue Laurier Ouest
Montréal (Québec) H2V 2K3
Tel: 1-514-277-8807
Fax: 1-514-278-2085
Email: info@flammarion.qc.ca

HONG KONG

City Discount Subscription Service, Ltd.
Unit A, 6th Floor, Yan's Tower
27 Wong Chuk Hang Road
Aberdeen, Hong Kong
Tel: 852-2580-3539
Fax: 852-2580-6463
Email: citydis@ppn.com.hk

KOREA

Hanbit Media, Inc.
Chungmu Bldg. 210
Yonnam-dong 568-33
Mapo-gu
Seoul, Korea
Tel: 822-325-0397
Fax: 822-325-9697
Email: hant93@chollian.dacom.co.kr

PHILIPPINES

Global Publishing
G/F Benavides Garden
1186 Benavides Street
Manila, Philippines
Tel: 632-254-8949/632-252-2582
Fax: 632-734-5060/632-252-2733
Email: globalp@pacific.net.ph

TAIWAN

O'Reilly Taiwan
1st Floor, No. 21, Lane 295
Section 1, Fu-Shing South Road
Taipei, 106 Taiwan
Tel: 886-2-27099669
Fax: 886-2-27038802
Email: mori@oreilly.com

INDIA

Shroff Publishers & Distributors Pvt. Ltd.
12, "Roseland", 2nd Floor
180, Waterfield Road, Bandra (West)
Mumbai 400 050
Tel: 91-22-641-1800/643-9910
Fax: 91-22-643-2422
Email: spd@vsnl.com

CHINA

O'Reilly Beijing
SIGMA Building, Suite B809
No. 49 Zhichun Road
Haidian District
Beijing, China PR 100080
Tel: 86-10-8809-7475
Fax: 86-10-8809-7463
Email: beijing@oreilly.com

JAPAN

O'Reilly Japan, Inc.
Yotsuya Y's Building
7 Banch 6, Honshio-cho
Shinjuku-ku
Tokyo 160-0003 Japan
Tel: 81-3-3356-5227
Fax: 81-3-3356-5261
Email: japan@oreilly.com

SINGAPORE, INDONESIA, MALAYSIA, AND THAILAND

TransQuest Publishers Pte Ltd
30 Old Toh Tuck Road #05-02
Sembawang Kimtrans Logistics Centre
Singapore 597654
Tel: 65-4623112
Fax: 65-4625761
Email: wendiw@transquest.com.sg

AUSTRALIA

Woodslane Pty., Ltd.
7/5 Vuko Place
Warriewood NSW 2102
Australia
Tel: 61-2-9970-5111
Fax: 61-2-9970-5002
Email: info@woodslane.com.au

NEW ZEALAND

Woodslane New Zealand, Ltd.
21 Cooks Street (P.O. Box 575)
Waganui, New Zealand
Tel: 64-6-347-6543
Fax: 64-6-345-4840
Email: info@woodslane.com.au

ARGENTINA

Distribuidora Cuspide
Suipacha 764
1008 Buenos Aires
Argentina
Phone: 54-11-4322-8868
Fax: 54-11-4322-3456
Email: libros@cuspide.com

ALL OTHER COUNTRIES

O'Reilly & Associates, Inc.
1005 Gravenstein Hwy North
Sebastopol, CA 95472 USA
Tel: 707-829-0515
Fax: 707-829-0104
Email: order@oreilly.com

O'REILLY®

TO ORDER: **800-998-9938** • **order@oreilly.com** • **www.oreilly.com**
ONLINE EDITIONS OF MOST O'REILLY TITLES ARE AVAILABLE BY SUBSCRIPTION AT **safari.oreilly.com**
ALSO AVAILABLE AT MOST RETAIL AND ONLINE BOOKSTORES